NOV 0 3 2010

WAR AND SEX

WAR AND SEX

A BRIEF HISTORY OF MEN'S URGE FOR BATTLE

JOHN V. H. DIPPEL

Ⓟ Prometheus Books

59 John Glenn Drive
Amherst, New York 14228-2119

Published 2010 by Prometheus Books

Inquiries should be addressed to
Prometheus Books
59 John Glenn Drive
Amherst, New York 14228–2119
VOICE: 716–691–0133
FAX: 716–691–0137
WWW.PROMETHEUSBOOKS.COM

14 13 12 11 10   5 4 3 2 1

Library of Congress Cataloging-in-Publication Data

Dippel, John Van Houten, 1946–
    War and Sex : a brief history of men's urge for battle / by John V. H. Dippel.
        p. cm.
    Includes bibliographical references and index.
    ISBN 978–1–61614–188–2 (cloth : acid-free paper)

U22.3.D576 2010
353.0201/9—dc22

                                                                2010014742

Use of "Fulfillment" and "Comrades" courtesy of Ann Charlton, neice and copyright holder for Robert Nichols, coauthor with William Charlton of *Putting Poetry First: A Life of Robert Nichols, 1893–1944.*

Printed in the United States of America on acid-free paper

To Penny,
who knows why

CONTENTS

INTRODUCTION

*W*ar or sex—it's never been a simple "either-or" choice. In fact, making war and making love have a long, tangled, intimate history. Aristophanes would have us believe it was once otherwise, having Lysistrata convince the women of Athens to forego sleeping with their husbands until they ceased from making war. But his play was a comedy and a fantasy, not to be mistaken for real life. In more recent times, Freud posited a duality of *eros* and *thanatos* in the human psyche: the drive to live and create life versus the death instinct. Writing after the horrific slaughter of World War I, trying to make sense of it, he could only explain this monstrous bloodletting as a mass succumbing to the latter impulse. During the 1960s, the mantra "Make love, not war" made sense to the hippies and made some converts to their antiwar cause, but it was no more in touch with human reality than what the Greek playwright had envisioned over two millennia before. Clearly, if it were that simple a choice, wars would have stopped a long time ago, and we all would be wondering where all the soldiers have gone.

If anything, history teaches us that human nature is much more complicated and contradictory: the need to make love and the need to make war are deeply intertwined. It was the lovely Helen, after all, whose fabled face launched "a thousand ships" and brought about the Trojan War. Indeed, gaining access to women has long been one of the major reasons why men have girded their loins for battle. Along with food and more land, warriors have always fought for the rewards of sex, female submission, and genetic immortality. The Romans grabbed—not necessarily raped—the Sabine women and fought off their men because, according to legend at least, the new Italian arrivals lacked wives of their own to perpetuate their race. The Vikings similarly took the females of conquered peoples back with them, as slaves, to the hyperborean Norselands or else entered into marriages with them on foreign shores. In our own day, the taking of women by force, or willingly in war's environment of chaos and imminent death, is seen as the soldier's version of the *droit de seigneur*—one of the spoils that goes to the victor. Then there are the female rewards that go to the warriors who prove their fitness as protectors and, thus, as mates. These old ways survive today in the warring customs of the Yanomamö people of the Amazon rainforest, who fight mostly out of sexual jealousy and then gratefully allow their triumphant headmen to sleep with as many women—and father as many children—as they want. But even in the "civilized" world, in our own time, returning war heroes turn female heads and quicken their hearts as mere men in mufti cannot.

But even milquetoast males benefit from a nation's going to war. To prevail under arms, a society has to undergo an internal transformation—a process of militarization—that elevates the qualities we associate with males (courage, self-sacrifice, stoic perseverance) while demoting those thought of as "feminine" (compassion, cooperation, kindness). This reordering reinstates a gender hierarchy: men become the admired sex. If they have previously lost some of their distinctive masculine identity or value to society, they can now collectively regain these attributes simply by virtue of their gender.

Going to war, in short, alters the power relations between men and women. Females are loath to object to this shift in status because their security, too, is at stake. Disgruntled males can take advantage of this to further their own ends. On the home front, assertive, competitive females are "put back in their place"—that is, in the home, taking care of the kids. Women encountered by soldiers during war are apt to be abused, humiliated, or violated—a psychological displacement of male frustration and anger over female usurpation of their prerogatives back home. There is even a plausible connection between the desire for war and the desire to restore male dominance. Many modern "wars of choice" (that is, those not waged in response to attack or imminent danger) have occurred after women in the bellicose nation have gained new rights and freedoms. When these conflicts have ended with victory, this successful outcome has halted or even reversed the trend toward full female equality and put men firmly back on top. In this sense, men "win" doubly, on and off the battlefield: winning a war turns the "battle of the sexes" in their favor.

The wars examined in this book—the Civil War, several regional conflicts at the end of the nineteenth century, World War I, World War II, the Vietnam War, and the ongoing confrontation between Islamic fundamentalists and Western nations—all conform to this pattern. Each was preceded by substantial progress for women in gaining rights and opportunities—the "woman's rights" movement of the antebellum era, the suffragette protests of the early twentieth century, the expansion of women's economic and domestic power in the 1930s, the stirrings of "second wave" feminism in the 1960s, and the growing acceptance of women as equals (even in uniform) in recent decades. And each of these wars has resulted in setbacks for females in the victorious nations—and greater progress for those on the losing side, where men have been discredited. Seen in this light, wars are not just about defeating external foes or protecting national security. They are also fought—consciously or unconsciously—to resolve domestic tensions and conflicts over the proper roles for men and women. War is, to paraphrase Claus von Clausewitz, the continuation of sexual politics by other means.

To raise the question of whether or not young volunteers or societies as a whole grasp all the implications of their decisions to fight a war is to dive into the murky waters of human motivation. A historian does so at great peril and with a full recognition that the view below the surface will be cloudy and incomplete. No single reason can possibly explain why we choose to do what we do—why we go off to war any more than why and with whom we fall in love. Much of our reasoning remains rooted in the realm of the unconscious. However, conceding this point does not mean that all inquiry into motivation is fruitless. Why each of us makes these fateful decisions is likely unknowable (even to ourselves), but the factors that induce *groups* of individuals (or entire countries, for that matter) to embrace war can be discerned, indirectly, by examining the gender (im)balance of power that may have made fighting appealing and then assessing how these circumstances (unfavorable for hierarchically minded men) were altered by winning on the battlefield.

It is my contention that many young, single soldiers stand to gain a "reproductive advantage"—a leg up over their peers in the Darwinian competition for sexual partners, mates, and, ultimately, for children. This appears to be a strong, unconscious but rational motive for signing up. It remains unconscious because it is not socially (and personally) acceptable for them to think in this way. It is rational because wartime service does offer these men a plausible way to overcome the liabilities that would otherwise hamper them in this sexual competition—too little education, poor income prospects, and an insufficiently masculine image. Many males from low socioeconomic backgrounds grasp that volunteering offers them a good chance to fulfill their biological destiny. They weigh the risks of being killed against these potential benefits—and decide to sign up. Is this the only reason why they do so? No. But, as I hope this book will demonstrate, it does help to explain why so many men—in different countries, and at different times—find war attractive.

For nations, the expected gains from war are similar. Like individuals, nations can find themselves in a fierce struggle for survival. For them, success is measured by their ability to remain strong and grow. A large and expanding population is the key to attaining this goal. However, in the modern era, as societies have evolved economically and politically, a nation's need to increase and multiply has been thwarted by an equally compelling desire on the part of its citizenry to conserve and prosper. Starting with the industrial age, the peoples of Western Europe and North America have dramatically reduced their birth rates, to the point where many of them are no longer producing enough offspring to ensure their survival, let alone their ability to win wars. As the perils of "depopulation" have become apparent, national leaders and their followers have trumpeted the virtue—indeed, the patriotic necessity—of producing more children, reflecting the Social Darwinian belief that human capital is a nation's greatest asset. This awareness was especially potent in the late nineteenth and early twentieth centuries—during the era of mass armies but before the advent of weapons of mass destruction. So, when it has come to the question of going off to war in this democratic era (when kings and queens no longer unilaterally decide), the reproductive aspirations of nation and citizen-soldier have often coincided.

This study of how growing gender equality and a concomitant decline in fertility creates resentment and hostility among some groups of men and encourages them to see war as a strategy for improving their reproductive fortunes has proceeded within certain a priori limitations. First is our imperfect knowledge of human motivation: it can be inferred from the historical record but never proven. It is not a matter of fact, but of insightful theorizing. Second, this book has focused on wars for which sufficient data exist for us to understand the social, economic, and political forces that preceded them and helped to cause them. Only with such information available is it possible to gauge how much simmering conflict between the two sexes may have underlain these more readily apparent reasons. Third, by and large I have looked at wars from the perspective of nations that did not *have* to fight—that is, those that were not responding to attack or imminent danger. (American reactions to the attacks of December 7, 1941, and September 11, 2001, are two exceptions.) For, under those other circumstances, the reason for fighting is less psychologically complex: it is strictly a matter of survival. This difference—I would argue—is one reason why the conventional gender distinctions reinforced during wartime—the men fight, and the women are protected—are not seen as vitally important when a nation's very existence is at stake. The Soviet Union during World War II and contemporary Israel are cases in point.

In other words, this book approaches war not as a condition arbitrarily imposed upon a people, but as social choice made in light of domestic pressures and needs having to do with gender relations. This consensual view of war reflects conditions of the modern world. In our day, popular urges help build momentum for war. Communication and the democratic political process amplify their power. During war, the release of these urges transforms soldiers and the peoples they serve. Depending upon the outcome, these wartime experiences then reshape postwar society and the lives of its returning warriors. For sexually disadvantaged young men—who make up the great bulk of volunteers—this outcome can lead to marriage and fatherhood. For them, the impulse to war is really the impulse to life.

Chapter 1

THE WAR BETWEEN THE SEXES, AKA THE CIVIL WAR

In the spring of 1840, eight young American women set sail for London to help change the world. They were in a joyful mood. One of them had just gotten married, and so this voyage across the Atlantic was also her honeymoon. She was tiny—only about five feet three—with twinkling blue eyes that conveyed a girlish mischievousness. She was a free spirit who loved to kick up her heels and dance. But, beneath this lighthearted façade, this bride had a steely nature. Whenever she played a game like chess she always fought hard to the bitter end and never gave her opponent any quarter. If she lost, she was devastated.[1] Mercurial in love, she had toyed with the affections of the man who had proposed to her—first accepting his proposal, then breaking off their engagement in a panic about losing her freedom, and then changing her mind again, abruptly accepting his offer of marriage.[2]

The couple had married in a rush because her handsome suitor was on his way to England: he had slyly used his invitation to a gathering there to persuade her. Because she simply *had* to go, too, she had said yes. She was not about to step back into the shadows and trust things to men. After digging in her heels she got the Scottish minister in Peterborough, New York, to back down and leave out the word *obey* from the vow she had to make to her betrothed, as she was not about to be subjugated to the will of any man, even one she loved this much. Her husband—ten years her senior—acquiesced. His bride clearly adored him and the work he was doing, and that was enough for him to love her back. He could never have imagined that someday *she* would be more famous than he.[3]

When twenty-four-year-old Elizabeth Cady Stanton (as she now

15

agreed to be called) stepped on board the packet ship *Montreal* in New York harbor a few days later, she could see the course of her life taking shape. The man who guided her up the gangplank, Henry Brewster Stanton, was already a celebrity in the abolitionist movement. His oratory and pen were persuasive in a way few men of his day could match. Elizabeth had been smitten with him from the moment he opened his mouth.[4] Now she was his partner—in her commitment to ending slavery, if not experience, fully his equal. Here was a man who stood on the right side of issues that mattered most to her, like her stodgy, slaveholding, Calvinist father who had frowned at her courtship with an abolitionist, who believed only men should go to college, who regretted that she was not a boy, who wished she could replace the son, Eleazar, he had lost just before his graduation from college, when Elizabeth was only eleven. Now she and her new husband were heading out in the world to fight the battle to end this scourge together. Henry was to attend the World's Anti-Slavery Convention in London, and she would, of course, be at his side. Men and even some women from both sides of the Atlantic would be attending. If the occasion arose, she, too, would speak. They would buck each other up, Henry and she.

Soon Elizabeth discovered that James G. Birney—the child of a slaveholder just like she was, a Southerner who had freed his own slaves and was now running for president as the Liberty Party candidate—was a fellow passenger. He, too, was bound for the convention. Elizabeth saw in him a kindred soul, but she was soon disappointed by his persistent patronizing, by his insisting she needed "toning down"—whatever that meant—before they reached England. The polite and gracious Birney turned out to be just as hopeless about women as her father, telling her it was not "ladylike" to ascend to the top of the ship's mast in a chair, as the male passengers did, or to call her husband "Henry" when others were in earshot. He was not, she ascertained, a believer in equal rights for women. Rather than brood over this, Elizabeth spent much of the remaining weeks at sea preparing for the questions on slavery she felt sure that, as the wife of a delegate, she was bound to be asked. She was more than ready to do so when the *Montreal* became becalmed within sight of the English coast, so she coaxed Henry and Birney into being lowered into a pilot boat to strike out for land ahead of everyone else.

Their lodgings in London were the "gloomiest" Elizabeth had ever experienced, but her mood brightened with the arrival of eight wonderful ladies from Philadelphia and Boston who—*mirabile visu!*—were also attending the antislavery gathering as delegates. They were a fine, upstanding, well-spoken group—Lucretia Mott, Sarah Pugh, Abby Kimber, Elizabeth Neal, and Mary Grew in plain Quaker outfits and with equally modest demeanors; Bostonians Ann Green Phillips, Emily Winslow, and Abby Southwick a bit livelier and outspoken.[5]

The New England women told a story about how they had been prevented from holding the annual meeting of their Female Anti-Slavery Society a few years before because of the threat on the part of some unconscionable men to disrupt the proceedings. There had been a big fuss in the newspapers about this beforehand: "trouble and violence" were bound to occur at this incendiary gathering, the ladies had been warned. But this had not cowed them: they had let their consciences and God's guidance dictate what they should do. They had written to one paper saying, "The cause of human freedom is our religion," and that they intended to go ahead and hold their meeting at a more welcoming venue elsewhere in the city. But this had only stirred up another hornet's nest, with handbills being nailed up outside city hall denouncing their plan and outrageously inviting members of the public to vie for a prize of one hundred dollars to go to the first person who laid "violent hands" on the "infamous foreign scoundrel" George Thompson, an English abolitionist who had been invited to speak before the ladies' group.[6] That evening the place was packed with angry, red-faced, snorting men, some thumping bullwhips, intending to thrash the speaker and cart him off to South Carolina, where he was likely to be lynched. The proslavery men hurled rotten tomatoes and vegetables at the president of the society, Mary Parker, until Mayor Lyman himself strode into the room and told the ladies to leave before there was bloodshed. In the face of such threats, prudence had prevailed, and they had gone back down the steps and out onto the street where a howling throng awaited them, full of "rage and contempt." There were other men waiting there—supposed friends who, just days before, had proclaimed themselves enemies of slavery—but now, sensing the crowd's wrath and revealing their own hypocrisy, did not lift a finger to help them. William Lloyd Garrison, a last-minute replacement for the anxious Thompson, had barely escaped with his life.[7] What they had sadly learned from this incident, the ladies from Boston stressed, was that in the future they would have to rely more upon themselves. Men were too easily swayed from the cause, too undependable.

Elizabeth was more than delighted to meet for the first time in her life women who shared her belief in equality between the sexes. (She wished Henry was more inclined toward this view.) She was particularly taken with Lucretia Mott—an older Quaker woman, the daughter of a Nantucket whaling captain, a friend of Garrison's, a fine organizer, deeply religious, a mother of five.[8] She was just a sprite of a woman, shorter than Elizabeth, thin as a bird. She was accompanying her husband, James, to the convention. Mrs. Mott was already a battle-hardened veteran, having faced hostile mobs and once narrowly avoided having her house set ablaze.[9] She had made a name for herself by forming an antislavery society in Philadelphia and then inviting free blacks in the city to come and speak before it. She was the only female delegate planning to address the assemblage, and Elizabeth, listening to her fellow lodger in the evenings in the abolitionist Mark Moore's boarding house, sensed here was a woman who stood head and shoulders above the rest of them—here was a woman she could model herself on. The ladies' enthusiasm for the forthcoming proceedings received two unexpected jolts. First, calling this a "world" conference turned out to be a gross exaggeration: the British were obviously in charge, and the Americans and the few from other countries were expected to play only minor parts. But that was a small disappointment compared to the other disheartening news: before the convention had a chance to meet, its British planning committee—emboldened by several American clergymen—had voted to bar females from taking an active part in the proceedings.[10] Although this came as a surprise, it was not unusual for men in the antislavery movement to close their ranks to females. When William Lloyd Garrison had founded the American Anti-Slavery Society (AASS) in Philadelphia seven years before, he had wanted it to include women, but the organization had never gotten around to inviting any to join. That was why Lucretia Mott had gone ahead and formed a group for women in the City of Brotherly Love. By the end of the decade, some forty women's societies in New England were working to end slavery. Many male abolitionists felt they could accomplish more by keeping these bodies apart—thereby not alienating potential new members by being seen as too tied to the "woman question." Frankly, they, too, disapproved of females being in politics. When a female was nominated to serve on the business committee of the AASS in 1840, this was the final straw: conservative-thinking men stormed out of the convention and formed their own organization. It expressly barred members of the fair sex from participating.[11]

The evening before the convention was to start, some gentlemen came around to the ladies' lodgings to dissuade them from showing up and provoking trouble. The Rev. Nathaniel Colver, representing the First Free Baptist Church in Boston, declared it to be his opinion that women were "constitutionally unfit for public or business meetings." When he was reminded that this was just what proponents of slavery said about blacks, he grew angry and left the boarding house.[12] The women agreed they would not be deterred. On the following morning they strolled through the bright, cheerful streets of London, heading toward the ornate Freemasons' Hall. News of their impending arrival caused the predictable stir: "The excitement and vehemence of protest and denunciation could not have been greater, if the news had come that the French were about to invade England."[13] The arbitrary decision to silence them prompted some male delegates from across the Atlantic to protest. Responding to some nudging from his wife, Ann, Wendell Phillips—a leading abolitionist from Boston—rose to denounce the women's exclusion and proposed that all duly chosen delegates be seated.[14] (Mrs. Mott had modestly proposed that no such case be made.) The Harvard-educated lawyer pointed out that male members of his antislavery association considered women as equals and declared, "We think it is right for women to sit by our side there [in the States], and we think it is right for them do the same here."[15] William H. Ashurst rhetorically asked, "Are not these women as competent as yourselves to judge of the principles of Christianity, and to bring forth the best affections of our nature?" The Englishman Thompson chimed it by reminding them all, "For years, the women of America have carried their banner [of abolitionism] in the van, while the men have humbly followed in the rear."[16] But such heartening remarks only produced the retort that "all order would be at an end" if the "promiscuous [mixed with men] female representation be allowed," and "God's clear intention violated."[17] The invitation to the convention, it was allowed, had been extended only to "gentlemen." An English cleric named Burnet implored the ladies to accede to the "prejudices and custom" of his native land and accept the committee's ruling; otherwise it would be better if the convention was called off and all returned home.[18] Another minister opined that "women will be badly off when they have nothing but their rights, and the men also."[19] Even a majority of the male American delegates, including many clergy, did not support seating the women, as it was not the custom in their societies to honor this practice.[20]

So, in the end, the profemale contingent lost its fight. In a show of solidarity, Phillips and a late-arriving Garrison opted to sit among the ladies and remain silent as well. The females were ushered to seats behind a bar and curtain, like members of the choir, so that the sight of them would not distract or discomfort the men. The male delegates opposed to the presence of women in the hall considered this a major concession.[21] In recognition of her preeminence among the segregated females, Mrs. Mott—dubbed by one Irish newspaper the "Lioness of the Convention"[22]—was given an elevated chair, from which she could observe what was being said on the other side. (Subsequently, she was the only woman at the convention to appear in the official painting commemorating it.)[23] During the breaks, other women flitted about her like moths. Elizabeth Cady Stanton was one of the most indignant over this turn of events. Before she and Lucretia Mott left London shortly afterward, they agreed that this kind of treatment of their sex should not—and would not—continue. It was high time that men be taught the "first principles of 'Human Freedom.'"[24]

Even after she returned to New York, Mrs. Stanton's anger had not ebbed. At her urging, she and Mrs. Mott made a pledge to call together a gathering of women, when the time was appropriate, to take up the issue of their rights. However, the moment did not become propitious for eight long years, as Mrs. Stanton was busy raising her first four children (learning in the process not to count upon men),[25] and Mrs. Mott was chronically beset by neuralgia and occupied by speeches up and down the eastern seaboard on the evils of slavery.[26] By chance, in 1848, Mrs. Mott was visiting her sister in the same town, Seneca Falls, New York, where Mrs. Stanton was then living. Elizabeth was feeling isolated and overwhelmed by the demands of running a rural household full of rambunctious young children while her husband was traveling around the country leading the fight against slavery.[27] At the same time, the rebuff that she and the other women had experienced in London still rankled. Meeting with Lucretia and several other women in a nearby town, Elizabeth poured out all her frustrations. In response, the women agreed to call together a convention five days hence—the first ever to be held in the United States on the subject of women's rights. This was to be totally independent from the struggle to free the slaves.

Thanks to public notices and word of mouth, more than three hundred women—and, unexpectedly, some men[28]—traveled to Seneca Falls for this historic gathering. Most of them came from nearby towns; many were Quakers well steeped in the creed of equality and committed to making it a reality in America.[29] Others were drawn there because of the Finger Lakes' reputation for unorthodox ideas and causes. Some, like the black abolitionist Frederick Douglass, came straight from the first meeting of a new political movement—the Free Soil Party—in nearby Buffalo, freshly imbued with a democratic, reformist spirit.[30] Still other women were motivated by economic freedoms they were beginning to enjoy due to the recent developing of manufacturing in the region. To link their campaign for women's rights to this broader context, the "Declaration of Sentiments" that Elizabeth Stanton drafted over two stifling midsummer days and evenings, July 19 and 20, wisely parroted the document Thomas Jefferson had penned nearly three-quarters of a century before:

> We hold these truths to be self-evident: that all men *and women* [italics added] are created equal; that they are endowed by their Creator with certain inalienable rights; that among these are life, liberty, and the pursuit of happiness; that to secure these rights governments are instituted, deriving their just powers from the consent of the governed.[31]

Emulating Jefferson's format, the document listed a series of grievances against men, stating, "The history of mankind is a history of repeated injuries and usurpations on the part of man toward woman, having in direct object the establishment of an absolute tyranny over her." At that time, such thoughts were provocative and ran counter to common practice in the United States. Eight years after the antislavery convention in London, women were still not welcome as speakers at most public gatherings. Indeed, the persons assembled at the Methodist chapel in Seneca Falls had respected this unwritten rule by choosing the experienced James Mott, not his wife, to preside over the proceedings. (For no woman had ever wielded the gavel in America before.) There was much to complain about. In 1848, American women could not own property, sign contracts, serve on juries, or—generally speaking—hold jobs once they married. Furthermore, they could not vote or run for office. They were, in fact, second-class citizens—many, many rungs above black slaves and freedmen in terms of individual freedoms, but still shut out of the world of public affairs. Most Americans wanted things to remain that way. When word of the gathering in this tiny New York village spread across the country, it met with contempt and condemnation. Some newspaper editorial writers tried to outdo each other in mocking its grandiose "declaration." (Two years later, the *New York Herald* would characterize the first National Woman's Rights Convention as a "motley gathering of fanatical mongrels" and "fugitive lunatics.")[32] Conservative preachers, including the Presbyterian one in Seneca Falls, denounced Stanton ("Infidel!") and the convention from their pulpits, and many ordinary citizens, male and female, made fun of it.[33] According to the occasionally unreliable Elizabeth Stanton, a number of the women who had affixed their signatures later changed their minds in light of the hostile reaction they had encountered and turned a "cold shoulder" toward this cause.[34] Overall, the reports out of Seneca Falls prompted a mixed reaction, certainly in the press.[35] Some papers hailed the convention as a historic point for the nation. By no means a zealot, the influential Horace Greeley, editor of the *New York Tribune*, noted that if Americans truly believed in what the Declaration of Independence said, then they would just have to accept equal rights for women.[36]

It seems that at this moment in the country's history, the idea that the fair sex ought to be afforded parity with men was radical, but not outlandish. Much had already occurred to lay the groundwork for the gathering in upstate New York. Most recently, women's involvement in the abolitionist movement had given them a voice in national political affairs and a greater awareness of their own capabilities. Across the country, female speakers were castigating "Demon Rum" and urging audiences to go out and smash bottles and plateglass windows in their local taverns. Several well-known women, such as Lucretia Mott, had gone on to assume prominent positions as speakers and writers in the antislavery cause. It was no exaggeration to state that women exercised a great deal of moral authority in building and sustaining this movement. Spending so much time and energy advocating for black emancipation naturally led some female abolitionists to examine their own situation more critically and to ponder how it might be improved. As would happen more than a century later, during the turbulent 1960s, this introspective process had led to several meetings dealing with the rights of women prior to the historic one held at Seneca Falls.[37]

A few books had also been published on the subject, including *An Appeal to the Women of the Nominally Free States*, which was written by the abolitionist Angelina Grimké and appeared in 1837. The following year, her sister and fellow activist Sarah Grimké published *Letters on the Equality of the Sexes, and the Condition of Woman*. This volume employed quotations from the Bible to make the case that men and women had been created equal and thus ought to lead their lives in "harmony and love," with neither sex holding "dominion" over the other.[38] Books like these drew upon earlier affirmations of the need for parity in marriage, notably William Thompson's 1825 *Appeal of One Half the Human Race, Women, Against the Pretenses of the Other Half, Men*. Here the egalitarian Thompson, writing collaboratively with his companion Anna Doyle Wheeler, laid out a seminal indictment of this institution ("Man, by law, superstition, and opinion, commands: woman, in marriage, by law, superstition, and marriage, obeys")[39] calling for both partners to enjoy the same rights instead.

While still far outside mainstream thought a quarter century after it was penned, Thompson's revolutionary credo was having an impact on the legal restrictions faced by American women. State legislatures as far flung and disparate as Maine and Mississippi had recently voted to allow women to own property, and a few had made it legal for females to draw up their own wills. On another front, women were demonstrating that they possessed independent minds and were eager to put these to use. In the 1830s, several seminaries (later called "colleges") came into existence to educate young women, and Oberlin College established a "Female Department," inviting "young ladies of good minds, unblemished morals, and respectable attainments" to study toward degrees alongside men—the nation's first experiment with coeducation at an institution of higher learning.[40] Just half a year after the conclave at Seneca Falls, Elizabeth Blackwell, the daughter of a liberal-thinking English industrialist, made history by becoming the first person of her sex to earn a medical degree in the United States.[41]

These legal and educational advances, in turn, had been made possible by a growing recognition that women could play more roles than wife and mother. A major factor in changing attitudes on this subject was the Second Great Awakening. This revivalist movement swept through Protestant congregations like a wildfire in the 1830s, inciting ministers and their parishioners to embrace with renewed passion and fervor the importance of doing good works in the service of God. Churches became the locus of ambitious social reforms ranging from picketing saloons to feeding the poor, from freeing the slaves to securing new rights for women. A populist ethos took hold within organized religion—particularly on the independent-thinking western frontier—as hundreds of thousands of new believers joined the ranks of Methodists and Baptists or created splinter denominations of their own.[42] They brought into these churches a disdain for established authority and a willingness to run things by themselves. Their infectious, reform-minded energy soon spilled over into the larger society. This activist spirit provided married women, in particular, a rationale for social engagement. (Some would eventually even become ordained as ministers.)[43] Their taking part in church services and community campaigns for greater social justice opened up new horizons in the lives of many of these middle-class wives. The lessons of their experiences were passed on to their daughters, many of whom came of age around the time of the gathering at Seneca Falls.

Behind this religious ferment lay an even more powerful force in the shaping of nineteenth-century America—the Enlightenment. In many ways, the emotionally charged Second Great Awakening was a reaction to this affirmation of natural rights, with its emphasis on reason and secular values. Jefferson and other Deist framers of the Declaration of Independence had minimized the potentially divisive issue of religious faith in order to forge a new nation.[44] But the political theories of a philosopher like John Locke also gave justification for an individualistic experimentation with new freedoms within the churches from the 1830s onward. In the words of one historian of this trend, "The crucible of popular theology combined odd doses of high and popular culture, of renewed supernaturalism and Enlightenment rationalism, of mystical

experiences and biblical literalism, of evangelical and Jeffersonian rhetoric."[45] Locke's belief in rational inquiry as the ultimate arbiter of human
behavior led him to view relations between the sexes from this perspective as well. In his *Two Treatises on Government*, the English philosopher
had had this to say about marriage:

> But the husband and wife, though they have but one common concern,
> yet having different understandings, will unavoidably sometimes have
> different wills too; it therefore being necessary that the last determina-
> tion, i.e., the rule, should be placed somewhere; it naturally falls to the
> man's share, as the abler and the stronger. But this reaching but to the
> things of their common interest and property, leaves the wife in the full
> and free possession of what by contract is her peculiar right, and gives
> the husband no more power over her life than she has over his; the
> power of the husband being so far from that of an absolute monarch,
> that the wife has in many cases a liberty to separate from him, where
> natural right, or their contract allows it.[46]

The fact that Elizabeth Stanton elected to couch her 1848 appeal for
women's rights in the idiom of the Declaration of Independence reveals
not only her astute political acumen, but also the enduring power of this
Enlightenment credo to arouse her fellow Americans to action.

The problem for Stanton and other progressive women of her day
was that this philosophy was "more honor'd in the breach than in the
observance." Two generations after its founding, the American republic
was still rent by paradoxes present at its creation—by contradictions the
Founding Fathers could not bring themselves to resolve, for fear of dis-
banding in disarray, their work unfinished. Competing allegiances to
"freedom" and "equality" were left in limbo. Furthermore, those who
were supposed to be innately "equal" were patently not so, and
"freedom" was just as clearly not enjoyed by all. The most egregious
default on revolutionary promises was by omission: leaving the matters
of voting and citizenship, as well as a host of other individual rights, up
to the states. They were free to pass laws restricting suffrage as they saw
fit. The Constitution did not state that blacks or women were *not* entitled to vote (or to be free, for that matter): it only prevented any extension of basic rights from being dictated by the federal government. (In
fact, women had once exercised the franchise in one state—New

Jersey—until that right was rescinded in 1807.)[47] Thus, the abolitionists and advocates of "woman's rights" might fight gamely for their respective causes, but the obstacles placed in their paths were formidable: they had to either work to have new laws passed at the state level or have the Constitution amended. And either course of action would run up against inhospitable political realities. In many states, the opponents of female suffrage and black freedom controlled the legislature. In addition, throughout the antebellum era, a majority of the Supreme Court—which had the final word on constitutional matters—was predominantly made up of supporters of slavery and enemies of female suffrage.[48]

Generally speaking, the American people wanted to maintain the status quo. Indeed, many were vehemently against freeing the slaves or making women the equals of men. This could be expected of those with a direct personal interest in these matters—slaveholders and male politicians, for example. But, in fact, hostility to giving these two groups basic rights was widespread. A barometer of public opinion on these two issues was the percentage of votes cast for political parties that espoused either emancipation or female suffrage in the decades leading up to the Civil War and, in the case of voting rights, up to 1920, when the Nineteenth Amendment was finally adopted. The only national party before 1864 to call for freeing the slaves—the Liberty Party—chose James G. Birney as its presidential candidate in both the 1840 and 1844 elections, but he garnered only about 7,000 votes in his first campaign—or three-tenths of 1 percent of all ballots.[49] Birney's larger tally of 60,000 votes four years later was largely attributable to popular opposition to annexing Texas, not to slavery. When Gerrit Smith—Elizabeth Stanton's first cousin—ran on the same party's ticket in 1848, he received just over 2,500 votes. Coincidentally or not, Smith and his party had embraced the cause of female suffrage during that campaign—one in which Lucretia Mott had been his running mate. She was the first woman ever to be given this honor. The unpopularity of awarding women the vote can similarly be gauged by its showing at the ballot box. If anything, this crusade seems to have met with greater opposition than freeing the slaves. Aside from the Liberty Party in 1848, *no* national party came out in favor of giving females the vote until Theodore Roosevelt ran on the Progressive line in 1912.[50] In 1870—two years after passage of the Fifteenth Amendment, guaranteeing *black males* the franchise—a Democratic congressman from

Maryland, speaking on the floor of the House of Representatives, could declare:

> Sir, who but a veritable fanatic could have believed, ten years ago, that the question, "Shall women be allowed to vote?" would so soon come to be considered throughout the greater portion of our country as one to be seriously entertained, gravely pondered on, and nicely decided, by the various political assemblies, law-making bodies, and judicial tribunals of the land? There is probably not one gentleman, in either branch of this our national Legislature—nay, of any Legislature in the whole country, North or South, who would not at that time, ten brief years ago, have laughed to scorn the proposition of woman suffrage; or, rather, he would have felt with regard to it like the big man who used to let his little wife whip him every day, because she liked the sport and it did not hurt him. . . . A monstrous army is now coming down upon us—a hundred thousand "whirlwinds in petticoats"—which we must meet firmly, or be overwhelmed by the storm.[51]

In 1881, eleven years *after* the first African American was elected to the US Senate, virtually all the senators who rose to speak in response to a proposal to create a special committee on women's suffrage made "haste to declare their unalterable opposition to any and all measures designed to give the ballot to women," even though no such legislation was actually under consideration. One Kentucky member of the chamber stated that he did not wish "ignorant colored women . . . [to] take and use the ballot, to the infinite confusion of social order." An Alabama colleague then jokingly suggested that women only be allowed to vote if *both* heads of a household agreed to this—an impossibility given the widespread animosity among men toward such a step.[52] Comments such as these might appear to exaggerate the intensity of opposition to giving women the vote, but they actually closely mirror sentiments aired outside the halls of Congress. Lucy Stone, whose fabled oratorical powers drew crowds numbering several thousand to hear her speak and earned her the sobriquet "morning star" of the women's rights movement, also had to walk past "hoodlums" lurking outside the halls where she was to hold forth. On occasion they would hurl insults at her, break windows, and, once inside, unleash a barrage of items in her direction, including—on one memorable summer night in 1848, in East Bridgewater, Massachusetts—"a profusion of coppers, dried apples, smoked herring, beans, and tobacco quids."[53] At another event of hers, on Cape Cod, a mob stormed the platform on which Stone had been waiting to speak and assailed her companion, Stephen Symonds Foster, tearing his coat apart. Stone somehow managed to charm one of the attackers into escorting her outside, where he gallantly lifted her onto a tree stump so that she could give her talk.[54] During her early years as a crusader for temperance, abolition, and women's rights, Susan B. Anthony also regularly faced unruly and raucous crowds that tried to shout her down, as she stirred up "deep-seated and ingrained prejudices bred into the very natures of men," some of whom felt that female activists like her were "committing a sin against God and violating His laws."[55]

Such vituperative reactions to female speakers like Stanton, Mott, Stone, and Anthony raise the question *why*. Was male hostility (and it *was* almost exclusively male, at least in its public expression, since women opposed to these progressive causes also did not approve of their sex's voicing its disapproval) aimed at *all* the radical changes being proposed? Was it focused more on one issue—say, women's rights—than on any other? Was this anger directed particularly at females because they were defying deeply held beliefs about how they ought to behave? The motives of a mob are rarely crystal clear, even to its members. What is known is that all three major social campaigns of nineteenth-century America—for temperance, the end of slavery, and women's rights— provoked strong opposition, but intense emotions and violent reaction were far more characteristic of the latter two movements. One explanation for this difference is that, while the crusade against alcohol ostensibly sought to change *behavior*, those on behalf of slaves and women sought to alter social *status*. Shutting down saloons and making the consumption of spirits illegal would not cause any group (except drunken husbands who abused their wives) to lose power or empower another. In addition, while all three movements had a moral basis, no one defended intoxication on such grounds, as one *could* argue for preserving slavery or denying women a role in public affairs. In other words, prohibition might take away one's "right" to order a drink, but it did not threaten basic values or the social order in the way that emancipation or female suffrage did. Both of these movements struck at the core of race- and gender-based power in the United States.

The overriding importance of maintaining this power structure can be glimpsed through the prism of the 1853 World's Temperance Convention, which was held in New York's Metropolitan Hall. "All friends" of this movement had been invited to attend, and among those accepted were several female leaders in the fight for women's rights as well as temperance, including Susan B. Anthony and Lucy Stone. Women were a relatively new and controversial presence in this group, however, and it soon became apparent they were not universally welcomed. At a preliminary planning session in May, attending members agreed that male and female delegates would be seated at the fall convention, but when it was proposed that the thirty-three-year-old Anthony—then serving as secretary of the "Daughters of Temperance"—be named to the convention's business committee, there was an uproar. Most of the strenuously objecting men were members of the clergy. One insisted that women should stay at home where they belonged—not attend meetings.[56] Withdrawing to meet separately, a group of three ministers decided that females should be excluded from the session in September. The women present and their male supporters then walked out. One Presbyterian minister said he was glad to be "rid of the scum of the Convention."[57] The president of the gathering, Mayor Amos C. Barstow of Providence, Rhode Island, noted that "women in breeches" were a disgrace to their sex and only produced mischief.[58]

Two days later, the women and sympathetic men held their own rally at the Broadway Tabernacle, at which Stone, Anthony, and others spoke defiantly against their being left out. The New York *Commercial–Advertiser* declared that a "battle of the sexes" had begun. The editor of the *New York Sun* chided: "The quiet duties of daughter, wife, or mother are not congenial to those hermaphrodite spirits who thirst to win the title of champion of one sex and victor over the other. . . . Could a Christian man, cherishing a high regard for women and for the proprieties of life, feel that he was promoting women's interests by being introduced to a temperance meeting by Miss Susan B. Anthony, her ungainly form rigged out in bloomer costume and provoking the thoughtless to laughter and ridicule by her very motions upon the platform?" At the subsequent annual meeting of the Woman's State Temperance Society, in Rochester, male members (who had previously been welcomed) monopolized the discussion, disparaging women's rights and prompting Anthony and Stanton to resign from the organization they had founded. When Anthony attempted to speak at the World's Temperance Convention that fall, she was hissed and booed and forced to leave the platform without uttering a word.[59] As a result of this furor, the temperance movement eventually split into two wings—one male, the other female.[60] The issue of women's role in public affairs would remain divisive for many decades. Even for women fighting the scourge of alcohol, female suffrage did not evoke much passion.

What both advocates and opponents of temperance correctly perceived was a connection between it and the other major social issues of the day. Some leading women in the fight for prohibition, notably Stanton, saw this as primarily a way to raise awareness of the evils of male domination and degradation of women.[61] And many women joined this cause not only because they considered drink immoral, but because it was contributing to abuse by their husbands. On the other hand, some Americans, particularly in the South, opposed the temperance movement not only because it seemed to be supportive of women's rights but also because of its perceived ties to the movement to free the slaves.[62] In fact, many Southerners worried about links between various "isms" they saw taking hold in the North—"abolitionism, prohibitionism, Fourierism, Mormonism . . . and feminism."[63] In the coming century, opponents of extending the suffrage would also worry that giving women the vote would hasten the arrival of prohibition. Just as some in the women's rights movements saw parallels between their oppression and that of the slaves, so did slave owners and many other Southerners consider challenges from females and blacks as a coordinated attack on white male privilege and preeminence.[64] As was noted earlier, even some men in the antislavery movement objected vociferously to assertive, politically engaged females. Both sides, in other words, saw common threads running through the American social fabric and took their positions on individual issues with this broader awareness in mind. This was how Harriet Beecher Stowe framed her sentimental indictment of the slave system in *Uncle Tom's Cabin*—the hugely successful book that Abraham Lincoln allegedly credited with having swung public opinion against the slave trade and thus brought about the Civil War.[65] Although it nominally dealt with the lot of downtrodden slaves on Simon Legree's plantation, Stowe's novel also illuminated how cruelty toward blacks was intertwined with excessive drinking and the "'enslaved' status of women in patriarchal society."[66] Indeed, some critics have contended that *Uncle Tom's Cabin* was an implicit attack on male dominance and oppression.[67] (Perhaps not coincidentally, its female readers were the most moved by it.)[68] Stowe intimated as much herself, in a prepublication letter in which she said her novel would give "the lights and shadows of the 'patriarchal institution' . . . [showing] the *best side* of the thing, and something *faintly approaching* the worst."[69] Against this evil, the author posits an idealized matriarchy, redolent with Christian virtues of hope, charity, self-sacrifice, and love. In an 1854 "Appeal to the Women of the Free States," Stowe, an ardent advocate of women's rights, made the argument that slavery was inconceivable without the male sex: "There is not a woman in the United States, when the question [of slavery] is fairly put to her, who thinks these things are right."[70]

For progressive-minded women who wanted more freedoms, the linkage between their cause and emancipation of the slaves was revealing and strategically important. As the historian David Brion Davis has observed, these similarities had become apparent to some women involved in the antislavery movement during the last decade of the eighteenth century. Demands for female rights during the French Revolution had contributed to this awareness.[71] In becoming more familiar with the slaves' plight, these women had become more conscious of how they were subjugated by men. As Abby Kelley, a Massachusetts Quaker and radical reformer, would write in 1838, "in striving to strike [the slave's] irons off, we found most surely that we were manacled *ourselves*."[72] By stressing this analogy, protofeminists like Kelley and the Grimké sisters not only helped other women to clarify their thinking and motivated them to join the struggle for legal equality; they also hitched their wagon to a more established and accepted movement. In the 1830s, abolitionism was certainly not a widely embraced cause in the United States, but at least (in the North) it had an organizational structure; a base in states across the Northeast and into the Midwest, particularly in Protestant churches; a raft of prominent speakers like Wendell Phillips, Frederick Douglass, Henry Stanton, and the Rev. Charles G. Finney; fiery editorialists like William Lloyd Garrison as well as savvy legal advisers; and a steady flow of income from generous benefactors to support its activities.[73] By affiliating with antislavery forces, supporters of women's rights could tap into these resources and reach a wider audience than they could by operating independently. There was also a logical affinity between the two movements, as both were advancing human equality, even if they had different priorities in pursuing this objective.

Women's rights advocates could also gain more visibility for their own agenda. The attempt on the part of Elizabeth Cady Stanton, in particular, to accomplish this goal would create friction within abolitionist ranks, as occurred in 1860, when she took advantage of a speech before the AASS to point out that, while freeing the slaves was her "first care," she and other women in this movement were also "working out our own salvation, and hastening the triumph of Love and Liberty over all forms of oppression and cruelty throughout the earth."[74] Stanton pressed this point, despite its contentiousness, because she understood the leverage that was being afforded her through meetings such as this one. The unpleasant truth she and her allies had to quietly acknowledge was that women's rights was a broadly unpopular cause. The fact owed more to demographics than intensity of sentiment. Almost all adult American males had a wife, but relatively few owned slaves. By 1800, an entire region of the country had disavowed slavery or prohibited it, for an economic rationale for owning slaves did not exist in the North. So there was almost no self-interest there in perpetuating the "peculiar institution" (even if there was almost no desire to abolish it either). On the other hand, the emancipation of women was a prospect that struck fear in the hearts of millions of married men—North or South, East or West, young or old, rich or poor—as the statements quoted above amply demonstrate. Here was a social revolution that would change all of these men's lives in a very personal and intimate way. Here was emancipation within their own homes. Throughout the nineteenth century, few men favored this, as witnessed by the minuscule number who lent their support to this cause.[75]

Looking around them in the early decades of the nineteenth century, well-to-do, white Protestant males of English stock saw several developments inimical to their interests that appeared to be converging and gaining momentum. The first of these was political—popular revolutions on both sides of the Atlantic that had overturned established, centrally controlled regimes and replaced them with loosely constituted republican governments, based upon the principles of liberty, equality, and fraternity. These uprisings had dealt a major blow to the previously reigning belief that birth, wealth, and social class should be the determinants of political (and economic) power. The same revolutionary spirit had then caught fire among slaves in the Caribbean. Locke's theories of natural rights and basic human dignity had sufficiently penetrated public thinking to induce the American government to outlaw the slave trade, in 1807, and for England to abolish the chattel system, in 1833. Now there were movements afoot in the United States to do the same, and women were simultaneously agitating for freedoms of their own. In England, the middle classes had won the right to vote. Socially as well as economically, the founding elite was now being challenged: in America, a frontier parvenu like Andrew Jackson had moved into the White House and invited an inebriated plebs to pay him a visit.

Unwelcome multitudes from Ireland and Germany were washing up on the eastern seacoast and taking away jobs from native-born Americans. What was more dismaying, in this "virulently Protestant" young republic, was the fact that most of these immigrants were Roman Catholics, loyal to the pope and therefore not to be trusted. Some incensed nativists also detected a hint of "femininity" in these huddled masses—a "laziness" and passivity borne of their faith that God would provide and alien to the American masculine spirit.[76] So the Irish, in particular, were greeted with harsh words and raised fists. Anti-immigrant violence erupted with alarming frequency from Ohio ("Down with the Roman Butcher!") to Maine.[77]

Overall, mob rioting—against slavery and for slavery, against immigrants and among immigrants, against exploiting banks and flawed elections, against those who advocated women's rights—reached its apex in 1835, when it seemed the nation was devolving into a state of anarchy.[78] Any group or cause perceived as remotely "foreign" was fair game for the angry throngs, as Joseph Smith and his small band of followers discovered when they tried to establish their Church of Latter-day Saints, first in Ohio and then in Missouri. Xenophobia targeted Mexicans south of the border and helped to whip up enthusiasm for sending troops across the Rio Grande under the banner of Manifest Destiny. The major expression of this territorial aggrandizement—migration westward—was a retort to enemies, foreign or domestic, who would deny the exceptionalism of white Protestant manhood. This pushing back of the frontier had revived this guiding force while also fostering a more egalitarian environment: out West, Americans seemed to respect their neighbors more for their individual qualities than their bloodlines. This leveling process was accelerated by the coming of manufacturing to cities and towns in England and the United States, which had created new economic opportunities and upward mobility. Freed from the ceaseless, inescapable toil on farms, married women were starting to earn money of their own, gaining some financial independence and a new sense of their human capabilities.

Economics, in fact, was now the driving force behind most of these transformations. One could see how it all played out by looking at a place like Seneca Falls. It had been first settled by whites in the 1790s, along an eponymous waterfall on the Seneca River, near the northern end of Cayuga Lake. By 1818, a canal had been constructed, linking Seneca Falls to the Erie Canal and facilitating the transporting of goods across the state and beyond. With the arrival of the Rochester-Auburn Railroad, in 1841, the market for these items greatly expanded. After affordable land had become available, a number of companies were attracted to the village, to take advantage of its waterpower for manufacturing purposes. Initially there was only a woolen mill, but soon distilleries, tanneries, flour mills, and factories dotted the river's banks. In the 1840s, several pump manufacturers relocated to Seneca Falls, making it a major center for production of fire engines.[79] Local industries provided numerous new jobs—for immigrant laborers and blacks who came to build the canal as well as for the residents of the village, mostly young and single, but also including a number of married women. It was among this pool of women that the ideas of Elizabeth Cady Stanton and Lucretia Mott first took hold, where the "Declaration of Sentiments" was born.

This was, in short, an Age of Emancipation—a liberating of body and soul among the less advantaged—and its unfolding made men, accustomed to taking their position of power for granted, nervous and apprehensive. Economically they might have felt reasonably secure that they could preserve their unchallenged status, but in terms of social and political power, they were not so sure. Anxiety about preserving white male power was particularly strong in the South. There, dependence on the slave system brought with it a constant worry about white safety and security. Despite tight controls, the possibility of slaves rising up in rebellion could not be discounted. With blacks now accounting for more than half the population in Louisiana, Mississippi, and South Carolina, and over a third of all residents in the Deep South in 1840, many whites felt they were living on top of a racial powder keg: in an instant, they could be engulfed by the unrestrained violence of unfettered human chattel. The uprising led by Nat Turner at a plantation in largely black Southampton County, Virginia, in 1831—which resulted in the deaths of fifty-five whites—seemed a grim harbinger of what might happen someday on a much larger scale. But maintaining the South's rigidly hierarchical social system also depended upon the subjugation of women. The need Southern white men felt to protect, defend, and be responsible for their wives, mothers, sisters, and children was an essential component of their masculine identity—and a basic justification for their dominating domestic life. It is fair to say that the Southern way of life would collapse if the two supporting pillars of slavery and female dependence were to topple. For, if they did, white males would have no more means of demonstrating their central importance as guardians of society.

While the term *patriarchy* is often used loosely to describe any social order in which men control the power structure, there is no question that it applied accurately to the antebellum South. For one thing, male primacy was written into law. In the mid-1830s, every Southern state except Louisiana still operated under British common law, which—among other things—meant that a husband was held legally responsible for his wife. He had to show up in court if she was accused, say, of slander or not paying her debts. When a woman married, her property was transferred to her husband, and she had no further control over it. Getting married thus involved giving up many freedoms and accepting a form of infantilization in return for being well taken care of.[80] Although these same laws were also in effect in the North, the restrictions on women's freedoms were greater south of the Mason-Dixon Line due to distinctive social customs there. In the South, marriage was a woman's destiny and chief obligation. An unmarried female was considered a "stale maid" and an embarrassment to her family. Because of the great importance of marriage and the lack of other options, Southern girls found mates early on.[81] It was not uncommon for them to marry—after obtaining their fathers' consent—by the age of fourteen or fifteen. Once they had said their vows, these young brides were expected to honor their husbands and bear children, soon and often. The fertility rate in the antebellum South was very high: in the absence of contraception, having six or eight offspring in rapid succession was typical, especially among the planter class.[82]

The life of a Southern wife in this social stratum was almost completely dedicated to her domestic duties. (These often included managing the family's slaves.) They were not supposed to take part in political or civic matters, or even express strong opinions on these subjects, since a sign of intelligence on their part could be distressing to their husbands.[83] Instead, women were put on a pedestal, as exemplars of moral purity. Their virtue was to be defended at all costs. On the plantations, white men and women inhabited largely separate spheres, but men held sway. But this belief in the God-given right of men to govern the lives of women was prevalent among the lower classes as well.[84] Like slaves and children, Southern females had to acquiesce to having little freedom. Their subordination was part and parcel of the larger social order. As one historian has summed up the reigning outlook, wives were "expected to recognize their proper and subordinate place and to be obedient to the head of the family. Any tendency on the part of any member of the system to assert themselves against the master threatened the whole, and therefore slavery itself."[85]

Around the time of the American Revolution, evangelical preachers had undermined this hierarchy by speaking before mixed gatherings of blacks, women, tenant farmers, and young people. Planters had looked askance as "allegiance and discipline switched from the patriarch and the family to the clergyman and the congregation."[86] Gradually, however, these ministers had accommodated themselves to Southern mores and abandoned their "subversive" role. But potential greater exercise of freedom by Southern women continued to disconcert their menfolk. Projecting their own notorious sexual proclivities onto their wives, they envisioned that widespread promiscuity and the end of monogamy would ensue if women were given rights like those enjoyed by men.[87] Given the precariousness of their hold over slaves, white Southern males were particularly sensitive to *any* possible challenges to the social status quo, and females clamoring for equality—as some of them were doing up in the North—was unnerving. This new development made many of these men become even more defensive of their way of life and more prepared to defend it—with force if necessary—against attacks from without. When their honor was at stake, they would not hesitate to give their lives to uphold it.

By the middle of the nineteenth century, women were asserting their independence in more subtle but equally consequential ways as well. The female firebrands in the antislavery, temperance, and nascent women's rights movements constituted an unheralded vanguard of their gender; their protests grew up of a broader and more gradual evolution in women's opportunities and roles since the advent of the industrial age. A need for more highly trained workers and an egalitarian, post-Enlightenment outlook encouraged the education of girls as well as boys.[88] Schooling made many of the former feel they could hold their own intellectually with the opposite sex. The free time and extra energy that activists found to devote to their campaigns also benefited apolitical, middle-class, educated women: thanks to greater prosperity, they now had more time to read books, become conversant with current issues, discuss these in letters, and involve themselves in church and community activities. Less well-off working women also improved their lot as a result of the extra money they brought home; many came to see that their lives had value outside the home. These added dimensions to women's lives prior to the Civil War caused a shift in their priorities. Raising a family was no longer all-consuming. Three signs of this change were an increase in the proportion of single women, later marriage, and a related decline in the fertility rate after 1840.[89]

Within the family, wives were shouldering greater responsibility for educating young children than they had during the colonial era (when farming fathers were more apt to be present).[90] This early "feminization" of domestic life made some men uneasy: they missed the ruggedly masculine "old days" when their forbears had chopped down trees in New England forests, tilled fallow soil, hunted for game, and bravely kept Indians at bay.[91] Their hankering for isolation, manly adventure, and heroics was apparent by the tremendous popularity of James Fenimore Cooper's Leatherstocking Tales, a series of frontier novels that appeared between 1823 and 1841. A stanza of Byron's set the tone for one of them, *The Deerslayer*:

> *There is a pleasure in the pathless woods,*
> *There is a rapture on the lonely shore,*

> *There is society where none intrudes,*
> *By the deep sea and music in its roar;*
> *I love not Man the less, but Nature more,*
> *For these, our interviews, from which I steal*
> *From all I may be or have been before,*
> *To mingle with the Universe and feel*
> *What I can ne'er express, yet cannot all conceal.*[92]

This longing also made western migration appealing—as an escape from an overly "civilized" (or "feminized") society.[93] It is not surprising that this impulse was particularly strong among young single males, whose economic and marital prospects in the East were not particularly good since they outnumbered their female counterparts by a sizable margin.[94] Along with a disquieting feeling that women had gained too much influence in the family came complaints about the rejection of traditional femininity by activist women. Many men in both the North and the South disdained such females as perverted sexual hybrids—"hens that crow" in the words of one newspaper editorialist.[95] These "mannish" women violated basic gender stereotypes and thus seemed to go against nature. But these females were also disturbing because they made men unsure about what really distinguished them from the opposite sex—and because they were challenging men over this issue. Partially in response to this assertiveness on the part of some of their female peers, a few prominent Americans in the 1840s urged their fellow men to become more manly by exercising and playing sports.[96]

For a whole host of reasons, tensions were mounting between the sexes at the same time that the two competing sections of the country—free states and slave states—were moving inexorably toward direct confrontation. (This was happening despite an aversion to war among political leaders in the North and the South.) There were no firm alliances within these polarized regions—very few Northerners, for example, endorsed women's rights. Yet the view existed in the Southern states that there was a conspiracy of like-thinking Yankees aligned against them. Abolitionists and female "agitators" were seen as in league and were thus damned with the same epithets. Rightly or wrongly, the politics of race and the politics of gender were seen as intertwined. It is symptomatic of this reality that Rep. Preston Brooks, Democrat of South Carolina, repeatedly brought down the gold tip of his cane on the head of Sen. Charles Sumner, Republican of Massachusetts, on the floor of the Senate on May 22, 1856, not solely because of their opposing views on slavery in Kansas, but also because Sumner had had the temerity to malign the character of Brooks's kinsman and fellow South Carolinian, Sen. Andrew Butler, a few days before by mocking his sense of chivalry, claiming he had chosen the "ugly" and "polluted" "harlot of Slavery" as his mistress.[97] Emotions on both sides leading up to the Civil War were no doubt amplified by sexually inflammatory slurs of this kind. The South prided itself on its code of honor, and opponents of its policies could not resist pointing to the hypocrisy that—to them—lay embedded within it. (The equivalent verbal riposte of proponents of slavery was to label their adversaries "nigger lovers.")[98] Sexual deviation or licentiousness was a charge commonly fired across the Mason-Dixon Line, as it was leveled at other groups, such as blacks and immigrants, to discredit them.[99] Slaves, for example, were accused of "debauchery." These verbal strategies clearly suggest the potency of gender norms and how they were mobilized to denounce one's enemies and "inferiors." The implication was that such sexual deviation placed those tainted by it beyond the pale of civilized society and unworthy of being taken seriously.

To what extent gender issues shaped the perceptions of Northerners and Southerners toward one other, solidified their mutual animosity, and made both sides more willing to go to war is difficult to determine. Since attitudinal polls did not exist back then, there is no way to quantify the impact of particular issues on the two regional psyches. Indeed, very little is known about how ordinary citizens in the North and the South regarded each other—and what inclined them to engage in fratricidal slaughter. While hundreds, if not thousands, of books have been written on the political and economic causes of the War between the States, almost none of them touch upon the individual psychological factors that made this conflict desirable, if not irresistibly compelling, to the hundreds of thousands of young men who willingly enlisted to fight in it.[100] The reasons most often cited for precipitating the Civil War are those that resonated among the ruling elites, but these did not necessarily motivate all able-bodied volunteers. This is certainly the case with slavery. Very few men in New York, Ohio, or Vermont signed up because they wanted to free blacks living on plantations a thousand miles away from their homes.[101] In places that had strong commercial ties with the South, such as western Pennsylvania, few residents wanted to see the chattel system abolished. On the contrary, "the slightest hint that the war might become a crusade to end slavery cast a pall over local events."[102] The goal of freeing the blacks was so unpopular in the North that many in the Union army angrily thought of quitting when they learned President Lincoln had issued his Emancipation Proclamation.[103] The soldiers' disdain, or lack of concern, for blacks was indicative of prevailing Northern sentiment. Most in the region uttered the word "abolitionist" with the same contempt they would display in pronouncing the phrase "free love." In the South, the preservation and the extension of slavery were viewed by political leaders and the planter class as the sine qua non of regional survival. Not surprisingly, a significant percentage of volunteers for Robert E. Lee's Army of Northern Virginia were slave owners who "couldn't imagine life without" the slave system.[104] But only 6 percent of Southern whites owned slaves (in 1830), meaning that the rest of the population had no direct economic stake in the system's continuation.[105] Of course, many nonslaveholders aspired to own slaves and also realized that freeing blacks would be detrimental to their future well-being. In worrying about what would happen if the North won, a large number of Confederate soldiers did mention slavery—but only as the fate that would await *them* at the hands of the Yankees.[106]

Preserving the Union—the reason given by President Lincoln and the Congress for going to war—was also cited frequently by Northern volunteers—at least by the better-educated and literate ones.[107] But statements to this effect in surviving letters and diaries may not reveal the whole truth: soldiers are rarely candid about their innermost feelings, especially when describing them after the fact to their loved ones back home. Nor are they fully aware of their motives for signing up. As occurs in practically all modern wars, a visceral emotional reaction to being attacked—the so-called *rage militaire*—did prompt a wave of enlistments on both sides after the initial bombardment of Fort Sumter.[108] But this subsided quickly, after about two months of fighting.[109] Thereafter, the number of Northern volunteers rose when the Union army lost battles and fell when it won them.[110] This fact suggests that love of country remained a powerful factor in the decision to volunteer, even if many who enlisted had only shallow patriotic roots: some 23 percent of Union troops had been born in foreign countries.[111] It did seem to matter a great deal, as Cyrus F. Boyd, a twenty-five-year-old Iowa native, observed after he enlisted in October 1861: "Everyone seems to be activated by the purest and most patriotic motives," he jotted down in his diary, "and those who are going seem to be moved by a sense of duty." (Like many other Northern soldiers, Boyd had ambivalent feelings about the black race: a supporter of Lincoln in the 1860 election, he favored abolition but did not accept that slaves were his fellow human beings.)[112]

Deep emotional attachment to one's nation (and region) counted for a lot in this conflict since only one side could emerge from it intact: it was literally a war for survival. Pride in one's state often created the most intense form of allegiance, given their separate colonial heritages. This bond carried more sentimental importance in the South than the North. "Old Virginia," a volunteer from the Blue Ridge Mountains in Lee's army, wrote in his journal "whither she goes I'll follow."[113] Confederate soldiers took their duty to safeguard their territory personally, seeing themselves as protectors of their families and homes.[114] If slaves gained their freedom, they feared, their wives would be in danger of being raped. Yankee troops could not be expected to behave liked civilized persons. An 1861 recruitment flyer in Tennessee implored men to sign up, asking rhetorically, "Shall we meet until our homes are laid desolate; until sword and rape shall have visited them?"[115] Ironically, safeguarding their own freedom entailed perpetuating its denial to others—chiefly, to slaves, but also to women. From the perspective of Northern volunteers, the Civil War was also about reasserting control: the South was betraying the country, mocking its social compact with the nation, threatening its very existence by a willful act of rebellion. This attempt to break away was analogous to an unruly child's disobeying its father—or a wife's defying her husband by leaving a marriage—or demanding more rights. Such defiance of their authority was something men of the North would not stand for. For they stood for preserving "domestic tranquility" in both senses of this phrase. Viewed in psychological terms, their rallying to preserve the Union could be seen as expressing an unconscious desire to restore their authority over women as well.[116]

Men on both sides felt their manhood was being put to the test—and they welcomed this. In the months before the war started, the South was abuzz with excitement over the prospect of war. In North Carolina, while women were busy sewing flags and uniforms, "even the small boys were hoping for the time to come when they might be allowed to shoulder rifles and go off to shoot 'Yankees.'" When the news came of the attack on Fort Sumter, one young man tossed his hat in the air, exclaiming, "Hurrah for South Carolina. I'm going to be a soldier now."[117] Southerners posited this test in terms of honor: it fell within the parameters of the code that they had been raised to uphold and that had a long, storied history in their part of the country.[118] Since the early frontier days, backcountry settlers had relied upon their own guns to defend their animals and property and had become accustomed to responding to insults with violence.[119] They felt that Yankees lacked this ennobling quality: instead, they were, as one preacher in New Orleans put it in a May 1861 speech, guilty of "barbarism" and "wicked and cruel aggression."[120] Cold-blooded and devoid of moral principles, Northerners only cared about money.[121] A Georgia volunteer was disgusted to find Yankee prisoners-of-war "all low flung and vulgar."[122]

Of course, in their own eyes, Union soldiers had ideals, too. They, too, believed in the masculine ideals of "courage, manliness, and self-control" and felt their time had now come to live up to them. They, too, were willing to place that obligation ahead of their own well-being.[123] They accepted that their sacrifice might be necessary for a greater good to endure.[124] They agreed with Oliver Wendell Holmes that war was "man's destiny," and many went off to battle ready for their rendezvous with it.[125] William Wheeler, a bachelor graduate of Yale, told a former classmate that he hoped his "useless, selfish life" might somehow be "expiated" if he were to die for his country.[126] Not all potential recruits saw the war in these terms, however. Especially in the North, many were more pragmatic minded, worried about their own safety and eager to profit materially from serving in uniform. For them, major inducements to join were enlistment bonuses, the promise of steady pay, and the assurance they would serve under experienced officers, not prone to recklessness. Money was a major incentive to join voluntarily.[127] Wages offered by the Union army—about twelve dollars a month—were enough for a bachelor but not sufficient to persuade a married man with children to step forward.[128] Group pressure also played a role: men tended to enlist together with others in their towns and villages, and those who held back risked being branded cowards.[129] Members of minority groups, such as free blacks and Irish American Catholics, signed up to attest their commitment to the nation, display ethnic pride, and gain greater acceptance.[130] Later in the war, fear of being drafted also made many Northerners decide to enlist.[131]

All these reasons may partially explain why soldiers signed up to fight in the Civil War—or, at any rate, how they justified this decision to themselves, friends, and loved ones. But what is missing from these explanations is the influence of preexisting attitudes, personal experiences, and elements of the Zeitgeist in predisposing young men to enlist. Choosing to risk one's life in war does not happen spontaneously, on the spur of the moment, even though, at times, it may appear this way. In the months and years preceding the Confederate shelling of Fort Sumter, talk of the two sections of the country eventually fighting each other was in the air, and men of military age would have had plenty of opportunity to ponder their options.[132] (Over four months elapsed between the date that South Carolina seceded from the Union and the commencing of hostilities in April 1861.) While it is clearly not possible to unravel all of the factors that might have affected the decisions of individual men, several *generational* circumstances arguably had a broad impact on making war attractive—in one region or the other, or in both. One of these was the volatility of the times. As was noted earlier, the antebellum era was marked by increasing disorder and violence. In addition to widespread rioting, men were resorting to their fists, clubs, axes, rifles, and the hangman's noose with alarming frequency. In the South, crowds lynched rebellious slaves with impunity. In the West, vigilantes imposed their own law in gold-mining camps.[133] In other parts of the frontier, men regularly settled disputes with duels. In the swamps of southern Florida, intrepid bands of Seminole Indians fought off federal troops for seven years. Spurred by the fiery abolitionist John Brown, Kansans went on a killing spree over the slavery issue in 1854, leaving two hundred dead by the end of the year. These sporadic eruptions showed that the forces of law and order were not adequate to maintain peace and security in many parts of the country. They also reinforced a belief that force was the only effective way to resolve conflict. This conclusion made a prospective sectional war over slavery seem not only inevitable but also the best way to settle this issue, once and for all.

The three major social crusades of the antebellum period—temperance, abolitionism, and women's rights—tended to foment violence because each threatened to overturn a way of life. White males realized they had much to lose if these movements succeeded: a ban on alcohol consumption would take away one of their most valued diversions and "domesticate" them against their will; the end of slavery would elevate black men so that they could compete for jobs (in the North) and extract revenge against their white masters (in the South); and equal rights for women would undo the clearly demarcated sex roles that most men saw as essential to preserving their masculinity. As emphasized by the sociologist Michael Kimmel, nineteenth-century American men partially defined their manhood by a "repudiation of the feminine, a resistance to mothers' and wives' attempts to civilize them"[134]—what Twain's Huck Finn had feared.

Mob hostility to these three causes was only the most flagrant form of a pervasive male opposition to changes in the gender status quo. Major writers of this period depicted a broad disdain for females who violated these norms, even if these men of letters did not always personally agree with this point of view. Herman Melville, for example, created in *The Confidence Man* a female character named Goneril—described by one critic as a "Medusa" figure of "female monstrosity," who "casts spells on or devours others, particularly men"[135]—although he was generally sympathetic to women's demands for more rights.[136] Edgar Allan Poe had no sympathy for women's rights advocates, bemoaning, in one anonymous 1859 essay, a future in which "woman is left to lord it over us, and the sceptre of her tyranny reigns permanent."[137] Poe's short stories also revealed a predilection for subjugating females, with a decided preference for dead ones.[138] Novelists like Melville and Cooper often dealt with the "woman question" by avoiding it—writing tales of exploration in which females were largely absent. (Melville's *Billy Budd* did implicitly take up gender-role tensions in portraying the clash between a feminized Budd—who is likened to a "beautiful woman in one of Hawthorne's minor tales"[139]—and a cruel and vindictive Claggart.) Even an eventual convert to abolitionism like Henry David Thoreau was disinclined to treat women as equals, finding them intellectually inferior.[140] Of course, misogyny was not the only reaction to women's advances in the first half of the century: authors and intellectuals like Emerson, Hawthorne, Walt Whitman, and Bronson Alcott championed this cause, along with male New England abolitionists Garrison, Phillips, and Henry Ward Beecher.

It remains irrefutable, however, that most leading figures in American cultural life during the antebellum era did not favor parity between the sexes.

Feelings on this issue ran deep on both sides. So did emotions on the slavery question, on alcohol, on immigrants, on war with Mexico, on Manifest Destiny, and a host of controversial issues. But none of these had quite the same impact on the daily lives of millions of Americans that the proper and appropriate roles for women did. Considerable unhappiness, ridicule, consternation, anger, condemnation, and antipathy were evoked by the very mention of "woman's rights" in the decades before the Civil War. Much of this negative reaction on the part of men had to be restrained: the dicta of polite society prevented them from speaking frankly. Northern men coming of age then were even less likely to voice any misgivings about the aspirations of women for more education and freedoms. Most of these young men were either courting or hoped soon to start doing so, and it would not have been particularly politic to reveal such opinions, at least not in educated circles in the North. But, inwardly, many were unhappy about this new female assertiveness and glad for an opportunity to squash it and restore traditional gender roles. The coming of war in 1861, with its attendant elevation of the masculine virtues of courage and self-sacrifice, provided this opportunity. This was even truer in the South, where war was seen as the ultimate test and validation of manhood. Indeed, regional differences figured prominently in how young men reacted to stirrings of what later would come to be known as "feminism." Below the Mason-Dixon Line, support for female rights was practically nonexistent.[141] Southern gentlemen were aghast at reports of Northern women taking part in meetings, holding forth on matters about which they had no business having an opinion, let alone trying to convince others to join the fight with them. Wrote George Fitzhugh, a proslavery Virginia lawyer, in response to Harriet Beecher Stowe:

> Nothing proved the dissolution and demoralization of antebellum Free Society more than the emergence there of women who assumed a masculine character and bestirred themselves with cant about their "rights." It was unnatural and offensive. . . . Woman naturally shrinks from public gaze, and from the struggle and competition of ordinary life. She

has but one right, and that is the right of protection. . . . But if she insists upon a public role as her right, is coarse and masculine, man will loathe and despise her, and end by abusing her.[142]

The Yankee "she-man" Fitzhugh and many of contemporaries envisioned with horror made a mockery of the Southern ideal of womanhood, and of the chivalric code that upheld it. Linked as it was in their minds with the abolition of slavery, this Northern version of the opposite sex posed a grave threat to Southern values and way of life. This coupling of dangers reinforced the region's willingness to fight for its integrity—moral as well as territorial. Southern men would have to stand up and protect both their own status and their womenfolk if the North did not stop meddling in their affairs. Despite Lincoln's election in 1860 on a Republican platform promising not to interfere with slavery in existing states, many Southerners were convinced that abolitionist sentiment was well entrenched in the North and that a Northern victory would spell the end of the slave system. (John Brown's raid on Harper's Ferry in October 1859 convinced many remaining doubters that this would happen.)[143] But white men in the North had no more desire to free the slaves than they did to give women the vote. Reading *Uncle Tom's Cabin* may have stirred many hearts, but it did not convert the North to the abolitionist cause. The resentment and frustration felt by many Northern men over the demands that were being made on behalf of slaves and women could not as easily find a release as they could in the South. Aside from those who stormed abolitionist meetings or threw garbage at "hermaphrodites" wearing bloomers, Northern males did not generally vent their unhappiness over these movements so overtly. They respected the social taboo against directing violence at women.[144] For their anger to be expressed it had to be aimed at another target. They could not vilify the South on these grounds, because its white inhabitants shared their views about emancipated women and blacks. But they could contemplate going to war against this region by transferring to it their bottled-up negative feelings about social pressures for change in the North.

There is historical evidence that such emotional projection can occur. For instance, the incidence of lynching in the South between the 1880s and 1920s was inversely correlated with the price of cotton. When prices fell, producers released their anger on helpless blacks.[145] Displacement of repressed aggressive impulses is, in fact, a widely acknowledged psychological process.[146] This can often be aimed at "outsiders" when the actual cause is an "in-group" off-limits to direct attack, as women and other "protected" groups normally are. This kind of transference would help to explain the sudden outpouring of hostility toward the South once the war started. Previously, many in the North may have disparaged their Southern countrymen as economically backward or mocked them—as Frederick Olmstead had—as prone to "swell, strut, bluster, and bully," but few had expressed hatred of those living below the Mason-Dixon Line.[147] There had been no previous public demonstrations calling for war against the South. The Confederate shelling of Fort Sumter seems to have been only the trigger releasing feelings that had been building up for some time. It is entirely plausible that the origins of this anger lay not below the Mason-Dixon Line, but much closer to home.

As was noted above, Northern outrage over slavery had been enflamed by Harriet Beecher Stowe's *Uncle Tom's Cabin*. Ostensibly, this was because of its moving descriptions of the callousness and cruelty shown by Simon Legree and his fellow plantation owners toward their slaves. But Stowe's novel was not only about the evil of slavery. Its larger moral protest was aimed at any system of power that subjugates particular groups, denies its members their rights, and treats them abusively and inhumanely. In the 1850s, black slaves were not the only group in America to be so oppressed, and white slaveholders were not the only group acting so oppressively. The Southern planters were merely the most egregious and repellent example of a white male power structure that Stowe objected to and in her other writings condemned. Because she could anticipate that most of her readers would be Northern white, middle-class women—as turned out to be the case—the New England novelist cast her tale of the slave system in a way that would emotionally engage this particular audience.[148] If many married women in this category could not relate directly to the plight of slaves, they could see parallels between the degradation of Southern blacks and the harsh, inconsiderate, and condescending treatment *they* received at the hands of their husbands. As one commentator on the novel has succinctly expressed it, slavery had a "familial analogy."[149]

Much of the emotional power of *Uncle Tom's Cabin* stems from this implicit association between the oppression of slaves and women. The reader may come to understand that the root of evil lies not in slave-holding per se, but in the construct of male power that allows slavery to exist. In her novel, Stowe contrasts the loving married relationships between slaves like George and Eliza with the hierarchical, distanced ones between planters and their wives. She further distinguishes white patriarchy, with its reliance on rigid control and violence, from its more open and caring black version. Tom represents an alternative male authority figure to the aggressive, bullying Legree.[150] Full of good sense, dignity, stoic forbearance, and "fraternal love," Tom is presented as a "sort of patriarch" on religious matters, but one who exercises his influence through his "cultivation of mind" and skill as a reader of the Bible.[151] These characteristics earn him genuine respect. While he is an enslaved black man, Tom stands as a paragon of the Christian gentleman Stowe and other progressive-minded Northern women hoped would become ascendant in the future, replacing the coldly controlling type with which they were well familiar.

By contrast, Tom's owner, Shelby, acts heartlessly in deciding to sell Tom, not bothering to inform his wife in advance and thus deepening her unhappiness. Shelby's wife—a stand-in for Stowe[152]—empathizes with the plight of the "poor, simple, dependent" slaves she has tried to raise as Christians and attempts to prevent Tom from being sold to pay off some debts. Imploring her husband to break off the deal with a slave trader, she says she will sacrifice anything to keep Tom together with his parents, to end this "cruel business." But Shelby will not relent. Instead, he tells his wife that he and the other planters only become resentful "when women and ministers come out broad and square, and go beyond us in matters of either modesty or morals."[153] For Shelby, life depends on conducting business, and business—in the end—has precious little to do with morality or compassion. By drawing this contrast, *Uncle Tom's Cabin* aligns white women with the oppressed slaves—against overbearing white males. In other words, the novel fosters an interracial alliance based on Christian religious principles, while isolating and castigating a ruthless capitalist ethos that ignores these values. However, since it was overtly a condemnation of slavery, this denunciation of male power remained veiled. The moral indignation felt by female readers of Stowe's novel could be safely focused on Southern planters, instead of on Northern businessmen, clergy, and domineering husbands. *Uncle Tom's Cabin* thus tapped into a wellspring of buried resentment without forcing these readers to become fully aware of the real source of their outrage. Northern mothers and wives who were profoundly moved by *Uncle Tom's Cabin* would use their moral influence to urge their sons, husbands, and brothers to go to war to end the slave system, not realizing they were actually making a case for their own liberation. The most potent propaganda tool for promoting war against the South was, at heart, a protofeminist tract.[154] Ironically, many men who volunteered for the Union army were electing to fight for a cause that was ultimately counter to their own best interests. In going off to restore federal authority over a rebellious Confederacy, they were inadvertently furthering another kind of revolution against their own authority back home.

However, in the short term, the commencing of hostilities between the North and the South was anything but beneficial to the campaign for women's rights. War abruptly halted this movement's advance just when it seemed that its ultimate goal of full and equal rights for women was close at hand. In 1860, battle-hardened after over a dozen years in the forefront of the struggles for women's rights and temperance, Elizabeth Cady Stanton—then in her mid-forties, her hair prematurely but luxuriantly white, her last child no longer a toddler—could look back with satisfaction at the progress that she had helped to achieve. Some fourteen states had recently changed their laws so that the property rights of wives were respected. Women could now sue for damages in court. Colleges and other institutions that closed their doors to women were under attack. The movement started in Seneca Falls in 1848 had spread throughout the North, holding annual conventions and collecting funds to spread its message further. In towns and villages from New Hampshire to Wisconsin, small bands of women were meeting to air their grievances. In New York, Stanton and her even more single-minded ally, Susan B. Anthony, were pressing the case for female suffrage, child custody, and the right to keep the money they earned. A few years before, in 1854, Stanton had addressed the state legislature in Albany, not mincing her words: "We demand the full recognition of all our rights as citizens of the Empire State. . . . We are moral, virtuous, and intelligent, and in all respects equal to the proud white man himself."[155] Her use of the word "white" was telling: Stanton did not want to ally her cause too closely with that of enslaved blacks, who, she readily acknowledged, were not the equal of her own race. (Some years later Stanton would grouse about women like her being treated the same as "Patrick and Sambo and Hans and Yung Tung who do not know the difference between a Monarchy and a Republic, who would never read the Declaration of Independence or Webster's spelling book.")[156] Despite the New York lawmakers' failure to heed her plea, progressive women in America could congratulate themselves on having gained more ground in the past decade than in any comparable period in the republic's history.

Then the war came. Stanton was briefly flummoxed: what would this mean for her cause? The Christmas before, ever-prudent Henry had written her to "keep quiet & let the Revolution go on," and she came to see both the wisdom and the necessity in that piece of advice.[157] She foresaw that a Northern victory would end with the slaves being freed, and then women would be emancipated as well.[158] Helping the Union to prevail was now what mattered most. Stanton welcomed this new opportunity: she told her closest confidante, Anthony, it was "impossible for her to think or speak on anything, but the War."[159] She stopped giving speeches about the plight of women. It was now, as an unhappy Anthony would sum up a few years later, "a war for the negro."[160] Just as would happen at the outbreak of World War I—in England and the United States—agitation for female suffrage abruptly ceased. Tens of thousands of Northern women stopped fighting for their sex and started fighting for their country. Victory for the Union was almost universally regarded as more important than winning new freedoms for women. That struggle could wait until the South had been defeated. In their patriotic devotion and eagerness to make sacrifices for the common good, female activists now strove to emulate the men who were grabbing rifles and heading off to war. As Stanton would later—somewhat hyperbolically— describe this response, "While he [the male soldier] buckled on his knapsack and marched forth, she planned the campaigns that brought the nation victory; fought in the ranks when she could do so without detection; inspired the sanitary commission; gathered needed supplies for the army; provided nurses for the hospitals; comforted the sick; smoothed the pillows of the dying; inscribed the last messages of love to those far away; and marked the resting places where the brave men fell."[161] Women also raised considerable sums of money for the Union cause.[162]

Stanton's followers in the newly formed Woman's Loyal National

League followed her example and threw themselves into this new crusade.[163] Four months after President Lincoln issued his Emancipation Proclamation, they endorsed the black man's right to vote. Stanton did not trust the president to follow through after the war and voted in 1864 for John C. Frémont instead.[164] Eventually, these activists collected over three hundred thousand signatures in support of this cause and had two black freemen deposit these bundled documents on the desk of a now mostly recovered but dumbfounded Senator Sumner.[165] They contained more signatures than had ever been submitted to Congress, on any issue. But while they were doing all this, the men who wrote the laws, sensing a masculine wind rising across the land, puffed up with war bravado, started to undo much that Stanton and Anthony had fought so long and hard to accomplish. Up in Albany, state legislators took back the rights they had only recently given women—first property rights, then the right to custody of their children following divorce.[166] Stanton fumed, but bit her tongue. She silently pondered her next move. It came, with her usual dramatic flourish, only months after the war had ended—in an article calling for *universal* suffrage. To further this end, Stanton joined forces with Anthony, Frederick Douglass, and Lucy Stone to establish the American Equal Rights Association. At the outset, it sought to link female and black suffrage. Later in 1866, Stanton, Anthony, and a group of her close female allies submitted a petition to Congress asking for a Constitutional amendment allowing women—"the only remaining class of disenfranchised citizens"—to have the vote.[167] This went nowhere. Her male friends told her they could not support this. Wendell Phillips declared flatly: "One question at a time. This is the negro's hour."[168] Stanton's cousin, the unwavering abolitionist Gerrit Smith, ignored her letter asking that, under the Fourteenth Amendment, representation in Congress not be decided only by the number of a state's *male* residents.[169] (This would mark the first time that the word *male* would appear in the Constitution.) The House and the Senate went ahead and voted for this amendment without including the words "female" or "universal." Women would have to wait half a century for their chance. By then, Susan B. Anthony would have been dead fourteen years, Elizabeth Cady Stanton nearly twenty, and Lucretia Mott forty years.

Advocates for women should have expected this rebuff. Male support for female suffrage was minimal before the war, and the rush of testosterone and masculine pride once Northern men slipped into blue uniforms and started to fight for the nation's survival made women's claim to equal citizenship seem even more outlandish and inappropriate. Instead, many liberals now rallied vociferously behind the antislavery movement: it was transformed from a "sentimental" cause, courtesy of *Uncle Tom's Cabin*, into a vigorous masculine campaign, destined to triumph on the battlefield.[170] Stanton's gamble that standing firm with the abolitionists might bring women, along with blacks, some fruits of victory did not pay off. Because of the war, the "woman problem" was now on the back burner of American politics. Gender relations reverted to traditional form. As one historian has put it, the call to arms revived "long-standing notions of male protection and female submissiveness."[171] This pattern ran deep and close to the surface in the South, but in the North it had lost some of its relevance as middle-class society had been somewhat "feminized" in the decades leading up to the War between the States. With military service having been left to professional soldiers since the Revolution, few American men had experienced the exhilaration and satisfying rewards that came with combat. On the contrary, many of them, particularly those in the educated and moneyed classes, had come to wonder what "masculinity" really meant and how it was distinguished from drawing room conversations about the nature of God. The coming of war dispelled these questions.

Ralph Waldo Emerson was typical of the Northern elite and its wartime "conversion" to manly values. Descended from a long line of Unitarian ministers, he had been elected class poet at Harvard; written love poems to a classmate coincidentally named Gay;[172] helped to run a school for young ladies; married briefly—only to lose his young wife to tuberculosis two years later; lived with his mother in his thirties before finding a second wife; and made a literary career for himself as a lecturer and with writings on nature, self-reliance, and transcendentalism—an intellectual movement in which he was a primary driving force. A pacifist, Emerson had given a lecture in 1838 that dismissed war as belonging to an early phase in humanity's development: "Nothing is plainer," he had affirmed, "than that the sympathy with war is a juvenile and temporary state."[173] He was an advocate of women's rights and a close friend of Margaret Fuller, the leading "feminist" thinker of her day. Like many men of his social position, Emerson opposed slavery but did not embrace abolitionism—until shortly before the war began.[174] Then he underwent a surprising, dramatic transformation. He noted in his journal that the times now called for "genuine, sincere, frank & bold" action, for a new "masculine morality," with less heed to be paid to that quaint antebellum notion of "sentiment." He stopped supporting equal status for women and started talking about the virtues of "muscular Christianity" as an antidote to what he now saw as an overly "feminized" society.[175] According to his friend Nathaniel Hawthorne, Emerson was now "breathing slaughter like the rest of us" after having been in a funk for some time until the first crack of rifles had reverberated inside his head.[176]

For the men who fought in the war and survived, it was a life-altering experience. Like all wars, the initial euphoria gave way to disillusionment and bitterness as the battles dragged on for years and the casualty lists grew longer without the quick, glorious victories the recruits on both sides had foreseen when they had marched through their hometowns on the way to the front.[177] Cyrus Boyd, an orderly sergeant with the Fifteenth Iowa Infantry, found himself engulfed in the butchery of modern war during the Battle of Shiloh in April of 1862. After more than a day of incessant attacks by Confederate forces, Boyd and his comrades were driven back into a flat roadbed nicknamed the "Hornet's Nest" because of the constant hum of rifle bullets whizzing by their heads. All around him he could hear the groans of the dead and dying. Boyd came across one soldier who had been torn in half by a cannon ball. Another had had his head shot off. "War is hell broke loose and benumbs all the tender feelings of men and makes of them brutes," Boyd found time to record in his diary on April 9. "I do not want to see any more such scenes and yet I would not have missed this for any consideration."[178] In this last, incongruous comment, Boyd inadvertently conveyed a sentiment shared by many of his fellow soldiers: war *was* exhilarating. Even after having engaged Southern troops in fierce fighting for two days in October 1862, near Corinth, Mississippi, Boyd had not lost his emotional attachment to the cause he was defending. Looking out from his fortified position once the guns had finally fallen silent, he recorded: "How glorious the old flag looked as it again floated over the works in the smoke and breath of battle."[179] In his mind as well as those of many other soldiers, the random slaughter attendant upon this war had not invalidated the rewards it would bring to the victors—to individual men and to the countries they loved so dearly.

The positive benefits of partaking of this conflict included sexual ones. Young men who had previously had no or little relations with women found abundant opportunities for such diversions during the lull between battles. In what has been characterized as the greatest growth period in the sex industry in the United States, prostitutes and camp followers swarmed around military barracks: one survey of this phenomenon found that almost a quarter of a million Union soldiers—or one in ten—were treated for venereal disease.[180] In cities near where troops were billeted for long periods of time, brothels sprang up as opportunistically as they have in all wars, and men frequented them with the same abandon those about to face death always evince.[181] As many as one in twenty of the women who migrated to the United States during the Civil War were forced into prostitution to meet this demand and help others reap the profits from it.[182] Sex and liquor were the two palliatives that kept morale from slipping. (They also interfered with fighting the war: after the Battle of Corinth, Cyrus Boyd found his camp full of "fastwomin'" who were "demoralizing" many of his fellow soldiers and "with the help of bad whisky will lay many of them out."[183] At another point, he observed that "whiskey and sexual vices carry more soldiers off than bullets.")[184] Boyd also experienced how popular a man in uniform was with the ladies, confessing in his diary that he had had his pick among the local ladies while he was based in Keokuk, Iowa. The greater freedom to indulge in these pleasures stalled the temperance movement temporarily and challenged Americans' puritanical views on sex.

Perhaps for this reason, but more likely because of the heightened fragility of life and desire for personal perpetuity, Americans produced a surprising number of children in the decade that encompassed the Civil War. Despite the long disruptions of marriages and engagements and the great loss of life during the war—some 620,000 men[185]—the nation's population grew by over 7 million during the 1860s.[186] Not surprisingly, most of this increase occurred in the victorious Northern states.[187] Those below the Mason-Dixon Line experienced a significant drop in fertility and did not return to prewar levels until the 1880s.[188] This was largely attributable to the dearth of eligible men. In one town in South Carolina, for example, 613 of the 2,137 young men who enlisted did not come back. Many of them left widows behind.[189] The contrast between the two sections suggests this "baby boom" may have been one of the benefits of being on the winning side. Union soldiers who returned home physically intact brought with them the aura of conquering hero, and this—plus the fact that their postwar circumstances were economically propitious—encouraged married couples to have children. (As in other wars, some couples also made the decision to propagate *before* the soldier-husband went off to war. As often happens at the start of hostilities, there was a sharp spike in the marriage rate circa 1861.)[190] The number of marriages also increased after the separations and delays necessitated by war, but, here, too, the North benefited more than the South. In Massachusetts, for example, the marriage rate rose from 20.15 per 1,000 persons in 1860 to 22.15 in 1866.[191] In the South, the deaths of so many men of marriageable age, postwar economic hardship, social disruption, and a generally pessimistic outlook made marriage and producing offspring less inviting.

If Northern men gained from the war *as men*, their counterparts down South suffered a devastating reversal of fortune. The linchpin of Southern manhood was its protective role. This rationalized white male dominion over both females and slaves, who were vulnerable and defenseless on their own and had to be taken care of. (Wartime letters written between Confederate president Jefferson Davis and his wife, Varina, frequently use the word "helpless" in referring to the plight of Southern women and children, even though the word hardly applied to her.)[192] Defense of the nation and defense of family were inextricably entwined in the Southern ethos.[193] Appeals for volunteers to hold back invading Yankees were couched in terms of guarding the "softer sex" from harm.[194] The enemy was as wont to ravage their wives and daughters as it was to destroy their farms and cities. So, when Northern armies breached the Mason-Dixon Line and thrust deep into Southern territory, the consequences were personal as well as military. When the great test of Southern manhood finally arrived, it turned into a fiasco. Already badly demoralized and mentally defeated, the men of the South did not put up much resistance. Many, in fact, lay down their arms and fled.[195] Thus, when Gen. William T. Sherman's army left in its wake a swath of smoldering plantations, twisted railroad tracks, stripped storehouses, and flattened fields as it marched from Atlanta to Charleston in late 1864, it also left the South's chivalric code in tatters. This invasion, as one historian has put it, "was like a driving motor behind the collapse of the old patriarchal, slaveholding household structure."[196] Union soldiers later added to the insult by insisting on singing bars from "Marching through Georgia" with stanzas like these:

> "Sherman's dashing Yankee boys will never reach the coast!"
> So the saucy rebels said and 'twas a handsome boast
> Had they not forgot, alas! to reckon with the Host
> While we were marching through Georgia.[197]

Even worse, with their men absent or impotent, a number of Southern women were raped: some 250 Union soldiers were court-martialed for this crime.[198] Many thousands more females suffered other indignities at the hands of Northern troops—having their homes invaded and occupied, being reduced to living in fear for their lives and those of their children. More generally, however, women in the Deep South lost confidence in their men's ability to take care of them, and this only deepened male feelings of inadequacy and failure on the battlefield, much as veterans might later proudly talk of upholding their honor.[199] Southern manhood was shattered.[200] What further emasculated these men was that many of their wives, out of necessity, had stepped into the breach and taken up responsibilities that were quintessentially male: keeping marauding Yankees at bay with a cocked rifle and stubbornly asserting their Southern pride. Many lamented they weren't men, that they couldn't go off and join the fighting.[201] Other women volunteered to tend wounded soldiers, in local hospitals or in their homes. A few even served as spies for the Confederacy. Because of their wartime actions in defense of their region, Southern women seemed temporarily to have exchanged places with men—an unthinkable state of affairs in this part of the country. The old order was temporarily suspended.[202] "Our whole world is demoralized— turned topsy-turvy," one mother told her daughters.[203] While men had been exposed as "braggarts and hypocrites," their wives had kept the South together in its final months.[204] The most damning image of this subversion of traditional gender roles was that of President Jefferson Davis disguising himself as a woman, wearing one of his wife's black shawls, running to evade capture by Union forces in May 1865.[205] This incident, immortalized (and exaggerated) in endless retelling, pictorial form, and even song, made a bitter mockery of all that Southern white males had once professed to be.[206] Not only had white males proved incapable of protecting their womenfolk, they also had to endure the humiliation of seeing newly emancipated black men being affirmed as their equals—both as free men and as brave soldiers.[207] The old racial and gender hierarchies lay in shambles.

This tremendous psychological setback came hand-in-glove with the South's costly defeat at the hands of the Union armies. After more than holding their own early in the war, Rebel forces were gradually worn down and overwhelmed by a superiorly equipped opponent. In battle after battle, they suffered grievous losses of life. By the time all the guns finally fell silent, after Lee surrendered at Appomattox, 18 percent of all Southern males between the ages of thirteen and forty-three lay dead—three times the percentage in the North—even though significantly more Union men had perished during the conflict.[208] This destruction of life and dismantling of white male power during the war was followed by federal military occupation, the adoption of a constitutional amendment granting voting rights to black males and simultaneous suspension of these rights for senior Confederate officials, and the arrival of hated "carpetbaggers" from the North, to oversee the writing of new state constitutions. In all senses of the word, the region—and its men—lay defeated. Even though many Southern wives would dutifully "stand by their men" and help them to regain their self-respect in the following decades, it would take a long time for this to happen.[209] Indeed, one could argue that white Southern males have never fully recovered what they once had. They would remain loyal to a "Lost Cause."

Clearly the impact of seeing so many men blown apart or shot at close quarters was sobering and deeply distressing; it left lasting emotional scars, including feelings of guilt and a revulsion against further violence.[210] But the fact that the war continued to be celebrated in literature for several decades afterward (Stephen Crane's 1900 *Red Badge of Courage* being the most notable example)[211] testifies to its positive impact on the Northern male psyche—perhaps because the reality was sanitized in the letters written home and in the stories survivors would later tell. John William De Forest's realistic novel *Miss Ravenel's Conversion from Secession to Loyalty* (1867) well captured this masculine metamorphosis.

An affluent and pious son of a Northern cotton manufacturer and a captain with a Connecticut regiment during the war, De Forest alluded to some of his own war experiences in telling the tale of an effete Northerner named Edward Colburne ("bookish, temperate, and sentimental"), who ends up competing against a far more physically imposing Southerner, a Virginia graduate of West Point fighting on the Confederate side, for the affections of the eponymous Lillie Ravenel. The lady in question prefers men who fight, and it is only by becoming a skilled and ruthless warrior that Colburne can ultimately win her heart.[212] While by no means a representative story of how men responded to the mayhem and bloodshed they encountered during the war, De Forest's novel tapped into a more general feeling among American men that the Civil War had redeemed their manhood and proper place in society. The historian John Stauffer has illustrated how men's positive image of themselves was revived by describing the outrage ignited by an article in the *Atlantic Monthly* by Harriet Beecher Stowe revealing that the poet Byron had committed incest.[213] Some 15,000—presumably male—readers cancelled their subscriptions out of dismay that this "male liberator and freedom fighter par excellence" would be cast in such a light. Some branded Stowe's article "revolting and obscene."[214] Shock, grief, and revulsion over the war's "harvest of death" on a scale never seen before may have been one Northern response to the war, but a resurgence of male heroism was clearly another.[215]

This enduring glorification of martial accomplishments helped to shape the nationalistic outlook of succeeding generations. After more than a decade of repressing memories of its horrors, Northerners started to look back on the Civil War as the seminal event in their lives: the battlefield became the defining metaphor for life.[216] Northern politics was essentially militarized, with parties approaching each election campaign as if it were another war. A "tough-mindedness" distinguished public discourse, setting it apart from the "feminine" talk in the home. Even the way middle-class boys were now taught to cultivate stoicism, loyalty, physical strength, and courage showed the impact of this conflict.[217] Uniforms were worn by groups like the Salvation Army as a testament to their manliness.[218] War veterans routinely made appearances at major civic events. Military service cemented men's importance and legitimized their right to lead the nation. Every occupant of the White House from

1869 to the end of the century—except for Grover Cleveland—had fought for the Union side.[219] By the mid-1890s, expressions of American patriotism routinely referred to the example set by soldiers during the Civil War. At a Harvard Memorial Day address in 1895, on a field named for six of the university's fallen alumni, Oliver Wendell Holmes Jr., who had left Harvard his senior year to serve with the Massachusetts militia, observed, "But in the midst of doubt, in the collapse of creeds, there is one thing I do not doubt, that no man who lives in the same world with most of us can doubt, and that is that the faith is true and adorable which leads a soldier to throw away his life in obedience to a blindly accepted duty, a cause in which he little understands."[220] When Theodore Roosevelt addressed Congress after the end of the Spanish-American War, he conjured up a similar image of those who had "saved" the Union—men without whose "steadfast prowess in the greatest crisis in our history, all our annals would be meaningless, and our great experiment in popular freedom and self-government a gloomy failure."[221]

Even when war itself was not on the horizon, it was employed as a metaphor for the therapeutic value that exertion and struggle can lend to a society that has lost its bearings and innermost convictions. Thus, even the philosopher William James, who had been tempted to join the Union army but ultimately chose not to, and who later held more pacifistic views, drew upon his country's legacy of the "warlike type" to inspire his twentieth-century readers to reinvigorate American society, in his 1906 essay "The Moral Equivalent of War."[222] Here James contended that "militarism is the great preserver of our ideals of hardihood, and human life with no use for hardihood would be contemptible." The salutary effect of the Civil War on Northern consciousness is also evident in the proliferation of war memorials and monuments attesting to the courage shown and sacrifices made by Union troops and their leaders.[223] Its enduring appeal to those who fought in the Union ranks is further reflected in their attendance of reunions for many years afterward.

As far as relations with the opposite sex are concerned, men in the North and the South took somewhat different paths. In the South, because of the loss of so many husbands and prospective marriage partners, many women now had to support themselves. There were simply not enough men to go around. This need spurred the creation of educational institutions for females including a number of teacher-training schools. In the ensuing decades, several formerly all-male universities such as Duke (then Trinity College) also admitted women—mostly ones from the middle class. In addition, a small number of women entered into businesses and took over managerial duties. Some ventured into the still male-dominated sphere of politics. A few offered their services as teachers in freedmen's aid societies formed to prepare emancipated blacks for citizenship.[224] But, for women as a whole, the woeful state of the Reconstruction-era economy, together with the persistence of strong cultural norms regarding gender roles, greatly limited their chances for greater independence and more rights. Most were not inclined to take advantage of these—to compete with men in the wider world; they preferred to play their time-honored roles of wife and mother.[225] Hence, men's exclusive control of the public sphere was barely challenged. By and large, Southerners did not interpret the region's defeat as compelling evidence that their social norms had to be reexamined and reformed. Only a small minority of educated women questioned the status quo. There was no campaign for female suffrage in the South until the last decade of the nineteenth century.[226] Indeed, only one state in the Deep South—Arkansas—ratified the Nineteenth Amendment before its adoption in 1920.[227]

Meanwhile, conservative white men fought hard to gain back their primacy in Southern society. To reestablish their control over blacks, they resorted to intimidation and mob violence. Established by Tennessee Confederate veterans shortly after the war ended, the Ku Klux Klan vowed to restore white supremacy and went about doing this by attacking and murdering recently freed blacks and the white Northerners who had come south to help them. Across the region, an average of 150 lynchings took place every year during the last decade of the century.[228] Many of these purported to be in response to sexual assaults on white women. Resorting to vigilante justice signaled that white men were still determined to uphold the old patriarchal code of Southern chivalry. After the end of Reconstruction, conservative whites also regained control over state legislatures and passed bills restricting the rights of women. In 1878, South Carolina, for example, nullified a post–Civil War measure allowing marriages to be dissolved because of cruelty or desertion.[229]

In the North, fighting and winning a war emboldened conservative-minded men to reverse or slow the trend toward greater gender equity. As was mentioned above, laws granting married women the right to own property and keep their children following divorce were stricken from the books in New York early in the war. While most states eventually did pass legislation allowing wives to keep their wages and other sources of income, their custody rights remained severely limited: by the end of the century, only nine states had given both divorced parents equal rights to their offspring.[230] With the focus on securing black suffrage after the war, the question of female voting rights remained shelved. The first statewide referendum on giving women the franchise was voted down in Kansas in 1868. In the following three decades, only one western territory, Utah (1870), and one state, Idaho (1896), would approve female suffrage.[231] (During the same period, eleven western and midwestern states extended the vote to male aliens who were intending to become citizens.)[232] In 1869, bitter over lack of progress toward achieving female suffrage, Stanton and Anthony formed the National Woman Suffrage Association, which condemned the Fourteenth Amendment for denying females the franchise and dedicated itself wholly to advancing the cause of women. Now free to speak her mind in the aftermath of a bloody war, Stanton turned her fury on the "man's government" that had caused it, denouncing this "destructive force" for being "stern, selfish, aggrandizing; loving war, violence, conquest, acquisition; breeding discord, disease, and death."[233] But her new group and its cause were swimming against a powerful masculine tide. When a bill on women's voting rights was finally brought before the Senate, in 1887, it was overwhelmingly rejected, by a 34–16 vote. It would take another thirty-three years before women in all of the states secured the vote.

In many ways, there was a legal backlash against women in the remaining decades of the century. Courts took a more harsh view of female criminals, sentencing many who were convicted of killing their children to be executed.[234] Divorce laws were tightened in many states, in reaction to an increase in the number of marriages that were being dissolved—two-thirds of them at the behest of the wife.[235] All told, over one hundred bills were adopted in less than two decades to help prevent the resulting decline in the birth rate.[236] (A woman's entitlement to equal rights in divorce had been advocated by Elizabeth Stanton as early as the 1850s. It was a cause that had subsequently been embraced by many women in the temperance movement. During Reconstruction, South Carolina legislators made divorce possible in cases of desertion or infidelity, but when Southern males regained control in 1878, they passed a law saying only the state legislature could grant a divorce, in exceptional cases.)

In the medical field, male doctors expressed their hostility toward professional women by attacking midwives and by seeking to regain control over the birthing process. In his presidential address in 1871, the head of the American Medical Association, Dr. Alfred Stillé, denounced these "rivals" to men, who were then overseeing a large percentage of births, branding them "monstrous productions."[237] Female physicians encountered even more pronounced resistance. More generally, women were denounced for having abortions and using contraception—freeing their sexuality from men's control.[238] Such reactions stemmed largely from men's anxiety that the opposite sex was continuing to gain ground in the battle for gender equity. Growing numbers of American women were attending college (mostly outside the South) and consolidating their guiding influence in primary education.[239] Females were working in more fields, particularly ones previously closed to them. They even sought elected office: between 1870 and 1910, female candidates ran for office in 480 elections across the country, despite their inability to vote.[240] In the last three decades of the nineteenth century, many Northern men felt a renewed urge to stop these advances, as the War between the States had reminded them how fundamentally different the sexes were: in the words of one historian of gender relations, "The Civil War had perhaps dramatized the crudest source of identity, the sexual distinction between fighting men and nonfighting women."[241]

In these differing sectional responses, we can see how the experience and outcome of war affected civilian society. In the South, defeat on the battlefield led to a weakening of white male power on the domestic front and opened the door for women to seek more rights and economic opportunities, but custom and economic restraints then held back all but a small number of females from capitalizing upon this situation. The traditional, hierarchical relationship between genders was largely restored, even though men now had a much diminished sense of their own worth, marred by feelings of guilt and failure. In the North, victory empowered men and gave them renewed confidence in their own abilities to control their own destiny and block female progress on many fronts. But, despite this reinforcing effect, Northern men were only temporarily able to slow women's movement toward equality. The forces driving economic growth and prosperity were stronger than male opposition to the gender-related changes that industrialized Northern society was undergoing in the last third of the nineteenth century. The need for a more highly trained and well-educated workforce—a need that men alone could not meet—required more women to step forward and contribute. In this larger sense, a pragmatic and forward-looking Abraham Lincoln had realized what was at stake for America when the South seceded—not just freedom of opportunity for the slave, but for all Americans. When he spoke before Congress on the historically freighted date of July 4, 1861, he made this perfectly clear: for the North, he said, this was "a struggle for maintaining in the world that form and substance of government whose leading object is to elevate the condition of men; to lift artificial weights from all shoulders; to clear the paths of laudable pursuit for all; to afford all an unfettered start and a fair chance in the race of life." When Elizabeth Cady Stanton, at her home in Seneca Falls, read those words in the newspaper, she must have smiled.

Chapter 2

NOT-SO-GREAT WARS— CUBA, SOUTH AFRICA, JAPAN

Appropriately enough, the last major European war of the nineteenth century was fought on the Continent's periphery. For the Great Powers, it was a remote, if vexing, sideshow. In the summer of 1877 the Russian army had battered the Balkans like an unwelcome hailstorm and was now threatening to march all the way to Constantinople and seize the Turkish capital. In London, an intemperate Queen Victoria daily harangued her prime minister, Benjamin Disraeli, about England's hesitance to intercede and turn back the tsar's forces: "There is not a moment to be lost or the whole of our policy of centuries, of our honour as a great European Power, will have received an irreparable blow!" she fulminated. "Oh, if the Queen were a man, she would like to go and give those Russians, whose word one cannot believe, such a beating! We shall never be friends again till we have it out. This the Queen feels sure of."[1] Her subjects, hoping to make amends for the disastrous slaughter of the famed Light Brigade in the Crimea nearly a quarter century before, likewise succumbed to chauvinistic indignation, chanting at rallies outside Parliament:

> We don't want to fight,
> But, by Jingo! if we do,
> We've got the ships,
> We've got the men,
> We've got the money too![2]

But the British impulse to go to war was stillborn. The Russians and Turks hastily signed an armistice, and, after less than a year of fighting, the conflict in the Balkans was over. The fatuous cartoons about carving up "the turkey" disappeared from the newspapers, Alexander's troops slogged back home, and a strange silence fell across Europe. No cannon roared, no crack of rifles resounded, no cries of "Charge!" wafted across the fields and forests of the Continent; no men ran forward, stumbled in their tracks, and fell; no torn, bloody corpses piled up on the sodden earth. And, even more strangely, the lull persisted. For the next twenty-five years, not a single conflict took place within nine time zones of Paris, not a single soldier died in battle. With each passing year, memories of war receded, the grass grew taller around the simple white crosses and weathered cemetery stones, and the thousands upon thousands of bodies desiccating beneath faded into oblivion. The battles that had claimed these lives lost their emotional resonance and became mere geographical curiosities—quaint, Baedecker names like Königgrätz, Sevastopol, and Mars-la-Tour. All these remnants of once-glorious causes belonged to a distant past. War itself seemed an enshrined relic. And this was not just wishful thinking. Ever since Napoleon had been defeated at Waterloo and banished to exile, Europe had been enjoying a largely uninterrupted state of peace—a *Pax Britannica*—not seen since the first decades of the eighteenth century.[3] An elaborate patchwork of treaties, strategic territorial swaps, and governmental transformations, originally worked out by the Congress of Vienna in 1815, had stilled the reflex to settle international disputes by calling out the cavalry and had established a precarious but stable balance of power that was to last—with only brief interruptions—for fully a century. Beneath this sheltering diplomatic umbrella, the powerful nations of Europe doggedly pursued their ambitions by less violent means. A hunger for foreign trade and overseas investment fueled territorial expansion, and England, France, Germany, and Russia scrambled to secure their own places in the sun—from the tip of South Africa to the ports of China and Japan. Fear and envy of rivals' successes and a desire to surpass them incited a global Darwinian competition to plant the flag and uphold national pride.

At home, back on the Continent, relations between the sexes were also changing, albeit subtly, during an era of peace. While the days of dashing heroes on horseback fast might have disappeared, well-positioned men still ruled society as if by divine right. They still exercised considerable power, but did so with restraint and a sense of diminished grandeur. The weight of recent, tumultuous history bowed them down. If the first half of the nineteenth century was defined by the audacious campaigns of Napoleon, the second belonged to Otto von Bismarck—a wealthy lawyer, twice an unsuccessful suitor, one-time reserve officer, and dour master of realpolitik who steered Germany toward unification by shrewdly manipulating events instead of riding slipshod over them. As the economies of England, France, and Germany grew more prosperous, the middle class in these countries flourished. For its growing members, the focus of daily life shifted away from war and international intrigue toward domestic matters—acquiring a good education, making a proper marriage, building a family, and living a comfortable, orderly, and civilized existence under the peaceful, unruffled conditions that characterized the early Victorian Age. Middle-class men and women alike abided by a shared sense of propriety, moral probity, and proper manners. Men were expected to behave as "gentlemen," and their wives as "ladies." Life unfolded like a well-crafted script, with few surprises or setbacks. Or so it seemed. This sentimental, somewhat treacly optimism of midcentury was well captured by the poet Robert Browning (albeit ironically) in his 1841 dramatic piece "Pippa Passes":

> The year's at the spring,
> And day's at the morn;
> Morning's at seven;
> The hill-side's dew-pearled;
> The lark's on the wing;
> The snail's on the thorn;
> God's in his Heaven—
> All's right with the world!

Middle-class men made their living by going out into the world in suits—to well-appointed offices in banks, brokerage houses, law firms, trading companies, and shops.[4] Their less well-off male counterparts further down the economic ladder trudged off to the factories, warehouses, and shops that had sprouted across the smoky urban landscape as industrialization took hold, and millions of workers abandoned their farms and rural homesteads to seek their fortune in these burgeoning metropolises.[5] During the first half of the nineteenth century, London doubled in size, and nearly a quarter of England's population was clustered in its ten largest cities. Berlin went through a similar expansion—increasing its population from 702,000 in 1867 to 1.5 million some thirteen years later—after becoming the capital of imperial Germany, and metropolitan Paris grew by threefold in the five decades after 1835.

Because these urban centers and their workspaces were large, crowded, and impersonal, living in them had the adverse effect of reducing the human stature and singularity of their residents. Instead of being known and respected by their neighbors and coworkers, as had been the case in the countryside, most city dwellers lived largely anonymous, isolated existences. Few cared about them or valued what they did. The size, complexity, and way of life in these sprawling metropolitan areas inevitably made individuals feel uprooted and insignificant. Furthermore, industrial labor was belittling to workers. The pride that had once come with one's craftsmanship and farming skills was not in evidence on the shop floor, where the daily routine was repetitive and impersonal, based on producing quantities of interchangeable goods rather than ones of individually distinctive quality. Men—and the unmarried women who managed to land factory jobs—derived no personal satisfaction from performing the tasks expected of them. Men, in particular, keenly felt the loss of self-validation they had once derived from their physical strength, which had traditionally set them apart from their fellows and, more important, from women. (The mingling of the sexes in the workplace further dispelled any notion of a male "mystique.") Now females were competing against them—displaying the same competence and, in some industries, taking away jobs because they would perform them for less money. These developments, as well as the moral questions raised by the presence of attractive single women in the factories, were deeply disturbing to working-class men.[6] They constituted a direct challenge to the notion of male superiority.

Urban life also broke the close bond between family and work that had existed for centuries. Now the two spheres were largely isolated from each other. Sequestered in their respective realms for much of the time, men and women led separate lives. Most men—except those belonging to the idle upper class—were absent during the day, earning a livelihood, and thus had to entrust the running of the home, including care of the children, to their wives.[7] They were caring, involved fathers, but, of necessity as well as inclination, in a limited way. With few exceptions, married women stayed at home: this was their sole domain. They made most of the day-to-day decisions within it, yet remained ultimately subject to their husbands' will.[8] Under English law, for example, a wife was regarded as a possession of her spouse rather than as an independent human being. If she did work, the husband garnered her earnings, and if the couple divorced, he was given custody of the children.[9] Of course, not all English women—or men—were content with these legal and social imbalances. As early as the 1860s, progressives like John Stuart Mill argued that marriage should not be a hierarchical arrangement between unequals, but rather a bond between caring "companions."[10] However, this was to remain a distinctly minority viewpoint for several decades to come.

With the economic value of their offspring diminished by the move from the land early in the industrial era, families throughout Western Europe began to produce fewer children in the second half of the century; wider use of contraception and declining infant mortality rates due to better nutrition and health measures also contributed to a drop in the birth rate after it had risen considerably over the preceding decades.[11] As late as 1871, 42 percent of women in England had six children or more; within less than thirty years, the average number of births had fallen to 3.5.[12] Because they had fewer mouths to feed—and greater expectation that their progeny would survive into adulthood[13]—parents tended to invest more resources in the few children they had. This greater concern about their welfare was also reflected in the passage of child labor laws to safeguard the health and well-being of society's youngest and most vulnerable workers.[14]

Of growing importance in an urbanized, highly competitive world was the need for more education. With class no longer the sole arbiter of economic status, young men could rise through the ranks of society by dint of ambition and drive, and, in the struggle to surpass their peers and succeed in this dynamic environment, having a keen, finely-honed mind could make all the difference. Because men were absent from the home so much, their traditional role of teacher for those children not enrolled in school was handed over to their wives.[15] More significantly, it now became the mother's responsibility to develop the moral fiber of the little ones left in their charge. Husbands returned in the evenings to make sure this was being accomplished.[16]

As men ventured into the rough-and-tumble world of commerce and industry, soiling their hands literally or figuratively by the unsavory tasks they had to perform—and the compromises they had to make[17]—to put food on the table, their wives acquired an aura of moral purity and uprightness.[18] Husbands looked up to them as a "Mother Angel."[19] Within their domestic dominion, married women nurtured the values that were being eroded in the wider world.[20] They upheld the conscience of a society—its "moral vision of life"[21]—that otherwise would be in danger of losing this guiding compass. A woman possessed the power to inspire purity within less innately spiritual males.[22] For the sake of social stability, a mother's guiding hand was critical, and its impact long-lasting. Summarized one midcentury American paean to this formidable maternal power: "As the mother's rule at home is, so, in a large measure, will be the characters of her children. By the mother is determined the future of her offspring. She may bend their natural impulses to good, or permit young life, in its first eager activities, to take on evil forms that will forever after mar the beautiful aspects of humanity."[23]

While mothers were being placed upon a pillar of virtue, European and American men of the latter half of the nineteenth century suffered a moral devaluation, as well as loss of influence within the family. They came to be seen as weak and subject to unhealthy, uncontrollable appetites.[24] Between William Carlyle's homage to "Great Men," in his widely read *On Heroes and Hero Worship and the Heroic in History*, which appeared in 1841,[25] and Leo Tolstoy's publishing of *War and Peace* a quarter century later, Western society entered a new Zeitgeist. Whereas Carlyle and many of his contemporaries had believed history was guided by the achievements of eminent, almost superhuman leaders,[26] the Russian novelist saw these same figures as mere cat's-paws of blind, impersonal forces—namely, the collective mass of humanity.[27] A seminal milestone in this transformation of nineteenth-century consciousness was Charles Darwin's *On the Origin of the Species*.[28] Darwin postulated that all living creatures, including humans, had assumed their present guise not as the result of some divine scheme, but due to "complex and little known laws of variation" governing their adaptation to changing environments.[29]

This notion of limited control over events (which would be expanded, by Freud, to include much of human behavior) tended to belittle and undermine the power of men because they were the sex entrusted to rule society by dint of their "masculine" rationality. If, in fact, their actions did not alter the course of events or improve the conditions of society, why should their power continue to be so esteemed and honored? To a large degree, moral authority derived from power: might *was* right. But this held true only if power was efficacious. If it wasn't, the male claim to superiority was discredited. If the world was no longer governed by an omnipotent, paternal God, then men's analogous role as patriarchs was deflated.[30] Masculine virtue was also called into question by the whiff of hypocrisy that surrounded male sexual mores during the last quarter of the nineteenth century. Increasingly exposed to the frank sensual temptations of a materialistic urban environment, and torn between a rigid Victorian moral code demanding sexual restraint and their own repressed desires, many (mostly young, single) men of the middle and upper classes took to leading double lives.[31] Ostensibly proper in their behavior, they secretly shed this aura of respectability and surrendered to more primal impulses, seeking out prostitutes and mistresses.[32]

At the start of the last third of the century, European and American societies remained nominally patriarchal, but rapidly changing social realities were quietly chipping away at masculine authority. In addition to being marginalized within the family and consigned mainly to a breadwinning role, men were encountering other developments that damaged their masculine self-image. At work, they were losing mastery over their fate: middle-class businessmen, employees, professionals, and shop owners were coming to realize (as factory workers long had known) that their material success did not depend wholly on their own efforts, but, largely, on forces beyond their control.[33] In a Darwinian world, some would win out, but others fail. Their economic and social status—like their masculinity—was not a given, but something to be constantly earned. Second, as was noted above, men were siring fewer children. This trend developed in the wake of the massive migration to urban centers across much of Western Europe as more lucrative economic opportunities opened up there.[34] In these growing cities and towns, both men and women had a chance to earn more money than on the farm and raise their families' standard of living. However, to stoke this upward mobility, women had to be freed from many years of being pregnant and looking after small children. And families had to become smaller, to conserve resources. Hence, there was a greater willingness to rely on birth control or abortion to reduce the number of children.

From a biological perspective, this decline in fertility was potentially worrisome to men (as it was to nations as a whole), but any reproductive concerns they might have had were somewhat nullified by the greater expectation that their offspring would survive to have children of their own and thus perpetuate the family line. More troubling was the reality that fewer women, especially in the middle classes, were now getting married during their prime child-bearing years.[35] For example, the 1851 census in England found that a third of women between the ages of twenty and forty were still—in the language of that day—"spinsters."[36] Some of these women were "superfluous"—the result of a male-female imbalance then prevalent in most of Europe in part because of higher mortality rates among boys and young men.[37] But others—likely the great majority of these women—remained single by choice. Rather than focusing on finding a husband and starting a family, they were seeking personal fulfillment independently, breaking new ground by demonstrating what women were capable of accomplishing on their own.[38] Many did so by acquiring more schooling. In terms of education, females were starting to catch up with their male counterparts. This was particularly so in the United States, where the first college for women, Mt. Holyoke, had been established as early as 1837. Less than fifty years later, a third of college students in the United States were female.[39] By 1870 more women were graduating from American high schools than men, and, according to census figures from a decade later, a higher percentage of females was literate. Progress on this front was slower in Europe: few French women attended normal (teacher-training) schools until the second half of the century,[40] and secondary schools were not established for them until the 1880s. (This extension of educational opportunities was spurred by a belief that Prussia's superior school system had contributed to its victory over France.)[41] But, by the end of the century, female enrollment in France's teacher-training institutions rivaled that of males, and, in England, similar colleges were attended predominantly by young women.[42] Secondary schools for girls in Prussia (limited to those whose families could pay the fees) did not receive official status until the

1870s. With the founding of Queens College in London (1848) and other independent secondary schools, greater educational opportunities for young, middle-class English women gradually materialized. These resulted in the establishment of the first college for females, Girton, at Cambridge in 1869.

Participating in public affairs was a major aspect of this emancipation from the home. The emergence of major activist groups such as the Women's Christian Temperance Union (founded in 1874) provided many middle-class women with a powerful international forum for airing common concerns and pursuing a decidedly feminist agenda: along with campaigning against the ills of alcohol, the WCTU fought to free women from (male) exploitation and oppression around the world. Such civic involvement naturally brought women into the political arena. As was noted earlier, American women began running for office even before they could vote. Scattered protofeminist groups in European countries like France and England also fought to reform social institutions, secure better-paying jobs, and gain more political rights for women.[43] Two American suffragette leaders even ran for the presidency.[44] As one American supporter of this trend summed up not long after the Civil War, "The main object in life for the Coming Woman will be not so much the mating as the making of herself."[45]

In England, the inclination to remain single and marry late—or not at all—was most pronounced in cities where women could be hired as domestic servants, or in the northern part of the country, where they could find employment in the textile industry.[46] Having an income of their own gave these young, unmarried females a freedom and autonomy that unsettled many conservative-minded men, in England as well as on the Continent, where a similar development was taking place.[47] This growing female self-reliance seemed to invalidate the traditional (male) belief that women were essentially helpless creatures, wholly dependent upon men for their security and livelihood. Most Europeans and Americans—men and women alike—feared that some females were gaining too much power and challenging male prerogatives. Women who "abandoned" their roles as wives and mothers were blamed for various social ills. Some English opponents of working women claimed that their "defective mothering" was responsible for their country's ominously increasing infant mortality rate.[48] As the century was coming to a close, conservative politicians, writers, and physicians in England and elsewhere accused married women of fomenting "race suicide" by not having as many children as they once had.[49] In some quarters, female gains provoked derision. Magazines like the *Saturday Review* lampooned British women who insisted on giving speeches in public despite a ban on their doing so.[50]

The French public, still wedded to the "separate spheres" philosophy of gender roles, did not warm to the suffragist cause. Almost all men and women in France subscribed to the notion that the two sexes had biologically complementary natures, and this reality should inform relations between them, including the marital one. Marriage was a woman's "natural" role, and women who remained single a disturbing oddity.[51] (Because of this traditionalist outlook, fully 42 percent of French women married by the age of twenty-one, versus only one out of four in England.)[52] Men were supposed to assume their rightful place in society as providers, husbands, and fathers, while women, temperamentally unfit of thinking independently, should focus on loving their husbands and children.[53] Many, especially on the right, blamed the nation's 1871 defeat by Prussia (and France's falling birth rate) on the "weakness of French gender categories" and hoped to "remasculinize" society through war, which they and conservative elements in many European countries and the United States regarded as "chivalric, heroic and regenerative of men and nation."[54] The Third Republic reestablished the power of parliament vis-à-vis the monarchy but did not extend the vote to women. Opposition to taking this step also remained strong in Germany, Italy, Belgium, and other countries on the Continent.

Women encountered similar hostility in the workplace. Their insistence on entering the "masculine" world of offices and factories was considered "unfeminine." Male workers worried about losing their jobs to women (especially during strikes), or having their wages cut as the result of an influx of females.[55] Unions in England, France, Germany, and the United States fought to keep women from becoming members.[56] In the professions, women made some nominal gains (such as Britain's 1876 Enabling Act, which allowed females to be licensed as physicians) but faced stiff opposition to any substantive changes in their status. Universities in England, for example, continued to exclude female medical students. As late as 1881, when Queen Victoria was celebrating her forty-fourth year on the throne, there were only a total of twenty-five female doctors in the British Isles.[57] (The entire German Reich had only 138 on the eve of World War I.) Single women who did overcome these obstacles, in various lines of work, had to deal with public scorn and dismay over their achievements: many considered a female who put career ahead of marriage and family to be sexually "unnatural."[58]

It was not only female social, political, and economic gains that threatened men and put them on the defensive. So did the new emphasis on sexual propriety and control in the second half of the nineteenth century. In an age when female "purity" was held up as the moral exemplar, the male sex drive began to look excessive, brutish, and unsavory: as one historian has observed, "maleness itself seemed to carry a certain odor of contamination."[59] In countries such as England, middle-class men were expected to conquer their lust through sheer willpower. The same held true in the United States, where, after the Civil War, "the Northern middle class clung to ideals of family stability, female purity and male self-control."[60] Like women of their station in life, English "gentlemen" were supposed to sublimate basic, animalistic instincts in deference to higher principles.[61] Women were taught to be wary of sexual advances and keep suitors at bay. Even their husbands were not to be encouraged to have frequent relations with them. (Wives were also warned about the danger of venereal disease.) This "culture of abstinence"[62]—together with heightened fears about the negative health consequences of giving birth and the adverse economic impact of having numerous children— deterred many women from marrying, increased the marriage age, decreased the frequency of sexual intercourse in marriage, extended the spacing between births, and, consequently, reduced the number of children born in middle-class families.[63] These factors contributed to the sharp drop in fertility in England and several other Western European countries after 1860.

Many middle-class men found these self-imposed sexual restraints trying. The often long periods of courtship preceding marriage meant that couples postponed having intercourse until well into their twenties, even later.[64] This produced a considerable amount of frustration. As the twenty-six-year-old Sigmund Freud wrote with a mixture of regret and self-congratulation to his fiancée, Martha Bernays, three years after their engagement (which would last for another year), he had adopted a "habit of continuous suppression of natural drives" since they had met—an experience that would help shape Freud's theory of sexual repression.[65] Freud's premarital experience was hardly exceptional for men of his social class. Until they married, most had few sexual outlets. Since masturbation was condemned as morally degrading and harmful to their health, single middle-class males in the Victorian era either had to ignore this admonition, become resigned to prolonged celibacy, or seek out prostitutes. It is no wonder that the number of women practicing this profession in cities like London, Berlin, and Paris reached unprecedented levels during this period.[66] Although such short-term dalliances may have served to release sexual tension, they did not alleviate the conditions that had made prostitution flourish—namely, a shortage of "legitimate," or socially acceptable, sexual partners. Nor did the abundance of prostitutes erase the stigma of associating with these women of easy virtue, and the inner conflict and guilt that this behavior often aroused.

The central fact remained that much of late nineteenth-century Europe and North America was sexually repressed. This reality had several negative repercussions for the relations between males and females, as well as for men's self-image. Men were seen—and saw themselves— as weak, morally inferior creatures, prisoners of corrupting, carnal cravings. Their sexual urges were socially inappropriate, unwelcomed, and had to be "overcome" through self-denial. Groups advocating male "purity" called for masculinity to be expressed by exercising restraint.[67] Power in men's dealings with the opposite sex did not lie in their own hands: fulfilling their desires was dependent upon the reluctant consent of impassive spouses or the payment of cash to prostitutes. Under these strictures, male frustration could easily lead to resentment, hostility, anger, even aggression against women.[68] Some men felt women were treating them contemptuously and condescendingly and reacted by lashing out—verbally or physically.

These ill feelings were reinforced by an underlying anxiety that the balance of power between the sexes was tipping in favor of women.[69] All of a sudden—or so it seemed—females were "invading" male territory and taking away large chunks of it, stripping men of much of their self-esteem and power. The strict division between male and female spheres was breaking down and thus imperiling a masculine identity based upon an exclusive, innate right to perform certain roles (such as earning an income) and exercise certain rights and responsibilities (such as voting). Educated, "liberated" females ("he-women" was one of the mildly derogatory terms for them) who asserted a desire to perform these same functions were seen as violating a fundamental principle of human nature and therefore widely condemned by bourgeois society—by men and most women alike. Middle-class males may have made fun of this new type of woman, but, deep inside, they were more than a little worried about what it portended. Equal status for women ran directly counter to their view of life. When the House of Lords reconsidered a bill granting custody of children to either surviving parent (instead of only to the father), in 1885, one member, the Marquess of Salisbury, condemned it as "the greatest interference with the rights and privileges that men valued more than they did their own lives."[70] A few years earlier, in response to suffragist complaints about the light sentences meted out to men who murdered adulterous wives—one was convicted of manslaughter and given just four days in prison—the home secretary, Sir William Harcourt, said he did not think "such conduct as that [her adultery] calls for much sympathy from the educated women of England."[71] When, in Paris in 1871, some women insisted on donning the uniforms and red sashes of the Communards and fighting beside them, the military officer who later prosecuted these activists for taking part in this uprising went as far as to denounce them for seeking to bring about the end of Western civilization through female emancipation.[72] In Washington, a congressman from Maryland made no bones about his animosity toward women's suffrage: "The little wife has attained to such strength and size that her blows now make the big man wince; the wee finger-nails have grown to talons, and tear now where they only tickled before; and if the good well-natured fellow does not look well to his guard, he will be throttled, stretched on his back, and brought to such terms as he dreamed not of, a short while ago."[73]

This heady mix of anger and angst surfaced in a number of literary and theatrical works of the day.[74] These included several novels by Émile Zola that depicted women as dangerous and devious threats to men's status—even their manhood.[75] The English novelist Walter Besant took a tongue-in-cheek approach in belittling ascendant female power in his 1883 fable, *The Revolt of Man*. In it, Besant depicted a topsy-turvy world in the near future, in which women have usurped all of the powerful roles once held by men. Meanwhile, men stay at home and cook, spin yarn, and take care of children. Above all else, they are valued for their good looks and "amiable disposition." They are expected to please women and thus invite their attention as suitors; they are taught to display "modest retirement" and a "graceful obscurity" befitting their sex. This role reversal has led to a sorry state of affairs: women have shown themselves to be inept at keeping society moving forward: under their tutelage, railroads and factories have ceased operating, the economy has stagnated, religion has been abandoned, and the population declined precipitously. The novel's "revolt"—by an "Army of the Avengers"—is an attempt by a disgruntled mob of men to reclaim the power they have lost, reassert their sexual dominance, and dispel the notion that women are their natural rulers.[76] The American novelist Henry James expressed the same unhappiness and ill-at-ease with emancipated females in his nearly contemporaneous novel, *The Bostonians*. It deals with the competition between a Southern lawyer (and Civil War veteran) named Basil Ransom and Olive Chancellor, his cousin and fervent feminist, for the affections and loyalty of a young woman, Verena Tarrant, who is the latter's protégée in the feminist movement. (James implies that Olive's attachment to Verena is sexual as well as political.) Articulating skepticism about feminism that recalls James's own, Ransom is put off by his cousin's stern, fanatical manner and by how she has used her influence to manipulate and control the younger woman and keep her away from men:[77]

> The women he had hitherto known had been mainly of his own soft clime, and it was not often they exhibited the tendency he detected (and cursorily deplored) in Mrs. Luna's sister [Olive]. That was the way he liked them—not to think too much, not to feel any responsibility for the government of the world, such as he was sure Miss Chancellor felt. If they would only be private and passive, and have no feeling but for that, and leave publicity to the sex of tougher hide![78]

Later in the novel, when speaking to Miss Birdseye—a "ticklish spinster" and former abolitionist—Ransom dismisses her idea that Verena only has value because of her political views: "My dear madam . . . does a woman consist of nothing but her opinions? I like Miss Tarrant's lovely face better, to begin with."[79] At another point,

Ransom confides to Verena wistfully and somewhat bitterly, "The whole generation is womanized; the masculine tone is passing out of the world; it's a feminine, a nervous, hysterical, chattering, canting age, an age of hollow phrases and false delicacy and exaggerated solicitudes and coddled sensibilities."[80] (A few years after he finished writing *The Bostonians*, James received a letter from his older brother, William, lamenting, "There is a strange thinness and femininity hovering over all America.")[81] Toward the end of the century, anxiety over female empowerment and its threat to male control adopted a darker and more ominous tone, notably in Bram Stoker's wildly popular 1897 novel, *Dracula*. In it, the "New Woman" of the day was not only taken to task for assuming male prerogatives (for example, in courtship) but also—in the guise of the count's "vampirized" female victims—portrayed as sexually voracious, predatory, and life-threatening.[82]

Books like these reflected the attitudes of many men (and women) on both sides of the Atlantic during the last two decades of the nineteenth century. So did more scholarly tracts, such as one written by the German psychiatrist Paul Julius Möbius titled *On the Physiological Deficiency of the Female* (1900).[83] These dissections of the "woman problem" echoed earlier jeremiads against the advancement of the fair sex, maintaining that males and females were constitutionally different and unequal and ought to remain that way.[84] Society's creating of separate spheres for men and women—public versus private, working world versus the home, "corrupt" versus "pure"—had given concrete expression to this dichotomous thinking. But now, with new economic possibilities springing up and a more materialistic ethos emerging in Europe and the United States, this role division was no longer functioning as it once had. As women probed and broke through the boundaries of their "precincts," in search of equality, they were throwing down an implicit challenge to the traditional notion that certain values, behaviors, rights, responsibilities, freedoms, and ways of life were inherently and exclusively "male."

Within the home, husbands were also losing some of their legally sanctioned authority and stature. Laws passed in late Victorian England gave more rights to married women, reflecting the fact that they were now better educated and more capable of managing their own affairs than their counterparts of previous generations.[85] Although women could still not sue for divorce, newly adopted measures made it easier for those who had been beaten by their husbands to become legally separated.[86] (By contrast, French wives gained the right to divorce in 1884. Two years later they were allowed to open bank accounts without their husbands' approval.)[87] Magazine articles and cartoons began to poke fun at fossilized "patriarchs" (much as Clarence Day would do, early in the next century, in his autobiographical account of his upper middle-class New York childhood in the 1890s, *Life with Father*). This breach of the gender barrier not only endangered male power, it also violated a central cultural belief that biology was destiny—any blurring of distinctions between men and women warred with their God-given human nature. According to time-honored precepts, Creation was intentionally hierarchical: humans held sway over lower life forms, and, in a parallel fashion, men ruled over women.[88] This was an immutable fact. If humans insisted on ignoring these constraints, they would only bring on their degeneration—a reversal of the evolutionary progress Darwin had outlined in his *Origin of the Species*—weakening Western society and leading to its decline.[89] Concern about this prospect had surfaced around midcentury, in the writings of the French psychiatrist Benedict-Augustin Morel and his disciple, Valentin Magnan.[90] To prevent this change in gender relations from occurring, European nations had to root out any such deviant elements (including "manly" women, homosexuals, criminals, immigrants, Jews, drug abusers, and "immoral," "morbid" artists).[91] Men, in particular, had to take steps to reassert their masculinity and disengage themselves from contaminating and debilitating influences—namely, women.[92]

One drastic way to do this was to withdraw from their presence and seek solace, security, and self-fulfillment in all-male communities. And they did so, en masse. In the United States, migrating westward was largely a decision made (at least initially) by young single men.[93] The US census for 1870 put the combined male population of the states of California, Nebraska, Nevada, Oregon, and Texas, plus the territory of Colorado at 880,552, whereas only 786,545 females resided there several decades after these lands had been first settled by Americans and European immigrants.[94] Certainly, men of this age group and marital status flocked to the frontier because they could more easily uproot themselves—and were possessed of a hankering for adventure, an inchoate restlessness, and a desire to make their fortune on the untrammeled expanses beyond the Mississippi. But another reason why young men heeded Horace Greeley's advice and headed west was to escape the ever-encroaching, constrictive influence of females. Mark Twain alluded to this impulse in describing Huck Finn's yearning to "light out for the Territory" in order to thwart his Aunt Sally's intent to "sivilize" him.[95] This male need to evade (female) socialization by "running away" has continued to be a major theme in American literature and film, stretching chronologically from the novels of James Fenimore Cooper to Jack Kerouac's *On the Road*. Nor is this a uniquely American preoccupation. During the Victorian era, large numbers of unattached male youths in England, France, Germany, and other European countries fled the encroaching company of women—and sought better economic opportunities—by migrating to overseas colonies, joining the military, or by doing both.[96] In England, for instance, the out-migration of young single men after 1870 contributed to the gender imbalance and subsequent decline in the marriage and birth rates, especially in the middle and upper classes.[97] For example, by the 1890s a disproportionately large number of English émigrés—26.5 percent—came from this social background.[98] Many of those leaving their native land—2 percent of the populations of England and Ireland—headed to Australia, where a total of 38,000 new arrivals from Europe came ashore annually between 1876 and 1890. The great bulk of those immigrants arriving around midcentury had been single males looking to strike gold.

Within Europe itself, there was a growing inclination for men to regard marriage not as their inevitable destiny, but as only one option open to them.[99] For many single middle-class men, the idea of remaining a bachelor gained appeal. The institution of bourgeois marriage came under attack in a slew of literary and critical works, including plays by Ibsen and Strindberg. Critiques like these made relations between the sexes appear fundamentally problematic, perhaps better avoided. In reaction to the encroaching presence of women in their lives, more and more men—married ones and bachelors alike—drew back, into all-male enclaves. In the words of a recent historian, "In the late Victorian period disillusionment with domesticity and the hankering after a bracing men-only world were what attracted many to careers overseas."[100] Without resorting to the extreme step of leaving their countries, many upper-class married men sought a refuge from their increasingly female-dominated households by spending evenings at private "gentlemen's" clubs and other establishments where women were not admitted.[101] The number of such clubs in London's West End increased by half between 1850 and 1900.[102] One historian has recently described this trend as a "flight from domesticity"—a sign of growing male "irritation with the rigid and exclusive association of domestic space with femininity." Increasingly, many middle-class men came to feel their wives and children to be "fetters" and a "straitjacket," rather than a comforting, supportive presence in their lives.[103] To meet the need for an alternative social life, all-male associations and organizations proliferated, attracting both single and married men. For example, in the United States, there was a "massive expansion of fraternal groups" such as the Odd Fellows, Ancient Order of United Workmen, and Freemasons over the three decades prior to 1900. One observer from that era estimated that one in every three males over the age of nineteen was a member of the latter organization in the United States.[104] The number of Masonic lodges in England increased by 2,329 between 1870 and 1912.[105] One of the primary reasons for joining the Freemasons, according to a contemporary historian, was to find "a masculine refuge from a feminized domestic sphere."[106] Even within their homes, men of means erected havens of their own: after midcentury, English country houses routinely included a set of rooms reserved for them and their male guests—to play billiards, smoke cigars, or read the newspapers.[107]

The other, related male response to what many considered a "feminization" of their societies was to revive "manly" virtues—traits that women supposedly lacked and thus could not call upon to compete against men and further aggrandize themselves. These attributes included courage, competitiveness, discipline, stoicism, aggressiveness, self-reliance, physical strength, and a willingness to sacrifice one's self for a higher cause. Coincidentally, these were the same "masculine" qualities that were then becoming more valued by society as rivalries among the Great Powers for global economic and political dominance intensified. By amply demonstrating these virtues, men in Europe and the United States could redraw a clear boundary line between the sexes and once again attest to the vital role they alone could play in elevating national stature. Returning to these core values would simultaneously constrain female aspirations and refurbish a badly damaged male identity. It would also help men reassume their position of unquestioned authority in the home. A revitalized and reempowered virility would stop the birth rate from falling and give nations the population boost they needed to compete successfully on the international stage. Furthermore, a reinvigorated masculine ethos would enable the next generation of young men to fight and prevail in the international conflicts this competition might produce. For a strong masculinity to have an impact, it had to be instilled during a boy's formative years.[108] In England, the United States, Canada, and other Western countries, there were growing concerns that the existing school system was not accomplishing this goal. Instead, educating boys in single-sex institutions—most notably in England's prestigious boarding schools—appeared to be hindering the development of their male identity and virility. (This was just the opposite of what educators had originally hoped to accomplish by separating boys from girls.)[109] Moralists bemoaned what they saw as widespread masturbation and ensuing homosexuality in these institutions—signs not only of moral lassitude but of insufficient willpower.[110] (The poet Robert Graves, who attended three such elite public schools in the years leading up to World War I, faulted them for teaching him to despise the opposite sex and consider girls as "something obscene.")[111] These practices threatened the well-being of the nation and therefore had to be eliminated.[112] While such signs of "effeminacy" might have been attributed to the intimate male bonding promoted by single-sex schools, some critics blamed stifling, overprotective mothers for not encouraging their sons to take part in appropriately masculine pursuits while they were growing up.[113] Other targets for their attacks were female teachers, who, by 1890, accounted for two of every three figures of authority in American classrooms and had become commonplace in English ones as well, particularly at the elementary level.[114] This trend, combined with the prolonged absence of fathers, was alleged to be denying boys adequate male role models.[115]

As was discussed above, prominent English and American figures had begun to advocate a "muscular Christianity" earlier in the century, as an antidote to the loss of manliness and "effeminacy" associated with the era's sedentary, office-bound way of life.[116] Carlyle, for example, had stressed the masculine qualities of heroic leaders in his seminal work on this subject. The belief was that participating in sports enhanced both physical and spiritual development, while also solidifying male gender identity. As similar worries about an attenuated "maleness" surfaced during the late Victorian period, this emphasis on competitiveness, courage, and athletic prowess attracted more devotees. The English novelist Thomas Hughes publicized the value of "muscular Christianity" in his widely read autobiographical chronicle of university life, *Tom Brown at Oxford*.[117] On the other side of the Atlantic, Protestant churches heralded manliness and physical activities as ways to make their "feminized" faith more attractive to men.[118] At the same time, boys' schools in Europe and North America introduced athletic pastimes—competitive sports and regular exercise—to build their characters, improve their health, and attest to their masculinity.[119] A variety of new games, including rugby, cycling, tennis, badminton, and hockey in England, responded to this growing need for physical activity.[120] These and other sports brought out qualities of manliness such as stoicism and self-sacrifice that could not be expressed in their domestic and working lives. In addition, they gave men a much-welcomed excuse for getting out of their homes.[121] Under the influence of his father, Theodore Roosevelt came to embody the virtues of the "strenuous life," first by exercising regularly (to build up his asthma-weakened constitution) and then by taking up boxing (to deal with bullies) as a youth.[122] First introduced by various military forces, the teaching of gymnastics was widespread by the middle of the century: three decades later, there were clubs and federations in Germany, Belgium, Poland, France, Switzerland, Russia, Denmark, Sweden, England, and the United States. In many schools, military instructors were hired to run drills and gymnastics classes. Instruction of this sort aimed at reviving male energy and strength at a time when they seemed to be sorely flagging and thus rendered nations vulnerable to defeat. The British were particularly eager to improve the fitness of their young men so that they could avoid a repetition of the military's embarrassingly poor showing in the Crimean War.[123] Glorification of male physical capabilities reached its zenith with the revival of the Olympic Games, in Athens in April of 1896.

In the final decades of the nineteenth century, physical training was, in fact, a way of readying a nation for war.[124] With each passing year, major conflict was becoming inevitable as the Great Powers contended over colonies and sought to gain the upper hand militarily. According to the then widely accepted theory of Social Darwinism, war provided the ultimate test of a nation's collective will and fitness for survival. As the psychologist and philosopher William James conceded in "The Moral Equivalent of War" (1906), war was the "gory nurse" who taught men to rise above themselves and act as one. Only the strongest would survive its test—and deserved to do so.[125] So, to fortify themselves for this coming struggle, Europe's dominant nations began to beef up their armed forces. In 1889, the British announced plans to add seventy vessels to their navy over the next four-and-a-half years. France and Russia quickly countered by committing themselves to even more ambitious maritime expansion. Even smaller countries became caught up in this fervor to prepare for battle. Across the Continent, civil society had long been embracing quasimilitary values and practices. Novelists and short-story writers presented characters in uniform in a flattering light. Long before the poems of Rudyard Kipling inspired countless British youth to fight for Queen and country, adventure writers like the Irish-born Thomas Mayne Reid (a favorite of the young Theodore Roosevelt) and England's G. A. Henty had penned tales such as the *Rifle Rangers* (1850), *The Young Buglers* (1880), *Held Fast for England* (1893), and *With Kitchener at Soudan* (1903), glamorizing war and heroics for their youthful readers.[126] True tales of manly adventure regularly appeared in the weekly *Boy's Own* paper, read by as many as two-thirds of English schoolboys.[127] These positive literary depictions represented a major change from early in the century, when fictional soldiers and sailors were often figures of ridicule.

In France, military preparation societies had been organized after the nation's defeat by Prussia in 1871: they had the mission of readying young men for war by training them in gymnastics and marksmanship and by rekindling patriotic feelings.[128] Popularized by Queen Victoria, sailor's suits became fashionable for boys in England—and later in Germany—to wear. Toward the end of the century, many youth—some only of elementary-school age—enthusiastically joined the ranks of military cadets and took part in parades and marching drills. In Ontario, local militias were formed to impart the importance of chivalry, patriotism, and group loyalty to Protestant youth then just coming of age. The Canadians wanted to affirm their continuing loyalty to England in the wake of their country's having gained its independence from the British

Empire in 1867. These units attracted many young men, especially those living in rural parts of the province, who were looking to attest to their masculinity at a time when more and more women were entering the workforce.[129] But this training also served the more practical purpose of readying young Canadians for combat service, much as did the discipline, self-sacrifice, male camaraderie, and teamwork learned by upper-class British youth on the playing fields of Eton, Harrow, and Rugby.

The late-century emphasis on male physical fitness, male bonding, male exclusivity, and male commitment to a higher cause arose from a largely overlooked demographic reality: as the nineteenth century was coming to a close, a historically unprecedented percentage of young European men (as well as women) was still single. Throughout the Continent, the same pattern of late marriage—and marriage by fewer people—had become well-entrenched by the nineteenth century. According to 1881 figures, 6 of 10 French women had recently celebrated their twenty-fifth birthday without a spouse, and a third were still single when they turned thirty. And France had the *lowest* mean female marriage age of sixteen countries in Europe. In 1871, two-thirds of English females twenty-five and under were without husbands. At the turn of the century, between 12 (France) and 15 (England) percent of all women in these two countries had never married.[130] In the United States, the median marriage age for women rose from 23.0 to 23.8 between 1850 and 1890.[131] The percentage of American females who were still single by the age of twenty rose from half of those born at midcentury to two-thirds of the cohort born in the last decades of the century.[132] Since some women of child-bearing age married men who were older than they were, an even higher proportion of males had no wife well into their twenties. Since cohabitation was then very rare, very few of these single men had produced any children either. In other words, they were not only sexually frustrated but also reproductively unfulfilled. Denied the daily companionship of a wife, and the socialization as well as sense of purpose that comes from being married and having children, they naturally sought out the companionship of other young men in the same situation—unattached, lonely, and eager for social contact and a certain level of otherwise-lacking intimacy. For many married men of the middle class, unhappy in homes where their wives held sway, spending time with a group of their peers—in a club or gymnasium—provided a more agreeable social outlet. This desire for male friendship (as a substitute, or anti-dote, for family life) can help account for the rise in popularity of team sports, men's clubs and fraternal organizations, group physical activities, the armed forces, and quasimilitary associations that were based upon—and thrived because of—their gender exclusiveness.

This late-century male bonding had consequences beyond an under-mining of European and American domesticity. The feelings of solidarity that were formed made these men prone to emotional or irrational impulses. Much as Freud would describe in *Group Psychology and the Analysis of the Ego* (citing the French social psychologist Gustave Le Bon), an individual who joins a group "acquires a sentiment of invincible power which allows him to yield to instincts, which had he been alone, he would perforce have kept under restraint."[133] Among young males, forming groups tends to promote competition, a heightened or hyper-masculinity, and aggressive behavior.[134] Violence can result when some seek to regain control over others and their self-esteem.[135] Concerted male aggression can give individual males a way to overcome feelings of inadequacy and insignificance, such as those experienced in Europe and the United States during the second half of the nineteenth century, when their value to society seemed to be rapidly diminishing. A need to assert primal male strengths as a "bulwark" against this "machine age" and its "feminizing" tendencies thus developed toward the end of this period. One of its goals was to reaffirm manliness at its most element level—to reverse the decline of population through a display of fecund virility. There was, in countries like Germany, much talk of a "New Man" emerging from the husk of an older and debased version.[136] Through the revival of this avatar, not only men but society itself could experience a "regeneration"—or return to a healthier, more authentic, premodern state. The most efficacious way for this to happen was through that quin-tessential test of manliness—war.

Thus, at the dawn of the twentieth century, pressures to expand empires and to reestablish male dominance led to the clash of armies at several different points around the world. In the Caribbean and Pacific, American expeditionary forces engaged the armies of Spain; on the southern tip of Africa, British and allied armies fought Dutch-descended Afrikaners, in the (Second) Boer War; and on the Pacific Rim, the armies of Japan and Russia did battle on land and at sea—all harbingers of far more bloody conflicts to come. At first, all of these conflicts were wildly popular: each spoke to a pent-up desire to display national prowess. Egged on by a jingoistic, "yellow" press, Americans were in such a hurry to free Cuba from the Spanish and carry out "an entirely selfless mission for humanity," that they did not pause to consider whether the sinking of the *Maine* in Havana harbor on February 15, 1898, was a provocative act of war or a fabricated pretext.[137] (For their part, Spaniards were just as quick to denounce the United States for interfering in Cuba and to declare that their nation's honor and valor would only be vindicated by defeating inferior adversaries in what they saw as a just cause.) But beneath all the high-minded idealism, Americans were also looking for a collective shot in the arm—a boost to their morale and pride after a recent economic downturn, in 1893. "War fever" was scarcely limited to young men eager to sign up. A reporter for the *New York World* queried one hundred women in different parts of the country and then wrote a piece entitled "American Women Ready to Give Up Husbands, Sons and Sweethearts to Defend Nation's Honor."[138] Political leaders like President McKinley felt pressure from "jingoes" to "assume a manly posture and appear to espouse manly policies." National honor was at stake. War was also bound to give a flagging American manhood a much-needed lift.[139] The country was also eager to flaunt its newly attained status of world power by inflicting a defeat on the relatively weak Spaniards, so the historian Richard Hofstadter would later contend in his doctoral dissertation analyzing how Social Darwinism motivated the United States to go to war.[140] Whatever the reason, American men were almost universally enthusiastic about this opportunity to fight for their country.[141]

Patriotic fervor animated would-be volunteers from all different classes, occupations, backgrounds, and regions. When the First Regiment Massachusetts Heavy Artillery was mustered into voluntary service early in the war, its complement of forty-eight officers included a dozen college graduates, among them nine Harvard men. (Another twenty-six of its alumni served as enlisted men in the 703-man regiment.)[142] The morning they were to board a train for their duty station in Boston, the men of the First clustered in their armories, a "seething whirlpool of enthusiasm."[143] After thirty-nine-year-old Theodore Roosevelt, then serving as assistant navy secretary, was given the green light to recruit "wild riders and riflemen" for his band of "Rough Riders," he was "literally deluged with applications from every quarter of the Union."[144] The American public's support for this four-month-long "splendid little war"[145] remained strong throughout largely because it was so short, so successful (Cuba, Puerto Rico, Guam, and the Philippines were annexed by the United States) and so relatively bloodless—only 358 men died in combat out of a force of 306,760.[146]

A similar euphoria swept over most of the British Empire when war broke out against the Boers in the fall of 1899, with passions enflamed by saber-rattling writers like Rudyard Kipling.[147] At its epicenter, the city of London pledged 1,000 volunteers for this patriotic, imperialist cause and attracted more than that number of eager candidates (all of whom were bachelors) within three weeks. Many of these young men came from the "better classes": they included some 45 bank employees, 62 lawyers and barristers, over 200 men who worked on the city's stock exchange, 47 engineers, 591 clerks, and 11 "medical men," in addition to a large working-class contingent.[148] As would happen in later wars, British nationalistic fervor would scarcely brook any opposition.[149] Groups and prominent individuals who opposed the Boer conflict endured scathing hostility. Antiwar feminists were a principal target of this opprobrium: their humanitarian concerns and desire for peace isolated them and made them appear unpatriotic. For criticizing government policy and arguing that England should unilaterally bring its troops home, Emily Hobhouse, a member of the South Africa Conciliation Committee, was branded a traitor, and, when she attempted to return to Africa, in late 1901, the military forcibly prevented her from setting foot on shore.[150] More generally, the outbreak of war had the effect of muting the voices of women (and men) who perceived a connection between women's rights and international peace.

But, these voices were only a small minority. Throughout the empire as well as in England itself, enthusiasm for this imperialistic cause was strong, if not universal. Most Australians, new members of the "imperial family," quickly caught the rapidly spreading "war fever": ministers delivered sermons on the God of Battles, poets penned sonnets praising heroic warriors, and a vast array of men responded with gusto to a British request for troops.[151] Many more tried to enlist than were needed: "Squatters and solicitors, bank directors and dock labourers, lawyers and lamplights" queued up to be among the twenty-thousand-man force

Australia was shipping across the Pacific.[152] Canadians of British heritage were passionate about this "manly adventure" and considered those who did not embrace their sentiment to be traitors. A total of 8,300 young men enlisted to serve in this remote conflict, and although only 242 died in it, Canada would later erect more monuments to their sacrifice than they would for the victims of any other war.[153] Even non-Anglo subjects of Queen Victoria's dominion embraced this cause: in Natal, the thirty-year-old Mohandas Gandhi organized a volunteer ambulance team of over one thousand of his fellow Indians to aid imperial troops, despite anti-Indian hostility among their countrymen that had led to his being beaten and nearly lynched by an angry British mob upon returning to Durban two years before.[154]

But popular support, particularly among the educated middle class, ebbed as the conflict dragged on without any decisive victories. News leaked out that Boer women and children as well as black African civilians were being held in concentration camps under barbaric conditions, with many dying of starvation, and that soldiers of the Crown were torching Boer farms and summarily executing captured enemy prisoners.[155] What had started out a manly lark turned into an ugly disgrace, a display of incompetence and brutality on a horrific scale. Furthermore, British males had shown themselves to be unfit to fight, mainly as a result of inadequate nutrition.[156] Of the twenty thousand men who had volunteered for the army, only fourteen thousand had passed the obligatory medical exam[157]—due to "heart troubles, weak lungs, rheumatic tendency, flat feet, or bad teeth."[158] The rejection rate was the highest in cities like Manchester, where poor health and living conditions were commonplace.[159] By the end of the war, three out of five would-be volunteers from these industrial towns were found unqualified to serve.[160] The loss (mostly to disease) of some 22,000 lives, out of a total force of 448,435, came as a shock. A postwar commission fueled fears that Britain's men were not up to the task of fighting future wars, as did publications such as *The Decline and Fall of the British Empire*, which dwelt upon masculine weakness and decadence. By some estimates, as many as one in ten people in England was not getting enough to eat.[161] "Degeneracy" was believed to afflict men of all stations in life: if working-class men suffered from poor health, then the socially elite were weak and effeminate—no match for the emancipated, self-reliant modern woman and incapable of reproducing themselves in sufficient numbers.[162] Rather than being a renaissance of British manhood at the dawn of a new century and nearly fifty years after the nation's debacle in the Crimean, the Boer War seemed to teach the same discouraging lesson: instead of glorious victories, the empire could henceforth expect only more "disaster and humiliation."[163]

Both of these conflicts tested naïve notions of warfare and its rewards, with mixed results. (The Russo-Japanese War falls into a different category since it was fought largely by conscripts.) On the one hand, the Spanish-American War seemed to conform to nineteenth-century expectations of what war was all about and how it was to be waged. Cavalry charged up hills and overran dug-in positions, warships bombarded each other, armies besieged fortified cities, commanders exchanged formal letters about terms of surrender, the (racially) "superior" side won and, through a formal peace treaty, claimed its territorial spoils. For most Americans this easy victory demonstrated not the need for a new approach to war—or fear of it—in a more technologically advanced age, but the reality that the United States was now a formidable military presence among the European Great Powers. (For Spain, of course, the outcome had the opposite consequence: its once paramount, far-flung empire was now gone forever.) On the other hand, the prolonged, costly resistance of ragtag bands of Boer guerillas to the mighty British army and its imperial allies confounded several assumptions: instead of being "honorable" and "decent," soldiers from great civilizations (such as Britain's) could behave like beasts, carrying out "scorched earth" policies; and, instead of being fought by organized forces under conventional rules of engagement, war could consist of commando raids and ambushes and be decided by surprise and stealth more than by planning and predetermined battlefield execution.[164] Perhaps most disconcerting of all—as the Russians would learn in being defeated by an ascendant Japanese military—triumph did not automatically come to the forces from the more "advanced" (that is, Western and white) nation. These painful lessons did not, however, translate into a rejection of war or of the idea that it provided the most valid test of a nation's strength and power. Patriotism was not rejected. Rather, the British ordeal in South Africa (as well as the Russian humiliation in the Pacific—the first modern defeat of a Western power by an Asian one) provoked dismay and outrage over the poor leadership, fighting condition, tactics, and strategy of its forces.[165] War per se was not the problem but actual performance under fire.[166] In order to improve this, both England and Russia undertook major military reforms that helped prepare them for the greater challenges of World War I.

The Boer War did not dispel fears of a "crisis of masculinity": under fire, the men of the British Empire had not measured up.[167] In several of the participating countries, concerns were voiced about how well boys were being prepared for manhood in an industrial age. In England, some worried that unhealthy urban conditions were producing less fit young men.[168] This would explain why it had taken three years for the vaunted, professional British army to subdue badly outnumbered Boer farmers. By remedying this situation, the quality of future soldiers (as well as workers) could be enhanced.[169] After the war, the British government launched a "national efficiency" campaign. It made the point that healthy, well-fed children and adolescents were essential for the nation's well-being.[170] During parliamentary elections in 1906 and 1910, Liberals embraced this point of view, seeing a link between the nation's imperial ambitions and social reform: England needed to improve living conditions for the poor and breed a "vigorous and industrious and intrepid" younger generation if it was going to dominate the world in the new century.[171] Subsequently, efforts were made to reduce deaths from infectious diseases in English cities.[172] With the same goal of producing a "virile race," the Conservative government and such private organizations as the Women's League of Service for Motherhood promoted what amounted to a "cult of motherhood."[173]

Across the Atlantic, many Canadians worried about the "weakening" of their society due to an influx of immigrants over the previous decade.[174] These newcomers—mainly from Ireland and the European continent—were supposedly diluting national strength. In order to prevail in coming wars, the nation had to reverse this trend by increasing the size of its native-born population. In some European countries, the continuing decline in fertility was now seen as a national security threat. While Germany had been assiduously repopulating over the past decades, France and Britain had seen their birth rates drop dangerously low.[175] From a high of 304 children for every 1,000 married women between the ages of 15 and 45 in 1871, the number of babies born in England had fallen to

234 in 1903. By the end of the nineteenth century, the nation was adding only 115,000 persons to its population each year, compared to some 600,000 annually in Germany.[176] Having begun the century as the European nation with the largest population (30 million), France had only added another 10 million by 1900 and fallen far behind its Teutonic rival by this measure. For a few years during the mid-1850s, the number of deaths in France had exceeded the number of births.[177] Half of French administrative districts had higher death than birth rates, and many villages had been deserted. Because of this "demographic weakness"—made all too apparent in its 1871 defeat by Prussia—France saw itself at a severe disadvantage in confronting the Reich militarily in the future.[178] In 1911, only 34.9 percent of the French population was under the age of 21—the smallest percentage in Europe—compared with 43.7 percent of Germany's.[179] As early as 1906, Germany could thus field an army of 1.2 million, whereas France could only muster a 318,000-man force.[180] Fear of this more powerful foe was revealed in contemporary cartoons that depicted France as a helpless maiden about to be ravished by an aggressive German soldier.[181] Many blamed this "depopulation" on emancipated young French women (*demi-vierges*, or "half-virgins") who, because of undue focus on their own personal advancement and pleasure, were neglecting their primary duties as mothers.[182] Anxiety over this state of affairs spurred the formation of several organizations dedicated to convincing French wives to have more children. At the same time, groups dedicated to ending alcoholism, prostitution, birth control, and public nudity welcomed such a development as advancing their causes. Émile Zola, a leading proponent of this cause and a cofounder of the National Alliance for the Growth of the French Population, was working on a novel about the joys of a large peasant family (*Fécondité*) when he died in 1902.[183] But the pronatalist movement, made up mostly of doctors, economists, lawyers, journalists, writers, academics, and demographers—in other words, the intellectual elite—had little impact on public attitudes or practices. Most French men and women resented such outside interference in their reproductive decisions.[184] Liberal politicians did not support laws to encourage motherhood, and it was not until 1913 that the legislature adopted measures giving assistance to large families and pregnant women.[185]

English and Canadian leaders and commentators worried that their troops' disappointing performance in the Second Boer War was also partially attributable to a shrinking population base.[186] If British forces were to maintain the imperial colonies and win future conflicts, this downward trend had to be stopped. A flurry of books, such as Sidney Webb's 1907 book, *The Decline in the Birth-Rate*, laid out this problem in detail.[187] (In an earlier article, Webb, a liberal economist, had rhetorically asked, "What is the use of an Empire if it does not breed and maintain in the truest and fullest sense of the word an imperial race?")[188] So did a National Birth-Rate Commission in a report submitted on the eve of World War I. Conservative writers warned that Germany and the United States were outstripping England in population growth, and that this trend boded badly for maintaining the empire's economic and political preeminence. If population was power, England's was slowly seeping away.[189] Similarly alarmist studies found that the greatest reduction in births was occurring among the educated middle and upper classes: England was essentially relying on a morally abject, impoverished, and racially alien minority to perpetuate itself.[190] The solution to this problem was for the intellectually and genetically superior elements of society to become more fecund. A nascent eugenics movement encouraged men to be more "virile" and to marry women who were also physically fit. At the same time, following France's example, a pronatalist movement gained ground in both England and Canada.[191] Women were told it was their "national duty" to marry and produce children.[192] As one historian has recently written in regard to Canada, "Many family reformers believed that the nation would need a large, healthy pool of future male citizens to provide both the army and the economy with the right quantity of soldiers and workers."[193] This view was also advanced in Italy, by the prominent anthropologist Guiseppe Sergi. In his 1900 book, *The Mediterranean Race: A Study of the Origin of European Peoples*, he argued that an expanding population was crucial to achieving "national regeneration," reversing Italy's evolutionary decline, and ending its international humiliation.[194] To achieve this shared demographic objective—at a time of slowly rising unemployment early in the century—experts in Canada, Britain, France, and several other European countries encouraged women to forego taking jobs in factories and offices and instead stay at home and produce more children. "New Women" were castigated for becoming so educated that they looked down on the prospect of becoming pregnant and raising a family. Proposals were put forward to make motherhood more appealing, by providing maternal health insurance and free meals for young children.[195]

To ensure that becoming full-time mothers did not result in "coddling" of their sons, new, more vigorous ways of childrearing were advocated. These were firmly rooted in Victorian notions of gender. The two sexes were inherently different and had to be raised accordingly. (In the United States, the psychologist Granville Stanley Hall advanced this point of view in his highly influential 1904 book, *Adolescence*.)[196] Boys needed more physical outlets and more time on their own, away from females, especially their mothers.[197] They needed to become toughened mentally and morally as well. It was with this goal in mind that Robert Baden-Powell, who—at twenty-three, the youngest colonel in the British army—had led the defense of Mafeking in the Second Boer War, organized the Scouting movement.[198] In other words, boys coming of age in the brand-new twentieth century had to preserve the gender boundaries their fathers had embraced a few decades previously in their attempt to avoid "feminization" in a domestically oriented Victorian world. If anything, the experience of fighting a war overseas—and the prospect of waging one closer to home—lent greater urgency to these arguments for shoring up masculinity. The Social Darwinism of Herbert Spencer, who had coined the phrase "survival of the fittest," took on even more relevance.[199] A robust manliness was now deemed essential for people to thrive and triumph over their adversaries. Because of this recognition and humanitarian concern for the plight of the urban poor, physical education became an integral part of a public school education in countries such as England and the United States. Theodore Roosevelt appeared to be delivering the coup de grace to nineteenth-century female empowerment and striving for equality when he opined, "There is no place in the world for nations that have . . . lost their fiber of vigorous hardiness and masculinity."[200]

All this talk about male "vigor" and the need to expand the native population did not, however, translate into a baby boom. The nations that had come away from turn-of-the-century battlefields as big winners did not halt the decline of their birth rates. For example, Japanese women born between 1881 and 1885 (who would have been in their prime childbearing years at the time of their country's defeat of Russia) had a mean of 4.571 children. This rate remained fairly constant over the next twenty years before falling sharply in the 1930s and 1940s.[201] And this was true for a society in which "every woman is expected to become a wife."[202] Similarly, the number of children born to American women around 1900 (between three and four each) did not rise in the aftermath of the Spanish-American War. In this reproductive regard, winning a war did not prove to be an unmitigated success.

European ruling elites also discovered that "masculinizing" their societies to gear up for a major war would not happen as easily or as completely as they had wished. In various countries, a growing number of women were implicitly rejecting the values and aspirations of the dominant patriarchal order. More and more of the younger ones were ignoring suggestions that they settle down and raise a family; instead, they were thronging into the workplace. Many were no longer content to perform only domestic service.[203] Despite criticism that working mothers were to blame for the poor health of the nation's youth, growing numbers of British women opted for white-collar positions in shops and offices, postponing marriage to do so.[204] Working together through the Women's Trade Union League (WTUL), females from all social classes gained better conditions and higher wages, and these successes drew more women into the workforce. By 1902, the WTUL had roughly fifty thousand members and had attracted the attention of American labor figures interested in developing the same kind of organization. (They did so the following year.) The clerical union in Britain first welcomed women in 1911, and four years later females constituted 9 percent of total union membership in the country.[205]

Meanwhile, women were entering the labor market across the Channel as well as in the United States in impressive numbers. Employers in the United States began offering training courses to give women the skills they would need for jobs in industry, undeterred by any fear of "trespassing beyond the bounds of femininity." Still, women were largely limited to certain fields that were considered sufficiently "genteel": the federal census of 1900 found that only 43 of the 294 fields in which women were working had more than five thousand female employees.[206] Benefiting from greater educational opportunities, more American women entered the professions, gaining tenuous footholds in medicine, law, and science by the turn of the century.[207] With females constituting a third of all workers by 1880, Germany could boast the largest women's labor movement in the world, even though women enjoyed few political rights. In France, female participation in the textile industry increased significantly in the new century.[208] The number of women working in these factories in the area of Lille, on the border with Belgium, is estimated to have risen from 16,503 to 60,596 between 1882 and 1896.[209]

With more education and worldly experience, "emancipated" women in Europe and the United States pressed for political equality—the right to vote. Suffrage movements made headway in the years leading up to World War I, although that goal eluded them. (Only Finland made the franchise universal, in 1906.) British "feminists" (the term first came into use around 1900) made the case most vociferously and militantly, under the leadership of Emmeline Pankhurst and later, her daughter, Christabel, and the Women's Social and Political Union (WSPU) they had founded a year after the Second Boer War had ended. But a broad spectrum of organizations joined in the chorus calling for equal political rights for women. Suffragist movements sprang up in Sweden, France, Germany, and Denmark.[210] In the United States, twelve states—Colorado, California, Idaho, Washington, Wyoming, Utah, Oregon, Arizona, Kansas, Michigan, Illinois, and Montana—voted to extend the franchise to women prior to World War I. But most men (and many women) remained adamantly opposed to making the sexes equal and thus blurring the lines between their "natural" roles. This opposition was now also firmly grounded in war psychology. Only "masculine" nations could prevail in the conflict that many Europeans saw as unavoidable, and any undercutting of the authority or power of men would leave them vulnerable to defeat. As the prominent foe of English suffrage, Lord Cromer, asked rhetorically in 1910: how "can we hope to compete against such a nation [Germany] if we war against nature, and endeavour to invert the natural role of the sexes?"[211]

In spite of much public consternation and hostility, women in Europe and the United States were making slow but steady progress on many fronts during the first decade of the new century. In this rejoined battle of the sexes, they held the upper hand. Two interconnected developments—higher rates of employment and lower rates of fertility—were on their side.[212] Not only did society need their contributions to the workforce as more jobs suited to their skills and aptitude came into existence (and as companies sought to keep wages low), but also women were in a better position to respond to this need because they were having fewer babies than even a generation before.[213] This fertility decline was accelerating for three reasons. First, due to a variety of factors including increased education and a better standard of living, more middle-class women were remaining single.[214] (In England, for example, during the period 1851 to 1931 an average of 43 percent of all females ages twenty-five to twenty-nine were unmarried.)[215] Second, those who eventually did get married were waiting longer to take this step.[216] Third, thanks to wider use of effective birth control devices and less frequent sexual activity, married women were choosing to forego pregnancies more than they had at the end of the previous century. As a result of these developments, the native-born populations in some European countries were barely replenishing themselves. The decline in births was most pronounced among the middle, upper, and well-educated classes. France had been dealing with this sobering reality for some time: one analysis of birth statistics has found that not a single cohort of French females born after 1826–1830 had borne enough children to keep the population from shrinking.[217] In England, the number of births per female fell from 3.5 in 1901–1905 to 2.8 in the years 1911–1915.[218] (The replacement number is 2.1.) A decade later, more than one in five English women in their twenties would be childless.[219] The crude birth rate in Germany declined from 34.3 per 1,000 persons in the period 1901–1905 to 31.7 in 1906–1910, and 26.3 between 1911 and 1915.[220]

Having fewer (or no) children to bring up and supporting themselves gave many middle-class women of the Edwardian Age more freedom than their mothers had enjoyed and more than most of their male contemporaries thought was appropriate. These social changes were an affront to their traditional views on gender—namely, that males should be the providers and decision makers in a marriage, and women should be submissive to them and bear all the children that they—the husbands—wanted. Male trade unions similarly regarded the influx of female workers into factories with paternalistic consternation and tried to thwart it. But, at the dawn of a new era, this masculine viewpoint appeared to be losing ground to a more "modern" outlook on gender relations. Rather than more Teddy Roosevelts, the new century seemed to be producing more "degenerate" or inadequate males. The passing of Europe's dominant matriarchal figure, Queen Victoria, in 1901, had not paved the way for a male resurgence. Edward VII, who succeeded her to the throne at the age of fifty-nine, was wildly popular but past his prime—scarcely a paragon of vigorous manliness. ("Bertie" had been under his mother's thumb and grown up undisciplined and lazy, with a sense of inadequacy poorly concealed by his infamous philandering. According to an early biographer, Lytton Strachey, when Bertie, at age seventeen, had read the duties that he would be expected to fulfill as Prince of Wales, he had burst into tears.)[221]

Across the Channel, Edward's sickly, emotionally unstable nephew "Willy" (Wilhelm II) had, as a boy, compensated for a withered left arm by building sand castles and wearing sailor suits. He had been judged by his demanding tutor "neither particularly inclined nor particularly suited for serious study."[222] Ruling and top military circles in Wilhelmine Germany were known for their homosexual dalliances and intrigues.[223] The kaiser himself—a "soft, effeminate, and highly strung" man—was allegedly involved in these.[224] In Austria, the army was also wracked by homosexual scandals, notably one involving the head of its counterespionage service, Col. Alfred Redl, and the Russian military attaché in Vienna. The French army captain Alfred Dreyfus was (falsely) accused not only of passing secrets to the Germans, but also of being a sexual "deviant"—a sign of the fragility of masculinity in his country at the turn of the century.[225] The sensational trials of the Anglo-Irish poet and wit Oscar Wilde for "committing acts of gross indecency with men" had repulsed fin-de-siècle society in England and abroad for laying bare an aspect of contemporary reality most found abhorrent and had pretended did not exist. Now it was even being argued—by Havelock Ellis—that masculinity and heterosexuality were not identical.[226] The ensuing Boer War had suggested that even "normal" men might be insufficiently masculine to perform well in battle. While some men across Europe were working out in gymnasia and, in effect, prepping for war, others, already tested in the fray, were proving to be effete, decadent, and feckless—not exactly the sort a nation could depend upon.

At the same time these revelations were jolting the European and American male psyche, more educated young women were seeking to define themselves in new ways, on their own terms—politically, economically, socially, and sexually.[227] After being castigated and driven into the shadows during the recent chauvinistic wars, feminist concerns regained traction in countries like England, and found a greater resonance. Given impetus by the creation of the Women's Social and Political Union (WSPU) in 1903, British suffragettes launched a more militant, determined effort to secure the vote, building upon the pioneering work of Susan B. Anthony in the United States. Across the Channel, in France, disparate groups backing women's suffrage coalesced into a national movement in 1909, and several women ran for the national legislature on this issue. In many European countries, young single women were becoming a more visible, if still underpaid, part of the workforce. By 1910, women made up a considerable percentage of those working in manufacturing—37 percent in France, 34 percent in Britain, 33 percent in Italy, 32.5 percent in Belgium, and 23 percent in Germany.[228] Many other women found employment in the growing service sector. In Germany, for example, they could be found staffing the counters of urban shops, offices, and department stores to a degree not evident just a few years before. The same held true in France, where a third of employed females worked in offices, although the largest number—over 3 million—were engaged in farming in this still largely rural society.[229]

The impact of female emancipation during the Edwardian era is evident in the cultural works it produced—for example, the plays of Ibsen (notably *A Doll's House*, which made its London debut in 1889) and George Bernard Shaw (*Pygmalion*), the novels of Thomas Hardy (*Tess of the D'Urbervilles* and *Jude the Obscure*), the short stories and plays of Arthur Schnitzler, and the expressionist paintings of Edvard Munch, Egon Schiele, and other artists of their generation. In addition, English female writers produced an abundance of novels portraying "rebellious heroines, independent women, and unhappy wives" and dealing frankly with female sexuality and the oppressiveness of marriage.[230] On many fronts, "liberated" women were refusing to accept the limitations on outlook and behavior that their male-dominated societies were seeking to impose upon them. This new female assertiveness even made inroads in faraway (and still patriarchal) Japan, where some enlightened circles believed that educating women would further national progress.[231]

There was, no doubt, a connection between this resurgent feminism and the failure of turn-of-the-century males to live up to expectations as protectors of the nation and procreators of the race. Both "failures"—evident, for the British and Russians, in the Boer and Japanese conflicts, respectively, and, for the French and other Europeans, in their relentlessly plummeting birth rates—telegraphed weakness and decline. In so exposing their shortcomings, men had lost the legitimacy of their claim that they performed a unique, irreplaceable role in society. Instead of recapturing the power and status they had ceded during the last decades of the previous century, European males seemed to have only lost more. Now, with war brewing on the Continent, pressure was once again mounting for them to "do their duty" and uphold their national honor. For this to happen, their societies would have to be militarized, and men returned to positions of authority. But the countervailing force of a growing feminism, stridently demanding more rights and parity between the sexes, threatened to prevent this masculine restoration from taking place. These two diametrically opposed social imperatives—male dominance and female equality—were now on a collision course, proceeding ahead at high speed. The course of events in the next few years would give one or the other an edge and tilt the outcome in their favor. For the growing numbers of emancipated women, hope lay in consolidating their recent gains by securing the vote and attaining sexual freedom. For men wishing to roll back these feminist advances, hope lay elsewhere—on the battlefields of glorious wars they could only dimly imagine, in prevailing during the life-or-death struggle that years of training on the playing fields, among bands of their brothers. Years spent developing habits of discipline, courage, and self-denial in service of lofty ideals that reflected their male essence had prepared them. For these young men, the battle of the sexes would be decided not at the ballot box or in the bedroom, but on another, more "manly" front—on ground that was familiar, well-trodden, and of their own choosing.

Chapter 3

ALL THE KING'S HORSES—WORLD WAR I

I t all happened in a few horrific seconds. As the lead horses careened by, a tall, slender, well-dressed woman with bright red hair and green eyes bent down, slipped under the wooden rail that held bystanders at the Derby back, and boldly stepped in front of the trailing three steeds as they rounded Tattenham Corner. One brushed past her, oblivious in its frantic haste. The woman then seemed to open her arms in a welcoming embrace as the king's horse, Anmer, bore down upon her, going full tilt. The force of the impact hurled horse, jockey, and the woman forward onto the churned turf.[1] Four days later, on June 8, 1913, Emily Wilding Davison, a militant suffragette, died from her massive internal injuries. The news stunned a British nation not accustomed to such violent death—certainly not a woman's.

It was not clear what Davison had intended—had she meant to kill herself this way, or was it just a terrible accident? Some claimed that the forty-year-old former teacher had gone to the annual Epsom Derby, where she knew the royal family would be in attendance, to stage an incident like this, to force the king *finally* to grasp how much women like her wanted the vote. Yet Davison had purchased a round-trip rail ticket. Perhaps she had only meant to grab the horse's bridle, to disrupt the race. Perhaps she had thought all the horses were already past when she stepped onto the track. Perhaps she had only made up her mind at the last minute to sacrifice herself.[2] To those who admired her, the details did not matter. Whatever her intentions, Davison was a martyr to the cause. By doing what she had done, she had lived up to the motto of the Women's Social and Political Union—"Deeds Not Words"—and paid the ultimate price.

Davison's funeral was a well-staged spectacle. Thousands showed up to pay their respects. The procession stretched for three-quarters of a mile through the streets of London—a long, silent cortege befitting a war hero, made up mostly of women—the older ones in black, the younger ones in white dresses bound by black armbands, holding purple irises and white lilies as their scepters. Some in the throng of onlookers booed, but the rest looked on respectfully, curiously.[3] Carriages full of flowers escorted the black-draped dray, and banners lofted high above the marchers gave expression to the sentiments on the marchers' minds. One quoted the words of the Latin poet Horace, uttered so often in the past by loyal British subjects—*Dulce et decorum est pro patria mori* (How noble and glorious it is to die for one's country).[4] Little could any in the crowd that June day in 1913 imagine how many times this phrase would be repeated in the coming years.[5] The weekly organ of the WSPU, the *Suffragette*, put a memorial to Emily Davison on the front cover of its next issue—a drawing of her transmogrified into an angel, standing on the Epsom track, with arms raised in the same expectant way, with a halo over her head made up of the words "Love That Overcometh."[6]

Mainstream opinion was less kind to her. The *Times* curtly dismissed Davison's extreme action as "not likely to increase the popularity of any cause with the ordinary public. Reckless fanaticism is not regarded by them as a qualification for the franchise."[7] The *New York Times* sounded the same disdainful note, branding her protest a "suffragist outrage." The newspaper's initial report on the incident seemed to express more sympathy for the royal thoroughbred (which recovered fully and went on to race again) than for the dying woman. It was easy for most English men and women to agree that Davison, an Oxford-educated teacher, was "mad." Her motto was Benjamin Franklin's perversely provocative "Rebellion against tyrants is obedience to God." Something of a loose cannon in the suffrage movement, she had behaved outrageously many times before—heaving rocks at the chancellor of the exchequer, David Lloyd George; setting pillar (mail) boxes on fire; going to prison numerous times; barricading herself in a cell; going on hunger strikes; enduring forced feedings; assaulting a Baptist minister she mistook for Lloyd George; hurling herself down a prison staircase and injuring her spine; and hiding overnight in the House of Commons so she could claim it on the 1911 census as her place of residence. Whatever hopes the

WPSU and its charismatic leader, Emmeline Pankhurst—an admirer of Joan of Arc—might have had that Davison's death would make the authorities more sympathetic to their cause did not materialize. Many of her fellow Britons were angry that the king's jockey, Herbert Jones, had been injured in the collision.[8] The Liberal government of Prime Minister Herbert Asquith did not waver in its opposition to giving women the vote, even though many MPs of his party now favored this policy.[9] This incident dismayed even many supporters of female suffrage.[10]

Davison's purported suicide was seen as only the latest and the most egregious of a series of highly public and symbolic actions taken to draw attention to the campaign to win the vote. In recent years, frustrated at the lack of progress toward their goal, members of the militant WPSU had adopted increasingly outlandish tactics, such as jumping onto the prime minister's car, breaking windows of government buildings, carving the phrase "Votes for Women" in golf greens, setting fire to empty country homes, physically confronting officials, chaining themselves to buildings, and destroying works of art.[11] In February 1913, a middle-aged suffragette from Leeds named Leonora Cohen had flung an iron bar at a case at the Tower of London containing the Crown Jewels, causing little damage but forcing the closure of museums throughout London.[12] These incidents had not helped the movement either.

More fundamentally, the suffragettes' rash behavior violated prevailing notions of what women were and how they should conduct themselves.[13] In their militancy, these radicals were crossing the line that defined one sex as separate and different from the other, overturning one of Edwardian society's fundamental principles. (This outlook was evident on the other side of the Atlantic, where critics of female suffrage had long contended that so "masculinizing" women would lead inevitably to the demise of civilization.)[14] Women who insisted on putting activism and careers ahead of marriage also posed a threat to the nation's—and the empire's—future because they were relinquishing their primary duty to produce children. This "selfish" decision was contributing to what some saw as a looming "race suicide": a shrinking "white" England would soon be numerically overwhelmed by a rapidly expanding population of inferior peoples. Furthermore, many conservative opponents of female suffrage saw proof in these militant tactics that they were right: women *were* too emotionally unstable and intellectually undeveloped to play a role in public affairs. This was to be reserved for men. In the words of one MP, "[The vote] is a badge, not of superiority, but of difference, a difference of masculine character and coercive power, a difference which is adapted for the governance of alien races and for the safeguarding of our Empire."[15] For all these reasons, the suffragist protests outraged most of the British public, especially tradition-minded men who perceived this aggressive feminism as challenging if not usurping their own masculine prerogatives. On the eve of World War I, this was a particularly sensitive issue since, in many European countries, the definition and value of "manliness" was then very much in question. Many men were experiencing doubts about what their roles in this new century should be and what they could contribute to modern society.

This was certainly the case in England, where the status of males seemed endangered. For one thing, working-class males were experiencing a number of economic setbacks. Increasing international competition and stagnating productivity had led some British companies to find ways of containing costs. In the first decade of the century, wages failed to keep pace with inflation—a situation aggravated by a recession in 1908.[16] In response to these developments, industrial workers had gone on strike in unprecedented numbers.[17] But the vast majority of these strikes had failed to reach their objectives.[18] In 1912, for example, a million coal miners had walked out in their campaign for a minimum wage, shutting down the entire industry for six weeks and crippling Britain's economy. The miners had only agreed to go back to work after the Liberal government had consented to introducing a bill granting this demand, but that promise had not been kept. Instead, the power of this English labor group had begun a long, slow downhill slide as the importance of coal mining in the country decreased.[19] This turn of events, coupled with the similar failure of dock and transport workers in London to organize a general strike that year, had "struck a hard blow at syndicalism."[20] In the following year, labor unrest had continued to spread in Britain, with another 688,000 workers joining picket lines. But, when they returned to work, conditions for these underpaid workers did not improve significantly. That year—1913—workers stayed off the job a record 40 million work days.[21]

On the international stage, the nation's manliness also seemed to be in eclipse. At the 1912 summer Olympic Games, held in Stockholm,

British athletes stumbled badly after having dominated the competition four years before on their home turf. This time, with little public backing or government financial support, instead of 156 medals, they came away with only 41. Backers of the games bemoaned this performance as a national disgrace.[22] Many worried about the implications of another poor showing four years hence, when the games were to be held in Berlin.

Politically, England lacked strong, decisive leadership. The Liberal prime minister, Lord Asquith, was considered weak, dependent on the votes of the Irish Parliamentary Party to maintain his majority control in the House of Commons. Asquith was constitutionally indecisive and inclined to change his position on major issues (such as female suffrage). He was also held in check by the conservative House of Lords, which vetoed many bills passed by Liberal MPs. In 1913, the prime minister hesitated to impose Home Rule on Irish Unionists for fear of inciting a civil war in Ireland, and sought, instead, to compromise on this volatile issue—another indication that the government was not capable of taking a firm stand and sticking to it. The new king, George V, had not brought an infusion of masculine vigor when he assumed the throne following the death of his father, Edward, in June of 1911. Already forty-four at the time; slight and knock-kneed; a fastidious, conservative dresser with a well-trimmed beard and equally well-manicured hands, the new monarch was most known for being an avid stamp collector. His expert marksmanship—the king famously shot twenty-one tigers on a trip to India and more than a thousand pheasants during one six-hour stretch on an aristocrat's country estate—did little to change this opinion of him.[23]

With their masculine power and stature in question on many fronts, insecure, frustrated Englishmen had little patience or tolerance for aggressively assertive suffragists. The militants' use of violence to attract attention to their cause was particularly unnerving. It is not surprising that some men resorted to physical force against these protesting females, who seemed to have shed all vestiges of womanliness. Often this kind of response was officially sanctioned. British police were wont to push and punch demonstrating suffragettes, or knock them roughly to the ground. On one occasion, when a group of women tried to invade Parliament, officers committed what amounted to sexual assault in restraining them.[24] Treatment of imprisoned suffragettes was also physically and sexually degrading. The women were held and force-fed by having a hose inserted in their mouths or noses. During some confrontations, police officers would stand back indifferently while bands of young hooligans pummeled suffragettes with mud, cursed, or assaulted them. While militants accounted for only a tiny fraction of English womanhood—never numbering more than five thousand—they aroused deep fear and animosity because their methods, as much as their objective, were profoundly disturbing to the social order. If these women were to prevail, many felt, England would only slip more rapidly into an irreversible decline. As Virginia Woolf would recall in the 1920s, the suffragists were a highly polarizing force in her country:

> No age can ever have been so stridently sex conscious as our own; those innumerable books by men about women in the British Museum are a proof of it. The Suffrage campaign was no doubt to blame. It must have roused in men an extra desire for self-assertion; it must have made them lay an emphasis upon their sex and its characteristics which they would not have troubled to think about had they not been challenged.[25]

Elsewhere in Europe, the movement for female suffrage did not arouse such strong passions. To the north, the Scandinavian countries had quietly granted women the right to vote earlier in the century. In more religiously and socially conservative nations further south, few favored female participation in public affairs. Most men and women were content with the gender status quo and would continue to feel this way for several decades to come. (France and Italy, for example, did not grant women the vote until the mid-1940s.) On the Continent, only Germany and Holland experienced significant progress in women's rights prior to World War I. In both cases, these advances came through political consensus building rather than street confrontation. This reflected a less polarized environment, in which there was little pressure for radical reform. Germany may have had the third-largest women's movement in the world (after Britain and the United States), but in 1908 only about 2,500 women belonged to the German Union for Women's Suffrage. This organization was pejoratively described by a writer for the *New York Times* a year later as "particularly backward" due to laws prohibiting women from participating in political activities.[26] When, also in 1908, this ban was lifted, and young

German women were finally allowed to attend university, much of the motivation for pursuing greater gender equity evaporated. In the second decade of the century, German suffragists, under attack from women's religious groups, renounced their support for abortion rights and sexual freedom and adopted a pronationalist position. After they did so, social conservatives had a hard time labeling them objectionable. Dutch feminists, operating in a more hospitable milieu, capitalized upon the convening of the International Woman Suffrage Alliance in Amsterdam in 1908 to make their case. These activists subsequently persuaded an array of political parties as well as the public to embrace it: women in the Netherlands received the franchise in 1917.[27] They were the first outside the Nordic countries to gain this right.

Although men on the Continent had less cause to fear militant feminism, they still had considerable worries about their own masculinity at a time when the boundaries separating the two genders were becoming fluid and ill defined. As the young, psychologically troubled Viennese philosopher Otto Weininger wrote in 1903, just before shooting himself in the heart: "The real world, from the point of view of sex, may be regarded as swaying between two points, no actual individual being at either point, but somewhere between the two."[28] Some European men reacted to pronouncements like this, as one historian has put it, "with an aggressive restatement of the old values," by lifting weights, donning uniforms, or hunting deer, while others succumbed to "male maladies" and "weak nerves."[29] In countries such as Italy, France, and Germany, renewed emphasis was placed on upholding male honor (and displaying courage) by fighting duels.[30] An estimated two hundred of these were fought in France alone between 1875 and 1900.[31] In other words, masculinity was reaffirmed along virile, heterosexual lines, rejecting any and all homosexual tendencies as incompatible with what it meant to be a man.[32] The "modern" notion of flexible male and female identities was widely regarded as both a symptom and a cause of Western society's feared impending demise. This link between insufficient manliness and cultural decline was a theme explored in many works of literature (as well as paintings) of the early twentieth century. The German novelist Thomas Mann, for example, took up this theme in his first novel, *Buddenbrooks* (1901), in which he dealt with the concerns of the eponymous family patriarch, Thomas Buddenbrooks, for his "sickly, unassertive, and shy" son, Hanno, who is more drawn to music than to taking over the family business.[33] Mann would make the connection between art, degeneration, and sexual deviance more explicit in his 1912 novella, *Death in Venice*. Perhaps the most significant treatment of homosexuality and decadence during this period was Marcel Proust's *A la recherché du temps perdu* (Remembrance of Things Past), the first volume of which appeared in 1913.

Other artists and intellectuals stressed the negative impact of modernism on society and the individual, particularly males. By succumbing to vast, impersonal forces such as industrialization and rule of the masses, the nations of Europe and the United States had been sapped of their collective vitality and ability to chart their own destinies.[34] The masculine impulse to control and dominate had yielded to a "feminine" passivity—acceptance of a more natural (or amoral) governing order. In sexual terms, this cultural development had weakened the male libido and allowed "degenerate" impulses to come to the fore. Society was succumbing to these debilitating influences because its manly fortitude had deteriorated. This alarming male "inversion" was as abhorrent to most Europeans as the "unnatural" women who were forsaking marriage and motherhood to work, live independently, usurp masculine prerogatives, and experiment sexually. Modern men were seen to be grievously lacking in discipline, self-reliance, aggressiveness, and virility.[35] Concern over this development was particularly great in France, where a link was perceived between male sexual "perversion" and reproductive failure.[36]

There was ample evidence of this disturbing trend in what many perceived as widespread homosexuality. This tendency appeared only to have increased as the Edwardian era came to a close. It was most apparent in the Continent's capitals. In Berlin, for example, the number of gay bars had nearly doubled (from twenty to thirty-eight) in the decade preceding World War I, and as many as two thousand male prostitutes were then making a living there—despite the existence of strict antihomosexual laws in Germany and elsewhere.[37] In 1908, a visitor from Paris, the playwright Oscar Méténier, was struck by the visibility of gay society in the German metropolis, especially among the officer corps and other well-to-do social circles he encountered there.[38]

In England, unconventional sexuality was becoming fashionable among the intellectual elite. In a village near Cambridge, a group of free-thinking young men and women loosely affiliated with the Bloomsbury Group and bound together by the bisexual poet Rupert Brooke gathered to "escape modernism by recreating a rural myth and developed an original lifestyle founded on worship of the body, freedom of movement, nudity, and coed bathing." These "Neo-Pagans" devised a "new paradigm for relations between men and women based on frankness and a free discussion of sexual questions."[39] For members of this and other avant-garde circles of the day, which included writers like D. H. Lawrence, Virginia Woolf, Lytton Strachey, and E. M. Forster, homosexuality was not a taboo but simply another form of "natural" human sexuality. An equally if not more tolerant outlook flourished in Paris—the final refuge of Oscar Wilde—where homosexual relations were all the rage in many salons, and where gay expatriates such as Gertrude Stein and Alice B. Toklas could find a warm welcome without worrying about running afoul of the law. In other European cities, highly eroticized art—the paintings of Gustav Klimt and Pablo Picasso, the ballets of Sergei Diaghilev, the plays of Franz Wedekind, the short fiction of Thomas Mann, and the operas of Richard Strauss—simultaneously titillated and scandalized the public.[40]

Such experimentation signaled a new openness and freedom regarding sexual matters—an outright rejection of Victorian moral strictures and discomfort over bodily pleasures. Moreover, this willingness to explore same-sex relationships and bisexuality indicated that the nineteenth-century idea of two antithetically defined and mutually exclusive genders was no longer considered valid. Sexual identity was not a biological or cultural given, but a matter for individual exploration and realization.[41] For those men and women who felt constrained by the old norms, this new way of thinking was liberating and exhilarating. They could now pursue a lifestyle in sync with their sexual predilections, not grossly at odds with them. For most Europeans, however, the overt presence of "unnatural," ambiguous, or "deviant" forms of sexual behavior frustrated their desire for conformity and certainty regarding such matters. This latter need certainly characterized French society, which endorsed as "primordial," natural, and proper the polarity of the two sexes and, outside the salons of Paris, fiercely resisted any attempt to tamper with these clear distinctions.[42] What was now apparent to all was that, in matters of sex, human beings were far more complex and variegated than had once been believed. Here was another central component of modern life that defied easy classification and comprehension. To a large degree, the changes in sexual mores grew out of changes in how men and women in Europe and the United States had been socialized to see themselves and each other, over the preceding twenty-five years.

The late nineteenth-century "flight from domesticity" had occurred because many middle-class married men had found their once-supreme masculine stature to be diminished and devalued within the home. Absentee breadwinners, morally suspect and deprived of unequivocal paternal respect, they had come to feel unfulfilled and out of place inside the well-appointed houses and apartments they had procured with their rising salaries and careers. Changes in marriage laws that reduced the husband's power over his wife had also made family life less appealing.[43] So these men had looked elsewhere—mostly to other men—for companionship, stimulation, emotional attachment; one historian has likened this quest as a "vital, masculine counterpart to domestic life."[44] They had also sought to reconnect with a more primal and distinctive maleness by testing themselves physically, in competition with their peers.

At the same time, many single men—either indifferent to marital life or unable to find a spouse—had sought personal happiness in largely male enclaves overseas or on other frontiers.[45] The latter included far-flung corners of European empires as well as the remote and forbidding polar caps—the goal of several celebrated (and all-male) expeditions during the early years of the twentieth century. Urban centers, especially in America, were also turning into gathering points for unmarried males. As a consequence of immigration from Europe and the countryside, this group constituted 40 percent of the residents of large US cities between 1890 and 1920.[46] In essence, these dissatisfied American and European men had sought to re-create a "separate sphere" for themselves on terms more to their liking and better suited to their temperament. Furthermore, they had done so in such a way as to ensure that their newfound domains—the public school, the gymnasium, the club, the military, the Wild West—would remain quintessentially male, impervious to any female inroads.

Close male bonds were, of course, not a new phenomenon, on either side of the Atlantic. Since the advent of the industrial age, men and women had spent much of their time in single-sex environments, working and relaxing apart from each other, and these affiliations had promoted strong emotional attachments. Men routinely used affectionate terms in writing to their male friends, embraced them openly— even shared beds with them (as Abraham Lincoln had done for four years with a close Springfield friend named Joshua Speed). Rarely were these relationships homoerotic or physical in nature. Rather, because they did not have to worry about being labeled "homosexual" (a term that did not then exist), boys and young men simply felt free to express their affection in a frank and uninhibited manner, as photographs taken during the nineteenth century reveal.[47]

Several historical events and other social trends had encouraged the growth of more outlets for this kind of male bonding and intensified it. In the United States, the bitter divisiveness of the War between the States had fueled a desire for unifying participation in civic life in the following decades. As a result, fraternal organizations, with their secretive initiation rituals and quasifamilial atmosphere, had proliferated. By 1896, 5.5 million American men, out of a total of 19 million, belonged to one or more of these organizations—most notably the Odd Fellows (810,000 members) Freemasons (750,000), and the Knights of Pythias (475,000). Middle-class men were especially inclined to join.[48] Growth of such groups continued well into the twentieth century; membership did not peak until the 1920s.[49] Another major social impulse was the need to work collectively to address the problems of an industrialized, urban world and restore bonds that had been severed by it. There was, during the Progressive Era, a "yearning for the community values of small-town life, nostalgia provoked by the materials, individualism, and 'bigness' of the new America."[50] This longing for a lost "connectedness," as well as a renewed civic mindedness, had ignited an explosion of men's (and women's) charitable, religious, professional, social, political, labor, veterans, collegiate, athletic, ethnic, and community-based clubs and associations. (Boys in Europe and the United States searched for this kind of organic, premodern bonding in scouting and in groups like the *Wandervogel*—bands of German youth who hiked through fields and forests to commune with nature and each other.) Half of the mass organizations ever created in the United States came into being between 1870 and 1920.[51] Most of these maintained a strict gender exclusivity;[52] indeed, this was a major aspect of their appeal.

Education was another arena in which, to a certain degree, the sexes were kept apart. This separation was truer of Europe than the United States, where few students attended private, single-sex secondary schools (although many colleges and universities continued to be all male or all female).[53] Beyond the primary level, schooling in countries like England, Germany, and France was largely limited to males—and only to those (a small percentage) who came from affluent, socially prominent families. During the formative years after the age of thirteen, when they were becoming young men, these privileged boys spent most of their time exclusively with their peers, cut off from their families, their communities, and from the opposite sex. The intense male bonding that occurred in these secondary schools promoted not only a "cult of manliness"— with an emphasis on athletics, stoicism, discipline, and group loyalty— but also misogyny.[54] Girls were disparaged and held in contempt. Particularly at English public schools, this hothouse atmosphere also encouraged amorous male-male friendships and sexual experimentation. As Robert Graves, who had several homosexual "flirtations" during his final years at boarding school, later wrote, the main activities there had been "games and romantic friendships."[55] Orgies and sexual abuse were commonplace at these schools well into the twentieth century.[56] Emotionally, the ties formed at places like Eton and Harrow served both as models for subsequent heterosexual pairings and as substitutes for them. They also found an outlet at Oxford, where a Platonic ideal of male love had taken hold toward the end of the Victorian era under the aegis of John Addington Symonds, Walter Pater, and A. E. Housman. This idea of a "sacred bond" between men was related to, and intertwined with, another tradition—that of brotherly love between equals, as found among knights in medieval tales such as the *Song of Roland*.[57] Both kinds of ties promised young men an idealized spiritual and emotional experience that was stronger and more deeply rewarding than what they could find with a woman, or in merely sexual experiences with their fellow adolescents.[58] This hankering for male-male affection is also evident in numerous literary works of this period. These range from the highly rarefied—Walter Pater's interpretation of Castor and Polydeuces—to the popular—Arthur Conan Doyle's felicitous pairing of Sherlock Holmes and Dr. Watson.

Another significant component of boys' secondary education in some countries was the instilling of patriotism. This process legitimized male bonding by elevating the emotional connection from the personal to a much higher (and abstract) level. French education officials, anxious to help prepare the nation's young men for war after the humiliating defeat by Prussia in 1871, made sure that boys learned their obligation as citizens—namely, to sacrifice their lives for France, if that need should arise. From the first day of class, they were taught to "love France."[59] Their zealous teachers—known as the "Black Hussars of the Republic" because of the coats they wore—used songs, poems, maps, and flags to inspire this emotion.[60] In addition to taking courses in history that glorified their country's achievements (and overlooked its shortcomings), these students spent much of their days taking part in gymnastics and undergoing military drills. (In the early 1880s, a law was passed requiring all French boys ages twelve and over to join *bataillons scolaires*—quasimilitary organizations wherein participants wore uniforms, carried rifles, and marched in Bastille Day parades with the regular army.)[61]

Taking their cue from the emperor himself, German schoolboys were filled with love and admiration for the nation's heroes and "the very ground on which they walked."[62] Students annually celebrated the emperor's birthday and the anniversary of the Battle of Sedan, on September 1, 1870, when Prussia had inflicted a major defeat on France. They learned by heart patriotic poems about the past glories of their nation and studied history not to critique the past, but to absorb a nationalistic perspective. Schoolmasters commanded their young charges the way an infantry captain would a gaggle of raw recruits.[63] Devotion to the fatherland was cultivated at all levels in Germany's education system but was most prominent in the all-male secondary schools, or *gymnasia*. Open only to the sons of wealthy or professionally accomplished families, these served as conduits into the highly prestigious officer corps of the army and navy: students took exams to qualify for a year of volunteer service that could lead to acceptance into these elite bodies, as well as into technical schools and universities.[64] Institutionally and philosophically, education and the military were, in fact, closely connected. Both stressed duty, discipline, and service to the state. Boys eager to defend Germany in uniform passed seamlessly from one to the other. By contrast, English public schools were slower to embrace patriotic symbols and values. Around the turn of the century, one could only rarely find a Union Jack flying over or in front of any of their buildings, and schools in London expressly banned any festivities on Empire Day—the late Queen Victoria's birthday.[65] However, by 1907, more than twelve thousand elementary schools in Britain were celebrating this holiday.[66]

What nationalism was missing in the classrooms of that day was made up for by the youth organizations that flourished in the years prior to World War I, most notably the Boy Scouts. By 1910, more than 100,000 British boys belonged to one of the 3,898 troops then in existence.[67] Overall, two of every five boys born between 1901 and 1925 joined one of these groups, which featured uniforms and military-style drills and emphasized patriotic submission.[68] The Boy Scout Law, for instance, stated: "A scout is loyal to the King, and to his officers, and to his parents, his Country, his employers, and to those under his orders. We must stick to them through thick and thin against anyone who is their enemy or who even talks badly of them."[69]

In imperial Germany, love of country was as estimable a virtue as a mother's love. Its civilian leaders flaunted their own militaristic infatuation by showing up for ceremonial events in uniform. The kaiser, who hoped to cultivate a "manly spirit" among his people, was wont to set out from Berlin on a long journey merely for the pleasure of changing into his admiral's garb when he arrived at his seaside destination.[70] Enthusiasm for Germany's military might was so intense that an organization formed in 1898 to lobby for expansion of the navy promptly signed up over 75,000 members; by the end of the century, over a million Germans belonged to this *Flottenverein*, or Navy League.[71] A similar booster group for the Reich army, the *Wehrverein*, was created in 1912. Other European nations were not as easily swept away by this increasingly bellicose mood in the new century, although virtually all of them felt obliged to bolster their military forces.

In Russia, where mass patriotism did not have a long history, celebrations of the two hundredth anniversary of Peter the Great's momentous victory over the Swedes at Poltava and of the centennial of Napoleon's defeat, combined with nationalistic education and newspapers, managed to awaken this feeling and dispel the mood of defeatism ensuing from the country's recent defeat by Japan. But, despite three decades of patriotic indoctrination in the schools, most French men and women were not eager for war.[72] And the British public, particularly its socialist-leaning working class, remained immune to similarly chauvin-istic appeals during the Edwardian era.[73]

While not universally present, patriotic pride undoubtedly helped to cement male group-identification early in the twentieth century. The sense of solidarity and common purpose fostered by nationalistic groups helped to reverse what was considered an unhealthy trend toward excessive individualism and fragmentation in modern society. Many men sought this communion with other males rather than with members of the opposite sex because, in their view, women were innately different from them and thus could not offer the same kind of intimacy. Authentic, primal unity lay in brotherhood, not marriage. Emotional bonds among men strengthened a willingness to sacrifice for the greater good and desire to return to an earlier stage in human development, when identity and meaning were based in a (sex-defined) group, and when the roles of males and females were strictly separated within this social context. The coming of war in 1914 would allow such feelings to have full expression.

Friendships among men also added a sorely missing human dimension in a world dominated by large, impersonal institutions and rigid, divisive structures, such as class. Not coincidentally, these male affiliations also had the effect of distancing men from women, accentuating the differences between the genders, and reaffirming men's putative superiority. These objectives took on urgency as competition among Europe's Great Powers intensified, and the likelihood of war increased. For nations could not hope to triumph on the field of battle unless they possessed an ample supply of militarist virtues—strong leadership, aggressive fighting spirit, willing submission to authority, unquestioning devotion to the state, and the selfless, mutual affection of its soldiers. In some countries, these qualities had been strengthened in the decades preceding World War I. While their governments had been fostering patriotism in the schools and through public celebrations, writers in nations like Austria, Germany, England, and France had also promoted these virtues through idealized images of male camaraderie in times of war. Rudyard Kipling well captured these sentimental feelings in a turn-of-the-century poem entitled "Follow Me 'Ome":

There was no one like 'im, 'Orse or Foot,
Nor any o' the Guns I knew;

An' because it was so, why, o' course 'e went an' died,
Which is just what the best men do.

• • •.

'E was all that I 'ad in the way of a friend,
An' I've 'ad to find one new;
But I'd give my pay an' stripe for to get the beggar back,
Which it's just too late to do.

As war approached, men had to be prepared for the sacrifices it would require.[74] A number of "invasion novels" explicitly addressed this growing threat, to help sound the alarm.[75] The most influential of these was *The Riddle of the Sands*, written by the Irish nationalist Erskine Childers (1903). In addition to persuading Winston Churchill to establish several naval bases in Scotland, this book aroused many of its British readers from their self-indulgent idleness—what the narrator, Carruthers, refers to as his own "silly egotism"—to defend the nation. Inspired by the example of his old Oxford friend Davies, Carruthers abandons his clubbish aloofness and succumbs to a "strain of crazy chivalry more common to the knights-errant of the Middle Ages than to sober modern youths," when he agrees to help patrol the waters between England and Germany looking for warships.[76] In many books or poems like this, love for one's country and for a friend (or lover) do not come into conflict, as E. M. Forster would later claim they did, but rather reinforce each other.[77] Often, as in *The Riddle of the Sands*, this personal bond was between two men—a foreshadowing of what would need to occur at the front.[78]

The appeal of these male-male friendships was chiefly emotional: men enjoyed each other's company and did not hesitate to express the feelings of comradeship, admiration, respect, caring, and even love that intense, shared experiences awakened and reinforced. The question remains: why did such affectionate ties become so important in the decades leading up to World War I? One explanatory factor is the larger social context—the relations between males and females at that time. Simply put, during the late Victorian and Edwardian ages, the two sexes did not spend that much time together. Despite—or, rather, because of—

women's economic and social advancement, they continued to lead largely parallel lives as World War I approached. The male affiliations of this era, whether deepened on boarding-school playing fields or the ice floes of Antarctica, compensated for the absence of female companionship and romantic involvement. They offered men an emotional satisfaction and group identification that women could not give them. This estrangement of the sexes was reflected in the declining centrality of the institution of marriage in Western European and American society.

This was not a new phenomenon. Over the preceding several centuries, growing percentages of men and women had delayed getting married or foregone matrimony entirely. This tendency contrasts starkly with the situation in traditional societies, including nations in Eastern Europe, where nearly all individuals had married by their twenties. What appears to have caused this discrepancy is economic development. The inclination to marry late or not at all coincided with the rise of cities, massive migration there from the countryside, and the concomitant growth of capitalism, industrialization, and a wage-based economy.[79] These new economic circumstances gave women, in particular, greater opportunities to earn a living and made it less appealing for them to marry early and devote their lives to raising a family. (Having many children conflicted with desires for upward mobility.) The declining European and American marriage rates during the nineteenth century have to be seen in this context of this larger social transformation.

This trend was clearly becoming more pronounced as the century was coming to an end. Whereas, in 1875, nine of ten British women had been married by the time they reached the age of fifty, only about eight in ten had attained this status in 1901, and this proportion would continue to drop until the 1930s.[80] More generally, around 1900, between 10 to 20 percent of all females and 7 to 14 percent of all males in Western Europe and the United States were still single.[81] Why was this happening? The causes are not readily apparent. Statistics show that the greatest decrease in marriage occurred among persons in their twenties. Economic disadvantage might have accounted for this: smaller incomes may have prevented many young couples from marrying. But statistical data do not support such an explanation. In fact, an analysis of marriage trends suggests the opposite: in 1900, males in low-paying professions— farmers, miners, laborers, and shoemakers—married earlier than men belonging to the professional and "independent" classes. Indeed, it was the decreasing marriage rate in these latter groups that accounted for most of the overall decline. In England, for example, fewer well-to-do couples were exchanging vows than those in working-class neighborhoods: the birth rate among middle- and upper-class couples who married in the 1870s and 1880s had fallen by between one-third and two-thirds more than the rate among working-class couples. This class-based discrepancy only widened in the following decades. By 1911, families of doctors, lawyers, scientists, teachers, and the like were having an average of 3.4 children, versus 6.1 in working-class families.[82] Clearly, then, diminishing or insufficient economic resources do not explain the drop in marriage rates.

Population figures indicate that a gender imbalance may have contributed to this development. During most of the nineteenth century, many European countries had a surplus of females. In England, women outnumbered men by over a million in 1901.[83] This was due, in large part, to a higher male mortality rate as well as colonial outmigration.[84] France had a similar "excess" of females of all ages: the number had risen from 140,000 in 1870 to 650,000 in 1906.[85] Out of a population of some 64 million in 1910, Germany had 845,661 more women than men.[86] However, a closer scrutiny of demographic data reveals that it was actually *males*, not females, who faced greater odds in finding a mate. For among those age groups most apt to marry, single men were far more plentiful than single women. In 1900, approximately 48 percent of Western European males ages twenty-five to twenty-nine, but only 35 percent of females in this age group, were still unattached. The proportion of "excess" young bachelors was greatest—18 percent—in France; in Italy the gender difference was 16 percent, in Germany 14 percent, in Austria 13 percent, and in the Netherlands and Belgium 9 percent.[87] Only in England was there near parity: 47 percent of men ages twenty-five to twenty-nine versus 42 percent of women in that age group were still single.[88] This male "marriage deficit" could be partially explained by the tendency of some younger women to marry older men.[89] But there is no evidence that this inclination increased as the century was coming to a close.

What had changed were the options open to middle-class women. Much more than their mothers or grandmothers, many of them could choose to continue their education at a higher level, embark upon a career, and support themselves. They could also more readily seek fulfillment in public affairs—in volunteer organizations and social causes. These greater freedoms did not, however, increase their chances of marrying. On the contrary, there was an inverse correlation between the amount of schooling a woman received and the chances of her "settling down."[90] Furthermore, women who had jobs were less apt to find a husband.[91] (This rule also applied to working-class women who relocated to take jobs in gender-segregated industries such as textiles.)[92] As females around the turn of the century acquired educational, political, and economic capital, either they became less inclined to accept a suitor's proposal, or else men were less disposed to woo them. One can surmise it was a combination of both factors.

There is little question that a large number of middle-class European men found this recent elevation of female status disconcerting. These men were used to being in charge, at home as well as in the wider world, and now they were losing their control. In contemplating marriage, many of them looked askance at the new model of an egalitarian, "companionate" arrangement. They were apprehensive about the power, independence, and willfulness they associated with "New Women" in their circle of friends. Such anxiety emerged in the works of many European writers and artists on the eve of World War I. Often this was tinged with hostility. These feelings surfaced in the paintings of Edvard Munch (who portrayed females as blood-sucking vampires), Gustav Klimt, Oskar Kokoschka, Ernst Ludwig Kirchner, and Pablo Picasso, as well as the plays of Strindberg and Franz Wedekind and—somewhat later—the novels and poems of D. H. Lawrence.[93] A more blatant antifeminist polemic appeared in F. T. Marinetti's 1909 *Futurist Manifesto*, which glorified "war—the only cure for the world—militarism, patriotism, the destructive gesture of the anarchists, the beautiful ideas which kill, and contempt for woman."

Rather than be "unmanned" by giving up their defining roles as provider, protector, seducer, and teacher of females, many middle-class European males may well have elected to remain bachelors or, at least, postpone marriage until they attained a more dominant social and economic position vis-à-vis prospective partners. Their hesitation to embrace women as equals, plus the shortage of potential partners, can plausibly account for much of the decline in late nineteenth-century marriages. In search for friendship and affection, these men turned to members of their own gender. In doing so, they made a major sacrifice. But remaining single all their lives, as roughly one in six Western European men in 1900 elected to do, these males also gave up the chance to have an active sexual life.[94] For most unattached middle-class men of this era—aside from those who frequented prostitutes—the notion of sex outside of marriage was unthinkable. While a few of their contemporaries were experimenting sexually and finding happiness in an uninhibited lifestyle, the vast majority of these men (and women) were still bound by Victorian moral conventions.

Before the Great War, sex remained a largely forbidden subject. The candid, groundbreaking writings of Freud and others on human sexuality had not yet permeated European and American societies. Freud's seminal *Three Essays on the Theory of Sexuality* (which denied that homosexuality was related to "degeneracy") first appeared, in the original German, in 1905, but was not translated into English until five years afterward. Havelock Ellis, author of *Studies in the Psychology of Sex* (the first volume of which was published in 1900), was largely unread in the years before the war and was thought of mainly as a purveyor of pornography.[95] Only a highly educated elite had ever even heard of these authors. Among the wider public prevailed a reticence to talk about sex and condemnation of those who indulged in it outside of marriage. As a consequence, it is estimated that only about 8 percent of American women born in 1900 had sex before the age of twenty. (This percentage would triple among women born between 1910 and 1919.) In his landmark study of female sexuality, conducted in the 1940s and published in 1953, Alfred Kinsey found that half as many American females born in the 1890s had had premarital relations as the cohort born in the decade after 1900. And almost all women in both age groups who had had premarital sex had done so with their fiancés, usually in the year before they married. Kinsey also discovered that well-educated, middle-class women were more apt to have their first sexual experiences at a later age than working-class, less-educated individuals.[96] In his earlier study, *Sexual Behavior in the Human Male* (1948), Kinsey had traced a similar pattern of postponed intercourse among more-educated men born around the turn of the century. Whereas 98 percent of those men surveyed who had only an elementary school education had had premarital sex, only about 67 percent of those with at least a high school diploma had.[97] Since sexual intercourse was so closely connected with marriage, a shortage of potential marriage partners—for whatever reason—doubtless contributed to this infrequency of sex among middle-class men.

Because extensive sexual activity was so uncommon among middle-class men who belonged to the generation that would fight World War I, it is not surprising that so many of them sought, as compensation, friendship, affection, even love for other men. Whether those men coming of age around 1914 found happiness despite foregoing heterosexual intercourse during most of their youth cannot be definitively answered, but it does not take a great leap of the imagination to infer that they did not. Single middle-class men were, in effect, forced to repress their sexuality and accept a nonsexual substitute.[98] One consequence was that a growing number of these young men were frustrated in fulfilling their biological imperative to sire children. During the first decade of the twentieth century the birth rate in many European countries dipped dramatically. In England and Wales, for example, it fell 25 percent from what it had been just ten years before, and by 1910 it was down fully a third from its peak of 36.3 births per 1,000 inhabitants in 1876.[99] With fears of war mounting, England was only increasing its population by 1 percent annually. France, where contraception was widely practiced, continued to lead in this dubious demographic distinction, producing only 21 babies for every 1,000 persons (or every 500 men) by the end of the century.

Even German women were not having babies at the same rate they had just a few decades back. The chances of a German man having any progeny were thus also declining. In 1914, there were 11,936,803 males ages eighteen to forty-five in that country. The year before, 1,894,598 babies had been born. This meant that only about one man in six within this prime childbearing age group became a father on the eve of the war. More tellingly, since just 54 percent of German men were married around this time (in 1910), of this pool of 6,445,440 potential fathers, only some 27 percent—or 1.7 million—had a child just before World War I.[100] (Another 137,284 babies—or 2.5 percent of the total—were born out of wedlock.)[101] These relatively low marriage and birth figures reflect a long-term trend in Germany and other countries. Between the

1830s and the 1860s, for example, the number of Prussian Protestant births per 1,000 inhabitants had fallen from 18.93 to 17.6, and among Prussian Catholics from 17.58 to 16.99.[102]

Much of this steep drop in the European birth rate is directly attributable to a simultaneous increase in the number and percentage of young single women who were working.[103] In August 1914, nearly 30 percent of England's labor force was female. Over three-quarters of these women were single.[104] Some 3.2 million females were working in industry, and another 1.6 million in domestic service, out of a total female population of roughly 23 million.[105] The number of German women ages fourteen to forty-nine who were working in 1907 amounted to 32 percent of all females ages ten and older.[106] In some countries, the percentage of gainfully employed females had risen sharply since the turn of the century (and would continue to increase during the war). For example, American women made up only 14.7 percent of the US work force in 1880, but 24.8 percent by 1910. By contrast, during a similar span, the proportion of German women working rose less dramatically, from 29.2 percent to 33.8 percent. Over this period, the number of births per 1,000 inhabitants declined from 39.3 to 29.8 in Germany and from 35.2 to 29.2 in the United States. In England and Wales, the birth rate decreased from 33.5 per 1,000 during 1881–1885 to 25.8 in 1909. In terms of percentage, the drop-off there (23 percent) was significantly greater than in Prussia (14.9 percent).[107] Since the proportion of women ages thirty-five to forty-five who were married remained fairly constant in these three countries (around 80 percent in Germany, 90 percent in the United States, and 60 percent in England), it seems apparent that the decrease in births resulted largely from the decision of couples (but usually of wives) to limit their offspring.[108]

Across Europe and the United States, with more people than ever now living in cities, where the economic value of children was greatly reduced, a desire to improve their standard of living, combined with the availability of contraception and abortion, induced millions of (mostly middle-class) women to reduce their fertility. One consequence of this trend, of course, was that the same number of married men in Europe and the United States were having either fewer offspring than in recent decades or none at all. Indeed, in modern Western history up until then there had not been a comparable period in which the reproductive prospects of so many men had worsened to this extent. As a result, they had as much reason to worry about biological survival as did their nations as a whole. Just as governments and allied organizations were responding to this birth "deficit" by promoting motherhood as the likelihood of war grew, so did individual males at this time feel the pressure to change the outlook of their wives so that they would have more children. Both national and individual virility needed to be reasserted.

Because of these dovetailing needs, women who opposed this pronatalist sentiment thus came under fire, particularly from traditionalist (or patriarchal) circles. The liberated lifestyle of the century's "New Women" dismayed conservative and religious elements not just on moral or sexual grounds, but because it was these women who were perceived to be ignoring their primary female duty to bear children and thus encouraging others to follow their example. This anxiety about the falling birth rate can be seen in attacks on feminists on both sides of the Atlantic for acting "against nature" and not cultivating their womanly charms. Edward Alsworth Ross, a progressive sociologist who feared large-scale Asian immigration into the United States would result in "race suicide," denounced American women he felt were losing their sexual attractiveness and becoming "squat, splay-footed, wide-backed, flat-breasted, broad-faced, short-necked—a type that lacks every grace that we associate with woman."[109] Some of his contemporaries, who regarded suffragists as a miscreant "third sex," predicted that feminists would stop having babies entirely as soon as they got the vote. (To show this was not the case, a parade of suffragettes marching up New York's Fifth Avenue in 1915 featured a wagon loaded with infants.)[110]

In England, the falling birth rate took on class implications: by not becoming pregnant in sufficient numbers, educated middle- and upper-class women were not perpetuating the nation's elite. Instead, the nation was being engulfed by a tide of "mediocrity": "quantity" was triumphing over "quality." This trend was quantified by a study conducted by the National Birth Rate Commission in 1914. The British Empire could not—it was argued—continue to flourish if the "less fit" reproduced in far greater proportion than the elites.[111] To sustain national glory, women of "good blood" had to renounce their newfound independence and return to the bedroom. The popular media reflected this growing unease with infertile "masculine women" by frequently publishing short stories about such characters and featuring them in cartoons, dressed mannishly in top hat and tails and smoking cigarettes. At the same time, many American and European men worried about females who were too flagrantly heterosexual—who freely displayed their bodies and sought out men for casual affairs. Such unabashed temptresses mocked male prerogatives by seizing the initiative in sex and by refusing to couple intercourse with marriage and reproduction.

In a more general way, women were threatening to men because of the inroads they had made since the 1880s into previously all-male domains and their persistent demands for even more rights and greater equality. While the suffragettes in England were the most obvious manifestation of this assault on male privilege, they represented merely the leading edge of a much more profound realignment of power between men and women in European and American societies. The movement to emancipate women from subservience to men had spread even to socially conservative Japan. There, since the 1890s, females had become a major presence in the workforce. In fact, they made up a higher proportion of industrial labor—60 percent—than anywhere else in the world.[112] Japan also had its own (albeit small) feminist movement, which gained visibility and raised eyebrows with the appearance of its literary journal, *Seito* (Bluestocking), in 1911. (One of the poems published in that inaugural issue heralded the power of female creativity: "All the sleeping women / Are now awake and moving.") These Westernized "New Women" provoked much derisive comment in Japan, but, nonetheless, marked the dawning of a new protofeminist consciousness in this archetypically male-dominated society.[113]

In terms of gender relations, several conditions were conducive to going to war.[114] First, there was growing male frustration and anger at female assertiveness in many arenas and its negative impact on men's self-esteem and sexual (as well as reproductive) control. Second, many men felt it necessary to reverse this trend and reassert masculine dominance. And finally, because of their estrangement from women, many of these same men had developed a longing for some other kind of intimate union—fulfillment through a loftier, richly rewarding, exclusively male cause that would allow them to transcend their individual selves as well as their dependence upon the opposite sex.[115] While World War I clearly had a whole host of geopolitical, economic, and nationalistic causes, to understand its popular appeal, one has to take these psychosexual needs into account.[116] These gender-related factors—not hatred of the enemy or a lust for imperial conquest—provided much of the collective emotional impetus that made this conflict not only acceptable but also desirable. As has already been noted, manifestations of these needs can be found just before and at the outbreak of hostilities. A hunger for communal, if not racial unity is evident in the sentiments of many writers and intellectuals across Europe on the eve of war. In many ways this yearning for an earlier organic community—what the Germans termed *Gemeinschaft*—instead of a mechanistic and more formally structured society, or *Gesellschaft*, was a flat renunciation of the modern world and the sense of alienation it had brought about.[117] Adumbrated by the operas of Richard Wagner and the philosophical works of Schopenhauer and Nietzsche, a Germanic longing for an organic wholeness found expression in twentieth-century writers as disparate as Thomas Mann and Rainer Maria Rilke.[118]

But this quest for wholeness was by no means limited to only one nation. Appalled by the petty divisiveness and materialism of his day, the Irish poet W. B. Yeats sought a "unity of being" through his lyrical reimagining of heroic Celtic myths and legends.[119] The French philosopher Henri Bergson and French writers such as André Gide and Anatole France ("Wandering re-establishes the original harmony which once existed between man and the universe") echoed their German counterparts, as did such English writers as H. G. Wells, who described the return of a primordial oneness in his science-fiction novel *In the Days of the Comet* (1906): "The air was changed, and the Spirit of Man that had drowsed and slumbered and dreamt dull and evil things, awakened, and stood with wonder-clear eyes, refreshed, looking again on life. . . . I had come out of the individual pit in which all of my shy egotism had lurked, I had overflowed to all humanity, I had seemed to be all humanity."[120]

For many members of Europe's elite, the coming of war came like an answer to this intellectual and artistic prayer. The poet and critic Edmund Gosse hailed the "union of hearts" that the conflict had brought to England. An expatriate who had resided in England for many years, Henry James was initially sickened that his adoptive nation was going to war, but then found compensation in the fact that "in an hour, here, all breaches instantly healed, all divisions dropped . . . so that there is at once the most striking and interesting example of united purpose."[121] Overnight, the internal divisiveness that had plagued the country in recent years disappeared.[122] ("We were all Britishers!" exclaimed one army recruiter in 1914.)[123] Implicitly, this bond was primarily among men, for it was they who were now going to be called upon to defend their nation, and they who would benefit most directly from this ennobling experience.

But women were not immune to this Zeitgeist, even "liberated" ones. The German feminist Gertrud Bäumer rhapsodized that "the limitations of our egos broke down, our blood flowed to the blood of the other, we felt ourselves one body in a mystical unification."[124] Fresh back from a stint of teaching at New York University, the German philosophy professor Rudolf Euken observed: "We experienced a powerful upswing in our souls; the life of the whole became directly the life of the individual, everything stale was swept away, new fountains of life opened themselves up. We felt ourselves taken above ourselves, and we were full of burning desire to turn this new consciousness into action."[125] In England, the eminent Greek scholar Gilbert Murray wrote of "the quickened pulse, the new strength and courage, the sense of brotherhood, the spirit of discipline and self-sacrifice" he had detected among his students at Oxford.[126]

In Germany, a similar mood was evident, if not universally felt.[127] The "August spirit" of patriotic bonding was hailed by the kaiser when he declared in his Berlin palace on the day of war mobilization: "From this day on, I no longer recognize parties. Only Germans."[128] All workers in the Reich subsequently agreed not to go on strike, and all political parties to refrain from criticizing the government, for the duration of the war. In France, a "Union sacrée" was forged to preserve the same kind of unity. The British chancellor of the exchequer, Lord George, told a London audience in July that the coming war would be "terrible," but that something "infinitely greater and more enduring" would emerge from it—"a new patriotism, richer, nobler, and more exalted than the old. I see among all classes, high and low, shedding themselves of selfishness."[129]

Not every statesmen was so sanguine about what the war would bring, but those who harbored doubts seemed helpless to check their people's appetite for war. (All countries were not so susceptible to this "fever": the French were notably muted in their response to the events of August.[130] The Italians were also decidedly reluctant to rush off to war. And British workers and socialists were initially opposed to their country's becoming involved.)[131] To many, war promised a mass salvation, an Armageddon in which they would prevail. This conviction brought them closer together, and being together made them feel stronger, larger than themselves. As the Austrian writer Stefan Zweig observed on the streets of Vienna that August, "Strangers spoke to one another in the streets, people who had avoided each other for years shook hands, everywhere one saw excited faces. Each individual experienced an exaltation of his ego, he was no longer the isolated ego of former times, he had been incorporated into the mass, he was part of the people, and his hitherto unnoticed person, had been given meaning."[132] Wrote the German equestrian and writer Rudolf Binding some years afterward, "On the streets and avenues, men looked each other in the eye and rejoiced in their togetherness."[133]

Even if the outbreak of war was not greeted with rapture in all circles and in all countries, it did seem to mark the end of the "old order of things" in Europe.[134] While materially rewarding, the modern age had brought a plethora of social problems and led many to feel their lives had no purpose. Now, in a moment of euphoria, all these misgivings seemed to have been dispelled. What could not be achieved singly could now be attained collectively. Many Europeans saw the coming confrontation as a "tonic" that could cure a hopelessly corrupt and effete society.[135] More than any previous major conflict, the Great War drew upon this pervasive desire to create a better world through a revitalizing common effort. The (male) unity that had fueled militarism would also be furthered by it. The ties that had connected men in university fraternities, sports teams, offices, civic organizations, political parties, secret societies, and churches would now reach their apotheosis in the brotherhood of the trenches. For "solidarity" was not just a rallying, propagandistic slogan, but a willing commitment of individuals to join with each other, help each other, and, if need be, die for each other.

This impulse coursed through society like an epidemic. After England declared war on Germany on August 4, 1914, most of the public quickly succumbed to "war fever," after having remained on the fence about the conflict on the Continent earlier that summer.[136] In Austria, many young men of military age shared the euphoria of a twenty-five-year-old failed artist named Adolf Hitler, who fell to his knees in a street in Vienna and "thanked Heaven from an overflowing heart for granting me the good fortune of being permitted to live at this time."[137] Bertrand Russell estimated that nine out of ten of his countrymen looked forward to the war's "carnage" with delight.[138] An overwhelming number of young British men responded unhesitatingly and enthusiastically to the call to arms—the largest volunteer enlistment in history. (England was the sole Great Power to depend upon volunteers at the start of the war.) Their reasons for signing up were varied, depending to some extent on social and economic circumstances. Among the educated middle class there was a strong sense of patriotic obligation. For recent graduates of public schools and elite universities, fighting for their country seemed a logical—and welcome—extension of the sporting competitiveness they had come to love.[139] Some of them (as well as many of their German counterparts) also had idealistic hopes that fighting together in a "sacred mission" would transform their generation; they would transcend class barriers to create an egalitarian "front community" and, when they returned home, a better, more unified society.[140] Others were attracted to the prospect of killing because it promised an emotional release—a boyish thrill and a joy that could not be found in a materialistic, repressive British society.[141] Many working-class men enlisted because they sensed that war would give them an opportunity not only to serve, but also to transform their lives, to free them from a stifling and banal existence.[142]

This desire to escape their individuality and become part of a larger entity—the army—was pervasive.[143] Recruiting stations in London and other cities were not able to handle the flood of men who sought to sign up in response to Lord Kitchener's call to arms.[144] This massive turnout proved essential, as nearly four out of every ten would-be working-class recruits were found unfit to serve because of poor health.[145] Nonetheless, out of a pool of 12 million available men of military age, more than 2.5 million managed to pass the physical and join the ranks during the first eighteen months of the war—300,000 in the rest of August alone, far exceeding what Kitchener had asked for.[146] All told, approximately one in four eligible men volunteered during the war.[147] As a result of such a massive response, and despite heavy casualties suffered early on, England did not need to resort to the draft to meet its manpower needs until

1916.[148] This impressive display of patriotic fervor was encouraged by the new practice of recruiting volunteers for a particular unit from the same city or town. These were so-called "Pals" battalions. These had been created shortly after the outbreak of hostilities to help the War Office process the unexpected flood of volunteers. During the first two years of the war, over 650 of these battalions had been constituted—a force of more than half a million men.[149] Reflecting a spirit of local pride that had been growing in England for several decades, volunteers came not only from the same town, but also from the same public school, factory, company, or sports club.[150] The first Pals battalion consisted of London stockbrokers, but many subsequent ones were made up of industrial workers from places like Manchester and Glasgow. Consequently, these units were bound together by a high degree of masculine esprit and camaraderie.[151] Members of Pals battalions were fighting not only for the glory of England but for their "lads," whom they would not want to let down.[152] The bonds between men serving in these battalions were naturally stronger than those between recruits who were randomly assigned to units, and they thus helped build a spirit of self-sacrifice as well as pressure to enlist.

Economic factors—namely, England's rising unemployment rate in the summer of 1914[153]—also induced many young men to sign up, as did boredom, a desire for adventure, fear of being deemed a coward, anger over alleged German atrocities, a sense of duty, and sincere, innocent patriotism. The emotional power of these ties should not be underestimated. They factored significantly, for instance, in the decision of so many youth from the middle and upper classes (who had no economic incentive) to volunteer.[154] The sacrifice of these elites is evident in the long list of names of British MPs, including dozens from the House of Lords, who died during the conflict, visible at the war memorial inside the Parliament building. Nearly 15,000 graduates and students of Oxford served, mostly as junior officers, and one in five of them died, compared with one in eight of all soldiers.[155] Because the officer corps of other warring nations such as Germany and Russia was similarly made up of men from the same social background, they were also disproportionately represented on the front lines and suffered more casualties, proportionately, than men from the lower or working classes.[156] (Across the Atlantic, a desire to serve was just as evident among the "better" classes: of the roughly 36,000 Harvard alumni and students alive in 1914, nearly a third—11,319—signed up for the armed forces.)[157] Overall, a much higher percentage of young men in white-collar positions ended up joining the army than ones employed in industry or farming, but this class discrepancy can be explained by the higher rejection rate of men from lower economic circumstances due to poor health.[158] Among the other belligerent Great Powers—namely, Germany, Austria, Russia, and France—compulsory military service obviated the need for volunteers, but youthful eagerness to defend the nation was not diminished by its being required. (The willingness to fight was sustained by an almost universal belief, on all sides, that the war would end, victoriously, by Christmas.)

Many of the young men who marched off to the trenches of France in 1914 and 1915 were gladly—even fatalistically—offering up their lives because they felt part of something larger that gave meaning to their lives. This identification could be as abstract as love of country or as concrete as affection for their fellow soldiers. As a chronicler of morale among the Second Scottish Rifles has written, "Deep down inside most of them [new recruits] there was a feeling that the true purpose of life was to serve some cause in an all-male community."[159] As often happens in war, the latter attachment became more important in the heat of battle. A twenty-year-old British lieutenant, preparing to lead his men against the Germans at the Somme, wrote to his parents: "Tomorrow morning I shall take my men—men whom I have got to love, and who, I think, have to love me—over the top to do our bit." Under counterattack during this battle, an officer in the Royal Dublin Fusiliers jotted down similar thoughts: "I cannot sleep for thinking of my fellow officers; I can scarcely grasp the fact that I shall never see some of them again . . . in the freshness of youth they have gone off to another world."[160] But a more generalized love motivated many as well. "We are caught up in a love that is more lasting, more sincere [than one for a woman]," wrote a French soldier named Henri Malherbe, at Verdun. "We give ourselves to liberate the nations, these splendid prisoners, the oppressed peoples, for noble ways and generous ideas."[161] Writing after having observed the Italian army, two Belgians noted: "The war has done what peace could not have accomplished except with the help of centuries. It has brought together all the Italians from Abruzzi and Piedmont, from Sicily and Venetia, uniting them in the same spirit of self-sacrifice; it has brought them all the same suffering; they all work painfully to the same end, and all have the same aspirations. It is thus that a nation is created and strengthened—they are all Italians now."[162]

In unity, European males who put on the uniform found redemption and rejuvenation. They also found—on the battlefield—opportunities for the ultimate expression of their deeply felt affection for other men, through common suffering, nursing of the wounded, and a willingness to die for each other. One English chaplain expressed these comradely feelings in a poem titled "Passing the Love of Women":

> Yes, I've known the love ov a woman, lad,
> And maybe I shall again,
> But I knows a stronger love than theirs,
> And that is the love of men.
>
> •   •   •
>
> The love of a woman draws to 'eaven,
>   An' 'eaven of 'uman bless,
> To the eyes that sing, the arms that cling,
>   And the long, long lovers' kiss.
> But your comrades keeps on callin' ye,
>   Callin' ye back to 'ell,
> To the fear o' death and the chokin' breath,
>   Drawn thick with a sickly smell.[163]

Their affinity for one another even extended to the enemy they were fighting and trying to kill. Facing each other across No Man's Land, soldiers forged an emotional bond based on common adversity.[164] It was most evident during the spontaneous Christmas truce of 1914, when English and German soldiers at Flanders serenaded each other and exchanged gifts—much to the dismay of their commanding officers.[165] In this sense, World War I was the culmination of a masculine withdrawal into a "separate sphere" in response to female narrowing of the "gender gap." By engaging in warfare these men were erecting an unbreachable barrier (much like the trenches) between them and the opposite sex: war was by definition a strictly male affair, and by answering its call, they were attesting to the unique contribution that men alone could make to the nation and, indeed, civilization itself. This assertion of male primacy carried over to—and was amplified on—the home front. One of the most direct and significant consequences of the commencement of hostilities was the total militarization of the warring nations. If the kaiser had proclaimed that he now only recognized Germans, the rest of warring Europe was implicitly declaring, "From now on, we recognize only men." For war not only demanded the physical courage and fighting spirit of men, it also required a return to the social values that were associated with males—most important, hierarchical power, discipline, and submission to authority. In regard to relations between the genders, the coming of war seemed to necessitate a revival of the status quo ante. This meant a renunciation of a feminism that had piqued most Europeans, male and female, for some time. Thomas Mann, speaking for the German bourgeoisie but also for most of European society, seized the onset of hostilities to issue a diatribe, "Thoughts on War," in which he distanced himself from his own feminine tendencies by projecting this "weakness" on to Germany's enemy, France, while allocating a warrior role to himself (as an artist). In the words of one critic, Mann wrote this essay to vent his "personal visceral hatred for ultra-femininity that trades on charming helplessness but in reality wants to dominate and destroy the male."[166]

Instead of fighting for their rights, female activists (as well as labor unions, political radicals, and other dissenting minorities) were now expected to put the national good ahead of their own demands.[167] And so they did.[168] This abrupt change of course is eminently apparent in the behavior of feminists in England and elsewhere in the wake of the various declarations of war. Emmeline Pankhurst's weekly, the *Suffragette*, which had lionized Emily Davison as a second Joan of Arc just over a year before, now changed its name to *Britannia* and adopted the motto "For King, for Country, for Freedom." Pankhurst herself, hoping to gain some postwar benefit from demonstrating her organization's patriotism but also worried about the survival of democracy, proclaimed: "Our country's war shall be our war."[169] After the government agreed to release all militants from prison, she ordered members of her WSPU to refrain from further acts of violence and throw their support behind the war effort. She also called for the abolition of trade unions.[170] Pankhurst and her daughter, Christabel, began giving talks to urge young men to join the army. (Previously, Christabel had blamed the war on men's love of "comradery," contending it would not have started if men and women enjoyed equal status.)[171] In 1917 the two women would form the Women's Party, which advocated the total destruction of Germany and Austria.

While not all suffragettes went along with this abrupt about-face (motivated by Pankhurst's intense, lifelong patriotism), most did. The momentum in England to grant women more political rights abruptly came to a halt, as it did in France, Germany, and, later, in the United States. (At the outset, American feminists opposed the conflict, fearing it would glorify the masculine warrior ethos and weaken their argument that the sexes should be treated as equals.[172] Later, the progressive Women's Peace Party split over US involvement, with some branches concluding that joining this "national crusade" would pave the way for female suffrage, while others felt the war would distract attention from this cause.)[173] For the time being, the nation's needs were greater than those of its disenfranchised women. German women's organizations summarily renounced their feminist agenda and helped to mobilize for the war. Elsewhere, some female activists now turned their animosity on young men who had not volunteered for service, handing out white feathers to them on the street. They joined a national campaign against anyone who objected to the war: many pacifists were put in jail, and politicians who dared to criticize government policy were booed as traitors. Feminine persuasiveness was also harnessed to spur enlistment. Young British women were wont to be "dazzled" by men who put on the uniform and reward their war-bound fiancés and boyfriends who did so with more intense affection.[174] One of the most popular English posters of the day showed a mother with her two children looking earnestly out a window at a column of departing troops, beside the caption "Women of Britain Say—GO!" Perhaps most significantly, many females in Britain withdrew from the public arena and embraced traditional domestic roles as mothers and homemakers, believing that doing so was their form of patriotic service: they would protect and sustain the home front while men were away fighting on the war front.[175] Women's magazines such as *Women's World*, *Mother*, and *Home* constantly reminded their readers of the pleasures to be derived from homemaking.[176] Even feminists supported this new emphasis. Articles appearing in *Common Cause*, the organ of the National Union of Women's Suffrage Societies

(NUWSS), covered topics such as "Mothering Our Soldiers" and the value of mothers.[177] This division of gender roles early in the war marked a return to the Victorian era's doctrine of "separate spheres."[178]

In the spirit of national sacrifice, other English women went to work, some taking over for men as tram and railroad conductors. On July 17, 1915, over thirty thousand women marched through the streets of London demanding their rights—not to vote, but to serve. Having made their point, seven hundred thousand of them signed up for jobs in the most dangerous of wartime industries—munitions. (They soon acquired the sobriquet "Munitionettes.") Many more thousands took positions in other factories made vacant by the first wave of enlistments. Between July 1914 and January 1918, the number of women working in England rose by 50 percent—from 3.2 million to 4.8 million. Female union membership tripled between 1914 and 1920.[179] Other women elected to support the war more directly, volunteering as cooks and, later in the conflict, as drivers, clerks, mechanics, telephone operators, bakers, and gardeners in the Women's Auxiliary Army Corps (WAAC). By the end of the war, 37.7 percent of Britain's labor force was female, and 46.7 percent of women were working—historically unprecedented proportions.[180]

Elsewhere, women were also involved in promoting the war cause, in various ways and to varying degrees. For instance, Canadian women became recruiters and received brooches for every ten men they convinced to sign up.[181] Several thousand of them shipped off to Europe as nurses, while others produced munitions.[182] Many more ran farms to keep the nation's food production going. Their counterparts in another corner of the empire—Australia—filled in for absent men in offices and shops, urged men who were still civilians to enlist, and helped out through the Red Cross and other women's organizations. Generally, however, women did not take on more "masculine" roles: the government would not allow females to perform war-related tasks. French females, already well represented in industry before the war, did not undergo any dramatic transformation after August 1914, but continued the gradual expansion of their presence in the labor force that had been going on for several decades.[183] The war did open up new employment opportunities. By 1918, some 430,000 of them were employed in war-related factories, while 63,000 women had assumed the more traditionally female role of nurse.[184] (As in Britain and the United States, some saw wartime service as a way to gain equal rights. But they met resistance from a conservative French public that was loath to elevate the status of females.)[185] From 1911 to 1921, the number of those who were working rose from 7.7 million to 8.6 million, or only about 11 percent.[186] Despite being paid much less than men, Austrian women responded in large numbers to the need for labor, and their presence in factories and other previously male-dominated sectors of the economy grew substantially.[187] In Germany, many married women assumed traditionally "female" wartime roles, such as organizing groups to raise money for the troops.[188] Some single females gave up domestic positions to work in war factories, while others took paid positions in the home, but the overall number of employed women did not increase as much as it did in some belligerent countries.[189] By contrast, as many as 48,000 Russian women volunteered to serve as munitions carriers and nurses on the eastern front, and late in the war, after the overthrow of the tsar, some were organized into military units, including two St. Petersburg battalions known as the Legion of Death. Their response to the call to duty helped to shame Russian men, many of whom were reluctant to serve, into signing up.[190] (Emmeline Pankhurst showed up in St. Isaac's Cathedral to lend moral support upon the battalion's departure to the front.) Shave-headed and dressed like male soldiers, three hundred of these female recruits fought valiantly against the Germans near Smorgon in July of 1917.

Across the Atlantic, suffragists followed the example of their British "sisters" and abandoned their crusade for the vote as soon as the United States entered the war, hoping to advance their cause by demonstrating that they, too, were patriots. The suffragist leader Harriet Stanton Blatch, daughter of Elizabeth Cady Stanton, urged her followers to go to work so that the nation might prevail:

> To win the war we must have man-power in the trenches sufficient to win it with. To win, every soldier, every sailor, must be well fed, well clothed, well equipped. To win, behind the armed forces must stand determined peoples. To win, the people of America and her Allies must be heartened by care and food.
>
> The sun shines on the fertile land, the earth teems with forests, with coal, with every necessary mineral and food, but labor, labor alone can transform all to meet our necessities. Man-power unaided cannot

supply the demand. Women in America must shoulder as nobly as have the women of Europe, this duty. They must answer their country's call. Let them see clearly that the desire of their men to shield them from possible injury exposes the nation and the world to actual danger.

Our winning of the war depends upon the full use of energy of our entire people. Every muscle, every brain, must be mobilized if the national aim is to be achieved.[191]

Many American women responded to these calls by volunteering for war-related tasks such as growing their own gardens, knitting socks, or buying Liberty Bonds. They worked together in organizations like the National League for Women's Service to help meet servicemen's need for clothing, food, books, and stateside recreation.[192] Some trained to be nurses and ambulance drivers, and 13,000 joined the US Navy, mostly as clerks.[193] But many others—some 2 million, all told—assumed the place of men in the nation's factories, transportation systems, and in other areas of the economy, earning higher wages than they had before the war, gaining new skills and financial independence. Between 1910 and 1920, the number of female clerks in the United States rose by 330,000, those holding manufacturing jobs by 300,000, and those employed as book-keepers, cashiers, accountants, and sales clerks by nearly 350,000. Many of these women gave up jobs as domestic servants, seamstresses, and milliners to take advantage of these better-paid opportunities.[194]

Much has been written about how the new economic opportunities that came with the outbreak of war empowered women in the warring nations. There is no doubt that World War I had a major impact on the lives of millions of these women, by exposing them to new work chal-lenges and environments. In England alone, an estimated 2 million women replaced men in factories, offices, the transportation sector, and other traditionally male spheres of the economy. In terms of numbers, the war did not have such a significant impact in other countries. In France, the upswing in female employment was less pronounced: the war only extended a trend that had been going on for some time.[195] In Ger-many, the estimated 17 percent wartime rise in the number of women who were earning wages was roughly what it had been over previous four-year intervals going back to the 1890s.[196] The major change for German women was their movement into war-related industries as the shortage of male workers grew during the conflict.[197] The same held true for American women: their representation in the workforce before the war (20 percent in 1910) did not increase significantly, but mainly shifted from the "female" sphere of the economy into war-related positions.[198] Still, World War I clearly changed women's (and society's) perception of what women were capable of accomplishing and contributing. But, on the other hand, it did not represent any fundamental change in the power relationships between the two genders. Despite their advances, women were still second-class citizens in these war-mobilized societies. Several contextual factors conspired to limit the social significance of so many women entering the labor market during the war years.

First, in taking over the jobs once held by men, these women were not so much changing society as acceding to its masculine ethos. As the outbreak of war called for the militarization of countries like France, England, Italy, Austria, Russia, and Germany, so did this transformation bring with it a resurgence of masculine values. In order to fight effectively, the nations needed to act collectively *more like men* than they had in recent years. Men's roles were what mattered most now, and to fulfill all of them, given the manpower needs of the armed forces, the assistance of women had to be enlisted: in this emergency situation, they had to be masculinized as well. Thus, it was permissible (although not welcomed) for women to operate a lathe, collect tram tickets, or even to serve (as nurses) on the front. But while some women could take on these normally male responsibilities, they remained subordinate to—and a poor substitute for—the real, but absent men they were replacing.[199] In the hierarchy of power and prestige, men remained at the pinnacle due to their newly assumed, higher status as warriors and protectors. Soldiers were the saviors of the nation. Before the war, serving in the military had carried a social stigma, but now this was bathed in a heroic glow.[200] In other words, as some historians have pointed out, while women made advances by moving into once predominantly male (and hence more valued) positions, men simultaneously rose in stature: thus, the power relationship between the two sexes did not really change.[201]

Nor did the attitudes of most men toward females working in *their* world. Resentment and hostility were most overt in labor unions, which first opposed women coming into the factories and then fought to keep them from staying there. Workers worried that less well-trained women would work for a lower wage and thus reverse the gains males had made in this regard.[202] These fears were well founded. Companies receiving military contracts in Germany and other countries attracted many female employees with pay offers that were better than what they could earn in other sectors of the economy, but less than what men expected to receive for doing these jobs.[203] But, more generally, European and American men accepted the more equal status of women only begrudgingly—as a necessary, but temporary evil. Most felt uneasy about the newfound economic power and personal freedom gained by the opposite sex. An influx of females into the labor force confounded their expectations of how women should behave. As would be the case at the end of World War II as well, displeasure over this trend was evident in the eagerness of employers, male employees, and most politicians to remove women from the workplace and send them back to their homes as soon as the conflict had ended and the soldiers had returned. Writing in April 1919, a correspondent for a Leeds newspaper would not bother to conceal his delight over the firing of female bus conductors and subway motormen, whom he branded "shrewish" and "aggressive" for treating passengers with "uncivility" and "callous disregard."[204]

But men worried not only about females gaining a foothold in the workplace; with their new independence from male control, women were also seen as a sexual threat. This applied to wives left at home by husbands headed for France, as well as to single women unrestrained by peacetime mores.[205] In several countries, authorities reacted almost hysterically to the prospect of so many liberated female libidos—an overreaction that, as one historian has noted, suggested "deep-seated unease about women generally."[206] The first week of the war, the English parliament passed a Defense of the Realm Act (DORA), which imposed a number of constraints on the public for security purposes but also imposed a curfew, barring women from being out on the street after seven in the evening. The intent of this measure was to limit prostitution and other "immoral" sexual activity, which would have an adverse affect on morale at the front, as well as on public morality.[207] Promiscuity also endangered the social order on the home front.[208]

English authorities were not alone in lamenting wartime sexual improprieties.[209] Voices were raised across Europe about the ill consequences of young women doing their "patriotic duty" by sleeping with soldiers.[210] The migration of large numbers of single women into cities in Germany, France, and other countries, combined with the upheaval, fluidity, and uncertainty of wartime existence, did result in an increase in both prostitution and illegitimate births during the war.[211] The German government sought to curtail infidelity among abandoned wives (and sustain troop morale) by urging neighbors of those who hosted frequent male visitors into their homes to report these wives as putative prostitutes.[212] In some areas of the German Reich, so many babies were born out of wedlock that authorities stopped using the word *illegitimate* on birth certificates.[213] More than one out of four newborns in Freiburg came from an illicit relationship, some of them between local women and French prisoners of war. Starting in 1917, a single woman who became pregnant was allowed to use the appellation "Frau" and assume her lover's name if he died on the front.[214] However, the percentage of such births in Germany did not actually grow as much as some had predicted or feared.[215] Paris was widely known for its private homes featuring *cabinets particuliers* that allowed for sexual dalliances under the veil of middle-class respectability. Infidelity among the wives of servicemen was perceived to be deplorably common in places as diverse as Budapest and Alsace-Lorraine.[216] But here, too, popular perceptions of sexual impropriety tended to exaggerate these developments, which were concentrated in the large cities.[217] Illegitimate births, for example, accounted for only 8.3 percent of the total in England throughout the war years, while in France the proportion only increased from 8.5 percent in 1914 to 14.2 percent in 1917.[218]

In all countries, consorting with prostitutes led to an upturn in the incidence of venereal disease.[219] British authorities, who had ignored this problem early in the war, grew so alarmed by the rate of infection (some sixty thousand cases by 1918) that a law was adopted making it a criminal offense to pass on syphilis or gonorrhea to members of the armed forces.[220] This measure reminded critics of the infamous nineteenth-century Contagious Diseases Acts, which had likewise sought to restrict female sexual behavior. At the same time, Lord Kitchener exhorted men under his command to show restraint.[221] But such measures were not very effective. A 1916 study by an English royal commission concluded that between 8 and 12 percent of males and 3 to 7 percent of females living in working-class neighborhoods of London had contracted a venereal disease.[222] German authorities, who had foreseen this kind of development, launched informational campaigns warning soldiers about the dangers of sexually transmitted diseases, while moralistic civic organizations called for a crackdown on "vagabond" women. These efforts, combined with the military's distribution of condoms, kept down the number of cases in German cities.[223]

At the same time, the warring governments took steps to preserve families during the conflict. But this help came with strings attached. In order to recruit married men in greater numbers, Whitehall agreed to extend subsidies to all wives of soldiers, instead of just a limited number. From just over a thousand at the start of the conflict, the number of wives in England receiving these allowances jumped to half a million by November 1914. Although they provided economic security to spouses in great need, these family subsidies also reinforced wives' dependence upon their spouses. To make sure that recipients did not abuse this assistance, the War Office went so far as to threaten to revoke them in cases of "immorality"—when the wife was found to be drinking, neglecting her children, or committing crimes. (French authorities also sought to restrict alcohol consumption among women, particularly married ones.)[224] The government even proposed that police observe these married women to make sure they were behaving properly, but protests deterred it from adopting this form of Orwellian surveillance. Still, wives could lose their allowances if they were found to have committed adultery.[225] By threatening to take them away, the state was committing itself to upholding sexual propriety (and male control).

It was not only economically and sexually that women's exercise of their wartime freedom threatened the existing order. In some countries, women also challenged the authority of the state. Left largely on their own in the countryside, Italian women, outraged over food shortages and the prolonged absence of their men, led the peasant revolts that sprang up sporadically starting in the winter of 1916. They also organized factory strikes over unfair treatment of workers.[226] Similarly, many newly educated but still disenfranchised Russian women became prominent figures in the wartime struggle to throw off tsarist rule in their country. But these isolated female revolts were the exception to the general rule of patriotic submission and accommodation that both men and women followed as their countries mobilized for war. In fact, even though the European conflict gave many women an unprecedented amount of freedom, it needs to be kept in mind that these opportunities to work and earn more money, to live independently, to enjoy greater sexual openness, and, more generally, to assume empowering, masculine roles reflected a necessary response to the exigencies of the moment rather than some new social consensus about how women should act or be treated. This freedom was given to them grudgingly, and only temporarily, predicated upon the overriding need to meet the grave challenges of the most devastating conflict that Europe had ever experienced.

Wartime attitudes toward women were ambivalent, as the belligerent nations attempted to sort out what the appropriate roles for females should be. These conflicting views are evident in the images used in war propaganda posters. In some instances, the female figure was portrayed in a heroic, aggressive manner, as a symbol for the nation itself as it rallied to defeat its enemies. This was a common motif in English and French posters, such as the 1917 British "National Service" one depicting Britannia as a female warrior clad in armor, standing upon a bluff pointing toward the Continent, holding up a windswept Union Jack, and urging a throng of men in civilian attire to go forth and join the fray.[227] But, as noted earlier, females could also be used as sexual enticement for would-be volunteers.[228] The most well-known placard of this sort—used to recruit men for the US Navy—showed a fetching young woman wearing a revealing sailor suit and smiling provocatively, next to the caption: "Gee! I Wish I Were a Man. I'd Join the Navy." Underneath ran the sexually suggestive message: "Be a Man and Do It." Here young men were led to fantasize about having such a woman as a reward for signing up while simultaneously imagining her as a masculine poseur or comrade.[229] Traditional male and female prototypes merge into this one somewhat disconcerting but also appealing image, which seems to suggest that making war and making love are not mutually exclusive choices, but compatible.[230]

More commonly, however, females were shown as the potential innocent victims of war—helpless, passive creatures who could only be saved by the heroic actions of brave men. A typical example of this is a poster used to convince Irish men to sign up: it shows two German soldiers in spiked helmets, brandishing bayonets, breaking into a house where a defenseless mother, child, and old man can only await their fate, while a tall, strong man of the house belatedly stands erect to meet this surprise threat. "Is *Your* Home Worth Fighting For?" the poster asks. This kind of imagery was intended to arouse the protective instincts of young males by implying it was they alone who could safeguard the nation.

Early in the war, sexually charged propaganda appealed to this reflexive tendency by conjuring up disturbing visions of defenseless women being raped by the enemy, as was alleged to have taken place in German-occupied Belgium.[231] The impression that sexual atrocities had been widespread there was promulgated in the government's 1915 Bryce Report, which devoted 238 pages to detailing such alleged incidents. Outrage over these purported incidents gave the war against Germany a moral purpose while also appealing to masculine protective instincts.[232] In still another guise, women could offer comfort and solace to men who went off to fight for them. Frequently, these women were shown as angels or nurses: one of the best known of the latter category appeared in an American Red Cross poster from 1918 showing a hooded nurse ("The Greatest Mother in the World") cradling a diminutive, wounded soldier on a gurney in a way that is highly suggestive of Michelangelo's *Pieta*.[233] As diverse as these pictorial renderings of females were, they shared one basic trait: women were presented as idealized objects of male fantasies. Their presence was justified only to the extent that it inspired, encouraged, and fulfilled men's longings. Aside from performing these functions, women had no reason to exist—and, it was implied, made no unique, vital contributions to society. In other words, the coming of war reduced women to support roles while it reaffirmed that males were the existentially essential gender.

Females who emulated males by joining the armed forces offended heightened sensitivities about sex roles and faced general condemnation. In countries like Germany and England, women initially responded as enthusiastically as men to the outbreak of war and just as eagerly sought to volunteer their services. Commenting on this phenomenon, the head of one English hospital remarked that "If Kitchener had asked for half a million women, he would have been oversubscribed by first post." But they discovered they were only welcome in traditionally feminine capacities, on the home front. The idea of women wearing uniforms was generally repellent, and those who put them on were apt to be disparaged as "men-women" or "promiscuous."[234] Germany, as well as other warring nations, did not allow women to do so, except as nurses. In England, female opponents of extending the suffrage were particularly vociferous in condemning women who joined the military.[235] From the perspective of the trenches, feelings toward women could easily turn more acerbic: soldiers facing death in the next charge across No Man's Land had little sympathy for those—male or female—who did not share and could not understand their stark, brutish, violent world.[236]

Theirs was the only true reality, and whatever way of life continued back home in places like Manchester, Pisa, Leipzig, Avignon, or Kiev seemed nothing but a grotesque charade.[237] Anger at a front-line enemy they rarely saw was easily transferred to "enemies" on the home front.[238] So far as this civilian world they had left behind was associated with women, so did they earn the animus and contempt of these front-line troops. Affections they may once have had for sweethearts back home were undermined by this growing gap between their experiences and were replaced, in many cases, by a stronger bond with their fellow soldier-sufferers.[239] As the Oxford-educated poet Robert Nichols wrote after surviving combat at the Somme:

> Was there love once? I have forgotten her.
> Was there grief once? Grief yet is mine.
> Other loves I have, men rough, but men who stir
> More grief, more joy, than love of thee and thine.
>
> Faces cheerful, full of whimsical mirth,
> Lined by the wind, burned by the sun
> Bodies enraptured by the abounding earth,
> As whose children we are brethren: one.
>
> •   •   •
>
> O loved, living, dying, heroic soldier,
> All, all my joy, my grief, my love, are thine.[240]

In some instances, this repudiation of womanly love in favor of a comradely one was the outgrowth of a long simmering misogyny, articulated by men under arms whose sexual orientation made them more apt to regard females cynically. Wilfred Owen revealed his bitterness toward women who had inveigled men into enlisting in his poem "Disabled." The narrator, a soldier who joined "to please the giddy jilts," can now, bound to a wheelchair, only mordantly observe "how the women's eyes/Passed from him to the strong men that were whole."[241] Owen's "Dulce et decorum" had originally been dedicated to his fellow poet Jessie Pope to convey his contempt for her jingoistic verses.

D. H. Lawrence expressed a similar disdain for women in his 1915 poem "Eloi, Eloi, Lama Sabacthani" ("O Lord, O Lord, why hast Thou forsaken me?"), in which he asks, with bitterness: "And why do the women follow us satisfied / Feed on our wounds like bread, receive our blood / Like glittering seed upon them for fulfillment?" As one commentator on this poem has observed, Lawrence appears to link the narrator's fear of dying in war with anger at women "as if the Great War were a climactic episode in some battle of the sexes that had already been raging for years." As the war experience unmanned men, literally and psychologically, it ceded greater sexual power to women, who otherwise might be subordinated to the male will.[242] (After the war, this theme of emasculation would be taken up in novels like Hemingway's *The Sun Also Rises* and poems such as T. S. Eliot's *Wasteland*, which deals extensively with the sexually wounded Fisher King.) Equally strong resentment at women for having goaded men into fighting can be found in Richard Aldington's postwar short story "The Case of Lieutenant Hall." Here women become a synecdoche for civilian society, which has remained blind to the realities of modern warfare: "I don't want ever to touch a bloody woman," an emotionally broken Hall rants. "Didn't they urge us into that hell, and do their best to keep us there?[243]

As was the case with Owen, Sassoon, Robert Graves, and several other soldier-writers, this hostility toward women also reflected their homoerotic inclinations. These tended to be intensified under fire, as men hunkered down in the trenches experienced an elemental interdependence with their comrades. Subliminal homosexual feelings would emerge in some poems by Sassoon ("In Barracks") and Owen. Typical of the latter's expressions of tenderness toward his fellow soldiers is this stanza from his "Greater Love":

> Red lips are not so red
> As the stained stones kissed by the English dead.
> Kindness of wooed and wooer

Seems shame to their love pure.
O Love, your eyes lose lure
When I behold eyes blinded in my stead!

But the war also had a way of merging male and female identities, of infusing all relationships with an erotic charge. It was as if, outside the gender strictures of society, men were free to explore a broader notion of love. Shared gratitude for being alive, for having endured so much together, engendered a new kind of physical intimacy—a closeness that "stood in opposition to and as a triumph over death."[244] Writing to his girlfriend from France, a British soldier named Frank Cocker described how one of his fellow soldiers had abruptly embraced him and kissed him twice, declaring that the first kiss came from the friend's fiancée and the other from his mother. A somewhat taken aback Cocker then returned this "tender salute," saying *this* kiss was from him.[245]

• • •

In sum, any advances made by European and American women during World War I have to be seen in the context of the process of militarization and the resurgence of masculinity that accompanied it. The war gave those who opposed equality between the sexes a strong rationale to stem the social pressure that had been pushing in that direction. Mobilization for war was, in the words of the German social historian George Mosse, "an invitation to manliness" and, simultaneously, a rejoinder to the contention that women were as valuable to society as men.[246] If the Great War had not been brought about by a need to demonstrate this point, it certainly provided an excellent test of its validity. Immersion in the *Stahlbad* (steel bath) of combat gave German youth, for one, a chance to harden themselves and shed any vestiges of effeminacy.[247] But war also lured young men from other nations eager to demonstrate their manliness. H. G. Wells hailed this resurgence of masculinity in his 1916 novel, *Mr. Britling Sees It Through*, in which the eponymous main character declares with satisfaction, on the eve of war: "He loved England now as a nation of men."[248] Vera Brittain's fiancé, Roland Leighton, felt compelled to join the fray in part because contemporaries he had contemptuously considered "effeminate" had already been wounded while he had not yet experienced combat.[249] Similarly, Rupert Brooke, anxious to distance himself from his own homosexual proclivities, wrote enthusiastically how the coming of war had awakened British youth and allowed them to leave behind a world "grown old and cold and dreary" and the "sick hearts" and "half-men" who lacked courage and a sense of honor.[250] Another English poet, Richard Aldington, would point out in his postwar novel *Death of a Hero* that a fear of appearing "womanly" had motivated many of his generation to volunteer.[251] This same sexual anxiety was evident in other books of this era, including Henri Barbusse's war memoir, *Under Fire*, and short stories by Wyndham Lewis ("The French Poodle") and William Faulkner ("All the Dead Pilots"). More broadly, there is no question that this conflict altered men and women's views of each other as well as the gender balance of power by reimposing traditional roles and social structures. So, in this sense, the very fact that a war took place meant a "victory" for tradition-minded men and women who saw the future of civilization endangered by a blurring of gender lines. (How, ultimately, the war experience affected the relationships between men and women is another matter.)

In addition to its spiritual "regeneration," social unification, and masculine "revival," World War I yielded one other major benefit for the generation of men who fought its battles. This was its stimulating impact on sexuality, marriage, and the birth rate. Paradoxically, an orgiastic spasm of violence like none ever seen before would produce more life than death in its wake and help the nations of Europe to renew and perpetuate themselves.

War cauterizes morality and unleashes more basic human impulses. "War fever" can easily turn into sexual frenzy. The overflowing of joyful emotions—the sheer hysteria—which so often accompanies news about a nation's going to war loosens the libido and lessens the restraints that otherwise inhibit its expression. Whether caught up in excitement of that moment, or subconsciously worried about impending death, young men and women seek out sexual release and biological fulfillment with striking abandon. War is a powerful aphrodisiac. So it was in Europe, in the late summer of 1914.[252] So, at least, does anecdotal testimony attest. In Paris, young French women eagerly offered themselves to departing soldiers—an act that the German sex researcher Magnus Hirschfeld would later describe as not so much motivated by patriotism as "a sort of war nymphomania which was observed in every land."[253] Their English counterparts succumbed to an indiscriminate "khaki fever."[254] In Budapest, "women fell into a feverish delirium of enthusiasm, as though the senses had, with one move, thrown off the repressive chains of all social and economic scruples."[255] Their sexual lust seemed to ape the lust for war and killing that had taken hold in the men they were embracing. For them, fighting and making love were intimately intertwined: they both promised an ecstasy greater than what they had found in life thus far.[256] Roland Leighton unwittingly acknowledged this connection when he told his mother before leaving for France in 1915: "Je suis fiancé. C'est la guerre."[257] Ernst Jünger, who, at the age of nineteen, volunteered for the German army on the day of mobilization, found little difference between war and love. "We had set out," he wrote in his memoir *Storm of Steel*, "in a rain of flowers, in a drunken atmosphere of blood and roses."[258] As was true for many soldiers of his generation and of others who experienced war, combat was akin to the sex act; Jünger described not only the horrors of modern conflict but also the exhilaration it brought: "We will force open the closed door and enter by force into the forbidden land," he wrote in a postwar novel, *Feuer und Blut* (Fire and Blood).[259] Conversely, sex was another form of conquest—the recruit's expectation, the warrior's due. Men heading off to the trenches took full advantage of the open arms of adoring females. Whether they were prostitutes or innocent young women caught up in the mood of liberated sexual passion did not appear to matter. Those without sweethearts flocked to brothels: places like New Orleans's French Quarter were inundated with recruits shortly after the United States entered the war.[260]

Practically overnight, a bellicose Europe became highly sexed. After a prolongation of Victorian mores and a retreat into all-male intimacy, men were *back*—handsome, bold, courageous, and eminently attractive. The weak, effeminate, questionably masculine male of the fin de siècle disappeared in the first flash of artillery, as the virile, noble, and heroic man returned to the scene. (Symbolically, Oscar Wilde's younger son, Vyvyan, joined the army in 1914 to help erase the stain his father had left on the family name.[261] Ironically, Wilde's lover, Alfred Lord Douglas, also joined the chorus of "remasculinized" men, writing in a 1915 essay of his delight that "Literary England" was now being cleansed of "sex-mongers and pedlars of the perverse.")[262] Some even blamed this effeminacy as well as "emasculating" feminists for inviting the Germans to go to war against England in the first place.[263] With a widespread repudiation of feminism came a rediscovery of heterosexual differences—and attractiveness. Under more lax wartime conditions, many young women in England, on the Continent, and in the United States became more sexually charged and open about fulfilling their desires. Some flocked to training camps for brief liaisons with departing soldiers. Feminine fashions came back in style and flat bosoms, once favored by the Continent's "New Women," gave way to more ample figures. The first bra, created by an American named Mary Phelps-Jacobs, was patented in 1914. During the war, hemlines rose to midcalf—higher than ever before.[264] With so many women working (and men away), dress became more practical, less restrictive: corsets were out, flesh-colored stockings were in. While some wore uniforms and other military-style garb, more affluent women in fashion-conscious cities like Paris dressed in an elegant and revealing manner that would remind returning soldiers of what they had been fighting for—and missing.[265] Young boys no longer wore dresses or epicene Lord Fauntleroy suits. Instead they aped their fathers and older brothers by donning more manly trousers or shorts. And, of course, millions of males put on sleek, well-cut uniforms—a sartorial metamorphosis that caused women's heads to turn and hearts to beat a little faster. This sight, overlaid with thoughts of heroic deeds to come, gave recruits an almost irresistible sex appeal. To what extent a desire to acquire this might have influenced young men to enlist is impossible to gauge, but they certainly could not have been ignorant of its positive effect on the opposite sex.

If becoming soldiers made men more desirable, doing so could also improve their chances of marrying and having children. This "edge" would particularly benefit poor, uneducated, or physically unattractive men who might not, under normal circumstances, find marriage partners. At the time of World War I, such "undesirable" men throughout Western Europe faced greater than usual odds in finding a mate because of the growing shortage of single females in their age group. But so did middle-class young men: their chances were diminished since so many potential spouses in their social stratum were electing not to marry but rather to pursue careers and support themselves. For both of these male subgroups, serving in uniform to defend their country could make an important difference in attracting marriage partners. While such a putative advantage cannot be documented, there is intriguing evidence of it in one salient demographic characteristic of the men who chose to volunteer for enlistment shortly after war was declared. Since all Continental armies drew on conscripts to fill their ranks, this evidence can only be gleaned from looking at the type of man who signed up for the British army—the only all-volunteer force (until 1916). Every one of the 2.5 million men who joined during this period had one trait in common—they were all single. (Married men were not accepted into the army until early in 1916, when a government report indicated that as many as half a million of them were prepared to serve.)[266] While unmarried men may have their own economic and social reasons for finding wartime service attractive (such as not having to worry about dependents), they were also distinguished by not having found a spouse and still, presumably, hoping to do so. This desired outcome may help explain the strong appeal of enlisting to young single men. Just by passing the medical exam, they were giving evidence of their physical well-being—an important consideration for prospective brides.

More support for the competitive edge that donning a uniform gives can be seen in the response to the call to duty of one particular subset of single men who were usually themselves at a reproductive disadvantage vis-à-vis their peers. These were men of short stature. It is well documented that this group often loses out in competition with other males, since women tend to prefer taller mates.[267] Since their height is a given, these men are inclined to display aggressive behavior to compensate for it and bolster their status and sexual attractiveness.[268] Enlisting for war is one way to do this. During the Great War, a large number of short men—under the minimum height set by the military, which was five feet four inches in England at that time[269]—circumvented restrictions on their serving by joining so-called Bantam Battalions.[270] They were formed in Britain and Canada, as well as in Germany, largely in response to the eagerness of so many short men to fight for their country and the government's dismay that large numbers of them had been rejected for duty at a time when the need for fresh troops was great.[271] Some four thousand men joined these units in England. Many of these "bantam" volunteers came from the country's north—specifically from mining communities. Their units were sent to the front lines, where they served with great courage and distinction—valued because their small stature made them difficult targets for enemy snipers and because they could take on jobs such as laying mines that taller soldiers could not so easily accomplish. Unfortunately, there is no statistical evidence about how well survivors of these "Bantam Battalions"—or, for that matter—veterans as a whole fared in the postwar marriage market, as compared to men who did not serve.

The first consequence of war appeared to be a matrimonial frenzy. Men who were already engaged or in a serious relationship impulsively proposed and were accepted on the spot. One had the impression that *everyone* was rushing to the altar. To accommodate the need for weddings before units crossed the Channel, the Archbishop of Canterbury gave permission for Church of England offices to remain open at all hours. Marriage services went ahead, even when the prospective bridegroom had only a few hours to spare before leaving for France.[272] This marital enthusiasm continued well into 1915, with soldiers being granted forty-eight-hour passes so that they could hastily walk down the aisle.[273] Observing a similar marital surge in Paris, the Spanish novelist Vincente Blasco Ibáñez unscientifically concluded that half the city's population was taking part.[274] But statistics indicate this was a grossly misleading observation. The marriage rate in England and Wales did rise early in the conflict—from an average of 15.4 per 1,000 persons during the previous decade to a historic high of 21.8 in September 1915; by one estimate, as many as 200,000 men and women got married who would have remained single if there had been no war.[275]

But this "marriage boom" was short lived and not nearly as dramatic as it appeared. Most belligerent nations did not experience any wartime increase. If anything, with so many young men going off to fight, the number of weddings soon declined. Germany saw the number of marriages drop early in the conflict—from 460,608 in 1914 to 279,076 in 1916—before a slight upturn to 352,453 marriages in 1918.[276] In Italy, Belgium, France, and the Netherlands, many fewer couples walked down the aisle in 1914 than did in 1912. It was only until *after* hostilities ended, and millions of single men returned home, that the marriage rate rose dramatically.[277] Whatever reproductive advantage military service would bring did not manifest itself immediately. Likewise, the number of babies born in these nations did not reverse its long decline while the war was going on. Instead, as might be expected, it fell further. In Britain, for example, the number of births decreased from 879,000 in 1914 to 663,000 in 1918.[278] Nearly 1.9 million German babies were born in 1914, but fewer than 1 million three years later.[279] France, Belgium, and Italy also experienced sharp declines in their birth rates.[280]

There are several explanations for these declines. First, the war removed millions of men from the arms of their wives and lovers. This exodus thus limited births to the issue of illicit liaisons, of men unqualified for military service, or of women who had divorced their absent husbands or lost them at the front—a much-diminished reproductive pool. Second, many married couples continued to practice birth control, ignoring government admonitions to procreate for the good of the nation during a time of war. The continuing drop in the birth rate was especially worrisome in Germany, as it was now in danger of depopulation.[281] In 1915, the German Interior Ministry, alarmed by the great loss of life on the front and its implications for the nation's future well-being, released a memorandum blaming "sexual immorality" and contraception for depressing the birth rate. The government subsequently made it illegal to promote birth control or abortion.[282] The Federation of German Women promoted the idea of a "Women's Year of Service" to convince more women to bear children.[283] A wife's patriotic duty to give birth was likened to what her husband was doing for the Reich on the front. To make pregnancy more economically viable, the Social Democratic Party pushed for extending maternal subsidies and child welfare support to all mothers. Likewise, the French suffragist leader Marguerite De Witt Schlumberger admonished her followers to perform their patriotic duty and "give to the nation the children who would replace those who died."[284] The pronatalist publication *La femme et l'enfant* ran a series of illustrations designed to promote maternity. One showed an oversize German baby (with emblematic helmet) threatening a much smaller one, in an adjacent bassinet, with a rattle. The caption read: "One of the profound causes of the present war has been our low birth rate." Another depicted a female warrior (representing France), holding a scale with two suspended babies: the larger one was labeled "1818," the smaller "1918." In the background were a number of cemetery crosses. The question posed was: "What do I do to replace all of those who have fallen if this continues?"[285] But all of this encouragement of motherhood through subsidies and support programs, as well as new pronatalist laws, failed to have any impact: by the end of the war, the German birth rate was half what it had been in 1913, despite vigorous efforts by the state to promote reproduction as national service.[286] These included subsidies for children between the ages of three and thirteen and a reduction of the taxes levied on large families. Similar concerns about this decline and efforts to encourage maternity fell on deaf ears in England, France, and other warring countries.[287]

Third, many women were reluctant to bring unintended pregnancies to term—either because they had resulted from rape or fleeting sexual encounters, or because economic or family circumstances were not favorable to raising a child. The fact that so many married women now held jobs in war-related factories contributed to this disinclination.[288] Overall, the effect of the war's coming was to put off the decision to have children: the situation at hand was too volatile and its outcome too uncertain for couples to make such a commitment to the future. From a long-term perspective, however, what the war accomplished was to nurture a desire to form families and have children once it was over. On this reproductive front, Europe's warring men may not have won an immediate victory, but at least the promise of one.

Early on, when the massed armies of Europe's Great Powers eyed each other with nervous excitement over the walls of their respective trenches, it seemed that, no matter the outcome of the battles that lay ahead, the circumstances they collectively faced, as men, had taken a turn for the better. A sense of purpose had reentered their lives: they had a cause worth fighting and dying for. They had already found, in the camaraderie of the front lines, a worthy outlet for their affections—a love more selfless and true than women might have to offer in its stead. More important, in light of the disturbing fluidity in male and female identities that had developed over the preceding decades, they had a strong sense of who they were, as men, and why they existed. Whatever claims middle-class women might have made to equal stature now seemed revealed as ludicrous. The "sex war" threatened by insurgent feminism was now a thing of the distant past.[289] Relations between the genders had returned to "normal," and European manhood was now confronting another, more glorious kind of conflict. Here, facing death against other men, in rising to this test of their mettle, these soldiers had ample opportunity to demonstrate what they had to offer their nations. In reaffirming their virility, they were also rekindling their sex appeal. The emotional intensity and precariousness of war made heterosexual relations more imperative: the chance for lovers to mate might not come again. As individuals, departing soldiers and abandoned wives could defer the joys of parenthood until they were reunited yet separate from each other, with hopes that bearing children would be one of the happy consequences of this great national sacrifice. These hopes were extended to countless young couples who, without the coming of war, might not have fallen in love or made such a familial pledge to each other.

For each of the warring countries, the war portended a Darwinian test of fitness: in daring charge and countercharge across No Man's Land, the superiority of one people over another would be graphically decided by the most graphic and unambiguous of measures—by the yards gained and the tally of bodies strewn in the mud. Reproductive vitality was both an indicator of the outcome and a consequence of it. Nations that possessed this manly vigor would defeat those that lacked it. This linkage was made transparent in a French postcard that circulated during the war. It showed Kaiser Wilhelm scrutinizing a cabbage through a looking glass as if trying to read signs in it. The caption declared: "Ma victoire est dans la choux." As one scholar has recently pointed out, this can be interpreted to mean that the German emperor is expressing confidence his country will triumph as long as this French vegetable (commonly associated with the birth of boys) remains barren—in other words, as long as his adversary fails to produce more soldiers.[290] But the relationship between war and sex was reciprocal: displaying virile potency on the battlefields of France would—or so it was believed—carry over to the bedroom. Victory would produce pride and optimism about the future, inspiring men and their wives to produce more babies and thus sustain national power for another generation.

This was the naïve view of 1914. Things would not turn out as the idealistic young men in their brand-new uniforms and their loved ones back home had wanted them to turn out. This "war to end all wars" would not prove to be the apotheosis of European and American manhood, but only ignobly hasten its dismantling as a cultural bastion. Instead of receiving honor and redemption, the men arrayed on these fields would undergo dismemberment and disillusion, emasculation and despair. For all of them, as well as for the nations they served, war would bring only defeat. No matter what the peace treaties said, or the leaders claimed, or the newly redrawn boundary lines showed, there would be no real victors this time.

Chapter 4

MAY THE BETTER MAN WIN—THE ROAD TO WORLD WAR II

In terms of scale and impact, the "Great War" or "World War" of 1914–1918 certainly earned its ironic sobriquet.[1] It was "great" in many ways—in geographical scope (battles were fought on four continents, from Verdun to Gallipoli, from Gorizia to Tsingtao); in the number of countries involved (thirty-four); and in its death toll (an estimated 15 million victims, of which 8.5 million were men in uniform).[2] While statistics can scarcely do justice to the enormity of human suffering and loss caused by this conflict, they do capture its historical uniqueness. No previous war had ever claimed as many victims in a comparable period of time.[3] During these four years, more soldiers died than in all the wars fought in the nineteenth century combined. For many countries, the carnage was staggering: 1.3 million French soldiers died, or an average of 930 a day, out of the 8.4 million who served.[4] The bodies of 300,000 of its dead were never found.[5] A little more than one in four of France's soldiers returned home unscathed.[6] One of every six Germans, Austrians, and Russians fell on the battlefield, while a small country like Serbia lost more than a third of its fighting men.[7] More than 2.5 million German soldiers who survived were disabled.[8] England lost nearly 9 percent of all males under the age of forty-five, but more than one-third of soldiers ages twenty to twenty-four.[9] Nearly 30 percent of all British troops were killed or wounded.[10]

If one includes the numbers of soldiers and sailors who were wounded, counted as missing, held as POWs, or who died as a result of disease or imprisonment, the human cost of this "War to End All Wars" becomes even more apparent. This grim total amounted to 90 percent of Austrian,

76 percent of Russian, 73 percent of French, 65 percent of German, 47 percent of Serbian, 39 percent of Italian, 36 percent of imperial British, and 35 percent of Belgian troops—all told, 37.5 million men out of the 65 million who were mobilized.[11] And this figure does not include veterans who suffered for the rest of their lives from shell shock or other forms of war-induced mental illness. In England and Germany, there were, according to some estimates, 200,000 and 300,000 of these psychiatric casualties, respectively.[12]

The true measure of loss lay not in the numbing numbers but in the youthful lives disrupted, disoriented, disillusioned, disabled, or destroyed. But in assessing these human consequences of the conflict, one encounters pitfalls: at the personal level, the evidence necessarily becomes subjective and thus subject to varying historical (and literary) interpretation. However, since the appearance of a spate of memoirs, diaries, novels, and poems about the war in the 1920s, a widely shared view has emerged that the war was a historically pivotal, catastrophic experience, which gave rise to a modern sense of reality. This perception has influenced how succeeding generations (in the United States and most of Europe) have come to regard this conflict.[13]

Because its scale was so enormous, its devastation so unprecedented, its outcome so inconclusive, and its meaning so highly debatable, the Great War has come to be regarded as the most defining of modern conflicts—one that rudely and utterly shattered European illusions about the nature of civilization, progress, morality, patriotism, God, and the meaning of life.[14] During this clash of armies, one *Weltanschauung* perished, and another came to life. In the postwar "mood of disenchantment," enthusiasm for war evaporated with the same alacrity with which it had seduced millions of Europeans, as, with the zeal of the newly converted, they now raised high the banner of pacifism.[15]

War was now a monstrosity to be avoided at all costs. Certainly this was how many writers and artists of that time portrayed its impact—in the macabre battlefield paintings of Otto Dix, the drawings of Georg Grosz; the poems of Siegfried Sassoon, Wilfred Owen, and Isaac Rosenberg; the novels of Erich Remarque, Ernest Hemingway, and Ford Madox Ford; and the memoirs of Edmund Blunden, Robert Graves, and Charles E. Montague. Judged by these works, the war was an infernal revelation. Never had the gossamer veil of hope and illusion been so rudely ripped away and the ugliness of life and the pointlessness of death so starkly revealed. In 1914, soldiers had marched off to the trenches believing in God, country, and the sustaining power of both, but returned—if they did at all—bereft of any such faith. Completely unprepared for what lay in store for them, they were transformed into what the poet T. S. Eliot, writing about the postwar generation, would call "hollow men." For the remainder of their lives they inhabited a debased reality. The indelible memories of No Man's Land blighted their souls and took hold of them like a demon, obliterating all other conceivable realities—past, present, or future. They became, as William Blake had prophesied, what they had beheld.[16] They were witnesses transfixed by what they had seen and their inability to make sense of it. Through words and images, they could only register their pain and anguish, over and over again, like Kurtz (in Joseph Conrad's turn-of-the-century novella *The Heart of Darkness*), who dies muttering enigmatically "The horror! The horror!" Typical of these battlefield witnesses is the French-English Henri Barbusse, who, having signed up in his forties, entered hell during an assault on German lines:

> Abruptly, across all the width of the opposite slope, lurid flames burst forth that strike the air with terrible detonations. In line from left to right fires emerge from the sky and explosions from the ground. It is a frightful curtain which divides us from the world, which divides us from the past and from the future. We stop, fixed to the ground, stupefied by the sudden host that thunders from every side; then a simultaneous effort uplifts our mass again and throws it swiftly forward. We stumble and impede each other in the great waves of smoke. With harsh crashes and whirlwinds of pulverized earth, towards the profundity into which we hurl ourselves pell-mell, we see craters opened here and there, side by side, and merging in each other. . . . The stridor of the bursting shells hurts your ears, beats you on the neck, goes through your temples, and you cannot endure it without a cry. The gusts of death drive us on, lift us up, rock us to and fro. We leap, and do not know whither we go.[17]

But the war's trauma was not confined to those who had experienced it firsthand. Like an epidemic, it spread over great distances and infected the imaginations of artists and writers who had never slipped on a uniform or glimpsed the trenches. Representative of this group was Virginia Woolf, whose empathy for those who had fought and been scarred by what they had witnessed at the front coalesced in the figure of Septimus Warren Smith in her 1925 novel, *Mrs. Dalloway*. As his name suggests, Septimus is a Victorian innocent, an early volunteer who "went to France to save an England which consisted almost entirely of Shakespeare's plays and Miss Isabel Pole in a green dress walking in a square." Under fire, he preserves his equilibrium by numbing himself—by becoming unable to feel. But afterward, when he returns to London (a "world without meaning") accompanied by his Italian bride, Lucrezia, this becomes a liability, as he cannot love her. Even literature no longer offers him any comfort. The only sensation he experiences is a recurrent, paranoid fear—terror evoked by death-haunted visions. Ultimately, Septimus can only escape these hallucinations and find peace by taking his own life: he hurls himself out a window and is impaled on a spiked railing.[18] While combat did not destroy his body, it killed his soul, and without it he does not really exist. Septimus's suicide only acknowledges this fact, making him another of the war's casualties.

The psychically maimed veteran occurs frequently in postwar literature.[19] Less grotesque than veterans with grievous physical wounds, he speaks for that part of the war generation that ostensibly had survived intact, but was, in fact, emotionally crippled. His destiny is to remain forever stuck in a mental No Man's Land, unable to resume a "normal" life. What he has seen and experienced is ineffable. His anguish lies in an inability to bear witness.[20] Like the men missing arms or legs, the veterans immobile in their wheelchairs, these inwardly disabled veterans have been emasculated, no longer able to feel.[21] They cannot relate to other people. As the listless, aptly named Krebs (German for "cancer") has come to realize in Hemingway's story "Soldier's Home," they only want to hear lies about the war, not what it was really like for him. His emotional truth—that he doesn't love anyone—is just as unpalatable.

While this view of the Great War was widely held at the time, and perpetuated through works of art, it does not fully reflect how European and American societies were affected by this conflict, and how they responded to it. The notion that the war ended one era and ushered in a "modern consciousness," that it created a set of "abrupt disjunctions" between past and present, arises from a particular perspective—namely, that of the educated middle class.[22] Despite being a small minority in the warring armies, it was this social stratum that was most influential in shaping public awareness of the war.[23] However, as historians like Joanna Bourke have pointed out, this "disillusionment thesis" is not universally applicable.[24] The idea that Europe was "changed, changed utterly" by the war appears simplistic. For one thing, many of the aspects of society we tend to label "modern" were already present long before the war. Conversely, there was more continuity between the pre- and postwar eras than this thesis will admit.[25] This observation applies as much to veterans as it does to the general populace. Not all men returned from France as emotionally inert as Septimus Smith and Harold Krebs, or as cynically pessimistic as John Dos Passos, who mocked in his trilogy *U.S.A.* the Wilsonian credo of "peace and freedom and canned goods and butter and sugar."[26] Instead, many came back whole and unscarred, eager to resume the lives that had been interrupted by military service and fulfill their deferred ambitions to fall in love, marry, and raise a family. Women, too, hungered after the stability of marriage and motherhood, even though some of them were reluctant to give up the greater freedom and employment opportunities that the war years had brought them. Their determination to achieve these domestic objectives—and success in doing so—is evident in the short-lived marriage and baby "booms" that occurred soon after the war ended. Furthermore, these pent-up desires of young people were part and parcel of a more general longing for "normalcy" once the conflict was over.

However, as has already been noted, the Europe that existed before the war was not exactly a paradigm of traditional attitudes and mores. Radically new thinking about how society should be organized and how political, economic, social, and sexual power should be distributed within it had entered public awareness long before the guns of August erupted in a roar. Although still peripheral and highly controversial, these unorthodox philosophies were part of the prewar Zeitgeist and thus made the idea of going back to some halcyon, homogeneous era a conservative's pipedream. Instead, it is more accurate to see the Great War as a testing ground for a variety of competing ideologies, including ones dealing with masculinity and the relations between the sexes. The war experience accelerated these social currents, put them under greater stress, brought them more into open conflict—strengthened them in some ways, while weakening them in others. The course that European and American society would follow afterward would be determined by this complex interplay of forces. No single point of view would emerge triumphant from this clash of ideas any more than any single army could unequivocally celebrate victory on the Continent's battlefields.

"Masculinity" was clearly put to the test in this conflict. In fact, it could be argued that the Great War was fought, in part, because of this issue.[27] As was pointed out earlier, mounting pressures to reaffirm a vigorous, aggressive manliness in the face of feminist advances contributed significantly to a building popular groundswell of support for going to war in 1914. Many men fervently hoped to demonstrate their unique male strengths and regain a lost, elevated stature by volunteering. They welcomed the outbreak of fighting. With their comrades at the front, they experienced a liberating euphoria, finding a collective purpose and a deep emotional bond that gave meaning to their lives. For many others, however, the war was deeply disillusioning: it had not proven to be the "proper arena for the successful, significant display of masculine ardor" they had expected.[28] Instead of feeling free, heroic, and ennobled, they were horrified and emotionally shattered by what they saw at the front. They returned home bitter and disenchanted, their maleness further diminished. Both of these reactions helped to shape the outlook of the surviving members of the war generation during the rest of their lives. These responses also perpetuated sharply contrasting models of masculinity and exacerbated tensions over gender roles during the interwar period. The unresolved conflict between these models and over male-female relations would eventually make war attractive once again a few decades later as the ultimate means of reasserting male supremacy.[29] War would offer the definitive solution that peacetime society could not. The clash between these two masculinities can be vividly seen in the front experiences of two German soldiers.

Born in 1895, Ernst Jünger grew up in a well-educated, middle-class family in the north German city of Hanover, where his father, Ernst Georg, who had earned a doctorate in chemistry, worked as a pharmacist. As a young boy, Jünger found himself temperamentally at odds with the scientifically based, progressive philosophy espoused by his father. A poor student at math and generally unhappy in the classroom, he felt alienated from other boys at boarding school. He was more drawn to

Nietzsche and the poems of Byron and wont to take long hikes through the nearby heath with his older brother or a band of youths who belonged to the *Wandervogel*, or "Wandering Birds" movement then popular throughout Germany.[30] In his schoolboy poems, Jünger voiced a desire to escape the strict confines of bourgeois society and travel to distant, fantastical lands. When he was barely eighteen, emboldened by having read Henry Morgan Stanley's *In Darkest Africa*, Jünger ran away from school to join the French Foreign Legion, in Algeria. (After only three months his father managed to get him out.) He was intensely patriotic, having memorized Horace's "Dulce et decorum est pro patria mori" by the time he was nine years old. He felt part of a long tradition of German patriots whose greatest hope and honor was die for their Fatherland. After war broke out, he went downtown to watch a regiment march by proudly while girls decorated them with flowers. Jünger was so struck by the soldiers' enthusiasm that he volunteered for the infantry the next day, August 1.[31]

Sent to the Western front as an enlisted man in December 1914, the nineteen-year-old Jünger was wounded by artillery fire the following spring. After recovering, he attended officer training school and was commissioned as a lieutenant. He returned to the front as a reconnaissance officer. In this position of leadership, he grew deeply attached to the men under him: "So bound together are we by experience, work, and blood that it wouldn't be possible for us to be any closer."[32] During a battle in August 1916 Jünger was wounded a second time, but he returned to action, not being able to imagine "anything more beautiful than the fiery smoke of battle and the wild, manly deed."[33] In March of 1917, fresh back from leave, he rejoined his regiment in France just in time to undergo a ferocious bombardment by the British, which caused massive casualties. Afterward Jünger helped unearth three dead German soldiers from gaping shell holes. One had had his head blown off and his neck was like a "great sponge of blood." The entrails of another flowed out of his body. Stunned by what he had seen, Jünger hastily gulped down a couple of cherry brandies and then went back to the officers' mess, where he found solace: "It was here, among the spirits of the undaunted dead, that the will to conquer was concentrated and made visible in the features of each weather-beaten face. There was an element at work here that the very horror of the war underlined and even spiritualized, an element not seldom found among the men with whom one lay in the shell-holes—sporting joy in danger, and a chivalrous impulse to see things out."

That winter Jünger found more sustaining inspiration in the works of the great nineteenth-century Russian novelists—Gogol, Dostoyevsky, and Tolstoy. With his regiment playing a key role, the German army launched a major offensive against British forces in March 1918. By now Jünger had developed a fatalistic view of his chances of survival: "Death had lost its meaning," he wrote during an earlier lull in the fighting, "and the will to live was made over to our country; and hence each one was blind and regardless of his personal fate." Holding a revolver in one hand and a bamboo riding cane in the other, Jünger raced toward the British positions: "an overwhelming desire to kill winged my feet." Later he would reflect, "Where would be the success of war if it were not for individuals whom the thrill of action intoxicates and hurls forward with an impetus not to be resisted?" But his admiration for the English as fellow soldiers curbed this impulse. Once, during a British counterattack in August 1918, he came upon a wounded enemy soldier lying in a hollow and put the revolver to this man's temple, but when the soldier pulled out a photograph of him and his family, Jünger swallowed his "moral rage" and stalked away.

Later, a man in his regiment was shot through the stomach and Jünger, nearly overcome with grief, mutely watched him die beside him. Soon thereafter, he was himself shot above the heart by one of his own men, who had mistaken him for an Englishman. He was then struck in the back of his head. With blood pouring out, he shook off thoughts of impending death and gathered his remaining strength, "possessed by one idea, to hurry forward and join in the fight." Finally taken to a field hospital, Jünger felt only regret to be out of action and irritation at the presence of females, in the guise of nurses (even though he insisted he was no misogynist): "One sank, after the manly and purposeful activities of war, into a vague atmosphere of warmth." With the war now at an end for him, having been wounded seven times in combat, he consoled himself by realizing how, having shed blood for Germany and its "greatness," he now was closer to his country than ever before. For his performance at Cambrai, Jünger was awarded the "Blue Max"—his country's highest military honor. At twenty-three, he was one of the youngest—and few surviving—men ever so honored.[34]

Erich Remark was born in Osnabrück three years after Jünger, into a working-class Catholic family of French ancestry. His father was a struggling bookbinder—not a strong male role model. Declining economic fortunes forced the family to move often while he was a boy, and Remark spent much of his time alone, reading and daydreaming. He developed an interest in fish and butterflies and a quietly rebellious temperament. He studied to become a teacher—his mother's wish for him. Tall, open-faced, and handsome, he attracted women, but he preferred reading Rilke and Hermann Hesse to courting them. In 1914, several of his schoolmates volunteered for the army right away, while Remark, only sixteen at that time, continued his studies, even though he, too, had succumbed to the patriotic fervor of the day and the manic desire to help Germany fight for the "salvation of civilization." Over the next two years, he saw this initial appetite for war wane as the number of "fallen" soldiers steadily climbed. By the time Remark was drafted, in November 1916, stories about the horrors of the front had reached Osnabrück and soured him on the glory of war. He had no illusions about what lay in store for him.[35]

After finishing basic training, Remark was dispatched to France, to help maintain and rebuild German trench defensives. He quickly discovered how lives were wasted because of incompetent martinets—bullying, sadistic men who cared only about their own power. The only war Remark and his fellow soldiers wanted to fight was against these petty tyrants. They were the real enemy, and he developed an intense hatred for them. At the same time, he came to see the soldiers on the other side of No Man's Land as fellow sufferers, worthy of his sympathy and friendship. Standing guard over a group of Russian prisoners, he realized how little separated them from him. It was only the leaders of their respective countries that sought this war and would benefit from it. For the ordinary soldier the war was meaningless.

While serving in northwest Belgium, he came under an artillery barrage for several days in what turned out to be his only exposure to combat. He carried a wounded comrade to the rear, only to discover his friend was already dead when he got there. Remark was then hit by shrapnel and sent back to the rear to recover. After several weeks at a hospital in Germany, he learned that his mother had died of cancer. Writing poems and playing the piano at hospital concerts, Remark did the best he could to delay his return to the front. But the war ended before he had to do so. Returning to Osnabrück, he resumed his teacher training, embittered by the staggering human costs of this conflict. He continued work on a novel, *Traumbude*, about an artistic circle during the prewar era. To develop his own independent literary persona, he changed his name from Erich Paul Remark to Erich Maria Remarque. (Altering the spelling of his last name restored its French roots.) Taking various jobs as a bookkeeper, librarian, and salesman for gravestones, he did all that he could to put memories of the war behind him. In the following years, he fell in love with an actress named Jutta Zambona, moved in with her, and eventually married her. However, Jutta's unfaithfulness (and, reputedly, his impotence) caused the marriage to break up, and in despair, Remarque returned to the subject that fit this dark mood—the war. He finished *All Quiet on the Western Front* in six weeks. He dedicated the novel to "a generation of men who, even though they may have escaped its shells, were destroyed by the war."

The fact that Remarque and Jünger could create such strikingly different accounts of the war and its impact is, perhaps, not as remarkable as the fact that both found large, highly receptive, and admiring audiences for their work in the decades that followed. *All Quiet on the Western Front* sold a million copies in Germany the first year after it was published, in 1929, and another 300,000 copies during a similar period in both England and France. Remarque's argument that the Great War had been fought at the expense of ordinary men for the benefit of the wealthy and powerful gained credence not only in his own defeated country but throughout Europe and the United States, because it articulated a growing conviction that there had been no winners in this conflict: both sides had suffered grievously and unnecessarily. War was a disaster for ordinary people, brought on by self-aggrandizing leaders who had manipulated naïve young men with patriotic lies so that they would fight against each other in defiance of their common humanity and peace-loving nature. The way to avoid future wars, Remarque implied, was to organize societies along more egalitarian lines—upholding justice, mutual respect, and equality for all. His humanistic message resonated with various mass movements—pacifist, socialist, and communist—that were gaining strength during the 1920s and 1930s. They shared an aversion to war as contrary to the best interests of the great majority of ordinary people. Remarque's reaction to World War I resonated most powerfully among young, sensitive intellectuals and members of the well-educated middle and upper classes who had made up a large portion of the officer corps. For it was these youth who had their grand illusions about the glory of warfare so horribly shattered. Born into aristocratic and privileged families; taught at public schools to believe in lofty, chivalric ideals; screened from most of life's daily unpleasantries; imbued with *noblesse oblige* to serve their country, these soldiers were least prepared for the frightful realities of the trenches—and most apt to feel betrayed and demoralized by what they experienced there.[36] Mingling with ordinary soldiers from the lower classes had helped many of them realize that artificial social divisions mattered little in the face of common suffering and indiscriminate death and opened their minds to a future in which these distinctions might disappear.[37]

Ernst Jünger and his vision of war as a searing, uplifting rite of masculine passage found a smaller, but more passionate following in the postwar era.[38] Mostly this was in his own nation and in its former ally Austria, where defeat had left a sour taste and a simmering desire to erase this blot on national honor by fighting and winning another war.[39] Soldiers trudged home to these countries broken in spirit as well as body and desperate for rehabilitation.[40] As the historian George Mosse has pointed out, a need to justify the sacrifice made on the battlefield induced many German veterans and other memoirists to envision the war as a "sacred event" and create a cult of martyrdom around those who had "fallen" for the sake of their country.[41] Many veterans and younger men who were attracted to right-wing quasimilitary groups after 1918 and later to the Nazi Party devoured Jünger, seduced by his message of personal transformation under fire. This was conveyed not only in his war memoir, *In Stahlgewittern* (*Storm of Steel*), which was published in 1920, but also in a series of essays Jünger wrote in the 1920s for various nationalistic magazines, such as *Der Vormarsch* (*The Advance*) and *Die Standarte* (*The Regiment*). All of these writings celebrated the perseverance of the heroic male warrior in an age dominated by impersonal, "machine" power.[42] In a 1923 piece, Jünger praised the nascent NSDAP for fusing nationalism and socialism and seeking to guide Germany toward a revolutionary renaissance under dictatorial leadership.[43] These words of praise induced Adolf Hitler to send Jünger a signed copy of

Mein Kampf and propose a get-together, but Jünger was scornful of the Nazis' racist ideology (which he considered crude and small-minded), and the meeting never took place.[44]

While Jünger's ecstatic celebration of modern war for reinvigorating male "courage and passion" was an extreme position, which relatively few Europeans of his generation were inclined to adopt, his nostalgia for the camaraderie and unified purpose at the front was evident among veterans on both sides.[45] These positive aspects of the war experience helped to justify an otherwise senseless slaughter. This redeeming sentiment can be gleaned in poems written during the war, such as Robert Nichols' "Comrades" (1915), about some soldiers' rescue of their mortally wounded, beloved officer:

> They lifted him.
> He smiled and held his arms out to the dim,
> And in a moment passed beyond their ken,
> Hearing him whisper, "O my men, my men!"

It can also be found in these stanzas from Ivor Gurney's "To Certain Comrades":

> Living we loved you, yet withheld our praises
> Before your faces.
> And though our spirits had you high in honour!
> After the English manner,
> We said no word. Yet as such comrades would,
> You understood.
> Such friendship is not touched by death's disaster,
> But stands the faster.
> And all the shocks and trials of time cannot
> Shake it one jot.[46]

Poems like these express the prewar hope that bonding under fire would satisfy men's need for an intense emotional attachment, free of gender antagonism.[47] The poignant irony, of course, was that so many of these intimate wartime bonds among men were destroyed almost as soon as they were forged.[48] They were what the war gave, and what the war took away. The decades-long quest for a separate male sphere of activity from which women would be excluded and in which men could openly enjoy the free, unrestrained pleasure of each other's company and affection had finally succeeded, but only briefly, in an environment *outside* of society—one based upon violence, suffering, and death. Since this war world existed as a temporary alternative to—or escape from—ordinary civilian life, its ambience could not be sustained once the guns fell silent, and the men came home. Still, the appeal of male oneness persisted. The war may have ended, but longing for the emotional intensity it had made possible had not. Whereas, for veterans like Remarque, the Great War had exposed the ugly side of masculinity—its vanity, cruelty, barbarity, and arrogance—other former soldiers looked back fondly on the ties they had forged and the deep satisfaction these had given them. In his memoir of the war published half a century afterward, the British volunteer George Coppard (who had lied about his age to enlist in August 1914) recalled: "Of my memories of life in the trenches, the one thing I cherish more than anything else is the comradeship that grew up between us as a result of the way of life we were compelled to lead."[49]

Even for those who had died, the feelings of love did not abate. As one of the officers of the Canadian Great War Veterans' Association stated in 1921, "[Comrade] to us means fellowship of a most sacred kind formed by ties that cannot be broken but are written in blood, ties that we formed in days of trial that cannot be broken now by anything else, ties that are sacred to those who have gone and to those who still live."[50] The importance so many survivors of the war placed on these ties is evident in the popularity of veterans' groups in the 1920s and 1930s. (Significantly, these organizations did not separate former officers from enlisted men, but, by treating all veterans alike, stressed the unifying commonality of their front experiences.) Rather than turn their backs on the war and "move on," considerable numbers of demobbed men joined these organizations and attended their reunions. In Canada, for example, some 40 percent of the 732 veterans of the Calgary-based 137th Battalion signed up in 1920. By the 1930s, fully a quarter of all of that country's surviving ex-soldiers—150,000 men—belonged to the Canadian Legion.[51] To the south, the American Legion was established in 1919, in part, to "preserve the incidents and memories of our association in the Great War" and to "consecrate and sanctify our comradeship by our devotion to mutual helpfulness."[52] By 1931, membership had reached 1 million, out of the 2 million men who had worn the American uniform overseas during the Great War. Similarly, *Stahlhelm*, the largest association of German frontline soldiers, was formed in 1918 to "join together veterans of the front back home and to sustain the loyal comradeship developed in battle." It had attracted half a million veterans by the late 1920s—many of whom were also active supporters of right-wing political groups such as the Nazis. An even larger number of former soldiers—over 3 million—had joined the major French veterans' association by this point.[53] Although a desire to lobby for welfare benefits accounted for some of the motivation for joining these associations, the emotional aspect was not at all insignificant. Former soldiers joined these organizations—and stayed involved in them for decades—because they still valued the sense of togetherness forged under fire.

Some observers hoped similar fraternal bonds would form the basis for a rejuvenated and more egalitarian postwar society.[54] Most prominent of these was the English writer D. H. Lawrence, who explored the prospects for a "blood brotherhood" or "eternal union" between men in three of his novels written after the war—*Women in Love* (1920), *Aaron's Rod* (1922), and *Kangaroo* (1923).[55] For Lawrence, ties between men offered a wholeness and completeness that intimacy with women could never equal. In *Women in Love*, the two main male characters, Birkin and Gerald, wrestle with one another in search of this union. Afterward, lying exhausted, they reflect on their feelings. Birkin finds the experience strangely fulfilling:

"One ought to wrestle and strive and be physically close. It makes one sane."
"You think so?"
"I do. Don't you?"
"Yes," said Gerald.
There were long spaces of silence between their words. The wrestling had some deep meaning to them—an unfinished meaning.
"We are mentally, spiritually intimate, therefore we should be more or less physically intimate too—it is more whole."
"Certainly it is," said Gerald. Then he laughed pleasantly, adding: "It's rather wonderful to me." Then he stretched out his hands handsomely.[56]

In Lawrence's novels, the closeness men seek includes a physical dimension, much as it does in the writings of T. E. Lawrence dealing with his wartime exploits in the Arabian Desert. This frankness harkens back to the casual, unself-conscious affection men of the Victorian era expressed for each other. In a sense, the two Lawrences were inheritors of the Greek ideal of male love as revived a generation before at Oxford by A. E. Housman, Walter Pater, and John Addington Symonds. (Homoerotic feelings were also a major element in the prewar German youth movement.) The fact that neither Lawrence personally experienced the hetacomb of the trenches allowed both men to honor this ideal while many veterans of their generation had come to abandon it after witnessing the slaughter of their comrades.[57] Significantly, however, the bond these two writers yearned for cannot endure. In *Women in Love*, Gerald dies of an illness in the snows of the Alps, and Birkin, seeing his friend devoid of spirit and vitality, can only feel "chiefly disgust at the inert body lying there."[58] As countless soldiers discovered on the front, the melding in brotherhood was intense, but fleeting, and ultimately elusive.[59]

Postwar male bonding had many positive attractions, but it also offered an escape—escape from the control and power of women. Much as late Victorian, middle-class men had retreated from their "feminized" homes to the friendly confines of their clubs and golf courses, so did their counterparts a few decades later continue to seek contentment and autonomy outside the company of females. World War I had served, in part, as an outlet for this impulse, but had only given Europe's young men a brief respite from their long-unresolved conflict with the opposite sex. In returning home, these veterans encountered a society in which women, owing to wartime necessity, appeared to have gained more rights and assumed more liberties than ever before. For many ex-soldiers, this was an unwelcome development, and unhappiness over it is manifest in postwar writings as well as in comments that appeared in the press. One German army officer would sourly note, "Whatever virtues were once found among the Germans seemed to have sunk once and for all into the muddy flood. . . . Promiscuity, shamelessness and corruption ruled supreme. German women seemed to have forgotten their German ways."[60] Dismayed veterans were bitter about this overt disavowal of the values they had gone off to fight for. They brought back from the trenches a "we-against-them" attitude and readily transferred this polarizing animosity to females who appeared to have usurped their roles while they were away. Many also blamed women not only for blithely and enthusiastically supporting the war but also for having contributed to the fatal "unmanning" of young men in the years leading up to it. Peacetime "feminization and masculine degeneracy" had prevented soldiers from performing well on the front.[61] Many of these former soldiers now wanted to reclaim their masculine prerogatives; they felt their service had earned them a more elevated status and respect. They felt emboldened to impose an aggressive, dominant masculinity on civilian society and to dislodge women from their recently won, more emancipated position. They wanted the postwar world to mirror the disciplined, hierarchical one they had known in uniform—in which females played only marginal roles. Many older men (born in the Victorian age) and ones who had not fought in the war joined in this effort to return to more traditionally structured gender relations.

Now that women were no longer "doing their bit" for the nation, negative attitudes about their having invaded what were still considered "male domains" could be openly expressed. Authors on both sides of the Atlantic presented female characters whose power threatened the men in their lives. D. H. Lawrence did so in *Women in Love*, further elaborating his fear of domineering (if loving) women first evident in his semiautobiographical *Sons and Lovers*.[62] Lawrence displayed deep resentment toward assertive women in short stories such as "Tickets Please" (1918) and "Monkey Nuts" (1919). The American writer William Faulkner (who had dreamed of being a pilot during World War I but never managed to become one) also evinced misogynistic views in several of his postwar stories, as well as in a number of his early novels—notably *Soldier's Pay*.[63] (In the latter, the female protagonist, Cecily Saunders, betrays a dying war veteran, much as Faulkner himself felt he had been treated by his childhood sweetheart; Cecily is portrayed as a "deceiving, traitorous Eve.")[64]

Ernest Hemingway, who had actually been wounded in the war, created male characters who had undergone a similar "emasculation" and who consequently became emotionally passive, under the thumb of strong female figures. (The sexually attractive but mannish Brett Ashley, in *The Sun Also Rises*, is a chief example.) Numerous other writers and artists took up the theme of the weak, dependent, and powerless male after the war: Franz Kafka is perhaps the best-known chronicler of this crippling male angst; Pablo Picasso (even before the war, in *Les Demoiselles d'Avignon* and *Three Women*) captured it best on canvas.

Artistically rendered fear of strong, seductive, and threatening females reflected a broader cultural feeling that men had failed the test of their manhood afforded by the war. Unease over this, in turn, fed a pervasive feeling that Europe had lost its bearings in the war and was now lacking in purpose, confidence, and conviction. The French poet Paul Valery and several of his contemporaries coined the phrase "Age of Anxiety" to encapsulate this postwar feeling of ennui.[65] Women were held partially responsible for this: they had first urged men to fight, then taken over power in their absence, and finally refused to surrender this once the soldiers came back. Women seemed to be both the cause and the beneficiaries of men's fall from greatness. In the masculine-centric thinking of the day, the decline of Western civilization and the decline of male power were assumed to be one and the same thing. Fear and loathing over these developments was most pronounced in societies where traditional masculine dominance was most closely aligned with the national ethos and the structure of political power. Germany was the most obvious case. Here attacks on married women who entered the workforce or refused to leave it were particularly virulent. So were diatribes against single women who defied conventionality with provocative displays of their sexuality. For young male Germans, this latter group was the more threatening, as these women held the power to seduce and sap men of their "martial masculinity"—that is, their autonomy, stoicism, and self-reliance. After the war, these "New Women" replaced the Americans and the British as the designated enemy of Teutonic manliness. Members of the paramilitary *Freikorps* were appalled by a "vaginal potency" that sought literally and figuratively to swallow them up and destroy the masculine integrity that they had constructed free of female "contamination" and "decomposition."[66] Rejecting the allure of females, these men, echoing Jünger, preferred the "voluptuousness of blood."[67] In addition to trends within their own society that favored giving the opposite sex more power (abortion rights, access to more jobs, as well as the vote), ultraconservative men who flocked to the *Freikorps* in the 1920s despised egalitarian ideologies such as Russian Bolshevism, which they associated with aggressive and manly females.

In tradition-bound, imperial Japan, the ruling military elite and the population that largely supported it were just as hostile toward recently empowered, middle-class women in their country and just as eager to thwart their exercise of personal freedom.[68] The small number of well-educated Japanese women who had begun advocating free love and challenging patriarchal marriage before the war faced harsh opposition.[69] Authorities imposed harsh penalties on women who had illegal abortions, for example. Japanese nationalists were adamant about promoting motherhood for military reasons—to increase the nation's population so the country would be in a better position to fight and prevail in anticipated future wars.[70] Like Germany and Italy, Japan generally reacted negatively to the democratic, individualistic tendencies in the postwar decades; right-wing elements sought, instead, to revive a "collective consciousness" and group conformity to strengthen their societies.[71] There was little room in their visions of national glory for liberated women or dissenting political philosophies.[72]

In the 1920s and 1930s, a residual longing for male unity was exploited politically, in Japan and several European countries. In Weimar Germany, extreme right-wing groups like the Nazis regarded veterans' groups and affiliated paramilitary and political organizations as the vanguard for the social revolution they wanted to bring about, relying upon unity, equality, militant struggle, and self-sacrifice to produce a victory that had been denied on the battlefield. For these nationalists, the war was not a disaster to be disavowed, but a "transformative instrument"— a testing ground for the values and personal qualities required for their revolution to succeed.[73] All of these traits were traditionally associated with males. In fact, the fascist movements that emerged in the aftermath of World War I were unabashedly masculine. Their ideology was decidedly "chauvinist," promising to restore men to their "rightful" position of dominance.[74] Their leaders spoke openly and often about cultivating the "New Man." This mantra had first echoed before the war and helped induce some young men to enlist, particularly in Germany.[75] The promise was that combat would discipline and harden these men and insulate them from weakening, feminine influence and feelings such as fear and sexual love: by killing and destroying they would fulfill their greatest human potential. They would become "men of steel."[76]

Once the war was over, this same "martial masculinity" was held up not only as an inspiration for self-doubting, socially and economically insecure men but also as the embodiment of the values felt to be lacking in the nation as a whole.[77] Right-wing movements sought to harness manliness for their own purposes. Male stoicism and discipline would serve as a "symbol of self-control and purity" for the process of revitalization and resurgence they hoped to lead.[78] Veterans were seen as models of this sorely needed, "traditional" masculinity. They would lead the way toward a "remasculinization" of society, completing the transformation they had begun during the conflict. (The Nazis used emotionally evocative terms such as *Frontsgemeinschaft* ["community of the front"] and *Arbeitsfront* ["labor front"] to link the masculine unity they were offering with what soldiers wanted to believe they had found in battle—an ideal "comradeship.")[79] To invert Clausewitz, politics would become a continuation of war by other means. By asserting the superiority of male attributes, a country like Germany could regain the primal strength that the enervating evolution of "civilization" had taken away. By transferring their love and allegiance to the Fatherland, men could break free of feminine control and regain the dominance they had once enjoyed.[80] In Italy, Mussolini also stressed the central role of the "New Man" in creating a new fascist order.[81]

This linkage between a revitalized manhood and political power was made explicit by the Nazi ideologue and later propaganda minister Joseph Goebbels, who proclaimed that Nazism was "in its nature a masculine movement."[82] Women were to play no part in this new German political life. As a contemporary historian has put it, "In gender terms, fascism was a naked reassertion of masculine supremacy in societies that had been moving towards equality for women."[83] It is thus not at all surprising that the membership in this German movement—like parallel ones in Austria and Italy—was overwhelmingly male throughout its existence: between 1925 and 1932, fewer than 8 percent of those who belonged to the NSDAP were women, and not until late in the war did the female proportion reach one-third. And this was a party of *young* men: seven of ten male members were under the age of forty. [84]

In light of the war's tremendous losses and what seemed to be almost universally acknowledged as its pointless folly, this celebration—indeed, deification—of men's unique attributes and bonds may appear incongruous. After all, wasn't the "lesson" of the Great War that modern conflict was a disaster for civilization? And weren't men (male leaders, at least) responsible for encouraging this madness? Virginia Woolf was certainly not alone, in her pacifist epistolary essay *Three Guineas*, in condemning the male "habit" of fighting, in decrying men's finding "happiness and excitement" in participating in war, whereas women (and a few, exceptional men, like Wilfred Owen and the Bishop of Birmingham) demonstrably did not.[85] Many of Woolf's contemporaries—men and women alike—blamed the war on male camaraderie. Reversing her earlier support for Britain's participation, the suffragette leader Christabel Pankhurst now condemned male dominance for making an ill-begotten conflict inevitable.[86]

But clearly this gender-based opprobrium fell on many deaf ears: in spirit, if not in deed, the attraction of the war experience continued to stimulate some male imaginations long after the last soldiers had slouched home to their waiting villages, cities, and towns. In fact, in some quarters, the "warrior spirit" emerged from this conflict seemingly intact and unquenchable. It represented another mythologizing of the brutal and harsh war realities—the antithesis of the "disillusionment" view.[87] This involved honoring the dead as heroes and perpetuating their memory through solemn ceremonies and equally glorifying monuments. The countries where this adulatory outlook was most likely to take hold were those that had been regarded as bellicose and excessively "masculine" before 1914, but where this warrior ethos had not delivered a military victory—that is, in Germany and Austria.[88] Not coincidentally, these states were also ones with no strong, historical commitment to individual freedoms or rights. In the former, Ernst Jünger may have represented an extreme in his assessment that serving on the front had been an "incomparable schooling of the heart," but many of his German male contemporaries shared his eagerness to redouble the struggle to restore "male" values to their once preeminent place in society.[89] For, instead of accomplishing this, the Great War had not only frustrated this long-festering ambition but pushed its realization even further into the future. On the field of battle, its soldiers had failed to deliver. Their nations were defeated.

Unlike other European countries, Germany and Austria (or, more properly, the Austro-Hungarian Empire) suffered severe damage to their national pride and identities after the war, when the victorious Triple

Entente powers (Great Britain, France, and Russia) subjected them to territorial as well as financial evisceration. Both were compelled to pay staggering war reparations. Under Article 231 of the Treaty of Versailles, Germany was held accountable for the war. To prevent a repetition of its bellicosity, a number of restrictions were imposed upon its military, including the conversion of its once proud and might army into a rump volunteer force of no more than 100,000 men. The size of its navy was similarly limited. Both Germany and Austria had to surrender large chunks of land—most notably, Austria's southern Tyrol and Germany's West Prussia as well as Alsace and Lorraine, abutting France.[90] The two former allies were also forbidden from uniting without the permission of the League of Nations (which, of course, would never grant this request). Summarily ending their imperial heyday, these territorial truncations forced the two countries to accept a strategically and psychologically diminished status. From now on, stripped of all grandeur, they were mere "republics." These humiliating actions, coupled with an ensuing hyperinflation, massive unemployment, and widespread hunger, came as a second national trauma—on the heels of the "stab in the back" allegedly delivered by Social Democratic politicians and "unpatriotic" Jews, which had denied Germany the battlefield victory its generals thought they had won. In 1922, Austria endured an even more crushing blow when, facing imminent bankruptcy, it had to surrender its short-lived sovereignty and become a ward of the equally young League of Nations. Taken together, this series of setbacks amounted to national emasculation. (While it had fought on the winning side, Italy also experienced a blow to its national pride and ambitions when it was not awarded greater international stature and prestige afterward. Popular frustration over this outcome played into the hands of Benito Mussolini and his militaristic fascist movement.) Much of Adolf Hitler's growing popularity in the late 1920s and early 1930s derived from his denunciation of the Versailles treaty and implicit promise to nullify it.[91]

The common threads connecting all of these right-wing groups were national—that is, male—humiliation and need to overcome this and dominate through incessant, warlike struggle.[92] When he founded the Italian fascist party in 1919, Mussolini made a connection between the "revolution" begun with his country's entry into the war four years before and the political one he was going to bring to fruition under his leadership.[93] As defenders of their countries' honor, Austrian and German veterans took this personally. Rather than accept defeat, however, many of them were drawn to political movements and ideologies that reassured them that ultimate victory still lay within their grasp.[94] They were joined by young men born too late to have served on the front, but equally attracted by the aura of militant masculinity and naked power surrounding groups like the right-wing, paramilitary *Freikorps*—a private army boasting half a million members less than a year after the war ended. These movements made no promise of "democratic" evolution, for they considered the institutions and egalitarian principles of democracy to be debilitating and alien to their national character, much as the novelist Thomas Mann did in espousing a "special way" for his country in his 1918 polemic *Betrachtungen eines unpolitischen* (Reflections of an Apolitical Man). An authoritarian system, Mann argued, "is and remains the one that is proper and becoming to the German people, and the one they basically want."[95] Nationalistic groups called for a "conservative revolution," which would sweep away Germany and Austria's hapless postwar experiments with parliamentary democracy and restore a more unified, centrally controlled political system, deriving its legitimacy from the collective consent of the *Volk*. Right-wing militants believed in rigidly separating the two sexes and relegating women to a subordinate, maternal function so that a virile "community of men" could emerge to lead this revolution.[96] Disgruntled former soldiers drew upon the masculine solidarity and confrontational, frequently violent methods learned during the war to advance their militant cause. Like their older brothers who had fought in the trenches, many of the young German males drawn to groups like the *Freikorps* had a "hunger for wholeness" and eschewed what they saw as the hypocritical norms of modern, bourgeois society. They yearned to rise up as one, to destroy this reason-based culture of their fathers and to replace it with one built upon youthful solidarity and submission to a revered authority.[97] They sought to infuse civilian life with a "new ruthlessness" and raw, primitive energy that brooked of no dissent or compromise.[98] They wanted, in essence, to militarize the home front and create new, totalitarian states resembling "war machines."[99]

Like an army in the midst of a battle, civilian society required a strong, exemplary leader who could inspire the utter devotion and self-sacrifice upon which victory depended. In the eyes of many German and Austrian veterans, when they surveyed the chaotic economic, political, and social conditions in their home countries, the absence of such a figure was a fatal, damning flaw. The fractious and incompetent political parties that characterized the postwar era were patently too feckless to accomplish what had to be done to restore national greatness. What was desperately needed—many believed—was an indomitable, almost superhuman "strong man," who would embody and actualize the collective will of his countrymen. (In militaristic Japan, this role was played by a godlike, infallible emperor.) Psychologically, such a figure would serve the inverse purpose of a scapegoat, taking on not others' guilt, but all their hopes and dreams. This deeply emotional longing provided much of the impetus for German men to join the Nazi Party during its formative years. The surviving testimonials of several hundred of these early members reveal how powerful a pull the "Führer myth" and its attendant "personality cult" had on them. Wrote one of the "old guard": "My ideal was a movement which would forge national unity from all working people of the great German fatherland. The realization of my ideal could happen through only one man, Adolf Hitler."[100] In Italy, admiration for Mussolini was likewise a more conducive reason for farmers and members of the working class to back his policies than any ideological affinity for fascism. In these emotion-driven nationalistic affiliations, all politics was personal. (Interestingly enough, fanatical, quasireligious faith in these larger-than-life leaders was not based upon their previous records of achievement or their social backgrounds. Both Hitler and Mussolini came from modest origins and during the war had only held the rank of corporal.)

What becomes clear is that the Great War did not resolve the problem of masculinity in the early twentieth century, but gave greater clarity and validity to two diametrically opposed notions of what this ought to be and how it should be expressed. Each interpretation was fortified by a myth extracted from the experience of the war.[101] One held that the reality of modern combat had rendered notions of "heroism," "glory," and even "patriotism" obsolete, contemptible. The other found in the same front experience a path to (male) salvation. While one disavowed war for victimizing its participants, the other hailed it for bonding them together and allowing them to create a superior kind of being.

Although these sharply contrasting responses dealt most directly with what it meant to be a man in the modern age, they also held implications for how men should behave in the postwar world as well as how society should be structured. There were implications for relations between the sexes as well. Jünger's ideology was unequivocally and proudly masculine. According to it, women played only subordinate, distracting, and enervating parts in the grand, heroic drama of human struggle and triumph. In his wartime writings, Jünger revealed an unconscious association between the enemy forces he, as a warrior, had to subdue and the female body. Both had to be subdued, ravaged, and conquered. For example, in *Feuer und Blut*, he wrote: "But now we will rip away this veil instead of gingerly lifting its corner. We approach as conquerors, armed with all the means of power."[102] For Jünger it seemed that the feelings aroused by war were more intense and meaningful than those any female could awaken in him: war—a world without women—was the ultimate aphrodisiac. In his 1926 *Der Kampf als inneres Erlebnis* (War as Psychological Experience) he recalled: "The baptism of fire! There the air was so laden with overflowing manliness that every draw of breath intoxicated, that one would have to weep without knowing why. Oh, hearts of men, who can feel that! . . . Supple, lean, sinewy bodies, striking faces, eyes in a thousand horrors turned to stone under helmets. . . . Jugglers of death, masters of explosives and flames, magnificent beasts of prey, they moved quickly through the trenches."[103] Jünger's honoring of the male body with this lavishly rhetorical language does not mean that he harbored homoerotic feelings, only that in the fusion of this body with acts of courage he perceived a higher fulfillment than heterosexual intercourse could offer him.[104]

Remarque's view of women and sex differed from Jünger's as much as did his reaction to the front experience. Yet for Remarque, too, the power struggle between men and women affected how he saw war, and vice versa. In fact, what triggered his urge to write about the war (after having not done so at all for nearly a decade afterward) was a falling out with his then wife, Jutta Zambona, after only two years of marriage. Although he claimed to have started this book to get his mind off her infidelities, a close reading of *All Quiet* suggests that he was transferring his vulnerability, anger, and passivity in this relationship onto the canvas of his war experience. Compared to Jünger's harrowing brushes with death, this was relatively thin material: Remarque had only one real exposure to combat before being wounded and invalided back to Germany to recover. Perhaps for this reason, but more likely because of his marital difficulties, he presents the war as a clash not between opposing armies but among soldiers fighting on the same (German) side—namely, the abuse inflicted upon ordinary soldiers by arrogant, egotistical, and cruel superiors, and the soldiers' response to this. In sharp contrast to Jünger, Remarque portrays the war as an emasculating ordeal. The only emotional compensation that his autobiographical character Paul Bäumer can find is the comradeship of his downtrodden fellows. There is a distinctly homoerotic element to their relationships, particularly the one between Bäumer and a considerably older soldier named Stanislaus Katczinsky, or "Kat." Remarque's description of a group of soldiers bathing also suggests this sensibility. The novel portrays a loss of masculine assertiveness and aggression during wartime, and their replacement by a quasifemale passivity and forbearance.[105] Bäumer's encounter with a French prostitute, for example, has a decidedly "feminine" tone:

> Her fingers close around my face. Close above me are her bewildering eyes, the soft brown of her skin and her red lips. . . . I—I am lost in remoteness, in weakness, and in a passion to which I yield myself trustingly. . . . I feel giddy, there is nothing here that a man can hold on to. We have left our boots at the door, they have given us slippers instead, and now nothing remains to recall for me the assurance and self-confidence of the soldier.[106]

His account mirrors memoirs of other soldiers, including those of his fellow German Franz Schauwecker, in stressing solicitous, motherly caring for one's comrades as the most important emotional dimension of life in the trenches.[107] Masculinity, these soldiers learned, could expand during wartime to encompass "soft" qualities otherwise deemed inappropriate and "womanly."

This impact of the war on male sexuality raised great concerns, both while the fighting was still going on and during the decades that followed. Early in the conflict, psychiatrists from several countries noted that the reactions of many soldiers to combat—what came to be called "shell shock"—closely resembled symptoms of hysteria. Subsequent analyses of these psychiatric casualties, conducted by the medical anthropologist W. H. R. Rivers and his British colleagues, concluded that they were suffering from a form of trauma or neurosis.[108] Their condition was frequently accompanied by sexual impotence. While courageous warriors were associated with "tumescence," victims of this trauma were paralyzed by fear and unable to perform.[109] Exposure to combat could also cause soldiers to regress and become emotionally and sexually attached to other men.[110] This overwhelming experience could drain men of their "normal," heterosexual desires. This theory gained credence particularly among German psychiatrists and sex researchers such as Magnus Hirschfeld.[111] Moreover, the belief that frontline combat had adversely affected "normal" male sexuality and made men "neurotic" added to a more general worry that men had returned from the trenches diminished by the helplessness and passive suffering they had experienced there and depicted so vividly by writers like Remarque. Fear of dying had made men "hysterical," subjecting them to a mental condition previously associated only with women. This diagnosis weakened the argument that males were inherently tougher than and different from females. If the war had been fought to restore such gender distinctions, or to "regenerate" Europe's males, it had obviously failed to accomplish this. War had not cured their "neuroses," only exacerbated them.[112] At the same time, many women had gained strength and self-confidence from having run households by themselves or supported their families.[113] Because of these unexpected developments, one of the requirements of the postwar era would be for men to reassume their traditional, active roles as lovers, husbands, and fathers.

There were strong social pressures for this to happen. The war had caused so much social upheaval and disorienting change that most Europeans were desperate to restore some semblance of stability in its aftermath. A return to traditional gender roles would facilitate this.[114] Men, it was felt, had to be "domesticated" again to eradicate the brutalizing, dehumanizing influence of their war experiences. By the same token, women were now expected to give up their wartime jobs and return to the feminine domain of the home.[115] This realignment would make postwar life more "normal." Freud's "death instinct" would yield to a psychologically healthier eroticism.[116] More complementary roles for men and women would prevent a return of the "sex war" that had plagued England in the years leading up to World War I and allow a state of "gender peace" to be established. Some hoped that better relations between the sexes would inhibit the impulse to make war.[117] New government policies encouraged young women to focus on domestic life. More information was made available on raising healthy children, as were subsidies to support them: children were now seen as crucial to the nation's future strength and well-being. Married women were told that motherhood was their most important function.[118]

Public acceptance of these traditional gender roles for men and women was reflected in the popularity of books extolling the virtues of married life. In England, volumes like Marie Stopes's *Married Love* (1918) and Theodoor Van de Velde's *Ideal Marriage: Its Physiology and Technique* (1926) were snatched up by hundreds of thousands of young people hoping to enjoy a physically and emotionally fulfilling marital life. Lecture halls in cities like Berlin filled to hear Van de Velde's words of advice on improving sexual technique.[119] In his writings and talks, the Dutch gynecologist argued that couples needed to strike a harmonious balance in their relationships, while admonishing men to keep the upper hand: Van de Velde, who had run away from his own childless, unhappy marriage with one of his patients, warned prospective brides that the main reason for conflict arising in a marriage was the wife's efforts to dominate her husband; it was "natural" for her to defer to him.[120] In the 1920s, American women were receiving more mixed messages about their primary responsibilities in life. New opportunities to attend college and work professionally had opened up for them, but pressures to marry and raise children were also mounting.

Governments were eager to restore the gender status quo ante. The first step in this process was to give men their jobs back and make them once again the family breadwinners. In England, Parliament wasted no time in making room for returning soldiers. In 1918, it approved the Restoration of Pre-War Practices Act, designed to ease women out of their jobs. In short order, it had its intended effect.[121] By the end of 1919, 750,000 British women had left their jobs; most married ones had gone back to their homes. A recession in 1920 pushed even more out of work.[122] Only a small number of wives were affected by these developments since most had not abandoned domestic life during the war. They had taken care of the family, serving as a "constant bulwark against radical innovation," while their men had been away fighting for the country. Once the war was over, new rights were granted to married women to make it more attractive for them to remain at home. Parliament approved several pieces of legislation favorable to wives, such as the 1923 Matrimonial Causes Act, which gave wives the same right to sue for divorce on the grounds of adultery that their husbands already enjoyed.[123] Some of these laws, such as the 1918 Maternity and Child Welfare Act, were designed to encourage married women to have more children and help replenish the males lost during the war.[124] In the United States, the importance of encouraging motherhood during a time of declining births rate was apparent even before the war, when Congress voted, in 1914, to make Mother's Day a national holiday.

With 8 million German men returning from the front, looking for work, the fledgling government in that country forced women to leave war-related jobs to make room for these veterans, and they complied. Virtually all the gains in income and status they had made between 1914 and 1918 were erased; by 1925, hardly any married women were left in the workforce.[125] Likewise, in France, the minister for employment first asked married women in November 1918 to voluntarily give up their positions to make room for returning male workers. Those who did not go along with this recommendation were then fired en masse the following January.[126] By contrast, employed women in the United States largely surrendered their jobs without much protest, having realized from the start that these were only temporary. As in England, male industrial workers were happy to see them go, having feared that their wages would be reduced by the continuing presence of females.[127]

The general feeling throughout Europe and across the Atlantic was that the war had made it necessary for women to venture outside their normal sphere of activity, and it was now time for them to go back to their proper place, just as men were doing. Public sentiment was now strongly supportive of marriage and the family. Men and women alike desired a return to gender "normalcy." Although the coming of war in 1914 (and the armistice four years later) had brought a brief libidinal release and given young females in particular more sexual freedom than they might have had in its absence, four long years of separation between soldiers and their sweethearts had intensified mutual longings to form stable, lasting relationships, marry, and start families as quickly as possible. Right after the conflict ended, this delayed biological urge ran strong among veterans of all nations, regardless of their views on politics and how they had reacted to the war experience. Just as overwhelmingly, single European and American women yearned to fulfill their domestic responsibilities. Thus, the vast majority of females left the workforce voluntarily. While some wartime polls had found English working women strongly in favor of staying in the labor force after the conflict ended, this sentiment had changed by Armistice Day.[128] Although some women objected to these massive layoffs—marching over to Westminster in 1918 to protest having to give up their lucrative factory jobs—most did not.[129] The same was true of Germany and other belligerent nations.[130] By and large, unless they had lost loved ones, British, French, German, Austrian, Italian, Belgian, and American women did not see the war as having fundamentally altered their lives. On the contrary, they were eager to enjoy the pleasures of domestic life. They regarded the period 1914–1918 as a necessary but regrettable hiatus in their young lives— and, by and large, rejoiced when it was over.[131] Most females of marriageable age willingly adopted a *"Kinder, Küche, Kirche"* ideology, which stressed traditional femininity and motherhood. By 1921, there were fewer women working in England than there had been a decade before.[132] If anything, the French were even more willing than their neighbors and allies to see the lines drawn more clearly between the sexes and undo the harm done by their wartime blurring.[133]

Restoring and upholding time-honored gender differences not only served the domestic focus of postwar Europe; it was also a natural reaction to the war experience. In undergoing a necessary process of militarization, the warring nations had emphasized the central importance of manly courage, discipline, and self-sacrifice. These traits set men apart from the opposite sex, and women's working in factories and even serving in uniform had not effaced belief in fundamental gender differences. War itself had only made these differences appear even more pronounced and insurmountable. The ability of normally mild-mannered fathers, sons, and brothers to endure the horrors of the trenches—and to kill others with abandon and even relish—indicated that males were innately different from females. The unchecked violence of men during combat and the "aggression and anger" many displayed once it was over were dismaying.[134] The "primal man" Freud saw nakedly revealed in the Great

War was a frightening creature—certainly not one with whom most women could feel any kinship.[135] On the contrary, he was a force against which they needed to guard themselves.[136] As a consequence, many feminists in England, who had previously been deeply committed to the notion that men and women should be treated equally since they were basically alike, began to rethink this premise. It now seemed more plausible to suppose that biology made the two sexes distinct and complementary.[137] Once again, the doctrine of "separate spheres" appeared to make sense. As Freud would express it a few years after the war, "Anatomy is destiny."[138] If women were going to attain all the freedoms and opportunities to which they were entitled, this did not mean these had to be the *same* as those enjoyed by men. Thus the so-called "New Feminists" who emerged in the 1920s focused their attention on gaining rights that were gender-specific—mainly those that guaranteed better conditions and protection for mothers, children, and working women.[139] One such advocate was Dora Russell, the second wife of the philosopher Bertrand Russell. A Cambridge-educated writer, pacifist, and feminist, Russell wrote an influential essay in 1925 applauding the contributions of working mothers and urging they be allowed to determine the number of children they wanted to have.[140] (Many other postwar feminists opposed abortion as inimical to motherhood.) Securing these rights would give these women "real equality" with men.[141]

This new set of priorities supplanted the earlier emphasis on political equality—that is, suffrage—once Parliament voted in February 1918 to grant the vote to women over the age of thirty—ostensibly to reward their wartime service to the country, but also to mollify feminists and forestall a revival of their militant tactics.[142] English feminists who persisted in demanding rights more associated with men, such as working in factories or entering professions like law and accounting, found the tide of public opinion now running more strongly than ever against them.[143] Opposition to married women working remained strong.[144] Single females seeking to keep war-related jobs after the armistice faced censorship in the press and hostility at the workplace. They were expected to return to their domestic "cage." A somewhat hyperbolic headline in June of 1919 fumed about a "Scandal of the Proposed Retension of Flappers while Ex-Soldiers Cannot Find Jobs."[145] The same resentment is evident in the frequent, derisive postwar comments made by British men about women who had held normally male positions during the war.

Another pressing reason why women were urged to turn their attention to marrying and raising families was the heavy loss of life in the war. With such a significant percentage of the male population under the age of twenty-five having been killed or disabled, European countries now had to rely upon a greatly diminished pool of potential fathers to marry and sire sufficient children to reverse the Continent's plunging birth rate.[146] (In England, for example, it would fall by 50 percent between 1900 and 1930, with 75 percent of this decline occurring after the war.)[147] Already in short supply prior to the war, prospective fathers were now even scarcer. So, too, were married men: of Germany's some 2 million war victims, a third had been married, leaving an equal number of widows.[148] The 1925 census revealed a surplus of 2 million such women in the Weimar Republic. The French had good reason to worry about this situation, having lost such a high percentage of their young men from an already small cohort. (One-fourth of France's dead soldiers were under the age of twenty-four.) During the parliamentary debate on the Versailles treaty in October 1919, Premier Georges Clemenceau warned that if France did not have more children in the coming decades, it would be "lost."[149]

War deaths had worsened this problem in England, too. It now had considerably fewer potential fathers. Three years before the fighting started, there had been 88 English men twenty-five years old for every 100 females of that age; but by 1921 there were only 81.[150] In other words, at least one in five would-be brides and mothers would not be able to find marriage partners—*if* every single one of them decided to get married. (If they didn't, of course, there would likely be even fewer babies.) This increased gender imbalance endangered the national well-being: many commentators feared that England would not be able to make up for its father "deficit" and produce enough male offspring to reverse the downward fertility trend and supply enough soldiers to fight Europe's next conflict. It was estimated that it would take Britain and Germany until 1930 to replace the manpower they had lost.[151] German officials also fretted about an imminent "race suicide" if the birth decline was not stemmed.[152] The size of an army was still deemed crucial to national defense: some speculated that Germany might never have invaded France if the latter had had a larger population.[153] Moreover, many world leaders in the twentieth century, including Hitler, regarded a larger pool of "quality" individuals as being just as important an outcome of war as increased territory.[154]

Marital trends during and right after the war were encouraging. In England, the prospect of dying young, alone, and—for many—without having had heterosexual relations had spurred thousands of bachelors about to board ships headed for France to tie the knot and consummate their relationships. Between August 1914 and June 1917, an estimated 200,000 more couples said their vows than would have if Archduke Ferdinand had not been assassinated.[155] A few years after the armistice, this matrimonial urge returned—with a vengeance. Young (and not so young) Britons were falling madly in love again—with domesticity. The sharp drop in marriages caused by the war was offset by a matrimonial "boom" starting in the early 1920s. The biggest change in marital plans occurred among men in their twenties. They were racing down the aisle in far greater numbers than they had at the end of the Edwardian Age. Over 20 percent more men ages twenty to twenty-four were married in 1921 than had been a decade earlier, versus 13.8 percent more females. Among those ages fifteen to nineteen (including men too young to have taken part in World War I), the increase in matrimony was more dramatic—up 117.7 percent for males, but only 54.9 percent for females. The proportion of older English men (ages forty-five to seventy-five) who were married also jumped over 20 percent.[156] Overall, the number of marriages per 1,000 inhabitants in England and Wales rose from 15.0 in 1910 to 20.2 in 1920.

British males were only modestly more eager to marry compared to their peers on the Continent. The marital spike was greatest in France, where the marriage rate rose from 15.6 to 31.9 over the same ten years. In Hungary, the rate jumped from 17.4 to 26.2, in Italy from 15.6 to 28.2, in Austria from 15.1 to 26.6, and in Germany from 15.4 to 29.0.[157] By 1925, 40.8 percent of the German adult population was married, compared to 36.1 percent in 1910.[158]

This marriage "fever" caused pronatalists to smile, for they foresaw a dramatic upswing in the number of births. But this did not happen, for two reasons. First, the nuptial "boom" directly after the war was not sustained. Instead, the rate quickly dropped back to prewar levels. By 1924, the number of marriages per 1,000 inhabitants was back down to 17.6 in France, 14.2 in Germany, 15.6 in the Netherlands, 15.3 in England and Wales, 16.2 in Austria, and 15.8 in Belgium.[159] (In the United States, the rate fell from 12.0 in 1920 to 10.4 in 1924, and it continued downward to a pre–World War II low of 7.9 in 1932.[160] This brought the number of births for the first time below the number needed to sustain the existing population.)[161] Put another way, 894,978 couples married in Germany in 1920, but only half that number—440,071, or roughly the same as just before the war started—four years later.[162] This greater foregoing of matrimony translated into a much larger proportion of bachelors (and bachelorettes) in the later years of the Weimar era: whereas only about 11 out of every 100 German men ages thirty-five to forty-five were still single in 1924, roughly 19 percent of them were unmarried in 1931.[163] A third fewer women ages twenty to twenty-five had found a husband than had done so in 1910–1911.[164] This tendency to defer marriage was evident in many other countries as well: in the 1930s, 86 percent of British men ages twenty to twenty-four still had not found wives; neither had 79 percent of Frenchmen in this age bracket, 90 percent of the Dutch, and 93 percent of the Swiss.[165] The fertility rate throughout Europe (for both warring and nonwarring nations) essentially reverted to what it had been on the eve of the war. In Belgium, it was 22.3 per 1,000 population in 1913 and 22.2 in 1920; in France, the comparable figures were 28.8 and 27.0; in England and Wales, 24.1 and 25.5; in Austria, 29.7 and 22.7.

Because so many more couples were getting married in 1920 compared to 1913, these figures indicate that the number of children per marriage was considerably lower *after* the war than before. Contrary to expectations, there was no "baby boom," just a continuation of the "bust." Only a few countries, such as Italy, experienced a sharp upswing in births after the war, but this did not end the long-term trend toward smaller families.[166] Overall, European women had fewer children during the 1920s than in the decade leading up to war: postwar British brides, for example, had only an average of 2.4 children, versus 3.5 for their predecessors.[167] Young working-class German housewives, influenced by the thinking of the "New Women" and leftist political parties such as the communists, started having just one child each. More generally, women marrying in the second half of the 1920s were bearing fewer than two children each, compared to nearly five for brides in 1905.[168] A similar reduction in family size took place in England: whereas only 20 percent of marriages commenced in 1860 had produced two or fewer offspring, that figure jumped to 67 percent by 1925.[169] During the Weimar period, the average working-class household had only 3.9 members. By 1929, the birth rate in Germany was 25.9; by the time Hitler assumed power, in 1933, it would be 14.7—the lowest in Europe, and half what it had been at the turn of the century. This rate was 31 percent below what was necessary to keep the German population growing.[170] One-third of all couples in Berlin had no children.[171] Across the Channel, by the mid-1930s the average British woman was having fewer than two babies—an all-time low.[172] The birth rate in the United States also plummeted during the 1920s and 1930s. By 1940, one in five married women did not have any children at all, as compared to one in ten at the turn of the century.[173]

Why did this happen? There is no simple answer to this question. Rather, this continuing downward trend can best be explained by a confluence of several interrelated economic, political, and social factors that had existed before the war and that came into greater play once it had ended. First of all, most of Europe was facing considerable hardship. The Great War had not produced any clear "winners"—no great bounty in terms of territory or other vital resources, no psychological boost, no sense that the future would be better than the immediate past. Emotionally, Europe was spent, its belief in itself depleted. An optimistic mood conducive to marriage and starting a family simply did not exist. The postwar reality was sobering and inhibiting. Most former warring nations faced huge debts, massive unemployment, industrial contraction, widespread poverty, declining trade, labor unrest, starvation, political instability and violence, bank failures, hyperinflation, and financial insecurity.[174] Even more important for recently married couples, housing was in short supply, especially in German and Russian cities and towns.[175] All of these developments made having and raising a large family difficult and undesirable.

As the decade progressed, and the impact of the Great Depression spread, the birth rate fell to new lows. Financially strapped couples simply could not support more children. Greater availability of contraception made it easier to plan family size and live within one's means. In fact, this was the second major factor depressing fertility. In some European countries, birth control was now entwined with politics. The com-

mitment of socialists and Marxists to equality between the genders translated into a reluctance of these two groups to regulate female sexuality:
there was to be no more double standard (although this principle was not
always honored). Russian Bolsheviks, for example, made abortion fully
legal, although the party leadership was not happy with this decision.[176]
Furthermore, having to bear many children restricted a woman's
freedom and her ability to earn as much as a man. Abortion offered liberation from the drudgery and slavish dependence on male breadwinners. So in countries where the left held sway, the right to terminate
pregnancies grew more widely accepted, as did other rights for women.
Without question, the most important of these was the franchise.
Women won this right toward the end of or after the war not only in
England and the United States but also in Russia, Canada, Austria, Hungary, Ireland, Poland, Germany, Belgium, Holland, and Sweden, as well
as several other smaller European nations. In Japan, buoyed by these
feminist victories, an effort to enact women's suffrage gained enough
support for a bill legalizing this was brought before parliament; it passed
twice in the lower house but was defeated in the upper one.[177] (Japanese
women did not get the vote until after World War II.) In the 1920s, the
Diet did vote to allow women to participate in political meetings,
sparking the creation of numerous all-female organizations.

Symbolically, having the vote altered how women saw themselves—
no longer as "second-class" citizens, but as equals with men in political
matters. Practically, the vote gave the other half of the population a voice
in the shaping of public policy. Article 109 of the liberal Weimar constitution of 1919, for instance, affirmed that "Men and women have the
same fundamental civil rights and duties."[178] In the spirit of this pledge,
111 female candidates were elected to the brand-new German parliament in 1920, and thousands more entered the law, medicine, and other
professions. At the same time, the League for the Protection of Mothers
took up the abortion cause, going so far as to argue that the state should
pay for this procedure.[179] Although females did not gain this right to
choose (except when the mother's life was in danger), the fact that abortion had entered Germany's social agenda in the 1920s attests to the
more tolerant climate of the Weimar era. By the end of the war, abortion—while still illegal—was an inescapable fact of life: as many as
200,000–400,000 of these procedures were being performed annually.[180]

The war was an indirect cause of such a change in behavior. (Another was the virtual collapse of the staid, fossilized Wilhelmine order.) The "failure" of touted male warriors to defend the nation had discredited patriarchy and the tightly controlling sexual mores that accompanied it. Taking their place—particularly in the major cities—was a free-wheeling libertinism: on the streets of Berlin, prostitutes were as commonplace as police officers and far more solicitous. Their brazen appearance was part and parcel of that city's transformation into what an aghast but undeniably fascinated Stefan Zweig dubbed "the Babylon of the world." This refugee from imperial Vienna had to reach far back into the past to find an equivalent of this gender-bending decadence: "Even the Rome of Suetonius had never seen such orgies as the pervert balls of Berlin, where hundreds of men costumed as women and hundreds of women as men danced under the benevolent eyes of the police."[181] The city was a sexual cornucopia. In the words of a recent historian, "Everywhere, it seemed, male and female bodies were in motion and on display as never before."[182] Berlin's licentiousness was less a reason why so few *Kinder* were being born in the 1920s as an indication of how lightly its citizens were taking their obligation to obey the biblical admonition to "be fruitful and multiply." Conditions were too unpredictable to make that kind of a commitment to the future. The unsettled and unsettling political climate in the capital, with bands of communists and *Freikorps* trading shots at each other on street corners, also mitigated against couples electing the traditional route of marrying and starting a family: too much was up in the air.

Across Europe, rebellion on all sides, not continuity, was the slogan of the day. First there had been the bloody overthrow of the tsar in Russia. Then, in 1919, inspired by the success of the Bolshevik Revolution, socialist-minded French workers demonstrated for better conditions and wages, producing violence and fears of a general strike.[183] A year later Italian socialists organized their own large-scale strike (forcing the government to call in Mussolini's Blackshirts to restore order). In solidarity with locked-out coal miners who were facing wage cuts, some 1.75 million British workers went on the picket lines in 1926, causing the Labour government to fear it might soon have a proletarian revolution on its hands. Marches and other protests by unemployed veterans, union members, and radical groups like the communists created a "Red Scare" in the United States. All of this turmoil discouraged the starting of families.

Sexual experimentation and a concomitant reluctance to settle down prematurely were not just European phenomenons. Even in tradition-bound Japan, the 1920s saw a further loosening of gender restrictions on young women. Postwar prosperity fueled a consumerism that attracted many young urban "New Women": magazines and stores cultivated their desire for a more liberated and cosmopolitan lifestyle and the Western values and individual fulfillment that went with this.[184] These included equality with men, education, and sexual freedom.[185] Across the Pacific, American youth were also tasting the forbidden fruit of sexual pleasure and finding it intoxicating. As in Europe, it was as if the "live for today, for tomorrow we may die" philosophy had been carried over from the war years. Young single women continued to work in the United States to roughly the same degree as before the war, and many of them used their burgeoning economic power to indulge themselves materially and sexually.[186] The crusade for birth control, led by the impatient and implacable Margaret Sanger (product of an upstate New York family of eleven children), attracted a large following.[187] Her calling for female sexual autonomy and fewer debilitating pregnancies resonated with working-class women.[188]

Even though America, too, hungered for a return to domestic "normalcy," more and more young people were disinclined to limit their sexual experience to the marital bed. In the 1920s, the prewar campaigns to eradicate prostitution and venereal disease seemed as hopelessly out of touch as a prominent family in New York City without a telephone: the stern, finger-wagging matrons of the "Social Hygiene Movement" had been replaced by the insouciant, unflappable flapper sipping bathtub gin. Premarital intercourse was becoming an accepted fact of American life: surveys of respectable, middle-class women found many more of them reporting having had greater experience than their mothers and even older sisters had confessed to fantasizing.[189] Along with increased early sex came, for *some* women, later (or no) marriage—and fewer children.

In the United States, there was little change in female marital and employment patterns after the war. The median age for women to marry actually decreased slightly between 1910 and 1920 (from 21.6 to 21.3), and the percentage of women who were single also declined somewhat—from 43 to 41 percent.[190] In Europe, however, the tendency to postpone or forego marriage entirely grew stronger during the interwar era: the proportion of never-married individuals reached a historic high in the 1930s.[191] This greater European disinclination to settle down early and start a family likely stems, in part, from the pronounced economic and political uncertainty that hovered over the Continent between the two wars. However, it also reflects a long-term trend for more single women in Europe and the United States to work outside the home.[192] The coming of peace in 1918 generally did not so much accelerate this tendency for these women to postpone marrying and having a family as it allowed a decades-old pattern to be restored.[193] For example, the percentage of English women ages twenty-five to twenty-nine who were still single remained roughly the same—over a third—as it had been since the mid-1850s.[194] In other words, it is inaccurate and misleading to attribute sole or even primary responsibility to the war experience for altering patterns of marriage and work in Western countries. Rather, it was a combination of more education and greater economic opportunities for women, plus more widely practiced birth control, that was driving these profound social changes. In the decades following World War I, the participation of women in the workforces of Europe and the United States continued its gradual but steady increase. The real change for women after the war was not in the numbers employed, but in *where* they worked: many foreswore traditional female jobs in textiles and domestic service in lieu of better-paying ones in offices, industry, and commerce.[195]

Regardless of its specific causes, the continuing decline in European fertility deeply distressed those political groups and governments bent upon regaining national strength through repopulation and utilizing this manpower advantage against their foes in future conflicts. There was already considerable concern about the growing Bolshevik "menace" in the east and the vulnerability of Western Europe to such threats.[196] This feared was stoked by a 1920 book entitled *The Rising Tide of Color against White World-Supremacy*. Its British author, Lothrop Stoddard, pointed out that "white" Europe had suffered so many casualties in the Great War that the "brown" and "yellow" peoples to the east now posed a grave threat: these "surplus" populations—a "rising flood of color"—would now surge westward and conquer a war-weakened white race, shown to be incapable of reproducing itself fast enough to remain strong.[197]

This alarmist view resounded especially in right-wing circles and countries ruled by bellicose, nationalistic regimes during the 1920s and

1930s: there the doctrine of social Darwinism still held sway. Belief in incessant struggle for survival and in the national glory and racial supremacy that victory would bring informed their population policies. As one recent study of this issue has put it, these aggressive nations regarded "political problems as biological problems and human history as natural history."[198] A healthy, growing population was the key to power and domination.[199] Hence, a "battle for the birth rate" had to be waged.[200] The Italian dictator Mussolini, for instance, saw that his dream of a New Roman Empire could only be attained by dramatically reversing the steep decline in fertility.[201] As pronatalists had urged earlier in the century, he believed that Italians had to revive their "instinct to propagate" for the nation to grow strong and assert itself internationally.[202] Under his rule, Italy tightened its antiabortion law, imposing prison sentences of between two and five years for those convicted of having terminated a pregnancy.[203] It was made a crime to distribute information about contraception. Unmarried men were taxed at more than double the rate of married ones. To push women into marriage, the government fired all females who had begun working for the national railway during World War I. Women were limited to holding those positions traditionally occupied only by females. Mussolini also ordered prostitutes off the streets, with the reasoning that, derived of this visual temptation, bachelors would be more likely to seek sexual satisfaction in marriage—and father more children. His fascist regime also offered some carrots to go with these sticks: family allowances were allotted on the basis of the size of the household. Couples were offered marriage and birth loans, and wives were given maternity insurance.[204] During his early years in power, Mussolini kept close tabs on demographic trends in individual provinces in Italy and repeatedly exhorted local authorities to boost their birth rates.[205]

German authorities and nationalists were just as determined to make up for the deaths of so many of their country's young men by restricting birth control and encouraging maternalism. (The war had claimed roughly 30 percent of the twenty-one- to twenty-four-year-olds who had fought in it.)[206] Many right-wing elements also believed that a growing population was essential to restoring and expanding German power in the world. They wanted women to quit their jobs and go back to their homes to "fulfill their destiny of producing and educating more children for the nation."[207] During the 1920s, nationalist groups jockeying for power, such as the fledgling Nazi Party, sought to ensure the country produced enough German soldiers to win the next war. Hitler and his followers were bent upon enlarging the nation's "Aryan" stock while simultaneously reducing the size of "inferior" and "undesirable" races.[208] The Nazi leader saw the coming struggle for world power in biological terms. In *Mein Kampf*, first published in 1925, he laid out his theory of competition among nations, postulating that success depended upon gaining additional land (*Lebensraum*) for a population to flourish and grow. Weaker, inferior races would be driven off this land or exterminated.[209] In World War II, his insistence on conquering Slavic and Jewish populations in the east expressed this race-driven, Darwinian thinking. In the fall of 1941, Hitler would tell intimates that he wanted to seize territories beyond the Reich in order to ensure Germany's "racial survival and expansion." He went on to explain, "The law of selection justifies this incessant struggle, by allowing the survival of the fittest."[210] Once the war had ended, an abundant supply of "pure" German babies would perpetuate the dominance of what Hitler regarded as a genetically superior *Volk*.[211]

In the Weimar Republic, encouraging fertility was not just a Nazi objective. In 1926, an otherwise liberal-minded Reichstag voted to continue the criminalization of abortion—a policy that dated back to the unification of Germany in 1871.[212] In the early years of the Weimar Republic, "New Women" who flaunted their sexual freedom and refused to marry and have children were castigated as "degenerate" and harmful to the national interest. (Openly gay men and their advocates like Magnus Hirscheld were detested even more.) At the same time, public and private organizations strove to elevate the status of mothers. Christian women's groups, as well as the feminist *Bund deutscher Frauenverein* (Federation of German Women's Associations), endorsed motherhood as a woman's ultimate fulfillment.[213] Germany's first marriage counseling center opened its doors in June of 1926, and in the following year a Law for the Protection of Mothers took effect, providing these women both pre- and postnatal benefits.[214]

These measures—part of the new government's generous social welfare program—were not particularly successful, however, as many young German women were not enthusiastic about relinquishing their sexually liberated postwar lifestyle for the more stable pleasures of married life and motherhood. Small financial inducements were not great enough to change their minds.[215] Lower- and working-class married women could ill afford more mouths to feed. They needed to earn a decent income as much as they wanted to maintain their sexual freedom. When the Social Democrats proposed a twelve-week maternity leave, they found that most wives could not afford to take this time off.[216] Those in their twenties and early thirties preferred to cultivate the image of the "New Woman"—independent, mannish, "slender, athletic, erotic, and amaternal."[217] With backing from the socialists and communists, some women's groups campaigned, instead, for more control of their bodies.[218] This was seen as critical to liberating working-class women from poverty.[219] Up until the Nazi takeover of power, the movement to legalize abortion steadily gained ground. The number of these procedures continued to rise, up to 1 million a year (among some 31 million women) in the latter years of the Weimar Republic.[220] By 1930, the publication of the National League for Birth Control and Sexual Hygiene had more than 15,000 subscribers. At that time, condoms were widely available at urban vending machines: one Berlin company sold 25 million a year.[221] The next year a rally in Berlin's Sportpalast drew a massive turnout to hear fired-up communist speakers proclaim, "Your body belongs to you!"[222] This was one of some 1,500 rallies in favor of birth control held in 1931, in part in response to Pius XI's denunciation of the practice the preceding December.[223]

Once Hitler came to power, in 1933, this era of sexual freedom abruptly ended. The reforms put in place by Weimar politicians—a relaxing of the laws on abortion, contraception, and homosexual activities—were summarily wiped off the books.[224] Nazi preoccupation with increasing Germany's low fertility rate led to the implementation of drastic measures designed to promote motherhood and restrict birth control. Henceforth, sex was to be linked with procreation, not self-indulgent pleasure. Women were told that raising a family was their primary obligation—their necessary and ennobling self-sacrifice for the good of the nation.[225] Organizations like the Mother Service Department were created to teach women how to be better mothers.[226] At the same time, new restrictions were imposed on contraception and abortion, although the Nazis were not consistent in opposing these practices, forcing mentally or physically impaired women to terminate their pregnancies.[227] In March 1993, a government decree sanctioned the closing of health clinics that had provided advice on family planning. In May of that year, the new government outlawed newspaper advertisements for contraceptive devices and abortion services. (During World War II, conviction for the latter could result in a death sentence.) A special tax was levied on unmarried adults. Prostitutes were driven off the streets and threatened with prison if they returned. On the other hand, government loans were made available to couples wishing to marry but financially unable to do so. Each new child reduced the amount that had to be repaid. Mothers were given special awards for having large families, and Nazi propaganda trumpeted the contributions to building the "master race" these women had made. The sole emphasis of the new regime was to reverse completely the Weimar philosophy of "preventing the reproduction of the strong . . . and shoring up the families of the weak." From now on, in the name of "racial hygiene," the fittest were to have as many children as possible, while the "unfit" were to have none.[228]

The military leaders of imperial Japan were just as committed to demonstrating their nation's power and superiority through war. And for them, too, population growth was the sine qua non for dominating the Asian Pacific: it was also unmistakable evidence of the nation's "potency."[229] To produce enough soldiers, colonial administrators, and commercial workers to build and sustain Japan's "Greater East Asian Co-Prosperity Sphere," the Japanese people would have to reproduce in far greater numbers than they had been doing in recent decades, despite a short-lived "baby boom" directly after World War I. From the 1880s to the early 1920s, the number of children per mother fell from 4.6 to 2.7.[230] Then, during the period 1925–1939, the number of babies born per 1,000 women plummeted by 25 percent—from 75.7 to a century low of 56.2—first due to greater prosperity, but then because of the Depression and Japan's invasion of Manchuria (which removed many potential fathers from their wives).[231] The latter event, as well as a realization that war in Asia was going to spread, prompted Japan's rulers to take firm action to increase the population. The government's goal was to propagate a racially "pure" population both at home and in recently conquered territories.[232] Within a few years, the birth control movement was "all but extinguished."[233] Abortion was severely punished. In 1932, women were enlisted in the crusade to militarize Japan through creation of the

National Defense Women's Association (which, its name notwith-standing, was run entirely by men). By the end of the decade, this organization, together with the Patriotic Women's Association, had a combined membership of 11 million women, out of a total female population of some 35 million. Japan thus indoctrinated its women far more extensively than either Nazi Germany or fascist Italy.[234]

Only a small, educated elite of men and women clung to their antiwar belief that limiting the size of Japan's population would prevent overcrowding—and thus avoid a wider Asian conflict.[235] As imperial forces extended their control across China in the 1930s, the government adopted the slogan "Bear More Children and Increase the Population."[236] The prime minister, Tojo, led a campaign to increase the country's fertility. His wife, who had borne seven children, declared that "having babies is fun." The government encouraged couples to marry early, set up "matchmaking agencies," and asked companies to give bonuses to employees who had babies. Women who had ten or more children were promised free education for their offspring.[237] A long-term goal was set of doubling the number of Japanese—to 100 million—by 1960.[238] This proved a difficult target to pursue, however, as Japan depended more heavily on single female industrial workers than countries in Europe did at that time.[239] During the war, the Japanese birth rate did increase for a while, but it soon fell back.[240] This conflict between desires to increase the population and expand factory production was not resolved until late in the war, when a pressing need for airplanes and other weapons compelled the government to drop its pro-baby policy.[241] But this change had little demographic impact.[242]

Less belligerent countries that had suffered major losses of life also realized that it was in their best interests to replace their dead youth as soon as possible: the war's adverse impact on already low birth rates was cause for grave concern since it made these countries prone to attack and defeat. In response to these fears, they promulgated policies to boost fertility. France—still the most demographically vulnerable European power—was particularly proactive in this regard. (In the half century since having been defeated by Prussia in 1871, France had only increased its population by 3 million; its aggressive neighbor, Germany, had added 20 million during this period.) It was estimated that females under age thirty outnumbered males in this group by 6 to 4. Between 1.5 and 3.5

million *jeunes filles* were without husbands.[243] The French government as well as numerous pronatalist groups in that country (such as the newly formed *Group parliamentaire pour la protection de la natalité et de la famille*) drummed home the message that married couples had an obligation to reproduce because of heavy war losses.[244] Maternity was portrayed as another form of national service. These efforts to encourage parenthood were more aggressive than those before the conflict, as the population decline appeared to have reached crisis proportions: it was feared not only that France would become easy prey for hostile neighbors eager to "finish it off" but also that its economy would not have enough workers, and the country would have to rely upon immigrants to support itself.[245] The nation's future was at stake. One wartime propaganda postcard had depicted a couple embracing above four infants, with the caption "*Ne nous oubliez pas*"—"Don't forget us."[246] Concomitantly, the French public grew strongly critical of young women who refused to marry. They were branded "selfish," hedonistic, and unpatriotic.[247] By having sex without having children, they were seen as abrogating their maternal duties and inverting the proper hierarchical relationship between males and females. One survey found that working single women, along with a general decline in moral standards, increased cost of living, and disruptions brought on by the war were blamed for France's continuing "depopulation."[248] To end this threat, these women had to give up their wartime freedoms and marry. In July 1920, a conservative-dominated French parliament, which included a large contingent of veterans supportive of pronatalist initiatives, passed a law banning abortion, the sale of contraceptives, and the dissemination of information about birth control.[249] At the same time, the government proselytized about the joys of having children. To make motherhood more financially attractive, married women were paid a government stipend to stay at home and raise their offspring.[250]

But most of these governmental policies or social pressures made little difference. The women of Western Europe defiantly refused to surrender the reproductive, social, economic, and political freedoms they had gained since the end of the Great War. Even in countries where the penalties for practicing birth control and abortion were extremely harsh, and where the incentives for marrying and having children were extremely attractive, the trend in fertility generally did not improve. Almost everywhere, women had even fewer babies during the 1920s and 1930s. Even fascist Italy did not manage to sustain its total fertility rate (or average number of children born to women over the course of a lifetime): this fell from approximately four in 1920 to three in the mid-1930s.[251] Between 1936 and 1940, the Italian birth rate remained fairly constant at roughly 23.4 per 1,000 inhabitants.[252] From a postwar high of 957,782 births in 1920, the number of British babies born annually dropped by nearly 40 percent—to 580,413 in 1933.[253] In Soviet Russia, the average woman went from having more than six children in 1920 to four at the end of the 1930s.[254] France's birth rate reached an all-time low of 620,000 in 1936.[255] In the United States, 400,000 fewer babies were born in 1935 than in 1910.

Nazi Germany was the rare but telling exception to this trend: the government's relenting campaign to bolster the marriage and fertility rates, combined with improvements in the economy and a resulting more positive outlook, resulted in a significant uptick in the number of couples walking down the aisle starting in 1933. Predictably, a few years later nearly 30 percent more women gave birth than in 1932.[256] German families continued to produce this many children into the early years of the war—a time when many husbands were away on the Western and Eastern fronts. What can account for these anomalous marital and fertility "booms"? The Nazi regime naturally claimed all the credit, citing its campaign to promote motherhood and the economic incentives it had given young couples to start a family.[257] But it seems more plausible that German couples opted to have more children when their personal financial circumstances made this feasible, after the high unemployment and poverty associated with the Depression eased. However, one should not overlook the psychological and emotional impact of Hitler's coming to power and giving millions of Germans reasons to hope for the future. A resurgence of national pride may well have influenced couples' decisions to start or expand their families. While such an explanation has to remain speculative in the absence of any public-opinion data, there are intriguing parallels in the temporary rise in births that took place in Italy and Austria prior to World War II. Italian births jumped almost 30 percent in 1937—the year after Mussolini's forces conquered Ethiopia; Austria's rate nearly doubled in the wake of the Nazi *Anschluss* in 1938.[258]

Barring such favorable circumstances, efforts by European governments to increase their populations were largely ineffectual: their ability to influence individuals' reproductive and marital decisions was very limited. From the perspective of male-female relations, the lesson learned was that women now exercised a formidable power in determining a nation's population and, hence, its future strength and power. Married women were much less under the control of their husbands than they had been a generation or two before. They were choosing to limit their births for personal reasons that conflicted directly with the state's (and their husbands') goal of having more babies. It was evident that men could no longer impose their will in this arena. Their wives were standing up to them. Both collectively and individually, this was a direct affront to male power. Coming in the wake of the Great War, this assertion of female prerogative seemed only to remind many European males of their failure to achieve a clear-cut victory in that conflict and thereby to regain the stature afforded to their fathers and grandfathers in earlier epochs. Loss of control over female sexuality was painfully emblematic of a larger "emasculation."

One could argue, more broadly, that the inadequacies of European manhood revealed on the front lines in Belgium and France were both responsible for—and the consequence of—a discernible drift away from well-defined gender roles and responsibilities and toward greater fluidity regarding definitions of "male" and "female." This ambiguity was anathema to groups such as the Nazis, which were dedicated to a "remasculinization" of their societies as a way of regaining the pride, unity, and power they felt Germany had lost—first at Versailles, and then in the chaos and excessive self-indulgence of the Weimar Republic. For such hypermasculine groups, the falling birth rate served as an irritating reminder of how little power they now possessed—and a focal point for seeking to restore their dominance. During the late 1920s and early 1930s, frustration over their failure to accomplish this objective played into the hands of leaders like Hitler, who galvanized male resentment over their loss of reproductive control and then, once in power, implemented policies to end this state of affairs and restore "patriarchal" marriage.

Female political gains added to male unease and unhappiness. These advances occurred in a time of democratization in many European countries. The postwar granting of more freedoms and rights to individual citizens was a reaction to the incompetence of unelected leaders—kings and generals alike—displayed during World War I. The blame for this seemingly pointless and inconclusive slaughter was placed on these nineteenth-century authority figures, and thus removed from the millions of their followers who had welcomed the war with gusto. Now it was time for "the people" to organize and run society along lines that respected their interests and not those of some hopelessly out-of-touch, aristocratic elite. Granting women the vote was a crucial step in this political transformation of European countries (as well as the United States). For women were not only half the population; they were also seen as a reliable counterweight to what many perceived as pernicious *male* aggressiveness, anger, and violence. With their voices being now heard, the chances of a repetition of this military fiasco would be greatly diminished. An infusion of "female" values into the public sphere would produce a more humane, just, and peaceful society, less susceptible to radicalism of the left or right. And, indeed, women voters did create momentum in that direction. Throughout most of the interwar era, they generally preferred centrist parties at the ballot box, wary of all extremists.[259] In Germany, for example, female voters were less attracted to the Nazis than men were. This discrepancy narrowed over time, however. By the time of the September 1930 parliamentary election (in which women constituted a fifth of the electorate), women were only slightly less supportive of Nazi candidates compared to men. More tied to traditionally conservative values, women did give Hindenburg the edge over Hitler in presidential voting in November 1932.[260] Female voters outnumbered males in Austria (as they did in Germany), bolstering major parties such as the Christian Social Party vis-à-vis its more nationalistic alliance partner, the German People's Party.[261]

On the national and international levels, women formed organizations dedicated to disarmament and world peace, as well as to promoting social welfare. In several countries, including Germany and Russia, women lobbied successfully for reforms of laws of particular interest to them, such as those pertaining to children's well-being and divorce.[262] These various female initiatives across Europe represented a rebuke to "patriarchal" policies of the recent past and thus evoked dismay and hostility among male-dominated groups and parties, which wanted women to stay out of political life and tend to their families instead. In public life as in the bedroom, women increasingly appeared to be having things their way—at the expense of nostalgic male longings for the old gender order.

Anger at the pace and direction of change in the modern world was amplified by men's inability to do much about these developments. Even more intolerable to radical traditionalists, who wanted nothing less than to destroy the modern society in which they were being forced to live, was the masculine degradation they sensed was to be the ultimate outcome of this transformative process. Society was still very much engaged in a "sex war." But, now, as the result of a disastrous, ill-advised war, men appeared to have lost some of the key advantages they had once enjoyed—courage, honor, pride—and were having a hard time regaining the upper hand. Women appeared to be winning, and men were losing. The indicators were all too apparent. Greater female sexual freedom made a mockery of the male need for certainty about paternity. Female control of fertility thwarted men's desire for multiple progeny to fulfill their biological obligations. Female suffrage ended male suzerainty over the policies and operations of the state. But perhaps the most ignominious setback European and American men had to endure in the interwar years was not inflicted on them by women, but by a far greater and impersonal force—a faceless, indomitable force beyond their comprehension, utterly devastating to their self-respect and identity. This was the inflexible law of supply and demand, which now turned against them. It created yet another disaster—the Great Depression.

For centuries, men had lived and died by the credo that work was the measure of their worth, and setting its value lay largely in their own hands. In the recent past the "civilized" nations of the world had experienced occasional doubts concerning this faith—brought on by "panics," "bubbles," and other startling economic hiccups—as they moved toward better tomorrows.[263] The flow of history seemed inexorably progressive. Year by year, life was getting better for more and more people, certainly since the dawn of the industrial age. This steady advance was a testament to the superiority of Western nations, to the male leadership entrusted with guiding them, and to the (largely) male workforce that provided the brains and the muscle responsible for this improving standard of living. The Depression destroyed this belief, just as it shattered the lives of millions of people around the world who had never envisioned such a turn of events. In terms of its traumatic impact, materially and psychologically, the Depression was the economic equivalent of the Great War. Starting with Wall Street's crash in October 1929, the financial carnage quickly spread around the world. Banks failed, businesses went bankrupt, companies and factories laid off millions of workers, trade shrank, factories closed their doors, farmers abandoned their fields, incomes plummeted, and families struggled desperately to stay intact as paychecks disappeared, and gaunt, unemployed men stood in line outside soup kitchens. The human toll was staggering. In the United States, a quarter of the labor force was idle by 1933, but the numbers were higher in the industrial sector. Over a million families lost their farms. Between 1929 and 1932, the income of the average American family fell by 40 percent. A quarter of the population had no money coming in at all. Two million men were reduced to wandering across the country in search of work.

On the other side of the Atlantic, the situation was even worse in Germany. There, more than a third of workers were out of jobs.[264] If one included their dependents, the number of Germans without a source of income approached 13 million, or a fifth of the entire population.[265] As many as half a million unemployed and destitute men were living on the streets.[266] Inflation, brought on by the need to pay off war loans and exacerbated by exorbitant reparations, decimated the savings of the middle class and its faith in the future. While almost all suffered, the sense of despair was deepest among working men; they had been expected to provide for their families, and their failure to put food on the table was a tremendous blow to their self-respect and identity as breadwinners. A study by the German economist Siegfried Kracauer (*The Salaried Masses*) found many middle-class men on the verge of giving up. "'Three years earned nothing. Future? Work, madhouse or turn on the gas,'" responded one man to Kracauer's questionnaire. "'I am spiritually broken and sometimes entertain thoughts of suicide,'" admitted another. "'Moreover, I have lost confidence in all men.'"[267]

The economic collapse dealt a coup de grace to the fragile Weimar Republic, as its elected officials had no answers, no understanding of what had to be done. Individual frustration and anger over this economic chaos and uncertainty played into the hands of a rhetorically gifted Hitler: his speeches denouncing Weimar's economic and political failures captivated anxious German voters in September 1930 and swelled the ranks of the NSDAP (National Socialist German Workers Party) delegation in the Reichstag from 12 to 107. Many of those who pulled the lever for the Nazis were disgruntled, first-time, younger voters, but older

Germans who had never warmed to the idea of a republic were even more fervently behind Hitler's party. To a wide array of Germans, men and women, young and old, workers and lower- to middle-class voters, the Nazis appealed as the "catch-all party of social protest."[268] Much of this discontent was with Germany's staggering economy: unemployed and underpaid members of the middle class voted for Hitler's party in large numbers.[269] The Nazi vision of a revitalized and triumphant Germany appealed in particular to young and middle-aged, economically hard-pressed men, who longed for a new identity and heroic redemption. Frustrated by the setbacks and disarray of the Weimar Republic, they wanted to throw off the old ways and fashion a new kind of society. These men, many of whom had joined nationalistic paramilitary groups after the war, made up the demographic core of the Nazi Party, as they did for Germany as a whole. Not having been reduced in size by the war, the birth cohorts of 1900 and 1914 had remained large: by 1933, persons ages twenty to forty-five made up 41.5 percent of the German population—considerably more than in 1925.[270] They represented a formidable force for radical change.

Impatient with parliamentary maneuvers, NSDAP stormtroopers stirred up unrest and violence in the streets to intimidate their opponents and muscle their way into power. The Nazis precipitated the breakdown of civil order as a catharsis that would enable their "new order" based on willpower, naked use of force, and ironclad determination to triumph. The Germans who celebrated Hitler's rise so rapturously had a quasireligious faith in these qualities and in the messianic Führer who epitomized them. This collective Germanic hunger for triumph—to prove to themselves and the world how great a nation this was, how unjustly they had been treated since the war, and how mighty and glorious they could now become—swept away all restraint and reason and made possible Hitler's fantasy of a fascist *Götterdämmerung*.

The great majority of German men and women sensed personal redemption in the torch-lit parade snaking through the heart of Berlin on the eve of Hitler's assuming the chancellorship on January 30, 1933. This victory was as much theirs as his: their fates were now one. For many conservative-minded men, the national "regeneration" promised by Hitler encompassed their own need to validate a long-suffering, long-tarnished masculinity. The blow to their self-esteem dealt by Germany's defeat in 1918; the indignities inflicted upon them since by Weimar's moral and sexual laxity, as well as by their wives' unwillingness to have more children; the anxiety caused by the rise of alien ideologies like communism; and, finally, the diminution of their stature as breadwinners brought on by the Depression—all of these insults to their manhood now seemed, in a bright flash, to have evaporated. The contest between two postwar masculine models—one assertive, chauvinistic, hierarchical; the other accommodating, nurturing, egalitarian—now appeared to have been settled in their favor. Undesirable, "inferior" males—homosexuals, left-wing radicals, Jews—were now either hauled off to concentration camps, driven abroad, or subjected to persecution. It came as no surprise that Erich Maria Remarque was one of them. Among the thousands of banned volumes tossed onto a bonfire outside Berlin's opera house that May were several copies of his *All Quiet on the Western Front.*[271] (Remarque himself had to flee the country to avoid arrest and, putatively, a worse fate: his sister, Elfriede, was beheaded during World War II as a stand-in for him.) Ernst Jünger, by contrast, was greatly honored, as an inspiration to a new generation of German warriors. Both Adolf Hitler and Joseph Goebbels admired his writing greatly and sought to make him a highly visible icon in the Nazi movement. Jünger was even offered a Nazi seat in the Reichstag. Disapproving of the Nazis and foreseeing disaster under their rule, he consistently resisted these overtures, quietly left Berlin for the small Saxon city of Goslar to study insects, and withdrew from public life after the Nazis came to power.

The postwar era in Europe had begun with another struggle among men—to redefine who they were and how they should act in light of a conflict that had failed to live up to hopes of restoring their masculine stature. Rather, the war experience had allowed its combatants to arrive at one of two vastly different conclusions about their identity and place in society. One reaction led them to see themselves as part of that society, linked to others through a common humanity and common predicament in the modern era—that is, under threat from destructive forces that could best be held at bay by collective, democratic action. These veterans chose reconciliation over conflict, peace over war. Adherents of the other interpretation, not accepting this premise, saw the struggle for dominance and control continuing: it was the very nature of existence. Some would succeed, while others would fail. Their challenge was to see that they—as individuals and as nations—came out on top in this competition. For this to happen, uniquely masculine attributes of courage and perseverance would have to be inculcated and developed to a higher degree. Men would have to be heroic warriors, as they had been in other ages. By dint of their unified power, they might turn back the clock to these times and reconstitute human society in their own grandiose image.

The battle between these two masculine types had gone back and forth. Right after the war had ended, a desire on the part of most European men and women to return to time-honored gender roles had given assertive masculinity an early victory. Married men had reclaimed their prewar jobs and role as family provider. Many single veterans had been able to marry and father children in large numbers. Women had largely accepted a subordinate, dependent position in the home. But antithetical elements at play in postwar Europe (and America) had then undermined this male "restoration." In the defeated nations of Germany and Austria, men were burdened by the onus of military defeat. But veterans of all nations bore psychic and physical scars that impaired their acting firmly and confidently: they were not the same as they had been before 1914. The granting of female suffrage in many countries made women equal citizens and gave them a greater voice in public affairs. They also enjoyed new sexual and marital freedoms (such as greater ease in obtaining a divorce): these gains weakened men's control over them and increased fears about an unfettered female libido. Because of these greater freedoms as well as inimical economic conditions, the marriage and then the birth rates had fallen sharply, returning to prewar levels. Finally, the Depression had put millions of men out of work, humiliated them, and forced them to depend, in many cases, on their wives to keep the family together. Collectively, these developments had given rise to feelings of powerlessness and insecurity among many men in Western Europe and the United States. Right-wing, male chauvinist organizations like the Nazi Party responded to these feelings with promises of military—and male—resurgence. Their movement repudiated the alternative masculine model for its purported surrender to democratic, feminist, and international pressures. They called for a return to hierarchical, masculine power. The victory of fascist movements in Germany, Italy, and Japan gave them a strong platform on which to realize this organizing principle domestically and then to assert it beyond their borders. The Darwinian struggle to dominate through the use of force was rejoined as the military of these nations rebuilt, expanded, and prepared for the inevitable next war. In this confrontation, men would not create a solidarity based on gender to oppose and defeat a threatening female challenge, as they had in the Great War. Instead, the two masculinities would do battle with each other to settle the still unresolved issue of how men were to exist and thrive in a modern world in which their prerogatives and position could no longer be taken for granted, but had to be earned.

Chapter 5

DEMOCRACY WINS, MEN LOSE—FROM WWII TO VIETNAM

In the late 1930s young American men were not itching for a fight. War was not something they either sought or wanted. Europe's troubles were not theirs. Like the great majority of their countrymen, they preferred to stay out of the widening conflict overseas. Isolationist sentiment ran deep and wide and remained largely unaffected by explosive international events. After Italy invaded Ethiopia in 1935, FDR spoke for the country as a whole when he vowed, "Despite what happens in continents overseas, the United States shall and must remain, as long ago the Father of Our Country prayed that it might remain—unentangled and free."[1] While the president would soon change his mind and abandon isolationism as fascist powers flexed their military muscles on the Continent, most of his fellow citizens did not.[2] When Hitler's armies unleashed a blitzkrieg against hapless Poland four years later, a Roper poll found that two-thirds of those Americans surveyed would rather see the Nazis prevail than go to the aid of the descendants of Kazimierz Pułaski (who had saved George Washington's life during the Battle of Brandywine) and Tadeusz Kościuszko (who had fortified Philadelphia against a British attack).[3] Even as late as January 1941, long after the fall of the Low Countries and the Battle of Britain, only 12 percent of Americans thought the country should enter the war against Germany and Italy.[4] Worried primarily of their own security, they believed that the wide Atlantic would keep their country safe, and that by remaining free, democratic, and peaceful, the United States could present an attractive alternative to a bellicose Nazi Germany, even though a growing number of Americans believed—incongruously—that Hitler would eventually

211

attack them, too.[5] This neutralist sentiment was evident in public support for the military—which was virtually nonexistent. At the start of World War II, the American army was the eighteenth largest in the world, smaller not only than those of Europe's major powers, but also of such lesser military stalwarts like Switzerland and Sweden. On a per capita basis, Germany had twenty times as many trained, battle-ready soldiers as the United States.[6] So, on a strictly pragmatic level, going to war against to this juggernaut was deemed inadvisable, if not foolhardy.

The sudden, devastating attack on Pearl Harbor on December 7, 1941, abruptly changed this laissez-faire outlook. It made the idle prattle on the nation's front porches and in the halls of Congress about putting "America first" and staying out of Europe's affairs irrelevant. The country was now in the war, like it or not. As happens whenever a foreign enemy strikes without warning, outrage, anger, and shock over this audacious act had the galvanizing effect of a lightning bolt. The nation united as one to defend itself and avenge its grievous humiliation. Across the United States—in big cities and villages too small to show up on maps, on leafy college campuses and in soot-dusted factories, in shantytowns and town squares, up and down the rocky New England coast and across the sun-baked Great Plains, in the foothills of the Rockies and in the Florida Panhandle, singly and in groups—young men responded unhesitatingly to the president's clarion call to arms. A disproportionate number of these volunteers came from the South—the bedrock of national honor and glory, the region most sensitive to slight and humiliation.[7] In the tiny Arkansas hamlet of Lepanto, for example, the entire high school football team marched down to the local recruiter's office to sign up for the navy; the one member who was rejected attempted to commit suicide out of fear he would be judged "yellow."[8] In metropolises like New York, Los Angeles, and Chicago, the lines of would-be enlistees stretched for blocks and overwhelmed the staffs hurriedly set up to process them. Some rural as well as urban recruitment offices had to stay open twenty-four hours a day to handle the load. In the first month after Pearl Harbor, over half a million men raised their right arms and took the oath of allegiance.[9]

They signed up for a myriad of reasons. Some stepped forward without hesitating because they felt the nation was at imminent peril of a Japanese invasion and needed every available able-bodied man to repel it. Many men in their late teens and early twenties joined because they saw America's declaration of war as their generation's rendezvous with destiny: the moment they had been waiting for. Since childhood, they had heard stories about adventure and glory on the fields of France, or in the forests at Antietam, and now—jejune, highly impressionable, and innocent of war's reality—they were eager to undergo the same exhilarating rite of passage into manhood. Many were hobbledehoys like eighteen-year-old William Manchester, whose father had joined the Marines in 1917 and quickly become disillusioned with military life, partially for having taken a burst of shrapnel on the Western Front. Still he remained a Marine to the end of his days, proud to slip into his dress blues once a year for parades through town, anxious to have his book-besotted stripling of a son carry on the family's tradition of military service, imploring young Bill with a silent, parting stare on his deathbed in early 1941 to avenge him. But it was Manchester's Virginia-born mother who had imparted to her son—a frail and timid lad, the chronic victim of schoolyard bullies—a vision of heroic sacrifice. She, a Northern transplant who had been taught Sunday school by J. E. B. Stuart's widow and who continued religiously to don a black dress in mourning every Confederate Memorial Day, inspired him to yearn "for valor," to convince "the likes of Lee and the Little Colonel to be proud of me." So, thanks to this reinforcing parental heritage, when the news about Pearl Harbor came over the airwaves in Manchester's hometown of Springfield, Massachusetts, there was no stopping him.[10]

Some were restless youngsters, trapped in impoverished and dead-end lives, sensing that war would bring them escape, a reprieve, and a fresh start. Typical of them was a scrawny and parentless Audie Murphy, who had grown up on farms in rural northeastern Texas absorbing like an acolyte the war stories of old men and, from the time he reached puberty, daydreamed of taking part in battles where "bugles blew, banners streamed, and men charged gallantly across flaming hills . . . where the dying were but impersonal shadows and the wounded never cried; where enemy bullets always miraculously missed me, and my trusty rifle forever hit home." This dream encapsulated his desire to cast off the stifling poverty his sharecropper family had known for generations. When his chance came to make it come true, after December 7, Murphy didn't stop to question it. Cocky and "looking for trouble," he set his sights on the Marine Corps. The problem was, he was only fifteen years old. Waiting until he turned eighteen was out of the question—the war would be over by then, he feared—so young Audie had one of his sisters forge a different date on his birth certificate so he could enlist. All that work came to naught when the Marines then rejected him because, at five feet five, he was too short and underweight to boot. Undeterred, Murphy settled for second best and signed on with the infantry, hoping he'd get to fly gliders. Nicknamed "Baby" by his buddies in basic training after he passed out once in formation and urged by his dubious commanding officer to become a cook instead of a combat soldier, Murphy absorbed these blows to his pride and kept his eyes fixed on getting into the action. Two and a half years later, for having single-handedly repelled a German tank and infantry attack with withering machine-gun fire in France, he would be honored with the Congressional Medal of Honor and be feted as America's most decorated war hero.[11]

Others volunteered to outgrow other inadequacies—self-described "mama's boys" like nineteen-year-old Robert Rasmus, who saw war as his one great chance to cut free from apron strings and become a man in the fiery cauldron of combat: "I was going to gain my manhood then," Rasmus would later explain. "I would forever be liberated from that sense of inferiority that I wasn't rugged. I would prove that I had the guts and the manhood to stand up to these things."[12] War offered the ultimate test of masculine prowess, and many young men followed Audie Murphy's example in seeking out the most exciting and dangerous assignments they could find. Clarence ("Bud") Anderson, the son of a "hardy and determined old Swede" who had lost all his money in the Depression, had nurtured a passion for flying since the day he had read about Charles Lindbergh's historic solo flight across the Atlantic. At seventeen he enrolled in a flight-training school in Sacramento, and after the Japanese bombs came raining down on Hawaii, he wasted no time signing up to be an army pilot. Assigned to the 357th Fighter Group, based in England, he thrived on the deadly encounters with the *Luftwaffe* fighters that rose angrily to engage him over the Continent and scored over sixteen kills, making him one of his country's top aces. "I was no fighter by nature," he would write in his memoirs. "But I enjoyed competing; and . . . dueling with airplanes was a way of compensating for my slender build and testing myself against anyone. . . . Combat was exciting, addictive, a test of our mettle and manhood—a crucible in which men became a cut above the rest."[13]

Some young men were initially hesitant to go off to war but changed their minds once serving became inevitable. They, too, succumbed to an urge to validate themselves. Richard Winters, a graduate of Franklin and Marshall who had joined the army several months before the United States entered the war so he could avoid the draft, finally decided to sign up for the paratroopers because of their elite status and esprit: he wanted to challenge himself and serve with "the best." On D-Day, he would be the only man on board his plane to survive its crash landing near Normandy.[14] Lloyd Wells, the son of a Missouri pipe fitter, was also initially reluctant to serve. Like many of his ambitious contemporaries, he had other aspirations. He resented being drafted in June of 1941 because this meant he would have to interrupt his studies. When the war broke out, he worried about being killed. A "somewhat bookish, more than a little immature, shy . . . tender and callow fellow," weighing a slender 120 pounds, he had no desire to "do his bit" for his country, let alone become a hero, but when his orders for Europe finally came down these reservations gave way to his sense of adventure and desire to "prove" himself, and Wells walked up the gangplank of his troopship "without regret."[15]

This need for American men to dispel doubts about their abilities and demonstrate their masculinity by going off to war stemmed, in part, from a male failure to provide for their families during the Great Depression. This failure had had a devastating effect on their self-image and self-respect, as it had on their European counterparts. Men now looked in the mirror and saw the face of dejection and defeat. For her 1940 book, *The Unemployed Man and his Family*, the Barnard sociologist Mirra Komarovsky interviewed several dozen middle-aged men in New York City who had lost their jobs and found that most had lost their moral authority in the home as well. Deprived of their livelihoods, these men felt like a "fallen idol." Their dominant position in the family was gone: they were no longer true men. Some wives (and children) openly regarded them with contempt because they could not put food on the table.[16] The denigration experienced by unemployed men, or those who had to wander about the country in search of work, made them poor role models for their sons. Many of these young men came of age in the late 1930s with disturbing images of their fathers' shortcomings, and these memories sometimes prevented them from developing self-confidence and a strong, positive male identity. Although powerful mother figures were treated sympathetically in novels such as *The Grapes of Wrath*, their newfound strength was worrisome to many Americans who thought fathers should dominate in the home. The role reversal was unnatural and humiliating to men—and their sons. (The father of Norman Mailer, for instance, became unemployed during the 1930s and ceded control over the family to Mailer's mother. As the novelist would recall later in life, "It was a nuclear family . . . my mother was the center of it, and my father was one of the electrons.")[17] When they reached working age, these youths also learned for themselves how humiliating it could be to not find work and thus be unable to marry and start their own families.

Social scientists, writers, and assorted pundits also worried that males who had grown up without a strong father figure during the Depression era—or, even worse, with a powerful mother—would not be masculine enough to assert their authority or to shoulder the roles that society normally assigned to them. One of the most important of these was that of soldier and defender of the country. American men, in other words, might not be up to defeating the Germans and the Japanese. This concern about "weak" and "emasculated" men was a leitmotiv running through many articles, short stories, and books that appeared in the early 1940s. Deprived of a father's steady, stern authority, boys were being coddled by their mothers and were thus unprepared for the rigors of manhood. So determined a researcher named Doris Drucker after asking male college students about their attitudes toward authority in 1940: most came from mother-dominated households and appeared to lack a sense of values or direction.[18] Lamented one male journalist later that year, "Men have been maneuvered into a position where it is impossible for them to think of anything but women and their wants. . . . We live in a daintier world than did our fathers, but also in a far less virile world." Western democracies had been transformed into "state matriarchies," and all that men could do about this was to "grow long hair or shake their fists at the planets."[19] Writing early in the war Margaret Mead expressed her fears that the failure of American parents to instill confidence and pride in their sons might have "maimed" them and made it impossible for them to muster the inner strength needed for victory on the battlefield. Having been given mixed messages about violence, they now might not be sufficiently aggressive to defeat their adversaries.[20] American mothers were fingered as the culprit for this erosion of masculinity in Philip Wylie's 1942 influential polemic, *Generation of Vipers*. He lambasted "mom's" need to control the men in her life and advised his male readers to evade her clutches before it was too late by pursuing such "dangerous and exciting" pursuits as hunting and going to war.[21] (Already a decade earlier, child psychiatrists had started to blame "overprotective," domineering, or emotionally repressed mothers for producing neurotic male offspring.)[22]

The tendency for more wives to work outside the home to bring in needed income was eyed with misgiving.[23] Throughout the Depression years, most American men (and women) continued to believe that supporting a family should be primarily a male responsibility. In a 1938 Gallup poll, three of four persons agreed that a wife should not take a job if she had a husband capable of providing for her.[24] For this reason, prominent professional women like the first female cabinet member, FDR's secretary of labor, Frances Perkins (whose husband was incapacitated by bipolar disorder), were not hailed as new role models. While more acceptable, the presence of legions of young, single, attractive women in professional offices, universities, businesses, and stores in the late 1920s and early 1930s could also be unsettling and even threatening to men of that era.[25] A number of popular movies like *Mr. Deeds Goes to Town* (1936), *My Man Godfrey* (1936), *The Awful Truth* (1937), *Holiday* (1938), *Bachelor Mother* (1939), and *Ball of Fire* (1939) portrayed such strong and independent women favorably. But others—*Alice Adams* (1935), *Jezebel* (1938), *Kitty Foyle* (1940), and *The Philadelphia Story* (1940)—laid out a more critical point of view. Several films, including George Stevens's *Quality Street* (1937), *Gunga Din* (1939), and *Woman of the Year* (1942), in which a feminist Tess Harding, played by Katharine Hepburn, was ridiculed for being unable to make breakfast, as well as Howard Hawks's *Bringing Up Baby* (1938) and George Cukor's *The Women* (1939), broadly satirized male and female characters who had strayed from their traditional gender roles and implicitly advocated a return to these norms.

As the prospect of war loomed, the need for such a gender realignment grew more urgent. If the United States was going to become involved in this conflict, young American men had to be persuaded to see themselves as strong, assertive, heroic figures, willing to put aside their private concerns for the good of the country. Mindful of men's lingering doubts about their manliness, the American government stressed the redeeming heroic qualities of soldiers in its prewar recruitment efforts. Men could become better, more esteemed persons and join a long-honored tradition by rising to the challenges of this day.[26] Casting off any pretense of political neutrality, the movie industry became a willing partner in this campaign to foster an idealized, self-sacrificing image of American men, ready to do battle with their country's enemies. In the years leading up to the war, Hollywood directors devoted much of their time to making movies about self-sacrificing, stoic heroes instead of debonair men-about-town like those portrayed by Fred Astaire and Cary Grant.[27] Stars like Gary Cooper and John Wayne came to dominate the silver screen. Cooper was most persuasive in his portrayal of the World War I hero, Sergeant York, in Howard Hawks's eponymous 1941 film. Cooper's portrayal of the laconic but principled Tennessee backwoodsman moved many of its young male viewers. They saw themselves in York's slow, reluctant metamorphosis from conscientious objector to calm and deadly sharpshooter in the Argonne Forest. The film's producers went out of their way to promote *Sergeant York* as a patriotic exhortation to the younger generation, staging a parade down Broadway at the time of its premiere, led by its glamorous star and a phalanx of veterans of the Great War.[28] Other propagandistic American movies of this prewar era dwelled upon the sinister, ruthless character of the Germans and Japanese to arouse feelings of hatred and persuade indecisive men to join the anticipated fight against these foes. In these films, the lines between "good" and "evil" were clearly drawn, and audiences responded as they were expected to do.[29]

Such exhortations to be more virile squarely addressed the uneasiness about the fighting readiness of American men after the setbacks and shortcomings of the 1930s. In addition to restoring some of the pride and stature they had lost because of this prolonged adversity, wearing a uniform would also alleviate another persistent cause for concern: it would provide men with a dependable, solid income for as long as they served. Unemployed men could thus become the primary breadwinner once again. Jobs were still in short supply at the start of the new decade. FDR's policies had not ended the nation's high unemployment. Nearly

15 percent of workers—some 8 million persons—were still looking for work by the end of 1940.[30] This situation made the military attractive, especially for low-wage workers. For them, America's declaration of war on December 8 came as a godsend—a chance to earn a decent wage, eat three meals a day, wear warm clothes, and sleep every night under a dry roof. Thus, after a long, bitter decade of scratching out a living, coal miners from West Virginia, hog farmers from Arkansas, longshoremen from Brooklyn, and lettuce pickers from the Sacramento Valley flocked to recruiting offices.

Even before the war, men looking for better-paying jobs had regarded the army as an attractive option. After President Roosevelt signed the Selective Training and Service Act of 1940, a poll found that three-quarters of men ages sixteen to twenty-four would be willing to wear a uniform for at least one year. When a signup for the draft was instituted, in October of that year, some 16 million men came forward and registered, more than meeting the army's manpower goals.[31] This willingness to serve at a time when the United States was still firmly against going to war indicates that an economic rather than a patriotic motive was responsible. The tremendous labor needs associated with participating in World War II proved this reasoning was not misguided: from 1940 to 1943, the unemployment rate in the United States fell from 14.6 percent to 1.9 percent. Almost all of this decrease was due to men going into the military, the number of which grew by 11 million during this period.

Earning a good salary in the army or navy gave some young men another advantage: they could now support not only a wife but children, too. This consequence was a vitally important consideration, particularly as the effects of the Depression had not yet worn off. During the 1930s, the birth rate in the United States had hovered around the replacement level, as married couples made the economically based decision to have fewer (or no) offspring in light of their diminished financial circumstances. At the same time, hundreds of thousands of men and women who might in better times have formed long-term relationships, married, and started families opted to remain single and childless. Young white men between the ages of twenty and twenty-four were particularly disadvantaged in their search for mates. In 1940, for every four of them who were unmarried there were only about 2.7 available females in their age group. Put another way, over 72 percent of men ages twenty to twenty-four were single, versus only 35 percent of women. (In the twenty-five to twenty-nine age bracket, only 22.8 percent of females were still unmarried, versus 35 percent of men.)[32]

Young men, in brief, had relatively poor marital and reproductive prospects. This was particularly so for those who had no jobs—roughly 5 percent of males ages twenty-five to thirty-four. The coming of war improved this situation dramatically, in several ways. First of all, many couples in love, wishing to tie the knot before they were torn apart by the war, hurriedly exchanged vows. Hundreds of thousands of marriages took place that would not have without the massive wartime call up. Second, the rumor that married men would not be drafted caused a brief, sharp spike in applications for marriage licenses.[33] Third, in order to help families stay together during wartime, the government began in 1942 to provide subsidies to wives whose husbands were drafted. These payments—equal to half what the average woman could earn in industry at that time—made soldiers financially attractive marriage partners. (Some feared that unscrupulous gold-digging women, dubbed "Allotment Annies," would take a stroll down the aisle just to receive these payments, hoping their absent spouses would not return alive from the war.)[34] In response to these more favorable circumstances, the United States experienced a marriage "boom."

Marriages increased by an impressive 20 percent during the war years (and would soar by nearly 50 percent in 1946). It has been estimated that 3 million more Americans joined in matrimony during World War II than would otherwise have done so.[35] An analysis of census data shows that men who served in the military were more likely to wed than those who did not (and were also—if they married during the war—more apt to divorce afterward).[36] There was clearly a marital "payoff" for serving. Since the first big jump in marriages took place in 1940—before any government subsidies were being offered—it appears likely that fears of separation and a desire to have children beforehand, along with an improving economy, were the major motivating reasons. And, just as happened in Japan, Germany, and several other belligerent nations early in the conflict, the birth rate in the United States increased in the wake of these war-related nuptials. This rise can also be attributed to improving economic circumstances and the greater number of new marriages, but the Selective Service's policy of not drafting fathers—honored until December 1943—was a contributing factor as well.[37] After being constant at approximately 17 births per 1,000 persons in the 1930s, the fertility rate went up to 19.4 in 1940 and 20.4 by 1945.[38] This rise represented the first phase of the postwar "baby boom," which would reach a high of 25.3 births per 1,000 in 1957.

In sum, while young Americans had many reasons for answering the call to arms after December 7, 1941, a pervasive feeling of inadequacy—as protectors, providers, and prospective husbands and fathers—underlay many of them. Enlisting in the army and navy had a salutatory effect on all of these perceived deficiencies. Men's image of themselves turned from negative to positive as they assumed the role of warrior, coming to the nation's aid. All of a sudden, men were highly esteemed. (As Roosevelt's future administrative assistant, Jonathan Daniels, noted with delight, the country was "magnificently male again.")[39] The greater income and higher standard of living that came with dependable government paychecks and regular promotions in the military helped millions of unemployed or poorly paid men feel good about themselves—and attract brides. The intense feelings of the moment—and uncertainty about the future—led many couples to marry, and others to have children. On the whole, American men may have been reluctant warriors—after the first burst of enthusiasm to sign up in late 1941 and early 1942, the military had to depend upon the draft to fill its ranks, and numerous men tried to avoid army combat duty by enlisting in other branches[40]—and they may not have had the same intense feelings of humiliation, anger, and insecurity that their German contemporaries had experienced in the wake of that nation's defeat in World War I. But the economic downturn of the 1930s, the near collapse of the capitalist system, and a loss of respect and status in the family had all inflicted wounds upon the American male psyche—wounds that a revived patriotism, men's new importance as soldiers, the nation's united response to the Japanese attack on Hawaii, and the economic and sexual/marital opportunities associated with entering the war seemed likely to heal. While they had not looked for this fight, it appeared to offer them a kind of salvation: consciously or not, they could sense many benefits for them in joining the effort to defeat Hitler and the Japanese.

The United States government could not, of course, appeal to would-be volunteers in these subtle and self-serving terms. To rally its young men for a long and trying struggle against its powerful adversaries, it needed a broader and more honorable message—one that would give the entire nation a sustaining rationale for making the human and material sacrifices the conflict in Europe and Asia would require. The war had to be presented not just as a struggle for international power—certainly not, as some groused, a war on behalf of capitalism—but as a life-or-death struggle to defend and preserve what all Americans regarded as sacred and inviolable. It had to be seen as a clash between two fundamentally and irreconcilably incompatible ways of life—between freedom and slavery, between fascism and democracy. In this struggle, the United States could not fail because its foes were innately "evil" and bent upon world conquest. It was do-or-die: as Vice President Henry Wallace put it, "There can be no compromise with Satan."[41] Instead, the United States had to prevail in order to ensure the triumph of liberty and democracy not just within its own borders, but all over the world. This was to be a crusade fought for the good of all humanity.

Facing a nation skeptical of war, the president had already resorted to his considerable rhetorical skills and mellifluous voice to drive this message home. Addressing a joint session of Congress (and, through his radio microphones, millions of ordinary Americans in their living rooms) on January 6, 1941, Roosevelt proclaimed the "Four Freedoms" for which the country was prepared to fight (freedom of speech, freedom of worship, freedom from want, and freedom from fear), concluding:

> This nation has placed its destiny in the hands and heads and hearts of its millions of free men and women, and its faith in freedom under the guidance of God. Freedom means the supremacy of human rights everywhere. Our support goes to those who struggle to gain those rights and keep them. Our strength is our unity of purpose.
>
> To that high concept there can be no end save victory.

The First Lady echoed these same sentiments in a radio talk she gave that fall, as German armies were sweeping across Russia and the fate of free Europe appeared to be hanging in the balance. Despite these disturbing developments, Mrs. Roosevelt sounded a defiantly optimistic note: "A wind is rising throughout the world of free men everywhere and they will not be kept in bondage. The rivers flow in the democracies that now exist through to those who are held temporarily in slavery and on to the deluded human beings who are voluntary slaves. . . . The rivers flow so swiftly they cannot be turned back, and the new beds which they make for themselves are the pattern of new ideas which the people who believe in freedom in the world are fashioning today."[42] The struggle would be hard, but the outcome would not be in doubt. Democracy would triumph.

To make this case stick and rally the people behind it, the Roosevelt administration needed the help of professionals, and so the newly established Office of War Information (OWI) turned to the myth makers of Hollywood. They were asked to put aside artistic independence and integrity for the duration of the war and lend their services to help to win it. Henceforth, films would be produced and put on silver screens all over the country to remind the American public about what was at stake and why they had to back the war effort wholeheartedly. At the same time, this new crop of Hollywood productions would be expected to depict what Americans were being asked to sacrifice and die for. The sobering realism of some Depression-era movies, depicting America as a down-and-out country, riddled by greed, crime, poverty, and class and racial tensions, would have to disappear—to be replaced by an idealized portrait of a nation pulling together as one and fully living up to its professed ideals. Movie makers were to focus on presenting "an unprecedented class and cultural consensus as the very essence of the American way."[43] The OWI would contribute to this effort by producing films and radio programs of its own and by having photographers document the nation's mobilization for war in ennobling black-and-white photographs.

Along with exhorting Americans on the home front to help out by remaining vigilant, conserving vital resources, watching what they said, and working in war-related factories to build the nation's "arsenal of democracy," this well-coordinated propaganda campaign emphasized that individuals from different walks of life, from different races and backgrounds—men and women alike—were overcoming these barriers to devote themselves to a common purpose. The great strength of American democracy lay in this universally shared commitment to achieving justice, equality, and tolerance for all. Soon after the United States entered the war, this theme was reflected in the films emanating from the Hollywood studios. One early, emotionally powerful example was *Mrs.*

Miniver, starring Greer Garson, which won the Academy Award for best picture in 1942. Its portrayal of English villagers putting aside traditional class divisions to beat back a Nazi invasion was intended to prepare American audiences for the same challenge. The 1939 book on which it was based had been widely read, and President Roosevelt had credited it with convincing many Americans to change their minds and back the war. He had the film's closing speech by the village's vicar, telling his parishioners in their bomb-shattered church that this conflict was "not only of soldiers in uniform; it is a war of the people, of all the people," broadcast over the Voice of America.[44] A host of subsequent movies like David Miller's *Flying Tigers* (1942), Mark Sandrich's *So Proudly We Hail* (1943), and Alfred Hitchcock's *Lifeboat* (1944) similarly dramatized this need for Americans to pull together, whether they were pilots flying missions over Japanese-occupied China, nurses stationed on the Philippines, or survivors of a torpedoed ship adrift in the North Atlantic. In such films, selfishness was the vice that had to be overcome, while inclusiveness, fairness, self-sacrifice, and a democratic humanism the virtues that ultimately mattered most.

This litany of values spoke loudly and directly to groups that up until now had felt isolated and denigrated in American society—denied its promise. Among these were the nation's nearly 13 million black citizens, many of whom had never voted, sat on a bus next to a white person, or been given a decent public education. They were still struggling to find a modicum of dignity and respect in a nation where Jim Crow laws defined them as second-rate, unreliable, and mostly worthless. The words of the president and his minions now gave them hope that this degrading situation might finally be changing. They believed that this time the words were not empty and meaningless, but a bona fide pledge to take firm action to make the world more just and democratic. They, too, might finally enjoy the freedoms of which FDR had spoken. If only out of necessity, doors long closed to blacks would be opened. Many young black men saw the war as an opportunity to demonstrate that they were worthy of these freedoms and to gain more economic and political rights once they returned home. Rebuffed by policies that kept them out of elite branches like the Marines and considered them constitutionally (that is, racially) incapable of holding up under fire, they went ahead and joined the segregated support units that would take them, so they could play their part in this historic conflict. All told, some 125,000 black soldiers and airmen would serve overseas during World War II, and many thousands more on stateside bases. The same trust in Roosevelt's words and desire to prove their worth induced countless gay men and women to step forward and take the oath of allegiance, in spite of official policy that deemed them psychologically unfit to do so.[45]

Women, too, had an important part to play in the defense of America, and both Hollywood and the federal government made sure not to overlook or minimize their potential contributions. OWI photographs taken early in the war featured women assembling the cockpits of C-47 bombers à la "Rosie the Riveter," stitching parachutes, packing tomatoes in Puerto Rico, and wiring electrical devices for Douglas Aircraft.[46] To show that women could also be brave, heroic figures in the fight against fascism, a number of movies cast them in such inspirational roles. In *Mrs. Miniver*, for example, the eponymous main character confronts a downed German flyer in her garden and manages to disarm him and call the police. In *So Proudly We Hail*, the nurse played by Veronica Lake sacrifices her own life to save those of her close friends. For married women on the home front, such dramatic gestures might be unrealistic, but these women, too, could help their country make it through the war by taking charge of their families and keeping them intact until their husbands returned from overseas. Such was the theme of films like *When You Were Away* (1944), which showed a pampered, upper middle-class housewife named Anne Hilton (Claudette Colbert) at first tearful and overwhelmed by her husband's being called up for active duty, but slowly learning to cope with running her household and looking after her two daughters without a man around to help her.

For all the propagandistic hyperbole about female factory workers with sleeves rolled up and polka-dot kerchiefs on their heads, the real-life experiences of an Anne Hilton were far more representative of what most American wives had to contend with during World War II. Fully seven of every eight married women stayed at home throughout that period, as did more than half of all females of working age.[47] While the number of wives in the labor force increased significantly between 1940 and 1945 (up from 800,000 to 5 million), only about 16 percent of these women ended up on the factory floor.[48] Most held traditionally female positions in offices, hospitals, stores, and schools.[49] Those who took over for men on the assembly lines—as they had been encouraged to do and as the public came to favor[50]—faced prejudice and hostility for moving into a previously all-male domain. With unconcealed schadenfreude, an article that appeared in *Newsweek* in June 1943 revealed that women were not measuring up to men, physically and psychologically, on the job: "By and large," this piece reported on a recent study, "women are less emotionally stable, more sensitive to weather conditions, attitudes of associates, and more environmental influences which men take in stride."[51] This negative assessment was widely endorsed: in a Gallup poll conducted that year, fewer than 30 percent of husbands surveyed said they approved of their spouses working with machinery in a factory.[52] Even greater animosity greeted those women enlisted in the armed services. After the United States declared war, Congress debated heatedly for five months before voting to allow them to serve in uniform, as members of the Women's Auxiliary Army Corps (WAAC), and that was only the start of women's struggle to gain acceptance in this role. Many men felt that "women in uniform were an insult to the collective machismo of the American male."[53] Male soldiers were the most vehement opponents, in no small part because WAACs were slated to take over clerical and support roles, freeing up that many more men for combat duty. Public perception of women in khaki as promiscuous hussies kept the army from reaching its enlistment goal of 1.5 million: by 1943, only 50,000 women had signed up, and this original target was never reached.[54]

This intense opposition to females assuming male roles was part of a larger unease with women working throughout their adult lives. The long-held belief that females should set their sights on becoming wives and mothers, not "career women," held firm. While few objected to young single women taking jobs before they found husbands, those who refused to give up these positions afterward were sharply criticized: they were accused of neglecting their families, especially the children whose care had been entrusted to them. Working mothers were chastised for being "selfishly materialistic."[55] And it was not only men who felt that way. During the war years, young single women wholeheartedly gave top priority to domestic duties when contemplating their futures: asked by *Fortune* magazine in 1943, only 6.2 percent of women between the ages of twenty and thirty-five said they would forego getting married for the sake of their careers. Although another 17.8 percent hoped to balance family and careers, fully three-quarters of those surveyed declared it was their primary ambition to marry, raise children, and run a household.[56] This preference helps to explain the ridicule aimed at "liberated" cinematic characters like Tess Harding in *Woman of the Year*. Anticipating its film noir treatment of the 1950s, Hollywood turned out several movies late in the war that cautioned against unbridled female power. These included *Double Indemnity* (1944), *Detour* (1945), and *Mildred Pierce* (1945).[57] By contrast, wartime films such as *Casablanca* presented females who were motivated by love, instead of the "male" virtue of courage, as positive role models.

Rather than have women compete with them in their worlds of provider and protector, American men wanted to treat women as "equal, but different." The coming of war had revived two complementary and somewhat conflicting notions about how the two sexes should relate to each other. One, derived from the overarching need to see America as the bastion of democracy, stressed the basic sameness of all groups—young and old, black and white, rich and poor, male and female. All were Americans, and this national identification was what mattered and what united them as they faced dangerous foreign enemies. The other, based upon the war's need for fighting men, put more stress on gender distinctions: men would defend the country in battle, not women. The best way for men to reconcile these two imperatives was to accept females as an integral and vital part of the way of life they were being called upon to defend, but restricted to spheres that were properly female, just as men should be allowed to hold sway in masculine domains. In other words, World War II, much as the Great War before it, reinstated the doctrine of "separate spheres." Throughout the conflict, most married (and unmarried) couples lived by this implicit compact, as they took on responsibilities that were deemed appropriate and defining for their respective genders. The war years elevated the status of women by providing more opportunities, in and outside the home. But, as had happened a generation before, their assuming these new roles generally did not so much close the gap in power between them and men as offer them autonomy and control in arenas that men had temporarily vacated. The more lasting lesson of the war was that both men and women properly belonged in those spheres of life that were best suited to their strengths, where they had the most to contribute. This recognition would do much to shape American gender roles during the 1950s and early 1960s.

While a spate of propagandistic books, films, and photographic images was doing much to build public support for the war effort by reinforcing the values that were in jeopardy if the nation lost, soldiers, sailors, airmen, and Marines assigned to battlefields on three continents to do the actual fighting had little time to absorb these propaganda messages. They were too busy cleaning their rifles, digging foxholes, and ducking enemy bullets to reflect upon the higher national credo that had sent them there. After the first wave of enlistments, most had joined for pragmatic reasons—or simply been drafted. Some saw the military as a good job—a place to earn good money and learn a trade.[58] The *Saturday Evening Post* ran a series of articles on "What I Am Fighting For" and concluded that GIs overseas were more focused on building a house or buying a sports car than on making the world safe for democracy.[59] When the writer John Hersey, on assignment on Guadalcanal in the fall of 1942, posed the same question, one Marine grinned, "Jesus, what I'd give for a piece of blueberry pie." One of his buddies told the correspondent for *Time* and *Life* he just wanted to "get the goddam [sic] thing over and get home."[60]

If American fighting men could not fully understand Roosevelt's Four Freedoms or name any of the provisions of the Atlantic Charter, they were, nonetheless, discovering what democracy meant by serving together in this common cause to defend it. In expanding exponentially from a small peacetime professional force into a massive military machine of over 12 million men, the US armed forces underwent a major social transformation as well. The influx of millions of civilians, unaccustomed to military ways and temperamentally unsuited to them, changed the internal dynamics of the various services, particularly the army. Instead of being shaped by the institution they entered, the new recruits had a profound impact upon it. They democratized it. The rigidly hierarchical and authoritarian army described by the writer James Jones in his novel *From Here to Eternity* was turned into a far more egalitarian one. The old style of professional leadership, which broke the spirit of recruits through intimidation and physical harassment, soon disappeared. In the words of one GI, "The top-kick [first sergeant] is a man to respect, but his pedestal is gone. . . . Men who try to play the movie version of the hard-boiled non-com often find themselves broken or refused a rise rank."[61] To some degree, this was the result of design. Like schools, the family, and other institutions, the military was now expected to live up to America's democratic principles and incorporate these into its practices. Troops were also to receive indoctrination in these principles so that they, too, would be better representatives of the society—both in uniform and when they returned to civilian life. Even though this mission clashed sharply with the restriction of personal rights and unquestioning obedience to higher-ups upon which all militaries depend, the US Army was tasked with teaching enlisted men about the "integrity of the individual and belief in democracy." Specially designated "Information and Education" officers were instructed to avoid heavy doses of propaganda and encourage "full freedom of discussion" among their charges.[62] Furthermore, stateside soldiers were allowed to hold periodic gripe sessions, during which they could air complaints about everything from the quality of mess food to the privileges reserved for their officers. If a soldier wanted to, he could seek redress all the way up the chain of command. As one military guidebook summed up, this "free man's army" belonged to the troops.[63]

This directive foundered upon three hard realities. First, the officers assigned to oversee this education in democracy were poorly trained and uninspired to do this job. They treated their work as a joke and a waste of time, as did their basic-training commanders.[64] Second, soldiers felt the same way. To them, all this talk about why America was fighting was just more army "b.s." A private undergoing training at Fort Bragg, North Carolina, wrote that whenever he and his fellow recruits heard phrases like the "American way of life," they responded with lusty Bronx cheers.[65] When another GI, at a camp in Texas, had asked one of his lieutenants if he could tell the men why they were going off to war, he got the same response.[66] Third, recruits in this wartime army were simply too independent minded, too smart, too mature, and too well educated to meekly buy whatever the military was trying to sell them. Without question, they were quite a different breed from General Pershing's doughboys. The *average* enlisted man in World War II scored better than 83 percent of their predecessors on standardized tests.[67] Fully 41 percent of this generation of GIs had graduated from high school, and another 11 percent had attended college. It was not unusual to find a Harvard,

Yale, or Princeton graduate in the ranks of a rifle company. To mollify public opinion, Congress had set the minimum draft age at twenty, but the reluctance of local boards to call up men that young resulted in the average age for an enlisted man being twenty-six.[68] These more mature recruits were not easy to mold into the strictures of military life. Ones who had been to college were the least compliant. They muttered about incompetent "lifers" and mocked their NCOs, company commanders, and commanding generals as stupid, pompous, vain, and petty-minded.[69] They had little use for a system that gave men of little ability and intelligence the power of life and death over them. More generally, American men raised to value freedom simply could not stomach the army way of life: "The distinctions between his authoritarian military life and democratic home-town existence arouse an understandable jealousy and pain," noted a writer for *Collier's* in the spring of 1944.[70] For the future literary critic and memorialist Paul Fussell, who was plucked off the idyllic campus of Pomona College to train as an infantry officer, it was all just "chickenshit"—something to which he developed a lifelong aversion.[71]

Because it drew so many men, from all parts of the country and from all income levels, the military became a microcosm of the larger society. Because all these diverse men had to live and fight together, functioning as a team, the differences that might otherwise have divided them fell away. Down East lobstermen shared bays with scions of Tidewater plantations, and shop clerks from Indianapolis dug latrines beside sons of Italian immigrants from Brooklyn. The army's policy of assigning men to one unit for the duration of their overseas service strengthened these personal ties: GIs came to see their "buddies" as their closest friends and care for them deeply, regardless of differences in background. In this regard, day-to-day life in uniform was more instructive about the virtues of "democratic life" than anything the GIs might have picked up by listening to one of FDR's speeches. Across Europe and on remote Pacific islands, American soldiers survived weeks of constant combat, under terrible, inhuman conditions, largely because of these intense bonds with the other men in their small units. As many memoirs, novels, and other accounts of the war consistently pointed out, these mutually supportive and "communal" ties gave real meaning to their war.[72] When wartime Hollywood movies such as Howard Hawks's 1943 *Air Force* showed members of bomber crews and infantry squads forgetting about individual concerns and helping each other to achieve victory, the celluloid propaganda was not far from the actual truth. Serving in the war cemented personal bonds that lasted a lifetime (or until an enemy bullet ended them) and created an enduring generational solidarity.

As World War II taught millions of American men to depend upon each other in order to survive, it also drove home the fragility and insignificance of individual lives. On battleships, on beaches, and on open fields, men died violently in massive numbers, wantonly, and without any apparent purpose being served by their deaths: they appeared to be only fodder for an enormous, impersonal war apparatus, which needed this constant fuel to keep going. In an instant, a soldier standing a few feet away would be blown apart and reduced to scraps of flesh and bone. About to head off for Anzio, Audie Murphy saw "jeeps drawing trailerloads of corpses . . . stacked like wood," their arms and legs bobbing grotesquely. Some of his best friends had been "blown all to hell."[73] On the island of Corregidor, Corporal William Manchester, long shorn of any visions of glory, miraculously survived an incoming Japanese shell, but the fifteen Marines with him were not so lucky: "Everywhere I groped, I felt only gobs of blood, shards of shattered bones, ropy intestines, and slimy brains."[74] Another young Marine, Eugene Sledge, had shipped out for the Pacific early in 1944 believing God would protect him, only to discover it was sheer luck that separated the quick from the dead. Thrashing through a swamp on the island of Peleliu, he stumbled upon dead Americans with their heads and hands cut off. On all sides lay putrefying, maggot-filled bodies. Some Marines had been killed by their comrades in this blind fury of combat. Averting his eyes briefly from these horrors, Sledge lost all of his former belief in the war.[75]

Raised to think that individuals were unique and precious, and that they were in control of their own destinies, many men who had these combat experiences realized this was not true. Swarms of men, overrunning other swarms, might change the tide of battle, but the ordinary soldier was only a piece of flotsam on this vast tide. This was how one well-meaning, caring company commander came to perceive modern jungle warfare, in James Jones's novel *The Thin Red Line*:

> It was a horrifying vision: all of them doing the same identical thing, all of them powerless to stop it, all of them devoutly and proudly believing

themselves to be free individuals. It expanded to include the scores of nations, the millions of men, doing the same on thousands of hilltops across the world. And it didn't stop there. It went on. It was the concept—concept? The fact; the reality—of the modern State in action.[76]

His reaction was much like that of William Manchester, who had to admit to himself after enlisting that he had been reduced to "a tiny cog in the vast machine which would confront fascism."[77] It was the same sobering recognition that Lt. Paul Fussell reached, while awaiting his orders to go overseas: "We were meant to be expended, and that's why there were so many of us."[78] Against the forces that gripped them, these men were helpless, their fates no longer in their own hands. In the words of the poet Randall Jarrell, they had to accept the prospect of dying "as the dice are thrown on a blanket; / As the leaf chars or is kindled; as the bough burns."[79]

If anyone could be blamed for this unremitting and often pointless slaughter, it was the incompetent and ignorant commanders who—it seemed—sent waves of men into battle as carelessly and casually as they would sweep crumbs off the kitchen table. Combat-hardened soldiers came to fear such vainglorious officers as their real enemy—egotistical authority figures to be wary of and ignore. Manchester captured the foolhardiness of such commanders in relating an incident on the beaches of Tarawa: a brash new lieutenant nicknamed "Tubby" exhorted Marines huddled together like sheep to stand up and follow him "over the wall," only to be immediately gunned down when he rose to lead this doomed, Hollywood-style charge.[80] In Norman Mailer's *The Naked and the Dead*, animosity toward his commanding officer leads a power-hungry sergeant to hold back information about the location of Japanese troops so this lieutenant will expose himself to enemy fire and be shot.[81] In Robert Lowry's novel *Casualty*, the narrator, an enlisted man named Joe Hammond, reviles his commanding general as a "weak-kneed conniving creature." Drunk one night, Hammond unleashes his full fury at the officers he has come to know: "He hated what they were, what they stood for, and what they wanted in life."[82] Inept, self-deluding commanders were ridiculed in other war novels, such as Thomas Heggen's *Mister Roberts* and Herman Wouk's *The Caine Mutiny*. Years later, in his book *Wartime: Understanding and Behavior in the Second World War*, Fussell would vent much of his pent-up anger at the "blunders, errors, and accidents" committed by higher-ups that led to so many troops being needlessly killed. While many junior and senior officers served with distinction during the war and were held in high esteem by their men, there is no doubt that the problem of "bad" leadership was systemic.[83] Military authorities verified this when they surveyed enlisted personnel toward the end of the conflict.[84]

Being killed was only the worst of fates to be feared. Many soldiers who didn't die during battles suffered severe psychological damage from these experiences. What psychiatrists had labeled "shell shock" during the Great War reappeared as "psychoneurosis" in this conflict. Pushed to and beyond the breaking point under constant bombardment or during close-hand combat, a large number of GIs succumbed to a kind of paralysis. They refused to fire their weapons and cowered in their foxholes. An influential study by the military historian S. L. A. Marshall found that only about 15 percent of front-line troops he interviewed in the Pacific had actually used their rifles when engaged with the enemy. Marshall attributed this behavior not so much to cowardice and fear as to an inbred American aversion to killing.[85] Whatever its causes, the failure of so many GIs to perform under fire was a cause for much alarm. During World War II, nearly twice as many soldiers were incapacitated by "battle fatigue" or "psychoneurosis" as were killed. Of the 800,000 men who saw combat, some 37 percent had to be given discharges because they could no longer function as effective soldiers.[86] In 1944, more GIs were released from duty because of psychiatric disability than were drafted.[87] Despite the military's earlier efforts to weed out men who might not hold up under the stress of battle, the rate of psychiatric casualties among American troops in this war was four times as large as it had been in World War I.[88] As much as field commanders attempted to characterize those who broke down as "spoiled brats" and "mommies' boys," it became apparent that the tendency to collapse under combat stress was endemic: even the bravest soldiers would break after prolonged exposure to fire.[89] Even more disconcerting, the incidence of "collapse" among American troops was later determined to have been much greater than among their German and Russian counterparts.[90]

Men who would later be hailed as exemplars of the "greatest generation" were not immune to other forms of unheroic conduct during World War II. About 6 percent of soldiers—roughly the same proportion as in the previous war—deserted, generally because they could not adjust to military life, did not believe in the war, distrusted their commanders, or could not continue to take the stresses of battle.[91] In the course of the war, a total of forty-nine men were sentenced to be executed for abandoning their units, although only one, Pvt. Eddie Slovik, actually suffered this fate.[92] In addition, American soldiers showed themselves to be less than the exemplars of moral probity and sexual fidelity that many back home believed them to have been. A large percentage of troops serving in Europe—married and single alike—had sexual relations with women they met there.[93] Many of these were prostitutes, while others were women aching for affection and sexual release amid the violence and chaos of wartime. While countless GIs received devastating "Dear John" letters while at the front, it appears that at least as many men in uniform also cheated on their wives and girlfriends.[94] Some of these affairs left married men with lingering feelings of remorse, as were suffered by Tom Rath, the main character in Sloan Wilson's 1955 novel, *The Man in the Gray Flannel Suit*: back in suburban Connecticut, Rath contemplates returning to the woman and a son he has left behind in Italy.[95] Some GIs were guilty of more grievous sexual misconduct: like soldiers in all wars, they committed rape. An estimated 17,000 sexual assaults took place at the hands of GIs stationed in England, France, and Germany.[96]

All of these male "failures" to measure up—failures of leaders to act wisely and in the best interests of their men, failures of soldiers to withstand harrowing combat conditions, failures of men to behave like decent human beings amid barbarous butchery, failures of husbands and fiancés to honor their pledges of faithfulness—gave soldiers returning home in 1945 no great cause for pride or satisfaction. They may have won the war and won the admiration of their families and hometowns, but most did not look back on their war experience happily. No matter what the newsreels proclaimed, or their town fathers declared, they did not feel like conquering heroes. They had seen what war really was like close up, and they had no desire to see any more. Whatever visions of glory that may have convinced some of them to enlist after Pearl Harbor had long since evaporated like some liquor-induced phantasmagoria. Mainly they were glad to have returned alive and in one piece. Despite their subsequent reputation, these veterans did not see themselves as exceptional or heroic. Because so many men had served and known what war was really like, this generation was not inclined to glorify the experience. Its members saw themselves as ordinary, imperfect men, eager to resume ordinary lives that had been interrupted by a trying but necessary interlude overseas. They wanted to look forward, not backward. And this was the country's mood, too. Once the two-day celebrations of victory over Japan were over, once the soldiers had come back home, most Americans were more than ready to put the war years behind them and move on. Unlike countries such as the Soviet Union, the nation did not feel the need to dwell at length, or with great spectacle, on its heroic sacrifices and triumphant warriors.[97]

If American veterans of World War II treasured anything from their war years it was the comradeship of their fellow soldiers. This bond had sustained them through the worst of the fighting, when the outcome was most in doubt, and when their lives hung in the balance. Memoir after memoir that appeared during the postwar years made this eminently clear.[98] Veterans recalled with still-raw emotion the trust and affection that had existed between them and other members of their "bands of brothers." Sledge wrote in his account of Pacific combat: "A man felt that he belonged to his unit and had a niche among buddies whom he knew and with whom he shared a mutual respect welded in combat."[99] The beloved war correspondent Ernie Pyle, who was to die on the island of Ie Shima near the end of the war, similarly observed: "The ties that grow between men who live savagely together relentlessly communing with Death, are ties of great strength. There is a sense of fidelity to each other in a little corps of men who have endured so long, and whose hope in the end can be so small."[100]

Much as had happened in the aftermath of World War I, the feelings of "pride, loyalty, comradeship, selflessness, even love" forged at close quarters in combat gave veterans not only nostalgia for such male bonds but also hope for the future. Such fraternal ties could serve as a model for constructing a more democratic postwar society and eliminating the selfish materialism and greed former soldiers found rampant in their cities and towns when they came back in 1945. No postwar novel or film better captured the importance of this soldierly esprit right after the war than William Wyler's 1946 movie, *The Time of Our Lives*. In it, three veterans return to their hometown of Boone City ill-equipped to fare well in its class-ridden and money-driven milieu. One of them has previously worked as a soda jerk, and another (played by an actual veteran) has lost both of his hands in a shipboard fire. Misfits in their families as well as their communities, the three men have only each other to turn to for comfort and advice. Thanks to this friendship, they manage to restore other relationships, rebuild their lives, and move forward.

Negative attitudes toward figures of rigid authority in the military carried over into the postwar era and made veterans distrustful of "patriarchal" civilian leaders. Instead, they—along with most Americans— liked more avuncular or grandfatherly ones, such as the sixty-two-year-old Dwight Eisenhower, who was handily elected president in 1952. This preference derived from a postwar consensus that authoritarian regimes and their megalomaniacal dictators had brought about a disastrous and costly war and that, in the future, all efforts would have to be made to prevent any such figures or their hierarchical, ideologically driven movements from coming to power in the United States. The nation as a whole became hypersensitive to vertical power structures. Even the military itself was not above criticizing the "arbitrary social distinctions" that normally characterized relations between enlisted men and officers and pondering a major reorganization to bring it more in line with a "democratic way of life."[101] A major focus of this concern was the Soviet Union and its expansive, threatening form of communism.

The era's strong aversion to powerful authority was evident in seminal tracts of the 1950s such as Theodor Adorno's *The Authoritarian Personality* (1950) and Hannah Arendt's *The Origins of Totalitarianism* (1951). It was also reflected in policies adopted by schools across the country as part of a concerted campaign to inoculate young children against totalitarian thinking. By 1948, forty-four states had adopted laws requiring that the Constitution be taught at the elementary-school level.[102] In the spirit of John Dewey, schooling was now regarded as the best preparation for democratic citizenship. Wrote the head of elementary education in the state of New York, "The very foundation of American society rests on the premise that individuals of different backgrounds can work together for the common good."[103] Antiauthoritarian thinking also guided how parents raised their children. The growing popularity of Dr. Benjamin Spock's *Baby and Child Care*, first published in 1946, also revealed Americans' disdain for "top-down" directives in lieu of freedom and common sense: "Trust yourself" was the good doctor's liberating mantra.

Postwar middle-class families were focused on the children. The US victory in World War II brought the nation unprecedented prosperity and an unequally unprecedented number of births. The population "payoff" for the nation was phenomenal. Between February and October 1946, the number of babies born monthly rose from 206,387 to 339,449—by more than 64 percent. By the time New Year's Eve rolled around, it became apparent the nation's mothers had set a new, all-time record of 3.4 million births. These additions to families kept coming in even larger quantities, surpassing 4 million annually over an entire decade, from 1954 to 1964.[104] This unanticipated "baby boom" felicitously coincided with the country's postwar economic growth: thanks to brand-new factories and highly profitable corporations, the per capita GDP in the United States reached $9,573 in 1950—nearly twice that of most Western European countries and the largest in the entire world. With an unemployment rate of only 5.3 percent, almost all veterans were able to land well-paying jobs, start or increase the size of their families, and—if they belonged to the growing middle class—move from the cities into newly established suburbs.

All of this economic progress was another direct benefit of the country's having armed itself and fought on the winning side in the war (while also having avoided being bombed or invaded). As Landon Y. Jones summed up in his book on the baby boom, the "flush of military victory, the staggering prosperity, the renewed faith in the future" all contributed to America's procreative splurge.[105] The linkage between these factors and the birth rate becomes clear when one compares the postwar "boom" in the United States with what happened in countries that lost the war, or that suffered so much destruction from it that their economies were in shambles afterward. In fact, the only other belligerent nations that experienced a surge in births comparable to what took place in the United States were Canada, Australia, and New Zealand—winning nations largely spared the physical and psychological damage caused by the war.[106] Other victorious countries had no such benefit: fewer babies were born in France between 1955 and 1960 than between 1950 and 1955, and the rate continued to decline thereafter. During the 1950s, the rate in England and Wales rose somewhat, from 15.9 to 16.5, but then declined again after the early 1960s. In the defeated nations of Germany, Italy, and Japan, birth rates did not conform to a single pattern, but the general trend was not upward. Japanese women continued to have fewer babies through the 1950s and beyond, with the rate falling from 66.7 births per 1,000 women in 1937 to 53.6 in 1950 and 37.5 in 1954.[107] Germany experienced a slight increase in births during the 1950s (rising from 16 to 17.8 per 1,000 inhabitants), but then the number of babies born plummeted in the mid-1970s. Italy likewise witnessed a small increase in fertility in the 1950s, followed by a decrease after 1960. Recent studies have indicated that the short-lived postwar baby "boomlet" in some Western European countries was due to policies that kept women out of the workforce.[108] In any event, the United States was the only major nation (in terms of population) to reap such a birth benefit from having taken part in World War II: this fact strongly suggests that both winning *and* being in a strong position economically once the fighting stopped were the factors most directly responsible for the postwar spurt in births.

The growth of America's families made domestic life the most important dimension of postwar society. Indeed, it was practically the *only* dimension: over 96 percent of females and 94.1 percent of males who came of age during World War II ended up getting married—the highest percentage ever in the United States. That same year, nine of every ten households consisted of a married couple, with or without children. Between 1947 and 1961, the number of American families increased by 28 percent.[109] The median age at first marriage at mid-decade was lower than it had been since records had been kept—20.1 for women and 22.5 for men. In 1950, half of the women aged twenty were already married, as were one of four among those eighteen years old. On top of this, couples were all reproducing at a rate not seen since early in the century. By 1957, the average family had 3.5 children. By 1960, 56.9 percent of families had at least one child under the age of eighteen living with them.

Burgeoning households in well-tended suburban tracts had become the engine driving a consumer-based economy as well as the center of popular culture. Men earning respectable, white-collar salaries were able to supply the cash needed to furnish these new homes with the latest appliances and other labor-saving devices, turning them into comfortable oases—retreats from the nuclear perils of the Cold War.[110] The children and wives who stayed at home when their fathers and husbands caught commuter trains into large metropolitan centers like New York, Chicago, Boston, and Philadelphia enjoyed a degree of leisure and freedom unknown to previous generations of Americans. They also experienced a great deal of autonomy: without the presence of grandparents or other relatives in the neighborhood, the nuclear family evolved into a largely free-standing unit—self-sufficient and self-preoccupied. Protected from the unpleasant realities of urban poverty, racial tension, class conflict, and external threat, suburban children grew up secure and well-fed, but also with plenty of opportunities to explore their benign environment and enjoy the largesse associated with their parents' vaulting standard of living. Because many fathers were absent during the day, these children of the affluent 1950s also came of age in a largely matriarchal world. "Mom" woke them in the morning and made them breakfast, helped them tie their sneakers and watched them play in the backyard; she taught them games like Parcheesi and sewed costumes for the Halloween parade; she baked them cookies and dabbed Unguentine on their skinned knees; she made them wash before dinner and sit in their chairs quietly until "Dad" had come in from the den and sat down, too.

The father's role in these postwar families was nominally primary, but, in fact, peripheral. Much lip service was paid to the importance of "Dad": he "knew best" and warranted respect and always had the last word in matters of discipline, but his being away most of the time when the children were awake meant that he had little time (other than on the weekends) to spend with his offspring, teach them his boyhood lore, and create a multidimensional relationship with them. Fathers who came back to families after the war had initially had a difficult time reintegrating into them. They were strangers to their young children and an unnecessary household addition to wives who had gotten along fine without them for two or three years—like a shiny new appliance for which there did not appear to be any pressing need. During the war, women's magazines had urged wives to prepare for "Daddy's" return and appreciate the "strength, courage, decisiveness" that men alone possessed.[111] Many mothers claimed to be more than willing to hand back to their husbands the male responsibilities they had temporarily shouldered, but things did not always turn out as planned. For one thing, middle-class wives were so accustomed to managing all the household duties that they felt no desire to have "Daddy" take over for them. In addition, many men were greatly changed by what they had seen and done in combat; they had trouble speaking about these experiences, and so a gulf opened up between them and the rest of their families, particularly their wives.[112] To some of them, the sullen man sitting across the breakfast table with a cigarette dangling out of the corner of his mouth was like an intruder. Some fathers found that their children, spared the rod in their absence, had become "spoiled" and unresponsive to parental directives. The old ways of disciplining a child by taking away privileges or sending him or her off to bed without supper had fallen out of favor. The expectation that "he made the rules, and the wife carried them out" had disappeared.[113] Many fathers resented this erosion of their authority. Mothers, on the other hand, being more attuned to the new trends in raising children, wanted to continue using this gentle, hortative way of making them behave. At the same time, many wives were reluctant to retreat into the background and surrender the independence they had known as single parents.[114]

The simple fact of the matter was that both mothers and fathers were unsure of what roles they would assume now that the family was reunited after such a long separation. Because their corporate jobs took them out of the home, many suburban middle-class fathers had trouble establishing a clear and consistent presence in it. Their lives were fractured by competing demands. Ironically, being absent during the day resembled their going off to war. It left them as out of touch on a daily basis as they had been for months at a time while serving overseas.

Taking care of children they scarcely knew posed numerous challenges. Leading childcare experts argued that fathers needed to become more involved with their offspring in order to make them psychologically well adjusted and thus more likely to grow up to be healthy adults, free of complexes and grievances. Without involved "dads," children were apt to fall under "feminine domination," more than one authority cautioned.[115] This masculine influence was also essential for the nation's future, to ensure a strong, healthy citizenry.[116] The advice columns similarly urged fathers to become "pals" with their sons and daughters before trying to discipline them.[117] To accomplish this, they had to "sit down with the children, talk with them, listen to them, play with them, and show that they enjoy them."[118] Fathers were supposed to offer words of praise instead of noncommittal grunts over the morning paper. Many husbands took up this challenge, flocking to courses on baby care, playing with their infants, giving them baths, and cooking meals.[119] Columnists for *Parents* magazine announced in 1952, "Today's husband isn't ashamed to be caught wearing an apron. He is perfectly willing to wipe a dish and pin a diaper."[120] *Life* proclaimed 1954 the year of the "domestification of the American man," noting that family life had been "elevated to a level of sacredness never before witnessed in our history."[121]

But these pronouncements represented more hope than reality. Postwar fathers were making efforts to be domestic partners, but this transition was not easy for them. It represented a big change from how they had been raised by *their* fathers, and many lacked a good model for performing paternal duties along more "enlightened" lines. Having been away for several years, veterans were unsure how to relate to their children and, frustrated, often threw up their hands and handed them back to their mother. In the years immediately after the war, some began to avoid their children and the home entirely, seeking solace in clubs and bars.[122] As they settled into stable, demanding jobs in the early 1950s, many middle-class fathers came to accept a secondary role in their families, ceding authority to their wives as they devoted more and more of their time to bringing home good salaries. As a result, they saw less and less of their children.

As new families were started, and others grew larger, work responsibilities grew concomitantly. So did the desire for greater affluence. Couples strove to keep up with "the Joneses." Wives encouraged their husbands to get ahead and bring home larger salaries. This was how men could demonstrate their worth.[123] This made work an all-consuming endeavor. Meanwhile, management of the household also became more demanding. With more children, mothers had to devote all of their time to looking after them. Wholly dedicated to their separate spheres, husbands and wives had little energy left over at the end of the day to share the other's world. When men came home tired and irritable they reached for a glass of Scotch or picked up the newspaper instead of making model airplanes with their sons. Wives stopped asking about the latest machinations in the office. Thus, out of necessity, the realms allocated to mothers and fathers grew more estranged and mutually exclusive. Inside the suburban home, fathers were reduced to being mother's helpers, reclaiming the kids on weekends the way divorced dads would do, but never quite with the same power now exercised by their spouses. Instead, they became marginalized, secondary figures in the neat, well-furnished houses they had paid for.[124] As an astute observer of American social behavior, Vance Packard noted fathers were merely an "appendage" of the family, shrunk to "insignificance" in its daily doings.[125] With Mom firmly in charge of this domain, and Dad issuing directives in his office, a new kind of marriage took root in these outlying postwar communities. Each parent contributed a complementary and uncontested expertise. The doctrine of "separate spheres" was back in force. But this arrangement only worked if the two partners largely kept out of each other's way. Paradoxically, these suburban marriages held together by the man and the wife staying apart for most of the time.

As a consequence, the presence of fathers in the home (like the presence of wives in a boardroom) seemed of dubious value—indeed, embarrassing. Awkward and out of place there, Dad invited derision. He descended into caricature. Radio programs were devised around the premise that "the American father is a man forty-five years old who can't get his shoes on the right feet, and whose pretense to have dignity and authority keeps his family in stitches."[126] Popular television shows of the early 1950s conveyed suburbia's unease with his presence: Clarence Day of Broadway fame degenerated into a moustache-twirling buffoon on the small screen version of *Life with Father*. Jackie Gleason's bus-driver persona, Ralph Kramden (mercifully, without kids), could only bulge his eyes and rant while a coolly competent Alice cleaned up his messes.[127] On the silver screen, Spencer Tracy, as *Father of the Bride* (1950), was reduced to grimly paying the mounting bills as his daughter's wedding unfolded like a Hollywood production in his living room. In the newspaper funnies, Dagwood Bumstead mainly spent his time preparing his signature sandwich and lounging about in his easy chair eating it. Cartoons in the *Ladies Home Journal* and other women's magazines lampooned husbands' inadequacies: they couldn't cook, vacuum, or lift a paintbrush without botching the job. These were the images that bombarded the consciousness of young boys and girls coming of age in the Eisenhower years. While these fictional fathers depicted the amusing foibles of married males in a domestic age, there were few contrasting masculine models for them to embrace. Strong, silent, stoic male figures who had rallied the country to war had all but disappeared from the movies and TV shows, and, if they did appear, it was usually to contrast them unfavorably with a new, more sensitive and compassionate hero. When John Wayne starred opposite Montgomery Cliff in Howard Hawks's *Red River* (1948), it was obvious he was a holdover from an earlier era—a patriarch whose harsh, driving manner no longer dominated; it was his adopted son, Matt (Clift), with his "soft heart," to whom the future belonged. In *Sands of Iwo Jima*, which was released the following year, Wayne reprised this role, playing a tough Marine sergeant who is as adept at fighting the Japanese as he is inept at being a father.[128]

In the mid-1950s, as the first members of the "baby boom" generation neared puberty, the relationship between American fathers and their sons became more problematic. So did the meaning of masculinity. This was so for two reasons. First of all, adolescent males were growing restive under the constraining wing of their stay-at-home mothers.[129] Not all young men of that day could pull away as graciously and lovingly as Ricky and David Nelson did in their weekly episodes of *Ozzie and Harriet*. A new sexual energy was yearning for expression, fueled by sensual, seemingly primitive rock 'n' roll music that turned teenagers into wildly gyrating hedonists. Possessed by this manic beat, and possessing the extra cash needed to buy the latest versions of it, teens were creating their own world, separating abruptly from their parents and looking for new male and female icons with which they could identify. Having a weak, ineffectual, even emasculated father was no longer something for adolescent males to dismiss with a laugh, as they had done a few years before while watching the ironically named *Father Knows Best*, but a cause for genuine dismay. Searching for a way to repudiate this risible figure and break free, they turned to peers who were already enacting their own rebellion on the screen. One was Marlon Brando, in dark glasses and black leather jacket, smugly triumphant astride a Triumph Thunderbird 6T motorcycle, in the 1953 biker flick, *The Wild One*.

But the rising male star who truly riveted his generation was the singular James Dean. In Nicolas Ray's 1955 film, *Rebel Without a Cause*, Dean played Jim Stark, a seventeen-year-old high school student who has just moved to Los Angeles with his parents. Like so many of his generation, Jim feels alienated and confused about his identity, including his sexuality, but he is unequivocal in his rejection of the weakness, hypocrisy, and willingness to compromise on principles he sees everywhere in the adult world, most depressingly in his own father. Frank Stark (Jim Backus) has long ago surrendered any semblance of masculine courage or conviction and now dotes impotently on his domineering wife. Rather than wear the pants in the family, he literally puts on an apron. Henpecked, not truly a man himself, he can offer his son no guidance about how to undergo a rite of passage into manhood, and so Jim has to discover this for himself. He is determined not to grow up to be like his father. ("She eats him alive and he takes it," Jim says, referring to his mother.) To do this, he has to test himself in what turns out to be a deadly game of chicken with a neighborhood tough. In order to fully become a man—sexually as well—Jim also has to leave his home and create a surrogate family with two of his peers—Judy (Natalie Wood) and Plato (Sal Mineo). Later, enraged at his father's continuing inability to stand up to his mother or understand him, Jim drags the older Stark into the living room and chokes him until his mother intervenes and pulls the two men apart. In the end, Frank does come through for Jim, comforting him in his despair after Plato's death: "Now, Jim, stand up. I'll stand up with you. I'll try and be as strong as you want me to be. Come on." While the movie ends soon after this scene of reconciliation, it left its young audiences more impressed by Jim's defiant attitude and the steps he takes to rebel against his parents. This need to go their own way to find themselves was the message that teens took away from the movie house with them.

Along with other young male idols of the mid-1950s and early 1960s (most notably, Clift and Brando), Dean portrayed gentle, sensitive youth, whose sexual identity was often ambiguous, bordering on bisexuality, indicative of the actors themselves.[130] Matinee figures whom a scornful John Wayne would dismiss as "trembling, torn T-shirt types" bore little resemblance to the rugged, imposing heroes who had populated the silver screen a generation before.[131] In revolting against their fathers, characters they portrayed were asserting their sexual freedom but defining this in a more complex, nuanced way. The cultural messages they were conveying were in conflict. On the one hand, these actors were urging their male contemporaries to stand up and be men. On the other hand, they were exposing (and not repudiating) frailties and vulnerabilities usually associated with females and "momma's boys." This ambivalence about masculinity was endemic in postwar America. Married men also appeared to have lost sight of who and what they were supposed to be, in large part because of the contradictory roles they were expected to play: aggressive, hard-driving executive by day, compassionate, caring father at night. The uneasiness with which the older generation regarded the younger's infatuation with rock 'n' roll, its undisguised sexual fervor, and its predilection for antisocial if not violent behavior was really a reflection of its own confusion about gender roles. (Youth gangs were a major concern during the 1950s, and some blamed weak, ineffectual fathers—like Jim Stark's in *Rebel Without a Cause*—for their prevalence.)[132] The youthful rebellions of Hollywood stars (and fictional characters like J. D. Salinger's Holden Caulfield) tempted older men as well, as they felt trapped in the "rat race" of the corporate life, paying a high price with heart attacks, bouts of impotence, alcoholism, and feelings of inadequacy. Like Frank Stark, they could relate to their sons and aspire to act like them.

Among these married men of the World War II generation, the impulse to rebel and act manly was satisfied mainly through fantasy. Late at night, when the house was quiet, they cracked open dog-eared copies of hardboiled Mickey Spillane crime novels or the latest James Bond thriller. There was no question which sex was in charge on those pages. Or else they sublimated their sexual yearnings by thumbing through Terry Southern's tongue-in-cheek *Candy* or Vladimir Nabokov's equally scandalous *Lolita*. In the movie theaters they toyed vicariously with infidelity through the character of Richard Sherman, joining with him in lusting innocently after Marilyn Monroe in the film version of the *Seven Year Itch* (1955), or, for that matter, in any movie in which she appeared. Monroe reinforced the sexual restraint of her uxorious male viewers even as she mocked it. Her amply inviting figure was the ne plus ultra of armchair allure in a decade during which Hollywood rediscovered the untouchable bosom and made it a substitute for adultery. In the repressive 1950s, elusive sex was something to which American men of all ages could relate. It was highly appropriate that nude photos of Monroe adorned the first issue of *Playboy* when it appeared on newsstands in December 1953: what was good for the father was even better for the son.

Social commentators fanned this rebelliousness. In books like David Riesman's *The Lonely Crowd* (1950) and C. Wright Mills's *White Collar: The American Middle Classes* (1951), they bemoaned the mindless conformity of a decade that had produced "organization men," but few free thinkers.[133] They excoriated the prevailing "myth of adjustment" that was telling young people nonconformity was synonymous with mental illness.[134] They rued the emphasis on security among college students.[135] They criticized the corporate life for pressuring men to "stay on the beam and on the team" at the expense of their individual masculine drives.[136] They lambasted husbands who allowed their wives to control them.[137] They worried that the distinctions between men and women were melting away.[138] They lamented a perceived increase in homosexuality.[139] They complained that fathers were spending too much time changing diapers and too little being "a masculine model that young males can imitate."[140] They contended that the contemporary husband was only a "silly boy."[141] They stressed the important differences between men and women and exhorted their male readers to assume the "strong-man part" in their marriages and not become "soft" or "sensitive."[142] They blamed "masculinized" wives and "feminized" husbands for causing the divorce rate and the incidence of homosexuality to go up.[143] They reminded men that an "accepted test of manliness is rigid emotional control," and that it was thus appropriate to let their wives take the initiative in expressing feelings.[144] While most of the articles and books dealing with the shortcomings of American men were more descriptive than prescriptive, they did help to promulgate the notion that masculinity was, once again, in "crisis." After having lapsed into domesticity once the war had ended, men now had to awake from their suburban complacency and assert their masculine qualities.

The other reason why masculinity was becoming a major social problem was that the United States was facing a growing threat to its national security in the form of Soviet communism. Fear of another, more devastating war had taken hold of the American public not long after Gen. Douglas MacArthur had accepted the surrender of Japanese forces on the deck of the USS *Missouri*, in Tokyo Bay, on September 2, 1945. The seeds of this fear had been planted by President Truman's decision to use the most awesome, lethal weapon ever devised—the atomic bomb—to bring the Pacific conflict to a close without having to invade Japan. While the bombings of Hiroshima and Nagasaki had accomplished that objective, it also left Americans anxious about the terrible power they had unleashed, and how it might someday be used against them. In the following months, newspapers carried maps showing concentric circles of destruction radiating outward from the centers of American cities. In November, *Life* ran a prospective account of how millions of lives would be snuffed out during a thirty-six-hour Russian missile barrage. As a historian of this period has put it, the months after the war were a "time of cultural crisis when the American people confronted a new and threatening reality of almost unfathomable proportions."[145]

Perhaps the greatest impact on the American state of mind was made by John Hersey's searing account of the destruction of Hiroshima, published in the August 31, 1946, issue of the *New Yorker*. For the first time, readers could learn about how the bomb had affected ordinary people on the ground in that Japanese city—a clerk, a doctor, a tailor's widow, a German priest—and empathize with their suffering. Realization that Americans were not immune from such horrors came in September 1949, when Truman announced that the Soviets had exploded a bomb of their own the month before. But, instead of spurring talk of bilateral disarmament, this event caused many Americans to place their hopes for a secure future in rapidly building a nuclear arsenal—not just to defend the country, but to launch a preemptive strike on the Soviet Union (or, in the summer of 1950, on North Korea).[146] The ensuing arms race between the two superpowers, designed to make nuclear war—thanks to the doctrine of "mutually assured destruction" (MAD)—unthinkable, gave the American public some feeling of security but did not banish the troubling thought that, someday, the country might find itself engaged in an exchange of intercontinental missiles that would make World War II look like a fight between toddlers in a sandbox.

The way most Americans dealt with this eventuality was not by panicking or resigning themselves to the inevitable, but by taking steps to protect themselves. Air raid shelters, marked by their slightly ominous black-and-yellow, triangular signs urging passersby to "take shelter in event of an attack," sprouted in the basements of urban buildings, while, in the suburbs, some families, with government encouragement, created fallout shelters in their basements, complete with sufficient stores of canned food and water to last for several weeks. Millions of school children routinely carried out air raid drills, giving them a welcome break from class if not a real sense of safety from atomic annihilation. These defensive measures—ill conceived as they may look in retrospect—did reassure citizens that *something* was being done to protect them, but, underneath, they remained worried. Fear of a nuclear holocaust, against which they were, in fact, helpless, lay beneath the surface of daily life in the 1950s, like some fatal disease—in remission, but never truly eliminated. Realizing that unacknowledged anxiety was as good a goad to get Americans into the cinemas and drive-in theaters as the pulchritude of a Marilyn Monroe, Hollywood studios churned out a host of productions dealing explicitly or implicitly with an enemy attack. These ranged from the ridiculous but still terrifying *Them!* (1954), in which the invaders were mutant ants, to the psychologically unsettling *Invasion of the Body Snatchers* (1956), to the more subdued by equally chilling *On the Beach* (1959), which portrayed the sad loneliness of the few survivors of a nuclear war.

A smaller, but just as important, group of films played upon Americans' hopes rather than their fears. They showed how, in the past, crises and great danger had awakened the fighting spirit in a few indomitable heroes, turning imminent defeat into victory. The coming of war to the Korean peninsula in June 1950 and the United States' subsequent participation in this conflict lent a dose of stark reality to this recurrent theme. Almost always these "heroes" who saved the day were men—self-contained, self-sufficient, and stoical figures like Marshal Will Kane, who postpones his retirement and intention to marry his Quaker fiancée in order to defend a peaceful Western town against a gang of four desperadoes, in the 1952 classic *High Noon*. Here Gary Cooper dusted off his persona of reluctant warrior, played most effectively before World War II in *Sergeant York*. Once again he struggled to meet competing urges—love and fighting, personal happiness and social threat—choosing, once again, to put the greater good ahead of his own. Kane's decision to remain and fight is more courageous because he has to do so alone: the rest of the townspeople are too passive and self-absorbed to help him. The lesson for contemporary audiences was that the security of America depended upon brave individuals willing to act when others weren't. Strength lay not in numbers, but in the steely resolve of the individual.

No figure in American folklore better embodied this independent-minded, rock-solid heroism than the "good gunman"—the solitary, enigmatic, and rootless stranger of the Wild West, who rides into town, confronts evil, defeats it, and then rides off silently into the sunset. In places where law and order spoke through the barrel of a rifle rather than from the bench, these Western heroes were indispensable. And so they seemed to be in the soporific, child-besotted 1950s. As an antidote to this conformist and nonconfrontational Zeitgeist they had no equal. Soon imitations of Gary Cooper and his high-noon showdown were showing up on the big screen—most famously, Alan Ladd as *Shane* (1953). Many of these gunslingers arrived covered in dust: they had become anachronisms even in their own day, and audiences were meant to regard them with a mixture of affection and consternation, as they did John Wayne in most of his postwar cowboy roles.[147] Perhaps because they ran the risk of coming across a bit oversized and overwrought on the big screen, Western heroes found a more fitting venue on television. There, in the living room, they became somewhat domesticated, more inclined to work cooperatively, in teams, than as lone wolves. In the era's most powerful medium, they became dominant and ubiquitous during the fifties: in any given week during 1959, American families had forty-eight westerns to choose among.[148] Shows like *The Lone Ranger, Davy Crockett, Gunsmoke, Have Gun—Will Travel, Wagon Train, Cheyenne, Wanted—Dead or Alive, Bronco, Bonanza*, and *Rawhide* drew millions of viewers. Among them were untold numbers of preadolescent and teenage boys, looking as much for a male role model as for an escape from their secure, but largely unchallenging world.

The fighting in Korea made war also a subject for popular culture, if not always one suitable for TV.[149] Many movies revisited World War II and presented its heroes as strong leaders who prevailed over cowardice and prudence by dint of sheer determination to win at all costs. Gregory Peck evinced this essential quality in *Twelve O'Clock High* (1949), as did Robert Ryan in *Men in War* (1957) and Montgomery Clift in *The Young Lions* (1957), to mention just a few.[150] Films about earlier wars shared with horse operas the underlying rationale of sounding an alarm: America faced major challenges abroad and could not afford to remain self-satisfied and disengaged from these threats. An important corollary to this message was that the country needed strong, bold, courageous young men to step forward and into the boots of these manly precursors. It would soon be their turn to follow their fathers into battle, displaying their mettle as the older generation had done. From this perspective, the constant airing of westerns and war stories during the 1950s can be seen as one continuous military recruiting advertisement.[151] (The TV series *West Point*, which aired the year after the success of the 1955 movie *The Long Gray Line*, was part of this indoctrination.)

The message sold well. At the peak of *Davy Crockett*'s popularity, at the end of 1955, Americans were buying five thousand coonskin caps a week and spending the equivalent (in today's money) of more than $2 billion on this talisman and related paraphernalia.[152] The sale of toy guns, holsters, and spurs in the mid-1950s brought in roughly the same amount.[153] War toys were also popular items: the sister of one Vietnam veteran has recently recalled how hundreds of "plastic green army men" collected by her brothers to "spin out their imaginary battles" populated the backyards in which they grew up.[154]

More tellingly, these programs and movies contributed greatly to the "militarization" of America toward the end of the Eisenhower years. With memories of the frustrating Korean stalemate fading, boys coming of age were easily caught up in this mood. Thanks to their demographics as well as their enthusiasm, more youngsters joined the Boy Scouts than ever before.[155] They also reacted positively to stories about the country's military forces, such as a 1959 piece in *Life* that rhapsodized about a new generation of "elite" Marines.[156] They accepted the revived truism that taking up arms for their country was a "natural step toward their culturally acceptable status of manhood."[157] Interest in attending one of the service academies increased. Early in the 1960s, following a new president's call for larger military, more young men signed up for the army than had done so a few years before.[158] As one historian of the Vietnam War has concluded, it is difficult to "exaggerate the extent to which young boys growing up in the 1950s and early 1960s were captivated by fantasies of warfare."[159] This youthful patriotism was part and parcel of a more general shift in the national temperament and self-awareness as the Eisenhower era came to an end. There was a growing sense that one generation was moving off the stage of history to make room for a younger and more energetic one. More particularly, this involved a new emphasis on masculine values and qualities—attributes necessary for the United States to compete successfully with what was regarded as a militant Soviet Union. To restrain the Russians and prevent them from gaining world dominance, America needed a more virile spirit. The appeal of this was evident in the appearance of well-muscled, handsome males with beards, tattoos, and eye patches—sailors, cowboys, policemen, jet pilots, and jackhammer operators—in ads for products ranging from cigarettes to sparkling beverages, from rental cars to razors. "Soft," suburban pitchmen like Ozzie Nelson were out, and the "he-man" was back.[160] Magazine racks in train stations now carried copies of *Playboy, True, Sir!, Esquire,* and *Saga* alongside *Parents* and the *Ladies Home Journal.*

The Harvard historian Arthur M. Schlesinger Jr. addressed the need for a revived American manliness in an influential essay he wrote for *Esquire* magazine in the fall of 1958. Echoing concerns previously expressed by David Riesman, Margaret Mead, Alfred Kinsey, and a host of prominent commentators that American women had become too dominant, had pushed their husbands too far, and "demasculinized" them, Schlesinger outlined this apparent "crisis" of masculinity.[161] He described how men had been "increasingly merged in the American household" and thus lost their distinctive gender identity. Meanwhile, their wives had gained more power by working outside the home. "They seem," he wrote, "an expanding, aggressive force, seizing new domains like a conquering army, while men, more and more on the defensive, are hardly able to hold their own and gratefully accept assignments from their new rulers." By using such language and such analogies, Schlesinger was likening women to the communist forces that were then challenging Americans at various flashpoints around the globe. Both "enemies" could only be defeated if men cast off their passive roles as "organization men" and asserted themselves vigorously in public life. "A virile life would be definite and hard-hitting," Schlesinger opined, "respecting debate and dissent, seeking clarity and decision."[162]

The liberal-Democratic historian did not spell this out in his article, but the person he had in mind to take the lead in the nation's masculine revival was none other than John F. Kennedy. After having been at first concerned about Kennedy's not being sufficiently liberal, Schlesinger had come around to recognizing the future president's potential to take the country in a bold new direction. To a striking degree, Schlesinger appeared—unconsciously—to link Kennedy's leadership ability with his sexual vitality. He perhaps first glimpsed this quality when he held his first long political conversation with the presidential aspirant at Hyannisport, on Cape Cod, in July of 1959.[163] At any rate, when Schlesinger wrote a second piece for *Esquire* ("The New Mood in Politics") the following January, the newly appointed political advisor used language that was unmistakably sexual: "new forces, new energies, new values are straining for expression and for release," he noted. The "politics of fatigue" was now passing from the scene, to be replaced by a new politics that was "spirited, articulate, inventive, incoherent, turbulent, with energy shooting off wildly in all directions."[164] Schlesinger's reaction to Kennedy was shared by many public service–minded men of his generation—the so-called whiz kids like Robert McNamara and Theodore Sorensen, who were drawn to Washington like moths to a flame to serve in the dynamic new administration. But an energized, youthful new leadership was also coming to the fore in other professional spheres—exceptional men (and a few women) such as those profiled in a 1962 *Life* photo essay on America's emerging leaders, all of whom were distinguished by their "tough, self-imposed standards of individual excellence," "zest for hard work," "dedication to something larger than public success," "boldness to try out new ideas," and "hard-bitten, undaunted hopefulness about man."[165]

With his admiration for James Bond, his love of competitive sports, his ample charm, shy smile, nimble wit, keen intelligence, and good looks, Kennedy set the bar for these ambitious and highly capable figures, while inspiring countless other Americans who heard him speak or caught a glimpse of him in person or on television. There was an abundance of charisma radiating from him, making Kennedy an inspiring icon for a baby-boom generation still in its teens. His youth and vigor were eminently seductive to both sexes.[166] For innumerable young men, Kennedy's dynamic manner, vision, and lofty language touched an idealistic chord deep within them. When the newly elected president stood hatless and coatless on the steps of the Capitol on a crisply cold January day in 1961 and declared that "the torch has been passed to a new generation of Americans—born in this century, tempered by war, disciplined by a hard and bitter peace, proud of our ancient heritage," they could be forgiven for thinking he was speaking directly to them, even if it was actually people of his own age he had in mind. When Kennedy wagged his finger, and in his cadenced, Boston Brahmin voice vowed to "pay any price, bear any burden, meet any hardship, support any friend, oppose any foe, in order to assure the survival and the success of liberty,"

America's youth took this pledge to heart as their own. And when the young president implored his fellow citizens to "ask not what your country can do for you—ask what you can do for your country," they could not resist taking this as an exhortation aimed directly at each and every one of them to join in whatever noble crusade their confident, irrepressible leader might choose to embark upon.

Kennedy's coming to power was, in some ways, just what many young American men had been longing for. Growing up in the "dull, placid, and sterile" 1950s, in mother-run homes, with fathers whom they saw little of and—often—did not admire greatly, many of these youth had lacked real-life models of assertive, self-confident manhood.[167] Their joining gangs can be seen as an attempt to compensate for this deficiency: the bravado, initiation rites, group loyalty, battles over "turf" rights, and "hypermasculinity" that were associated with these predominantly urban groups aped, in a puerile and distorted way, how "real" men were supposed to act. More broadly, the increasing rate of violence among male adolescents during this decade suggests a deep level of frustration and failure to mature into manhood.[168] Extensive media interest in this problem, the impact of movies like *Rebel Without a Cause* and *West Side Story*, and pronounced public concern also say much about how young males were widely perceived at this time—as having strayed from the conventional path leading from childhood into adulthood. And, in fact, a large proportion of American youth were having trouble making this transition. To some extent, this was because they regarded the world of grownups with disdain, if not outright rejection. Books like Paul Goodman's *Growing Up Absurd* (1961) catalogued their grievances with a postwar society that appeared to deny them any chance for a meaningful existence and that sought only to stifle their individuality and force them to "adjust" to preexisting and inflexible norms. Novels like *Catcher in the Rye* captured a lurking suspicion that all adults were "phonies," incapable of honest thoughts or deeds. The hypocrisy young people found pervasive in the older generation dismayed them and intensified the normal tendency of youth to disparage their elders and long to do better in their own lives. The idealistic rhetoric of Kennedy's inaugural address spoke to this hunger for authenticity and vigorous, masculine action.[169]

Its impact can be seen in the memoirs of young men who responded to these lofty words a few years later by joining the military and going off willingly to fight in Vietnam, as tens of thousands did until the conflict there grew bloody and intractable.[170] In 1960, Philip Caputo signed up for the Marines, partially out of boredom with life in suburban Chicago, but also due to a "missionary idealism" engendered by the "intoxicating spirit" of those days. He was searching for a "chance to live heroically," his appetite for this kind of experience having been piqued by watching John Wayne lead charges across Pacific beaches. The recruiters who showed up at Loyola University that year had had little trouble persuading him that war offered the "ultimate adventure." Caputo was already eager to prove to himself that he was tough and show his parents he could be responsible and act like a man. The recruitment slogan "The Marine Corps Builds Men" confirmed that he had found the way to do this.[171]

Ron Kovic, only fourteen when he watched Kennedy's inaugural, was even more impressionable, his head filled with images from *Sands of Iwo Jima*: he and his friends would spontaneously hum the Marine Corps anthem while watching it.[172] They turned his backyard in Massapequa, on Long Island, into a battlefield and carried out recon "missions" the way the Marine Guidebook instructed them to do. To build up his body, Kovic lifted weights and wrestled in high school. He cried each time he lost a match, as he had done whenever his Little League team had come up short. He dreamed he was playing for the Yankees, and, in this recurrent reverie, they never lost. This relentless competitiveness and testing masked feelings that somehow he still did not fully measure up as a man. Like Jim Stark, he didn't want to end up like his father, ringing up groceries bags at the local A&P. He wanted to be noticed and talked about. He wanted to be a "hero."[173]

William Calley, an unhappy insurance investigator, had less than five dollars left in his pocket when he got his draft notice in the mail. To turn his life around, he decided to try his luck in OCS. Short in stature, he was captivated by the six-feet-two army recruiter he encountered in Miami, who "looked like an American high school hero," and Calley signed up on the spot. Officer training gave him a confidence he had not possessed before and allowed him to overcome his inhibitions about killing people. Later to be charged with murdering unarmed civilians at My Lai, he, too, had already seen his share of movies like *To Hell and Back* and envisioned his pending service in Southeast Asia as a real-life re-run. "We will go to Vietnam and be Audie Murphys," he prophesied. "Kick in the door, run in the hooch, give it a good burst." When he received his orders for Vietnam in December 1967, Calley saw this as a long-denied opportunity to throw his modest weight around: "I'm the big American from across the sea. I'll sock it to these people."[174] He was not the only young American to succumb to what a psychiatrist who worked with Vietnam veterans has called the allure of "physical dominance."[175]

A desire to prove their worth and thereby assuage feelings of inadequacy or failure prompted many of Calley and Kovic's contemporaries to head over to their local recruiters.[176] (Worries about being insufficiently "manly" even troubled forty-four-year-old John F. Kennedy in his first dealings with the Soviet leader Nikita Khrushchev. After their confrontational first meeting, in Vienna in June 1961, a "shattered" Kennedy returned to his suite, where he ranted that the Russian premier had treated him "like a little boy." Kennedy vowed never to let that happen again.)[177] How much of this volunteer spirit was due to enthusiasm for the war is hard to determine. Unquestionably, many young men signed up simply to avoid being drafted, as often happens during a time of war.[178] But working-class enlistees later interviewed for a book about their motivation repeatedly cited a desire to become "somebody" by fighting for their country. A Polish-American named Billy Cizinski attempted to volunteer when he was only fifteen in part because his family situation was unstable, but also because he considered himself just a "dumb Pollack" who had to pick fights in order to win acceptance from his friends. Five-feet-five Frank Matthews, from a small town in Alabama, joined the Marines in order to show he could measure up: because of his lack of height, he felt he constantly needed to become an "overachiever just to feel like I had achieved at all." Another recruit, Richard Deegan, signed up largely because his father had once told him he "didn't have the balls to do it." Many of these Vietnam volunteers came from families in which the father was either absent or had a strained relationship with his son or sons.[179] Partially for this reason, some had had trouble maturing emotionally and had gotten into the trouble with the law. A number of these men looked to the army to help them grow up.[180] While many conceded that a major reason for joining the military was the absence of better options or reluctance to take their chances in the draft, these psychological factors should not be underestimated.

In addition to offering them a chance to demonstrate their manhood, the war in Vietnam met other basic male needs. One of these was finding mates. Generally speaking, earning a good, reliable income helps to make men attractive as marriage partners.[181] But, in the mid-1960s, such a desirable economic status was becoming more difficult to attain for many working-class youth who had not gone to college. With so many baby boomers entering the workforce, competition for jobs was intensifying. During this decade, unemployment among males ages sixteen to nineteen averaged 12.5 percent—far higher than among the population as a whole.[182] Recent changes in the labor market had put a greater premium than in past decades on having advanced education and higher skills. Furthermore, more women were attending and graduating from college than in previous generations, and they were vying successfully with their male peers for many entry-level white-collar positions, such as clerical ones.[183] In addition, married women were increasingly competing for jobs: between 1950 and 1970, the percentage of wives who were working outside the home rose from 23.8 to 40.8; for those with children under age eighteen, it more than doubled over those two decades—climbing from 18.4 percent to 39.7.[184] In particular, these women were making inroads into the service sector, taking away low-paying jobs from males.[185] The participation of females tended to depress wages in this part of the economy, thus contributing to a widening income gap between middle- and working-class men.[186] As a result of these developments, semiskilled young men looking for jobs in the middle of the decade were increasingly at a disadvantage in attracting potential mates. Certain demographic trends were worsening their predicament.

Historically, young single males have often outnumbered their female counterparts because of the tendency of some women in their teens and early twenties to marry older men. But this discrepancy was greater than usual in the early 1960s, mainly because so many women were continuing the pattern from the previous decade and marrying early, while their male contemporaries were having difficulty finding jobs and bringing in good incomes.[187] Domestic life remained a primary female focus, but women's choice of partners was changing: they were increasingly inclined to select older, more financially secure men. At the start of the decade, 70 percent of women were married by their twenty-fourth birthday, a much higher percentage than in 1940 (42 percent) or

1930 (50 percent).[188] More than 16 percent had walked down the aisle before they celebrated their twentieth birthday. In 1960, 16.1 percent of females ages fifteen to nineteen were married, compared to only 3.9 percent of males. In 1968, 410,574 women under the age of twenty became brides, but only 176,274 males in this age group wed. This inclination for women to marry at a young age was strongest in the South: there the number of teenage brides rose by 36 percent between 1960 and 1969. By the end of the decade, in 40 percent of all marriages in eight Southern states and Utah, the bride was under twenty. This meant that young single males in these states had to compete for spouses their age or younger from among a considerably smaller pool of still available females. Outside the South, men in this age group were facing a similar dilemma, although one not quite numerically disadvantageous. Nationally, in 1964, two and a half times as many female teenagers were getting married as males in the eighteen-to-nineteen age bracket. In 1969, a third of all women getting married were still in their teens, but only 14 percent of men. While 717,000 females under twenty had tied the knot, only 311,000 men their age had done so.[189]

Instead of marrying, settling down, and starting a family, more and more of these males were living by themselves. In 1950, some 254,000 men ages twenty to thirty-four remained unmarried, but by 1960 nearly 2 million men between the ages of twenty and forty—one-fourth of the total number of men in this age group—were still single. The great majority of them had never been married. In desperation, many were turning to classified ads and dating agencies for help in finding spouses. Between 50,000 and 75,000 men were seeking psychiatric help because of their failure to accomplish this goal.[190] But their situation did not improve. By 1966–1967, 6.3 million males between the ages of eighteen and twenty-four were single, versus only 5 million females. In the age bracket twenty-five to thirty-four, there was a surplus of some 618,000 single men.[191] By 1974, the year after the last American troops left Vietnam, the number of unmarried men in their twenties and thirties had increased by 55 percent over what it had been in 1950. During the same time period, the number of single women increased by only 25 percent.[192] In the mid-1970s, unmarried males in the twenty-to-thirty-four age group still exceeded single females by over half a million. For every two men presumably in the marriage market, there were only 1.4 available females.[193] From a reproductive standpoint, single men faced even greater odds of fulfilling their biological urge to pass along their genes. For, in their lifetime, American fertility had taken a historically unprecedented nosedive. After reaching a peak of 4.3 million births in 1957, the baby boom had fizzled: the birth rate for married women fell from 122.9 per 1,000 persons that year to 105.6 in 1964.[194] By 1972, the birth rate in the United States fell below the replacement level.[195] A year later, the rate was down to 69.2—44 percent lower than its historic high in the mid-1950s.[196] Many young unmarried women were by then successfully relying upon contraceptives to limit unplanned pregnancies.[197] Married women were choosing to postpone and limit their births so that they could spend more years in the workforce. The once heralded baby boom had turned into a bust.[198]

Under these adverse circumstances, single working-class men in search of a wife and children faced an uphill struggle. The odds of their achieving either goal were not good, compared with what they had been for their fathers: statistically, they were 33 percent less likely to marry, and, if they did, could count on having, on average, one fewer child. They had few resources to make them stand out among their peers in this fierce reproductive competition. One way for these economically disadvantaged young men to acquire more human capital and thus increase their desirability as mates was to join the military and serve in Vietnam. For most men, there was little or no financial gain from signing up, unless they were unemployed: pay for enlisted men was "abysmally low" early in the 1960s and remained at this level even after the United States began sending large numbers of soldiers to Southeast Asia.[199] However, there has typically been a marriage "payoff" for men who fight in wars and return victorious, most notably for Americans after World War II. Women are generally attracted to men who will make good protectors as well as providers.[200] Men thinking about enlisting in the sixties could assume—or at least hope—that this would be the case for them, too. Some observers of the Vietnam era certainly felt this was a reasonable expectation. George Gilder, a writer who had briefly served in the Marines, contended that most men joined the corps "in part as a virility rite, with women assumed as a reward."[201] Teenage soldiers who had little success with girls prior to enlisting did, in fact, gain a boost in appeal from wearing the uniform. The sister of Jim Schuler, who came to her Catholic girls' academy in his neatly pressed army uniform after returning from Vietnam, recalls that his appearance caused a "palpable thrill"—a "near-swooning adulation that made Jim smile with embarrassment and pleasure."[202]

Volunteers for this war clearly had a variety of reasons for doing so, but the generally low socioeconomic status of the great majority of these enlisted men suggests that most aspired to "get ahead," in one way or another, through wartime service.[203] In many ways, they had not yet grown up, discovered who they were, or been fully socialized. They had not yet acquired the skills or self-confidence to accomplish much in life. They badly needed to affirm their own worth.[204] Their quests for higher self-esteem, peer acceptance, and escape from a bad family environment were closely intertwined objectives and thus difficult to isolate from each other.[205] One can argue, however, that all these perceived benefits were prerequisites for attracting potential spouses, and that this was the ultimate and most desired "reward" for going off to war. That a large proportion of soldiers serving in Vietnam were susceptible to these motivations is evident in what is known about their group composition. First of all, two-thirds were volunteers (as compared to only one-third in World War II), indicating that at least that many were serving in Vietnam because they wanted to be there.[206] Until the war started to go badly for the United States, it was generally popular in the enlisted ranks. Second, the average age of these soldiers was twenty-two (not nineteen, as is often erroneously stated, but still significantly lower than the average age of twenty-six in World War II), making it statistically likely that most were still single.[207] This surmise is supported by the fact that only 17,539 married men were killed in Vietnam out of a total death toll (including those who died from nonhostile action) of 58,202.[208]

Signing up for Vietnam also appealed to many young men who had been raised in conservative, patriotic families with a history of military service and a respect for traditional values.[209] Their country was asking them to serve, and they did not shrink from answering this call to duty. They were doing what was expected of them and what they believed was right. By putting on a uniform, these volunteers were making a visible, personal statement about what America meant to them, and what they held dear about it. The values they were affirming were cultural as well as political. The 1960s was a time of sweeping change, with conventional mores being challenged by new, seemingly radical ways of thinking, speaking, dressing, and behaving. Institutions ranging from colleges and universities to the military to the family were coming under attack. Many tradition-minded youth, as well as their elders, found this new lifestyle and its hostile attitude toward authority alarming and threatening. Their way of life appeared to be as much in danger as American troops over in Vietnam. By joining the military, they were coming to its defense as well. They were also finding a clear purpose at a time when much in their lives was uncertain and confusing.[210]

One of the brewing cultural battles of the 1960s was over sexuality. Easy access to contraception, a surge in premarital sex, a sharp rise in the number of unmarried couples, an increase in births outside of marriage, a somewhat higher divorce rate, the prevalence of sexually charged images in the movies and popular magazines such as *Playboy*, talk of "women's liberation," and a concomitant trend toward gender equality were all disconcerting developments in the eyes of many conservative Americans.[211] Countless young men raised to believe in male superiority, male sexual prerogatives, and clear differences between the sexes took strong exception to these trends: just as they were entering manhood, expectations concerning gender behavior appeared to be changing, and not in their favor. More wives were not only working but also questioning their domestic "golden cage." Some suburban housewives were paying heed to Betty Friedan, whose *Feminine Mystique* was published the same year Kennedy was assassinated. In an interview that appeared in *Life*, she declared: "I don't like this self-pitying, trapped housewife bit. I think women who have been victims of the feminine mystique should do something about it, should attack the things they used to take for granted, should grow."[212] A few years later, advice columnist Joyce Brothers proclaimed that married women were "at last coming into their own as human beings" and urged more of them to follow this example.[213] For some women, this included walking out of bad marriages: the US divorce rate was starting to creep up, with one of every three marriages now ending in a courtroom. Many of these marriages had lasted for fifteen years or more.[214]

At the same time, younger single women were becoming more sexually active than they had been a decade before. They were either taking a cue from their mothers' own tentative steps toward independence or deciding to live their own lives according to different rules. In any event, the Pill and the diaphragm had found their way into female college dormitories early in the decade, although they were probably used less than Gloria Steinem believed to be the case after conducting a campus survey in 1962.[215] And this greater sexual freedom was by no means confined to academia. By 1967, with taboos about birth control fading, as many as one-fifth of women of childbearing age were regularly controlling their fertility.

This emerging female prerogative to choose when and with whom to have children would, in the ensuing decades, have a profoundly transformational impact on American life—on the importance of marriage, the size and structure of families, and on "sexual politics." Indeed, no single other development would so significantly and irreversibly tilt this balance of power in favor of women than the widespread availability and use of oral contraception.[216] But, in the mid-1960s, this shift was still in the offing. More couples were also choosing to become POSSLQs ("Persons of the Opposite Sex Sharing Living Quarters") instead of man and wife. The number of Americans cohabitating "in sin" rose by 20 percent in the 1960s.[217] Having enjoyed this amount of sexual freedom and experience, single women in their twenties were seemingly no longer the blushing, shy maidens of the 1950s.

But this impression was misleading: it made the first half of the 1960s appear more revolutionary than they actually were. In fact, most women—married and single alike—still cast a cold eye on infidelity and sought happiness in what the mainstream magazines referred to as the "Standard American Marriage." They wanted to be good wives, wanted to do what Dr. Brothers told them to do: "Go out of your way to keep yourself sweet and dainty."[218] In 1966, the *Saturday Evening Post* could inform its readers that most of them were content to "choose the traditional role." Fifty-two percent of married couples considered themselves "very happy" and another 25 percent "moderately happy." Only 5 percent admitted they weren't happy.[219] College women were still more focused on finding husbands than on forging careers. If they did have sex before marriage, it was most likely with the man they intended to wed. Even among emerging radical groups such as Students for a Democratic Society, females largely played an ancillary role—mimeographing manifestos instead of writing them, deferring meekly to the talkative and forceful men who ran the meetings. Reality for most American women lay somewhere between what Gloria Steinem hoped it was and what the mainstream magazines needed to believe it still was. The truth of the matter was that American marital and sexual mores were beginning to change but had not yet changed that much. The real sexual revolution was yet to come.

Some young men in the mid-1960s might have been enjoying the benefits of this female sexual emancipation, but not all of them were so open-minded or thrilled by this development. Many remained wedded to traditional mores.[220] They had qualms about this heady new freedom in the bedroom, even if their disdain was tinged with envy and frustration over not having partaken of it. [221] (They, too, ogled the *Playboy* center-folds, but only touched the slick paper.) They were not comfortable on the shifting sands of American morality. They sought more solid ground on which to build their lives. At a time when their contemporaries were experimenting with unorthodox lifestyles, they preferred the old familiar one. They wanted an identity that was straightforward and unambiguous. Since they were men who honored tradition, this meant an identity based upon conventional notions of gender. Traditional masculinity was at the core of their sense of being. To cultivate it, they sought to develop a "male mystique." Raised in the long gray shadow of World War II, they saw military service as a major milestone in this process. Fighting in a war overseas was even more defining. It was the rite of passage they had learned to hold sacred. It was answering the call to duty of a country that they believed always stood for and did the right thing.[222]

Volunteering for Vietnam was also a kind of strategic retreat from an increasingly turbulent American society—a way of removing themselves and regrouping on their own territory, under their own rules. For some of these conservative young men, going off to fight can be seen as their attempt to distance themselves from the sexual "revolution" that was taking place in the United States, establishing their manhood apart from women.[223] Becoming a member of an all-male military fraternity strengthened their commitment to male uniqueness and male dominance at a time when these traits were being questioned.

The relative youthfulness of troops sent to Vietnam suggests that many had not had sexual relations with women before enlisting.[224] In fact, many later confessed to having been virgins at that time. Army service afforded some of these GIs a way to avoid having to confront this lack of experience or, alternatively, an opportunity to make up for it.[225] Ron Kovic, for one, seems to have had little or no intercourse before joining the Marines when he was eighteen: he had listened to his priest's admonition that sex was a "sin."[226] But, in his memoir, he implies that he occasionally had sex while serving in the Marines. Many of the veterans treated for PTSD by psychiatrist Jonathan Shay told him they had had their first sexual encounters in Vietnamese brothels. This initiation reinforced preconceptions that sex was an emotionless act of conquest over passive female "sex objects," even if such experiences also left some young soldiers wary and fearful of women.[227]

Having their way with prostitutes or other Vietnamese women enabled some GIs to compensate for the powerlessness and fear they faced daily in the jungles of Vietnam.[228] However, in their dealings with these Vietnamese women, some soldiers released sexual frustrations caused not just by the dearth of other ("round-eye") females, but also by the growing independence and freedom that American women were assuming.[229] This gender animosity was apparent in the misogynistic language prevalent in the military at that time, starting in basic training when fresh recruits were called "ladies" and "pussies."[230] The sexual mistreatment and the rape that occurred with alarming frequency in Vietnam also attest to an underlying animus toward women in general.[231] Because Vietnamese women belonged to an alien culture and could easily be suspected of consorting with the enemy, it was more acceptable to project this anger onto them than direct it at women back home.[232] GIs dehumanized the Vietnamese women with whom they had sex by calling them "slope cunts" or "boom-boom girls."

In time of war, soldiers typically use abusive antifemale terminology to harden themselves, channel their rage, create a hypermasculine self-image, and build close, emotional bonds with their comrades. The common coinage of expletive binds men as intimates and assuages individual guilt over the attitudes that give rise to these words. Such language, in turn, "reframes" the reality they are confronting. Under the stress of combat, depersonalizing language can enable GIs to lose their inhibitions and regress. [233] Their actions become as primitive and brutal as their words. An anger and aggressiveness that are considered inappropriate in civilian life become valued assets under fire.[234] When violence is omnipresent, survival is at stake, adrenalin is flowing, and the rules of civilized behavior appear to have lost all meaning, soldiers can release bottled-up feelings of sexual inferiority, frustration, and rage at whatever females who happen to be in their vicinity.[235] They victimize in order to escape feeling of being victims. During the Vietnam conflict, powerful sexual urges, coupled with a previous failure to form normal, loving relationships with women, easily turned some American troops into sexual predators and rapists, as happened, most notably, at My Lai.[236] But the frequency of such abusive, degrading behavior suggests that an even deeper anxiety was being expressed: a fear of losing control over women as well as over their own lives.[237]

Sexually as in many other ways, Vietnam attracted young, single, immature, idealistic and tradition-minded Americans with the promise of affirming their masculinity. It offered them a chance to impose their will and reverse a flow of events that was undermining their stature and distributing their power to women. Vietnam lured them by seeming to hold the solution to their existential needs—to earn self-respect and honor among their peers, as well as admiration from the women they hoped to court and marry. In fulfilling these aspirations, they would achieve some degree of success. According to some studies, a slightly higher percentage of veterans of the Vietnam War ended up getting married than men who did not serve there, or men who did not go into the military at all; excepting those who saw extensive combat or came to suffer from PTSD, these veterans were as apt to stay in these marriages as nonveterans and to have more children than the latter did.[238] Given that most former GIs came from low socioeconomic backgrounds and had relatively few skills, only a high-school education, and limited job prospects, these marital and parental outcomes are somewhat surprising. They suggest that serving in this war, unpopular and unsuccessful as it was, did, in fact, yield some of the sexual and reproductive rewards its willing participants had hoped to gain from it.

In most other regards, of course, Vietnam would turn out to have been a horrendous illusion—the promised revival of muscular American masculinity, Kennedy's pledge to spread liberty around the world, the return to traditional values all failed to materialize as the United States and the soldiers sent abroad in its name ran up against the humbling limits of their power.[239] Many lost their innocence, their trust in their leaders, their faith in their country, and their immaculate vision;[240] committed crimes and witnessed other reprehensible and inhuman acts; tasted the bitterness of defeat; surrendered much of their authority and honor; endured and inflicted pain; became bitter and alienated; and acquired lasting psychic as well as physical scars.[241] These soldiers came back to an utterly changed country—one in which, as a result of this foreign misadventure and the domestic upheaval it accelerated, they would be less appreciated than before. This time, the gamble of waging war did not pay off—not as it had for their fathers. Much more was suffered than just the first defeat in America's history. The nation's self-confidence was gone, and the image of its men was in tatters. As Landon Jones, chronicler of the "boomers" has put it, "The optimism and hope that the generation took into the Vietnam years only made its eventual disenchantment more devastating. They had been young and idealistic and Vietnam made them old and cynical."[242]

Chapter 6

MEN ON THE ROPES— THE CONTEMPORARY FEMINIST CHALLENGE

As he pushed his way down the aisle, headed for the cockpit, Waleed al Shehri stumbled toward one of the crew members. It was a stewardess. Amid the roar of voices rising around him he could hear the high whine of her screams. In spite of all of the chaotic movements to his left and right, as passengers half rose in their seats and hands reached out to grab him, he could see her face distorted with fear, her body braced against a seat back, blocking him. For a brief second they locked eyes, and the look on her face became panic-stricken, but still she did not move. He lunged forward. He was very near her now. Then their bodies met. He felt hers, soft but unyielding. This forced intimacy with a strange woman in a uniform repulsed him. It was different than the other night when the whore had taken off her clothes in the hotel room—the first time in his life he had seen a grown woman naked. He had wanted her—to experience what it was like to lie with a female, once, before he died—but afterward he had hated her and her foolish chatter, and he and his brother had thrown her out into the hallway as one would discard a soiled towel. This time he felt no desire, only rage at her stubborn defiance—that it was a woman who stood in his way. Then he drew his arm back, tightened his grip on the box cutter, and plunged the blade into her uniformed midriff. She groaned and staggered and slid toward the carpet. He stepped over her. The way to the cockpit was now clear. His goal was in sight. God *was* good.

No one will ever know for sure if this is exactly how events unfolded on American Airlines Flight 11 early on the morning of September 11, 2001, when a group of five Arab hijackers seized control and diverted the half-loaded Boeing 767 southward, away from its scheduled route toward Los Angeles, to crash it into the North Tower of the World Trade Center. But from what is known from the phone calls made by another flight attendant, Betty Ong, during the time the aircraft was being commandeered, this scenario closely approximates what transpired. Several persons on board did attempt to prevent the takeover from happening. One was a former Israeli military officer named Daniel Lewin, a passenger in the first-class section who had been sitting a row behind Mohamed Atta and another hijacker and had tried to stop them from reaching the cockpit. His throat was cut, probably by one of the so-called muscle hijackers, making Lewin the first person to die on this fateful day. At least one member of the crew also was killed during the takeover. This was chief flight attendant Karen Ann Martin. She was stabbed to death near the cockpit.[1] Waleed al Shehri, along with his older brother Wail and a third native of Saudi Arabia, Satam al Suqami, were the three muscle hijackers on board the doomed flight, assigned the tasks of subduing the passengers and cabin crew and taking control of the plane's cockpit, so that Atta—the only conspirator on board that flight who had been trained to fly jumbo jets—could then guide the roaring Boeing airliner straight down the Hudson Valley to its unsuspecting target in Lower Manhattan.

The two brothers came from an impoverished border region of Saudia Arabia. They belonged to a prosperous Saudi family whose wealth, like that of Osama bin Laden's, derived from the construction business. They had been raised in the same strict, puritanical Wahhabi school of Islam, which forbids all contact between the sexes before entering into an arranged marriage. As far as can be ascertained, both Wail, twenty-eight, and Waleed, twenty-three, had obeyed this dictum even though they were not fanatical or particularly observant young men. Indeed, they had drifted into al Qaeda's plot to attack America more out of boredom and purposelessness in their lives than because of any deep-seated animosity toward the United States and the values it represented.[2] But the prospect of martyrdom—or was it the fleshly temptations of America?—had ended their sexual abstinence. While staying in the Park Inn Hotel outside Boston in the days preceding September 11, al Suqami and the al Shehri brothers had hired prostitutes.[3] It is likely, given the constraints imposed on their sexual impulses by their family's Islamic belief and from what is known about their activities during the years leading up to 9/11, that none of the three young Saudi men had had intimate relations with a woman ever before. Furthermore, they had almost certainly not had even casual girlfriends or friendships with young females outside their families. For them to have had any such relationships would have been anathema—cause for shame and ostracism, further diminishing their already low status as single males with no great talents or intelligence in a tradition-bound society like Saudi Arabia, where unemployment was rife and their prospects for marriage poor.

In this respect, al Suqami and the two al Shehri brothers were typical of the hijackers of 9/11. While no one background, set of circumstances, or motivation can be said to have characterized all nineteen of these men, the great majority of them did share a lack of experience with the opposite sex. For some, this was a matter of principle; for others, a lack of opportunity or inclination. (All but two of the muscle hijackers were single, as were most of the principal figures in the plot, including three of the four conspirators who flew the planes.)[4] Almost universally, sex was problematic for these would-be martyrs. Many of them regarded women as temptresses—threats to their religious devotion and to their murderous intent, but also to their tenuous masculinity. This hostile, misogynistic attitude frequently could be traced back to their early years. As a boy, Atta, the leader of the 9/11 operation, had been "painfully shy" around women (other than his mother, to whom he was "extremely attached") and, according to his father, had been called a "sissy." After he became more devout, the younger Atta spurned women for being incapable of matching his religious intensity. While studying in Germany, he avoided eye contact with women and informed female Muslims—through their fathers—that they were not welcome in the religion classes he was teaching. He made a point of not walking down a street in Hamburg frequented by prostitutes. In the will he wrote more than five years before boarding Flight 11, Atta requested that no females attend his funeral or visit his grave. He dreaded the "contamination" such contact would bring.[5] A conspirator from the United Arab Emirates, Marwan al-Shehhi, avoided speaking to women and hardly talked about them. Another member of Atta's Hamburg cell, Ziad Jarrah, was so offended by the "Western ways" of German women that he threatened to kill one of them.

Yet, prior to their suicidal attacks on American cities, many of the hijackers had a variety of sexual encounters with such "impure" women. On the evening of September 9, Atta and two companions went to the Pink Pony Strip Club in Daytona Beach, where they indulged in vodka and lap dances.[6] (Atta was wont to "knock back five or six stiff drinks in an evening.")[7] Likewise, two other plotters spent hundreds of dollars on pornographic videos and sex toys while staying in Florida during July 2001.[8] Yet these same men covered photographs of seminaked women in their hotel suite with towels.[9] In San Diego, a Saudi plotter named Nawaf al-Hazmi, frustrated in his efforts to find a bride on Internet sites, frequented a nude bar near the Islamic Center.[10] One of the men who would take over United Flight 93 spent part of his final weekend at an exotic club in Elizabeth, New Jersey.[11] Several other 9/11 hijackers contemplated paying for a female escort service the night before boarding their flight in Boston.[12] While such sexual release is common for males in their teens and twenties who do not enjoy "normal," intimate relationships with women (as it is with soldiers about to face death in war), the fact that these nominally devout Muslim young men—who claimed to revile the United States for its licentiousness—acted this way is puzzling.[13] Were the hijackers hypocrites? Were they really not true believers? Or were these brief sexual encounters somehow revealing about their underlying motives for taking part in this murderous mission?[14]

To resolve this issue requires an examination of Muslim views on women and sexuality, of the gender-related practices in Islamic societies, and of the personal circumstances and prior experiences that may have influenced what these men did during their final days. One possible explanation for their conflicted or repressed sexuality might lie in the tenets of Islam. The Qur'an is by no means coy or puritanical in dealing with relations between the sexes. In fact, more of its pages are devoted to this topic than to any other secular one.[15] By laying down numerous rules and guidelines, the Islamic holy text seeks to codify how men and women should treat one another. An overriding objective of the Qur'an is to impose structure and predictability on this central dimension of human behavior, which is inherently volatile, highly emotional, and thus not readily subject to reason or restraint.

Submission to the will of God is the essence of Islam and the key to happiness. So it behooves male and female Muslims to unquestioningly accept and obey the prescriptions contained in the Qur'an. The most important principle is the polarity of the sexes. Men and women are totally different beings: their natures complement one another. Males are identified with reason, order, and control. Females are associated with sexual passion, disorder, and a lack of control.[16] Desire conflicts with obedience to Islamic law and thus has to be disavowed: since women are the "concrete incarnation" of desire, they have to be brought under male control.[17] While, in theory, the two genders are equal in dignity, in practice males are given precedence, because their qualities allow them more readily to submit to Allah: their powers of reasoning and understanding make them spiritually superior. They are closer to God. This higher status affords males certain prerogatives denied the opposite sex. Their wives are to obey them or risk a beating.[18] Sexual intercourse is a husband's right, and a wife must accede; if she refuses to do so she is accursed.[19] Married women are supposed to repress their own desires. Their husbands are expected to keep their wives' innately powerful sexual urges under control, as they pose a threat to the rule of reason and the divine purpose of life.[20] Single women who have illicit sex (that is, outside of marriage) bring great shame upon their families and are subject to physical punishment, including death, for this breach of honor (*sharaf*).[21] Males who commit adultery or have sex before they marry incur no such penalties unless the woman is "under the jurisdiction of another man"—that is, one whose honor would be violated by such intimate relations.[22] Thus, it is permissible under Islamic law for men to frequent prostitutes. Men may have as many as four wives at one time, as long as they can support them, but women can only have one husband. A Muslim man can divorce his wife simply by declaring his intent to do so, but a married woman has to obtain her husband's consent or establish legally legitimate grounds, such as impotence, for taking this step. Males are awarded higher status in legal matters as well. In court, the testimony of one man counts the same as two testimonies by women. Men are normally given twice the inheritance that women receive. More generally, men are designated "guardians" and protectors for their spouses, and in return for exercising these responsibilities they are to receive passive compliance with their decisions.[23]

Fundamental to Islam is maintaining these and other distinctions between the sexes. To blur these lines is to defy a God-given propriety and duality.[24] Muslim society is organized so as to emphasize and maintain these gender differences. Any deviation from them, such as homosexuality, is harshly condemned.[25] Outside the family circle, males and females inhabit separate spheres and have little to do with each other. Where traditional Islamic values predominate, young people are not allowed to spend time together, form friendships, or have any kind of physical contact. From childhood on, boys and girls are taught to associate sex with sinfulness and to resist any temptation to lust. Both single and married women are to be kept out of the sight of unrelated men—either by staying largely within the home or by covering themselves so that only their hands and eyes are visible. Females who go out into the world—to work or engage in public affairs—risk losing their chastity.[26] The wearing of the *hijab* aims not only to safeguard female modesty but also to reduce the sexual allure of females and their power to seduce males. Of course, such shrouding of the female form can easily have the opposite effect of making the mysterious even more attractive.

At any rate, the segregating of Muslim communities by gender and the emphasizing of female sexuality tend to exacerbate sexual tensions and instill an inordinate (if indiscernible) preoccupation with sex. Men and women think of one another as sexual beings.[27] In this sense, the dictates of Islam war constantly with the predilections of human nature, and the true believer has to wrestle constantly to overcome the latter in seeking to honor the former.[28] This struggle is most intense and trying for youth. From before puberty through their most sexually charged years, young men and women have no sanctioned way to experience physical intimacy without first entering into marriage. While the custom of arranged marriages has facilitated sexual consummation at an early age, especially for women, the requirement that a prospective husband be able to provide for a bride had placed a major economic hurdle in the way. Up until the second half of the twentieth century, the prevalence of polygamy in Muslim societies also made it more difficult for young men to find wives, since older, wealthier males secured more than their fair share of marriageable females. On occasion, these good providers would ignore the admonition to have no more than four wives and establish "harems," further contributing to the scarcity of young single women and the prolonged bachelorhood of young males. This situation creates considerable sexual repression among these men in traditional Muslim societies. In recent decades their sex-related frustration has intensified. As is often the case, repression of this sort can create strong aggressive feelings, sometimes leading to violence.[29]

In recent decades, young men with limited means have become greatly disadvantaged in the Islamic marriage market. Their number has increased dramatically over the last thirty-five years, as countries in the Arab world have experienced growing rates of poverty and unemployment, despite the large revenues generated by their oil exports. By 1999, some 26 percent of the workforce in North Africa and the Middle East was unemployed; this was one of the highest such rates in the world at that time. And this situation has not improved since. Average personal wealth in the Persian Gulf states has not increased significantly from what it was in the 1970s. In Saudi Arabia—the home of most of the 9/11 hijackers[30]—per capita income instead fell dramatically between 1980 and 1988 and has remained at this much lower level. The proportion of persons living below the poverty line in several Arab nations in North Africa and the Middle East rose sharply in less than two decades. In Algeria, it jumped from 12.2 percent in 1988 to 22.6 in 1995; in Jordan, from 18.7 in 1987 to 24 in 1992; in Morocco, from 13.1 in 1990–1991 to 19 in 1989–1989, and in Yemen, from 19.2 in 1992 to 25.4 in 1998. Since the 1980s, real wages in most Arab countries have plummeted, most notably for persons working in the public sector. These negative trends have had the greatest impact on young people, particularly those living in rural areas or with little education or training. Low-skilled males in their twenties and early thirties have also been adversely affected by the growing educational attainments and participation of females in the labor markets of these countries. The latter trend has been a consequence of globalization and the changing nature of skills required in a more manufacturing-oriented world economy.

These two developments have transformed the Middle Eastern workforce. By 1995, a greater percentage of young women than men was employed in *every* Arab country except for Yemen. Periodic wars in the Middle East have also increased economic insecurity, stagnation, and inequality and made it more difficult for young men to obtain the material resources to marry, including the funds normally required by a bride's family in some countries.[31] The increase in female employment has created considerable resentment against women: some Arab men are apt to blame them for the downturn in their own economic fortunes.[32] A third social change that has extended male celibacy in some Muslim countries is the adoption of marriage reforms designed to limit the number of child brides. As a result of this policy, the average age of an Egyptian bride rose from 18.7 to 21.9 years from the 1930s to the 1990s.[33] Even though many rural women in countries like Egypt have disregarded these minimum-age laws, their continuing to marry early has been offset nationally by the decisions of young professional women in urban centers to postpone marriage. In addition, probably as a result of cultural traditions that give preference to male children and thus lead to higher child mortality rates for females, young Arab men outnumber women their age: by the mid-1970s this was the case in every Muslim country in the Middle East except Yemen.[34] This numerical imbalance makes the competition for brides that much more onerous. Because of all these economic and demographic factors, young Arab men have to wait a long time to marry: their average age when they finally do wed—in their mid- to late twenties—is one of the highest in the developing world.[35] Being out of work, with poor marital and career prospects, has deprived many youth in the Middle East (and other Islamic countries) of a sense of purpose, made them restless and—like similar "surplus" single male populations elsewhere in the world—susceptible to radical political slogans and active involvement in their militant causes.[36]

This worsening marital outlook for these Muslim youth has been compounded by the humiliation resulting from military defeats at the hands of Israel and the United States, as well as from the extended presence of American military forces in the region.[37] Leaders of groups like Hamas and al Qaeda have stated that the crushing Arab defeat during the Six-Day War in 1967 was what led them to embrace radicalism. A teenage Ayman al-Zawahiri, for instance, joined the Muslim Brotherhood shortly after this painful Israeli victory. In justifying the acts on September 11, Osama bin Laden contended "Our nation has been tasting humiliation and contempt for more than eighty years."[38] This long succession of setbacks has precipitated a "crisis of Arab masculinity."[39] Several generations of Muslim men have come of age with a sense of inadequacy and failure. They have not lived up to the expectations of Arab manhood. They have not protected their families and their villages. Israel has defeated them in a series of one-sided wars. Their lands are still dominated by foreign powers. Their governments have not delivered on a promise of greater freedom. Their leaders have not ful-filled the hopes of youth for social mobility, higher economic status, and career success with which they have grown up and for which their par-ents have labored and saved.[40] In light of these demoralizing circum-stances, many Muslim youth have looked elsewhere for validation. To reverse their fortunes, they have embraced the role of warrior—defender of the faith and of their sacred territory. Joining a jihad against the West has given these young men one final chance to affirm their masculinity in an inhospitable world.[41] This decision holds out another kind of reward as well. Fighters can expect sexual and marital benefits.

First, there is the promise of joyous eternal life. The Islamic vision of heaven—a paradise open to all true believers and those who perform good deeds during their earthly existence—abounds with sensual delight. For men, it is a frankly sexual paradise, where voluptuous, uninhibited young women are freely available to them.[42] As the Qur'an puts it, "theirs shall be the dark-eyed houris, chaste as hidden pearls: a guerdon for their deeds . . . virgins, loving companions for those on the right hand."[43] In their "final instructions," the hijackers of 9/11 were told they should be "filled with gladness, for there is nothing between you and your wedding but mere seconds."[44] For young men of little education who have been denied sexual experience and fear that they may never marry, the appeal of this erotic fantasy should not be underestimated, even if it is only a secondary motive for them.[45] The fact that radical Islamic groups use lavish descriptions of heaven to recruit teenage boys for suicide missions demonstrates this point.[46]

Sacrificing one's life can also—paradoxically—improve the likeli-hood of having children (that is, the "reproductive fitness") for the sur-viving male sibling and extended family members of a young martyr. A recent study has shown that this has been a clear benefit for middle-class Palestinian families whose sons have died in this manner. Radical organ-izations such as Hamas regularly pay the parents of martyrs a lump sum ranging in value from $25,000 to $100,000 or monthly payments of between $200 and $1,000. (Until the overthrow of his regime, Saddam Hussein had given the families of fighters killed by Israeli forces in the West Bank and Gaza an additional $10,000 each.)[47] Since the average Palestinian male only earns about $4,200 in a year, such a financial windfall can greatly boost a family's economic status and thus the prospects of its remaining male offspring being able to provide for a wife.[48] This benefit, however, only applies to middle-class families, since the financial "reward" is not large enough to make a real difference to poor ones. To what extent would-be suicide bombers might be altruistically motivated by these economic consequences has not yet been determined.[49]

Second, young Islamic men who join the struggle against Israel and its Western allies without intending to commit suicide and who survive can count on becoming more attractive marriage partners for having fought against these enemies. Their families, friends, and communities are likely to hail them as national heroes, and many shy, impressionable young females will see in such brave defiance the limning of their imagined beloved. This linkage between marriage and jihad was revealed following Israel's 2008 invasion of the Gaza Strip. The militant Islamist organization Hamas organized ten separate mass weddings between widows of recently killed fighters and men who aspired to take their places. Three hundred couples were joined in matrimony at one of these events, held in a sports stadium and sponsored by Hamas. The three chief goals were to provide new husbands for these women who had already lost one spouse to war, to give the unmarried militants brides, and to produce—through these new unions—more male offspring to continue the struggle against the Israelis. The new wife of one badly wounded Hamas fighter declared she had one wish for her new relationship: to go on a suicide mission across the border together.[50]

There is another reason why sexual issues predispose young Muslim men to go to war. This stems from how they perceive the West. In line with its dualistic thinking about gender, traditional Islam tends to regard the United States and Western Europe as fundamentally opposed to the Muslim world. As far as sexual mores are concerned, this means that the West is associated with nudity, provocative display of the body, homosexuality, premarital and extramarital sex, promiscuity, pornography, sexual deviation and excess of all kinds, an open and aggressive female libido, and, in general, a lack of restraint and discretion in matters of sex. This grossly simplified and distorted image follows a succession of mutual, historical misrepresentations on the part of both Islamic and Christian societies, dating back to the Crusades. As relatively recent as the eighteenth century, Western travelers to the Middle East returned to write accounts of a "decayed," poverty-stricken civilization—"feudal backwaters" populated by bloodthirsty "Musselmen" with few social graces and bad hygiene. Islam was described as barely a religion.[51] Once racist thinking took hold in Europe, Western commentators on this part of the world emphasized its "backwardness, degeneracy, and inequality."[52] This stereotypical outlook has been invoked to justify European intervention and occupation of the Middle East.[53] The sole characteristic that appealed to many of these uncomprehending foreign visitors was the sexual allure they found to be tantalizingly ubiquitous. They could as easily imagine themselves partaking of the sensual delights of an Arab harem as today's naïve young Islamic martyrs envision Paradise. This alien corner of the world devolved in their Western imaginations into a throbbing sexual fantasy.[54] This image of the Arab world as highly sexualized was widely promulgated by European travel writers and novelists in the late nineteenth and twentieth centuries.[55] Fantasies of willing female submission to the needs of foreign males were part and parcel of the overall perception that these lands existed mainly for Western exploitation and gratification.

Ironically, early Middle Eastern voyagers to the Western Hemisphere "discovered" a libertinism that was just as pervasive. The difference for them was that this spectacle was not so much tempting as appalling. For example, when the Egyptian teacher Sayyid Qutb came to the United States in the late 1940s to study its educational system, he was impressed by many aspects of American life but dismayed by its "primitiveness"—evident in its violent sports and its religious practices, but also in its sexual mores. Qutb depicted a United States that would have been scarcely recognizable to Americans of that era. He observed young people in Colorado and California surrendering without qualms or reservations to the "temptation of the body . . . stripped of all modesty."[56] The American woman shamelessly used her physical charms to seduce and control men. She understood what power lay in "round breasts, the full buttocks, and in the shapely thighs, sleek legs, and she knows all this and does not hide it. She knows it lies in clothes: in bright colors that awaken primal sensations, and in designs that reveal the temptations of the body—and in American girls these are sometimes live, screaming temptations! Then she adds to all this the fetching laugh, the naked looks, and the bold moves, and she does not ignore this for one moment or forget it." In a society obsessed with materialism, sex was simply another commodity to be bought and sold, Qutb concluded after a two-year stay in the United States.[57] Subsequently, he wrote an article for an Egyptian magazine, elaborating upon his assessment of the American female: "As soon as she gets closer to you, you feel her overpowering sexual drive devoid of any innocence, then she turns into flesh, mere flesh, but nonetheless real voluptuous flesh."[58] While Qutb was apparently not impervious to these physical temptations, his encounter with Western sexual freedom strengthened his belief that the United States was a morally debased and inferior country. As the most prominent intellectual figure in the Egyptian Muslim Brotherhood during the 1950s and 1960s, Qutb would help disseminate this one-dimensional view of the West and shape the attitudes of several generations of its members.[59] One of his chief fears was that America's "moral bankruptcy" might someday spread to Muslim societies.

Over the centuries, both the Arab and Western worlds have projected their own (forbidden) desires and fears onto the other—an example of the "splitting" of the personality, as explicated by Freud and other psychologists. According to this theory, persons who are incapable of integrating their "good" and "bad" qualities end up detaching from the latter by identifying them in others, convinced that their own selves remain unsullied by these undesirable traits. This process allows the individual to continue to believe in his or her superiority, while dismissing other persons as unworthy and inferior. Societies can also apply this "split" awareness toward nations that appear to threaten them: the duality of thinking (good versus evil) helps them to prepare for and justify war against these perceived enemies. This disposition has been apparent in recent times in the confrontations between nations of vastly different cultures—for example, the reciprocal demonization of the United States and Japan before and during World War II.[60]

The same psychological process has also taken place in the United States and in fundamentalist Islamic nations over the last several decades. Conservative religious elements in these societies have been concerned about a deterioration of traditional values due to the rise of powerful modernist forces.[61] For instance, the Iranian leader Ayatollah Ruhollah Khomeini once wrote of "the poisonous culture of imperialism penetrating to the depths of our towns and villages throughout the Muslim world, displacing the culture of the Qur'an."[62] Both East and West have seen in the other a challenge to their own values and have intensified their mutual hostility so that they can preserve what they treasure most—democracy, individuality, and freedom in the United States; moral probity, social cohesion, and respect for law and authority in the Muslim world. Another reason for this "splitting" is the need to preserve a collective unity based upon a strong group identity.[63] The vilification of foreign foes furthers this objective. It also serves to draw attention away from the shortcomings and defects of one's own society, thus preserving the status quo.

As noted above, the same process of dividing the world into "good" and "evil" can also help individuals justify attitudes and actions that otherwise would be socially unacceptable. Anger stemming from frustration and sexual tensions can be transferred from internal causes (such as cultural constraints or a shortage of sex partners) to external ones. These "outside" enemies become a more legitimate target for these negative feelings.[64] A discharge of pent-up rage can more easily occur when normally operating restraints are removed—for example, when an individual or group (such as the 9/11 hijackers) are living abroad. This venting may take a sexual form or be expressed through violence.[65] Inflicting pain on others simultaneously alleviates one's own suffering and reinforces the comforting conviction that all responsibility for what has gone wrong can be laid at the feet of others. The injured or wronged person ends up feeling pure, righteous, heroic, and guiltless for having "punished" the offending parties and thus having demonstrated his or her power to rectify previous injustices.[66]

Many persons who come to see the world in these black-and-white terms and act accordingly suffer from what psychologists have labeled a borderline personality disorder (BPD). They have an unstable identity and difficult relations with others. They are prone to rapid swings of emotion and impulsive behavior. These individuals suffer from feelings of shame, which they seek to relieve by blaming others. According to some psychologists, the origins of this disorder lie in a child's upbringing. In traditional patriarchal societies, the father is often absent, and the mother assumes primary responsibility for raising the children. She may pass on to them the anger and frustration she has experienced as a submissive and undervalued member of society. Offspring of such mothers sometimes fail to develop a strong sense of self; they remain socially withdrawn. They can easily be attracted to powerful figures who promise to exact revenge for their plight through acts of violence. There are a number of parallels between persons with this personality disorder and the Islamist extremists who have carried out suicide attacks against Western targets, including the 9/11 hijackings. This fact does not mean that individuals like Mohamed Atta suffered from BPD. It only suggests that such a psychological framework can provide valuable insights in seeking to understand the motives of fanatics who kill hundreds of innocent persons to "punish" their enemies.[67]

Regardless of their overall psychological make-up, many of the young men who seized four American airplanes on September 11, 2001, displayed a distinct animosity toward women—especially those females who had adopted Western ways of dress, manner, and lifestyle. Most of the hijackers had misogynistic attitudes and reviled the United States for its liberal sexual mores. As one conservative commentator has expressed it, "What disgusts them [conservative Muslims] are not free elections but the sights of hundreds of homosexuals kissing each other and taking marriage vows. The person that horrifies them the most is not John Locke but Hillary Clinton."[68] In the words of the eminent scholar of Islam Bernard Lewis, "The most powerful accusation of all [within the Muslim world] is the degeneracy and debauchery of the American way of life."[69] Since the sexual revolution, many Arabs have been appalled by Western "libertarianism" and worried about its threat to their own traditional mores.[70] Arab animosity is directed at practices that empower women and free them from the restrictions imposed by traditional Muslim belief. Open displays of the female body are regarded as grossly immoral.[71] Western women who are so liberated not only affront the gender roles clearly spelled out in the Qur'an, they also pose a direct challenge to male sexual domination, which is also a basic tenet of Islam. Women outside the control of men are alarming because their sexual vitality is felt to be greater than men's.

At the same time, conservative Muslims see themselves as protectors of women—against the sexual violations, degradation, and depersonalization they perceive in the West. This concern for Islamic womanhood is evident in the dedication of an instructional manual used by some members of al Qaeda. In translation, it reads, in part: "To the sister believer whose clothes the criminals have stripped off / To the sister believer whose hair the oppressors have shaved / To the sister believer who's [sic] body has been abused by the human dogs." This same document makes this same "sister" a pledge "to retaliate for you against every dog who touch [sic] you even with a bad word."[72]

While disdainful of women, misogynist men are also tormented by a desire to have sex with them. One way to resolve this dilemma is to turn females into objects of loathing—to perceive them as corrupt and contemptible while maintaining a sense of remaining "uncontaminated" by contact with them.[73] This psychological mechanism can explain the hijackers' hiring prostitutes and viewing sexually explicit materials before carrying out their missions. Moreover, many traditional Muslim men regard all women as "impure" and "debasing."[74] Islamic warriors preparing for battle—or young men planning to commit suicide mass murder—therefore withdraw from female contact so that they can fight in a "pure" state. For this reason, Mohamed Atta gave his fellow hijackers final instructions to "make sure that you are clean, your clothes are clean, including your shoes," before they ventured forth on the morning of September 11.[75] This view of women reinforces a tendency among Islamic fundamentalists to treat females as inferior beings, to be kept under the strict control of males and punished if they assert their independence or autonomy. Such freedom violates gender polarity in traditional Muslim (as well as Christian and Jewish) cultures. These societies thus seek to preserve "patriarchal" power and prevent women from gaining political, social, and economic rights.[76] A male desire to maintain separate gender spheres (and their own higher status) is evident in Pakistan's recent application of *Shari'a* law to acts of sexual misconduct and the extreme penalties—including stoning to death—which have been mandated for females who have relations outside of marriage.[77]

The sexual tensions and frustrations that may well have afflicted the 9/11 hijackers and other fanatical Islamic fundamentalists also arose from the clash between cultural conditioning and repression in their own countries and the rapid changes in moral, political, economic, and social norms elsewhere in the world. The spreading of Western mores made many young people in traditional Muslim societies aware of other models for sexual and social behavior and awakened a desire to experiment with them. Backers of the traditional order then sought to defend it by gaining power and using it to attack any elements that were inimical to the existing hierarchal, male-dominated social order. (The resurgence of traditional Islamic movements in countries like Iran and Egypt can be traced to popular disaffection with Western-oriented governments.) As the propagators of liberal sexuality, the United States and European countries incurred the wrath of the righteous. While the attacks of 9/11 and other terrorists acts against the West clearly have had political objectives[78]—namely, the withdrawal of foreign (non-Muslim) forces from the Middle East and an end to their support for Israel and "apostate" Islamic regimes in the region—the sexual dimension of the Western "threat" and "humiliation" remains an important motivating factor, certainly for many young male Islamic "holy warriors" whose personal (that is, sexual and reproductive) circumstances make them highly sensitive on this subject.

The sexual frustrations plaguing youthful Muslim men have made them contemptuous of the United States and hostile toward it, but also envious of the sensual pleasures so readily available there. Regardless of their own inner conflicts, Islamic fundamentalists do not see the West as having any conflicting values of its own. Instead, the West is a monolithic foe—the "Great Satan." This perception has suited the militants' need to create a one-dimensional caricature. In doing so, they have overlooked the fact that the United States is itself deeply divided over many basic cultural and moral issues. Indeed, certain elements in American political, social, and religious life hold views similar to the conservative forces that were calling for jihad against America and its European allies, whereas others were firmly opposed to all the mullahs and their followers advocated. Two subjects on which the United States did not have a clear consensus were sexuality and gender.

Much of the domestic controversy and dissension in this area dates back to the sexual revolution of the late 1960s. Starting then, the availability of contraception effectively decoupled heterosexual intercourse from pregnancy and childbirth. As regular use of the Pill by single and married women increased exponentially, the incidence of unintended births in the United States declined. So did the overall birth rate, although this trend had actually begun earlier (in the late 1950s) and thus was not solely due to greater use of contraception.[79] The impact of oral contraceptives on teenage pregnancies was most pronounced during the early 1970s, when these had become available to a large percentage of young women wishing to become sexually active but not to conceive a child. Between 1970 and 1973, birth rates for white American teenagers ages fifteen to nineteen fell by 22 percent.[80] (This rate rose by 9 percent in the 1980s, but then resumed its steep decline, dropping another 27 percent between 1991 and 2001.)[81] By 1975, the likelihood of a female American teenager bearing a child was more than 40 percent less than what it had been two decades before. Over roughly the same period, however, the rate of sexual intercourse among females in this age group jumped by 30 percent: in 1971, three in ten teenage American females were sexually active, but five years later 40 percent had had relations.[82] By 1992, nearly two-thirds of non-Hispanic white females had had intercourse by the age of eighteen, compared to only 54 percent of their male contemporaries.[83]

This growing discrepancy between the rates of intercourse and birth clearly demonstrates the impact of contraceptive devices. Since the Pill was by then the overwhelmingly most popular method in use, birth control was now primarily left up to females. Young single women were able to control their fertility to an unprecedented degree. Not only could they greatly reduce the chances of an unwanted pregnancy, they could also decide by themselves when and with whom they wanted to conceive a child.[84] This greater freedom led to a sharp decline in the proportion of overall births involving single teenagers during the last three decades of the last century: in 1970, this age group accounted for half of all births outside marriage, but by 1999, only 29 percent of such births were to teenagers.[85] Between the late 1950s and the early 1960s, the fertility rate for *all* teenage women had already fallen by more than one-fourth.[86] Because of this development, a quantum shift occurred in the balance of sexual power. What females gained in autonomy, control, and peace of mind, men lost in terms of their certainty over paternity and involvement in the choice to have a baby. As the anthropologist Lionel Tiger has put it, men were now "cut out of the reproductive agreement." These changes caused considerable male anxiety. Men could no longer regard their female sex partners as subject to their will. Nor could they expect to be informed of or to deal with the consequences of having unprotected sex. Not knowing if they have actually fathered a child made many American men uncertain of genetic continuity, or in Tiger's words, their "place in the march of generations."[87]

Young unmarried females were not the only ones able to prevent pregnancies more effectively. The Pill also made it possible for married women to postpone and limit births. Whereas, in 1970, 71 percent of wives had a child within the first three years of marriage, only 37 percent did so during this same period in 1990.[88] At the same time, American women were choosing to delay walking down the aisle, steadily pushing up the median age for first-time brides—from 20.2 in the mid-1950s, to 21.1 in 1975, to 24.8 in 1996, and 25.8 in 2004.[89] The median age for men to marry has risen concomitantly, from 23 in the late 1960s to 26 in 1990, to 27.1 in 1996 and 27.4 in 2004.[90] This delay in marriage during prime childbearing years has contributed to a falling American birth rate over the past four decades: it dropped from 18.4 per 1,000 persons in 1970 to 15.9 in 1980, to 16.7 in 1990, to 14.7 in 2000, and 14.0 in 2005.[91] Not only have families been having fewer babies, many have decided not to have any at all. The percentage of women in their late twenties with children at home has fallen from 73.6 in 1970 to 52.9 in 2007.[92] By this latter year, one of every five American women in their early forties had never had a child, compared with just one in ten in 1980.[93] As a consequence, the birth rate in the United States slipped below the replacement level in 1972 and has remained there since.[94] The size of American households also reached a historic low by the late 1980s.[95]

This predilection to marry later and have fewer children developed as young women were taking advantage of an array of new educational and employment opportunities. More females were going to college than ever before, continuing a trend that had started in the early 1960s. Between 1969 and 2000 the number of women attending college increased by 157 percent; for men, it rose by only 39 percent. From 1967 to 2000, the proportion of females ages eighteen to twenty-four enrolled at an institution of higher education jumped from 19.2 to 38.4, while the proportion of men *decreased*, from 33.1 to 32.6.[96] Female enrollment in higher education quickly caught up with that of men; by 1978 there were more women on college campuses than men.[97] Having more education translated into more lucrative job and career prospects. Consequently, a growing proportion of American wives were opting to stay in the labor force after they got married or return to work after having had children. The proportion of married women in the United States who were employed increased from 30.5 percent in 1960, to 40.8 in 1970, and to 51.2 percent in 1983. From 1970 to 1988, the percentage of employed married women with young children increased from 30 to 56 percent.[98] This trend contributed to a "feminization" of the American workforce: by 2005, 41 percent of full-time workers were female, up 9 percent since 1976. (By 2009, women were close to becoming a majority.)

As more wives were going off to work, fewer husbands were accompanying them. The percentage of married men who worked fell from 93 percent in 1940 to 79 percent in 1983. (In 2009, the proportion of American males over the age of twenty who had a job had reached a historic low of 68.2 percent.)[99] The greatest decline occurred after 1970, among men in their late fifties and early sixties.[100] Overall, female dependence on male breadwinners has decreased dramatically since the early 1960s, when 42 percent of American households relied completely on the husband's earnings. By 1988, only 15 percent of families did.[101] Between 1980 and 2006, the proportion of total family income from the earnings of wives grew from 26.7 to 36.5 percent.[102] At the end of the twentieth century, one of every four wives earned more than her husband.[103] Diverging trends have emerged in the wages earned by men and women over the last several decades. In mid-1990s, women were bringing home 7.6 percent more money than they had in 1979, but men's paychecks were 14 percent smaller.[104] During this period, female earnings rose— from $24,000 (in 2005 dollars) in 1970, to $34,000 in 2005. But male wages remained essentially stuck in the $40,000–45,000 range.[105] As a result, the wage gap between men and women has been narrowing: in 1979, men earned, on average, 37 percent more than their female counterparts, but by 2005, their paychecks were only 20 percent larger.[106] In the decade from 1979 to 1989 alone, female earnings increased 1.7 percent annually *more* than male earnings.[107]

Better economic circumstances for women led to a decline in the marriage rate.[108] Growing numbers of young females could support themselves without a husband, and so the financial rationale for tying the knot greatly diminished. (Having a bigger income also made it feasible for more women to end their marriages than had been the case in the past.)[109] Over this same period, the need to marry because of a premarital pregnancy also lessened, as there was greater public acceptance of cohabitation and births out of wedlock. (Academic use of the term *illegitimate* fell out of favor by the early 1970s.) In the late 1960s, nearly 70 percent of unmarried, pregnant teenage females between fifteen and nineteen ended up getting married before the birth of their first child, but this proportion had fallen to nearly 35 percent by 1970 and to 20 percent by the early 1990s.[110] Reflecting a broader trend in the industrialized world, marriage became a less central feature of American life. Between 1970 and 2007, the number of marriages per 1,000 Americans decreased from 10.4 to 7.3.[111] During a thirty-five-year period, this rate declined nearly 48 percent, from 76.5 per 1,000 unmarried women in 1970 to 39.9 in 2005.[112] More specifically, the percentage of young women who were still single by their twenty-fourth birthday shot up from 28.4 in 1960 to 35.8 in 1970, 50.2 in 1980, and 66 in 1994.[113]

More independence for women was responsible for several major changes in American mores and institutions. One of these was the rise in households headed by women—that is, without a male partner. Their number increased more than tenfold between 1970 and 1988—from 248,000 to 2.7 million.[114] By 1989, 16.5 percent of all households in the United States were solely supported by a woman, up from 9.2 percent in 1950.[115] Another significant development was an unprecedented increase in births to unmarried women. This occurred mainly among women in their thirties. The fertility rate for single females over thirty doubled between 1970 and 1993.[116] By 2006, nearly half of all births to women ages thirty and younger were taking place outside marriage.[117] Of the 4.2 million American women who gave birth the previous year, more than a third were divorced, separated, widowed, or never married.[118] To put these figures in historical perspective, only 4 percent of all births in the 1950s took place outside of marriage, but a third did so in 1999.[119] This trend results from a number of related economic and social factors—the decline in marriage rates as many couples have opted to live together without making a formal legal or religious commitment to each other; the greater likelihood of such nonmarital relationships breaking up;[120] the unwillingness or inability of men to accept their paternal responsibilities; and the choice more young women are now making to raise a child on their own, made possible by their greater financial independence.[121] In addition, a continuing high incidence of divorce has left a large number of women in the position of having to raise children without a partner. The greatest increase in the divorce rate took place in the 1970s, when it rose from 3.5 per 1,000 persons to 5.2 per 1,000.[122] In recent decades, more than four out of ten marriages have been dissolved. As a consequence, by 1989 more than one-fourth of all households with children were headed by a single parent, in nine in ten cases by the mother.[123]

This fracturing of the nuclear family was part of a general transformation of living arrangements in the United States since the early 1960s. Households have decreased in size and lost much of their familial (or marital) basis.[124] For example, family units consisting of unmarried couples (and their offspring) became—with over 50 million households—the majority in 2005.[125] In addition, the percentage of men in the United States who are single rose from 30 percent in the late 1960s to 42 percent by 2000; the percentage of single women climbed from 34 percent to 45 percent during the same timeframe.[126] As a result, by the end of the 1980s, more than 24 percent of all American households consisted of a single person, up from 13.0 percent in 1960 and 17.1 in 1970. In 1989, 13.1 million women and 8.8 million men were living alone. (Most of the excess number of women in this category is the result of their having outlived their husbands: among single persons ages fifteen to fifty-five, men slightly outnumber women.)[127] The number of single households had more than doubled since 1970.[128] By 1994, 7 percent of all men between the ages of fifteen and thirty-four were not in a shared living situation; this represented more than a 100 percent increase over the preceding twenty-four years.[129] Four years later, 712,000 males in the eighteen to twenty-four age group were living alone, versus 524,000 females.[130] Meanwhile, a growing proportion of Americans have been living with persons who are not members of their families.[131]

These dramatic changes in sexual mores, educational and employment opportunities, marital choices, and living arrangements have transformed American society in a number of ways. From a gender perspective, it appears that women have largely benefited from these changes, while men have not. In general, men now play much-diminished social and economic roles, as their nearly exclusive prerogative to perform these roles has ended, and women have taken their places. The impact of male displacement has been felt most acutely in the home: more than a third of all children are currently growing up without a father around.[132] By 2005, both parents were present in only 63 percent of American families, compared to 93 percent in the early 1950s.[133] By the time they have turned eighteen, more than half of all American children have experienced a paternal absence for a significant amount of time. These developments are associated with (but not necessarily the cause of) a number of poor social and emotional outcomes for boys. For example, nearly three of every four teenage murderers come from homes without fathers; fatherless children are eleven times more likely to become violent than ones with fathers; 70 percent of imprisoned male juvenile offenders grew up without fathers; 85 percent of male rapists who admit to being motivated by "displaced anger" are from fatherless homes.[134] Aside from such putative negative effects on children's well-being, the absence of fathers has greatly reduced the impact of male parenting and created what one authority on this subject has called a "culture of fatherlessness" in the United States.[135] Regardless of how this phenomenon is characterized, there is no doubt that many boys are currently growing up without a male role model. This fact has impaired their ability to mature and assume the roles of husband and father when they reach full manhood.

On top of having more tenuous ties to their offspring, a growing proportion of American husbands are not experiencing fatherhood at all. Due largely to the prevalence of working wives and the conflicts between raising children and holding full-time, demanding jobs, an increasing number of married couples are foregoing parenthood. In 2007, fewer than one in three couples had children under eighteen in their households—a sharp drop from the nearly 50 percent who were parents the year John F. Kennedy was elected president.[136] This shrinking likelihood of experiencing parenthood deprives those men affected of one of the pivotal aspects of being a man (as it deprives their female partners of the joys and satisfactions that come with being mothers). More broadly, the diminishing of paternal involvement further weakens a masculine identity already eroded by the decreasing of male breadwinning responsibilities.

The stagnation in male incomes in the United States since the 1970s has negatively affected masculine self-esteem: more and more men have been unable to earn enough to maintain the standard of living that they had known growing up. One recent study determined that income for men of all educational levels (except for those who have graduated from college) was less in 2005 than it had been for their fathers in 1980.[137] For young males of low socioeconomic status, this decline in earning power has translated into an increasing difficulty in finding women who will marry them. Numerous studies have shown a direct correlation between male income and both marital outcome and reproductive prospects within marriage. One study has concluded that employed fathers are twice as likely to "legitimize" their children via marriage as unemployed ones.[138] Because their earnings diminished by 25 percent from the 1970s to the late 1990s, one-third of men ages twenty-five to thirty-four were not financially well enough off at the end of the century to support a family.[139] Males with only a high school education were most adversely affected: their incomes fell relative to those who had graduated from college, so that the earnings gap between these two groups widened considerably. By 2005, the income "premium" for a college degree amounted to a difference of 63 percent, versus 30 percent in 1980. In other words, men without any higher education were much worse off economically vis-à-vis their better-educated peers than they had been a quarter century before.[140] This worsening of their financial circumstances put these less-educated men in a much less-competitive position in attracting potential spouses and starting a family. Consequently, many of these poor, less-educated American men have ended up living alone or cohabitating with a woman.[141] A surplus of single males in their twenties has added to these marital obstacles. In 2004, there were 120 men in this age group for every 100 women; for Hispanics, the gender imbalance was much greater—153 young men for every 100 women.[142] These alternative living arrangements, in turn, have made it less likely that men in this category will have stable long-term relations or father children. In other words, as men have become less successful wage earners, they have become less able to fulfill their basic sexual and reproductive needs.

As many little-educated, poorly skilled, and low-earning American males have lost stature as husbands, fathers, and providers, they have simultaneously faced an even more daunting challenge on another front—namely, female demands for equity in all spheres of life. This revolt against male domination and control came from a "second-wave" feminist movement, which emerged in the mid-1960s. In its origins, it had striking parallels with the first such movement of its kind in the United States back in the 1840s. Arguably, this new movement began with the publication of Betty Friedan's 1963 *The Feminine Mystique*, a critique of the limited career opportunities then available to middle-class, suburban housewives. This book appeared the year after Helen Gurley Brown's bestselling *Sex and the Single Girl* (which urged young, single, working women to seek sexual and career fulfillment just as men did)[143] and the same year as the report of President Kennedy's commission on the status of women, which focused national attention on female employment and the need for more gender equality in the workplace.[144] Learning—by participating in "consciousness-raising" groups—that many of their female friends and other peers were facing similar frustration and oppressiveness in their marriages as well as their professional aspirations, women who read Friedan's book began to examine how "patriarchy" informed many institutions in American life, from the family to the university, from churches to the corporate board room, and prevented them from realizing their full human potential. Soon the "women's liberation movement" was leveling sharp criticism at these institutions and creating organizations such as the National Organization of Women (NOW) and mass media like *Ms.* magazine to spread the campaign for women's rights across a broad canvas. Women sought greater sexual freedom through legal access to abortion and contraceptives; legal redress for rape; maternal leave and affordable childcare; financial equity in divorce settlements; equal pay, greater representation in labor unions, and more blue-collar jobs; increased access to higher education and professional careers in law, business, academia, the military, and medicine; and a larger role in political parties, voting, and governance. Across the country, supporters of NOW lobbied state legislatures to pass the Equal Rights Amendment (ERA), after it was adopted by both houses of Congress. In colleges and universities, profeminist faculty members fought successfully to make women's studies part of the curriculum.

At the same time, activists tried to change negative or demeaning male perceptions of women as "sex objects" and innately limited (and inferior to men) in their ambitions or intelligence. In September 1968, a group of feminists protested what one of their leaders termed the "degrading mindless-boob-girlie symbol" of Miss America at the annual pageant in Atlantic City, and some demonstrators from New York burned an effigy of "Traditional Womanhood" during an all-female antiwar rally in Washington, DC.[145] In March 1970, two hundred feminists occupied the offices of the editor of the *Ladies Home Journal* to protest the "sexism" of women's magazines.[146] Proponents of more rights for women also held symposia and other gatherings to draw attention to the plight of battered women and victims of rape. Some "women's libbers" turned the tables on men verbally, using derogatory terms to characterize male behavior they considered deplorable: men who clung to notions of male "superiority" were taunted as "male chauvinist pigs" or "sexists." Others were denounced as "oppressors" and "fascists." In general, men were put on notice that their words and deeds would be held up to close scrutiny and invite condemnation if they did not conform to the new feminist thinking.

By becoming aware of their common plight and developing pride in their unique capabilities and strengths as women, feminists forged a sense of "sisterhood," which helped their cause to grow and achieve many of its aims.[147] These included the passage of a number of landmark laws protecting the rights of women and affording them more equality in the home and at work.[148] Perhaps most importantly, the women's movement brought about a fundamental change in how American women viewed themselves and the roles they could play in life. This commitment to female empowerment not only transformed the lives of millions of women, it also forced countless men to reexamine their own biases about the opposite sex and to adopt a more "enlightened" outlook in dealing with females in their families, communities, and places of work. A feminine consciousness permeated many sectors of American society, dispelling the old assumptions about gender and replacing these with a more egalitarian and gender-neutral outlook. The ideology of women's liberation caused a seismic shift in relations between men and women. In a whole raft of arenas, men could no longer assume any a priori preeminence. Instead, it was now agreed that positions of prestige and power were to be awarded on the basis of merit, not gender.

While this sea change in gender relations was widely welcomed by many, but not all, women and by some men, it encountered much resistance as well. Many men were caught off-guard by the feminist critique. They had long harbored "sexist" attitudes without having considered whether these were fair to women—or based in reality. It was difficult for many to acknowledge their biases, overcome them, and become liberated "new men." This evolution was particularly challenging for men of the World War II generation. They had grown up with clear notions of what made men and women different, and few were willing or able to discard these notions overnight. Many of these middle-aged men and women were wary of society's going "too far" in allowing younger females to explore new roles and blur the line dividing the sexes.[149] Many businesses and companies, run by members of the "greatest generation," were opposed to giving women positions of responsibility and power.[150] One of the most outspoken "liberal" adversaries of feminism was the novelist Norman Mailer, whose lifelong preoccupations with machismo, violence, and tests of manhood prevented him from viewing feminism other than as a breach of the natural order and a threat to his omnivorous male sexuality.[151] (During a legendary confrontation with Germaine Greer and several other feminists in New York's Town Hall in 1971, Mailer declared he was an "enemy of birth control.")[152] Prominent male writers born in the 1930s, such as Philip Roth and John Updike, also clung to Mailer's belief that women were essentially sexual beings, whose company was best enjoyed in the bedroom rather than in the drawing room.

But even younger men who were politically radical and eager for a thorough-going social and economic revolution tended to draw the line at gender equality. Recalling the attitudes of male abolitionists in the 1840s, they, too, took their dominance for granted. They, too, continued to think of females as "sex objects" or faithful subordinates—"shit-workers" in their organizations, as one disgruntled female later recalled.[153] Leadership in radical groups brought with it "sex and the adoration of young women"—a truism that free speech activist David Lance Goines discovered (and took advantage of) at Berkeley in the early 1960s.[154] Sometimes it seemed as if political protest and sexual libido were two manifestations of the same revolutionary impulse.[155] In the fall of 1967, male students returning to the University of Wisconsin in Madison after taking part in a civil rights rally in Milwaukee marched on a women's dormitory, shouting "We want silk! We want pants! We want sex!" Obliging coeds tossed rolls of toilet paper and panties out the windows at them.[156] Males in groups like the Student Non-Violent Coordinating Committee (SNCC), Students for a Democratic Society (SDS), and the Black Panthers brushed off questions about how they were treating women. The black activist and SNCC leader Stokely

Carmichael famously (although not seriously) responded to a 1964 paper on the role of women in his organization by quipping, "The only position for women in SNCC is prone."[157] As the authors of a cultural history of the 1960s have put it succinctly, "Women were the niggers of the New Left."[158] When women in SDS and kindred left-wing groups openly declared their bitterness over their second-class treatment and their commitment to feminism—notably in Casey Hayden and Mary King's 1965 mimeographed manifesto "Sex and Caste"—their male lovers and comrades were "caught up short" and out of touch. They, too, had not really thought about women's reality before.[159]

Young men of a conservative mind-set listened to what the feminists were saying and watched what they were doing with more clarity. They allowed no revolutionary illusions to cloud their perceptions. Because their idea of masculinity was firmly grounded in the belief that the two sexes were inherently different and ought to remain that way, these traditionalists were enraged at the "libbers'" attack on male privilege and power and at the "swift collapse of male public dominance" in American society.[160] In their antifeminist tirades, these men resembled their British counterparts on the eve of World War I. They denounced feminist activists as "bra burners," "bitches," "Commie whores," "dogs," and "lezzies."[161] (The apparent absence of femininity in the feminist movement was particularly galling to these traditionalists.) They fought back not only with derisive language but also with intimidating displays of pique and outrage: construction workers in hard hats mocked their new female co-workers and openly ogled the smartly dressed ladies parading by their job sites; at feminist rallies, women speakers were sexually baited.[162]

Better-educated and more affluent males could be just as incensed over female inroads into their domains, as was evident in the angry reactions of some alumni (and faculty) at universities like Yale and Princeton to decisions making these hallowed male institutions coeducational.[163] Seven years after Dartmouth's trustees voted, largely out of financial necessity, to admit women, the cochair of the newly created women's studies department would lament that women were "still seen as guests of the place, not part of it; the majority of the students still view women as female objects for their pleasure."[164] The persistence of attitudes like this indicated that a large proportion of men found the "liberation" of women disturbing and threatening. And they had good reason to be fearful. Never before in American history had so many unhappy, angry women made such a concerted assault on the principle of male supremacy and on the men who upheld it. Never before had women so openly proclaimed their sexual freedom and the right to regulate their own reproduction. Never before had American men felt their control over the other half of the population slipping away, in so many ways. For working-class men in particular, the feminist challenge hit home economically as well as socially and sexually: for the first time ever, women were competing for their jobs—as plumbers, electricians, and road-equipment operators. Many of these male blue-collar workers responded with hostility and acts of sexual harassment. But male animosity stretched across class and occupation lines. As the journalist and author Anthony Astrachan would reluctantly conclude after interviewing almost four hundred men for his 1986 book, *How Men Feel: Their Responses to Women's Demands for Equality and Power*, "There are a lot of men out there who hate the idea of women working, especially in jobs outside the traditional service and clerical fields, and who hate the wider changes of which working women are a part."[165] With anger and confusion over feminist demands mounting, many tradition-minded young men sought to defend their remaining male prerogatives by identifying with groups that espoused the kind of gender distinctions they still strongly believed in.

As was pointed out in the previous chapter, the American military was one such institution, and during the late 1960s and early 1970s, the ongoing war in Vietnam offered these disgruntled young men, worried about their masculine status, a chance to wield power and demonstrate their value to society.[166] Many recruits were unhappy with the laissez-faire "youth culture" of the 1960s, with its permissive attitudes about sex and androgynous gender roles. They wanted to stand up for another kind of America and traditional mores. But it would be wrong to argue that many men enlisted or volunteered for duty in Vietnam in response to feminism: the women's movement was only nascent when the bulk of recruits were entering the armed forces, and most of these new soldiers had heard little about feminist demonstrations or demands. (Intriguingly, however, rates of rape and violent crime increased dramatically in the late 1960s and continued to rise until the early 1980s. To what extent these increases might be related to greater female freedoms, including sexual activity, is beyond the scope of this book to ascertain.)[167] It would be more accurate to say that a major reason for serving during this conflict was the chance this offered to assert traditional masculine values at a time when so much in American society—issues of politics, race, generational transition, and gender—was disturbingly in flux. Sexual anxiety no doubt became part of their general uneasiness with radical change, as soldiers based in the United States witnessed other members of their generation don tie-dyed T-shirts, headbands, and love beads, smoke pot, and fall into each other's arms—or, in Vietnam, read about the hippies' "summer of love." This casual cavorting grated against their conservative mores, while, at another level, it made them jealous. While they were risking their lives in the jungle, watching their buddies die in the burst of a Claymore mine, their long-haired coevals were condemning this war, calling them "babykillers," *and* having lots of sex. (One of the slogans of the antiwar movement that particularly irritated the GIs was "Girls say yes to boys who say no.")[168] This blend of envy and disdain is evident in the letter one soldier in Vietnam wrote to the Berkeley student newspaper in 1967: "You see, while you're discussing it [the war] amongst each other, getting in bed with dark-haired artists, substituting Mao for LSD . . . deciding who should really run the school, and all the myriads of other equally important stuff, some people are dying for lighting a cigarette at night, or 'cause the NCO in charge was drunk, etc., etc."[169] As a bulwark against this lifestyle, Vietnam volunteers affirmed the value of courage, risk-taking, heroism, and sacrifice. These were the virtues that made men strong, distinct, and special, and these soldiers were prepared to put their lives on the line to show this was still true.

The parallels between the unfavorable marital and reproductive prospects for working-class American men in the late 1960s and early 1970s and the dilemma faced by young Muslim youth in the Middle East and parts of southern Asia a generation later are striking. Both groups were dealing with economic and psychological setbacks. Both felt their masculinity was endangered. Both were torn between their sexual desires and a puritanical morality. Both were losing out in the competition to attract mates and sire children. Both needed a way to assert their self-importance to reverse this decline in their fortunes. Both sought in patriotic service and violent aggression a solution to their plight. And both found—to their dismay—that assuming the role of warrior did not produce the desired result. Fighting on the losing side only further deepened their feelings of impotence and undermined their self-confidence. For many Americans, the lesson of Vietnam was the folly of vain, arrogant, and deluded male leaders and the terrible human cost of wars that were fought primarily to uphold their power. Ordinary soldiers who went off to fight believing in what these leaders told them were sorely disillusioned by the reality they found in Southeast Asia. What they experienced did not bolster their masculine pride but rather suggest that the feminists were perhaps right. Masculinity *was* inherently aggressive, cruel, and domineering: wars were not fought for just causes, but to provide a collective outlet for these impulses.[170] Even male sexuality seemed justly maligned: its need to control and impose its will was akin to how men behaved in combat. This linkage was pointed out by feminist writers like Adrienne Rich, whose 1973 essay "Caryatid" argued that "the capacity for dehumanizing another which so corrodes male sexuality is carried over from sex into war"; the American bombing of North Vietnam was an act of sexual aggression, exposing the "congruity of violence and sex in the male psyche."[171] Soldiers who observed the abuse, degradation, and rape of Vietnamese women had to concede there was some truth to this assertion.

While most Americans were not prepared to blame the entire male sex for leading the country into such a disastrous war, there is no doubt that the military's failure to defeat the Vietcong and North Vietnamese forces brought about a thorough examination of the meaning and impact of masculinity in American society. More than ever before, the nation was facing a "crisis in masculinity." A good number of men, including many veterans, still believed in their country and the cause that had brought its troops to faraway Vietnam. But others looked back on their lives thus far and found them marked by "betrayals, losses, and disillusionments."[172] Their belief that their country was always right and always on the right side had been destroyed. These veterans directed their anguish and rage at higher-ups in government and the military—"all the men who had lied to us and tricked us," as Ron Kovic did at the Republican convention in Miami in 1972.[173] Instead of trying to salvage something positive from this defeat, disenchanted ex-soldiers like Kovic "recognized that their manhood lay in coming to terms honestly and agonizingly with loss."[174] They were not alone in assessing the war so critically. Many other Americans were now coming around to regard the hubris and vanity of their leaders as responsible for this debacle. (The attempted impeachment of Richard Nixon in 1974 can be seen as the ultimate repudiation of American wartime leadership.) Antiwar movies released in the late 1960s and early 1970s, including *The Dirty Dozen, Little Big Man, M*A*S*H*, and *Soldier Blue*, captured this recriminatory mood. The armed forces bore the brunt of the attack. Rather than the admired defenders of America's most hallowed values, the military and all who belonged in it now appeared to be the country's worst enemies—the massacres at places like My Lai as well as the loss of so many lives in what Lyndon Baines Johnson had once derisively labeled a "raggedy-ass little fourth-rate country" shook the nation's sense of its own righteousness and capabilities.[175]

As the troops straggled home from Southeast Asia in the early 1970s, there was a general (although not universal) feeling of revulsion in the country against men in uniform. Incidents of hippies spitting on them in airports, while exaggerated, stunned these GIs and revealed the depth of anger and revulsion against them on the part of some who had fervently opposed the war.[176] Conversely, former soldiers who threw away their medals on the steps of the Capitol or who testified about war crimes they had observed were seen as America's real heroes—men who had stood up for principle and risked their lives not to kill the enemy but to bring the war to a close. Young men who had resisted the draft were now—at least in some quarters—regarded as lone voices of conscience, not as cowards. Meanwhile, public support for the US military and operations overseas slumped.[177] Due to the unpopularity of the draft, the army was transformed into an all-volunteer force in the early 1970s. Fear of getting bogged down in another "quagmire" like Vietnam was evident in a disinclination to send troops abroad to fight: after a loss of over fifty-eight thousand lives in that conflict between 1964 and 1973, the number of US service members to die in foreign wars shrank to fewer than seven hundred in engagements in Grenada, Panama, Iran, Lebanon, and Iraq over the rest of the century.[178]

More generally, in the 1970s, men who rejected aggression, violence, and war were held in high esteem—as "good" Americans, to be distinguished (in another instance of "splitting") from the "bad" ones who had wantonly killed women and children and tarnished the nation's name half a world away. The 1978 movie *Coming Home* sought to lay out these polarized masculine types—pitting a paraplegic veteran named Luke

Martin (Jon Voight) against a hard-driving but mentally shattered Marine captain Bob Hyde (Bruce Dern) in vying for the affections of Hyde's wife, Sally (played by Jane Fonda). Sally's sexual awakening through her affair with Luke makes an implicit connection between love and the renunciation of a possessive, egotistical, and destructive form of male sexuality. The "new" postwar American man was one who was willing to drop this isolating "armor" and open himself up to feelings of compassion and connection with others—namely, women.

Another powerful testimony of this "conversion" process came in the form of Ron Kovic's memoir of his bitter disillusionment with war, *Born on the Fourth of July* (1976). In this book, Kovic—the Long Islander who, as a teenager, had dreamed of being a heroic Marine, only to be paralyzed by an enemy bullet that severed his spinal cord—tells of his getting together with other Vietnam veterans back in the States. In these meetings, he established deep emotional connections with complete strangers: "We were men who had gone to war. Each of us had his story to tell, his own nightmare. Each of us had been made cold by this thing. We wore ribbons and medals. We talked of death and atrocity to each other with unaccustomed gentleness."[179] Thirty-two years after completing his memoir, Kovic would write again about how his experience of the war changed him: "I became a messenger, a living symbol, an example, a man who learned that love and forgiveness are more powerful than hatred, who has learned to embrace all men and women as my brothers and sisters."[180] Many equally disillusioned veterans came to regard their previous concept of masculinity as a "fraud."[181]

Many Vietnam veterans suffered physical, mental, and emotional wounds from their combat experience. Like Kovic, their lives were changed forever—often in negative ways. Some could not readjust to society or maintain good relationships with their families, friends, lovers, wives, and children. Others suffered from depression, alcoholism, recurring nightmares about combat, and symptoms of posttraumatic stress disorder (PTSD).[182] Still others became cynical about their country and its motives. Groups of one-time warriors renounced war and worked together to prevent future ones. Some embraced a kind of manhood completely different from the ideal with which they had grown up. For American men, especially white, middle-class, heterosexual ones, this was a confusing time. Many were "disconnected and despairing."[183] If "machismo" was now discredited, what kind of men were they supposed to be? How should they respond to the recent social revolutions that had empowered women, gays, blacks, and other minority groups? How should they relate to women?

Anxiety about masculine identity is evident in a spate of books that were published in the mid-1970s, such as *The Male Dilemma* (1974) and *The Hazards of Being Male* (1975). Freed from rigid expectations regarding their gender roles, some men began to ponder new constructs of masculinity. Heeding the advice of the *Ladies Home Journal* editor John Mack Carter, they started to "re-examine their roles . . . to grow where they have been stunted, to move forward where they have been held back, to find dignity and self-fulfillment on their own terms."[184] Taking their cue from the feminists, they began to contemplate their own liberation, perceiving how the conventional male sex role had held them in an emotional straitjacket.[185] In the jargon of that day, they "got in touch with their feelings," became unafraid to show them. They acknowledged their "feminine side," grew less inclined to view men and women as biological opposites and more willing to accept that the two genders were—in many ways—equals. Their literary preferences shifted from Normal Mailer and James Jones to Joseph Heller (*Catch-22*). For their cinematic patron saint, they looked to an ironic and intellectual Woody Allen instead of the laconic John Wayne.[186]

During the late 1970s and into the 1980s, many of these "new men" (and their female companions) donned unisex clothes; dabbled in recreational drugs; indulged in casual sex; pursued unorthodox careers; flirted with "personal awareness" movements, cults, and religious sects; "dropped out" of society; questioned authority and raised children to do the same; and, in general, sought self-fulfillment above all else, morphing from socially conscious baby boomers into the "Me Generation." They grew indifferent to social norms and lax about honoring them. In sexual matters, an attitude of "live-and-let-live" permitted a general loosening of standards and the flowering of alternative gender identities. This tolerant environment made it possible for a gay rights movement to emerge, gain acceptance, and secure legal rights: between 1973 and 1998, the proportion of Americans favoring legalization of gay sex rose from just over 40 percent to nearly 60 percent.[187]

This grand experiment with new lifestyles and values in the late

1970s did not sit well with conservatives. Many of them were shocked by the new freedoms being flaunted in their families, in their neighborhoods, and on their television screens. They felt the country was undergoing an irreversible moral decline, losing its preeminence as a nation based on Christian virtues—as, in Vietnam, it had lost its presumed supremacy as a warrior nation. Yet, as much as traditionalists bemoaned these cultural developments and sought to roll them back, it seemed they were swimming against the tide of history. The forces demanding more individual freedoms—the right to live as they saw fit—were constantly winning the battles in court, weakening the institutions and moral bedrock that, in the past, had given American society stability, security, and continuity. For tradition-minded white men, these structures were closely associated with a gender and racial hierarchies. The progress women, blacks, gays, and other minorities had made in securing more rights was now endangering the foundation on which their masculine identity was based.[188] The "feminization" of the country had left them marginalized, angry, and frustrated.[189] In the late 1970s, this resentment fueled the rise of the Christian Right, which vowed to revive traditional "family values."[190] To bolster their political clout, conservative American men and women looked for someone who could sell this conservative message. They found their spokesman in the person of Ronald Reagan.

Reagan's candidacy in the 1980 presidential election (challenging what many perceived to be a "soft" and ineffectual Jimmy Carter) gave them hopes that a return to a more assertive masculine ethos might be in the offing.[191] Reagan's recitation of rhetorical questions at the close of his only debate with Carter, on October 28, 1976, struck the kind of defiant note they wanted to hear: "Is America respected around the world as it was? Do you feel that our security is as safe, that we're as strong as we were four years ago?" Such refrains, combined with Reagan's penchant for bold, unambiguous rhetoric in his stump speeches, helped win over many traditional Democratic voters in that election—many of whom were blue-collar, white males aggrieved as much by their poor masculine self-image as by their floundering economic situation.[192] Tired of being ridiculed for their "racist" and "sexist" views, these men found a more compatible, welcoming home within the Republican Party and gave Reagan 61 percent of their votes. At last, it seemed to many of them, a man's man was back in the White House.[193] This strong male tilt toward the GOP opened up a "gender gap" in presidential (and congressional) politics that persisted during subsequent elections.[194] Consistently since then, Republican candidates have appealed to traditional male voters by hinting that their Democratic opponents were less-than-manly "wimps."[195] While presenting their party as led by "decisive, tough, strong, and domineering men," Republicans have backed "profamily" policies favored by religious and social conservatives: these policies, which include opposition to abortion and premarital sex, appeal to men who want to reestablish control over female sexuality and roll back the advances made by feminists.[196]

While Reagan's posturing made him popular among white men, his foreign policy was still restrained by vestiges of the "Vietnam syndrome"—a reluctance to assert American power by dispatching troops abroad. Under his leadership, the United States showed a preference for "proxy" wars—covertly supporting the Contra rebels in Nicaragua with arms and money, for example. The United States did intervene directly in one country in the Western Hemisphere—Grenada—but this was a brief, surgical incursion with minimal loss of life.[197] When the human costs of flexing American muscle overseas became greater—as they did when 241 Marines died in a bomb blast in Lebanon in October 1983— Reagan was not willing to stand his ground and fight.

During the 1980s, there was, in short, a dearth of opportunities for American males to display their patriotism and warrior traits—physical prowess, emotional control, aggressiveness, and violence. In the absence of real-world outlets, some men found fulfillment in fantasy: Hollywood obliged their appetite for adventure, heroics, and redemptive triumph by turning out a slew of movies featuring tight-lipped, murderous male cartoon characters taking the law into their own hands and erasing the blot of America's Vietnam defeat by slaughtering a host of equally one-dimensional enemies. Among these were several highly successful films featuring "Dirty Harry" (Clint Eastwood), "Rambo" (Sylvester Stallone), and Arnold Schwarzenegger's futuristic (and mechanized) "Terminator."[198]

Top Gun—the 1986 story of the training of a renegade fighter pilot (played by Tom Cruise)—set a record for video sales and caused enlistment for both the Navy and the Air Force to soar. While movies such as these managed to both legitimize and sublimate male aggressive impulses, they did not provide a satisfactory masculine model for other

American men who were unhappy with the absence of meaning and pride in their lives. These were not men of action, but poets, intellectuals, and academics. But they, too, regretted contemporary America's lack of "manliness" and began to reflect upon how this situation had come about and how men might recover this core quality.

An important figure in this inquiry was the scholar Joseph Campbell, whose writings about myth, heroes, and their quest for self-discovery attracted a large readership (and, posthumously, a television audience) in the 1980s. An even more significant role was played by the poet Robert Bly. A leading opponent of the Vietnam War, Bly subsequently turned his attention to the problem of becoming a man in the modern world. In 1990, he published a book on this subject entitled *Iron John: A Book about Men*, which became a best seller. Here Bly argued that American boys were finding it difficult to become men because they lacked father figures. Since the 1950s, he reasoned, women had gained power as men had lost it. More and more boys were now growing up without fathers, socialized solely by their mothers. Trust between fathers and sons had been broken by the Vietnam War. Untutored and confused, many young soldiers in that conflict were thus no more than "brutal boys—undone, unfinished men." In addition, society no longer honored the same rites of passage that had once ushered them into manhood. In the wake of Vietnam, many boys had grown up to become "softer receptive" males—ones preferred by women.[199]

While Bly's book and the "mythopoetic" men's movement it inspired did not recommend any return to aggressive behavior such as war, his emphasis on males taking pride in their natural strengths, "wildness," and assertiveness did invite a positive reassessment of masculinity and offer some men a way to feel good about themselves at a time when traditional male values were under attack in American society. Many men, too, had come to see their nature as "problematic" and wondered what valuable contributions they could still make in a society that seemed to uphold feminine traits as more desirable and truly human. They considered many masculine roles, such as that of warrior, as obsolete and harmful. They worried that their gender might be inherently "abnormal" and "inferior."[200] While mocked in some quarters for its "wild men" rituals in the woods, Bly's movement gave some men a way to reestablish male bonding and generational connections. Perhaps more importantly, it gave them a powerful language with which to reimagine themselves and "raise their consciousness," as women had done before them.

But, in the ensuing decade, the men's movement did not flourish. In retrospect, it seems clear that this version of masculinity had little of substance to offer men. Gathering in the woods to beat drums and affirm their worth might have given participants a fleeting sense of positive worth, but the fact of the matter was that such affirmations had almost no impact on how male celebrants were actually leading their lives. Bly's hopes for the return of a benevolent patriarchy ran up against the hard, cold statistics put out by the Census Bureau, indicating that American fathers were becoming ever more inconsequential in influencing their children's lives. As the poet himself came to concede in his 1997 book, *The Sibling Society*, growing up to be a man (or a woman)—let alone a nurturing father—was becoming an undesirable goal in contemporary America, which seemed structured so as to arrest this normal process of maturation and perpetuate the state of adolescence. The nightmarish fiction of *Lord of the Flies*—in which there were no grown-ups around to set the rules and spoil the fun—had turned into fact.[201] Thus, the Bly-inspired retreats could only offer a brief respite—a chance for men to experience how different, in splendid isolation, their maleness and fatherhood might be, or might have been—but no solutions to this lingering male malaise back in the world. Like the short-lived "men's liberation" movement of the 1970s, this mythopoetic movement was more of a *cri de coeur* than a plan of action. And, like the cartoonish cinema of brawny male-action figures during the 1980s, it came across as deeply enamored of a mythical, heroic past that probably never really existed. If it had, the flow of history was certainly moving further and further away from it.

In terms of gender relations, American society was heading toward genuine parity in many areas (although it was still far behind most Western European countries in this regard), as the privileges once claimed by men were rapidly disappearing. By the end of the last century, American women were earning more college degrees than men, closing the gap in earnings, and gaining more power in public affairs and in the private sector than they had ever before. Even though many of these gains were occurring at a painfully slow pace, the momentum in the direction of equity seemed strong. But what many women saw as advances, a large percentage of men continued to experience as defeats. The American economy was redistributing wealth—mostly to the already affluent, but also a greater share to women than it had in the past—instead of creating significantly more prosperity for all. Overall, men's wages had remained stagnant while those of females had gradually increased.[202] This reality, coupled with greater social acceptance of new rights for women (such as abortion) and worsening marital and reproductive outcomes, had left many socially and economically disadvantaged men with a bad taste in their mouths.[203] Starting in the Reagan years, this resentment has taken the form of a backlash—sullen, stubborn opposition to policies and practices that favor working women—much as has occurred at other points in American history when significant progress for females was being achieved.[204]

The locus of American foreign policy and military power shifted dramatically in 1991, when President George H. W. Bush sent over half a million troops to Saudi Arabia to lead a multinational coalition of armies in expelling Iraqi forces from Kuwait. This highly successful ground campaign—completed in just over four days—ended Saddam Hussein's occupation of his neighbor, but, perhaps more importantly, brought to a close an era in American history. For nearly three decades prior to this war, no American army had engaged in major combat operations overseas—the longest period of peacetime in over a century. Those preceding years had been overshadowed by memories of Vietnam—a collective desire to avoid repeating the misjudgments and ignorance that had led the country into that unwinnable conflict. But this restraint in utilizing American military strength had come to be regarded, in some circles, as a dangerous liability: possessor of the most powerful armed forces in the world, the United States appeared to have been reduced to the status of helpless giant by the lessons it had extracted from Vietnam. While it had held back, other, hostile countries had grown strong and challenged America's supremacy. Thus, although the United States had not provoked this war, its triumph in the Persian Gulf was viewed by many—especially by many conservatives in the government, the military, and allied organizations—as ending this era of self-imposed impotence and ushering in a more proudly assertive one.[205] As President Bush proclaimed to a group of state legislators shortly after hostilities had ceased,

"The specter of Vietnam has been buried forever in the desert sands of the Arabian peninsula. It's a proud day for America and, by God, we've kicked the Vietnam syndrome once and for all."[206] Initially skeptical about going to war over Kuwait, the American public applauded this mission once it had ended with such a one-sided victory, costing so few lives.[207] The war's successful outcome greatly benefited President Bush (who received an 89 percent approval rating soon after it ended), the armed forces (which gained more positive press coverage and public approval),[208] its leaders (elevating chairman of the Joint Chiefs of Staff Colin Powell and coalition commander General Norman Schwarzkopf to the status of presidential contenders), and government spending on defense (which rose slightly despite a sagging economy).[209] The war did not spur interest in enlisting in the armed forces, but that was largely because of manpower cuts mandated by Congress during this post–Cold War era.[210] Furthermore, the professional American military was large enough to conduct operations in the Persian Gulf without new recruits.

The Gulf War of 1991 was historic in another sense: it was the first conflict in American history in which large numbers of women actively participated: they totaled forty thousand, or 6 percent of the US force.[211] Their presence marked a contentious if inadvertent break with long-standing tradition—the exclusion of female soldiers from combat. Because of the fluidity and rapidly unfolding nature of Operation Desert Storm, troops could not be separated into "frontline" or "rear-echelon" units, and so male and female soldiers from different units found themselves under Iraqi fire and firing back. Fifteen women died[212]—twice as many as in the Vietnam conflict, and more than seven times as many as in the Korean War.[213] These deaths, as well as the fact that women were fighting alongside men, were more accepted by the American public than Pentagon officials had predicted, largely because the number of fatalities was so small.[214] Although the reality that female soldiers were involved in a foreign war came as a surprise to many, the percentage of women in the armed forces had been increasing since the mid-1970s—from 1.6 percent of all personnel in 1973, to 8.5 percent in 1980, to 10.8 percent in 1989, and 12 percent at the time of the Gulf War.

This influx of women reflected several trends in civilian society—women's growing economic self-reliance, the greater need for two incomes in American households, and the impact of feminist thinking about gender equity. But, if the public was somewhat ready to go along with the reality of a fighting "GI Jane," the American military certainly was not.[215] By and large, members of the armed forces were strongly opposed to allowing members of the opposite sex to serve in combat positions.[216] To some extent, their objections were based on a more general opposition to women in the military: female soldiers would destroy the all-male esprit that binds an army together and makes serving in it appealing. But many officers and enlisted men also felt women would be an impediment during the stress and chaos of war: they would weaken the intimate, mutually supportive bonds that sustain men under fire. When one now-retired general was asked, in the 1970s, what his views on introducing female soldiers into combat units were, he replied, "Use nukes first."[217] Even after the Department of Defense opened up thousands of combat-related assignments to females in 1994, commanders dragged their feet at doing so.

The mingling of male and female soldiers in the Middle Eastern desert did not go well for many of the latter. Incidents of sexual harassment—verbal and physical—were widely documented: in a 1995 survey, nearly a quarter of women who had taken part in Operation Desert Storm reported they had been harassed, and over 3 percent said they had been assaulted. Another civilian study found even higher rates of sexual abuse during this combat mission.[218] It is generally believed that these known cases represent only a small percentage of actual incidents.[219] Such unwelcome encounters were a major cause of PTSD among female veterans.[220] Many went unreported because the female victims feared recrimination for bringing any allegations before their commanding officers. In the words of one female who served in the Persian Gulf, "Like most female soldiers, I learned the hard way that men dominate military culture. We are stuck in a culture that makes it difficult to report abuse because of reprisal."[221] The causes of this epidemic of sexual harassment are complex and controversial. Throughout history, war and rape have been closely linked. The mounting tensions and excess aggression aroused by fighting for survival can easily turn into sexual violence, and women can become sexual prey. Soldiers who feel vulnerable and helpless can unburden themselves of these feelings by depersonalizing and humiliating women (and men) through sexual assault. This restores their sense of power and control in a hostile, threatening environment. Male soldiers who have had problems establishing consensual sexual relations with women outside the military (or war zone) can see the battlefield as a kind of sexual free-fire zone, in which normal taboos and restraints fall away, and anything goes. Finally, there is the issue of sexual deprivation during war. Usually, the male sex drive—heightened by combat and the fear of death—can be satisfied by recourse to prostitutes and camp followers, but in the sexually puritanical Middle East, such women are generally not available.[222] Some veterans have used this rationale to explain the high frequency of assaults on their female comrades.[223] Whatever the cause, there is abundant evidence that sexual harassment and assault have emerged as major problems within the "coeducational" military the United States began to field in the Gulf War. Before the invasion of Iraq in 2003, while American troops were based in Kuwait, a large number of assaults occurred, and this rate has only increased during the US presence in Iraq and Afghanistan. A report released by the Department of Defense lists 2,924 reported cases of sexual assault throughout the military during 2008—more than 8 percent higher than in the previous year. The incidence among female troops in the two war zones more than tripled during this period.[224] As one female soldier who served in Iraq in a company with 1,500 men and only 18 women summed up, "I was fresh meat to hungry men."[225]

What is particularly disturbing about this trend is that it seems to have been largely an American problem within the multinational force. (Rape and assault have also been endemic among Iraqi security forces.) One could contend that members of other armies have had less access to uniformed female nationals and therefore commit these crimes less frequently. But, in fact, this is not wholly so. For instance, 1,600 female British military personnel were serving in Iraq and Afghanistan as of 2007, out of a total of roughly 12,000. This amounts to 13 percent, or nearly the same proportion of females as in the American forces. Yet cases of rape and harassment in the British military are markedly fewer.[226] Still, US soldiers are hardly the only ones around the world who harass and assault women in their ranks. Rates of sexual harassment and assault in the Israeli army are equally high, for example.[227] On the other hand, during World War II, women serving in the Red Army were rarely raped or otherwise assaulted by their male comrades. Rather, the latter developed a sisterly affection for their female counterparts and found sexual release mostly with willing nurses, telegraph operators, and other noncombatant "wives."[228] Red Army soldiers later vented their sexual hostility, exacted revenge, and inflicted humiliation by raping millions of female civilians, including even Russian ones, as they swept westward into the heart of Nazi Germany.[229]

One factor that appears to make sexual assault more common during wartime is a high degree of bottled-up hostility, either toward women in general, or, for racial reasons, toward the enemy nation. The predilection for rape among Japanese troops in China (20,000 assaults in Nanking alone in 1937), among American troops in Vietnam, and among Serbian forces in Bosnia during the early 1990s seems motivated by perceptions of their victims as "alien," inferior, and thus somehow less human and more liable for abuse. Defiling these women was a way to emasculate their foes, to thwart their reproductive aspirations. But the rape of women from one's own country, or from those from nations that are ethnically and religiously similar, seems to suggest a deeper, misogynistic basis: the rape victim is a stand-in for other females who have previously ignored, rejected, or ill-treated the "avenging" perpetrator. In Kuwait and Iraq, the sexual abuse of American women in uniform by males in their same units would appear to fall into this category. They were abreacting pain endured long before they set foot in the war zone.

Without question, the multinational coalition's victory over Saddam Hussein in 1991 greatly elevated the power and prestige of the United States. The aerial decimation of targets inside Iraq and General Schwarzkopf's blitzkrieg ground attack deep into enemy territory demonstrated the unsurpassed destructive might and strategic genius of the American military in a way the world had not witnessed since the dropping of the atomic bomb on Japan. General Schwarzkopf ("Stormin' Norman") was deified in the press, going from "mere general to genuine sex symbol faster than a speeding smart bomb," in the words of a *Newsday* feature writer.[230] It reaffirmed the prowess of American fighting men and their leaders. It won them the admiration of the nation. It largely erased haunting memories of Vietnam. It made Americans feel good about their country. This was, crowed Andy Rooney on *60 Minutes*, "the best war in modern history, not only for America, but for the whole world, including Iraq, probably."[231] But the war's positive impact on the country's psyche was only temporary. The triumph in the Gulf did not improve the deteriorating economic situation back in the States, where oil prices spiked and unemployment remained stubbornly high. After a brief recovery, the nation slipped back into recession. Its Daedalian fall from heroic heights was exemplified by the fate of George H. W. Bush: judged out of touch with his fellow Americans' plight, his polling numbers plummeted, and he lost his bid for reelection in 1992 to Bill Clinton, garnering less than 38 percent of the vote.

The military, too, lost its luster.[232] Continuing their post–Cold War downsizing, the armed forces grew even smaller—from slightly over 2 million active duty members in 1990 to 1.5 million five years later. During the coming decade, the glorious victory won in the Arabian Desert was not to be repeated. US troops were deployed for a while in Somalia and Haiti, and American planes bombed targets in Yugoslavia and Iraq, but, in general, the importance of the armed forces diminished. Images of victory gave way to ones of defeat. Dead Army Rangers were dragged through the streets of Mogadishu. An explosion tore through the garage under the World Trade Center in New York, killing six people, injuring over a thousand, and shaking the nation's confidence. The Pentagon was forced by a president who had spurned service in Vietnam to accept gay men and women in the ranks. Their civilian boss at the Department of Defense was an economist who, as a young antiwar Congressman, had gotten the public all stirred up about the Air Force's plan to test poison gas on beagles.[233] Women were making a lot of news. The secretary of the Air Force was a woman. So was the secretary of state. Hillary Clinton was acting like a "copresident." Blondes seemed to be everywhere. In response to early rumors about her husband's adultery with one of them, the president's wife declared, "I'm not some Tammy Wynette standing by my man."[234] But she did anyway. After it was revealed that he had had an affair with a White House intern, her husband's ranking as the most admired man in the world went up four points. Like Clinton, many men in the 1990s seemed boyishly adrift without a purpose, just looking for a little diversion. One of the most popular programs on television was *Seinfeld*, in which nobody really did anything but tell jokes. In another—*Frasier*—two snobbish psychiatrist brothers divested of spouses indulged their childish sibling rivalry over lattes. It was amusing, but equally pointless.

All this changed in a flash after 9/11. The nation was under attack and apparently helpless to defend itself. It badly needed people who could step forward and rescue the endangered, care for the injured, and track down and kill the persons responsible for this stunning attack on American soil. So it was reassuring to see, along with the horrifying images of people jumping out of the Twin Towers on September 11, the fire trucks roaring down to Lower Manhattan; the intrepid firefighters laden with gear ascending the massive buildings with no regard for their own safety or lives; the strangers comforting ash-covered fellow New Yorkers on the sidewalks; the once-derided mayor of New York, Rudolph Giuliani, stepping up to the microphones and cameras before anyone had any idea how many had perished in the explosion and surprising even his most ardent critics by revealing that he was not only human and compassionate, but fully in command. "Tomorrow," an obviously shaken Giuliani promised, "the effort will be at trying to recover as many people as possible and trying to clean up the horrible mess that was created by all of this."[235] With those comforting words and the thousands more he offered in the following days, Giuliani evolved from brash bully to symbol of perseverance and resilience. Stopping to honor the dead and missing in Union Square Park the next day, an artist mused aloud about how her view of the mayor had now changed. "I am not a supporter of Mayor Giuliani," she confessed, "but he was so elegant. I have newfound love for him. . . . He sounded like a real leader."[236]

Giuliani was only one of a host of leaders who were redeemed from obscurity and ill-repute by their words and actions in the aftermath of 9/11. President George W. Bush, who had sat speechless in a Florida classroom for seven minutes after he had been informed of the attacks, looking like an actor who had yet to figure out how to play his part, stood atop the still-smoldering debris pile three days later with a bullhorn in his hand and a grin on his face and told the throng of chanting ("USA! USA!") rescue workers, "I can hear you, the rest of the world hears you, and the people who knocked these buildings down will hear all of us soon."[237] And the nation rallied behind him and his promise of revenge. Bush's secretary of defense, Donald Rumsfeld—an indomitable wrestler in his days at Princeton, but now, at age sixty-nine, known more as a bespectacled bureaucratic in-fighter—underwent the same kind of improbably apotheosis. Blunt, bullish, and full of confidence, he became America's newest heartthrob. Gushed the *Philadelphia Inquirer*'s Beth

Gillin: "He's vigorous. He's direct. . . . No doubt about it, Donald Rumsfeld is a stud muffin."[238] From the president on down the chain of command, male leaders were firmly back in charge, and the public loved them. Retired generals dominated the air waves as they once had commanded troops in battle, offering sage advice to the president and their successors. Male anchormen reclaimed their prominence in the broadcast booths, as TV executives sensed the nation needed deep, masculine voices to steady its nerves. "Beefcake" images of male firefighters graced calendars, and establishment newspapers like the *New York Times* wrote about a more "muscular role" for the government.[239]

If America's manhood had suffered a direct blow in the toppling of the phallic Twin Towers, then this symbolic emasculation gave men added incentive to rise up and assert *they* were still standing. Through the voices of its talking heads, as Susan Faludi has pointed out, the country ached for a "new John Wayne masculinity"—a return to the days when men could be counted upon to rout the guys in black hats and make Dodge City safe again.[240] The same primal need to set things right transformed ordinary men into potential saviors. Those who dropped what they were doing to rush into Manhattan and join the tireless crews at the World Trade Center site, or who made the more risky commitment to sign up for the army or marines to hunt down bin Laden and his followers, were honored for their sacrifice and courage as much as those (again, men) who had risen from their seats on Flight 93 to storm the cockpit and try to prevent disaster on 9/11. Even the fabricated heroes of the small screen basked in heroic hues: as a stolid Jack Bauer, star of Fox Television's fortuitously well-timed antiterrorism thriller, *24*, saved America from a succession of 9/11-style plots, he seemed to carry the hopes of the entire country into each new episode, even as his methods for extracting information grew increasingly brutal and crossed the line into torture.[241]

As men returned to the forefront, women quietly left the stage. As in wars past, their role was to support—to stand by their men. Prominently visible female personages in the media served only to remind viewers of male inadequacies, so they had to go. Some even hinted that it was their having "feminized" men and made them "weak" that had left the country totally unprepared for these attacks.[242] America would now be better off if women now got out of the way and let men get the job done. The fact that female firefighters and police officers—despite their minuscule numbers in these traditionally male professions—had also gone to the aid of victims at the World Trade Center, and that three of them had died while doing so, was conveniently overlooked. It was the men who were being celebrated as heroes; it was the women whom they were rescuing.[243] This reversion to stock gender roles followed the script played out in wars past: it could be justified as helping to clarify the lines of responsibility for defending the country and to embolden men to assume the duties it was felt only they could perform—or, at least, perform well.

The strange thing was that few actually stepped forward and took the oath of allegiance. In the wake of 9/11, newspapers, magazines, and books abounded with stories of young men (and women) who had reacted spontaneously with patriotic outrage to these attacks and signed up to defeat the terrorists who had perpetrated them. Many of these volunteers came from unlikely places—the offices of Goldman Sachs, a professional football team, college campuses. And, while their eagerness to serve helped the various branches of the armed services to meet their enlistment quotas in the ensuing months and for several years afterward, there was no massive stampede to the recruitment offices, as had occurred after Pearl Harbor.[244] A spike of interest in serving after 9/11 quickly subsided.[245] Why didn't more Americans come forward in this hour of national crisis? Partially this can be explained by the Bush administration's response to the attacks. Instead of asking the American people to make sacrifices and join in a common effort after 9/11, the president urged his countrymen to carry on with their normal lives and leave the job of dealing with al Qaeda and its supporters up to the professional military.[246] As the United States prepared to attack first Afghanistan and then Iraq, little effort was made to persuade civilians to sign up for these planned operations. Governing this approach was the reality that the American military was now, for all intents and purposes, a separate force outside civilian society and independent of it. Asking ordinary citizens to don uniforms, pick up weapons, and fly across the world to help defeat the nation's enemies seemed as anachronistic as asking residents of an urban block to fill water buckets to put out a fire in their neighborhood. A sense of shared responsibility for defending the country no longer existed. This was no accident, but the outcome of a deliberate policy decision in the 1970s: after Vietnam, the government, wanting to isolate the military from the shifting winds of public opinion, had ended the draft and made service a matter of free will. The continuation of this policy suggested that the American public was happy to let career professionals wage wars for them, thus quarantining the suffering these would inevitably bring, as well as sparing the military much moral and political second guessing if these wars did not go well.

Mainly for this reason, the average citizen of military age—male or female—did not feel compelled to join up after September 11, even though the United States had just sustained a devastating, unprecedented attack on its continental homeland. For a time, the military did not appear to want or need tens of thousands of new recruits. The military responses to 9/11 being contemplated at the Pentagon did not involve large armies engaged in battle for years to come. Instead, the secretary of defense and his top generals envisioned rapid, decisive victories, to be achieved by a small, professional force. However, as the wars in Afghanistan and Iraq unexpectedly dragged on and casualties mounted, the need for additional troops became apparent. The Pentagon was then forced to step up its recruitment efforts. These focused on working-class youth, particularly in urban neighborhoods.[247] To help persuade young men and women to join, they were offered substantial enlistment and educational bonuses.[248] (However, advertisements for the military on television and high school visits by army and marine recruiters also stressed the heroic aspect of serving the country during wartime.) The Pentagon's pragmatic approach reflected two inescapable facts: first of all, the war in Iraq was not going well, and it was thus hard to "sell" it on patriotic grounds; and, second, the motives for young people to sign up for the military now had more to do with self-interest than during World War II and even the Vietnam conflict. (Army recruiters had implicitly acknowledged this individualistic state of mind when they adopted the slogan "An Army of One" before 9/11.) Although many had been moved by love of country to join after the September 11 attacks, this motivation had receded with the passage of time and the worsening of the situation in Iraq. By 2005, financial incentives were far more persuasive.[249] This strategy made sense, given that large numbers of volunteers came from lower socioeconomic backgrounds.[250] The sharp increase in the number of persons and families living in poverty in 2001 indicates how great the need for additional income was: there were 1.4 million more poor Americans and 400,000 more families in this situation than the year before; growing wage inequity meant that families at the bottom of the economic ladder were living off less than they had in 2000.[251]

Evidence of the war's economic appeal was found in interviews journalist Michael Massing conducted among army recruits stationed in upstate New York in 2008: most aspired to "make it into the middle class."[252] It is also manifest in several memoirs written by veterans of the Iraq and Afghanistan conflicts: in one of them a twenty-four-year-old Oklahoman with two young sons conceded that he and his wife saw the military "as a way to get out of poverty."[253] But the desire to get ahead by earning a better, more reliable salary masks another, less often stated reason: the wish to marry and have children (as well as provide for already existing families). There is evidence that being in the armed services after the September 11 attacks did provide this kind of marriage "bonus." Starting in 2002, the marriage rate among active-duty soldiers began to climb slightly, ending a long decline since the mid-1990s. More relevantly, the percentage of married recruits entering the military rose similarly, from a low of 9.9 percent in 2001 to 11.1 in 2005.[254] These trends ran counter to an overall increase in the percentage of unmarried Americans during this period.[255]

At the same time, the continuing segregation of the armed forces from civilian society had several major negative consequences. Perhaps the greatest of these was the armed forces' persisting insulation from and hostility toward certain trends in the "outside world." The most sensitive and controversial of these had to do with sex roles and gender identity. Sustained combat in Iraq and Afghanistan only intensified animosity against women serving there. The number of sexual assaults and incidents of harassment reached epidemic levels: according to several studies conducted in 2008, 30 percent of female veterans reported being raped while serving in the military, another 71 percent stated they had been sexually assaulted, and fully 90 percent had been sexually harassed.[256] An alarming proportion of female veterans of the Iraq and Afghanistan conflicts also suffer from PTSD, mostly as a consequence of being raped.[257] The motives for this kind of degradation at the hands of their fellow soldiers have not yet been adequately analyzed, but one can surmise that the stresses of prolonged combat, the lack of other sexual outlets, and a pervasive misogynistic environment are largely responsible. A number of male soldiers seem more determined than ever to humiliate women in their ranks, make their lives unbearable, and discourage other females from signing up. Their behavior betrays a basic fact about the US military: it remains philosophically and emotionally uncomfortable with the presence of women, especially in times of war. While there are recent signs that this resistant attitude is changing, the armed forces still have to figure out how to reconcile externally imposed obligation to accept females in the ranks as full and equal members within the exclusionary, masculine esprit and traditions.[258] Some men in uniform feel that the military's very essence and continuity as an institution are endangered by the pressures to accept women as participants in the waging of war—an enterprise they regard as a fundamental and essential expression of their male identity. By acceding to these demands, they fear surrendering what little still distinguishes them and justifies their existence. In rebuffing women, they are fighting for their own survival.

Their intense desire to hold female soldiers at bay finds itself on a collision course with the equally intense desire on the part of women to achieve parity in all spheres of American life. Having made remarkable progress in securing new opportunities in education, employment, and professional careers, in freeing themselves from second-class status, in gaining new rights and legal protection, and in attaining a degree of economic independence, women are eager to see all remaining obstacles to fulfilling their full potential fall away. Those who want to serve their country by fighting in its wars are advancing this common cause. The long struggle for gender equity, dating back at least to the women's rights movement of the nineteenth century, has now reached a critical juncture. The tensions generated by the two competing human needs traced in this book—on the one hand, to define one's self by what makes us different and, on the other hand, to avoid being held back by such definitions—have come to a head.

This debate over the proper role of women in the military carries both symbolic and real significance. Symbolically, it will clarify whether or not Americans still believe that biology should be a factor in determining how society is organized. It will settle the question, "Who can be a warrior?" As a practical matter, the resolution of this controversy will decide whose lives are to be put at risk and potentially sacrificed for the good of the nation—who will protect and who will be protected, who will die and who will live. Thus much is at stake. For those who favor greater female empowerment, integrating women into combat units would represent a major accomplishment—the chance to perform one of the most vital roles a society can entrust to its people. But, in the eyes of many traditionalist men, such a breach of a once sacrosanct divide between them and the opposite sex would spell the end of their uniqueness—the demise of the last defining trait of manhood. For them, this is a last-ditch struggle to preserve a sense of worth. With so much hanging in the balance, this is likely to be a long and painful confrontation. On its outcome may well hinge the shape of American society for some time to come.

NOTES

CHAPTER 1

1. Theodore Stanton and Harriot Stanton Blatch, foreword, *Elizabeth Cady Stanton: As Revealed in Her Letters, Diary, and Reminiscences*, ed. Theodore Stanton and Harriot Stanton Blatch (New York: Harper & Brothers, 1922), p. xvii.

2. Lori D. Ginzberg, *Elizabeth Cady Stanton: An American Life* (New York: Hill & Wang, 2009), p. 33.

3. Ibid., p. 87.

4. Ibid., p. 32.

5. For more details about Stanton's courtship, marriage, and trip abroad, see ibid., pp. 67–89.

6. Quoted in *Right and Wrong in Boston: Report of the Boston Female Anti-Slavery Society* (Boston: Female Anti-Slavery Society, 1836), p. 28.

7. For an account of this confrontation, see ibid., pp. 6–35. Cf. Jack Tager, *Boston Riots: Three Centuries of Social Violence* (Boston: Northeastern University Press, 2002), pp. 30–32.

8. Dorothy Sterling, *Lucretia Mott* (New York: Feminist Press, 1964), p. 121.

9. Peter Hinks and John McKivigan, eds., *Encyclopedia of Antislavery and Abolition* (Westport, CT: Westwood, 2007), p. 484. In 1838, Mott had also witnessed the tarring and feathering of the male president of Pennsylvania Hall, an antislavery forum in Philadelphia. Letter of Lucretia Mott to Maria Weston Chapman, May 13, 1840. Beverly Wilson Palmer, ed., *Selected Letters of Lucretia Coffin Mott* (Urbana: University of Illinois Press, 2002), p. 76. Cf. Carol Berkin, *Civil War Wives* (New York: Knopf, 2009), pp. 72–73.

10. Letter of Lucretia Mott to Maria Weston Chapman, July 27, 1840. *Selected Letters*, pp. 78–79.

11. Those who left the AASS also objected to Garrison's radical proposal to create a new federal government and write a new constitution that would forbid slavery. See, for example, Aileen Kraditor, *Means and Ends in American Abolitionism: Garrison and His Critics on Strategy and Tactics, 1834–1850* (New York: Pantheon, 1969).

12. Frederick B. Tolles, ed., *Slavery and "The Woman Question": Lucretia Mott's Diary of Her Visit to Great Britain to Attend the World's Anti-Slavery Convention of 1840*, supplement 23, *Journal of the Friends' Historical Society* (Haverford, PA: Friends' Historical Association and Friends' Historical Society, 1952), p. 29.

13. Document 4 (1:53–62), "World's Anti-Slavery Convention, London, England, June 1840," http://www.sscnet.ucla.edu/history/dubois/classes/995/98F/doc4.html (accessed September 20, 2009).

14. Sterling, *Lucretia Mott*, p. 116.

15. Palmer, ed., *Selected Letters of Lucretia Mott*, p. 81, note 8.

16. Remarks of George Thompson, *Proceedings of the General Anti-Slavery Convention* (London: Johnston & Barrett, 1841), p. 34.

17. Carrie Chapman Catt and Nettie Rogers Shuler, *Woman Suffrage and Politics: The Inner Story of the Suffrage Movement* (New York: Scribner's, 1926), p. 17.

18. "World's Anti-Slavery Convention."

19. Remarks of Rev. C. Stovel, *Proceedings*, p. 43.

20. Remarks of Rev. Nathaniel Colver, *Proceedings*, p. 27.

21. Letter of Lucretia Mott to Maria Weston Chapman, July 29, 1840, *Selected Letters*.

22. This was in the *Dublin Weekly Herald*. Quoted in Sterling, *Lucretia Mott*, p. 114.

23. Her presence in this painting was kept to a minimum due to the animosity of the artist, Benjamin Haydon, toward Mott. After having shown her and a black portrait artist around his studio, he vowed that her "infidel notions" disqualified her from having prominent visibility in his work and reduced her to a small "blob of paint" in the background. Sterling, *Lucretia Mott*, p. 120.

24. Letter of Lucretia Mott to Maria Weston Chapman, July 29, 1840. Mott was referring to Hebrews 5:12.

25. Elizabeth Cady Stanton, *Eighty Years and More: Reminiscences*, 1915–1897 (Lebanon, NH: University Press of New England, 1993), p. 120.

26. Catt and Shuler, *Woman Suffrage*, p. 19.

27. Stanton, *Eighty Years*, p. 145.

28. The invitation to attend had specified the meeting was to be for women only. Catt and Shuler, *Woman Suffrage*, p. 19.

29. At least one-quarter of the signers of the "Declaration" were Quakers, making them the largest single religious contingent. "The Birth of the Women's Rights Movement in Seneca County," p. 8, http://www.co.seneca.ny.us/history/Birth%20of%20the%20Women%27s%20Rights%20Movement%20in%20Seneca%20County.pdf (accessed September 18, 2009).

30. Henry Stanton helped to organize the Free Soil Party and campaigned for its presidential candidate, Martin Van Buren, during the 1848 election.

31. "Declaration of Sentiments," Seneca Falls Convention, 1848. This document was signed by sixty-eight women, including Lucretia Mott and Elizabeth Cady Stanton. Thirty-two men, including James Mott, signed a separate statement of support.

32. Quoted in Sylvia D. Hoffert, *When Hens Crow: The Woman's Rights Movement in Antebellum America* (Bloomington: Indiana University Press, 1990), p. 97.

33. Vivian Gornick, *Solitude of Self: Thinking about Elizabeth Cady Stanton* (New York: Farrar, Straus & Giroux, 2005), p. 45.

34. Stanton, *Eighty Years*, p. 149. Cf. Erik A. Bruun and Jay Crosby, eds., *Our Nation's Archive: The History of the United States in Documents* (New York: Black Dog & Leventhal, 1999), p. 295. There is no evidence that this actually happened.

35. One survey of seventy-one newspapers around the country found that those who had editorialized one way or the other about the Seneca Falls gathering were equally divided in their opinions. Judith Wellman, *The Road to Seneca Falls: Elizabeth Cady Stanton and the First Woman's Rights Convention* (Urbana: University of Illinois Press, 2004), p. 210.

36. Ibid.

37. Nancy Isenberg, *Sex and Citizenship in Antebellum America* (Chapel Hill: University of North Carolina Press, 1998), p. 5.

38. Sarah M. Grimké, *Letters on the Equality of the Sexes and the Condition of Woman* (Boston: Knapp, 1838), p. 4.

39. William Thompson, *Appeal of One Half the Human Race, Women, Against the Pretenses of the Other Half, Men* (New York: Lenox Hill, 1970), p. 64.

40. Robert S. Fletcher and Ernest H. Wilkins, "The Beginning of College Education for Women and of Coeducation on the College Level," *Bulletin of Oberlin College New Series* 343 (March 20, 1837), http://www.oberlin.edu/archive/resources/1937Bulletin/transcript.html (accessed September 19, 2009).

41. Blackwell graduated from nearby Geneva College in January 1849 first in her class. However, fellow female boarders in town refused to speak with her during her three years of residence there. Catt and Shuler, *Woman Suffrage*, p. 21.

42. Membership in Methodist churches doubled in the decade 1820–1830, and the number of Baptists increased by a factor of ten in the thirty years after the American Revolution. Nathan O. Hatch, *The Democratization of American Christianity* (New Haven, CT: Yale University Press, 1991), p. 3.

43. The first female minister, Antoinette Brown, was ordained by the Con-

gregational Church in 1853. Paula D. Nesbit, *Feminization of the Clergy in America: Occupational and Organizational Perspectives* (New York: Oxford University Press, 1997), p. 23.

44. Benjamin Franklin and Stephen Hopkins, of Rhode Island, are other signers identified with deism.

45. Hatch, *Democratization of American Christianity*, p. 35.

46. John Locke, *Two Treatises on Government* (London: Baldwin, 1824), p. 177.

47. For details, see Thomas G. West, *Vindicating the Founders: Race, Sex, Class and Justice in the Origins of America* (Lanham, MD: Rowman & Littlefield, 1997), pp. 75–77.

48. Between the founding of the nation and 1850, seven presidents were slaveholders, and four were not; slaveholders held the position of chief justice of the Supreme Court for forty-nine years, while nonslaveholders occupied it for only twelve. Furthermore, at no point during this sixty-year period were slave owners a minority on the Court. See remarks of George Washington Julian on "The Slavery Question," House of Representatives, May 14, 1850, in George W. Julian, *Speeches on Political Questions* (New York: Hurd & Houghton, 1872), p. 25.

49. The Republican platform of 1860 had opposed the extension of slavery to the western territories, as had the Free Soil platform of 1848, but neither had expressly called for the "complete extirpation" of this practice as the 1864 GOP platform did.

50. Roosevelt's campaign gave women a prominent presence in that campaign, including allowing Jane Addams to give the speech seconding his nomination at the party's national convention.

51. Remarks of Rep. Stevenson Archer, House of Representatives, 42nd Congress, 2nd Section, Appendix to the *Congressional Globe* (May 30, 1872), p. 632.

52. "Woman Suffrage in the Senate," *New York Times*, December 22, 1881.

53. Quoted in Andrea Moore Kerr, *Lucy Stone: Speaking Out for Equality* (New Brunswick, NJ: Rutgers University Press, 1992), p. 55.

54. Ibid.

55. Quoted in Ida Husted Harper, *The Life and Work of Susan B. Anthony*, 3 vols. (New York: Arno, 1969), 3: 1364. For several accounts of hostile crowd reaction to her speaking, see Harper, *Susan B. Anthony* (Indianapolis: Hollenbeck, 1898), p. 1.

56. Letter of Lucy Stone to The Una, May 1853, Mary Jo Buhle and Paul Buhle, eds., *The Concise History of Woman Suffrage* (Urbana: University of Illinois Press, 2005), p. 143.

57. Remarks of Rev. John Chambers, "World Temperance Convention:

Meeting of Delegates" (September 1–2, 1853). Votes for Women: Selections from the National American Woman Suffrage Association Collection, 1848–1921, American Memory, Library of Congress, http://memory.loc.gov/cgi-bin/query/r?ammem/naw:@field%28DOCID+@lit%28rbnawsan1898div4%29%29 (accessed September 15, 2009).

58. Remarks of Amos C. Barstow, ibid.

59. Harper, *Susan B. Anthony*, 1:101.

60. In 1873, the Women's Christian Temperance Union (WCTU) was founded. Many men in this movement felt their continued leadership was important for sustaining male dominance in society. To them, ending dependence on alcohol was the best way to restore masculine self-reliance and the ideal of the "self-made man." Because drink weakened their will, they thought of it as a "feminizing" force. Holly Berkley Fletcher, *Gender and the American Temperance Movement of the Nineteenth Century* (New York: Routledge, 2008), pp. 7, 15, 56.

61. Ibid., p. 41.

62. Ian R. Tyrrell, "Drink and Temperance in the Antebellum South: An Overview and Interpretation," *Journal of Southern History* 48, no. 4 (December 1988): 485–89. Even though some Southern men backed restrictions on alcohol consumption in order to help preserve their control over slaves and women, there were far fewer persons, proportionally, committed to temperance in that region than in the North. Fletcher, *Gender and the American Temperance Movement*, pp. 28, 48.

63. Severn Duvall, "Uncle Tom's Cabin: The Sinister Side of the Patriarchy," *New England Quarterly* 35, no. 4 (December 1962): 17.

64. During the 1850s, Anthony attempted to bring the antislavery and women's movements together. During an 1859 women's rights convention speech, she declared: "Where, under our Declaration of Independence, does the Saxon man get his power to deprive all women and Negroes of their inalienable rights?" See remarks of Susan B. Anthony, Ninth Women's Rights Convention (May 12, 1859), Elizabeth Cady Stanton, Susan B. Anthony and Matilda Joslyn Gage, eds., *History of Woman Suffrage*, 4 vols. (New York: Fowler & Wells, 1881), 1: 675.

65. The year it appeared, 300,000 copies of *Uncle Tom's Cabin* were sold, and the novel went on to become the second-greatest bestseller in the United States (after the Bible) in the nineteenth century. One historian has rightly observed that this one book "had a greater impact on Northern sentiment than the combined effect of all the abolitionist tracts that were ever published." David L. Lightner, *Slavery and the Commerce Power: How the Struggle against the Interstate Slave Trade Led to the Civil War* (New Haven, CT: Yale University Press, 2006), p. 127.

66. Robert S. Levine, "Fiction and Reform—I," in Emory Elliott, ed., *The Columbia History of the American Novel: New Views* (New York: Columbia University Press, 1991), p. 144.

67. See, for example, Jean Fagan Yellin, introduction, *Uncle Tom's Cabin* (Oxford: Oxford University Press, 1998), p. xxvi. See also LeAnn Whites, "The Civil War as a Crisis in Gender," in Catherine Clinton and Nina Silber, eds., *Divided Houses: Gender and the Civil War* (New York: Oxford University Press, 1992), pp. 3–21. After writing *Uncle Tom's Cabin*, Stowe took on another bastion of patriarchy—the Calvinist faith—in her novel *Oldtown Folks* (1869).

68. For the impact of Stowe's novel on women readers, see Claire Parfait, *The Publishing History of* Uncle Tom's Cabin, *1852–2002* (Farnham, UK: Ashgate, 2007), p. 26. One scholar has pointed out that *Uncle Tom's Cabin* was an example of the sentimental novel, which is written "by, for, and about women." Jane Tompkins, *Sensational Designs: The Cultural Work of American Fiction, 1790–1860* (New York: Oxford University Press, 1985), pp. 124–25.

69. Letter of Harriet Beecher Stowe to Gamaliel Bailey, March 9, 1851, quoted in Duvall, "Uncle Tom's Cabin," p. 4.

70. Quoted in Ronald G. Walters, "Harriet Beecher Stowe and the American Reform Tradition," in Cindy Weinstein, ed., *The Cambridge Companion to Harriet Beecher Stowe* (Cambridge: Cambridge University Press, 2004), p. 171. Stowe felt that all women would be devastated by a forced separation from one of their children, as happened to slave mothers. Largely for this reason, she believed that the wives of Southern planters were not supportive of the chattel system. Duvall, "Uncle Tom's Cabin," p. 19.

71. David Brion Davis, "Declaring Equality: Sisterhood and Slavery," in Kathryn Kish Sklar and James Brewer Stewart, eds., *Women's Rights and Transatlantic Slavery in the Era of Emancipation* (New Haven, CT: Yale University Press, 2007), p. 11.

72. Quoted in Bonnie S. Anderson, *Joyous Greetings: The First International Women's Movement, 1830–1860* (New York: Oxford University Press, 2001), p. 122.

73. Important financial backers were the Tappan brothers, Lewis and Arthur, and Gerrit Smith. Free blacks in the North also contributed to this cause.

74. Quoted in Stanton, *Elizabeth Cady Stanton*, 2:78. Many who were present later expressed their indignation that Stanton had used this occasion to associate emancipation with "a topic so foreign to the call" that had united them.

75. As late as 1902, male voters in New Hampshire rejected a referendum that would have given women in their state the vote.

76. Amy S. Greenberg, *Manifest Manhood and the Antebellum American Empire* (New York: Cambridge University Press, 2005), p. 98.

77. David Grimstead, *American Mobbing, 1828–1861: Toward Civil War* (New York: Oxford University Press, 1998), pp. 12, 98, passim.

78. There were a total of 147 riots in the country that year, with 46 of them being proslavery. Ibid., p. 4.

79. Walter Gable, "The Flats: A Brief History," unpublished manuscript, Seneca Falls Historical Society (February 14, 2005). See also Wellman, *Road to Seneca Falls*, p. 76.

80. Anya Jabour, *Scarlett's Sisters: Young Women in the Old South* (Chapel Hill: University of North Carolina Press, 2009), p. 180. Cf. Marilyn Yalom, *A History of the Wife* (New York: HarperCollins, 2001), p. 205.

81. Only "menial, tedious, or low-paying jobs" were available to antebellum Southern women. George C. Rable, *Civil Wars: Women and the Crisis of Southern Nationalism* (Urbana: University of Illinois Press, 1989), p. 29.

82. Yalom, *History of the Wife*, p. 212.

83. Anne Sinkler Whaley LeClercq, "Daily Life on a South Carolina Plantation, 1855–1983: A Scrapbook Memory from Three Generations of Women," in Susan Tucker, Katherine Ott, and Patricia P. Buckler, eds., *The Scrapbook in American Life* (Philadelphia: Temple University Press, 2006), p. 43

84. The conviction that all white men deserved unquestioned domestic authority forged a powerful bond that crossed class boundaries. Scott Stephan, *Redeeming the Southern Family: Evangelical Women and Domestic Devotion in the Antebellum South* (Athens: University of Georgia Press, 2008), p. 16.

85. Anne Firor Scott, *The Southern Lady: From Pedestal to Politics, 1830–1930* (Chicago: University of Chicago Press, 1970), quoted in LeClercq, "Daily Life," p. 43. Another historian has written, "The same outside forces that endangered slavery also endangered a man's control over his family and, thereby, his place in society." Walter B. Edgar, *South Carolina: A History* (Columbia: University of South Carolina Press, 1998), p. 294.

86. Stephan, *Redeeming the Southern Family*, p. 17.

87. Davis, "Declaring Equality," p. 12.

88. S. J. Kleinberg, *Women in the United States, 1830–1945* (New Brunswick, NJ: Rutgers University Press, 1999), pp. 58–62.

89. J. David Hacker, "Rethinking the 'Early' Decline of Marital Fertility in the United States," *Demography* 40, no. 4 (November 2003): 605–608. Nearly half of American women born in 1850 were still single by the time they turned twenty. This would increase to two-thirds of those born at the end of the century. Lee L. Bean, Geraldine P. Mineau, and Douglas L. Anderton, *Fertility Change on the American Frontier: Adaptation and Innovation* (Berkeley: University of California Press, 1990), p. 129. By far, the factor most responsible for the decline in the birth rate was a decrease in marital fertility. Warren C. Sanderson,

"Quantitative Aspects of Marriage, Fertility and Family Limitation in Nineteenth Century America: Another Application of the Coale Specifications," *Demography* 16, no. 3 (August 1979): 340.

90. By the 1850s, most responsibility for the raising of children was in the hands of women. Graham J. Barker-Benfield, *The Horrors of the Half-Known Life: Male Attitudes toward Women and Sexuality in Nineteenth-Century America* (New York: Routledge, 2005), p. 38. They held sway in what Alexis de Tocqueville referred to as their "moral precincts."

91. Many men felt they needed to leave home to find sexual autonomy as well. Ibid., p. 10.

92. Lord Byron, *Childe Harold's Pilgrimage*, canto IV: CLXXVIII.

93. On the eve of the Civil War, as many people lived outside the eastern states as did within that region. Fig. 2, "Regional Shares of Total Population, 1790–1910," Guillaume Vandenbroucke, "The American Frontier: A Hundred Years of Western Settlement," Research Report No. 7 (February 2007), Economie d'avant Garde, http://www.econ.rochester.edu/Faculty/Greenwood Papers/Frontier.pdf (accessed September 28, 2009).

94. In 1850, the population of the United States included 9.9 million white males and 9.1 million white females. The west was initially settled primarily by single males, creating a significant gender imbalance. Between 1850 and 1860, nearly 63 percent of mountain state residents were male. Barker-Benfield, *Horrors of the Half-Known Life*, p. 13.

95. Hoffert, *When Hens Crow*, p. 101.

96. Clyde Griffen, "Reconstructing Masculinity from the Evangelical Revival to the Waning of Progressivism: A Speculative Synthesis," in Marc C. Carnes and Clyde Griffen, eds., *Meanings for Manhood: Constructions of Manhood in Victorian America* (Chicago: University of Chicago Press, 1990), p. 189. Cf. Clifford Putney, *Muscular Christianity: Manhood and Sports in Protestant America, 1880–1920* (Cambridge, MA: Harvard University Press, 2001), pp. 20–21.

97. Charles Sumner, *The Crime against Kansas: The Apologies for the Crime—The True Remedy* (Boston: Jewett, 1856), p. 9.

98. This epithet was also used by Northerners who strongly opposed abolition. See, for example, "Remarks of Rev. J. C. K. Milligan, 20 Nov. 1883," *Reformed Presbyterian and Covenanter* 22:3 (March 1884), p. 89.

99. They were often accused of defiling "true womanhood." Mary P. Ryan, "Gender and Public Access: Women's Politics in Nineteenth-Century America," in Craig J. Calhoun, ed., *Habermas and the Public Sphere* (Cambridge, MA: MIT Press, 1993), p. 271.

100. Between 1.2 and 1.4 million men volunteered for the Confederate army; nearly 2.9 million signed up for the Union army.

101. According to one estimate, only one in ten Union soldiers fought to end slavery. Randall C. Jimerson, *The Private Civil War: Popular Thought during the Sectional Conflict* (Baton Rouge: Louisiana State University Press, 1988), p. 41. See also James McPherson, *For Cause and Comrades: Why Men Fought in the Civil War* (New York: Oxford University Press, 1997), p. 19.

102. Carol Reardon, "'We Are All in This War': The 148th Pennsylvania and Home Front Dissension in Centre County during the Civil War," in Paul A. Cimbala and Randall M. Miller, eds., *Union Soldiers and the Northern Homefront: Wartime Experiences and Postwar Adjustments* (New York: Fordham University Press, 2002), p. 5.

103. Gen. George McClellan, a Democrat, wrote to President Lincoln before the latter's issuance of the Emancipation Proclamation, saying, somewhat disingenuously, that "a declaration of radical views, especially upon slavery, would rapidly disintegrate our present armies." Quoted in Charles S. Wainwright, *A Diary of Battle: The Personal Journals of Colonel Charles S. Wainwright, 1861–1865* (New York: Da Capo, 1998), p. 85.

104. More than a third of enlistees in Lee's army either owned slaves or came from slave-owning families, whereas only one in four white males in the South fell into either of these categories. More than half of the officers who joined in 1861 owned slaves. Joseph T. Glatthaar, *General Lee's Army: From Victory to Collapse* (New York: Free Press, 2008), pp. 20–21.

105. Lee Soltow, "Economic Inequality in the United States in the Period from 1790 to 1860," *Journal of Economic History* 31 (December 1971): 825.

106. McPherson, *For Cause and Comrades*, p. 106. He cites several letters from Confederate soldiers expressing this fear.

107. Ibid., p. 8. McPherson's survey of diaries and letters by Civil War soldiers contains a disproportionate percentage of ones from this group.

108. Ibid., p. 17. Cf., Glatthaar, *General Lee's Army*, p. 14.

109. Mark A. Snell, "'If They Would Know What I Knew It Would Be Pretty Hard to Raise One Company in York': Recruiting, the Draft, and Society's Response in York County, Pennsylvania, 1861–1865," in Cimbala and Miller, *Union Soldiers and the Northern Home Front*, p. 78.

110. McPherson, *For Cause and Comrades*, p. 17.

111. Jordan Ross, "Uncommon Union: Motivation among Civil War Soldiers," *American Nineteenth Century History* 3, no. 1 (Spring 2002): 19.

112. Cyrus F. Boyd, *The Civil War Diary of Cyrus F. Boyd*, ed. Mildred Throne (Baton Rouge: Louisiana State University Press, 1953), pp. 1, 2. See also Reed Mitchell, "Soldiering, Manhood, and the Coming of Age: A Northern Volunteer," in Clinton and Silber, *Divided Houses*, p. 44.

113. Quoted in Glatthaar, *General Lee's Army*, p. 2.

114. Ibid., p. 33.

115. "Freemen of Tennessee! To Arms," recruitment flyer, May 17, 1861, http://www.paperlessarchives.com/cw_posters.html (accessed September 22, 2009).

116. Margaret R. Higonnet, "Civil Wars and Sexual Territories," in Helen M. Cooper, Adrienne A. Munich, and Susan M. Squier, eds., *Arms and the Woman: War, Gender, and Literary Representation* (Chapel Hill: University of North Carolina Press, 1989), p. 80. Writing about the phenomenon of civil wars in general, Higonnet argues that "the theme of civil war becomes a metaphor for reversals in emotional and sexual relationships; with striking frequency, gender roles under the pressure of social change become inverted," p. 82.

117. Quoted in Laura Elizabeth Lee Battle, *Forget-me-nots of the Civil War: A Romance* (St. Louis, MO: Fleming, 1909), p. 33.

118. McPherson, *For Cause and Comrades*, p. 24.

119. "Insults risk diminishing one's manhood unless responded to with force." Richard E. Nisbett and Dov Cohen, *Culture of Honor: The Psychiatry of Violence in the South* (Boulder, CO: Westview, 1996), pp. xvi, 53, passim.

120. Glatthaar, *General Lee's Army*, p. 29.

121. Jimerson, *Private Civil War*, pp. 127–28.

122. Quoted in Glatthaar, *General Lee's Army*, p. 60.

123. Earl J. Hess, *The Union Soldier in Battle: Enduring the Ordeal of Combat* (Lawrence: University Press of Kansas, 1997), p. 194.

124. Drew Gilpin Faust, *This Republic of Suffering: Death and the American Civil War* (New York: Knopf, 2008), p. 6.

125. Ibid., pp. 179, 194.

126. Quoted in Ross, "Uncommon Union," p. 27. This feeling of not having previously done much with their lives was a common theme in letters written by well-educated, middle-class Northern volunteers.

127. It also played a role in the decision to reenlist: men who had low incomes tend to do so more frequently than those with greater earning capabilities. See John Robertson, "Re-Enlistment Patterns of Civil War Soldiers," *Journal of Interdisciplinary History* 32, no. 1 (Summer 2001): 15–35.

128. Snell, "'If They Would Know,'" p. 82. Volunteers also earned about 10 percent more per month than draftees. Russell L. Johnson, "'Volunteer While You May!' Manpower Mobilization in Dubuque, Iowa," in Cimbala and Miller, *Union Soldiers and the Northern Homefront*, p. 41.

129. Reardon, "'We Are All in This War,'" p. 10. This meant that some communities, or parts of the North, supplied far more volunteers than others. See Johnson, "'Volunteer While You May!'" p. 35. Heavily Democratic areas like Dubuque were more likely to have ample numbers of volunteers.

130. Ross, "Uncommon Union," pp. 20–21.

131. Snell, "'If They Would Know,'" p. 108.

132. As early as 1850, observers like Horace Mann could foresee the South seceding if limits were placed on the extension of slavery. Mary Mann, *Life of Horace Mann*, vol. 1 (New York: Mann, 1891), p. 288.

133. William F. Brundage, *Lynching in the New South: Georgia and Virginia, 1890–1930* (Urbana: University of Illinois Press, 1993), p. 4.

134. Michael S. Kimmel, *Manhood in America: A Cultural History* (New York: Free Press, 1996), p. 60.

135. Beverly A. Hume, "Of Cuttle-Fish and Women: Melville's Goneril in *The Confidence Man*," in Elizabeth Schultz and Haskell Springer, eds., *Melville and Women* (Kent, OH: Kent State University Press, 2006), p. 202.

136. Schultz and Springer, "Melville Writing Women/Women Writing Melville," in *Melville and Women*, pp. 7–8.

137. "My Wife's Portrait, by a Gentleman of the New World," *Ladies Companion* 15 (1859): 255.

138. "Poe's representation of female characters reveals much more about the nineteenth-century male psychology and a patriarchal ideology that objectifies women as objects of beauty and pleasure." Leland S. Parson, "Poe and Nineteenth-Century Gender Construction," in J. Gerald Kennedy, ed., *A Historical Guide to Edgar Allan Poe* (New York: Oxford University Press, 2001), p. 202.

139. Herman Melville, "Billy Budd, Foretopman," in *Billy Budd and Other Stories* (New York: Penguin, 1995), p. 237.

140. See, for example, Thoreau's critical reaction to a female lecturer on "womanhood" in 1851. Henry David Thoreau, *Henry David Thoreau: A Year in Thoreau's Journal: 1851* (New York: Penguin, 1995), p. 327.

141. Angelina Grimké had been considered a "freak" by her friends in South Carolina. Gerda Lerner, *The Grimké Sisters from South Carolina: Pioneers of Woman's Rights and Abolition* (New York: Oxford University Press, 1998), p. 67. Cf. Berkin, *Civil War Wives*, pp. 23ff.

142. Stephen B. Oates, *The Approaching Fury: Voices of the Storm, 1820–1861* (New York: HarperCollins, 1997), p. 119.

143. Steven A. Channing, *Crisis of Fear: Secession in South Carolina* (New York: Norton, 1974), p. 119.

144. For the psychological basis for this, see John Dollard et al., *Frustration and Aggression* (New Haven, CT: Yale University Press, 1939), pp. 50–51.

145. "African Americans served as a convenient, vulnerable target against which whites could vent the anger and frustration created by blocked economic ambitions." Stewart Tolnay and E. M. Beck, *A Festival of Violence: An Analysis of Southern Lynchings, 1882–1930* (Urbana: University of Illinois Press, 1995), p. 70.

146. See, for example, Edward C. Tolman, *Drives toward War* (New York: Appleton, 1942), pp. 64–66, 83, passim; Alix Strachey, *The Unconscious Motives of War: A Psycho-analytical Contribution* (London: Unwin & Allen, 1957), p. 21; Franco Fornari, *The Psychoanalysis of War* (Bloomington: Indiana University Press, 1975), pp. xvii, passim; and Dollard, *Frustration and Aggression*, pp. 10, 44, passim.

147. Olmstead's comments quoted in Susan-Mary Grant, *North over South: Northern Nationalism and American Identity in the Antebellum Era* (Lawrence: University Press of Kansas, 2000), p. 81. In the North, many looked down on white Southerners as economically backward, but there was little hatred of the region. Prominent Northern visitors to the South came away with reinforced repugnance for the slave system, but better understanding of the rationale of its upholders. See, for example, William Cullen Bryant, "A Retrospective Glance," in *Prose Writings of William Cullen Bryant*, vol. 2, *Travels, Addresses, Comments*, ed. Parke Godwin (New York: Appleton, 1884), p. 408. Bryant pronounced the defenders of slavery with whom he spoke as "uncorrupted and pure in personal character."

148. Brandi McCandless, "Slavery's Destruction of Domestic Life in Stowe's *Uncle Tom's Cabin*," *Ampersand*, undated manuscript, http://itech.fgcu .edu/&/issues/vol2/issue1/utc.htm (accessed October 1, 2009).

149. Duvall, "*Uncle Tom's Cabin*," p. 12.

150. Legree represents the "devastating consequences of male dominance untempered by a recognition of the domestic claims of their is own family or that of the slaves." LeeAnn Whites, *Gender Matters: Civil War, Reconstruction, and the Making of the New South* (New York: Palgrave Macmillan, 2005), p. 23.

151. Cynthia G. Wolff, "Masculinity in *Uncle Tom's Cabin*," *American Quarterly* 47, no. 4 (December 1995): 598–99, 611.

152. Joan D. Hedrick, *Harriet Beecher Stowe: A Life* (New York: Oxford University Press, 1995), p. 121.

153. Harriet Beecher Stowe, *Uncle Tom's Cabin, or Life among the Lowly* (New York: Fenno, 1899), pp. 32, 36, 37.

154. Stowe's support for female equality emerged more clearly in her historical novel *The Minister's Wooing* (1859). Stowe encountered male hostility for writing this indictment of slavery because she was a woman. Hedrick, *Harriet Beecher Stowe*, p. 232.

155. Stanton, speech of February 14, 1854. Quoted in Catherine Clinton, *The Other Civil War: American Women in the Nineteenth Century* (New York: Hill & Wang, 1999), p. 78.

156. Stanton, "Manhood Suffrage," speech of December 24, 1868. Quoted in Davis, "Declaring Equality," p. 15.

157. Letter of Henry B. Stanton to Elizabeth Cady Stanton, December 12, 1860, Ann D. Gordon, ed., *Selected Papers of Elizabeth Cady Stanton and Susan B. Anthony*, 4 vols. (New Brunswick, NJ: Rutgers University Press, 1997) 1:456.

158. Ginzberg, *Elizabeth Cady Stanton*, pp. 103–104, 107.

159. Letter of Susan B. Anthony to Wendell Phillips, April 29, 1861, Gordon, *Selected Papers*, 1:464.

160. Remarks of Susan B. Anthony, Thirteenth National Women's Rights Conference, May 14, 1863, Gordon, *Selected Papers*, 1:489. See also Ginzberg, *Elizabeth Cady Stanton*, p. 107.

161. Stanton, *Elizabeth Cady Stanton*, pp. 195–96. Some four hundred women took part in the war disguised as men, mostly on the Union side.

162. Clinton, *Other Civil War*, p. 81.

163. At their May 14, 1863, gathering in New York's Church of the Puritans, the assembled members of the league also agreed that "there never can be a true peace in this Republic until the civil and political rights of all citizens of African descent and all women are practically established." Quoted in Garrett Epps, *Democracy Reborn: The Fourteenth Amendment and the Fight for Equal Rights in Post-Civil War America* (New York: Holt, 2006), p. 214.

164. Ginzberg, *Elizabeth Cady Stanton*, p. 115.

165. Gordon, *Selected Papers*, p. 511. Cf. Epps, *Democracy Reborn*, p. 214.

166. Kathleen Barry, *Susan B. Anthony: A Biography of a Singular Feminist* (New York: NYU Press, 1988), p. 149.

167. "A Petition for Universal Suffrage," 1866. Elizabeth Cady Stanton and Susan B. Anthony Papers Project, http://ecssba.rutgers.edu/docs/petuniv.html (accessed September 25, 2009).

168. Quoted in Davis, "Declaring Equality," p. 15.

169. Gornick, *Solitude of Self*, p. 80.

170. Stephen Kantrowitz, "Fighting Like Men: Civil War Dilemmas of Abolitionist Manhood," in Catherine Clinton and Nina Silber, eds., *Battle Scars: Gender and Sexuality in the Civil War* (New York: Oxford University Press, 2006), p. 21.

171. Nina Silber, *Gender and the Sectional Conflict* (Chapel Hill: University of North Carolina Press, 2008), p. 19.

172. Donald Yocovone, "Abolitionists and the 'Language of Fraternal Love,'" *Meanings for Manhood*, p. 90.

173. Ralph Waldo Emerson, "War," address to Boston Peace Society, March 1838, in *The Complete Writings of Ralph Waldo Emerson*, 2 vols. (New York: Wise, 1922), 2:1142.

174. Emerson supported the violent actions of the radical abolitionist John Brown, for example. Andrew Fiala, *Practical Pacifism* (New York: Algora, 2004), p. 16.

175. Emerson had been interested in promoting exercise since the 1840s,

particularly after a visit to England, where he found the average man to be a "wealthy, juicy, broadchested creature," well suited to rule the world. Quoted in Pitney, *Muscular Christianity*, p. 21.

176. John Stauffer, "Embattled Manhood and New England Writers, 1860–1870," in *Battle Scars*, pp. 122–24.

177. Even after the war started, some soldiers felt it would end in a matter of months. See, for example, "Diary of Ezekiel J. Sankey, Soldier," entry dated May 1862, http://civilwar.aea14.k12.ia.us/Resources/sankey_diary.htm (accessed September 23, 2009).

178. Boyd, diary entry for April 9, 1862, p. 42.

179. Ibid., entry for October 11, 1862, p. 75.

180. Robert K. Krick, foreword to Thomas P. Lowry, *The Story Soldiers Wouldn't Tell: Sex in the Civil War* (Mechanicsburg, PA: Stackpole, 1994), p. ix. See also Catherine Clinton, "'Public Women' and Sexual Politics during the American Civil War," in *Battle Scars*, p. 61.

181. A South Carolina soldier noted in a letter to his wife that so many women of easy virtue visited his camp in 1861 that "you would think there was not a married man in the regiment but me." Quoted in James I. Robertson, *Soldiers Blue and Gray* (Columbia: University of South Carolina Press, 1998), p. 119.

182. Kenneth C. Davis, introduction to *Don't Know Much about the Civil War: Everything You Need to Know about America's Greatest Conflict but Never Learned* (New York: HarperCollins, 1997), p. xviii.

183. Boyd, diary entry for July 16, 1862, p. 57.

184. Quoted in Mitchell, "Soldiering, Manhood, and the Coming of Age: A Northern Volunteer," p. 45.

185. Of these deaths, an estimated 414,000 were due to disease, and only about 200,000 to battlefield wounds.

186. By one estimate, the war's losses resulted in 1.2 million fewer births between 1861 and 1870. J. David Hacker, "The Human Cost of War: White Population in the United States, 1850–1880," *Journal of Economic History* 61, no. 2 (June 2001): 488.

187. In the 1860s, the populations of Southern states such as Alabama, Georgia, and South Carolina increased only marginally. By contrast, Illinois added over 800,000 residents, Massachusetts more than 200,000, and New York 500,000.

188. Between 1862 and 1866, Southern states experienced an annual fertility decline of 21 percent, versus only 10.9 in the North. But this difference was partially due to the fact that a higher proportion of Southern males were away fighting. Hacker, "Human Cost," p. 488. Between 1860 and 1870, the number

of births in Alabama and Virginia remained roughly constant, while it rose by 13 percent in Pennsylvania. However, some other Northern states, including Massachusetts and New York, also had no significant fertility increases during this decade. Table XX, "Persons Born in, and Surviving at, the Close of Each Census Year, with Proportion to All Living Persons, 1870–1860–1850," *Ninth Census*, vol. 2, *Vital Statistics* (Washington, DC: GPO, 1872), pp. 522–23.

189. Peter W. Bardaglio, *Reconstructing the Household: Families, Sex, and the Law in the Nineteenth-Century South* (Chapel Hill: University of North Carolina Press, 1998), p. 130.

190. Glenda Riley, *Divorce: An American Tradition* (New York: Oxford University Press, 1991), p. 78. Hastily entered into, many of these marriages ended in divorce.

191. "Persons Married Per 1,000 Population in Massachusetts," in William B. Bailey, *Modern Social Conditions* (New York: Century, 1906), p. 141.

192. See Hudson Strode, ed., *Jefferson Davis: Private Letters, 1823–1889* (New York: Harcourt, Brace & World, 1966). Varina Davis, an independent-minded and intelligent woman, played a leading role in rallying Southern women on the home front. She also proved to be a formidable fighter for her husband after he was arrested and imprisoned at the end of the war. See Berkin, *Civil War Wives*, pp. 172, 177–84, 168–88.

193. Silber, *Gender and the Sectional Conflict*, pp. xiv, 3, 6, 9, 13. Silber argues that the Southern image of womanhood was central to its defense of the region.

194. Nina Silber, *The Romance of Reunion: Northerners and the South, 1865–1900* (Chapel Hill: University of North Carolina Press, 1993), p. 194.

195. By one estimate, more than 100,000 Confederate soldiers—or one in nine—deserted during the war, as did roughly twice that number of Union troops. Ella Lonn, *Desertion during the Civil War* (Gloucester, MA: Smith, 1966), p. 226.

196. Whites, "The Civil War as a Crisis in Gender," p. 97.

197. Henry Clay Work, "Marching through Georgia," 1865.

198. Crystal N. Feimster, "General Benjamin Butler and the Threat of Sexual Violence during the Civil War," *Daedalus* 138, no. 2 (Spring 2009): 128.

199. Before he died, Gen. Robert E. Lee conceded he had lost everything but his honor during the war. Michael Fellman, *The Making of Robert E. Lee* (Baltimore: Johns Hopkins University Press, 2003), p. 300.

200. William F. Pinar, *The Gender of Racial Politics and Violence in the United States: Lynching, Prison Rape, and the Crisis of Masculinity* (New York: Lang, 2001), p. 268.

201. George Rable, "'Missing in Action': Women of the Confederacy," *Divided Houses*, pp. 135–41. In New Orleans, some Southern women defiantly

pinned Confederate flags to their dresses. Many letters and diaries written by women at that time mused, "If only I was a man."

202. Dana W. McMichael, *How Confederate Women Created Self-Identities as the Civil War Progressed: A Study of Their Diaries* (Lewiston, NY: Mellen, 2008), p. 23.

203. Quoted in Whites, "The Civil War as a Crisis in Gender," p. 96.

204. Silber, *Romance of Reunion*, p. 28.

205. For details of this incident, see Berkin, *Civil War Wives*, pp. 174–75.

206. Ibid., 30–31. Cross-dressing was not that uncommon in those days as a form of disguise. Abraham Lincoln, for example, had donned a shawl en route by train to Washington for his first inaugural, to thwart would-be assassins. One ditty about Davis's capture ran as follows:

> Jeff Davis was a warrior bold
> And vowed the Yankees should fail;
> He jumped into his pantaloons
> And swore he'd rule them all.
> But when he saw the Yankees come
> To hang him if they could,
> He jumped into a petticoat
> And headed for the wood.
> —"Jeff in Petticoats: A Song for Our Times" (1865)

207. Whites, *Crisis in Gender*, p. 3, passim.

208. Maris A. Vinvovskis, "Have Social Historians Lost the Civil War? Some Preliminary Demographic Speculations," *Journal of American History* 76, no. 1 (June 1989): 40.

209. David R. Goldfield, *Still Fighting the Civil War: The American South and Southern History* (Baton Rouge: Louisiana State University Press, 2004), p. 101.

210. Faust, *Republic of Suffering*, p. 34.

211. Crane had never experienced combat. His protagonist, Henry Fleming, overcomes his initial cowardice to prove himself under fire. Before that battle, he reflects, "A faith in himself had secretly blossomed. There was a little flower of confidence growing within him. He was now a man of experience. He had been out among the dragons, he said, and he assured himself they were not so hideous as he had imagined them. . . . They did not sting with precision. A stout heart often defied, and defying, escaped." Crane, *The Red Badge of Courage: An Episode of the Civil War* (New York: Appleton, 1917), p. 151.

212. Stauffer, "Embattled Manhood," pp. 125–26.

213. Stowe would expand this piece and publish it as a book, *Lady Byron Vindicated*, in 1870.

214. Ibid., p. 121.

215. Faust, preface, *Republic of Suffering*, p. xi.

216. E. Anthony Rotundo, *American Manhood: Transformation in Masculinity from the Revolution to the Modern Era* (New York: Basic Books, 1993), pp. 232–33.

217. Ibid., pp. 42–43.

218. Griffen, "Reconstructing Masculinity," p. 192.

219. Kristin L. Hoganson, *Fighting for American Manhood: How Gender Politics Provoked the Spanish-American and Philippine-American Wars* (New Haven, CT: Yale University Press, 1998), p. 25.

220. Oliver Wendell Holmes Jr., "The Soldier's Faith," address, Harvard University, May 30, 1895, http://people.virginia.edu/~mmd5f/holmesfa.htm (accessed September 29, 2009). After his death in 1935, two stained Civil War uniforms belonging to Holmes were discovered in a closet, along with a note saying the stains were from Holmes's own blood.

221. President Theodore Roosevelt, "Civil War Veterans," address to the 57th Congress, First Session, December 3, 1901, in. E. E. Garrison, ed., *The Roosevelt Doctrine* (New York: Grier, 1904), p. 123.

222. William James, "The Moral Equivalent of War," 1906. After the war, James blamed his father for keeping him out of the war, but, in reality, it was his own indecisiveness. James was tempted by witnessing a parade of departing Union troops through the streets of Boston in 1863. But he spent the remainder of the war studying medicine at Harvard. Louis Menand, *The Metaphysical Club* (New York: Farrar, Straus & Giroux, 2002), pp. 74–75.

223. For photographs of a large sampling of these monuments, North and South, see "American Civil War Monuments and Memorials," http://www.waymarking.com/cat/details.aspx?f=1&guid=cb16e588-fc05–418c-a3dab24949812966 (accessed September 29, 2009).

224. Judith E. Harper, *Women during the Civil War: An Encyclopedia* (London: Routledge, 2004), p. 169.

225. Rable, *Civil Wars*, pp. 2–4.

226. The participation of Southern women in "benevolent societies" before and during the war had not "produced anything resembling a feminist consciousness." Ibid., p. 16.

227. Legislatures in Missouri (1919), Kentucky (1920), and Tennessee (1920)—border states siding with the South during the Civil War—also approved this amendment prior to its ratification. Other Southern states passed this measure over the succeeding decades. The last state to approve this constitutional change, Mississippi, did so in 1984.

228. Bret E. Carroll, *American Masculinities: A Historical Encyclopedia* (Thousand Oaks, CA: Sage, 2004), p. 95.

229. James Bryce, *Studies in History and Jurisprudence* (New York: Oxford University Press, 1901), p. 831.

230. Mary Ann Mason, *From Father's Property to Children's Rights: The History of Child Custody in the United States* (New York: Columbia University Press 1996), p. 57.

231. In Utah, this right was taken away in 1887 and then restored in 1896.

232. Hoganson, *Fighting for American Manhood*, p. 22.

233. Stanton, *Selected Papers*, 2:195.

234. For a celebrated case, see Sarah Barringer Gordon, "Law and Everyday Death: Infanticide and the Backlash against Woman's Rights after the Civil War," in Austin Sarat, Lawrence Douglas, and Martha M. Umphrey, eds., *Lives in the Law* (Ann Arbor: University of Michigan Press, 2002), pp. 59–81.

235. Riley, *Divorce*, p. 79. During the fifteen years after the war ended, the number of divorces granted rose over 58 percent. Lack of financial support and cruelty were frequently the grounds cited, and wives filed five of six petitions on these bases. Women were also finding that being a wife and mother was not as wholly satisfying a role as it had once been.

236. Susan Faludi, *Backlash: The Undeclared War against American Women* (New York: Crown, 1992), p. 48.

237. Quoted in Barbara Ehrenreich and Deidre English, *Witches, Midwives, and Nurses: A History of Women Healers* (Old Westbury, NY: Feminist Press, 1973), p. 26.

238. Barker-Benfield, *Horrors of the Half-Known Life*, pp. 57–58.

239. By 1870, two-thirds of teachers in public and private schools were female. Ibid., p. 19.

240. Ibid., p. 133.

241. Ibid., p. 79.

CHAPTER 2

1. Quoted in L. S. Stavrianos, *The Balkans since 1453* (New York: Holt, Rinehart & Winston, 1963), p. 408. Disraeli's response was "It is something to serve such a sovereign."

2. Ibid., p. 408.

3. European armies were engaged in fighting during these decades, but on foreign soil. British forces, for example, suppressed a rebellion against their occupation of India in 1857, seized the Suez Canal, and made Egypt a protectorate a quarter century later. The Dutch fought against insurgents in present-

day Indonesia, and French troops helped the British to put down a rebellion in China.

4. Exceptions to this general rule were independent professionals, such as architects, doctors, and ministers, who maintained a study in the home. John Tosh, *A Man's Place: Masculinity and the Middle-Class Home in Victorian England* (New Haven, CT: Yale University Press, 2007), p. 60.

5. England led the way in this internal migration. In 1801, only about 20 percent of its population lived in towns and cities. By midcentury, over 50 percent did.

6. Joan W. Scott, *Gender and the Politics of History*, rev. ed. (New York: Columbia University Press, 1999), pp. 152, 155. Working women were often associated with prostitutes and unchecked sexuality. Charles Dickens took up this issue in his novel *Bleak House*, in which work is seen to corrupt female characters. See Martin A. Danahay, *Gender at Work in Victorian Culture: Literature, Art and Masculinity* (Burlington, VT: Ashgate, 2005), pp. 67–68.

7. In the United States, working-class men spent about sixty hours a week on the job, leaving them little time to interact with their children. However, middle-class fathers were more engaged with their offspring, serving as secondary caregivers. See Elizabeth H. Pleck, "Two Dimensions of Fatherhood: A History of the Good Dad–Bad Dad Complex," in Michael E. Lamb, ed., *The Role of the Father in Child Development*, 4th ed. (Hoboken, NJ: Wiley, 2004), pp. 36–38.

8. A middle-class Victorian husband was regarded as a failure if his wife displayed "insubordination" to him. Tosh, *A Man's Place*, p. 61.

9. A married English woman's right to own property independently was not affirmed until passage of the 1882 Married Women's Property Act. In the United States, custody cases began to favor mothers around the middle of the century. John Demos, *Past, Present, and Personal: The Family and the Life Course in American History* (New York: Oxford University Press, 1986), p. 58.

10. Speech of John Stuart Mill in Parliament, 1867, quoted in Tosh, *A Man's Place*, p. 53.

11. Ansley J. Coale and R. Treadwell, "A Summary of the Changing Distribution of Overall Fertility, Marital Fertility, and the Proportion Married in the Provinces of Europe," in Ansley J. Coale and Susan Cotts Watkins, eds., *The Decline of Fertility in Europe: The Revised Proceedings of a Conference on the Princeton Fertility Project* (Princeton, NJ: Princeton University Press, 1986), p. 22. In England, the birth rate had reached a peak of 36.3 births per 1,000 population in 1876, but then began to fall, as it would continue to do until the early 1930s. Richard A. Soloway, *Birth Control and the Population Question in England, 1877–1930* (Chapel Hill: University of North Carolina Press, 1982), p. 4. Rubber con-

doms were widely available in England by the 1870s, and "mass diffusion" of information on other methods of birth control began around the same time. Michael S. Teitelbaum, *The British Fertility Decline: Demographic Transition in the Crucible of the Industrial Revolution* (Princeton, NJ: Princeton University Press, 1986), pp. 200–201.

12. Michael Anderson, *British Population History: From the Black Death to the Present Day* (Cambridge: Cambridge University Press, 1996), p. 38.

13. During the first half of the nineteenth century, the infant mortality rate (the percentage of babies who died before their first birthday) in Europe and the United States was appallingly high: between 8 and 10 percent of those from well-to-do homes, who were well fed and taken care of, did not live a full year, while among the urban poor, the incidence of death before that age approached one in three.

14. The Factory Act of 1833, designed to protect children who worked in textile factories, was only one in a series of such reform measures adopted in industrial England. It made it illegal to employ children under the age of nine and restricted (to eight) the number of hours those ages nine to thirteen could work in a day. France enacted its first major child labor law in 1841, requiring that part of each day be set aside for educational purposes. Lee S. Weissbach, "Child Labor Legislation in Nineteenth-Century France," *Journal of Economic History* 37, no. 1 (March 1977): 269–70.

15. Mother was the "primary parent" by the early decades of the century. Demos, *Past, Present, and Personal*, p. 49.

16. A recent study of the role of middle-class, nineteenth-century English fathers has noted how the home was a comforting counterbalance to their demanding workplaces, concluding that "the Victorians placed a higher value on family than any other generation before or since." Tosh, preface, *A Man's Place*, p. ix.

17. According to one social historian, the world outside the home was considered "disordered, unstable, full of 'traps' and 'temptations' to vice in many forms." Demos, *Past, Present, and Personal*, p. 55.

18. James Fenimore Cooper captured this otherworldly moral purity of American women in his 1835 work, *Notions of the Americans* (Philadelphia: Carey, Lea and Blanchard, 1835), p. 105. Here his traveling companion remarks: "To me, woman appears to fill in America the very station for which she was designed by nature. In the lowest conditions of life she is treated with the tenderness and respect that is due to beings whom we believe to be the repositories of the better principles of our nature. Retired within the sacred precincts of her own abode, she is preserved from the destroying taint of excessive intercourse with the world. She makes no bargains beyond those which supply her own little

personal wants, and her heart is not early corrupted by the baneful and unfeminine voice of selfishness."

19. Tosh, *A Man's Place*, p. 78.

20. In England, this disparity was emphasized after passage of the Contagious Diseases Acts and the Criminal Law Amendment Act of 1885, which led to a crackdown on prostitution and made Victorians aware that some men, at least, fell far short of the dominant ideal of "social purity." Ibid., p. 154.

21. Ibid., p. 55.

22. E. Anthony Rotundo, *American Manhood: Transformation in Masculinity from the Revolution to the Modern Era* (New York: Basic Books, 1993), p. 107.

23. T. S. Arthur, ed., *Mother's Rule, or The Right Way and the Wrong Way* (Philadelphia: Peck & Bliss, 1859), p. 3.

24. Michael C. C. Adams, *Great Adventure: Male Desire and the Coming of World War I* (Bloomington: Indiana University Press, 1990), p. 6.

25. Carlyle wrote: "These are the leaders of men, these great ones; the modellers, patterns, and in a wide sense creators, of whatsoever the general mass of men contrived to do or attain; all things that we see standing accomplished in the world are properly the outer material result, the practical realisation and embodiment, of Thoughts that dwelt in the Great Men sent into the world." Carlyle, *On Heroes and Hero Worship and the Heroic in History*, ed. Clement K. Shorter (London: Ward, Lock, 1900), pp. 3–4.

26. Paternal authority was linked to that of God. Jensen, "From a Father-Dominated, through a Brother-Dominated, to a Mother-Dominated Society: On Changing Values in Modern Western Culture," in Ann Katherine Isaacs, ed., *Political Systems and Definitions of Gender Roles* (Pisa: Edizioni Plus, 2001), p. 218.

27. "The movement of nations is caused not by power, nor by intellectual activity, nor even by a combination of the two, as historians have supposed, but by the activity of all the people who participate in the event, and who always combine in such a way that those who take the largest direct share in the event assumed the least responsibility, and vice versa." Tolstoy, epilogue, *War and Peace*, trans. Rosemary Edmonds (New York: Penguin, 1982), p. 1425.

28. Another was Karl Marx's *Das Kapital*, which was first published in 1867. Marx also saw capitalist society ruled by structural contradictions rather than by the conscious actions of individuals.

29. Darwin, introduction, *On the Origin of Species by Means of Natural Selection* (New York: Avenel, 1979), p. 24.

30. Tosh, *A Man's Place*, p. 149. Cf. Ross Shideler, *Questioning the Father: From Darwin to Zola, Ibsen, Strindberg, and Hardy* (Stanford, CA: Stanford University Press, 1999), pp. 4, 19ff.

31. For a treatment of sexual mores and behavior in Victorian England, see Michael Mason, *The Making of Victorian Sexuality* (Oxford: Oxford University Press, 1994) and Mike Huggins and J. A. Mangan, eds., *Disreputable Pleasures: Less Virtuous Victorians at Play* (London, New York: Cass, 1994). For an opposing view of the era's morality, see Gertrude Himmelfarb, *The De-moralization of Society: From Victorian Virtues to Modern Values* (New York: Knopf, 1995). John Tosh has noted that it is largely a "myth" that married men of this period frequently cavorted with prostitutes; rather, their clients were mainly men too young to marry or "confirmed bachelors." Tosh, *A Man's Place*, p. 56. Anthony Rotundo also concludes that the large number of brothels in American cities suggests that some of their clientele were young, single men. Rotundo, *American Manhood*, p. 126.

32. The rise of prostitution—and venereal disease—in England resulted in passage of the first Contagious Diseases Act in 1864. In Paris and other French cities, brothels began to appear early in the nineteenth century. The same trend was evident in most Western European countries.

33. This grimly realistic worldview was vividly conveyed in the latter novels of Charles Dickens, particularly in his 1854 *Hard Times*.

34. This explanation was first advanced by the French social scientist Arsene Dumont in his *Dépopulation et civilization: étude démographique* (Paris: Lecrosnier et Babé, 1890). The economic rationale for limiting family size was further developed by the economist Paul Leroy-Beaulieu, in his *La question de la population* (Paris: Alcan, 1913). A study of declining fertility in the United States after the Civil War has also concluded that economics, not demographics, was the decisive factor. See J. David Hacker, "The Human Cost of War: White Population in the United States, 1850–1880," *Journal of Economic History* 61, no. 2 (June 2001): 486–89.

35. While most careers remained closed to them, American women did manage to enter the teaching profession in large numbers, thanks to the growth of female higher education. In 1870, two of three teachers in public and private schools were women. Graham J. Barker-Benfield, *The Horrors of the Half-Known Life: Male Attitudes toward Women and Sexuality in Nineteenth-Century America* (New York: Routledge, 2005), p. 19.

36. Gerry Holloway, *Women and Work in Britain since 1840* (London: Routledge, 2005), p. 17. A decade later, of the nearly 6 million adult women in England, 39.6 percent were either widowed or still single. Josephine E. Butler, *The Education and Employment of Women* (London: Brakell, 1868), p. 3. Among women ages twenty-five to twenty-nine, the percentage of those who were unmarried remained fairly constant between 1851 and 1931—namely, 39 percent in England and Wales, and 47 percent in Scotland. Teitelbaum, *British Fertility Decline*, p. 98.

37. Richard A. Soloway, *Demography and Degeneration: Eugenics and the Declining Birth Rate in Twentieth-Century Britain* (Chapel Hill: University of North Carolina Press, 1995), p. 11. In 1851, there were 104.2 females in England and Wales for every 100 males; by 1911, this gender imbalance had reached 106.8 to 100. See Patricia Jalland, *Women, Marriage, and Politics, 1860–1914* (Oxford: Oxford University Press, 1986), p. 255. Germany had a similar "excess" of females—17 million vs. 16 million males—at the middle of the century. Unmarried women were more prevalent among the bourgeoisie than the working class. Nancy R. Reagin, *A German Women's Movement: Class and Gender in Hanover, 1880–1933* (Chapel Hill: University of North Carolina Press, 1995), p. 101. For a discussion of the important impact of Britain's sex ratio on that country's marriage rate between 1851 and 1891, see R. I. Woods and P. R. A. Hinde, "Nuptiality and Age at Marriage in Nineteenth-Century England," *Journal of Family History* 10, no. 2 (1985): 120–21. This article concludes that much of this gender imbalance resulted from men and women migrating to different parts of the country to find work.

38. It is impossible, of course, to know why so many women remained single during the nineteenth century. Most of these women belonged to the middle or lower-middle classes. No doubt, some of them did not attract suitors because of their modest financial circumstances or lack of physical attractiveness. But a case can be made that many females of this socioeconomic status turned down proposals of marriage, chiefly because becoming a wife and mother would have conflicted with their values, opinions, and professional aspirations. They were strong-willed and well-educated women, not willing to subordinate themselves to a "patriarchal" husband. (One study has determined that only 28 percent of female college graduates in the second half of the nineteenth century married, as compared to 80 percent of all American women. See Gioia Diliberto, *A Useful Woman: The Early Life of Jane Addams* [New York: Scribner's, 1999], p. 60.) In looking at the lives of prominent female figures of the nineteenth century (while conceding they are not representative of all, or even most women, one finds supporting evidence for this view. Susan B. Anthony, Dorothea Dix, Mary Cassatt, Gertrude Bell, Anne Brontë, Emily Dickinson, Clara Barton, Louisa May Alcott, Florence Nightingale, Jane Austen, and Elizabeth Blackwell (the first American woman to graduate from medical school) all faced a conflict between their desire to pursue a career and a wish to marry and have children. All opted to forego marriage. Most of these women turned down proposals or else believed so strongly that marriage was detrimental to female independence that they did not seek or attract suitors. A minority of these "spinsters"—for example, the French novelist Rosa Bonheur—had a sexual preference for other women.

39. See Göran Therborn, *Between Sex and Power: Family in the World, 1900–2000* (New York: Routledge, 2004), p. 31.

40. Anne T. Quartararo, *Women Teachers and Popular Education in Nineteenth-Century France: Social Values and Corporate Identity at the Normal School Institution* (Wilmington: University of Delaware Press, 1995), p. 53.

41. James F. McMillan, *France and Women, 1789–1914: Gender, Society and Politics* (London: Routledge, 1999), p. 148.

42. Marcelline J. Hutton, *Russian and Western European Women, 1860–1939: Dreams, Struggles, and Nightmares* (Lanham, MD: Rowman & Littlefield, 2001), pp. 48–49.

43. French female activists concentrated on changing family law and securing more economic opportunities. See Marilyn J. Boxer, "'First-Wave' Feminism in Nineteenth-Century France: Class, Family and Religion," *Women's Studies International Forum* 5, no. 6 (1982): 551–59. English feminists sought greater educational opportunities in order to gain access to a wider range of professions. Female workers also formed associations such as the Society for the Promotion of Employment of Women (1859) and the Women's Protective and Provident League (1874), to fight for jobs and sexual equality at the workplace. In Germany, an early focus on religious emancipation gave way to feminist efforts to gain better education, better jobs, and more political rights during the last third of the nineteenth century.

44. The two unsuccessful candidates were Victoria Woodhull, in 1872, and Belva Lockwood, in 1884 and 1888.

45. Prentice Mulford, "The Hunt for Smugglers," *Atlantic Monthly* (February 1873), p. 202.

46. By 1851, an estimated 650,000 women were working in textile factories. They were the second-largest source of female jobs, after domestic service. Holloway, *Women and Work*, p. 27.

47. In France, for example, the number of working women rose from 4.6 million in 1866 to 6.8 million in 1901—a 47 percent increase. More than a third of French women were employed by 1906. Table 1, "Women in the Active Population," McMillan, *France and Women*, p. 161.

48. Holloway, *Women and Work*, p. 78. In 1875, it was estimated that one in eight English infants died before the age of one. This was 0.4 percent higher than the incidence in 1861–1870. Other European countries had even higher rates: 22 per 100 in France, Prussia, and Spain, for example. Peter Gay, *The Bourgeois Experience: Victoria to Freud: Education of the Senses*, vol. 1 (New York: Norton, 1999), p. 234. After having declined in the 1880s, the infant mortality rate in England climbed again, reaching 163 deaths out of every 1,000 infants by

1899. Anna Davin, "Motherhood and Imperialism," *History Workshop* 5 (1978), p. 11. This amounted to the loss of 120,000 lives annually.

49. The British socialist reformer Sidney Webb published an article on this subject in the *New York Times* in 1906. In this piece, he contended that some 200,000 fewer babies had been born in England and Wales between 1871 and 1901 because of the steep drop in the fertility rate. He noted that the decline was the steepest in factory towns where a large percentage of married women worked, and in places where women of the "servant class" were congregated. See "'Race Suicide' in Great Britain," letter to the editor, *New York Times*, October 28, 1906. One book, published shortly before World War I, predicted the "passing of this great Anglo Teuton people" due to the sharply declining birth rate. M. S. Iseman, *Race Suicide* (New York: Cosmopolitan, 1912), p. 5.

50. Holloway, *Women and Work*, p. 44.

51. McMillan, *France and Women*, pp. 155, 218. McMillan writes, "The maintenance of a gender order based on sexual difference was widely regarded as fundamental to the preservation of social stability."

52. Ibid., p. 163.

53. Judith Surkis, *Sexing the Citizen: Morality and Masculinity in France, 1870–1920* (Ithaca, NY: Cornell University Press, 2006), pp. 9, 51.

54. Margaret H. Darrow, *French Women and the First World War* (New York: Oxford University Press, 2000), pp. 10–11.

55. Ibid., p. 57.

56. For a discussion of male resistance in the English print industry, see Michelle E. Tusin, "Performing Work: Gender, Class, and the Printing Trade in Victorian Britain," *Journal of Women's History* 16, no. 1 (2004): 103–26. Union opposition to female membership in France during the 1870s is described in Carolyn J. Eichner, *Surmounting the Barricades: Women in the Paris Commune* (Bloomington: Indiana University Press, 2004), pp. 75–76. Animosity toward female workers in these countries as well as Germany is treated in Wendy Z. Goldman, *Women, the State and Revolution: Soviet Family Policy and Social Life, 1917–1936* (Cambridge: Cambridge University Press, 1993), p. 75. See Barker-Benfield, *Horrors of the Half-Known Life*, p. 19, for details on US male factory workers' antifemale attitudes.

57. Brian Harrison, "Women's Health and the Women's Movement in Britain, 1840–1940," in Charles Webster, ed., *Biology, Medicine and Society, 1840–1940* (Cambridge: Cambridge University Press, 1981), p. 51.

58. Holloway, *Women and Work*, p. 38.

59. Demos, *Past, Present, and Personal*, p. 55.

60. John D'Emilio and Estelle B. Freedman, *Intimate Matters: A History of Sexuality in America* (New York: Harper & Row, 1988), p. 107.

61. Michael C. C. Adams, *Great Adventure: Male Desire and the Coming of World War I* (Bloomington: Indiana University Press, 1990), p. 13. In the words of a contemporary social historian, Victorian England was not "a culture which was at home with its sexuality." Simon Szreter, *Fertility, Class and Gender in Britain, 1860–1940* (Cambridge: Cambridge University Press, 2002), p. 397.

62. Szreter, *Fertility, Class and Gender*, p. 367.

63. The average marriage age in England remained at twenty-five during the last third of the century. More than 10 percent of women over the age of forty-five at that time had not had experienced sexual intercourse. Statistics cited in Szreter, *Fertility, Class and Gender*, p. 393. A sampling of marriage registers conducted in 1890 found that the average professional man married at age 31.2. Tosh, *A Man's Place*, p. 172.

64. Tosh, *A Man's Place*, p. 109.

65. Sigmund Freud to Martha Bernays, August 29, 1883, quoted in Peter Gay, *The Bourgeois Experience: Victoria to Freud*, vol. 2: *Tender Passion* (New York: Norton, 1999), p. 11.

66. Exact statistics on the number of prostitutes in these cities are not available, and estimates vary widely. For example, the figure for London at midcentury ranged between 5,000 and 220,000. Paula Bartley, *Prostitution: Prevention and Reform in England, 1860–1914* (New York, London: Routledge, 2000), p. 2.

67. Angela V. John and Claire Eustance, "Shared Histories—Different Identities: Introducing Masculinities, Male Support and Female Suffrage," in Angela V. John and Claire Eustance, eds., *The Men's Share? Masculinities, Male Support, and Women's Suffrage in Britain, 1890–1920* (London: Routledge, 1997), p. 7.

68. From a Jungian perspective, male envy of female creative, life-giving power can lead to aggression. See Loren E. Pedersen, *Dark Hearts: The Unconscious Forces That Shape Men's Lives* (Boston: Shambhala, 1991), p. 77.

69. Tosh, *A Man's Place*, p. 183.

70. Quoted in Mary L. Shanley, *Family, Marriage and the Law in Victorian England* (Princeton, NJ: Princeton University Press, 1993), p. 149.

71. Ibid., p. 173.

72. Karen M. Offen, *European Feminisms, 1750–1900: A Political History* (Stanford, CA: Stanford University Press, 2000), p. 147.

73. Remarks of Rep. Stevenson Archer, May 30, 1872, quoted in Gay, *Education of the Senses*, p. 192.

74. The theme of sexual competition was common in late Victorian literature, both in the United States and in England. See Sandra M. Gilbert and Susan Gubar, *No Man's Land: The Place of the Woman Writer in the Twentieth Century*, 2 vols. (New Haven, CT: Yale University Press, 1988), 1:4.

75. In his *Germinal* (1885), a grocer who has had sex with several women as payment for overdue bills is castrated by an angry mob of females.

76. Walter Besant, *The Revolt of Man* (London: Chatto & Windus, 1897), pp. 23, 97, 150–51, 207, 275, 303.

77. James was worried about strident feminism, but his views on this subject were not identical with those of Ransom. Gilbert and Gubar, *No Man's Land*, p. 26.

78. Henry James, *The Bostonians* (London, New York: Macmillan, 1886), p. 11.

79. Ibid., pp. 25, 217.

80. Ibid., p. 137.

81. Quoted in Mark Gerzon, *A Choice of Heroes: The Changing Faces of American Manhood* (Boston: Houghton, Mifflin, 1982), p. 59.

82. Bram Stoker, *Dracula* (London: Constable, 1897), pp. 142, 458. For a recent discussion of Stoker's treatment of the "New Woman," see Joan Acocella, "In the Blood: Why Do Vampires Still Thrill?" *New Yorker*, March 16, 2009.

83. Other representative titles were *The War of the Sexes* and *The Sex Triumphant*. Gilbert and Gubar, *No Man's Land*, p. 18.

84. See, for example, Horace Bushnell, *Women's Suffrage: The Reform Against Nature* (New York: Scribner's, 1869).

85. Tosh, *A Man's Place*, p. 145.

86. Jon Lambertz, "Feminists and the Politics of Wife-Beating," in Harold L. Smith, ed., *British Feminism in the Twentieth Century* (Amherst: University of Massachusetts Press, 1990), p. 27.

87. McMillan, *France and Women*, p. 155.

88. The medieval notion of a Great Chain of Being, arranged with God, the Prime Mover, at the top and inanimate matter at the bottom, placed male humans just below the angels, but did not include females, who were considered to be of a lower order. No creature could alter its position in this fixed hierarchy.

89. For a discussion of European fears of "degeneracy" and response to them, see Leo Braudy, *From Chivalry to Terrorism: War and the Changing Nature of Masculinity* (New York: Knopf, 1993), pp. 322–25.

90. Robert A. Nye, *Masculinity and Male Codes of Honor in Modern France* (New York: Oxford University Press, 1993), pp. 74–75.

91. Max Nordau, *Degeneration* (New York: D. Appleton, 1895), p. 326.

92. From a psychological point of view, this reflects the need of young men to separate from their mothers so that they can become men. See, for example, Arthur Brittan, *Masculinity and Power* (Oxford: Blackwell, 1989), p. 32.

93. David T. Courtwright, *Violent Land: Single Men and Social Disorder from the Frontier to the Inner City* (Cambridge, MA: Harvard University Press, 1996), pp. 50, 59.

94. Twenty years earlier, males had outnumbered females in the western mountain territories by 46,000 (out of a total population of 175,000). Barker-Benfield, *Horrors of the Half-Known Life*, p. 13.

95. Twain's novel *Huckleberry Finn* ends with these sentences: "But I reckon I got to light out for the Territory ahead of the rest, because Aunt Sally she's going to adopt me and sivilize me, and I can't stand it. I been there before."

96. "The empire beckoned as the most unequivocal means of realizing the fantasy of a manly life free from feminine constraint." Tosh, *A Man's Place*, pp. 193–94. The gender imbalance in imperial colonies was great. In German South-West Africa, for example, there were only nineteen white European women for every one hundred German soldiers. Lewis H. Gann, *By the Rulers of German Africa, 1884–1914* (Stanford, CA: Stanford University Press, 1977), p. 227. However, many immigrants from Germany and some other countries tended to come in family units.

97. Diana Gittins, *Fair Sex: Family Size and Structure, 1900–1939* (London: Hutchins, 1982), p. 37. In the four decades leading up to World War I, more than a quarter of the men who attended Balliol College, Oxford, subsequently emigrated, half of them to India. Tosh, *A Man's Place*, p. 176.

98. Ibid., p. 179.

99. Ibid., p. 194.

100. Ibid., p. 176.

101. New laws and court rulings giving more rights to wives made the home less appealing to many late Victorian husbands. A major turning point was the Married Women's Property Act of 1870. Shanley, *Feminism, Marriage, and the Law*, p. 77.

102. Tosh, *A Man's Place*, p. 186.

103. Ibid., pp. 182, 172–73.

104. Robert Putnam, *Bowling Alone: The Collapse and Revival of American Community* (New York: Touchstone, 2000), pp. 388–89. Anthony Rotundo has estimated that between one-eighth and one-quarter of all American men belonged to fraternal organizations by the end of the century. Rotundo, *American Manhood*, p. 143.

105. This figure is cited in Tosh, *A Man's Place*, p. 187.

106. Robert A. Nye, "Kinship, Male Bonds, and Masculinity in Comparative Perspective," *American Historical Review* 105, no. 5 (December 2000): 1659, http://www.historycooperative.org (accessed September 15, 2009).

107. Tosh, *A Man's Place*, p. 182.

108. French secondary schools were expected to instill "heterosexual masculinity" in their male students. Surkis, *Sexing the Citizen*, p. 113.

109. The theory was that educating boys by themselves would make them

more "manly" and morally upright. This view of the English public school was popularized by Thomas Hughes's 1857 novel, *Tom Brown's School Days*. It stressed the role of competition in developing strong, successful males. J. A. Mangan, "Social Darwinism and Upper-Class Education in Victorian and Edwardian England," in J. A. Mangan and James Walvin, eds., *Manliness and Morality: Middle-Class Masculinity in Britain and America, 1800–1940* (Manchester, UK: Manchester University Press, 1987), p. 142.

110. The Austrian writer Robert Musil dealt with the homoerotic aspects of life in a military academy during the 1890s in his novella *The Confusions of Young Törless*.

111. Robert Graves, *Good-Bye to All That: An Autobiography* (Providence, RI: Berghahn, 1995), p. 25.

112. Michael S. Foldy, *The Trials of Oscar Wilde: Deviance, Morality, and Late-Victorian Society* (New Haven, CT: Yale University Press, 1997), p. 130.

113. This recrimination also occurred in the United States, in the 1850s. Mark C. Carnes and Clyde Griffen, *Meanings for Manhood: Constructions of Masculinity in Victorian America* (Chicago: University of Chicago Press, 1990), p. 189.

114. It has been estimated that the number of female teachers in England doubled between 1871 and 1911. Holloway, *Women and Work*, p. 122.

115. This was also a concern in Canada. Mark Moss, *Manliness and Militarism: Educating Young Boys in Ontario for War* (Oxford: Oxford University Press, 2001), p. 22.

116. Donald E. Hall, *Muscular Christianity: Embodying the Victorian Age* (Cambridge: Cambridge University Press, 1984), p. 20. Cf. Carnes and Griffen, *Meanings for Manhood*, p. 189.

117. Thomas Hughes, *Tom Brown at Oxford* (New York: Macmillan, 1895), pp. 107ff.

118. Clifford Putney, introduction, *Muscular Christianity: Manhood and Sports in Protestant America, 1880–1920* (Cambridge, MA: Harvard University Press, 2003), p. 2.

119. This emphasis on physical games and sports took hold in schools for middle-class American boys in the 1860s; it represented an extension of the "boy culture" that had developed in the preceding decades and given young boys an alternative to the female-dominated home life. See E. Anthony Rotundo, "Boy Culture: Middle-Class Boyhood in Nineteenth-Century America," in Carnes and Griffen, eds., *Meanings for Manhood*, pp. 15–36.

120. Sports became compulsory at English public schools between 1860 and 1880. John Springhall, "Building Character in the British Boy: The Attempt to Extend Christian Manliness to Working-Class Adolescents, 1880–1914," in Mangan and Walvin, eds., *Manliness and Morality*, p. 66.

121. Tosh, *A Man's Place*, pp. 188–89.

122. Theodore Roosevelt, *An Autobiography* (New York: Macmillan, 1913), p. 30.

123. See "British Disaster in the Crimea—the British War System," in Karl Marx, Eleanor Marx Aveling, and Edward Bibbins Aveling, *The Eastern Question: A Reprint of Letters Written 1853–1856 Dealing with the Events of the Crimean War* (New York: Routledge, 1994), pp. 506–12. While much of the blame for the army's performance was placed on outdated equipment and tactics, superannuated leaders, and inadequate logistics, the Crimean War experience gave impetus to the physical fitness movement in Britain, as a way of preparing for the next conflict. Peter Bailey, *Leisure and Class in Victorian England: Rational Recreation and the Contest for Control, 1830–1885* (London: Routledge, 1987), p. 135.

124. Adams, *Great Adventure*, p. 40.

125. The British journalist and economist Walter Hagenot developed this view of warfare in his book *Physics and Politics* (New York: D. Appleton, 1895). It was also promulgated by the sociologist Benjamin Kidd, in his bestselling *Social Evolution* (New York: Macmillan, 1894).

126. Henty's books, of which there were eighty, sold some 150,000 copies in England. Springhall, "Building Character in the British Boy," p. 62.

127. Gerard de Groot, *Blighty: British Society in the Era of the Great War* (London, New York: Longman, 1996), pp. 38–39.

128. David M. Pomfret, *Young People and the European City: Age Relations in Nottingham and Saint-Etienne, 1890–1940* (Aldershot, UK: Ashgate, 2004), p. 114.

129. "The idea of belonging to a socially desirable masculine unit was especially appealing to men threatened by the dislocations of industrialisation and the increased 'feminization' of society." Moss, *Manliness and Militarism*, p. 33.

130. Figures cited in Claire G. Moses, *French Feminism in the Nineteenth Century* (Albany: SUNY Press, 1984), p. 23.

131. David J. Hacker, "Rethinking the 'Early' Decline of Marital Fertility in the United States," *Demography* 40, no. 4 (November 2003): 609.

132. Lee L. Bean, Geraldine P. Mineau, and Douglas L. Anderton, *Fertility Change on the American Frontier: Adaptation and Innovation* (Berkeley: University of California Press, 1990), p. 129.

133. Sigmund Freud, *Group Psychology and the Analysis of the Ego*, trans. and ed. James Strachey (New York: Norton, 1959), p. 9.

134. The proclivity of groups of men to engage in antisocial, violent behavior has been observed, in recent years, among Asian societies with a higher proportion of males than females. These "excess" males have been labeled

"empty branches." See Valerie M. Hudson and Andrea M. den Boer, *Bare Branches: Security Implications of Asia's Surplus Male Population* (Cambridge, MA: MIT Press, 2004).

135. Anne Campbell, introduction to *Men, Women, and Aggression* (New York: Basic Books, 1991), p. viii.

136. George L. Mosse, "Masculinity and the Decadence," in Roy Porter and Mikulas Teich, eds., *Sexual Knowledge, Sexual Science: The History of Attitudes to Sexuality* (Cambridge: Cambridge University Press, 1994), pp. 252, 254.

137. David F. Trask, *The War with Spain in 1898* (Lincoln: University of Nebraska Press, 1996), p. 58.

138. *New York World*, March 6, 1898.

139. Kristin L. Hoganson, *Fighting for American Manhood: How Gender Politics Provoked the Spanish-American and Philippine-American Wars* (New Haven, CT: Yale University Press, 1998), pp. 2–4, 10–11, 15–42, passim. Many men felt women were taking on too visible a role in public affairs, to the detriment of the opposite sex. A "feminization of American politics" was taking place.

140. Richard Hofstadter, *Social Darwinism in American Life, 1860–1915* (Philadelphia: University of Pennsylvania Press, 1945).

141. Excitement about this war spread even to nonbelligerent nations, such as England. See "All England Excited," *New York Times*, April 23, 1898. The paper's correspondent in London observed, "In such a crisis the attitude of benevolent neutrals only partially conceals their undoubted desire to be in it themselves."

142. All told, 350 Harvard alumni served in the Spanish-American War, or one out of every hundred soldiers. John T. Bethell, "'A Splendid Little War': Harvard and the Commencement of a New World Order," *Harvard Magazine* (November/December 1998), http://harvardmagazine.com/1998/11/war.html (accessed September 18, 2009).

143. James A. Frye, *The First Regiment Massachusetts Heavy Artillery, United States Volunteers, in the Spanish-American War of 1898: United States Volunteers, in the Spanish-American War of 1898* (Boston: Colonial, 1899), pp. 24, 90, 93.

144. Theodore Roosevelt, *The Rough Riders* (New York: Review of Reviews, 1904), pp. 10, 11.

145. This was Roosevelt's assessment. But sentiment at his alma mater, Harvard, was divided on the merits of this conflict. Bethell, "'A Splendid Little War.'"

146. Of the entire American force, some 125,000 men had volunteered for the war. Statistics are found in Table 1, "Principal Wars in Which the United States Participated: U.S. Military Personnel Serving and Casualties," Hannah Fischer, Kim Klarman, and Mari-Jana Oboroceanu, *CRS Report for Congress: American Military Operations and Casualties: Lists and Statistics* (Washington, DC:

GPO, May 14, 2008), p. 2. However, typhoid and other contagious diseases did claim more than 2,000 American victims.

147. A notable exception was Ireland, where anti-British feelings translated into backing for the Boers.

148. Jonathan Schneer, *London 1900: The Imperial Metropolis* (New Haven, CT: Yale University Press, 2001), pp. 85–86.

149. Most initial opposition came from Ireland, where sympathies for the plight of the Boers were pronounced.

150. Heloise Brown, *"The Truest Form of Patriotism": Pacifist Feminism in Britain, 1870–1902* (Manchester, UK: Manchester University Press, 2003), p. 170.

151. Barbara R. Penny, "Australia's Reaction to the Boer War: A Study in Colonial Imperialism," *Journal of British Studies* 7, no. 11 (November 1967): 97.

152. Frank Wilkinson, *Australia at the Front: A Colonial View of the Boer War* (London: John Long, 1901), p. 3.

153. Moss, *Manliness and Militarism*, pp. 1, 43, 39.

154. Denis Judd, *The British Imperial Experience from 1765 to the Present* (New York: Basic Books, 1997), p. 155.

155. The dead included half of all Boer children under the age of sixteen. For public reaction to these atrocities, see Gil Merom, *How Democracies Lose Small Wars: State, Society, and the Failures of France in Algeria, Israel in Lebanon, and the United States in Vietnam* (Cambridge: Cambridge University Press, 2003), p. 61.

156. David Silbey, *The British Working Class and Enthusiasm for the War, 1914–1916* (London: Cass, 2005), p. 16. As a war correspondent, Winston Churchill wrote an article for the London *Morning Post* conceding that the "individual Boer, mounted and in a suitable country, is worth three to five regular soldiers. The only way to deal with them is to either get men equal in character and intelligence as riflemen, or failing that, huge masses of troops." Quoted in Henry Pelling, *Winston Churchill* (Ware, UK: Wordsworth, 1999), p. 63.

157. Joanna Bourke, *Dismembering the Male: Men's Bodies, Britain, and the Great War* (Chicago: University of Chicago Press, 1996), p. 13.

158. Davin, "Motherhood and Imperialism," p. 15.

159. In Manchester, 8,000 of 11,000 would-be recruits were rejected because of poor health. Bourke, *Dismembering the Male*, p. 13.

160. Soloway, *Demography and Degeneration*, p. 41. As many as 60 percent of men were ultimately found unqualified for service if one included those who were initially accepted by the military but then discharged on these grounds.

161. J. M. Winter, *The Great War and the British People* (Houndmills, UK: Palgrave, 2003), p. 17.

162. Pamela M. Fletcher, *Narrating Modernity: The British Problem Picture, 1895–1914* (Farnham, UK: Ashgate, 2003), p. 94.

163. Judd, *British Imperial Experience*, p. 157.

164. British generals looked down on the Boers from firing from hidden positions in trenches, but had to admire their use of concentrated firepower against numerically superior imperial forces. De Groot, *Blighty*, p. 23.

165. Public dismay at the defeat of the czar's forces led to the Russian revolutions of 1905 and 1917. In England, the long-ruling, pro-war Conservatives were thrown out of power in 1906.

166. Some observers did sense that the British Empire was about to emulate the "decline and fall" of its Roman predecessor by succumbing to "decadence." Soloway, *Demography*, p. 2.

167. Bourke, *Dismembering the Male*, p. 13. Recruits had literally not reached expected standards in terms of height, weight, and level of health. Soloway, *Demography*, p. 41.

168. Harry Hendrick, *Child Welfare: England 1872–1969* (London: Taylor & Francis, 1994), p. 93.

169. Michael S. Teitelbaum and Jay M. Winter, *The Fear of Population Decline* (Orlando, FL: Academic Press, 1985), p. 30.

170. Helen Brocklehurst, *Who's Afraid of Children? Children, Conflict and International Relations* (Aldershot, UK: Ashgate, 2006), p. 25. This point was made in the 1903 Report of the Royal Commission on Physical Training. Hendrick, *Child Welfare*, p. 93.

171. Remarks of Earl of Roseberry, former prime minister, 1902, quoted in Bernard Semmel, *Imperialism and Social Reform: English Social-Imperial Thought, 1895–1914* (London: Allen & Unwin, 1960), p. 63.

172. For a discussion of comparative mortality problems in Germany and England, see Jörg Vögele, *Urban Mortality Change in England and Germany, 1870–1913* (Liverpool: Liverpool University Press, 1998).

173. Les Garner, *Stepping Stones to Women's Liberty: Feminist Ideas in the Women's Suffrage Movement, 1900–1918* (Madison, NJ: Farleigh Dickinson University Press, 1984), p. 9.

174. Moss, *Manliness and Militarism*, p. 46. The population of Canada grew by 34 percent from 1890 to 1914, but most of this growth was the result of immigration: 3 million new arrivals took up residence between 1896 and the start of World War I. The great majority of these immigrants came after 1905.

175. In 1900, Germany had a crude birth rate of 36 per 1,000, while France's stood at only 21 per 1,000. Teitelbaum and Winter, *Population Decline*, p. 30.

176. Soloway, *Demography and Degeneration*, p. 6. France's fertility rate also

lagged far behind England's. Consequently, between 1800 and 1900, the French population only increased by 39.8 percent, versus 252 percent in England. Annette F. Timm and Joshua A. Sanborn, *Gender, Sex and the Shaping of Modern Europe: A History from the French Revolution to the Present Day* (Oxford: Berg, 2007), pp. 181–82.

177. William H. Schneider, *Quality and Quantity: The Quest for Biological Regeneration in Twentieth-Century France* (Cambridge: Cambridge University Press, 1990), p. 15.

178. After France's defeat in 1871, some fifty books were published dealing with the danger of depopulation. Marie-Monique Huss, "Pronatalism and the Popular Ideology of the Child in Wartime France: The Evidence of the Picture Postcard," in Richard Wall and Jay Winter, eds., *The Upheaval of War: Family, Work and Welfare in Europe, 1914–1918* (Cambridge: Cambridge University Press, 1988), p. 330.

179. McMillan, *France and Women*, p. 141.

180. Teitelbaum and Winter, *Fear of Population Decline*, p. 25.

181. Nye, *Masculinity*, p. 79.

182. Surkis, *Sexing the Citizen*, p. 113. The derogatory term *demi-vierge* was evoked by Marcel Proust. McMillan, *France and Women*, p. 142.

183. Ibid., p. 27.

184. Schneider, *Quality and Quantity*, p. 3.

185. However, in 1905 France did make it lawful for close relatives to marry and awarded patrimony to illegitimate male offspring. Nye, *Masculinity*, p. 81.

186. Surkis, *Sexing the Citizen*, pp. 17, 25.

187. An earlier book advocating population growth was J. R. Seeley's *The Expansion of England*, which came out in 1883. It argued that population growth was essential if England was going to hold onto its colonies.

188. Quoted in Davin, "Motherhood and Imperialism," p. 18.

189. Ibid., p. 10.

190. Soloway, *Demography*, pp. 12–14. At a 1904 gathering of British gynecologists, a speaker cautioned that marriages between members of the "better classes" were not producing offspring, and children born in the working class were taking their place in society. Davin, "Motherhood and Imperialism," p. 22.

191. Claire A. Culleton, *Working-Class Culture, Women, and Britain, 1914–1921* (New York: St. Martin's, 1999), p. 5.

192. Davin, "Motherhood and Imperialism," p. 13.

193. Moss, *Manliness and Militarism*, p. 46.

194. Maria Sophia Quine, *Population Politics in Twentieth Century Europe: Fascist Dictatorships and Liberal Democracies* (London: Routledge, 1995), pp. 28–29. Sergi's ideas would later be appropriated by Mussolini.

195. Davin, "Motherhood and Imperialism," p. 13.

196. Hall wrote of the separate destiny of females: "Biological psychology already dreams of a new philosophy of sex which places the wife and mother at the heart of a new world and makes her the object of a new religion and almost of a new worship, that will give her reverent exemption from sex competition and reconsecrate her to the higher responsibilities of the human race." Granville Stanley Hall, *Adolescence: Its Psychology and Its Relations to Physiology, Anthropology, Sociology, Sex, Crime, Religion and Education* (New York: D. Appleton, 1905), p. 652.

197. Moss, *Manliness and Militarism*, p. 48.

198. Baden-Powell had been influenced by Theodore Roosevelt's writings about building male character on the frontier. John M. Mackenzie, "The Imperial Pioneer and Hunter in the British Masculine Stereotype in Late-Victorian and Edwardian Times," in Mangan and Walvin, *Manliness and Morality*, p. 179.

199. Ironically, Spencer had opposed the war, regarding the Boers as "patriots" and condemning British efforts to annex South Africa as a "continuation of our practice of political burglary." Letter of Spencer to James Sully, December 10, 1899, in David Duncan ed., *Life and Letters of Herbert Spencer* (London: Methuen, 1908), p. 422.

200. Quoted in Howard K. Beale, *Theodore Roosevelt and the Rise of America to World Power* (Baltimore: Johns Hopkins University Press, 1956), p. 52.

201. Table 3, "Means and Variances of Children: Number (Total Births) Born to Various Women Cohorts and Ratios of Effective to Actual Population Sizes," Yoko Imaizumi, Masatoshi Nei, and Toshiyuki Furusho, "Variability and Heritability of Human Fertility," *Annals of Human Genetics* 33, no. 3(1970): 254.

202. Alice Mabel Bacon, *Japanese Girls and Women*, rev. ed. (London: Kegan Paul, 2001), p. 298. Bacon, the first Western woman to live in a Japanese home, wrote this account in 1890.

203. In 1900, out of the over 4 million British women who were working, 1.7 million were employed as domestic servants, while only 124,000 were teachers, and another 68,000 nurses.

204. Companies adopted the practice of firing female members once they married. The 1903 report of the Committee on Physical Deterioration blamed working mothers as the "main problem" to be resolved. Holloway, *Women and Work*, pp. 79, 116. But studies undertaken by the Birmingham Health Department, from 1908 to 1912 found that the rate of infant mortality was actually lower among working mothers than among those who stayed at home. Marjaana Niemi, *Public Health and Municipal Policy Making: Britain and Sweden, 1900–1940* (Aldershot, UK: Ashgate, 2007), p. 77.

205. Gittins, *Fair Sex*, p. 45.

206. Alice Kessler-Harris, *Out to Work: A History of Wage-Earning Women in the United States* (New York: Oxford University Press, 2003), pp. 176, 141.

207. Ibid., p. 116. But the vast majority of female professionals were to be found in nursing and teaching.

208. McMillan, *France and Women*, p. 149.

209. Patricia Hilden, *Working Women and Socialist Politics in France, 1880–1914: A Regional Study* (Oxford: Oxford University Press, 1986), pp. 22–23.

210. June Hannam, "Feminism: Women, Work, and Politics," in Gordon Martel, ed., *A Companion to Europe: 1900–1945* (London: Blackwell, 2006), p. 38.

211. Quoted in Garner, *Stepping Stones*, p. 9.

212. The proportion of women who worked rose sharply after 1900 in a number of countries, including Germany, but this upward trend stemmed from growth in the industrial sector. Gordon Martel, *Modern Germany Reconsidered: 1870–1945* (London: Routledge, 1992), p. 219.

213. With unemployment rising in Europe, employers were actively recruiting women since they would work for a lower wage. See William Henry Beveridge, *Unemployment: A Problem of Industry*, 3rd ed. (London: Longmans, Green, 1912), p. 247.

214. For a discussion of these reasons, see note 35. Another likely factor was the lack of contact between the sexes that resulted from the "separation of spheres" during the Victorian era. One study of the declining birth rate in the United States during the nineteenth century has concluded that a decrease in the marriage rate accounts for 26 percent of the drop in the birth rate, with the rest due to declining marital fertility. Warren C. Sanderson, "Quantitative Aspects of Marriage, Fertility and Family Limitation in Nineteenth Century America: Another Application of the Coale Specifications," *Demography* 16, no. 3 (August 1979): 340.

215. Soloway, *Demography and Degeneration*, p. 11.

216. For example, the mean age at which women in the United States married rose from 23.0 to 23.8 from 1850 to 1890. Hacker, "Rethinking the 'Early' Decline," p. 609. Whereas half of American women born in 1850 were still single by the age of twenty, two-thirds of those born in the last years of the century were unmarried when they reached this age. Bean, Mineau, and Anderton, *Fertility Change*, p. 129.

217. Philip Longman, *The Empty Cradle: How Falling Birth Rates Threaten World Prosperity and What to Do about It* (New York: Basic Books, 2004), p. 4.

218. Table 2.2, "Trends in Local Fertility Rate and Net Reproductive Rate, 1907–97, England and Wales, Scotland and Northern Ireland," David Coleman, "Population and Family," in A. H. Halsey and Josephine Webb, eds., *Twentieth-Century British Social Trends* (New York: St. Martin's, 2000), p. 35.

219. Elidh Garrett, Alice Reid, Kevin Shurer, and Simon Szreter, *Changing Family Size in England and Wales: Place, Class and Demography, 1891–1911* (Cambridge: Cambridge University Press, 2001), p. 3.

220. Cornelie Usborne, *The Politics of the Body in Weimar Germany: Women's Reproductive Rights and Duties* (Basingstoke, UK: Macmillan, 1992), p. 2.

221. Lytton Strachey, *Queen Victoria* (New York: Harcourt, Brace, 1921), p. 281.

222. Letter of Georg Hinzpeter to Crown Prince Frederick, April 2, 1873, quoted in John C. G. Röhl, *Young Wilhelm: The Kaiser's Early Life, 1859–1888*, trans. Jeremy Gaines and Rebecca Wallach (Cambridge: Cambridge University Press, 1998), p. 281.

223. Notables whose affection for young men was revealed included the industrialist Friedrich Krupp, General Count Kuno von Moltke, the kaiser's second son, and Prince Philipp zu Eulenberg, one of Wilhelm's intimate friends. See Marcus Funck, "Ready for War? Concepts of Military Manliness in the Prusso-German Officer Corps before the First World War" in Karen Hagemann and Stefanie Schüler-Springorum, eds., *Home/Front: The Military, War and Gender in Twentieth-Century Germany* (Oxford: Oxford University Press, 2002), p. 53. The emperor himself was later suspected of having homosexual proclivities. See John C. G. Röhl, "'The Emperor's New Clothes': A Character Sketch of Kaiser Wilhelm II," in *Kaiser Wilhelm II—New Interpretations: The Corfu Papers* (Cambridge: Cambridge University Press, 2005), pp. 47, 48, passim.

224. Modris Eksteins, *Rites of Spring: The Great War and the Birth of the Modern Age* (New York: Anchor Books, 1989), p. 87.

225. See Christopher E. Forth, *The Dreyfus Affair and the Crisis of French Manhood* (Baltimore: Johns Hopkins University Press, 2004).

226. Havelock Ellis, *Studies in the Psychology of Sex*, vol. 2: *Sexual Inversion*, 3rd ed. (Philadelphia: F. A. Davis, 1921).

227. For a discussion of women's search for sexual autonomy in the Edwardian era, see Margaret Jackson, *The Real Facts of Life: Feminism and the Politics of Sexuality, 1850–1940* (London: Taylor & Francis, 1994), pp. 6–33.

228. Fig. 10–3, "Women as a Proportion of the Manufacturing Labour Force, 1890s–1970s," Deborah Simonton, *A History of European Women's Work: 1700 to the Present* (London: Routledge, 1998), p. 223.

229. McMillan, *France and Women*, p. 161.

230. Jane Eldridge Miller, *Rebel Women: Feminism, Modernism and the Edwardian Novel* (Chicago: University of Chicago Press, 1994), p. 38.

231. Bacon, *Japanese Girls and Women*, p. 296. See also, Joanna Liddle and Sachiko Nakajima, *Rising Suns, Rising Daughters: Gender, Class and Power in Japan* (Bangkok: White Lotus, 2000), pp. 30, 33, 35. But the first college for women was not established until 1911.

CHAPTER 3

1. "Militant Throws King's Derby Colt," *New York Times*, June 4, 1913. For a video clip of the incident, see http://www.youtube.com/watch?v=TH_r6-JpO9Q (accessed July 14, 2009).

2. A recent article has concluded that Davison was prepared to die for her cause, but was not suicidal. Gay L. Gullickson, "Emily Wilding Davison: A Secular Martyr?" *Social Research* 75, no. 2 (Summer 2008): 461–84, http://findarticles .com/p/articles/mi_m2267/is_2_75/ai_n28048828/print (accessed July 15, 2009).

3. Men in the crowd gathered in Hyde Park removed their hats at the mention of Davison's name. Martin Pugh, *The March of the Women: A Revisionist Analysis of the Campaign for Women's Suffrage, 1866–1914* (Oxford: Oxford University Press, 2002), p. 204.

4. "Suffragists Honor 'Militant Martyr,'" *New York Times*, June 15, 1913.

5. The poet Wilfred Owen would use it ironically in his 1917 eponymous poem written after a gas attack on the Western Front, in France.

6. *Suffragette*, June 13, 1913.

7. "A Memorable Derby," London *Times*, June 5, 1913.

8. "Sensational Derby," *Morning Post*, June 5, 1913.

9. During the 1910 parliamentary election, Asquith had declared his willingness to support female suffrage, but changed his mind after he was reelected. This abrupt about-face infuriated members of the WSPU, who broke windows at his 10 Downing Street residence.

10. Pugh, *March of the Women*, pp. 205–206.

11. Gullickson, "Emily Davison." Among the artworks damaged was Velasquez's *Venus*, at the National Gallery.

12. "Suffragist Assails Tower Treasures," *New York Times*, February 1, 1913.

13. The term *suffragette* was then used to refer to members of the militant WSPU, as compared to the more moderate *suffragists* who believed in gaining the right to vote through peaceful protests and letter-writing campaigns. Many of the latter belonged to the National Union of Women's Suffrage Societies (WNUSS).

14. See, for example, Horace Bushnell, *Women's Suffrage: The Reform Against Nature* (New York: Scribner's, 1869).

15. Remarks of Harold Baker, 1912 parliamentary debate on the "Conciliation" Bill, March 28, 1912, http://www.johndclare.net/Women1_Arguments Against.htm (accessed July 6, 2009).

16. James E. Cronin, *Industrial Conflict in Modern Britain* (London: Croom Helm, 1979), p. 59.

17. In the textile industry, for example, the number of industrial actions rose

from about 50 in 1910 to nearly 300 in 1913. See Fig. 2.1, "Number of Strikes in the United Kingdom, 1888–1974," ibid., p. 18.

18. In 1910, only 16.3 percent of industrial strikes were successful, while 13.6 failed completely, and the rest resulted in a compromise with management. George H. Perris, *The Industrial History of Modern England* (New York: Holt, 1914), p. 512.

19. Coal production reached a peak in 1913. However, employment did not reach its high point until a decade later. Over the next fifteen years the number of miners fell precipitously. Michael Dintenfass, *Managing Industrial Decline: The British Coal Industry between the Wars* (Columbus: Ohio State University Press, 1992), p. 4.

20. Arthur L. Cross, *A History of England and Greater Britain* (New York: Macmillan, 1914), p. 1086.

21. David Silbey, *The British Working Class and Enthusiasm for the War, 1914–1916* (London: Cass, 2005), p. 17.

22. J. A. Mangan, *A Sport-Loving Society: Victorian and Edwardian Middle-Class England at Play* (London: Routledge, 2006), p. 266.

23. Kenneth Rose, *King George V* (London: Sterling, 2000), p. 87.

24. June Purvis, *Emmeline Pankhurst: A Biography* (London: Routledge, 2004), p. 150.

25. Virginia Woolf, *A Room of One's Own* (San Diego: Harcourt Brace Jovanovich, 1989), p. 99.

26. "Mrs. Catt to Rouse Women of Germany," *New York Times*, March 14, 1909. Richard J. Evans, "Liberalism and Society: The Feminist Movement and Social Change," in Richard J. Evans, ed., *Society and Politics in Wilhelmine Germany* (London: Croom Helm, 1978), p. 206.

27. For details on the Dutch suffragist movement, see Minike Bosch, "History and Historiography of First-Wave Feminism in the Netherlands, 1866–1922," in Sylvia Paletschek and Bianka Pietrow-Ennker, eds., *Women's Emancipation Movements in the Nineteenth Century: A European Perspective* (Stanford, CA: Stanford University Press, 2004), pp. 62–63.

28. Otto Weininger, *Character and Sex* (New York: Putnam's, 1906), p. 9.

29. Phillip Blom, *The Vertigo Years: Europe, 1900–1914* (New York: Perseus, 2008), p. 2.

30. See Margaret H. Darrow, *French Women and the First World War* (New York: Oxford University Press, 2000), p. 10.

31. Robert A. Nye, *Masculinity and Male Codes of Honor in Modern France* (New York: Oxford University Press, 1993), p. 185.

32. Raewyn W. Connell, *Masculinities* (Berkeley: University of California Press, 1995), p. 195.

33. Gerald Izenberg, *Modernism and Masculinity: Mann, Wedekind, Kandinsky through World War I* (Chicago: University of Chicago Press, 2000), p. 118. As Izenberg points out, the influence of Hanno's mother and of other women is blamed for Hanno's insufficient "manliness."

34. Mann would examine this problem in his 1918 tract, *Betrachtungen eines Unpolitischen*, or *Reflections of an Apolitical Man*.

35. This was particularly so in Germany. See George L. Mosse, "Masculinity and the Decadence," in Roy Porter and Mikulas Teich, eds., *Sexual Knowledge, Sexual Science: The History of Attitudes to Sexuality* (Cambridge: Cambridge University Press, 1994), p. 252.

36. Nye, *Masculinity*, p. 115.

37. Paragraph 175 of the German Criminal Code, adopted in 1871, had made sexual acts between men punishable by imprisonment. The Netherlands outlawed such acts in 1911. For more on homosexuality in fin-de-siècle Germany, see Modris Eksteins, *Rites of Spring: The Great War and the Birth of the Modern Age* (Anchor Books: New York, 1989), pp. 82–83.

38. Michael E. Nolan, *Inverted Mirror: Mythologizing the Enemy in France and Germany 1898–1914* (New York: Berghahn, 2006), p. 62. England enacted a similar measure—the Criminal Law Amendment Act—in 1885.

39. Florence Tamagne, *A History of Homosexuality in Europe*, 5 vols. (New York: Algora, 2006), 1:14.

40. Eksteins, *Rites of Spring*, p. 34. The May 1912 Paris performances of *L'Apres-midi d'un faune* by the Ballets Russes appalled audiences by their overt, bestial eroticism. Blom, *Vertigo Years*, p. 287.

41. Around the turn of the century, the notion of homosexuals as a "third sex" gained credence among sex reformers such as Karl Heinrich Ulrichs and Emil Hirschfeld. Tamagne, *History of Homosexuality*, 1:154.

42. Nye, *Masculinity*, pp. 5, 9. This French concern about preserving male and female spheres of power and dominance found an early expression in Jean-Jacques Rousseau's *Discourse on the Origin and the Foundations of Inequality among Men*, or *Second Discourse*. French conservatives attributed their country's weakness vis-à-vis Germany to French "divorce, female emancipation, the declining birth rate, and the degeneration of patriarchal authority in general." Darrow, *French Women*, p. 11.

43. The move away from a patriarchal model of marriage began in Europe with the Scandinavian countries, which adopted a more egalitarian view of the institution prior to World War I, in the wake of their having granted women the vote. See Göran Therborn, *Between Sex and Power: Family in the World, 1900–2000* (New York: Routledge, 2004), pp. 79–80.

44. Sarah Cole, *Modernism, Male Friendship, and the First World War* (Cambridge: Cambridge University Press, 2003), pp. 3, 23ff.

45. Graham J. Barker-Benfield, *The Horrors of the Half-Known Life: Male Attitudes toward Women and Sexuality in Nineteenth-Century America* (New York: Routledge, 2005), p. 13.

46. Bret E. Carroll, ed., *American Masculinities: A Historical Encyclopedia* (Thousand Oaks, CA: Sage, 2003), p. 46.

47. See, for example, David Deitcher, *Dear Friends: American Photographs of Men Together, 1840–1918* (New York: Abrams, 2001).

48. Mark C. Carnes, *Secret Ritual and Manhood in Victorian America* (New Haven, CT: Yale University Press, 1989), p. 1. The 5.5 million members included half of middle-class males.

49. Carroll, *American Masculinities*, pp. 177–78.

50. Robert Putnam, *Bowling Alone: The Collapse and Revival of American Community* (New York: Touchstone, 2000), p. 379.

51. Theda Skocpol, "How Americans Became Civic," in Theda Skocpol and Morris Fiorina, eds., *Civic Engagement in American Democracy* (Washington, DC and New York: Brookings Institution and Russell Sage Foundation, 1999), quoted in Putnam, *Bowling Alone*, p. 384.

52. A sampling of organizations founded after 1870 makes this evident: the American Red Cross, National Rifle Association, American Bar Association, Knights of Columbus, Women's Missionary Union, International Brotherhood of Electrical Workers, National Council of Jewish Women, National Congress of Mothers (later the Parent-Teacher Association), Veterans of Foreign Wars, International Ladies Garment Union, and Boys Clubs of America.

53. Virtually all public schools in the United States were coeducational by 1882. Of the 582 colleges in the country in 1870, 343 accepted only men, 70 were solely for women, and 169 coeducational. By 1890 the number of men's colleges had reached 400, while there were 465 coeducational colleges and 217 women's colleges.

54. The phrase "cult of manliness" appears in J. A. Mangan and James Walvin, eds., *Manliness and Morality: Middle-Class Masculinity in Britain and America, 1800–1940* (Manchester, UK: Manchester University Press, 1987), p. 1. The value of loyalty inculcated in the public schools easily transferred to military units during World War I.

55. Robert Graves, *Good-Bye to All That: An Autobiography* (Providence, RI: Berghahn, 1995), p. 41.

56. Tamagne, *History of Homosexuality*, pp. 107–108.

57. Jeffrey Richards, "'Passing the Love of Women': Manly Love and Victorian Society," in Mangan and Walvin, *Manliness and Morality*, p. 99.

58. See Linda Dowling, *Hellenism and Homosexuality in Victorian Oxford* (Ithaca, NY: Cornell University Press, 1996), pp. 36, 67. Through his reading of Plato as a student, Symonds had found a way to distinguish his "erotic dream of ideal male love" from the sordid homosexual acts he had witnessed at Harrow. See also Cole, *Modernism*, pp. 25–26.

59. John H. Grainger, *Patriotisms: Britain 1900–1939* (London: Routledge & Kegan Paul, 1986), p. 33.

60. Mona L. Siegel, *The Moral Disarmament of France: Education, Pacifism, and Patriotism, 1914–1940* (New York: Cambridge University Press, 2004), pp. 10, 25. By 1900, however, some teachers had grown disenchanted with nationalism and militarism.

61. E. M. Hartwell, "Military Drill and Gymnastic Culture in Physical Culture," *Boston Medical and Surgical Journal* 115, no. 11 (September 16, 1886): 253.

62. In an 1890 address, Kaiser Wilhelm II had asked schools to develop the "national" aspect of education "in history, geography, and heroic tradition." See Edward H. Reisner, *Nationalism and Education since 1789: A Social and Political History of Modern Education* (New York: Macmillan, 1922), pp. 210–11.

63. Blom, *Vertigo Years*, p. 167.

64. Only about one in 10,000 German boys ended up attending these secondary schools. Reisner, *Nationalism*, pp. 208, 212.

65. Grainger, *Patriotisms*, pp. 38–39.

66. Pamela Horn, "English Elementary Education and the Growth of the Imperial Elite, 1880–1914," in J. A. Mangan, ed., *Benefits Bestowed? Education and British Imperialism* (Manchester, UK: Manchester University Press, 1988), p. 48.

67. Brad Beaven, *Leisure, Citizenship, and Working-Class Men in Britain, 1850–1945* (Manchester, UK: Manchester University Press, 2005), p. 97. The Boys' Brigade, the second largest of these organizations, had as many as 61,000 members before World War I. John Springhall, "Building Character in the British Boy: The Attempt to Extend Christian Manliness to Working-Class Adolescents, 1880–1914," in Mangan and Walvin, *Manliness and Morality*, p. 57.

68. An exception was the Boys' Life Brigade, founded by a clergyman, John Brown Paton, in 1898. It was to include, he vowed, not "the least tinge of militarism." John Springhall, *Youth, Empire, and Society: British Youth Movements, 1883–1940* (London: Croom Helm, 1977), p. 44.

69. Quoted in Grainger, *Patriotisms*, p. 40.

70. Blom, *Vertigo Years*, p. 171. Kaiser William II, *My Memoirs, 1878–1918* (London: Cassell, 1922), p. 218. The kaiser felt that compulsory military service was the "best school for the physical and moral schooling of our people."

71. A British organization with the same name and purpose was founded in 1894.

72. Except for those on the right, the French people remained wary of taking this step. James F. McMillan, *Twentieth-Century France: Politics and Society in France 1898–1991* (New York: Oxford University Press, 1992), p. 37.

73. Rodney Hilton, *"Were the English English?" Patriotism: The Making and Unmaking of British National Identity*, ed. Raphael Samuel (London: Routledge, 1989), p. 27. Cf. John N. Horne, *Labour at War: France and Britain, 1914–1918* (Oxford: Clarendon, 1991), p. 42.

74. The British National Service League was established to mobilize a defense against an anticipated German invasion. It had a membership of 200,000 on the eve of the war. Brian Bond, *War and Society in Europe, 1870–1970* (Leicester, UK: Leicester University Press, 1983), p. 75.

75. These included William Le Quex's 1906 *The Invasion of 1910*.

76. Erskine Childers, *The Riddle of the Sands: A Record of Secret Service* (New York: Dodd, Mead, 1915), pp. 21, 88, 210.

77. In the late 1930s, Forster would write, "If I had to choose between betraying my country and betraying my friend, I hope I should have the guts to betray my country." *What I Believe* (Richmond: Hogarth Press, 1939).

78. The prewar poems of Rupert Brooke are an exception, revealing him to be torn between these two attachments. See, for example, his 1914 "Peace," which contains this stanza:

> Now, God be thanked Who has matched us with His hour,
> And caught our youth, and wakened us from sleeping,
> With hand made sure, clear eye, and sharpened power,
> To turn, as swimmers into cleanness leaping,
> Glad from a world grown old and cold and weary,
> Leave the sick hearts that honour could not move,
> And half-men, and their dirty songs and dreary,
> And all the little emptiness of love!

79. J. Hajnal, "European Marriage Patterns in Perspective," in D.V. Glass and D. E. C. Eversley, eds., *Population in History: Essays in Historical Demography* (Chicago: Aldine, 1965), p. 134.

80. Robert Woods, *The Demography of Victorian England and Wales* (Cambridge: Cambridge University Press, 2000), p. 89.

81. William B. Bailey, *Modern Social Conditions* (New York: Century, 1906), p. 137.

82. Richard A. Soloway, *Demography and Degeneration: Eugenics and the Declining Birth Rate in Twentieth-Century Britain* (Chapel Hill: University of North Carolina Press, 1995), p. 11.

83. Katherine V. Snyder, *Bachelors, Manhood, and the Novel, 1850–1925* (Cambridge: Cambridge University Press, 1999), p. 21. The ratio of females to males in England and Wales had remained between 1.04 and 1.05 throughout the nineteenth century. See Brian R. Mitchell, "Population and Vital Statistics: 2—Population (By Sex) and Intracensal Increases, British Isles, 1801–1981," *British Historical Statistics* (Cambridge: Cambridge University Press, 1988), p. 9.

84. Diana Gittins, *Fair Sex: Family Size and Structure, 1900–1939* (London: Hutchins, 1982), p. 37. In the ten years leading up to 1901, some 80,000 civilians emigrated annually from the United Kingdom. In the following decade the figure was 90,000. Most of these migrants were young males. See Joe Hicks and Grahame Allen, "A Century of Change: Trends in UK Statistics since 1900," Research Paper 99/111, Social and General Statistics Section, House of Commons Library, December 21, 1999, p. 6. Between 1870 and 1910, this outmigration had reduced the population growth of England and Wales by 21 percent. T. J. Hatton and Jeffrey G. Williamson, *The Age of Mass Migration: Causes and Economic Impact* (New York: Oxford University Press, 1998), p. 208.

85. Nye, *Masculinity*, p. 83.

86. *New International Year Book: A Compendium of the World's Progress* (New York: Dodd, Mead, 1917), p. 266.

87. Hajnal, "European Marriage Patterns," p. 102.

88. A decade later, however, the tables had turned in favor of men: for every 990 British bachelors ages twenty-five to twenty-nine, there were 1,000 single women of the same age. Table 2.15, "Number of Marriageable Females per 1,000 Marriageable Males, England and Wales, 1911 and 1921," Richard Wall, "English and German Families and the First World War, 1914–1918," in Richard Wall and Jay Winter, eds., *The Upheaval of War: Family, Work and Welfare in Europe, 1914–1918* (Cambridge: Cambridge University Press, 1988), p. 71.

89. For instance, on the eve of World War I, the mean age for German females to marry was just under 24, while it was 27.5 for males. Franz Rothenbacher, "Population Structure and Population Development in Germany," Grundseminar: "Sozialstruktur der Bundesrepublik Deutschland, 2005," http://www.mzes .uni-mannheim.de/users/rothenbacher/lehre_WS2005/population.pdf (accessed June 30, 2009).

90. Of the graduates of Bryn Mawr College between 1889 and 1903, 53 percent remained single. John D'Emilio and Estelle B. Freedman, *Intimate Matters: A History of Sexuality in America* (New York: Harper & Row, 1988), p. 189. This proportion held true for all female college graduates during the 1890s. Mary E. Cookingham, "Bluestockings, Spinsters and Pedagogues: Women College Graduates, 1865–1910," *Population Studies* 38 (1984): 351.

91. Woods, *Demography*, p. 93.

92. Ibid., p. 95.

93. For a discussion of this tendency, see Bram Dijkstra, *Idols of Perversity: Fantasies of Feminine Evil in Fin-de-Siécle Culture* (New York: Oxford University Press, 1986).

94. Roughly the same percentage of European women remained celibate. In 1900, the proportion of women ages forty-five to forty-nine who had never married was 10 percent in Germany, 15 percent in England, 12 percent in France, 19 percent of Swedish, and 11 percent in Italy. Therborn, *Between Sex and Power*, p. 145.

95. Vincent Brome, *Havelock Ellis, Philosopher of Sex: A Biography* (London: Routledge, 1979), p. 1.

96. Susan E. Harari and Maris A. Vinovskis, "Adolescent Sexuality, Pregnancy, and Childbearing in the Past," in Annette Dawson and Deborah L. Rhode, eds., *The Politics of Pregnancy: Adolescent Sexuality and Public Policy* (New Haven, CT: Yale University Press, 1995), pp. 32–33.

97. Alfred C. Kinsey, Wardell B. Pomeroy, and Clyde E. Martin, *Sexual Response in the Human Male* (Philadelphia: W. B. Saunders, 1949), Table 136, "Pre-Marital Intercourse: Accumulative Incidence," p. 550.

98. Barker-Benfield, *Horrors of the Half-Known Life*, pp. 5, 10.

99. Michael S. Teitelbaum, *The British Fertility Decline: Demographic Transition in the Crucible of the Industrial Revolution* (Princeton, NJ: Princeton University Press, 1986), p. 77.

100. Many of the unmarried German men came from the working classes. See Volker Rolf Berghahn, *Imperial Germany, 1871–1918: Economy, Society, Culture, and Politics*, 2nd ed. (New York: Berghahn Books, 2005), p. 49.

101. *New International Year Book*, p. 267. The proportion of illegitimate births was then 7.5 percent.

102. Table IX, "Marriages per 1,000 Population in Prussia, 1820–1867," Lawrence Schofer, "Emancipation and Population Change," in Werner E. Mosse, Arnold Paucker, and Reinhard Rürup, eds., *Revolution and Evolution: 1848 in German Jewish History* (Tübingen: Mohr, 1981), p. 83.

103. Teitelbaum, *British Fertility Decline*, p. 215. Cf. Gittins, *Fair Sex*, p. 13.

104. In 1911, the figure was 78 percent. Gerry Holloway, *Women and Work in Britain since 1840* (London: Routledge, 2005), p. 150.

105. Ibid., p. 132.

106. http://www.nber.org/chapters/c6304.pdf, p. 47.

107. *New International Encyclopedia*, vol. 23, 2nd ed. (New York: Mead, 1930), p. 207.

108. George R. Porter, *The Progress of the Nation* (London: Methuen, 1912), p. 13.

109. Edward A. Ross, *Changing America: Studies in Contemporary Society* (New York: Century, 1912), quoted in Laura H. Behling, *The Masculine Woman in America, 1890–1935* (Urbana: University of Illinois Press, 2001), p. 40.

110. Ibid., p. 39.

111. This argument was advanced in 1906, by the epidemiologists Arthur Newsholme and T. H. C. Stevenson. See Soloway, *Demography and Degeneration*, p. 18.

112. Joanna Liddle and Sachiko Nakajima, *Rising Suns, Rising Daughters: Gender, Class and Power in Japan* (Bangkok: White Lotus, 2000), p. 60.

113. Vera C. Mackie, *Feminism in Modern Japan: Citizenship, Embodiment, and Sexuality* (Cambridge: Cambridge University Press, 2003), pp. 47–48.

114. The argument that war would not accomplish anything was also being made, but not heeded. In 1911, the writer and pacifist Norman Angell published a pamphlet entitled "Europe's Optical Illusion," making the case that military victory would not translate into economic gain. As a book, this sold over 2 million copies and was translated into twenty-five languages, but did not deter the Great Powers from pursuing bellicose solutions to their international rivalry.

115. Men's alienation from women and from their families made war attractive. See Michael C. C. Adams, *Great Adventure: Male Desire and the Coming of World War I* (Bloomington: Indiana University Press, 1990), p. 109.

116. While conceding that the issue of reproduction was not a primary cause of the Great War, one historian has written, "Racist discursive strategies, which linked the biological reproduction of society to the 'survival' of the nation, did, however, contribute to the organization and protraction of a war that, originally intended to last a few short weeks, dragged on for four nightmarish years." This need grew, particularly in Germany, as losses on the front mounted. Elizabeth Domansky, "Militarization and Reproduction in World War I Germany," in Geoff Eley, ed., *Society, Culture and the State in Germany, 1870–1930* (Ann Arbor: University of Michigan Press, 1996), p. 431.

117. The salient differences between these two terms was first laid out by Ferdinand Tönnies, the father of German sociology. Tönnies wrote about these two kinds of human association in his 1887 work, *Gemeinschaft und Gesellschaft*. This gained wide readership when it was reissued in 1912.

118. Mann would argue the merits of Gemeinschaft versus Gesellschaft in his *Observations of an Unpolitical Man* (1918) as well as in later works such as *Doctor Faustus* and his "Joseph" tetralogy. Of the latter, completed during the Nazis' rise to power, Mann would write that it represented a step "from the bourgeois and the individual to the mythical and typical." Quoted in Harry Slochower, *Mythopoesis: Mythic Patterns in the Literary Classics* (Detroit: Wayne State University Press, 1970), p. 323. For evidence of Rilke's longing for a mythic

poetic unity, see his *Neue Gedichte* (1907). In 1914, he wrote a group of poems (*Fünf Gesänge*) heralding war for bringing a new order and unity to society.

119. In a 1904 speech delivered in New York's Carnegie Hall, Yeats distinguished the Irish from the English by describing his native country as a place where one could find "on the Western seaboard, under broken roofs, a race of gentlemen, keeping alive the ideals of a great time when men sang the heroic life with drawn swords in their hands." Quoted in Terence Brown, *The Life of W. B. Yeats: A Critical Biography* (London: Blackwell, 2001), p. 159.

120. H. G. Wells, *In the Days of the Comet* (London: Macmillan, 1906), p. 233–34.

121. Letter of Henry James to Henry James Jr., August 6, 1914, *The Letters of Henry James*, vol. 2, ed. Percy Lubbock (New York: Scribner's, 1920), p. 386.

122. Labor unrest, the suffragist campaign, and the struggle for Irish independence abruptly ended. According to some historians, the British people seemed to prefer fighting real (i.e., foreign) wars to bickering over these domestic matters. See, for example, Kathy J. Phillips, *Manipulating Masculinity: War and Gender in Modern British and American Literature* (New York: Palgrave, 2006), p. 1, and Susan K. Kent, *Making Peace: The Reconstruction of Gender in Interwar Britain* (Princeton, NJ: Princeton University Press, 1993), p. 12.

123. Quoted in George Robb, *British Culture and the First World War* (Basingstoke, UK: Palgrave, 2002), p. 5.

124. Gertrud Bäumer, "Frauenleben und Frauenarbeit," in Max Schwartze, ed., *Der Weltkrieg in seiner Aufwirking auf das deutsche Volk* (Leipzig: 1918), quoted in Jeffrey Verhey, *The Spirit of 1914: Militarism, Myth, and Mobilization in Germany* (Cambridge: Cambridge University Press, 2000), p. 5.

125. Rudolf Eucken, "Der Sturm bricht los!" *Deutsche Kriegswochenschau*, July 29, 1917, quoted in Verhey, *Spirit of 1914*, p. 5.

126. Quoted in Roland N. Stromberg, *Redemption by War: The Intellectuals and 1914* (Lawrence: Regents Press of Kansas, 1982), p. 43.

127. Jeffrey Verhey has found a greater range of response among Germans to the coming of war. See his *Spirit of 1914*. Niall Ferguson has identified a similarly mixed reaction in England. See his *The Pity of War: Explaining World War I* (New York: Basic Books, 1999), pp. 177ff. An eyewitness account of the public mood in August 1914 supports their contentions. See Hans Peter Hanssen, *Diary of a Dying Empire*, trans. Oscar O. Winther (Bloomington: Indiana University Press, 1955).

128. For a description of this event, see Hanssen, *Diary*, pp. 25–26.

129. Remarks of Lord George, Queen's Hall, London, September 19, 1914, *New York Times Current History of the War*, vol. 1:1, *What Men of Letters Say* (New York: New York Times, 1914), p. 343.

130. Darrow, *French Women and the First World War*, p. 53. The French public thought of the war as "hateful, odious, disrupting, inevitable—and near at hand." James Cameron, *1914* (New York: Rinehart, 1959), p. 68. It took the German invasion of Belgium to change public opinion.

131. Adrian Gregory has noted how British enthusiasm for the war has been overstated. The largest gathering held in response to the news of war was one mounted by socialists in Trafalgar Square to protest England's involvement. Gregory, "British 'War Enthusiasm' in 1914: A Reassessment," in Gail Braybon, ed., *Evidence, History and the Great War: Historians and the Impact of 1914–18*, (Oxford: Berghahn, 2005), pp. 67ff. Labor groups in both England and France abandoned their opposition to war a week after hostilities were declared, realizing their nations now faced a "national emergency." John N. Horne, *Labour at War: France and Britain, 1914–1918* (Oxford: Clarendon, 1991), pp. 42–43.

132. Stefan Zweig, *The World of Yesterday*, pp. 173–74, quoted in Hew Strachan, *The First World War: To Arms* (Oxford: Oxford University Press, 2003), p. 104.

133. Quoted in Bond, *War and Society*, p. 80.

134. Wolfgang J. Mommsen, "German Artists, Writers and Intellectuals and the Meaning of War, 1914–1918," in John Horne, ed., *State, Society and Mobilization in Europe during the First World War* (Cambridge: Cambridge University Press, 2002), p. 22.

135. Bond, *War and Society*, p. 72.

136. Cameron, *1914*, p. 62.

137. Quoted in James J. Sheehan, *Where Have All the Soldiers Gone? The Transformation of Modern Europe* (Boston: Houghton Mifflin, 2008), p. 62.

138. Quoted in Silbey, *British Working Class*, p. 20.

139. Julian Grenfell, the son of a lord and a graduate of Eton and Oxford, joined the British army in 1910. In October 1914, he wrote from France: "I adore war. It is like a big picnic but without the objectivelessness of a picnic. I have never been more well or more happy." He was killed seven months later by a shell fragment. Gerard de Groot, *Blighty: British Society in the Era of the Great War* (London, New York: Longman, 1996), p. 45.

140. Eric J. Leed, "Class and Disillusionment in World War I," *Journal of Modern History* 50, no. 4 (December 1978): 680. See also George L. Mosse, *Fallen Soldiers: Reshaping the Memory of the World Wars* (New York: Oxford University Press, 1990), p. 58.

141. Adams, *Great Adventure*, pp. 52, 85.

142. Eric J. Leed, *No Man's Land: Combat and Identity in World War I* (Cambridge: Cambridge University Press, 1979), pp. xi, 6–7.

143. Ibid., p. 55.

144. Peter Simkins, *Kitchener's Army: The Raising of the New Armies, 1914–16* (Manchester, UK: Manchester University Press, 1988), pp. 49, 52, 66.

145. Silbey, *British Working Class*, p. 101. According to the records kept by one recruiter, the rejection rate among unskilled laborers was close to 50 percent.

146. J. M. Winter, *The Great War and the British People* (Houndmills, UK: Palgrave, 2003), p. 27. Kitchener had hoped for an initial enlistment of 200,000.

147. Ferguson, *Pity of War*, p. 198.

148. Enlistment rates actually rose after reports reached England of defeats suffered by the British Expeditionary Force (BEF) at the end of August. Silbey, *British Working Class*, p. 23.

149. Peter Simkins, "Kitchener and the Expansion of the Army," in Ian Beckett and John Gooch, eds., *Politicians and Defence: Studies in the Formulation of British Defence Policy, 1845–1970* (Manchester, UK: Manchester University Press, 1981), pp. 100–101.

150. Simkins, *Kitchener's Army*, p. 82, 84.

151. One private noted that his fellow football players had joined "all full of sportsmanship and that sort of thing." A volunteer from Leeds, who had signed up for a Pals battalion after reading the names of other local men who had already joined in a newspaper, commented of his comrades-in-arms: "I never met a finer lot of fellows in my life." Peter Hart, *The Somme* (London: Weidenfeld & Nicolson, 2005), p. 41.

152. One recruitment poster played upon this feeling: "You're proud of your pals in the Army, of course! But what will your pals think of YOU?" Quoted in Ferguson, *Pity of War*, p. 206.

153. Gregory, "British 'War Enthusiasm' in 1914," p. 80.

154. Niall Ferguson has pointed out that most of the Germans and English who turned out to voice support of the war at urban demonstrations were from the middle class. Ferguson, *Pity of War*, p. 189.

155. Table 1.1, "Military Participation of Members of the University of Oxford in All Combatant Armies in the First World War," in Brian Harrison, ed., *The History of the University of Oxford*, 3 vols. (Oxford: Oxford University Press, 1984), 3:20. Of those who graduated between 1910 and 1914, 29 percent were killed in the war. Winter, *Great War*, p. 93. Significantly, among Oxford students at that time, a higher percentage of public school graduates joined than ones from lower socioeconomic backgrounds.

156. For example, 15.2 percent of British officers died in the war, versus 12.8 percent of enlisted men. This equaled 635,891 deaths, compared to 37,484 in the officer corps. De Groot, *Blighty*, p. 273.

157. Frederick S. Mead, ed., *Harvard's Military Record in the War* (Boston: Harvard Alumni Association, 1921), p. v.

158. Silbey, *British Working Class*, pp. 43, 47. Approximately 1 percent of these Harvard men died in the war, compared with 0.6 percent of all American men ages twenty-two to forty-nine. Frank B. Livingstone, "The Effects of Warfare on the Biology of the Human Species," in Morton Fried, Marvin Harris, and Robert Murphy, eds., *War: The Anthology of Armed Conflict and Aggression* (Garden City, NY: Natural History Press, 1968), p. 8.

159. John Baynes, *Morale: A Study of Men and Courage* (London: Cassell, 1967), p. 124.

160. Quoted in Hart, *The Somme*, pp. 105, 144.

161. Henri Malherbe, *The Flame That Is France*, trans. Van Wyck Brooks (New York: Century, 1918), p. 21.

162. Jules Destree and Richard Dupierreux, *To the Italian Armies* (New York: Unwin, 1917), p. 5.

163. G. A. Studdert Kennedy, "Passing the Love of Women," in *Lads: Love Poetry in the Trenches*, comp. Martin Taylor (London: Constable, 1989), pp. 147–48.

164. For many soldiers, the war itself was the enemy, along with the civilians who supported it. Leed, *No Man's Land*, pp. 106–107, 109–10.

165. For a full account of this fraternization, see Stanley Weintraub, *Silent Night: The Story of the World War I Christmas Truce* (New York: Free Press, 2001).

166. Izenberg, *Modernity and Masculinity*, p. 146.

167. Radical groups such as the Industrial Workers of the World (IWW, or "Wobblies") and the Socialist Party were subject to government repression during the war.

168. See Susan K. Kent, "The Politics of Sexual Difference: World War I and the Demise of British Feminism," *Journal of British Studies* 27, no. 3 (July 1988): 232–53.

169. Quoted in Jean Bethke Elshtain, *Women and War* (New York: Basic Books, 1987), p. 112. However, neither the government nor any members of Parliament had struck any such quid pro quo with Pankhurst's organization. Gail Braybon, "Winners or Losers: Women's Symbolic Role in the War Story," *Evidence, History and the Great War*, p. 89.

170. Paula Bartley, *Emmeline Pankhurst* (London: Routledge, 2002), pp. 183–84.

171. See her 1914 editorial, "The War" in *The Suffragette*. James Longenbach, "The Women and Men of 1914," in Helen M. Cooper, Adrienne Auslander Munich, and Susan Merrill Squier, eds., *Arms and the Woman: War, Gender, and Literary Representation* (Chapel Hill: University of North Carolina Press, 1989), p. 98.

172. See David M. Kennedy, *Over Here: The First World War and American Society* (New York: Oxford University Press, 2004), p. 30.

173. Erika A. Kuhlman, *Petticoats and White Feathers: Gender Conformity, Race, the Progressive Peace Movement, and the Debate over War, 1895–1919* (Westport, CT: Greenwood, 1997), pp. 73, 80, 101, 103. Many suffragists believed they had to serve in order to demonstrate that they were deserving of voting rights. Kimberly Jensen, *Mobilizing Minerva: American Women in the First World War* (Urbana: University of Illinois Press, 2008), p. 11, passim.

174. Samuel Hynes, *The Soldiers' Tale: Bearing Witness to Modern War* (New York: Penguin, 1997), p. 50. Hynes cites a London journalist who was moved to enlist after the three young women with whom he had an "understanding" became attracted to home-front soldiers.

175. Elizabeth Domansky, "Militarization and Reproduction in World War I Germany," in Geoff Eley, ed., *Society, Culture and the State in Germany, 1870–1930* (Ann Arbor: University of Michigan Press, 1996), pp. 436, 454.

176. Robb, *British Culture*, p. 61.

177. Kent, *Making Peace*, pp. 16–17, 22. After the war, the head of the NUWSS, Millicent Fawcett, wrote in her memoir *What I Remember* that "the care of infant life, saving the children, and protecting their welfare was as true a service to the country as that which men were rendering by going into the armies to serve in the field."

178. See, for example, Susan K. Kent, "Love and Death: War and Gender in Britain, 1914–1918," in Frans Coetzee and Marilyn Shevin-Coetzee, eds., *Authority, Identity, and the Social History of the Great War* (Providence, RI: Berghahn, 1995), p. 157.

179. Claire A. Culleton, *Working-Class Culture, Women, and Britain, 1914–1921* (New York: St. Martin's, 1999), p. 24.

180. Holloway, *Women and Work*, p. 144, and Deborah Thom, "Women and Work in Wartime Britain," in Wall and Winter, eds., *Upheaval of War*, p. 306. Just before the war, in 1911, 29.6 percent of the labor force was composed of females.

181. Kuhlman, *Petticoats and White Feathers*, p. 1.

182. German women seeking to serve at the front as nurses joined the Austrian army, as their own did not allow women to serve near a combat zone. Domansky, "Militarization," p. 437.

183. Darrow, *French Women*, p. 3. Before the war, between 35 and 40 percent of females worked, making France one of the world leaders in this regard. According to other sources, the number of employed French women actually fell during the war—from 1.5 million early in 1914 to 1.3 million in July 1918. See, for example, Jean Louis Robert, "Women and Work in France during the

First World War," in Wall and Winter, eds., *Upheaval of War*, p. 253. Data on this labor aspect are not highly reliable.

184. Darrow, *French Women*, pp. 141, 170.

185. Ibid., p. 239.

186. Steven C. Hause, "More Minerva than Mars: The French Women's Rights Campaign and the First World War," in Margaret Higonnet, Jane Jenson, Sonya Michel, and Margaret Collins Weitz, eds., *Behind the Lines: Gender and the Two World Wars* (New Haven, CT: Yale University Press, 1989), p. 105. Hause points out that the temporary employment gains made by French women during the war were surrendered after the conflict, as the number of working females declined.

187. Reinhard J. Sieder, "Behind the Lines: Working-Class Family Life in Wartime Vienna," in Wall and Winter, eds., *Upheaval of War*, p. 119. By 1916, 363,970 women were working alongside 920,702 men in the industrial, trade, and transport areas.

188. Robert L. Nelson, "German Comrades–Slavic Whores: Gender Images in the German Soldier Newspapers of the First World War," in Karen Hagemann and Stefanie Schüler-Springorum, eds., *Home/Front: The Military, War and Gender in Twentieth-Century Germany* (Oxford: Oxford University Press, 2002), p. 77.

189. For example, in Bavaria during the years 1914–1916, the number of previously unemployed females who were then earning incomes rose only 6.9 percent. Ute Daniel, "Women's Work in Industry and Family: Germany, 1914–1918," in Wall and Winter, eds., *Upheaval of War*, p. 272.

190. These female units were greatly admired in the United States. Reporting on their accomplishments spurred debate in the United States about the proper role of women during the war. Jensen, *Mobilizing Minerva*, pp. 62–64.

191. Harriet Stanton Blatch, *Mobilizing Woman-Power* (New York: Woman's Press, 1918), pp. 34–35.

192. For details of this wartime service, see Ida C. G. Clark, *American Women and the World War* (New York: Appleton, 1918).

193. At the end of the war 21,480 American women were serving in the Army Nurse Corps. Jensen, *Mobilizing Minerva*, p. 14.

194. For statistics on wartime female employment in the United States, see Table 5, "Increase and Decrease in the Number of Women Employed in the Principal Nonagricultural Occupations, 1910—1920," in Maurine Weiner Greenwald, *Women, War, and Work: The Impact of World War I on Women Workers in the United States* (Ithaca, NY: Cornell University Press, 1990), p. 14.

195. See Hause, "More Minerva than Mars," p. 102.

196. Ute Daniel and Margaret Ries, *The War from Within: German Working-*

Class Women in the First World War, trans. Margaret Ries (Oxford: Berg, 1997), pp. 43–44.

197. This was the case in the city of Freiburg, for example. See Roger Chickering, *The Great War and Urban Life in Germany: Freiburg, 1914–1918* (Cambridge: Cambridge University Press, 2007), pp. 141–42.

198. Jensen, *Mobilizing Minerva*, p. 14.

199. In Freiburg, Germany, male printers objected to women taking up positions beside them, complaining the females would lower the standard of their work. Chickering, *Great War*, p. 145.

200. Cf. Simkins, *Kitchener's Army*, p. 186.

201. For a discussion of this thesis, see Margaret R. Higonnet and Patrice Higonnet, "The Double Helix," in Higonnet et al., eds., *Behind the Lines*, pp. 33–34.

202. Holloway, *Women and Work*, pp. 138–39. This fear also took hold among male workers in the United States. Greenwald, *Women, War, and Work*, p. 237.

203. Chickering, *Great War*, p. 152.

204. Kent, "The Politics of Sexual Difference," p. 239.

205. The number of illegitimate births grew so rapidly in England that Parliament took up the issue of how to deal with the social consequences of this development. Magnus Hirschfeld, *The Sexual History of the World War* (New York: Panurge, 1934), p. 193.

206. Richard Bessel, *Germany after the First World War* (Oxford: Clarendon, 2003), p. 238.

207. Early in the war, British authorities also closed music halls, cabarets, theaters, cafes, and other places of public entertainment in an attempt to bring civilian life more in line with the serious reality of the front. Gary D. Stark, "All Quiet on the Home Front: Popular Entertainment, Censorship, and Civilian Morale, 1914–1918," in Coetzee and Shevin-Coetzee, eds., *Authority, Identity*, pp. 57–63.

208. Susan R. Grayzel, "The Enemy Within: The Problem of British Women's Sexuality during the First World War," in Nicole Ann Dombrowski, ed., *Women and War in the Twentieth Century: Enlisted with or without Consent* (London: Routledge, 2004), p. 73.

209. Prostitution and sex-related crime actually decreased during the first years of the war throughout Europe before increasing dramatically thereafter. In Paris, for example, the number of cases of syphilis rose by a third during the first year of the war. Hirschfeld, *Sexual History*, pp. 189, 192.

210. Leed, *No Man's Land*, p. 45. He cites the example of the Hungarian press in sounding the alarm about this trend.

211. In England and Wales, such births rose from 37,000 in 1914 to 57,000 in 1917. In France, the proportion of illegitimate births increased from 8.5 percent to 14.2 percent of the total during this period. Susan Grayzel, "Liberating Women? Examining Gender, Morality and Sexuality in First World War Britain and France," in Braybon, ed., *Evidence, History and the Great War*, p. 120.

212. Domansky, "Militarization," p. 448.

213. Neil M. Heyman, *World War I* (Westport, CT: Greenwood, 1997), p. 92. In the city of Freiburg, one-fourth of all births were not legitimate. Chickering, *Great War*, p. 355.

214. Chickering, *Great War*, p. 355.

215. In 1913, 9.77 percent of all German births were out of wedlock; by 1918, it reached a peak of 13.1. Bessel, *Germany after the First World War*, p. 233. Bessel points out that the number of illegitimate births per 1,000 unmarried women was actually lower in 1917 than in 1913.

216. Hirschfeld, *Sexual History*, pp. 36–37, 197.

217. Braybon, "Winners or Losers," p. 96. Braybon points out that accounts of female sexual economic freedoms during the war overlook the fact that most women's lives were not greatly changed. Many lurid descriptions of "orgiastic" behavior such as *Sexual Life during the World War* (1937) document male fears more than actual events. A British commission concluded in 1918 that women had not acted any more immorally during the war. Gail Braybon and Penny Summerfield, *Out of the Cage: Women's Experiences in Two World Wars* (London: Pandora, 1987), p. 113.

218. Grayzel, "Liberating Women?" pp. 120–21.

219. Among US armed forces, the rate of infection increased from 16 percent before mobilization to 40 percent afterward, according to one survey. Hirschfeld, *Sexual History*, p. 108.

220. Grayzel, "Enemy Within," p. 82. Robb, *British Culture*, p. 54. The rate of infection in Britain was seven times as great as in Germany. All told, Allied troops contracted 1.5 million cases of these diseases during World War I. John Costello, *Virtue Under Fire: How World War II Changes Our Social and Sexual Attitudes* (Boston: Little, Brown, 1985), p. 212.

221. Robb, *British Culture*, p. 54.

222. Grayzel, "Liberating Women?" p. 126. Some considered these conservative estimates.

223. See, for example, Chickering, *Great War*, pp. 355, 361. The incidence of VD only increased after the war, with so many soldiers returning. Bessel, *Germany after the First World War*, p. 236.

224. Grayzel, "Liberating Women?" pp. 116–17.

225. Susan Pedersen, "Gender, Welfare, and Citizenship in Britain during the Great War," *American Historical Review* 95, no. 4 (October 1990): 996–97.

226. Giovanna Procacci, "A 'Latecomer' in War: The Case of Italy," in Coetzee and Shevin-Coetzee, eds., *Authority, Identity*, pp. 20ff.

227. A French poster from 1917 entitled "Pour le drapeau! Pour la victoire!" showed a female figure with uplifted sword, helmet, and bare breast, holding a tattered tricolor, and urging soldiers to rise to battle. A similar image was used in a German propaganda poster: here the figure of Germanica stands with drawn sword waiting on a cliff to do battle with an approaching British fleet. Jay M. Winter, *The Experience of World War I* (London: Macmillan, 1988), p. 184.

228. Baroness Emma Orczy, author of *The Scarlet Pimpernel* and founder of the Active Service League, sought to persuade women not to associate with men who had refused to sign up. Robb, *British Culture*, p. 33. She also offered a military-style badge to women who convinced their male friends and relatives to do so. Nicoletta Gullace, *The Blood of Our Sons: Men, Women, and the Renegotiation of British Citizenship during the Great War* (London: Palgrave Macmillan, 2002), p. 87.

229. A similar use of females as a sexual reward for signing up was evident in a 1917 poster showing an attractive woman, in uniform with wind-tossed hair, saying "I Want You. . . . For the Navy."

230. A popular song of the day explicitly linked enlistment with sexual initiation. See Kent, "Love and Death," p. 159.

231. The German territorial violations of Belgium and France were feminized. Kent, *Making Peace*, p. 9. During the war Italian planes dropped leaflets over Austrian positions, warning that advancing Russian forces intended to ravage women in Hungary. Nancy Huston, "Tales of War and Tears of Women," *Women's Studies International Forum* 5, nos. 3–4 (1982): 278.

232. De Groot, *Blighty*, p. 7.

233. For this and other depictions of women in American posters of World War I, see Laura M. Rother, "World War I Posters and the Female Form: Asserting Ownership of the American Woman," master's thesis, Cleveland State University, June 2008, http://www.ohiolink.edu/etd/send-pdf.cgi/rother%20 laura%20m.pdf?acc_num=csu1211918047 (accessed June 12, 2009).

234. Culleton, *Working-Class Culture*, p. 68.

235. Jenny Gould, "Women's Military Service in First World War Britain," in Higonnet et al., eds., *Behind the Lines*, pp. 116, 118–19, 121.

236. Siegfried Sassoon conveyed this animus in his poem "Blighters," first published in a collection of verses on his war experiences and his antipathy toward war. Sassoon was a decorated soldier who tired of the war and its gruesomeness. His protests were covered in the press, but instead of being court

martialed for speaking out he was diagnosed with severe shell shock and hospitalized. While at a military hospital for treatment, he met Wilfred Owen. There he began to write scathing verses, revealing the wholesale corruption the war engendered. As Thomas Schilling writes, "Generals, politicians, civilians, maligners, profiteers, and even women in general are vilified in Sassoon's verse." Indeed, soldiers returning home were frequently dismayed to find their wives, lovers, and family members living in conditions they could scarcely imagine—a cause of considerable resentment, which Sassoon bitingly demonstrated. See Mary Louise Roberts, *Civilization without Sexes: Reconstructing Gender in Postwar France, 1917–1927* (Chicago: University of Chicago Press, 1994), p. 8; Thomas Schilling, "Wilfred Owen, Siegfried Sassoon, and the Great War Discourse on Shell Shock" (bachelor of science paper, MIT, June 2006), p. 26.

237. "I can scarcely realise that you are there in a world of long wards and silent-footed nurses, and bitter, clean smells, and an appalling whiteness in everything," wrote Vera Brittain's lover, Roland Leighton, from France, shortly before being killed at the age of twenty. "I wonder if your metamorphosis has been as complete as my own. I feel a barbarian, a wild man of the woods, stiff, narrowed, practical, an incipient martinet, perhaps—not at all the kind of person who would be associated with prizes on Speech Day, or poetry, or dilettante classicism." Quoted in Brittain, *Testament of Youth: An Autobiographical Study of the Years 1900–1925* (New York: Penguin, 1994), p. 216.

238. Leed, *No Man's Land*, p. 16.

239. Another example of this sentiment can be found in Wilfred Owen's poem "Greater Love," which contains these stanzas:

> Your voice sings not so soft,—
>> Though even as wind murmuring through raftered loft,—
>> Your dear voice is not dear,
>> Gentle, and evening clear,
>> As theirs whom none now hear,
>> Now earth has stopped their piteous mouths that coughed.

> Heart, you were never hot
>> Nor large, nor full like hearts made great with shot;
>> And though your hand be pale,
>> Paler are all which trail
>> Your cross through flame and hail:
>> Weep, you may weep, for you may touch them not.

240. Robert Nichols, "Fulfillment," in George Herbert Clarke, ed., *A Treasury of War Poetry: British and American Poems of the World War, 1914–1917* (Boston: Houghton Mifflin, 1917), pp. 166–67.

241. *World War One British Poets: Brooke, Owen, Sassoon, Rosenberg, and Others* (Mineola, NY: Dover, 1997), p. 23.

242. Sandra M. Gilbert, "Soldier's Heart: Literary Men, Literary Women, and the Great War," in Sandra Gilbert and Susan Gubar, eds., *No Man's Land: The Place of the Woman Writer in the Twentieth Century*, vol. 3: *Letters from the Front* (New Haven, CT: Yale University Press, 1996), p. 199.

243. Quoted in David Malcolm, *A Companion to the British and Irish Short Story* (Malden, MA: Blackwell-Wiley, 2008), p. 41. For a discussion of this tendency of veterans to project anger onto women, see Phillips, *Manipulating Masculinity*, p. 28.

244. Santanu Das, *Touch and Intimacy in First World War Literature* (Cambridge: Cambridge University Press, 2005), p. 118.

245. Ibid., p. 109.

246. George L. Mosse, *Nationalism and Sexuality: Respectability and Abnormal Sexuality in Modern Europe* (New York: Fertig, 1985), p. 114. In another book on the war, Mosse notes that the German youth movement earlier in the century had embraced a Greek ideal of manliness, based upon a "superbly formed body," self-control, modesty, restraint, decency, and fairness. See Mosse, *Fallen Soldiers*, p. 60.

247. Sabine Kienitz, "Body Damage: War Disability and Construction of Masculinity in Weimar Germany," in Hagemann and Schüler-Springorum, eds., *Home/Front*, p. 181.

248. H. G. Wells, *Mr. Britling Sees It Through* (New York: Macmillan, 1916), p. 14.

249. Brittain, *Testament of Youth*, p. 126.

250. Rubert Brooke, "Peace" (1914).

251. Phillips, *Manipulating Masculinity*, p. 25.

252. For many young women, the coming of war was associated with sexual awakening. See Kent, *Making Peace*, p. 9.

253. Hirschfeld, *Sexual History*, p. 26.

254. Robb, *British Culture*, p. 51.

255. Comments of the journalist E. Erdeley, quoted in Hirschfeld, *Sexual History*, p. 26.

256. Leed, *No Man's Land*, p. 8.

257. Brittain, *Testimony of Youth*, p. 135.

258. Ernst Jünger, *Storm of Steel*, trans. Michael Hofman (New York: Penguin, 2004), p. 6.

259. Quoted in Leed, *No Man's Land*, p. 114.

260. Costello, *Virtue Under Fire*, p. 211.

261. Robb, *British Culture*, p. 34.

262. Quoted in Kent, *Making Peace*, p. 42.

263. So contended Lord Sydenham, in a 1917 debate on a suffrage bill. Ibid., p. 14.

264. Robb, *British Culture*, p. 53.

265. Florence Brachet Champsaur, "French Fashion during the First World War," *Business and Economic History On-Line* 2 (2004): 12–13, http://www.h-net.org/~business/bhcweb/publications/BEHonline/2004/Champsaur.pdf (accessed July 1, 2009).

266. In planning for conscription in July 1915, Lord Kitchener had expressed his desire to limit this call up to unmarried men "as far as may be." Quoted in Simkins, *Kitchener's Army*, p. 145. Thus the Military Service Bill of 1916 excluded married men, as well as those engaged in war-related industries.

267. A recent study involving 4,500 Polish men between the ages of twenty-five and sixty concluded that "taller men are reproductively more successful than shorter men, indicating that there is active selection for stature in male partners by women." Men without children were an average of 3 centimeters shorter than those with at least one child. B. Pawlowski, R. I. M. Dunbar, and A. Lipowicz, "Tall Men Have More Reproductive Success," *Nature* 403 (January 13, 2000): 156.

268. See, for example, Vladas Griskevicius, Joshua M. Tybur, and Steven W. Gangestad, "Agress to Impress: Hostility as an Evolved, Context-Dependent Strategy," *Journal of Personality and Social Psychology* (forthcoming), http://www.carlsonschool.umn.edu/assets/125344.pdf (accessed June 28, 2009). Cf. J. A. Shepperd and A. J. Strathman, "Attractiveness and Height: The Role of Stature in Dating Preference, Frequency of Dating, and Perceptions of Attractiveness," *Personality and Social Psychology Bulletin* 15 (1989): 617–27, and J. E. Murray, "Marital Protection and Marital Selection: Evidence from an Historical-Prospective Sample of American Men," *Demography* 37 (2000): 511–21.

269. The average height for English males at the time of World War I was 5'7".

270. These units accepted men who were between 5'1" and 5'4". Martin Gilbert, *The Somme: Heroism and Horror in the First World War* (New York: Holt, 2006), p. 5.

271. Lyn MacDonald, *1915: The Death of Innocence* (London: Headline, 1993), p. 148. The German bantams were dubbed *Brotbeutelhupser* or *Fummelkork*. "German War-Slang," *Literary Digest* 59, no. 1 (October 5, 1918): 29. British military authorities agreed to lower the minimum height in light of heavy losses in November 1914. Paul Fussell, *The Great War and Modern Memory* (Oxford: Oxford University Press, 1975), p. 9.

272. MacDonald, *1914*, p. 203. Often the two-guinea marriage fee was waived.

273. MacDonald, *1915*, p. 151.

274. Hirschfeld, *Sexual War*, p. 35.

275. "Effect of War on Crime, Marriage, and Insanity," *Journal of Heredity* (1918): 365.

276. Table 26: "Marriages, Births, and Deaths in Germany, 1914–1924," Bessel, *Germany after the First World War*, p. 229.

277. For statistics on European marriage rates, see Brian R. Mitchell, *International Historical Statistics: Europe, 1750–2005* (New York: Palgrave Macmillan, 2007), pp. 100ff.

278. Grayzel, "Liberating Women?" p. 120.

279. "Marriage, Births, and Deaths," Bessel, *Germany after the First World War*, p. 229.

280. Mitchell, *International Historical Statistics*, pp. 100ff.

281. The crude birth rate in Germany fell from 31.7 per 1,000 in 1906–1910 to 17.9 in 1916–20. Cornelie Usborne, *The Politics of the Body in Weimar Germany: Women's Reproductive Rights and Duties* (Basingstoke, UK: Macmillan, 1992), p. 2. Most of the decline was the result of married couples deciding to limit their number of births. Usborne, "'Pregnancy Is the Woman's Active Service': Pronatalism in Germany during the First World War," *Upheaval of War*, p. 390.

282. Usborne, "'Pregnancy,'" p. 391.

283. Usborne, *Politics of the Body*, p. 67.

284. Quoted in Judith Wishina, "Pacifism and Feminism in Historical Perspective," in Anne E. Hunter ed., *On Peace, War and Gender: A Challenge to Genetic Explanations* (New York: Feminist Press, 1991), p. 88. One wartime French postcard showed an empty crib, stating "Now is the time to do our utmost." Marie-Monique Huss, "Pronatalism and the Popular Ideology of the Child in Wartime France: The Evidence of the Picture Postcard," in Wall and Winter, *Upheaval of War*, pp. 334–35, 340.

285. Roberts, *Civilization without Sexes*, figs. 15 and 16, following p. 87.

286. Usborne, *Politics of the Body*, pp. 17–19. Cf. Domansky, "Militarization," pp. 448–50. Germans, as well as the French, worried about the government interfering in their reproductive decisions more than they did about depopulation. Married women in war-impoverished countries like Germany were loathe to have more mouths to feed. Domansky, "Militarization," p. 450. Furthermore, government policies benefiting mothers ran afoul of public resentment at such favoritism: for example, women in Berlin who became pregnant were seen as selfish. Belinda J. Davis, *Home Fires Burning: Food, Politics, and Everyday Life in World War I Berlin* (Chapel Hill: University of North Carolina Press, 2005), pp. 39–41.

287. Grayzel, "Liberating Women?" p. 121.
288. Ibid., pp. 124–25. Cf. Usborne, "'Pregnancy,'" p. 397.
289. This phrase appeared in the 1913 book *Sex Antagonism*, by the reproductive biologist Walter Heape. Gilbert and Gubar, *No Man's Land*, p. 28.
290. Huss, "Pronatalism," pp. 333–34, 335, Plate 8.

CHAPTER 4

1. The term *Great War* appeared in print as early as August 31, 1914, in an article in the *New York Times*. Even before the conflict began, the phrase "world war" was in use as a descriptor for this anticipated conflict. In French it was known as "La Grande Guerre," and in German as "Der Grosse Krieg."

2. One historian has pointed out that the phrase "Great War" reflected a nineteenth-century, middle-class "preoccupation with growth, gain, achievement, and size." Modris Eksteins, *Rites of Spring: The Great War and the Birth of the Modern Age* (New York: Anchor Books, 1989), p. 177.

3. Only during the Battle of Lepanto in 1571, when Christian and Ottoman naval forces suffered some forty thousand fatalities during only four hours of fighting, had the death toll approached what it was during World War I. See Colin Thubron, "The Great Battle against Islam," *New York Review of Books* 56, no. 6 (April 9, 2009): 32, citing Roger Crowley's *Empires of the Sea: The Siege of Malta, the Battle of Lepanto, and the Contest at the Center of the World*.

4. Mary Louise Roberts, *Civilization without Sexes: Reconstructing Gender in Postwar France, 1917–1927* (Chicago: University of Chicago Press, 1994), p. 95. Laid end to end, the French war dead would have stretched three times as long as the distance between Paris and Berlin.

5. James J. Sheehan, *Where Have All the Soldiers Gone? The Transformation of Modern Europe* (Boston: Houghton Mifflin, 2008), p. 75.

6. Jay M. Winter, *The Experience of World War I* (London: Macmillan, 1988), p. 202.

7. Ibid., p. 207. Serbia had the highest percentage of deaths, followed by Turkey (27 percent) and Romania (25 percent).

8. Sabine Kienitz, "Body Damage: War Disability and Construction of Masculinity in Weimar Germany," in Karen Hagemann and Stefanie Schüler-Springorum, eds., *Home/Front: The Military, War and Gender in Twentieth-Century Germany* (Oxford: Oxford University Press, 2002), p. 187.

9. Sheehan, *Where Have All the Soldiers Gone?* p. 101. Winter, *Great War*, p. 81.

10. J. M. Winter, *The Great War and the British People* (Houndmills, UK: Palgrave, 2003), p. 79.

11. Britain alone had some half a million seriously disabled veterans, including 240,000 amputees and 10,000 who were blinded. In the 1930s, 1.1 million disabled or disease-stricken French war veterans were still receiving government pensions. These figures are cited in David Stevenson, *Cataclysm: The First World War as Political Tragedy* (New York: Basic Books, 2005), p. 448.

12. This statistic for England is cited in Sarah Cole, *Modernism, Male Friendship, and the First World War* (Cambridge: Cambridge University Press, 2003), p. 188. In some battles, shell shock accounted for as many as 40 percent of British casualties. According to another source, 80,000 men were being treated for this condition at the end of the war. George Robb, *British Culture and the First World War* (Basingstoke, UK: Palgrave, 2002), p. 48. In the decade after the war ended, 114,600 men applied for pensions based upon having mental disorders. Gerard de Groot, *Blighty: British Society in the Era of the Great War* (London, New York: Longman, 1996), p. 278. For the German statistic on shell shock veterans, see Paul Frederick Frank, "Hysterical Men: War, Neurosis, and German Mental Health, 1914–1921," PhD dissertation, Columbia University, New York (1966), p. 8.

13. See Samuel Hynes, introduction to *A War Imagined: The First World War and British Culture* (London: Bodley Head, 1990), p. ix. But these firsthand accounts are not always reliable in depicting what soldiers felt during combat. See Edgar Jones, "The Psychology of Killing: The Combat Experience of British Soldiers in the First World War," *Journal of Contemporary History* 41, no. 2 (April 2006): 234.

14. The appearance of Oswald Spengler's highly influential *The Decline of the West in 1918* gave a philosophical gloss to this pessimistic outlook.

15. Sheehan, *Where Have All the Soldiers Gone?* p. 104.

16. William Blake, "Jerusalem," in *Complete Writings*, ed. Geoffrey Keynes (Oxford: Oxford University Press, 1966), p. 674.

17. Henri Barbusse, *Under Fire: The Story of a Squad*, trans. W. Fitzwater Wray (New York: Dutton, 1917), pp. 253–54.

18. Virginia Woolf, *Mrs. Dalloway* (New York: Harcourt, Brace, 1925), pp. 130, 226, passim.

19. For example, in Rebecca West, *The Return of the Soldier* (1918), and Ford Maddox Ford, *Parade's End* (1924–1929).

20. It was determined at the time that the majority of victims of "shell shock" had not actually seen or taken part in front-line combat. However, subsequent analysis of soldiers treated for this condition has suggested this was not the case. See Jones, "Psychology of Killing," pp. 239–40. Many men developed

neuroses as a result of their efforts to repress war-related memories. See, for example, W. R. Rivers, "The Repression of War Experience," paper presented before the Royal Society of Medicine, December 4, 1917, http://www.first worldwar.com/features/rivers2.htm (accessed June 2, 2009).

21. Veterans missing limbs or unable to walk felt they were no longer men; dependent on others, they regressed to childhood. Kienitz, "Body Damage," p. 188.

22. These terms were used by, among others, the historians Modris Eksteins (*Rites of Spring*) and Samuel Hynes (*A War Imagined*). See Joanna Bourke, *Dismembering the Male: Men's Bodies, Britain, and the Great War* (Chicago: University of Chicago Press, 1996), p. 19. Hynes has claimed that the war altered "the ways in which men and women thought not only about war but also about the world, and about culture and its expressions." Quoted in Robb, *British Culture*, p. 1. Paul Fussell relied upon the literary works produced during and after the war to support his thesis about an emerging new consciousness. See his *The Great War and Modern Memory* (Oxford: Oxford University Press, 1975).

23. Commenting on this fact, one study of the literature of World War I concedes that "it is hard to think of any other war whose conclusion brought about such a rush of pacifist art and pacifist statements or which killed so many poets." Laurence Davies, foreword to Celia Malone Kingsbury, *The Peculiar Sanity of War: Hysteria in the Literature of World War I* (Lubbock: Texas Tech University Press, 2002), p. xiv.

24. A similarly more balanced view on the war's long-term social effects can be found in de Groot, *Blighty*.

25. For this perspective, see Phillip Blom, *The Vertigo Years: Europe, 1900–1914* (New York: Perseus, 2008), p. 2, passim.

26. John Dos Passos, *1919* (New York: Grosset & Dunlap, 1932), p. 247.

27. George Mosse, among others, has contended that the "quest for masculinity" was a major reason for the war. George L. Mosse, *Nationalism and Sexuality: Respectability and Abnormal Sexuality in Modern Europe* (New York: Fertig, 1985), p. 116.

28. Frans Coetzee and Marilyn Shevin-Coetzee, introduction, *Authority, Identity, and the Social History of the Great War* (Providence, RI: Berghahn, 1995), p. ix.

29. Marcus Funck, "Ready for War? Concepts of Military Manliness in the Prusso-German Officer Corps before the First World War," in Hagemann and Schüler-Springorum, *Home/Front*, p. 14.

30. Thomas R. Nevin, *Ernst Jünger and Germany: Into the Abyss, 1914–1945* (Durham, NC: Duke University Press, 1996), p. 26.

31. For these details on Jünger's early years, see Gerhard Loose, *Ernst Jünger* (New York: Twayne, 1974); Heimo Schwilk, ed., *Ernst Jünger: Leben und*

Werk in Bildern und Texten (Stuttgart: Klett-Kotta, 1988); Julien Hervier, *Details of Time: Conversations with Jünger*, trans. Joachim Neugroschel (New York: Marsilio, 1995); and John King, "Writing and Rewriting the First World War: Jünger and the Crisis of the Conservative Imagination, 1914–25," PhD dissertation, St. John's College, Santa Fe, NM, 1995.

32. Jünger, *Feuer und Blut: Ein kleiner Ausschnitt aus einer grossen Schlacht* (Berlin: Frundsbergverlag, 1935), p. 51. Author's translation.

33. Ibid., p. 38.

34. Jünger, *The Storm of Steel*, trans. Michael Hofmann (London: Allen Lane, 2003), pp. 134, 135, 141, 144, 254, 255, 259, 260, 278, 314, 315.

35. For details on Remarque's early years, see Hilton Tims, *Erich Maria Remarque: The Last Romantic* (London: Constable, 2003).

36. For a discussion of the impact of public school education on British soldiers, see Peter Parker, *The Old Lie: The Great War and the Public-School Ethos* (London: Constable, 1987), p. 17.

37. "The trenches of the Great War thus provided a breeding ground for a new idea, the notion that the front experience had forged a community of men in which all social and material distinctions disappeared." Stephen G. Fritz, *Frontsoldaten: The German Soldier in World War II* (Lexington: University Press of Kentucky, 1995), p. 207.

38. Jünger was read with delight by many young German men who had missed out on the fighting. Eric D. Weitz, *Weimar Germany: Promise and Tragedy* (Princeton, NJ: Princeton University Press, 2007), p. 114. Jünger's view of war changed as the conflict dragged on with more death and less clarity about its purpose. By 1917, his initial enthusiasm for battle had waned. When he published his war diaries in the 1920s, Jünger omitted passages that conveyed his sense of disillusionment. King, "Writing and Rewriting," pp. 142, 146. Cf. Jünger, *Feuer und Blut*, p. 38.

More generally, the perception that the war had dealt masculinity—and men—a grievous blow prevailed. "Something in these interwar struggles over masculinity helps explain how the victimized soldier not only survived in the form he did, but acquired the status of a historical truism." Leonard V. Smith, "Masculinity, Memory, and the French First World War," Coetzee and Shevin-Coetzee, *Authority, Identity*, p. 269.

39. An English translation of *In Stahlgewittern* did not appear until 1929.

40. Austrian soldiers felt they were "losers in every sense," and this negative self-image contributed greatly to their alienation from wives and families and to the high rate of divorce among veterans. Reinhard J. Sieder, "Behind the Lines: Working-Class Family Life in Wartime Vienna," in Richard Wall and Jay Winter, eds., *The Upheaval of War: Family, Work and Welfare in Europe, 1914–*

1918 (Cambridge: Cambridge University Press, 1988), p. 129.

41. See George L. Mosse, introduction to *Fallen Soldiers: Reshaping the Memory of the World Wars* (New York: Oxford University Press, 1990), p. 7, passim. Mosse notes that this urge to reshape actual experience into more reassuring myth dates back to nineteenth-century conflicts such as the German wars against Napoleon.

42. Cf. ibid., p. 56. In this conflict, most killing occurred without combatants actually seeing each other. Three times as many men died from artillery shells as from bullets. Jones, "Psychology of Killing," p. 237.

43. Elliot Yale Neaman, *A Dubious Past: Ernst Jünger and the Politics of Literature after Nazism* (Berkeley: University of California Press, 1999), p. 31.

44. Jünger did subsequently autograph a copy of *Feuer und Blut*, dedicating it to "the nationalist leader Adolf Hitler." Ibid., p. 31. The Nazi leader made numerous notations and underlined passages in this book at a time when he was thinking of writing his own war memoir. John Gross, "A Constant Reader," *New York Review of Books* 56, no. 8 (May 14, 2009): 9.

45. Fritz, *Frontsoldaten*, pp. 188–89.

46. *The Muse in Arms*, ed. E. B. Osborne (London: Murray, 1917), pp. 49, 130.

47. Cole, *Modernism*, pp. 2, 7, 18.

48. Ibid., p. 139. Cole points out that many literary works about the war deal with soldiers who have lost their comrades.

49. George Coppard, *With a Machine Gun to Cambrai: A Story of the First World War* (London: Stationery Office Books, 1969), pp. 172–73.

50. Quoted in Jonathan F. Vance, *Death So Noble: Memory, Meaning, and the First World War* (Vancouver: University of British Columbia Press, 1999), p. 129.

51. Ibid.

52. Preamble, Constitution of the American Legion, in George S. Wheat, *The Story of the American Legion* (New York: Putnam, 1919), p. 193.

53. De Groot, *Blighty*, p. 269. But only half a million English veterans had become members of the British Legion by the early 1920s.

54. One such optimist was William Paine, author of *A New Aristocracy of Comradeship* (London: L. Parsons, 1920).

55. Cole, *Modernism*, p. 235.

56. D. H. Lawrence, *Women in Love* (New York: Viking, 1933), p. 310.

57. T. E. Lawrence's guerrilla skirmishes in the desert had a distinctly romantic quality: they scarcely resembled what was taking place simultaneously in France. D. H. Lawrence, a pacifist, was declared unfit for service due to his poor health. So, initially, was T. E. Lawrence.

58. Lawrence, *Women in Love*, p. 543.

59. In *Aaron's Rod*, the desire to build a new world based on male friendship also founders.

60. Quoted in Richard J. Evans, *The Coming of the Third Reich* (New York: Penguin, 2004), p. 126.

61. This point of view was pervasive among right-wing elements in Weimar society. See Margaret H. Darrow, *French Women and the First World War* (New York: Oxford University Press, 2000), p. 8.

62. In a letter about this novel to the literary critic Edward Garnett, Lawrence wrote of Paul Morel's mother: "But as her sons grow up she selects them as lovers—first the eldest, then the second. These sons are urged into life by their reciprocal love of their mother—urged on and on. But when they come to manhood they can't love, because their mother is the strongest power in their lives, and holds them." Letter of Lawrence to Garnett, November 19, 1912, in D. H. Lawrence, *The Selected Letters of D. H. Lawrence*, ed. James T. Boulton (Cambridge: Cambridge University Press, 2000), p. 49.

63. In his 1918 story "Ad Astra," for instance, several American soldiers reminisce at the end of the war. They ridicule the "twaddle about glory and gentlemen" they had once believed, and one of them quizzes a German about his reasons for signing up: "'Why did you go, then?' Bland said. 'Did the women make you? throw eggs at you, maybe?'" Faulkner, "Ad Astra," *The Portable Faulkner*, ed. Malcolm Cowley (New York: Viking, 1967), p. 422.

64. In the 1920s, Faulkner tended to depict the "new women" of that era in disapproving, masculine terms: "boyish, breastless figure, skittish and . . . sexually frigid." Frederick R. Karl, *William Faulkner: American Writer* (New York: Weidenfeld & Nicolson, 1989), pp. 210–11.

65. See Valery, "Crisis of the Mind," *Athenaeum* (London), April 11, 1919, and May 2, 1919.

66. Klaus Theweleit, *Male Fantasies*, vol. 1: *Women, Floods, Bodies, History*, trans. Stephan Conway (Minneapolis: University of Minnesota Press, 1987), pp. 73, 126, 162, passim. Theweleit argues that "fear and hatred of women" was a more prevalent theme in novels written by *Freikorps* members than anti-Semitism. Theweleit, *Male Fantasies*, vol. 2; *Male Bodies: Psychoanalyzing the White Terror*, trans. Stephan Conway (Minneapolis: University of Minnesota Press, 1989), p. xi.

67. Quoted in Theweleit, *Male Bodies*, p. 188.

68. As the result of increased trade during World War I, Japan prospered and developed a consumer culture in the 1920s. Many urban young women consequently indulged their appetite for Western-style clothes and lifestyle. Barbara H. Sato, *The New Japanese Woman: Maternity, Media, and Women in Interwar Japan* (Durham, NC: Duke University Press, 2003), p. 27.

69. In 1911, shortly after the Tokyo premiere of Ibsen's *A Doll's House*, a literary magazine entitled *Seito* (Bluestocking) appeared. Its essays, poems, and short stories were all written and edited by women and embraced what could be called feminist causes. A primary focus was Japan's law on adultery, which made it a crime for wives, but not for husbands. At its height, *Seito* had three thousand subscribers. Joanna Liddle and Sachiko Nakajima, *Rising Suns, Rising Daughters: Gender, Class and Power in Japan* (Bangkok: White Lotus, 2000), p. 15.

70. Sabine Frühstück, *Colonizing Sex: Sexology and Social Control in Modern Japan* (Berkeley: University of California Press, 2003), pp. 128–29.

71. Paul Brooker, *The Faces of Fraternalism: Nazi Germany, Fascist Italy, and Imperial Japan* (Oxford: Clarendon, 1991), p. 6. In the face of growing police suppression, the Japanese Community Party was ordered to go underground in the mid-1920s. Mikiso Hane, introduction, *Reflections on the Way to the Gallows: Rebel Women in Prewar Japan* (Berkeley: University of California Press, 1988), p. 26. In February 1936, a group of disgruntled Japanese officers assassinated the premier Okada and several other high-ranking officials out of unhappiness with the government's "drifting away from the true spirit of Japan." Quoted in Joseph G. Grew, *Ten Years in Japan: A Contemporary Record Drawn from the Diaries and Private and Official Papers of Joseph G. Grew, U.S. Ambassador to Japan* (New York: Simon & Schuster, 1944), p. 170.

72. The Japanese government enacted a Peace Preservation Law in 1925, which put strict limits on "subversive" ideas and organizations. This law was first applied to left-wing students at Kyoto's Doshisha University. Richard H. Mitchell, *Thought Control in Prewar Japan* (Ithaca, NY: Cornell University Press, 1976), p. 72.

73. Sheehan, *Where Have All the Soldiers Gone?* p. 99.

74. Jill Stephenson, "Propaganda, Autarky, and the German Housewife," in David Welch, ed., *Nazi Propaganda: The Power and the Limitations* (London: Taylor & Francis, 1983), p. 119.

75. Mosse, *Fallen Soldiers*, pp. 58–59.

76. See Theweleit, *Male Bodies*, pp. 159–82.

77. Marcus Funck, "Ready for War? Concepts of Military Manliness in the Prusso-German Officer Corps before the First World War" in Hagemann and Schüler-Springorum, eds., *Home/Front*, p. 14.

78. Mosse, *Nationalism and Sexuality*, pp. 13, 16.

79. Mosse, *Fallen Soldiers*, p. 183. Cf. Thomas Kühne, "Comradeship: Gender Confusion and Gender Order in the German Military, 1918–1945," in Hagemann and Schüler-Springorum, eds., *Home/Front*, pp. 237ff. Fascism offered men the "will to oneness." Theweleit, *Male Bodies*, p. 101.

80. Joshua S. Goldstein, *War and Gender: How Gender Shapes the War System*

and Vice Versa (New York: Cambridge University Press, 2001), pp. 372, 373.

81. Mosse, *Fallen Soldiers*, p. 184.

82. Quoted in Martin Durham, *Women and Fascism* (London: Routledge, 1998), p. 168.

83. R.W. Connell, *Masculinities* (Berkeley: University of California Press, 1995), p. 193.

84. Jost Düllfer, *Nazi Germany, 1933–1945: Faith and Annihilation*, trans. Dean Scott McMurry (London: Arundel, 1996), p. 10.

85. Virginia Woolf, *Three Guineas* (Philadelphia: Harvest Books, 2006), pp. 9, 10, 11, 12.

86. James Longenbach, "The Women and Men of 1914," in Helen M. Cooper, Adrienne Auslander Munich, and Susan Merrill Squier, eds., *Arms and the Woman: War, Gender, and Literary Representation* (Chapel Hill: University of North Carolina Press, 1989), p. 104.

87. Mosse calls this the "Myth of the War Experience." Mosse, *Fallen Soldiers*, p. 7.

88. A pacifist movement came into existence in Germany shortly after the war ended, proclaiming "Nie wieder Krieg" ("No More War"), but it failed to attract many followers since this outlook was associated with the Versailles treaty and Germany's former enemies. Mosse, *Fallen Heroes*, p. 197.

89. Jünger, preface, *Storm of Steel*, p. xi.

90. All told, Germany had to surrender 13.5 percent of its prewar territory. Its payment to the Allies for having started the conflict amounted to 6.6 million pounds.

91. After becoming chancellor, Hitler made a point of denouncing the treaty in a speech before the Reichstag, on May 17, 1933. His occupation of the Rhineland in 1936 was a clear sign that he considered the treaty null and void.

92. Italian forces were ill-served by the vainglorious and incompetent leadership of Gen. Luigi Cadorna. Due to his poorly conceived attacks on the Austrian army, they suffered high casualty rates. With 689,000 dead, Italy actually lost a higher percentage of its population during the war than did England. Many of those who survived were deeply embittered by the war experience. See Mark Thompson, *The White War: Life and Death on the Italian Front, 1915–1919* (New York: Basic Books, 2009).

93. Benito Mussolini, remarks of March 18, 1919, cited in Paul O'Brien, *Mussolini in the First World War: The Journalist, the Soldier, the Fascist* (Oxford: Berg, 2005), p. 12.

94. A quasi-fascist veterans' group also emerged in France in the mid-1920s. It was called Crois-de-Feu ("Cross of Fire") and sought to emulate more-established counterparts in Germany and Italy.

95. Thomas Mann, *Reflections of an Apolitical Man*, trans. Walter D. Morris (New York: Frederick Ungar, 1983), pp. 16–17.

96. Mosse, *Nationalism and Sexuality*, p. 154.

97. Peter Gay, *Weimar Culture: The Outsider as Insider* (New York: Harper & Row, 1968), pp. 78, 81, 96.

98. Mosse, *Fallen Soldiers*, pp. 160–62.

99. Edmund Stillman and William Pfaff, *The Politics of Hysteria: The Sources of Twentieth-Century Conflict* (New York: Harper & Row, 1964), p. 121.

100. Quoted in Ian Kershaw, *The "Hitler Myth": Image and Reality in the Third Reich*, 2nd ed. (Oxford: Oxford University Press, 2001), p. 30.

101. In examining the testimonies of French war veterans, Leonard Smith has found a duality between works that portrayed soldiers as "brutes" and those that made them out to be victims. The "brute" enjoyed killing and found it morally acceptable, while the "victim" (such as Paul Bäumer in *All Quiet on the Western Front*) deplored the unnecessary loss of life. In many firsthand accounts of the war, the writer/veteran imposed a moral framework around his experience, depicting himself as an "embattled self." See Leonard V. Smith, *The Embattled Self: French Soldiers' Testimony of the Great War* (Ithaca, NY: Cornell University Press, 2007), pp. 7–8, 90, 197–98.

102. Quoted in Eric J. Leed, *No Man's Land: Combat and Identity in World War I* (Cambridge: Cambridge University Press, 1979), pp. 158–59.

103. Jünger, *Der Kampf als inneres Erlebnis*, pp. 40–41, quoted in Michael E. Zimmerman, *Heidegger's Confrontation with Modernity: Technology, Politics, and Art* (Bloomington: Indiana University Press, 1990), p. 52.

104. After the war, Jünger married and fathered two sons.

105. Although Remarque married twice and had numerous affairs with women, he was sexually passive and disengaged in these relationships. He disliked children and had no desire to become a parent. See Tims, *Remarque*, pp. 128, 185, 174, passim.

106. Remarque, *All Quiet on the Western Front*, trans. A.W. Wheen (Boston: Little, Brown, 1929), p. 150.

107. Kühne, "Comradeship," pp. 234–36. Schauwecker had enlisted in hopes of finding a classless society within the army. After the war he became a staunch nationalist and enthusiastic supporter of the Nazi movement. Eric J. Leed, "Class and Disillusionment in World War I," *Journal of Modern History* 50, no. 4 (December 1978): 688.

108. Juliet Mitchell, *Mad Men and Medusas: Reclaiming Hysteria* (New York: Basic Books, 2000), p. 128.

109. Two French psychiatrists, Louis Huot and Paul Voivenel, argued that men became more potent—and fearless—in combat and then returned to a

more normal state, emphasizing self-preservation, once it was over. Robert A. Nye, *Masculinity and Male Codes of Honor in Modern France* (Berkeley: University of California Press, 1998), p. 227. Early in the war, soldiers suffering from shell shock were treated the same as those with physical wounds: they were sent back to the front as soon as they were judged able to return. British as well as German physicians concluded these psychiatric casualties were merely "weak and selfish." Simon Wessely, "Twentieth-Century Theories on Combat Motivation and Breakdown," *Journal of Contemporary History* 41, no. 2 (April 2006): 271.

110. During the war, Max Hirschfeld, a German-Jewish physician specializing in sexual matters, received thousands of letters from German officers and men describing homosexual experiences they had had. Jason Crouthamel, "Male Sexuality and Psychological Trauma: Soldiers and Sexual Disorder in World War I and Weimar Germany," *Journal of the History of Sexuality* 17, no. 1 (January 2008): 71.

111. Ibid., pp. 61–64, 75–77. One conclusion was that the Great War had failed to "remasculinize" European men.

112. Frank, "Hysterical Men," p. 2. German physicians treating shell shock victims tried to restore them to health by giving them an opportunity to rest and recuperate. This approach failed, however, and so more aggressive treatments, including electrotherapy and hypnosis, were attempted, with some success.

113. Birthe Kundrus, "Gender Wars: The First World War and the Construction of Gender Relations in the Weimar Republic," in Hagemann and Schüler-Springorum, eds., *Home/Front*, p. 163.

114. "Britons sought to return to the 'traditional' order of the prewar world, an order based on natural biological categories of which sexual differences were a familiar and readily available expression." Susan K. Kent, "The Politics of Sexual Difference: World War I and the Demise of British Feminism," *Journal of British Studies* 27, no. 3 (July 1988): 247.

115. Susan K. Kent, *Making Peace: The Reconstruction of Gender in Interwar Britain* (Princeton, NJ: Princeton University Press, 1993), pp. 3, 97–100.

116. Freud felt that the so-called death instinct arose from men's failure to integrate feminine aspects of being with their dominant male ones. Loren E. Pedersen, *Dark Hearts: The Unconscious Forces That Shape Men's Lives* (Boston: Shambhala, 1991), p. 166.

117. Kent, *Making Peace*, p. 107.

118. As one historian has put it, "successful womanhood was becoming virtually synonymous with successful motherhood." Diana Gittins, *Fair Sex: Family Size and Structure, 1900–1939* (London: Hutchins, 1982), p. 52.

119. Weitz, *Weimar Germany*, pp. 297–98.

120. Kent, *Making Peace*, pp. 109–13. Van de Velde felt that men were naturally "active," and women "passive." He also argued that "antagonism" was an intrinsic part of the attraction between men and women. Theodoor Van de Velde, *Sex Hostility in Marriage: Its Origin, Prevention, and Treatment* (New York: Friede, 1931), pp. 9, 37.

121. Gerry Holloway, *Women and Work in Britain since 1840* (London: Routledge, 2005), p. 147.

122. Gail Braybon and Penny Summerfield, *Out of the Cage: Women's Experiences in Two World Wars* (London: Pandora, 1987), p. 132.

123. Pressure to liberalize England's divorce laws intensified after the war. Stephen M. Cretney, *Family Law in the Twentieth Century: A History* (Oxford: Oxford University Press, 2003), pp. 215–20.

124. Harold L. Smith, "British Feminism in the 1920s," in Harold L. Smith, ed., *British Feminism in the Twentieth Century* (Amherst: University of Massachusetts Press, 1990), p. 47.

125. Helen Tierney, *Women's Studies Encyclopedia* (Westport, CT: Greenwood, 1999), pp. 584–85.

126. Jennifer E. Milligan, *The Forgotten Generation: French Women Writers of the Inter-War Period* (Oxford: Berg, 1996), p. 11.

127. Maurine Weiner Greenwald, *Women, War, and Work: The Impact of World War I on Women Workers in the United States* (Ithaca, NY: Cornell University Press, 1990), p. 238.

128. In a 1916 survey of employed English women, 2,500 out of 3,000 polled said they wanted to keep their jobs after the war. Claire A. Culleton, *Working-Class Culture, Women, and Britain, 1914–1921* (New York: St. Martin's, 1999), p. 28.

129. Robb, *British Culture*, p. 64.

130. At the Krupp armaments factories in Essen, Germany, only about 500 women were still on the job by early 1919, of the 30,000 who had been there in 1917. Weitz, *Weimar Germany*, p. 21.

131. "One has to accept that after the war most women positively yearned to leave their wartime jobs and return home to husbands and family." De Groot, *Blighty*, p. xi.

132. Kent, "Politics of Sexual Difference," p. 239.

133. Darrow, *French Women and the First World War*, p. 7.

134. S. J. Kleinberg, *Women in the United States, 1830–1945* (New Brunswick, NJ: Rutgers University Press, 1999), p. 137.

135. Sigmund Freud, *Civilisation, War and Death*, ed. John Rickman (Toronto: Hogarth, 1953), p. 24.

136. With some 10,000 veterans returning home each day in 1919, their impatience over delays caused some anxiety about their "rebellious energy" leading to disorder and violence. Cole, *Modernism*, p. 211.

137. As the historian Susan Kent has noted, "the rhetoric of separate spheres had become infected with the rhetoric of war." Susan K. Kent, "Love and Death: War and Gender in Britain, 1914–1918," in Coetzee and Shevin-Coetzee, eds., *Authority*, pp. 171–72.

138. Peter Gay, ed., *The Freud Reader* (New York: Vintage, 1965), p. 665. Freud wrote this in 1924.

139. For example, the English feminist and progressive weekly *Time and Tide* promulgated the view that women should see themselves as different from men. Smith, "British Feminism," p. 50.

140. Dora Russell, "Hypatia," *The Dora Russell Reader: 57 Years of Writing and Journalism, 1925–1982* (London: Taylor & Francis, 1983), pp. 33–36.

141. Ibid., p. 48.

142. G. I. T. Machin, *The Rise of Democracy in Britain, 1830–1918* (London: Palgrave Macmillan, 2001), p. 140. Ironically, most females who had worked during the war were under this age and thus did not receive the vote at that time: Some 5 million out of the 11 million who might have been eligible were excluded. This limitation ensured that men would retain political control in England. Kent, "Politics of Sexual Difference," p. 236. These younger women had to be excluded in order for the bill to be approved by Conservatives in Parliament. For similar reasons, the Representation of the People Act also made it easier for some men—chiefly veterans and men still overseas on military duty—to cast votes. De Groot, *Blighty*, p. 312. When all women ages twenty-one and older received the vote in 1928, the feminist movement suffered a further setback. Smith, "British Feminism," p. 62.

143. Married British women did make some advances as a result of the Sex Disqualification (Removal) Act of 1919, which made it unlawful to bar them from some professions and the civil service. Robb, *British Culture*, p. 65.

144. For a discussion of this issue, see Gail Braybon, *Women Workers in the First World War*, 2nd ed. (London: Routledge, 1989), pp. 216ff. Braybon notes that even though most employers disapproved of married women working, they still hired them—at lower wages than they would have to pay other workers.

145. *Daily Sketch*, June 28, 1919, quoted in De Groot, *Blighty*, p. 263.

146. One demographer calculated that the absence and death of soldiers prevented 40 percent of the normal number of French babies from being born. The lack of leaves at the outset of the war contributed to this decline. Roberts, *Civilization without Sexes*, p. 95.

147. Maria Sophia Quine, *Population Politics in Twentieth-Century Europe: Fascist Dictatorships and Liberal Democracies* (London: Routledge, 1996), p. 18.

148. Elizabeth Domansky, "Militarization and Reproduction in World War I Germany," in Geoff Eley, ed., *Society, Culture and the State in Germany, 1870–*

1930 (Ann Arbor: University of Michigan Press, 1996), p. 443.

149. Quoted in Graziella Caselli, Jacques Vallin, and Guillaume J. Wunsch, *Demography: Analysis and Synthesis—A Treatise in Population* (Boston: Elsevier, 2006), p. 78.

150. Fig. 2.2, "English and German Families and the War," Richard Wall, "German and British Families and the First World War, 1914–1918," in Wall and Winter, eds., *Upheaval of War*, p. 66. For the age group twenty to twenty-four, a slight shortage of eligible females in 1911 (984 for 1,000 males) turned into a surplus (1,043 per 1,000 males) in 1921. Table 2.15, "Number of Marriageable Females per 1,000 Marriageable Males, England and Wales, 1911 and 1921." Ibid., p. 71.

151. "Effect of War on Crime, Marriage, and Insanity," *Journal of Heredity* (1918): 365.

152. Quine, *Population Politics*, p. 101.

153. Michael S. Teitelbaum and Jay M. Winter, *The Fear of Population Decline* (Orlando, FL: Academic Press, 1985), p. 40.

154. Matthew J. Connelly, *Fatal Misconception: The Struggle to Control World Population* (Cambridge, MA: Harvard University Press, 2008), p. 5.

155. "Effect of War," p. 365.

156. Table 2.16, "Change to Marital and Age Distribution of the Population, England and Wales, 1911–1921." Wall, "German and British Families," p. 72.

157. "Vital Statistics: Rates per 1,000 Population," Mitchell, *International Historical Statistics*, pp. 103, 105, 106, 109.

158. Cornelie Usborne, *The Politics of the Body in Weimar Germany: Women's Reproductive Rights and Duties* (Basingstoke: Macmillan, 1992), p. 90.

159. "Vital Statistics," in Brian R. Mitchell, *International Historical Statistics: Europe, 1750–2005* (New York: Palgrave Macmillan, 2007), pp. 103, 104, 105, 106, 109.

160. Table 3.1, "Marriage Rate, United States, per 1,000 Population," Hugh Carter and Paul C. Glick, *Marriage and Divorce: A Social and Economic Study* (Cambridge, MA: Harvard University Press, 1970), p. 41.

161. Connelly, *Fatal Misconception*, p. 83.

162. Table 26, "Marriages, Births, and Deaths in Germany, 1910–1924," in Richard Bessel, *Germany after the First World War* (Oxford: Clarendon, 1993), p. 229.

163. "Proportion Married, Germany (Empire and Federal Republic)," Franz Rothenbacher, "Population Structure and Population Development in Germany," seminar paper, "Sozialstruktur der Bundesrepublik Deutschland" (2005). German men were also marrying relatively late: in 1934, the average age

of grooms in the province of Brandenburg was 27.7. Clifford Kirkpatrick, *Nazi Germany: Its Women and Family Life* (Indianapolis: Bobbs-Merrill, 1938), p. 135.

164. Usborne, *Politics of the Body*, p. 90.

165. Table 4, "Proportions single at specified ages in several European countries in the period of the Second World War," J. M. Winter, "The Demographic Consequences of the War," in Harold L. Smith, ed., *War and Social Change: British Society in the Second World War* (Manchester, UK: Manchester University Press, 1990), p. 159.

166. Italy's birth rate jumped to 31.8 by 1920 in the wake of a spike in postwar marriages. However, poverty and poor health conditions reduced this potential increase in the population. Before the war, one-fourth of all Italian babies either did not survive to celebrate their first birthday or died before adulthood. Quine, *Population Politics*, p. 18.

167. Robb, *British Culture*, p. 65.

168. Elizabeth D. Heineman, *What Difference Does a Husband Make? Women and Marital Status in Nazi and Postwar Germany* (Berkeley: University of California Press, 1999), p. 6.

169. Gittins, *Fair Sex*, p. 33.

170. Kirkpatrick, *Nazi Germany*, p. 151.

171. Atina Grossmann, *Reforming Sex: The German Movement for Birth Control and Abortion Reform, 1920–1950* (New York: Oxford University Press, 1995), p. 4.

172. Michael Anderson, ed., *British Population History: From the Black Death to the Present Day* (Cambridge: Cambridge University Press, 1996), p. 38. This birth rate was not duplicated until 1980. The crude birth rate per 1,000 inhabitants bottomed out at 14.7 between 1936 and 1940. A. H. Halsey and Josephine Webb, eds., *Twentieth-Century British Social Trends* (New York: St. Martin's, 2000), p. 35.

173. Kleinberg, *Women in the United States*, p. 234.

174. Unemployment in the United States and England peaked at 25 percent in the 1930s. By 1932, the rate in Germany had climbed to nearly 30 percent. Britain's economic output fell by some 25 percent between 1918 and 1921 and did not recover its previous strength until the late 1930s.

175. Grossman, *Reforming Sex*, p. 10. Orlando Figes, *The Whisperers: Private Life in Stalin's Russia* (New York: Macmillan, 2007), p. 172.

176. Sheila Fitzpatrick, *Everyday Stalinism: Ordinary Life in Extraordinary Times: Soviet Russia in the 1930s* (Oxford: Oxford University Press, 2000), p. 142.

177. Liddle and Nakajima, *Rising Suns*, p. 15. For more on Japanese reform movements of the 1920s, see Hane, introduction, *Reflections on the Way to the Gallows*, pp. 24–26.

178. Quoted in Stephen Lee, *The Weimar Republic* (New York: Routledge, 1998), p. 114.

179. Ibid.

180. Usborne, *Politics of the Body*, p. 22.

181. Quoted in Otto Friedrich, *Before the Deluge: A Portrait of Berlin in the 1920s* (New York: Harper & Row, 1972), p. 178.

182. Weitz, *Weimar Germany*, p. 312.

183. W. Scott Haine, *The History of France* (Westport, CT: Greenwood, 2000), p. 144.

184. The middle class in Japan grew from 2.3 percent of the population in 1903, to 6.5 percent in 1918, to 10.5 percent in 1921. Sato, *New Japanese Woman*, p. 30.

185. Ibid., pp. 5–20.

186. In 1910, 23 percent of American women were working; in 1920, 21 percent were. Table 2.1, "Labor Force Participation Rates," Gary N. Powell and Laura M. Graves, *Women and Men in Management*, 3rd ed. (Thousand Oaks, CA.: Sage, 2002), p. 14.

187. Sanger came up with this definition of a woman's duty: "To look the world in the face with a go-to-hell look in the eyes; to have an idea; to speak and act in defiance of convention." *Margaret Sanger: An Autobiography* (Whitefish, MT: Kessinger, 2004), p. 110.

188. John D'Emilio and Estelle B. Freedman, *Intimate Matters: A History of Sexuality in America* (New York: Harper & Row, 1988), p. 232.

189. Ibid., pp. 203, 257.

190. US Bureau of the Census, "Estimated Age at First Marriage," *Current Population Reports* (2000). See also US Bureau of the Census, *Historical Abstracts of the United States, Colonial Times to 1970*, Series A 160–171 (Washington, DC: US Government Printing Office, 1989), http://www.unmarried.org/statistics.html (accessed September 12, 2009).

191. Göran Therborn, *Between Sex and Power: Family in the World, 1900–2000* (New York: Routledge, 2004), p. 162.

192. After the Great War, the proportion of working British women who were single remained about 77 percent. However, in Canada, there was a major shift away from careers to motherhood among women in their twenties, to make up for the men who died in the conflict. See Wendy Mitchinson, *Giving Birth in Canada, 1900–1950* (Toronto: University of Toronto Press, 2003), pp. 13–14.

193. In England, for example, the percentage of working women in 1921 was nearly the same as in 1911: 29.6 versus 29.5. Holloway, *Women and Work*, p. 149.

194. Michael S. Teitelbaum, *The British Fertility Decline: Demographic Transition in the Crucible of the Industrial Revolution* (Princeton, NJ: Princeton University Press, 1986), p. 98.

195. In Germany, the proportion of women working did not increase substantially between the prewar years and the 1920s. See Dagmar Reese, *Growing up Female in Nazi Germany*, trans. William Templer (Ann Arbor: University of Michigan Press, 2006), p. 173.

196. Teitelbaum and Winter, *Fear of Population Decline*, p. 40.

197. Lothrop Stoddard, *The Rising Tide of Color Against White World-Supremacy* (Honolulu: University Press of the Pacific, 2003), pp. 3–5, 7, 236. Stoddard warned that "above the eastern horizon the dark storm clouds lower, and the weakened, distracted white world must soon face a colored peril threatening its integrity and perhaps its existence." He saw Japan's victory over Russia in 1905 as the "beginning of the ebb" of power that would soon be facing "white" Europe. Ibid., p. 153.

198. Connelly, *Fatal Misconception*, p. 79.

199. After the Great War, the competition among European powers was based "increasingly on efforts to out-reproduce other nations." Domansky, "Militarization," p. 431.

200. Quine, *Population Politics*, p. 35.

201. Ibid., p. 18. This problem had worsened due to the deaths of some 680,000 men during World War I.

202. Mussolini drew on the earlier, prefascist writings of Guiseppi Sergi, who founded the Italian Eugenic Society in 1912, and Corrado Gini, who published *Demographic Factors in the Evolution of Nations* in 1912. Quine, *Population Politics*, pp. 27–30.

203. Giovanni Bognetti, "Italy," in Dennis Campbell, ed., *Abortion Law and Public Policy* (The Hague: Martinus Nijhoff, 1983), p. 83.

204. Martin Clark, *Modern Italy, 1871–1982* (London: Longman, 1984), p. 275. Victoria de Grazia, *How Fascism Ruled Women: Italy, 1922–1945* (Berkeley: University of California Press, 1993), pp. 44, 45, 86.

205. Connelly, *Fatal Misconception*, p. 79.

206. Table 1, "Deaths among German Soldiers, by Age, 1914–1918," Bessel, *Germany after the First World War*, pp. 9, 225.

207. Evans, *Coming of the Third Reich*, p. 117.

208. Quine, *Population Politics*, p. 41. This policy has been described as "racially qualified" population growth. The Nazis were not alone in adopting measures to weed out "undesirable" elements to make their nations stronger. During the 1930s, several Scandinavian countries adopted eugenic sterilization laws, while in the United States, many "feebleminded" or merely only "antisocial" women were sterilized during this decade. In fact, Hitler was an admirer of these American practices. Connelly, *Fatal Misconception*, pp. 80, 105.

209. Gerhard L. Weinberg, "The World through Hitler's Eyes," *Germany, Hitler, and World War II: Essays in Modern German and World History* (Cambridge: Cambridge University Press, 1996), pp. 34–35.

210. Quoted from *Hitler's Table Talk* in Richard J. Evans, *The Third Reich at War* (New York: Penguin, 2009), p. 171.

211. Domansky, "Militarization," pp. 461–63. The Nazi obsession with expanding the "Aryan" race led them to create "farms" for "selective breeding" between members of the SS and racially matched females, to encourage German couples to have children outside of marriage, and to adopt children from Slavic families with sufficiently "Aryan" features. See Dagmar Herzog, *Sex after Fascism: Memory and Morality in Twentieth-Century Germany* (Princeton, NJ: Princeton University Press, 2005), pp. 59–61.

212. This law made abortion a misdemeanor instead of a "crime against life" and reduced the term of imprisonment for committing or assisting with this procedure. Cornelie Usborne, *Cultures of Abortion in Weimar Germany* (Oxford: Berghahn, 2007), p. 5.

213. Usborne, *Politics of the Body*, p. 67.

214. Grossman, *Reforming Sex*, pp. 5, 10, 12, 13.

215. Usborne, *Politics of the Body*, p. 25.

216. Ibid., p. 49.

217. Weitz, *Weimar Germany*, p. 305.

218. Grossman, *Reforming Sex*, p. 208.

219. Lee, *Weimar Republic*, pp. 119–20.

220. Weitz, *Weimar Germany*, p. 305.

221. Evans, *Coming of the Third Reich*, p. 128. In 1938, one researcher estimated that Germans were using 75 million condoms annually. Herzog, *Sex after Fascism*, p. 25.

222. Grossman, *Reforming Sex*, p. 92.

223. Evans, *Coming of the Third Reich*, p. 129.

224. Groups advocating homosexual rights were summarily banned after February 1933.

225. In a 1935 Party Congress speech, Hitler declared: "The man upholds the nation as the woman upholds the family." Quoted in Kirkpatrick, *Nazi Germany*, p. 112.

226. This body, which was established in 1934, ran "motherhood" courses attended by some 670,000 women. Ibid., p. 75.

227. This "racially hygienic" policy was driven by the Nazi desire to create a "master race." See Gabriele Czarnowski, "Women's Crimes, State Crimes: Abortion in Nazi Germany," in *Gender and Crime in Modern Europe*, ed. Margaret L. Arnot and Cornelie Usborne (London: University College of London

Press, 1999), pp. 240–41. The Nazis were ambivalent about sexual matters in general. For a discussion of this topic, see Herzog, *Sex after Fascism*, pp. 10–63.

228. Evans, *Coming of the Third Reich*, pp. 376–77.

229. Frühstück, *Colonizing Sex*, p. 119.

230. Yoko Imaizumi, Masatoshi Nei, and Toshiyuki Furusho, "Variability and Heritability of Human Fertility," *Annals of Human Genetics* 33, no. 3 (1970): 354.

231. Table 91, "Female Births per 1,000 Women, 1925–1954," Irene B. Taeuber, *The Population of Japan* (Princeton, NJ: Princeton University Press, 1958), p. 234.

232. Connelly, *Fatal Misconception*, p. 79.

233. Helen M. Hopper, "'Motherhood in the Interest of the State': Baroness Ishimoto (Kato) Shiazue Confronts Expansionist Policies Against Birth Control, 1930–1940," in Hiroko Tomida and Gordon Daniels, eds., *Japanese Women: Emerging from Subservience, 1868–1945* (Folkestone, UK: Global Oriental, 2005), p. 40.

234. Brooker, *Faces of Fraternalism*, p. 212.

235. Frühstück, *Colonizing Sex*, pp. 119, 128. Cf. Michael A. Barnhart, *Japan Prepares for Total War: The Search for Economic Security, 1919–1941* (Ithaca, NY: Cornell University Press, 1988), p. 31.

236. Liddle and Nakajima, *Rising Suns, Rising Daughters*, p. 128.

237. Thomas R. H. Havens, "Women and War in Japan, 1937–1945," *American Historical Review* 80, no. 4 (October 1975): 928.

238. In fact, this goal was reached in 1967. Some demographers suggested early in the war that Japan would need as many as 200 million people to sustain its Greater East Asian Co-Prosperity Sphere. Irene Taeuber, "Demographic Research in Japan," *Pacific Affairs* 22, no. 4 (1949): 393.

239. In the 1920s and 1930s, some 60 percent of the Japanese industrial workforce was female.

240. From 3.6 children per woman in 1938, the rate increased to 4.5 in 1947, but then fell sharply. Griffin Feeney, "Fertility Rate in East Asia," *Science* 266 (December 2, 1994): 1519.

241. Taeuber, "Demographic Research," p. 128. In mid-1943, the Japanese government began encouraging women to work but did not coerce them to do so. Havens, "Women and War in Japan, 1937–1945," p. 916.

242. Between 1943 and 1945, Japan's population declined from 73.9 million to 72.1 million. But this was largely because of war losses. Table 1, "Population by Sex (as of October 1 of Each Year)—Total Population (from 1920 to 2000), Japanese Population (from 1950 to 2000)," Portal Sites of Official Statistics of Japan, http://www.e-stat.go.jp/SG1/estat/ListE.do?bid=000000090004&cycode=0 (accessed June 28, 2009).

243. Roberts, *Civilization without Sexes*, p. 154.

244. Starting in 1935, more persons were dying in France than being born. Marie-Monique Huss, "Pronatalism and the Popular Ideology of the Child in Wartime France: The Evidence of the Picture Postcard," in Wall and Winter, eds., *The Upheaval of War*, p. 56.

245. Roberts, *Civilization without Sexes*, pp. 102, 108.

246. Huss, "Pronatalism," pp. 47, 53–54.

247. Roberts, *Civilization without Sexes*, p. 120.

248. Huss, "Pronatalism," p. 52.

249. Ibid., p. 55. See also Robert C. Ostergren and John G. Rice, *The Europeans: A Geography of People, Culture, and Environment* (New York: Guilford, 2004), p. 90. The bill to ban the promoting of abortion and birth control passed the Chamber of Deputies in 1930 by the overwhelming majority of 521 to 55. Roberts, *Civilization without Sexes*, p. 94.

250. Under the Family Allowance Act of 1932, subsidies for married couples with children were made compulsory. Quine, *Population Policies*, p. 49.

251. Fig. 2, "Historical and Contemporary Fertility Trends, 1864 to 1995," Rachel Franklin, "Italian Fertility, 1846 to 1961: An Analysis of Regional Trends," draft paper, 43rd European Congress of the Regional Science Association, August 27–30, 1993 (Jyvaskyla, Finland), p. 15.

252. Table 1, "Birth Rates, by Region, per 1,000 Inhabitants, 1921–1945," de Grazia, *How Fascism Ruled Women*, p. 46.

253. Winter, *Great War and the British People*, p. 137.

254. Fig. 2.1, "Trends in Total Fertility Rate in Russia and Other Countries of Western and Eastern Europe, 1880–1990," Sergei V. Zakharov and Elena I. Ivanova, "Fertility Decline and Recent Changes in Russia: On the Threshold of the Second Demographic Transition," http://www.rand.org/ pubs/conf_proceedings/CF124/CF124.chap2.html (accessed June 29, 2009).

255. Huss, "Pronatalism," p. 62.

256. Births shot up from 971,174 in 1933 to 1,261,273 in 1935. Kirkpatrick, *Nazi Germany*, p. 166. The number of marriages per 1,000 inhabitants reached a high of 22.4 in 1939. Therborn, *Between Sex and Power*, p. 164.

257. Nazi propaganda linked having children with serving the nation. A typical postcard showed Hitler with a beaming mother holding a child, with the caption: "A Mother's Happiness." The German government awarded marriage loans of 1,000 marks starting in June 1933. But these relatively small amounts were unlikely to convince couples to have children. The loans may have encouraged a number of unmarried couples expecting a child to marry, however. For two points of view on this matter, see Kirkpatrick, *Nazi Germany*, pp. 128, 134, 166, and Quine, *Population Politics*, p. 114.

258. "Vital Statistics," Mitchell, *International Historical Statistics*, pp. 103, 106.

259. Social Democratic leaders worried that their female supporters had a tendency to pull the party in a more conservative direction. Weitz, *Weimar Germany*, p. 126.

260. Gisela Bock, *Women in European History*, trans. Allison Brown (Malden, MA: Wiley-Blackwell, 2002), pp. 204–205. The "gender gap" in voting for the Nazis decreased from 15.6 percent in 1928 to 1.8 percent in 1930. Christine Faure, ed., *Political and Historical Encyclopedia of Women*, trans. Richard Dubois (New York: Routledge, 2003), p. 332.

261. Karen M. Offer, *European Feminisms, 1700–1950: A Political History* (Stanford, CA: Stanford University Press, 2000), p. 291.

262. Divorce rates in Germany and Russia increased four- and fivefold compared to what they had been prior to the war. Annette F. Timm and Joshua A. Sanborn, *Gender, Sex and the Shaping of Modern Europe: A History from the French Revolution to the Present Day* (New York: Berg, 2007), p. 148. But, in Germany, the percentage of marriages ending this way remained small: only 20,000 more divorces were granted between 1913 and 1925 than in the previous twelve-year period. Usborne, *Politics of the Body*, p. 97.

263. Major depressions occurred in the nineteenth century—in 1819 and 1837 (confined to the United States) and between 1873 and 1896 (worldwide impact). But these did not affect as many people as the twentieth-century one.

264. If the 2 million "unofficially" unemployed Germans are included, the rate was closer to 40 percent. Weitz, *Weimar Germany*, p. 161.

265. Evans, *Coming of the Third Reich*, p. 236.

266. Ibid., p. 232.

267. Weitz, *Weimar Germany*, pp. 165–66.

268. Evans, *Coming of Nazi Germany*, pp. 261, 264.

269. The Nazis polled better among unemployed persons in this class than those in the working class. Conan Fisher, *The Rise of the Nazis* (Manchester, UK: Manchester University Press, 1995), p. 113.

270. The proportion of the German population under forty-five had been only 35.9 percent in 1911. Table 1, "Age Group 20–45 in Percent of Total Population of Germany," Herbert Möller, "Youth as a Force in the Modern World," *Comparative Studies in Society and History* 10, no. 3 (April 1968): 243.

271. At that time, Remarque was singled out for having betrayed his fellow soldiers in World War I. Evans, *Coming of the Third Reich*, p. 429.

CHAPTER 5

1. Quoted in Carl N. Degler, *Out of Our Past: The Forces That Shaped Modern America* (New York: Harper Brothers, 1959), p. 527.

2. However, even as late as the fall of 1940, when Roosevelt was running for his unprecedented third term, he told audiences, "Your boys are not going to be sent to any foreign war." Quoted in Clarence R. Koppes, *Hollywood Goes to War: How Politics, Profits, and Propaganda Shaped World War II Movies* (Berkeley: University of California Press, 1990), p. 19.

3. William B. Breuer, *War and American Women: Heroism, Deeds, and Controversy* (Westport, CT: Praeger, 1997), p. 17.

4. George H. Gallup, *The Gallup Poll: Public Opinion, 1935–1971*, 3 vols. (New York: Random House, 1971), 1:259.

5. David Gordon, "America First: The Anti-War Movement, Charles Lindbergh, and the Second World War, 1940–1941," paper presented at a joint meeting of the Historical Society and the New York Military Affairs Symposium, September 26, 2003, p. 1, http://libraryautomation.com/nymas/america first.html (accessed August 20, 2009).

6. Doris Kearns Goodwin, *No Ordinary Time: Franklin and Eleanor Roosevelt: The Home Front in World War II* (New York: Simon & Schuster, 1995), p. 23. Some 6.8 million German men had undergone military training, versus only about 500,000 Americans.

7. See James M. McPherson, *For Cause and Comrades: Why Men Fought in the Civil War* (New York: Oxford University Press, 1997), p. 25, and Richard E. Nisbett and Dov Cohen, *Culture of Honor: The Psychiatry of Violence in the South* (Boulder, CO: Westview, 1996), pp. 31, 53, passim. During 1942, Texas sent the largest proportion of its eligible male population to war, but Vermont and New Hampshire were next in line. "Texas Enlistments Top All States on Ratio Basis," *New York Times*, January 21, 1943.

8. William L. O'Neill, *A Democracy at War: America's Fight at Home and Abroad in World War II* (New York: Free Press, 1993), p. 129.

9. John M. Collins, "WWII NCOs," *Army* 55 no. 2 (February 2005): 59. In the month after the Japanese attack, over 55,000 signed up for the navy. "100,000th Man Enlists in Navy since Dec. 7," *New York Times*, February 2, 1942.

10. William Manchester, *Goodbye, Darkness: A Memoir of the Pacific War* (Boston: Little, Brown, 1980), pp. 16, 21, 22, 25, 26, 28, 33.

11. Audie Murphy, *To Hell and Back* (New York: Holt, Rinehart & Winston, 1949), pp. 6–8.

12. Quoted in Studs Terkel, *"The Good War": An Oral History of World War II* (New York: Pantheon, 1984), pp. 38–39. For similar comments on how fighting in World War II helped young American men grow up, see the questionnaires compiled in the World War II Survey Collection, US Military History Institute, Carlisle Barracks, PA.

13. Clarence E. Anderson, *To Fly and Fight: Memoirs of a Triple Ace* (New York: St. Martin's, 1990), pp. 16, 27, 30, 120–21.

14. Richard D. Winters, *Beyond Band of Brothers: The War Memoirs of Major Dick Winters* (Berkeley: University of California Press, 2006), p. 10.

15. Lloyd M. Wells, *From Anzio to the Alps: An American Soldier's Story* (Columbia: University of Missouri Press, 2004), pp. ix, 21.

16. Mirra Komarovsky, *The Unemployed Male and His Family: The Effect of Unemployment upon the Status of the Man in Fifty-Nine Families* (New York: Octagon, 1971), pp. x, 23ff.

17. Quoted in Mary V. Dearborn, *Mailer: A Biography* (Boston: Houghton Mifflin, 1999), p. 16.

18. Doris Drucker, "Authority of Our Children," *Harper's* 182 (February 1941): 276, 278–79.

19. Roy Helton, "The Inner Threat: Our Own Softness," *Harper's* 181 (September 1940): 338, 341.

20. Margaret Mead, *And Keep Your Powder Dry: An Anthropologist Looks at America* (New York: Morrow, 1943), pp. 121, 125, 141.

21. Philip G. Wylie, *Generation of Vipers* (New York: Holt, Rinehart & Winston, 1942), pp. 237–38.

22. One influential book on this subject was David M. Levy's *Maternal Overprotection*, which was published in 1943. For more on these fears about mothers, see Kathleen W. Jones, "'Mother Made Me Do It': Mother-Blaming and the Women of Child Guidance," in Mary Ladd-Taylor and Lauri Umansky, eds., *"Bad Mothers": The Politics of Blame in Twentieth-Century America* (New York: New York University Press, 1998), pp. 99–126.

23. Between 1920 and 1940, the proportion of married women living with their husbands who had been employed outside the home rose from 5 percent to 13.2 percent. Much of this increase was the result of the husband's being unemployed. Table 4, "Measures of Labor Force Participation, 1917–1940," Evan Roberts, "Married Women's Work in War and Depression, 1917–1940," paper presented at the Fifth European Social Science History Conference, Berlin, March 24–27, 2004, http://users.pop.umn.edu/~eroberts/evanroberts_esshc.pdf (accessed July 7, 2009). During the war, when so many millions of married men were serving overseas, the number of wives in the workforce rose more sharply—up by 2 million between April 1940 and March 1944. Karen

Anderson, *Wartime Women: Sex Roles, Family Relations, and the Status of Women during World War II* (Westport, CT: Greenwood, 1981), p. 4.

24. Gallup, *Gallup Poll*, 1:131. For a discussion of negative attitudes toward working wives, see Bernard Sternsher and Judith Sealander, *Women of Valor: The Struggle against the Great Depression as Told in Their Own Life Stories* (Chicago: Dee, 1990), p. xi.

25. Overall, the labor force participation of American females ages eighteen to sixty-four increased to 30 percent by 1940, up from 20 percent in 1900. Valerie K. Oppenheimer, "Demographic Influence on Female Employment and the Status of Women," *American Journal of Sociology* 78, no. 4 (January 1973): 947. During the war, the proportion of women over fifteen who were working rose from 28 percent to over 34 percent. Daron Acemoglu and David H. Autor, "Women, War and Wages: The Effect of Female Labor Supply on the Wage Structure at Mid-Century," *Journal of Political Economy* 112, no. 3 (June 2004): 499.

26. Recruitment posters such as Tom Woodburn's 1940 "The United States Army: Then—Now—Forever" linked the service of American soldiers in earlier wars with the contemporary crisis.

27. As many as 40 percent of the movies produced in Hollywood during the early 1940s featured heroes of this type. Lary May, "Making the American Consensus: The Narrative of Conversion and Subversion in World War II Films," in Lewis A. Erenberg and Susan E. Hirsch, eds., *The War in American Culture: Society and Consciousness during World War II* (Chicago: University of Chicago Press, 1996), p. 83. Grant went from playing sophisticated urbanites to action hero in such films as *Only Angels Have Wings* (1939) and *Gunga Din* (1939).

28. Koppes, *Hollywood Goes to War*, p. 39.

29. For a discussion of how the movie industry supported the war effort, see May, "Making the American Consensus," pp. 71–102.

30. The government reported that just over 8 million Americans were unemployed in March 1940.

31. Lee Kennett, *G.I.: The American Soldier in World War II* (New York: Scribner's, 1987), p. 7.

32. Table 5, "Marital Status of the Population Ages 15 and Older, by Age and Sex for the United States: 1890–1940," "Population: Vol. IV, Characteristics by Age, Part I: United States—Summary," *Sixteenth Census of the United States, 1940* (Washington, DC: Bureau of the Census, 1943), p. 16.

33. Robert J. Maddox, *The United States and World War II* (Boulder, CO: Westview, 1992), p. 188.

34. John Modell and Duane Steffey, "Waging War and Marriage: Military Service and Family Formation, 1940–1955," *Journal of Family History* 3, no. 1 (1988): 200.

35. Steven Mintz and Susan Kellogg, *Domestic Revolutions: A Social History of American Family Life* (New York: Free Press, 1988), p. 154. However, according to the Census Bureau, 1.185 million additional marriages took place. William Tuttle Jr., *"Daddy's Gone to War": The Second World War in the Lives of America's Children* (New York: Oxford University Press, 1993), p. 19.

36. Mintz and Kellogg, *Domestic Revolutions*, p. 195. See also Eliza K. Pavalko and Glenn H. Elder Jr., "World War II and Divorce: A Life-Course Perspective," *American Journal of Sociology* 95, no. 5 (1990): 1213–15. The US divorce rate increased during the second half of the 1930s but accelerated after 1940. It reached a peak of 18.0 per 1,000 marriages in 1947 (compared to 6.0 in 1933). Samuel H. Preston and John McDonald, "The Incidence of Divorce Within Cohorts of American Marriages Contracted since the Civil War," *Demography* 16, no. 1 (February 1979): 13. Some studies have concluded that the haste with which marriages were formed during the war explains this high divorce rate. See, for example, William L. Anderson and Derek W. Little, "All's Fair: War and Other Causes of Divorce from a Beckerian Perspective," *American Journal of Economics and Sociology* 58, no. 4 (October 1990): 901–22.

37. Selective Service awarded married men with children a 3-A deferment in 1942. But men who had gotten married (and had children) after Pearl Harbor had to prove they had not done so simply to avoid the draft. Growing manpower needs forced the Selective Service to change this policy. George Q. Flynn, *The Draft, 1940–1973* (Lawrence: University Press of Kansas, 1993), pp. 69, 74.

38. Table 1, "Population, Number of Births and Deaths, and Crude Rates: The Registration Areas, United States, 1900–1937," *Vital Statistics of the United States: 1937*, Part I, *Natality and Mortality Data for the United States* (Washington, DC: Government Printing Office, 1937), p. 16. The birth rate in the United States in the years leading up to the war was comparable to those of England and Wales, Germany, and France.

39. Quoted in Joe L. Dubbert, *A Man's Place: Masculinity in Transition* (Englewood Cliffs, NJ: Prentice-Hall, 1979), p. 230.

40. Two-thirds of the 7 million American soldiers in World War II were draftees. By comparison, only a quarter of troops who served in Vietnam were conscripts. Of course, the latter was a much smaller force—only about 2 million men, all told.

41. Quoted in Koppes, *Hollywood Goes to War*, p. 67.

42. Remarks of Eleanor Roosevelt, September 28, 1941, quoted in Walter White, *A Rising Wind* (Garden City, NY: Doubleday, Doran & Co., 1945), epigraph.

43. Quoted in May, "Making the American Consensus," p. 73.

44. Jan Herman, *A Talent for Trouble: The Life of Hollywood's Most Acclaimed Director, William Wyler* (New York: Da Capo, 1997), p. 235.

45. For a treatment of this subject, see Allan Berube, *Coming Out Under Fire: The History of Gay Men and Women in World War II* (New York: Free Press, 1990).

46. For images of American women at work, see "America from the Great Depression to World War II: Photographs from the FSA-OWI Collection, 1939–1945," Prints and Photographs Division, Library of Congress, http://www.loc.gov/rr/print/coll/052_fsa.html (accessed September 11, 2009).

47. Tuttle, *"Daddy's Gone to War,"* p. 71.

48. Michael C. C. Adams, *The Best War Ever: America and World War II* (Baltimore: Johns Hopkins University Press, 1994), p. 70. According to another source, only about one in ten working women held defense-related jobs. David M. Kennedy, *Freedom from Fear: The American People in Depression and War, 1929–1945* (New York: Oxford University Press, 1999), p. 778.

49. Kennedy, *Freedom from Fear*, p. 779.

50. By 1942, 60 percent of Americans felt it was a good idea for women to work in war-related factories. William H. Chafe, *The Unfinished Journey: America since World War II* (New York: Oxford University Press, 1995), p. 14.

51. "Yes, Women Are Different," *Newsweek* 21, no. 25 (June 21, 1943): 106.

52. John Costello, *Virtue Under Fire: How World War II Changed Our Social and Sexual Attitudes* (Boston: Little, Brown, 1985), p. 179.

53. Ibid., p. 41.

54. Ironically, the fears about WAACs having affairs with married soldiers were largely misplaced, as many turned out to prefer other women to men as sexual partners.

55. Richard E. Lingeman, *Don't You Know There's a War On? The American Home Front, 1941–1945* (New York: Putnam, 1970), p. 86.

56. "The Fortune Survey: Women in America," Part I, *Fortune* 28, no. 2 (August 1943): 16.

57. These were followed, in 1946, by *The Strange Loves of Martha Ivers* and *The Postman Always Rings Twice*, and, in 1947, by *Out of the Past*.

58. See, for example, letter of "Private S.F.," "Correspondence: We're in the Army Now," *New Republic* 104, no. 22 (June 2, 1942): 764.

59. John Morton Blum, *V Was for Victory: Politics and American Culture during World War II* (New York: Harcourt Brace Jovanovich, 1976), p. 64.

60. Quoted in John Hersey, *Into the Valley: A Skirmish of the Marines* (New York: Knopf, 1943), pp. 37, 73–74, 75. Similarly, the aspiring playwright Arthur Miller, working at the Brooklyn Navy Yard, found little evidence that sailors serving there knew what they were fighting for. See Kennett, *G.I.*, p. 89.

61. Dale Kramer, "What It's Like in the Army," *Harper's* 187, no. 1117 (June 1943): 18–19.

62. Benjamin C. Bowker, *Out of Uniform* (New York: Norton, 1946), p. 112.

63. Philip Wylie and William W. Muir, *The Army Way: A Thousand Pointers for New Soldiers Collected from Officers and Men of the U.S. Army* (New York: Farrar & Rinehart, 1940), p. 43.

64. David L. Cohn, "Should Fighting Men Think?" *Saturday Review of Literature* 30, no. 3 (January 18, 1947): 6.

65. Letter of "Private S.F.," p. 764.

66. Letter of "A.L.B.," "Correspondence: We're Still in the Army," *New Republic* 105, no. 1 (July 14, 1941): 736

67. Christopher Lasch, *Inequality: A Reassessment of the Effect of Family and Schooling in America* (New York: Basic Books, 1972), p. 63.

68. Kennett, *G.I.*, p. 22.

69. Only 23 percent of noncommissioned officers had finished high school, and very few had attended college. Samuel E. Stouffer, *The American Soldier*, Vol. 1, *Adjustment during Army Life* (Princeton, NJ: Princeton University Press, 1949), pp. 62–63.

70. Leo Cherne, "Now the Army Changes Men," *Collier's* 113, no. 2 (March 27, 1944): 69.

71. Paul Fussell, *Doing Battle: The Making of a Skeptic* (Boston: Little, Brown, 1996), pp. 65, 77, 174. When he left the army, Fussell swore "never to be under anyone's orders for the rest of my life."

72. See, for example, J. Glenn Gray, *Warriors: Reflections on Men in Battle* (New York: Harcourt Brace, 1959), pp. 26, 90, 114, 177.

73. Murphy, *To Hell and Back*, pp. 83, 94.

74. Manchester, *Goodbye, Darkness*, p. 70.

75. Eugene B. Sledge, *With the Old Breed at Peleliu and Okinawa* (Novato, CA: Presidio, 1981), pp. 146, 148, 156.

76. James Jones, *The Thin Red Line* (New York: Scribner's, 1962), p. 215.

77. Manchester, *Goodbye, Darkness*, p. 123.

78. Fussell, *Doing Battle*, p. 97.

79. Randall Jarrell, "Soldier (T.P.)," in *The War Poets: An Anthology of the War Poetry of the 20th Century*, ed. Oscar Williams (New York: John Day, 1945), p. 162.

80. Manchester, *Goodbye, Darkness*, p. 237.

81. Norman Mailer, *The Naked and the Dead* (New York: Holt, 1948), p. 602.

82. Robert Lowry, *Casualty* (New York: New Directions, 1946), pp. 38, 142.

83. Eugene Sledge, for example, grew deeply attached to his Marine commanding officer, a Bowdoin graduate named Andrew Haldane, who "had a rare combination of intelligence, courage, self-confidence, and compassion that commanded our respect and admiration." When Haldane was killed, on Peleliu, Sledge broke down, sobbing. Sledge, *With the Old Breed*, pp. 40, 140.

84. Stouffer, *Adjustment during Army Life*, p. 370.

85. S. L. A. Marshall, *Men against Fire: The Problem of Battle Command in Future Wars* (Gloucester, MA: Peter Smith, 1978), pp. 61, 72, 78.

86. Richard A. Gabriel, *No More Heroes: Madness and Psychiatry in War* (New York: Hill & Wang, 1987), pp. 74–75.

87. Robert Fantina, *Desertion and the American Soldier, 1776–2006* (New York: Algora, 2006), p. 116.

88. Bowker, *Out of Uniform*, p. 80.

89. Adams, *Best War Ever*, pp. 95, 97. A postwar study concluded that fully 98 percent of soldiers had showed "adverse psychiatric systems" after thirty-five days under fire. See Gabriel, *No More Heroes*, p. 119.

90. Ibid., p. 10.

91. Fantina, *Desertion*, p. 116.

92. Lawrence M. Vance, "The Execution of Eddie Slovik," http://www .lewrockwell.com/vance/vance34.html (accessed September 10, 2009).

93. One estimate is that most US troops in Europe had sexual intercourse once a month. Robert J. Lilly, *Taken by Force: Rape and American GIs during World War II* (New York: Palgrave Macmillan, 2007), p. 40.

94. One gains a sense of this perceived parity of sexual infidelity from the 1946 film *The Best Years of Our Lives*, in which a reunited married couple, Fred and Marie Derry, trade innuendoes about what each was doing apart from the other. The US military was so alarmed by the findings of its survey on soldiers' sexual behavior during wartime that this report was not released for nearly forty years. Costello, *Virtue Under Fire*, p. 99.

95. Sloan Wilson, *The Man in the Gray Flannel Suit* (New York: Simon & Schuster, 1955), p. 82.

96. This estimate is derived from the number of rape cases brought before military courts. Lilly, *Taken by Force*, p. 13.

97. Few movies, memoirs, or novels glorified the war or the men who fought in it. Audie Murphy's *To Hell and Back*, made into a film in 1955, was one of these.

98. So did various analytical accounts of men in combat, such as J. Glenn Gray's *Warriors*.

99. Sledge, *With the Old Breed*, p. 98.

100. Ernie Pyle, *Brave Men* (New York: Grosset & Dunlop, 1945), p. 197.

101. Such were the recommendations of a 1946 panel headed by Gen. James Doolittle, hero of a successful raid on Tokyo in April 1942. However, the top brass ultimately rejected this proposal. Stouffer, *Adjustment during Army Life*, pp. 379–80.

102. Tuttle, *"Daddy's Gone to War,"* p. 113.

103. Ibid., p. 116.

104. Figures cited in James T. Patterson, *Grand Expectations: The United States, 1945–1974* (New York: Oxford University Press, 1997), p. 77.

105. Landon Y. Jones, *Great Expectations: America and the Baby Boom Generation* (New York: Coward, McCann & Geohegan, 1988), p. 22.

106. Winter, "Demographic Consequences," p. 162. Japanese planes did strike northern Australia between February 1942 and November 1943, killing some 900 people and destroying a large number of ships and airplanes.

107. Table 91, "Female Births per 1,000 Women, 1925–1954," Taeuber, *Population of Japan*, p. 234.

108. Matthias Doepke, Moshe Hazan, and Yishah D. Maoz, "More Babies for Europe: Lessons from the Post-War Baby Boom," *Vox* (September 8, 2008), http://www.voxeu.org/index.php?q=node/1620 (accessed August 24, 2009).

109. Elaine Tyler May, *Homeward Bound: The American Families in the Cold War Era* (New York: Basic Books, 1988), pp. 20, 165.

110. For a discussion of how the American home, with its well-stocked bomb shelter, offered a safe haven during the 1950s, see ibid.

111. Hope R. Bennett, "Living without Father," *Parents* 18, no. 7 (July 1943): 21.

112. Movies like *Crossfire* (1947) and *The Men* (1950) dealt with the problems of adjustment for veterans. Several articles in popular magazines shortly after the war told of ex-GIs who had resorted to violence to express their resentment over their situations back home.

113. Quoted in Vance Packard, "Give the War Babies a Break," *American Magazine* 139, no. 5 (May 1945): 112.

114. See, for example, Therese Benedek, "Marital Breakers Ahead?" *Parents* 20, no. 9 (September 1945): 148.

115. Ruth Wall, "Let Daddy Take Over," *Parents* 26, no. 6 (June 1951): 37. Cf. O. Spurgeon English, "Father's Changing Role," *Parents* 26, no. 10 (October 1951): 44.

116. Emotionally immature and abusive fathers could produce bad children, like Adolf Hitler. Edward A. Strecker, "Pops and Popism," *Parents* 22, no. 5 (May 1947): 102.

117. Elizabeth B. Hurlock, "A New Role for Fathers," *Hygeia* 28, no. 1 (January 1950): 68.

118. Quoted in Juliet Danziger, "Life Without Father," *New York Times Magazine* (May 7, 1944), p. 16.

119. In 1949, the Visiting Nurse Service of New York began offering courses to expectant fathers on bathing, feeding, dressing, and changing infants. "School for Expectant Fathers," *Hygeia* 27, no. 10 (October 1949): 690.

120. O. Spurgeon English and Constance J. Foster, "How Good a Family Man Is Your Husband?" *Parents* 27, no. 9 (September 1952): 37.

121. Quoted in Michael S. Kimmel, *Manhood in America: A Cultural History* (New York: Free Press, 1996), p. 245.

122. Whitman M. Reynolds, "When Father Comes Home Again," *Parents* 20, no. 10 (October 1945): 70–71. Alcohol abuse was a major cause of postwar divorces among GIs. One historian has estimated that as many as 40 percent of such breakups in the 1950s stemmed from excessive drinking. Tuttle, *"Daddy's Gone to War,"* p. 220.

123. See Margaret Mead, *Male and Female* (New York: Morrow, 1949), pp. 188, 306.

124. Wrote the parent and child editor of the *New York Times Magazine*, "He removes himself from active participation in family life . . . because he has been talked into believing that in dealing with the Delicate Soul of a Child he is no match for his wife and the other experts." Dorothy Barclay, "Rights of Man around the House," *New York Times Magazine* (October 2, 1955), p. 48.

125. Quoted in Tuttle, *"Daddy's Gone to War,"* p. 112.

126. Robert M. Yoder, "Don't Shoot Father—Save Him for Laughs," *Saturday Evening Post* 221, no. 7 (August 14, 1948): 28.

127. Writing about television sit-coms, David Halberstam has noted, "Dads were good dads whose worst sin was that they did not know their way around the house and could not find common household objects or that they were prone to give lectures about how much tougher things had been when they were boys." Halberstam, *The Fifties* (New York: Fawcett Columbine, 1994), p. 509.

128. Wayne had similarly anachronistic roles in such 1950s films as *The Searchers*, *The Man Who Shot Liberty Valance*, and *The Wings of Eagles*.

129. It should be noted that many mothers did, in fact, work outside the home during the 1950s. By the end of the decade, 39 percent of women with children at home held jobs. In 1950, only 12 percent had. Anita Ilta Garey, *Weaving Work and Motherhood* (Philadelphia: Temple University Press, 1999), p. 2.

130. Dean and Clift were gay, and Brando bisexual, as was the older matinee idol Cary Grant. Other leading closeted gay actors of the 1950s included Rock Hudson, Anthony Perkins, Raymond Burr, Tommy Kirk, Richard Chamberlain, and Sal Mineo. Gary Cooper was also rumored to have had at least one male lover. See Larry Swindell, *The Last Hero: A Biography of Gary Cooper* (Garden City, NY: Doubleday, 1980), pp. 104–105.

131. Quoted in Steven Cohan, *Masked Men: Masculinity and the Movies in the Fifties* (Bloomington: Indiana University Press, 1997), p. 202.

132. Child psychologists associated absent or uninvolved fathers with the growing problem of juvenile delinquency in the 1950s. See, for example, Elizabeth H. Pleck, "Two Dimensions of Fatherhood: A History of the Good-Dad,

Bad-Dad Complex," in Michael E. Lamb, ed., *The Role of the Father in Child Development*, 4th ed. (New York: Wiley, 2004), p. 41.

133. William H. Whyte's *Organization Man* came out in 1957.

134. Robert Lindner, *Must You Conform?* (New York: Rinehart, 1956), pp. 45, 167–68.

135. Oscar Handlin, "In a Time of Distrust: Yearning for Security," *Atlantic Monthly* 187, no. 1 (January 1951): 25–27. Cf. Dorothy Thompson, "The Careful Men: Tomorrow's Leaders Analyzed by Today's Teachers," *Nation* 184, no. 10 (March 9, 1957): 11.

136. Louis Lyndon, "Uncertain Hero: The Paradox of the American Male," *Woman's Home Companion* 83, no. 11 (November 1956): 43, 107.

137. See, for example, Robert J. Moskin, "The American Male: Why Do Women Dominate Him?" *Look* 22, no. 3 (February 4, 1958): 78–79.

138. Ken Kraft, "Who's Whose?" *Collier's* 126, no. 5 (July 29, 1950): 10.

139. "A Delicate Problem," *Newsweek* 43, no. 24 (June 14, 1954): 100.

140. "Between a Boy and His Dad," *Look* 21, no. 13 (June 25, 1957): 169. A couple of years later, Margaret Mead would publish her concerns about men's involvement in the home undermining their masculinity. Mead, "Job of the Children's Mother's Husband," *New York Times Magazine* (May 10, 1959): 7, 66–67.

141. Bruno Bettelheim, "Fathers Shouldn't Try to Be Mothers," *Parents* 31, no. 10 (October 1956): 40.

142. Judson T. Landis and Mary G. Landis, "The American Male . . . Is He First-Class?" *Collier's* 130, no. 3 (July 19, 1952): 22–23.

143. Robert Coughlin, "Changing Roles in Modern Marriage: Psychiatrists Find Them a Clue to Alarming Divorce Rate," *Life* 41, no. 26 (December 24, 1956): 112. Helen M. Hacker, "The New Burdens of Masculinity," *Marriage and Family Living* 19, no. 3 (August 1957): 228–29. An estimated 10 percent of married men were impotent, according to one survey. Amory Clark, "His Sex Habits," *Cosmopolitan* 142, no. 5 (May 1957): 32.

144. David R. Mace, "Your Husband Will Never Tell You, But—" *Woman's Home Companion* 79, no. 5 (May 1952): 44.

145. Paul Boyer, *By the Dawn's Early Light: American Thought at the Dawn of the Atomic Age* (New York: Pantheon, 1985), pp. 14, 22.

146. In August 1950, more than a quarter of Americans polled were in favor of dropping an atomic bomb on North Korea to force that country to withdraw its forces from the south. By November 1951, over half of those surveyed supported battlefield use of atomic weapons. Stephen J. Whitfield, *The Culture of the Cold War*, 2nd ed. (Baltimore: Johns Hopkins University Press, 1996), p. 5.

147. In *The Searchers* (1956), for example, the relentless quest by Wayne's character to find his niece and avenge her kidnapping seems obsessive and out of place.

148. Garry Wills, "American Adam," *New York Review of Books* 44, no. 4 (March 6, 1997): 33.

149. It has been speculated that the increase in violence in TV shows during the early 1960s was intended to woo young male audiences away from movie theaters. Mitchell K. Hall, *Crossroads: American Popular Culture and the Vietnam Generation* (Lanham, MD: Rowan & Littlefield, 2005), p. 67.

150. Cultural ambivalence about such larger-than-life, driven figures can be seen in films like *Moby Dick* and *Mutiny on the Bounty*.

151. So confessed Darryl Zanuck, director of *Twelve O'Clock High*. For years, this movie was shown to Air Force cadets as a good example of how officers should handle their men in combat.

152. Randy Roberts and James S. Olson, *A Line in the Sand: The Alamo in Blood and Memory* (New York: Free Press, 2001), p. 245.

153. Vincent Tompkins, ed., *American Decades* (Detroit: Gale, 1994), p. 272.

154. Catherine Whitney, *Soldiers Once: My Brother and the Lost Dreams of America's Veterans* (Cambridge, MA: Da Capo, 2009), p. 21. The popularity of war toys continued into the 1960s: the 1966 Montgomery Ward holiday catalog featured Special Forces' "burp guns," pistols, grenades, dog tags, infantry badges, and berets—"everything for the little company commander to hide under the Christmas tree." Quoted in Jane Stern and Michael Stern, *Sixties People* (New York: Knopf, 1990), p. 206.

155. Robert Putnam, *Bowling Alone: The Collapse and Revival of American Community* (New York: Touchstone, 2000), p. 55.

156. "Stirring Spirit Lifted Higher," *Life* 47, no. 22 (November 30, 1959): 107.

157. Cynthia Enloe, *The Morning After: Sexual Politics at the End of the Cold War Era* (Berkeley: University of California Press, 1993), p. 56.

158. For example, during a three-week period in August 1961, following President Kennedy's speech saying he wanted to increase the size of the military to 2.7 million men, enlistments rose 39 percent over the same time frame the year before. "Army Enlistments Up," *New York Times*, August 27, 1961.

159. Christian G. Appy, *Working-Class War: American Combat Soldiers and Vietnam* (Chapel Hill: University of North Carolina Press, 1993), p. 60.

160. John P. Sisk, "Enter the Man's Man," *Commonweal* 59, no. 12 (December 19, 1958): 310.

161. Moskin, "The American Male," p. 77.

162. Arthur M. Schlesinger Jr., "The Crisis of American Masculinity," *Esquire* 50, no. 5 (November 1958): 63–65.

163. Arthur M. Schlesinger Jr., *A Thousand Days: John F. Kennedy in the White House* (New York: Mariner, 2002), p. 17.

164. Arthur M. Schlesinger Jr., "The New Mood in Politics," *Esquire* 53, no. 1 (January 1960): 58–60.

165. "A Red-Hot Hundred," *Life* 53, no. 11 (September 14, 1962): 4–9.

166. A male journalist would record that Kennedy was the "most seductive person I've ever met. He exuded a sense of vibrant life and humor that seemed naturally to bubble up out of him." Quoted in Patterson, *Grand Expectations*, p. 438.

167. J. Ronald Oakley, *God's Country: America in the Fifties* (New York: Norton, 1986), p. 427.

168. For trends in violent crime among male adolescents, see Thomas G. Moeller, *Youth Aggression and Violence: A Psychological Approach* (Mahwah, NJ: L. Erlbaum, 2001), pp. 5, 7.

169. Susan Faludi has observed that Kennedy's address was promoting a "government-backed program of man-making, of federal masculinity insurance." Faludi, *Stiffed: The Betrayal of the American Man* (New York: Perennial, 2000), p. 25.

170. By early 1966, army enlistments were not keeping up with expanding manpower needs, and the Pentagon began to worry about how it could continue to recruit enough men. See Russell Baker, "Observer: Filling the Ranks," *New York Times*, February 20, 1966. Later that year, the Department of Defense announced it was raising its draft quota in October to 46,200—the largest since the Korean War—due to a falling enlistment rate. Benjamin Welles, "October Draft is 46,200: Biggest since the Korean War," *New York Times*, August 5, 1966.

171. Philip Caputo, *A Rumor of War* (New York: Holt, Rinehart & Winston, 1977), pp. xii, 5, 6, 8, 14, 285.

172. Numerous soldiers who served in Vietnam had watched John Wayne movies and *To Hell and Back*. See Bob Greene, *When the Soldiers Returned from Vietnam* (New York: Putnam, 1989), p. 109, and Charles R. Anderson, *The Grunts* (Novato, CA: Presidio, 1976), p. 190. The psychiatrist Robert Jay Lifton found that many of the veterans he interviewed spoke of the "John Wayne thing"—their "death" as a civilian and "rebirth as a new military self" after they had entered the service. Lifton, *Home from the War: Vietnam Veterans—Neither Victims nor Executioners* (New York: Simon & Schuster, 1973), p. 187. More than any previous generation, the Vietnam one had its sense of reality shaped by images from films and television.

173. Ron Kovic, *Born on the Fourth of July* (New York: McGraw-Hill, 1976), pp. 43, 51, 55, 56, 63.

174. John Sack, *Lieutenant Calley: His Own Story* (New York: Viking, 1970), pp. 24, 26, 28, 31.

175. Theodore Nadelson, *Trained to Kill: Soldiers at War* (Baltimore: Johns Hopkins University Press, 2005), p. 15.

176. Cf. Jonathan Shays, *Achilles in Vietnam: Combat Trauma and the Undoing of Character* (New York: Atheneum, 1994), p. 9.

177. Quoted in Richard Reeves, *President Kennedy: Profile of Power* (New York: Simon & Schuster, 1993), pp. 166, 172. Lyndon Johnson also felt he needed to prove his manliness by prosecuting the war in Vietnam. See Chafe, *The Unfinished Journey*, p. 276. Cf. David Paul Kuhn, *The Neglected Voter: White Men and the Democratic Dilemma* (New York: Palgrave Macmillan, 2007), p. 77.

178. The enlistment rate rose 40 percent over what it had been in the previous year, as the army increased its monthly draft quotas in 1965. Jack Raymond, "Military Manpower: The Arithmetic Now," *New York Times*, January 2, 1966.

179. Appy, *Working-Class War*, pp. 67–68, 75, 82.

180. Whitney, *Soldiers Once*, p. 41. Whitney's brother, Jim, a troubled young man, had had several run-ins with the law and opted to enlist rather than go to jail. His father felt military service would "straighten him out. Make a man of him."

181. Recent analyses of the links between socioeconomic status and marriage rates confirm this. See, for example, J. Scott South and Kim M. Lloyd, "Marriage Markets and Non-Marital Fertility," *Demography* 29, no. 2 (May 1992): 250. Cf. Lionel Tiger, *The Decline of Males* (New York: Golden, 1999), p. 121.

182. Appy, *Working-Class War*, p. 45. This rate broke down to 12 percent for white males in this age group and 27 percent for blacks.

183. In 1960, a third of American women were attending college. A decade later it was over 40 percent. Martin A. Marty, *Daily Life in the United States, 1960–1990: Decades of Discord* (Westport, CT: Greenwood, 1997), p. 51. A 1973 report put out by the Nixon administration blamed the greater participation of women, especially married ones, in the workforce for growing wage inequality among males during the 1960s. Christopher R. Lingle and Ethel B. Jones, "Women's Increasing Unemployment: A Cross-Sectional Analysis," *American Economic Review* 68, no. 2 (May 1978): 86. As the proportion of females employed in the clerical sector increased, salaries declined. Albert W. Niemi Jr., "The Male-Female Earnings Differential: A Historical Overview of the Clerical Occupations from the 1880s to the 1970s," *Social Science History* 7, no. 1 (Winter 1983): 103.

184. Table 2, "Labor Force Participation Rates of Married Women, Husband Present, by Presence and Age of Own Children, 1950–83," Elizabeth Waldman, "Labor Force Participation from a Family Perspective," *Monthly Labor Review* (December 1983): 3.

185. This trend grew more pronounced in the 1970s. See Jane R. Wilkie, "The Decline of Men's Labor Force Participation and Income and the

Changing Structure of Family Economic Support," *Journal of Marriage and the Family* 53 (February 1991): 113.

186. This impact became discernible starting in the late 1960s. David S. Loughran, "Does Variance Matter? The Effect of Rising Male Wage Inequality on Female Age at First Marriage," Labor and Population Program, Working Paper Series 00–12, www.rand.org/labor/DRU/DRU2347.pdf (accessed September 2, 2009).

187. Willard L. Rodgers and Arland Thornton, "Changing Patterns in First Marriages in the United States," *Demography* 22, no. 2 (May 1985): 268. In the period 1959 to 1962, the marriage rate was 8.5 per 1,000 inhabitants, but in 1963 it reached 8.8.

188. Marty, *Daily Life*, p. 4.

189. A. M. Hetzel and M. Cappetta, "Teenagers: Marriages, Divorces, Parenthood, and Mortality," *Vital Health Statistics* 21, no. 23 (August 1973): 1–7.

190. "Where Are All the Men?" *Ladies Home Journal* 77, no. 11 (November 1960): 76, and Eleanor Harris, "Men without Women," *Look* 24, no. 24 (November 22, 1960): 124, 129.

191. Table 6: "Marital Status by Family Status, Age, Race, and Sex: 1966–1967," *Population Reports, C3.186, P-20, 171–180 (1966–67)* (Washington, DC: US Bureau of the Census, 1967), p. 15.

192. Frances E. Kobrin, "The Fall of Household Size and the Rise of the Primary Individual in the United States," *Demography* 13, no. 1 (February 1976): 132.

193. Ibid.

194. "Fertility Measurement," *Vital and Health Statistics, Document and Committee Reports, Series 4, No. 1–14* (Hyattsville, MD: NCHS, September 1965), p. 7.

195. Ben J. Wattenberg, *The Birth Dearth* (New York: Ballantine, 1987), p. 3.

196. *Trends in Fertility in the United States* (Hyattsville, MD: US Department of Health, Education, and Welfare, September 1977), p. 2.

197. For evidence of the impact of contraception on fertility in the 1970s, see John F. Kantner and Marvin Zelnik, "First Pregnancies to Women Aged 15–19: 1976 and 1971," *Family Planning Perspectives* 10, no. 1 (January/February 1978): 11–20. They contend that increased sexual activity among women in this age group did not result in more births due to greater reliance on birth control.

198. By 1963, more than a million American women were using the Pill. Seven years later, that number had risen to 12 million. The percentage of births out of wedlock grew from 4 percent in 1950 to 14.2 percent in 1975. Subscriptions to *Playboy* increased from 1 million in 1960 to 7 million in 1972. Marty, *Daily Life*, pp. 66, 67, 71.

199. Charles C. Moskos, *The American Enlisted Man: The Rank and File in*

Today's Military (New York: Russell Sage, 1970), p. 45. This was also true for married men.

200. See, for example, Tiger, *Decline of Males*, pp. 121, 221.

201. George Gilder, *Naked Nomads: Unmarried Men in America* (New York: Quadrangle, 1974), p. 24.

202. The army made Schuler, a high-school dropout, believe that he was "somebody special." Whitney, *Soldiers Once*, pp. 54, 160.

203. It has been estimated that as many as 80 percent of soldiers who fought in Vietnam came from poor or working-class families. Appy, *Working-Class War*, p. 85. A 1964 survey of enlisted personnel concluded that most GIs had signed up to get away from home, to travel, to be patriotic, to avoid the draft, or—the most cited reasons—to advance themselves. See Moskos, *American Enlisted Man*, p. 49.

204. In Bobbie Ann Mason's novel, *In Country*, the main character, Sam(antha) Hughes, discovers that her father, who died in Vietnam, was a "mama's boy" who found fulfillment in killing: he wanted to "get some notches on his machete." Mason, *In Country* (New York: Perennial, 1985), pp. 196, 222.

205. Many who served in Vietnam had absent fathers or poor relationships with them. This was confirmed by at least one infantry commander. William Broyles Jr., *Brothers in Arms: A Journey from War to Peace* (New York: Knopf, 1986), p. 135. A 1964 study of the military found that twice as many enlisted men had absent fathers when they were in their midteens as did officers. Moskos, *American Enlisted Man*, p. 41.

206. Volunteers also accounted for nearly 70 percent of American deaths in Vietnam. One survey concluded that only 11 percent of men who enlisted and then served in Vietnam had signed up to avoid the draft. Richard A. Kulka et al., *Trauma and the Vietnam War Generation: Report of Findings from the National Vietnam Veterans Readjustment Study* (New York: Brunner/Mazel, 1990), p. 23.

207. In 1967, the Department of Defense reported that 36 percent of enlisted personnel were married, but only 21 percent of those in the lowest four ranks. But these figures include both stateside troops and those serving overseas. Moskos, *American Enlisted Man*, p. 43.

208. These statistics are to be found at the US Department of Veterans Affairs Web site: http://www.va.gov (accessed September 4, 2009). It is not documented how many of these married men who died were career soldiers. The Pentagon ended its ban on drafting married men in October 1965.

209. This group included a large percentage of middle-class college students. Contrary to general thinking, these youth were not more antiwar than any other segment of American society by the end of the 1960s. A survey by two University of Michigan professors showed that students who had attended col-

lege actually tended to be more "hard line" on the war than both the general public and those with less education. R. W. Apple Jr., "Public Opinion Experts Contend Youth Has Not Opposed War as Much as Many Believe," *New York Times,* June 15, 1970.

210. John Wheeler, *Touched with Fire: The Future of the Vietnam Generation* (New York: F. Watts, 1984), p. 18.

211. By 1971, an estimated 28 percent of American females ages fifteen to nineteen had had premarital sex. Kantner and Zelnik, "First Pregnancies," p. 9. Another study found that, by age twenty, 40 percent of female college students had lost their virginity. Sexual activity levels among women of this age were approaching that of males. Mirra Komarovsky, *Dilemmas of Masculinity: A Study of College Youth,* 2nd ed. (Walnut Creek, CA: Rowman Altamira, 2004), p. 80.

212. "Angry Battler for Her Sex," *Life* 55, no. 18 (November 1, 1963): 87.

213. Joyce Brothers, "Why Shouldn't Husbands Dry Dishes?" *Good Housekeeping* 162, no. 3 (March 1966): 26.

214. Samuel Withers, "Some Guide Rules for Divorced Fathers," *New York Times Magazine* (September 29, 1963): 103.

215. Gloria Steinem, "The Moral Disarmament of Betty Coed," *Esquire* 58, no. 3 (September 1962): 97.

216. For a full elucidation of this thesis, see Tiger, *Decline of Males.*

217. 13 Table UC-1, "Unmarried Partners of the Opposite Sex, by Presence of Children, 1960 to Present," Historical Time Series, Families and Living Arrangements, US Census Bureau, http://www.census.gov/population/www/socdemo/hh-fam.html (accessed September 2, 2009).

218. Joyce Brothers, "Can Love Last Forever?" *Good Housekeeping* 160, no. 3 (March 1965): 76.

219. Sandford Brown, "May I Ask You a Few Questions about Love?" *Saturday Evening Post* 239, no. 27 (December 31, 1966): 24.

220. Overall, nonmarital sexual activity did not increase until the late 1960s. Milton J. Bates, *The Wars We Took to Vietnam: Cultural Conflict and Storytelling* (Berkeley: University of California Press, 1996), p. 133.

221. One study of the cultural aspects of the Vietnam War has pointed out that the sexual revolution was more "intragenerational" than intergenerational, pitting "liberated" young women against more traditionalist males. Ibid., p. 134. Another study, in 1970, concluded that single American women had grown more permissive over the preceding decade, so that their attitudes had come to resemble those of their male counterparts. See Harold T. Christensen and Christina F. Gregg, "Changing Sex Norms in America and Scandinavia," *Journal of Marriage and the Family* 32, no. 4 (November 1970): 616–27.

222. For evidence of this unquestioning patriotism among middle-class

youth, see Paul Lyons, *Class of '66: Living in Suburban Middle America* (Philadelphia: Temple University Press, 1994).

223. Wartime experience tends to conflate violence and sexuality. During the Vietnam era, for example, recruits were told to "love" both their rifles and their penises. Whitney, *Soldiers Once*, p. 45. According to one historian, a number of GIs became "double veterans" by having their first sexual experience with a captured Vietnamese woman (or prostitute) and then killing her. Cynthia Enloe, *Does Khaki Become You? The Militarization of Women's Lives* (London: Pluto, 1983), p. 34.

224. Catherine Whitney notes in her memoir of her brother that he and many of his fellow recruits were virgins. Whitney, *Soldiers Once*, p. 45.

225. There are no statistics on the sexual history of military recruits during the Vietnam era, but memoirs and other anecdotal accounts indicate that many men had little or no intercourse before signing up. Novels about the war also describe young soldiers losing their virginity with Vietnamese women. See, for example, Denis Johnson, *Tree of Smoke* (New York: Farrar, Straus & Giroux, 2007), p. 235.

226. Kovic, *Born on the Fourth of July*, p. 68.

227. Jonathan Shays, *Odysseus in America: Combat Trauma and the Trials of Homecoming* (New York: Simon & Schuster, 2002), p. 70.

228. Loss of control over their own lives and fear of dying unnecessarily led some GIs to turn on their own officers, who "would want to carry out all kinds of crazy John Wayne tactics, who would use their lives in an effort to win the war single-handedly, win the big medal, and get his pictures in the hometown paper." Anderson, *The Grunts*, p. 190.

229. Fear of a girlfriend or wife's being unfaithful was common. See, for example, Tim O'Brien, *The Things They Carried* (New York: Penguin, 1991), pp. 4–31, 110–25, 130.

230. Kovic, *Born on the Fourth of July*, p. 77. Cf. Nancy Sherman, *Stoic Warriors: The Ancient Philosophy behind the Military Mind* (Oxford: Oxford University Press, 2005), p. 74. When a recruit died of heat stroke during basic at Ft. Jackson, South Carolina, his fellow soldiers recited to their drill sergeant the reason he had died: "Because he was a pussy, Sergeant." Tobias Wolff, *In Pharaoh's Army* (New York: Knopf, 1994), p. 47.

231. For some indication of the frequency of rapes committed by GIs, see Susan Brownmiller, *Against Our Will: Men, Women and Rape* (New York: Simon & Schuster, 1975), pp. 104–105. See also Nick Turse, "The Vietnam War Crimes You Never Heard Of," History News Network, November 17, 2003, http://hnn.us/articles/1802.html (accessed September 7, 2009). No reliable statistics on this crime exist, however. For soldiers' testimony about rape, see

"Vietnam: American Holocaust," http://www.youtube.com/watch?v=Qwzf WRGnYbQ (accessed September 9, 2009).The callousness that GIs showed toward Vietnamese rape victims is captured in Michael Herr's *Dispatches*. After contemplating a dead female Viet Cong who had been raped, a Marine matter-of-factly remarked, "No more boom-boom for that mama-san." Herr noted that he had "made that same tired remark you heard every time the dead turned out to be women." Herr, *Dispatches* (London: Pan, 1978), p. 161. However, American women who served as nurses in Vietnam found GIs to be universally respectful toward them. Keith Walker, *Piece of My Heart: The Stories of Twenty-Six American Women Who Served in Vietnam* (Novato, CA: Presidio, 1985).

232. In *Dispatches*, Herr told of a "serious tiger lady going around on a Honda shooting American officers on the street with a .45." But it was unclear if this supposed killer was actually a woman. Herr, *Dispatches*, p. 40. The first enemy whom platoon leader Thomas Carhart killed turned out to be a female nurse, "very young and very beautiful." This was an experience that came back to haunt him in his dreams. Thomas M. Carhart III, "The Nam" (undated type-script), Special Collections, US Military Academy Library, West Point, NY. GIs also passed around Vietnam "legends" about prostitutes who concealed pieces of glass or razor blades in their vaginas.

233. Because of their youth, GIs in Vietnam were wont to regress when they had some free time; they would become "as rowdy as hell week at the Deke house and as macho as a street gang defending its turf. . . . They were boys at play when the war did not require them to be men." Peter Goldman and Tony Fuller, *Charlie Company* (New York: Morrow, 1983), pp. 65, 67.

234. Catherine Whitney has concluded that her brother "brought some of his demons with him into combat." Whitney, *Soldiers Once*, p. 158. Studies of the marital impact of combat duty in Vietnam indicate a higher divorce rate among men most exposed to fire. But the preexisting aggression of many of these men also made them effective fighters. Robert S. Laufer and M. S. Gallops, "Life-Course Effects of Vietnam Combat and Abusive Violence: Marital Patterns," *Journal of Marriage and the Family* 47, no. 4 (November 1985): 850. One study has concluded that the qualities that lead men to participate in combat later make them "poor marriage material." Cynthia Gimbel and Alan Booth, "Why Does Military Combat Experience Adversely Affect Marital Relations?" *Journal of Marriage and the Family* 56 (August 1994): 701.

235. During the war, Americans transferred their feelings of being threatened onto their enemies, who were seen as a kind of "bogeyman." Robert W. Rieber, introduction, *The Psychology of War and Peace: The Image of the Enemy*, ed. Robert W. Rieber (New York: Plenum, 1991), p. 7. Dave Grossman has argued that early exposure to video games and war movies had made Vietnam-era sol-

diers more prone to fire their weapons than their predecessors in World War II. Dave Grossman, *On Killing: The Psychological Cost of Learning to Kill in War and Society* (Boston: Back Bay, 1996) pp. 311, passim.

236. Tom Bissell, *The Father of All Things: A Marine, His Son and the Legacy of Vietnam* (New York: Pantheon, 2007), pp. 223–39.

237. Innumerable soldiers received "Dear John" letters while serving in Vietnam: one draftee recalled they were "as common as flies on sores." Norman L. Russell, *Suicide Charlie: A Vietnam War Story* (Westport, CT: Praeger, 1993), p. 127. Some reacted to this abrupt end to their relationships with a promise to get even. A Marine stationed at Khe Sanh whose wife confessed in a letter that the child she was expecting was not his threatened to "kill his old lady" when he returned home. Herr, *Dispatches*, p. 105.

238. Studies of the marital and parental outcomes of men who served in Vietnam have reached different conclusions. It appears that exposure to combat is a determining factor. One study has found that soldiers from units that saw only little or no combat had a relatively low divorce rate of 12 percent in the mid-1970s. James E. Westheider, *The Vietnam War* (Westport, CT: Greenwood, 2007), p. 165. Another study, conducted in the 1980s of 1,259 men who were of draft age in the 1960s, found that 84 percent of Vietnam veterans were married, versus 81 percent of non–Vietnam veterans, and 70 percent of men who had not served. Similar findings emerged from another survey during that decade. See Kulka et al., *Trauma and the Vietnam War Generation*, p. 27. Veterans had the lowest divorce rate—20 percent—compared to 27 percent among non–Vietnam veterans and 24 percent for men without military experience. Laufer and Gallops, "Life Course Effects," p. 845. These findings were confirmed by another study, based on interviews with veterans in Washington State. R. A. Vaughn Call and Jay D. Teachman, "Life-Course Timing and Sequencing of Marriage and Military Service and Their Effects on Marital Stability," *Journal of Marriage and the Family* 15, no. 1 (February 1996): 222–23. According to *Veterans of Foreign Wars Magazine*, eight of ten Vietnam veterans were still married to their first wives in 1985, and 90 percent of them had children. "Vietnam War Statistics." http://www.skytroopers.org/vietnam_war_statistics.htm (accessed September 14, 2009). Another book, published in 2002, asserts that the divorce rate among veterans is no greater than among men who were never in the military. Michael Lind, *The Necessary War: A Reinterpretation of America's Most Disastrous Military Defeat* (New York: Free Press, 2002), p. 175. However, the National Survey of Families and Households, conducted in the early 1990s, reported that Vietnam veterans had a 28 percent higher divorce rate than nonveterans. It seems that divorces involving former soldiers are apt to occur after many years of marriage.

239. It should not be overlooked that many Vietnam veterans looked back

proudly on their service and declared that they would serve their country again if called upon to do so.

240. As had been the case for some GIs in World War II, former Vietnam soldiers tended to blame their officers and higher-ups in Washington for waging the war badly and losing it. Shays, *Achilles in Vietnam*, pp. 127, 145, 154.

241. Ron Kovic, for example, returned home a paraplegic, after being paralyzed in a firefight in the DMZ. He became a fierce opponent of the war.

242. Jones, *Great Expectations*, p. 103.

CHAPTER 6

1. *The 9/11 Commission Report: Final Report of the National Commission on Terrorist Attacks upon the United States* (Washington, DC: Government Printing Office, 2004), p. 5.

2. Charles M. Sennott, "Before Oath to Jihad, Drifting and Boredom," *Boston Globe*, March 3, 2002.

3. One of the two women who were driven by taxi to the Park Inn later identified al Suqami, from an ATM photo, as closely resembling one of the men she had had sex with. FBI, "Working Draft Chronology of Events for Hijackers and Associates," Part C (2001), p. 264, http://www.historycommons.org/sourcedocuments/2001/pdfs/fbi911timeline106–210.pdf (accessed August 15, 2009).

4. One pilot, a Lebanese named Ziad Jarrah, had a Turkish girlfriend in Germany, whom he later married. *9/11 Commission Report*, p. 163.

5. Lawrence Wright has written, "The anger that this statement directs at women and its horror of sexual contact invites the thought that Atta's turn to terror had as much to do with his own conflicted sexuality as it did with the clash of civilizations." Wright, *The Looming Tower: Al Qaeda and the Road to 9/11* (New York: Knopf, 2006), p. 307.

6. Robin Morgan, *The Demon Lover: On the Sexuality of Terrorism* (New York: Washington Square Press, 2001), pp. xxii–iii. Cf. Wright, *Looming Tower*, p. 307, and Terry McDermott, *Perfect Soldiers: The 9/11 Hijackers: Who They Were, Why They Did It* (New York: HarperCollins, 2005), pp. 19, 22, 36, 54, 60, 82, 245–47.

7. Robert Fisk, *The Great War for Civilisation: The Conquest of the Middle East* (New York: Knopf, 2005), p. 853. Fisk was told this by the father of Ziad Jarrah.

8. This information was contained in a document prepared by the FBI entitled "Hijackers Timeline (Redacted)," cited in Paul Matt, "Newly Released FBI

Timeline Reveals New Information about 9/11 Hijackers That Was Ignored by 9/11 Commission," February 14, 2008, http://www.bibliotecapleyades.net/sociopolitica/esp_sociopol_911_44.htm (accessed August 13, 2009).

9. Christopher Reuter, *My Life Is a Weapon: A Modern History of Suicide Bombing*, trans. Helena Rags-Kirkby (Princeton, NJ: Princeton University Press, 2002), p. 8.

10. McDermott, *Perfect Soldiers*, p. 192.

11. "A Careful Sequence of Mundane Dealings Sows a Day of Bloody Terror for Hijackers," *Wall Street Journal*, October 16, 2001.

12. In the end, they decided against doing so either because they considered the price—over $400—too high, or because they did not have sufficient money. Shelley Murphy and Douglas Belkin, "Hijackers Said to Seek Prostitutes," *Boston Globe*, October 10, 2001.

13. Islamic fundamentalists, such as those who belong to Iran's ruling Party of Allah, frequently blame the "foreign enemies of Islam"—and pro-Western Arab leaders—for fomenting prostitution in their countries. Amir Taheri, *Holy Terror: Inside the World of Islamic Terrorism* (Bethesda, MD: Adler & Adler, 1987), p. 154.

14. For a fictional depiction of the sexual conflicts experienced by the 9/11 hijackers, see Andre Dubus III, *The Garden of Last Days* (New York: Norton, 2008).

15. Taheri, *Holy Terror*, p. 154.

16. Female sexual voraciousness is to be feared; a woman is considered an "omnisexual" being, her sexuality animated by "animal energy, irresistible, vibrating, and [which] makes the universe vibrate to a rhythm all its own." Fatna A. Sabbah, *Woman in the Muslim Unconscious*, trans. Mary Jo Lakeland (New York: Pergamon, 1984), p. 26.

17. Ibid., p. 113.

18. This is affirmed in Sura IV, verse 38, of the Qur'an.

19. *Sahih Bukari*, vol. 7, book 62, no. 121.

20. Women are believed to be capable of enslaving men sexually. Sabbah, *Woman in the Muslim Unconscious*, pp. 45, 50.

21. Beverley Milton-Edwards, *Islam and Violence in the Modern Era* (New York: Palgrave Macmillan, 2006), p. 116.

22. Raphael Patai, *The Arab Mind*, rev. ed. (New York: Hatherleigh Press, 2002), p. 130.

23. Qur'an, Sura IV, verse 34.

24. "Bivalence is the will of God." Abdelhuhab Bouhdiba, *Sexuality in Islam*, trans. Alan Sheridan (London: Routledge & Kegan Paul, 1985), p. 7.

25. "Sexual deviation is a revolt against God." Ibid., p. 31.

26. Patai, *Arab Mind*, pp. 135, 138.

27. Ibid., pp. 126, 134.

28. As Fatna Sabbah has summed up, "Muslim civilization is defined as an attempt to control pleasure." Sabbah, *Woman in the Muslim Unconscious*, p. 4.

29. Patai, *Arab Mind*, pp. 136–37.

30. Twelve of the thirteen "muscle hijackers" came from this country.

31. Kiren Chaudhry, "New and Recurring Forms of Poverty and Inequality in the Arab World." Paper presented at the Workshop on Devastated Economies, UCLA, February 4–5, 2005, pp. 5, 13, 15, 23, 26. By 2003, the rate of female enrollment at the university level was higher than that for males in Bahrain, Jordan, Kuwait, Lebanon, Qatar, and Saudi Arabia. http://www.apsanet.org/imgtest/TaskForce DiffIneqDevChaudry.pdf (accessed August 15, 2009). Paying a "bride-price" is generally expected in Palestinian courtships. See, for example, Aaron D. Blackwell, "Middle-Class Martyrs: Modeling the Inclusive Fitness Outcomes of Palestinian Suicide Attack," http://www.uoregon.edu/~icds/Evolution_FG_files/Blackwell_Suicide Attack.pdf (accessed August 9, 2009).

32. Barbara Ehrenreich, "A Mystery of Misogyny," *Progressive* (November 30, 2001), http://www.alternet.org/story/11996/a_mystery_of_misogyny/?page=entire (accessed August 9, 2009).

33. Suad Joseph and Afsaneh Najmabadi, *Encyclopedia of Women and Islamic Cultures*, 6 vols. (Boston: Brill, 2003), 3:251.

34. Patai, *Arab Mind*, p. 349.

35. Ibid., p. 130. Cf. Joseph and Najmabadi, *Encyclopedia of Women and Islamic Cultures*, p. 54.

36. In Asian societies such as China, these idle bands of young men are known as "bare branches." For a discussion of this phenomenon and the danger it poses to these countries, see Valerie M. Hudson and Andrea M. den Boer, *Bare Branches: Security Implications of Asia's Surplus Male Population* (Cambridge, MA: MIT Press, 2004). This excess of young males has also been linked to higher rates of violence in the United States. See David T. Courtwright, *Violent Land: Single Men and Social Disorder from the Frontier to the Inner City* (Cambridge, MA: Harvard University Press, 1996).

37. Many Palestinian youth were radicalized by seeing their fathers beaten or humiliated by Israeli soldiers during the first intifada against Israel, between 1987 and 1993. One study has concluded that some 55 percent of children witnessed acts of this nature. Consequently, many of these young men joined the second intifada that began in September 2000. Jacqueline Rose, "Deadly Embrace," *London Review of Books*, November 4, 2004, http://www.lrb.co.uk/v26/n21/rose01_.html (accessed August 10, 2009).

38. John Esposito, *Unholy War: Terror in the Name of Islam* (Oxford: Oxford University Press, 2002), pp. 18, 22.

39. See, for example, Monte Palmer and Princess Palmer, *At the Heart of*

Terror: Islam, Jihadists, and America's War on Terrorism (London: Rowman & Littlefield, 2004), pp. 20, 23.

40. A Beirut civil servant, the father of the hijacker Ziad Jarrah had spent thousands of dollars to send his son to a university in Hamburg, Germany. Fisk, *Great War*, p. 852.

41. Chaudhry, "New and Recurring Forms of Poverty," p. 26.

42. Herman Pleij, *Dreaming of Cockaigne: Medieval Fantasies of the Perfect Life* (New York: Columbia University Press, 2001), p. 210.

43. 3 Sura LVI, verses 56–58, *Holy Qur'an*, trans. M. H. Shakir (Elmhurst, NY: Tahrike Tarsile Qur'an, 1983), p. 538. Cf. "Reformist Saudi Author: Religious Cassettes Advocate Jihad by Emphasizing Martyr's Sexual Rewards," *Saudi Gazette*, November 17, 2005, cited in MEMRI, November 23, 2005, http://memri.org/bin/articles.cgi?Page=countries&Area=saudiarabia&ID=SP103205#_edn1 (accessed August 10, 2009).

44. McDermott, *Perfect Soldiers*, Appendix B, "The Last Night," p. 250.

45. The complex web of factors that have produced suicide bombers in Iraq is detailed in Mohammed Hafez, *Suicide Bombers in Iraq: The Strategy and Ideology of Martyrdom* (Washington, DC: United States Institute of Peace Press, 2007).

46. See, for example, Tamer Khawireh, "Islamic Jihad Promises Heaven to Teen Recruit," Associated Press, March 31, 2004, Jihad Watch, http://www.jihadwatch.org/archives/001356.php (accessed August 14, 2009). However, some commentators argue the attractiveness of this heavenly fantasy is exaggerated. See Abhinav Aima, "Grapes? Virgins? Does That Explain Suicide Bombers?" August 5, 2004, http://www.commondreams.org/views04/0805–02.htm (accessed August 12, 2009). It is perhaps most accurate to say that these acts of self-sacrifice are primarily seen as redemptive and as serving a higher, nationalist cause: the life of the individual takes on greater meaning through them.

47. "Hussein Pays Families of Palestinian 'Martyrs' $10K, Including Suicide Bomber," Associated Press, March 13, 2003.

48. Blackwell, "Middle-Class Martyrs," p. 4.

49. This hypothesis has been discussed by two economists analyzing the motives of suicide bombers. See Alan Krueger and Jitka Maleckova, "Does Poverty Cause Terrorism?" *New Republic* 225, no. 26 (June 24, 2002): 31.

50. Taghreed El-Khodary, "For War Widows, Hamas Recruits Army of Husbands," *New York Times*, October 30, 2008.

51. For these and other eighteenth-century Western observations about the Middle East, see Michael B. Oren, *Power, Faith, and Fantasy: America in the Middle East, 1776 to the Present* (New York: Norton, 2007), pp. 41, 43, 46.

52. Edward Said, "Latent and Manifest Orientalism," in Alexander Lyon Macfie, ed., *Orientalism: A Reader* (New York: New York University Press, 2001), p. 112.

53. See, for example, Jasmin Zine, "Between Orientalism and Fundamentalism: Muslim Women and Feminist Engagement," in Krista Hunt and Kim Rygiel, eds., *(En)gendering the War on Terror: War Stories and Camouflaged Politics* (Burlington, VT: Ashgate, 2006), p. 31.

54. Ibid., pp. 13–14. Cf. Edward Said, introduction, in Joseph A. Massad, *Desiring Arabs* (Chicago: University of Chicago Press, 2007), pp. 7, 9.

55. Nikki R. Keddie, *Women in the Middle East: Past and Present* (Princeton, NJ: Princeton University Press, 2006), p. 251.

56. Sayyid Qutb, "'The America I Have Seen': In the Scale of Human Values," (1951), pp. 6, 9, 12, 13. Kashf ul Shubuhat Publications. http://www.scribd.com/doc/6412907/Syed-QutubThe-America-I-Have-Seen (accessed August 15, 2009).

57. Ibid., pp. 13, 14.

58. Quoted in Gerges A. Fawas, *Journey of the Jihadist: Inside Muslim Militancy* (Orlando, FL: Harcourt, 2006), p. 154. In a subsequent book dealing with his experiences in the United States, Qutb declared he had been appalled by "this vulgarity which you call the 'emancipation of women.'" Quoted in Esposito, *Unholy War*, p. 124.

59. Ibid., p. 156.

60. For a discussion of how Japan and the United States developed striking similar negative images of each other, see John W. Dower, *War without Mercy: Race and Power in the Pacific War* (New York: Pantheon, 1986).

61. R. L. Euben, *Enemy in the Mirror: Islamic Fundamentalism and the Limits of Modern Rationalism: A Work of Comparative Political Theory* (Princeton, NJ: Princeton University Press, 1999), p. 15.

62. Quoted from Khomeini's "Message to the Pilgrims" in Esposito, *Unholy War*, p. 76.

63. Fathali M. Moghaddam, *From the Terrorists' Point of View: What They Experience and Why They Come to Destroy* (Westport, CT: Praeger, 2006), pp. 17, 26.

64. For discussions of displaced aggression, see John Dollard et al., *Frustration and Aggression* (New Haven, CT: Yale University Press, 1969), and Franco Fornari, *The Psychoanalysis of War* (Bloomington: Indiana University Press, 1975).

65. Patai, *Arab Mind*, p. 149.

66. For a treatment of this psychological process, see Ron Potter-Efron and Terry S. Trepper, *Handbook of Anger Management: Individual, Couple, Family, and Group Approaches* (London: Routledge, 2005), pp. 177ff.

67. For a brief discussion of the possible link between BPD and suicide terrorists, see Ami Pedahzur, *Suicide Terrorism* (Malden, MA: Polity, 2005), p. 35.

68. Dinesh D'Souza, *The Enemy at Home: The Cultural Left and Its Responsi-

bility for 9/11 (Garden City, NY: Doubleday, 2007), p. 16. He faults the US "cultural left" for having "fostered a decadent American culture that angers and repulses traditional societies, especially those in the Islamic world."

69. Bernard Lewis, *The Crisis of Islam* (New York: Modern Library, 2003), pp. 80–81.

70. Patai, *Arab Mind*, p. 150.

71. Ibid., p. 139.

72. "Al Qaeda Training Manual: Declaration of Jihad against the Country's Tyrants—Military Series," p. 7, http://fas.org/irp/world/para/aqmanual.pdf (accessed August 14, 2009).

73. John M. Davis, "Countering International Terrorism: Perspectives from International Psychology," in Chris E. Stout, ed., *Psychology of Terrorism: Coping with the Continuing Threat* (Westport, CT: Praeger, 2004), p. 124. Cf. Moghaddam, *Terrorists' Point of View*, p. 70.

74. Ehrenreich, "Mystery of Misogyny."

75. Fisk, *Great War*, p. 840.

76. Stephen Ducat, *The Wimp Factor: Gender Gaps, Holy Wars, and the Politics of Anxious Masculinity* (Boston: Beacon, 2004), p. 208.

77. This Hudood Ordinance came into effect in Pakistan in 1979. Recent cases of rape victims in Pakistan and elsewhere being punished for accusing their attackers have made evident the persistence of traditional attitudes regarding such violations of sexual mores.

78. Economic factors do not appear to be of major motivating importance. See Krueger and Maleckova, "Does Poverty Cause Terrorism?" p. 31. They point out that middle-class Palestinians are as likely to support suicide attacks against Israelis as persons of a lower socioeconomic status.

79. Births in the United States started to decline slightly in 1957, and half of the decrease in fertility took place by 1970. See Selma Taffel, "Trends in Fertility in the United States," *Vital and Health Statistics Series* 21, no. 28 (Washington, DC: US Government Printing Office, September 1977), pp. 2, 5.

80. This decline came on the heels of a 33 percent increase in "illegitimate" births among teenagers between 1965 and 1970. June Sklar and Beth Berkov, "Teenage Family Formation in Postwar America," *Family Planning Perspectives* 6, no. 2 (Spring 1974): 81.

81. Alison M. Spitz et al., "Pregnancy, Abortion, and Birth Rates among U.S. Adolescents, 1980, 1985, and 1990," *Journal of the American Medical Association* 275, no. 13 (April 3, 1996): 991. See also "New Report Revises Birth and Fertility Rates for the 1990s, Uses 2000 Census Population Estimates to Improve Accuracy," Centers for Disease Control, August 4, 2003, http://www.cdc.gov/nchs/PRESSROOM/03facts/revisesrates.htm (accessed August 18, 2009).

82. John F. Kantner and Marvin Zelnik, "First Pregnancies to Women Aged 15–19: 1976 and 1971," *Family Planning Perspectives* 10, no. 1 (January/February 1978): 11.

83. *Sex and America's Teenagers* (New York: Alan Guttmacher Institute, 1994), p. 164.

84. By 1976, reliance on condoms, douches, and withdrawal declined as the use of the Pill doubled over the 1970 rate. Marvin Zelnik and John F. Kantner, "Sexual and Contraceptive Experience of Young Unmarried Women in the United States, 1976 and 1971," *Family Planning Perspectives* 9, no. 2 (March/April 1977): 63.

85. Naomi Seiler, "Is Teen Marriage a Solution?" (Washington, DC: Center for Law and Social Policy, April 2002), p. 4, http://www.clasp.org/admin/site/publications_archive/files/0087.pdf (accessed August 18, 2009).

86. "Fertility Measurement: Vital and Health Statistics," *Document and Committee Reports* Series 4, nos. 1–14 (Washington, DC: US Government Printing Office, September 1965), p. 7.

87. Lionel Tiger, *The Decline of Males* (New York: Golden, 1999), pp. 35, 48.

88. Barbara Dafoe Whitehead and David Popenoe, "Life without Children: The Social Retreat from Children and How It Is Changing America" (New Brunswick, NJ: National Marriage Project, 2006), p. 12, http://marriage.rutgers.edu/Publications/2008LifeWithoutChildren.pdf (accessed August 22, 2009).

89. Table MS-2, "Estimated Median Age at First Marriage, by Sex: 1890 to the Present" (September 21, 2006), http://www.census.gov/population/socdemo/hh-fam/ms2.pdf (accessed August 22, 2009).

90. Chart 2, "Selected Marriage and Divorce Indicators, 1920–1989," Tallese Johnson and Jane Dye, "Indicators of Marriage and Fertility in the United States from the American Community Survey: 2000 to 2003" (May 2005), http://www.census.gov/population/www/socdemo/fertility/mar-fert-slides.html (accessed August 22, 2009).

91. "Live Births and Birth Rates, by Year," http://www.infoplease.com/ipa/A0005067.html (accessed August 22, 2009).

92. Table 2, "Percentage of Women with Own Children in the Household, 1970 and 2007," Whitehead and Popenoe, "Life without Children," p. 13.

93. Table 3, "Percentage of Women 40–44, Childless, 1970–2006, ibid., p. 14.

94. By 2006, the fertility rate among women in their midforties was 1.9.

95. Chart 1, "Number of Households, Married Couples, and Persons per Household, 1910–1989," James R. Wetzel, "American Families: 75 Years of Change," *Monthly Labor Review* 113, no. 4 (March 1990): 6.

96. From 1960 to 1970, the percentage of women going to colleges and universities as undergraduates rose from 30 to 40. Martin A. Marty, *Daily Life in the United States, 1960–1990: Decades of Discord* (Westport, CT: Greenwood, 1997), p. 51.

97. Thomas G. Mortenson, "What's Wrong with the Guys?" p. 1, http://www.postsecondary.org/archives/previous/GuysFacts.pdf (accessed August 23, 2009).

98. Cheryl D. Hayes, John L. Palmer, and Martha J. Zaslow, eds., *Who Cares for America's Children? Child Care Policy for the 1990s* (Washington, DC: National Academic Press, 1990), p. 17.

99. Heather Boushey, "Will Economic Trends Change Family Dynamics? Testimony to the Equal Opportunity Employment Commission," April 22, 2009, Center for American Progress Action Fund, http://www.american progressaction.org/issues/2009/04/eeoc_testimony.html (accessed August 23, 2009).

100. Elizabeth Waldman, "Labor Force Statistics from a Family Perspective, *Monthly Labor Review* 106, no. 16 (December 1983), p. 3, http://www.bls.gov/opub/mlr/1983/12/art2full.pdfhttp://www.bls.gov/opub/mlr/1983/12/art2 full.pdf (accessed August 23, 2009).

101. Jane R. Wilkie, "The Decline of Men's Labor Force Participation and Income and the Changing Structure of Family Economic Support," *Journal of Marriage and the Family* 53 (February 1991): 111.

102. Boushey, "Economic Trends."

103. Tiger, *Decline of Males*, p. 110.

104. Ibid., p. 5.

105. Table P-36, "Median Income of Full-Time, Year-Round Workers, 1995–2005: Historical Tables," *Current Population Survey* (Washington, DC: Bureau of Labor Statistics, 2006).

106. Mark Doms and Ethan Lewis, "The Narrowing of the Male-Female Wage Gap," *FRBSF Economic Letter* (June 29, 2007): 1, http://www.sf.frb.org/publications/economics/letter/2007/el2007-17.html (accessed August 24, 2009).

107. Solomon W. Polachek and John Robst, "Trends in the Male-Female Wage Gap: The 1980s Compared with the 1970s," *Southern Economic Review* 67, no. 4 (April 2001): 869. But during the previous decade the gap narrowed by only 0.39 percent annually, largely because most of the women entering the workforce then were low skilled and thus poorly paid.

108. See William P. Butz and Michael P. Ward, "The Emergence of Countercyclical U.S. Fertility," *American Economic Review* 69, no. 3 (June 1979): 327. The authors note that the rise in male wages in the 1950s similarly accounted for the "baby boom" of the postwar era.

109. Scott J. South, "Economic Conditions and the Divorce Rate: A Times-Series Analysis of the Postwar United States," *Journal of Marriage and the Family* 47, no. 1 (February 1985): 38. The proportion of divorces initiated by wives has since risen to roughly two-thirds.

110. Fig. 3, "Percentage of Premaritally Pregnant Women Aged 15–19 Marrying before the Birth of their First Child, 1930–1994," Seiler, "Teen Marriage," p. 5. Zelnik and Kantner, "First Pregnancies," p. 76.

111. Chart SF8.1, "The Decline in Crude Marriages between 1970 and 2007," Marriage and Divorce Rates, OECD Family Database (December 15, 2008), p. 4, http://www.oecd.org/dataoecd/4/19/40321815.pdf (accessed August 24, 2009).

112. Fig. 1, "Number of Marriages per 1,000 Unmarried Women Age 15 and Older, by Year, United States," Barbara Dafoe Whitehead and David Popenoe, "The State of Our Unions: The Social Health of Marriage in America, 2005" (July 2005), http://marriage.rutgers.edu/Publications/SOOU/TEXTSOOU2005.htm (accessed August 24, 2009).

113. Table 65, "Number of Women Never Married by Age: 1960–1994," in Marvin B. Sussman, Suzanne K. Steinmetz, and Gary W. Peterson, eds., *Handbook of Marriage and the Family* (New York: Plenum, 1999), p. 47.

114. Wetzel, "American Families," p. 5.

115. Ibid., p. 4.

116. Rosanna Hertz, *Single by Chance, Mother by Choice: How Women Are Choosing Parenthood without Marriage and Creating the New American Family* (New York: Oxford University Press, 2006), p. xv.

117. Table 1, "Percentage of Live Births to Unmarried Women, by Year, United States," Whitehead and Popenoe, "Life without Children," p. 6.

118. Jane L. Dye, "Fertility of American Women: 2006," Current Population Reports (August 2008): 2, http://www.census.gov/prod/2008pubs/p20–558.pdf (accessed August 19, 2009).

119. Seiler, "Teen Marriage," p. 4.

120. Breakups are twice as likely to happen in nonmarital relationships as among married couples.

121. In her study of sixty-five middle-class American women who have become single mothers, Rosanna Hertz found many such decisions came in the wake of failed relationships with the fathers. These women have found they no longer face any social stigma for deciding to raise a child on their own. See Hertz, *Single by Chance*, p. 19, passim. According to one study, nonmarital relationships involving children are five times as likely to dissolve as marriages with offspring. Georgina Binstock and A. Thornton, "Separations, Reconciliations and Living Apart in Cohabiting and Marital Unions," *Journal of Marriage and the Family* 65 (2003): 434.

122. Table 72, "Live Births, Deaths, Marriages, and Divorces: 1950–2003," *Statistical Abstract of the United States* (Washington, DC: US Census Bureau, 2006), p. 64, http://www.census.gov/prod/2005pubs/06statab/vitstat.pdf (accessed August 24, 2009).

123. Wetzel, "American Families," p. 11.

124. From an average size of slightly less than five persons in 1890, the American household shrank to a little over three members by 1970. Frances E. Kobrin, "The Fall of Household Size and the Rise of the Primary Individual in the United States," *Demography* 13, no. 1 (February 1976): 1342.

125. Sam Roberts, "To Be Married Means to Be Outnumbered," *New York Times*, October 15, 2006.

126. Chart 1, "Marital Status of American Adults," http://www.unmarried .org/statistics.html (accessed August 15, 2009).

127. Wetzel, "American Families," p. 11.

128. Table 1, "Households, by Type, in the United States, Selected Years, 1950–89," Wetzel, "American Families," p. 7.

129. P-20, "Marital Status and Living Arrangements," *Current Population Reports* (March 1994): 484.

130. Table B, "Marital Status and Living Arrangements of Adults 18 Years Old and Over: March 1998," *Official Statistics* (November 16, 1998), p. iv, http://www.census.gov/prod/99pubs/p20–514u.pdf (accessed August 18, 2009).

131. By the end of the 1980s, 29.1 percent of American households were made up of persons who were not related by blood or marriage. Wetzel, "American Families," p. 11.

132. This was as of 2000. Whitehead and Popenoe, "Life without Children," pp. 17–18.

133. Mortenson, "What's Wrong with the Guys?" p. 3.

134. For these statistics, see *Common Sense and Domestic Violence* 3 (January 30, 1998): 403–26.

135. Mortenson, "What's Wrong with the Guys?" p. 2.

136. Table 4, "Households with Children under 18, 1960–2007," Whitehead and Popenoe, "Life without Children," p. 20.

137. Fig. 6, "Income of Fathers (1980) and Sons (2005), by Education Level," Matt Homer et al., "Going Nowhere: Workers' Wages since the Mid-70s," p. 6, http://www.tcf.org/Publications/EconomicsInequality/GoingNowhereRC.pdf (accessed August 25, 2009).

138. For a summary of these findings, see Scott J. South and Kim M. Lloyd, "Marriage Markets and Non-Marital Fertility," *Demography* 29, no. 2 (May 1992): 249.

139. Tiger, *Decline of Males*, p. 137.

140. Whereas average wages for men who had graduated from high school declined from $40,000 in the early 1970s to $30,000 in 2005, those for male college graduates stayed fairly constant, at about $50,000 during this period. Homer et al., "Going Nowhere," p. 6.

141. Joshua R. Goldstein and Catherine T. Kenney, "Too Poor to Marry? A Cross-National Comparison of the SES Gradient in Marriage and Cohabitation," September 22, 2006, p. 1, http://paa2007.princeton.edu/download.aspx?submission Id=70825.

142. http://www.census.gov/Press-release/www/releases/archives/facts_for _features_special_editions/006116.html (accessed August 24, 2009).

143. For more details on Brown's book and its impact, see Jennifer Scanlon, *Bad Girls Go Everywhere* (New York: Oxford University Press, 2009). *Cosmopolitan*, the magazine Brown began editing after the success of her book, gave its female readers plenty of sexual tips in articles such as "The Etiquette of the Orgasm." Cited in Jane Stern and Michael Stern, *Sixties People* (New York: Knopf, 1990), p. 25.

144. Recommendations of the Presidential Commission on the Status of Women (PCSW), which was created by President Kennedy in 1960 and chaired by Eleanor Roosevelt, led to Congress passing the Equal Pay Act of 1963. This law created a framework for protecting women against discrimination in compensation based on gender.

145. The phrase referring to Miss America was coined by the one-time actress and feminist Robin Morgan. See "People and Events: The 1968 Protest," *American Experience*, PBS, http://www.pbs.org/wgbh/amex/missamerica peopleevents/e_feminists.html (accessed August 28, 2009).

146. For details on this sit-in, see Susan Brownmiller, *In Our Time: Memoir of a Revolution* (New York: Dial), pp. 84–92.

147. The term *sisterhood* was first widely used in the 1960s by a radical group of feminists known as "Redstockings." In 1970, an anthology of feminist essays appeared under the title *Sisterhood Is Powerful*.

148. These included laws giving women more financial equity in divorce, greater parity in intercollegiate athletics, more personal rights such as abortion, and protection from sexual harassment. In addition, female plaintiffs won a number of major court cases involving sexual discrimination, rape, and other crimes of a sexual nature.

149. Tom Brokaw, *Boom! Voices of the Sixties* (New York: Random House, 2007), p. 195. Brokaw found this attitude to be widespread among the women of the World War II generation he interviewed. He cites the example of Barbara Walters, who, after she became a prominent television interviewer, was instructed to allow her male counterpart, Frank McGee, to always ask the first question. Ibid., p. 196.

150. Female aspirants to managerial positions were often told these were not appropriate for women. Ibid., pp. 216–17.

151. Even toward the end of his life, Mailer remained steadfast in his espousal of "macho" stances, for example, lambasting the United States for being a "timorous giant" in its response to the attacks of 9/11. Oliver Burkeman, "Machismo Isn't That Easy to Wear," *Guardian*, February 5, 2002, http://www.guardian.co.uk/books/2002/feb/05/fiction.oliverburkeman (accessed August 29, 2009).

152. Quoted in Charles McGrath, "Norman Mailer, Towering Author with a Matching Ego, Dies at 84," *New York Times*, November 11, 2007.

153. Women members of groups like SDS were frequently required to assert their allegiance to these male-dominated organizations rather than to feminist ones. See interview with Cathy Wilkerson, February 17, 1985, Columbia University Oral History Collection, http://historymatters.gmu.edu/d/6916/ (accessed August 22, 2009). When several women sought to introduce women's issues during a fall 1967 gathering of SDS, they were "hooted down." Ron Chepesiuk, *Sixties Radicals, Then and Now: Candid Conversations with Those Who Shaped the Era* (Jefferson, NC: McFarland, 1995), p. 233.

154. Margot Adler, *Heretic's Heart: A Journey through Spirit and Revolution* (Boston: Beacon, 1997), p. 102. Adler recalls a 1984 speech by Bettina Aptheker, another Berkeley free speech activist, in which Aptheker—Adler's activist role model—admitted that many women in the movement were "seriously abused, physically and sexually," by both police and male campus radicals. Ibid., p. 104.

155. Some male members of radical groups like SDS regarded sex as a way of binding members together. One early SDS member once remarked, "The movement hangs together on the head of penis." Quoted in Todd Gitlin, *The Sixties: Years of Hope, Days of Rage* (New York: Bantam, 1987), p. 108. "The sexual intensity," Gitlin notes, "matched the political and intellectual; or was it the other way round?" Having sex was also a way of recruiting women into the movement, or what the feminist Marge Piercy called "fucking a staff into existence." Ibid., p. 371.

156. David Maraniss, *They Marched into Sunlight: War and Peace—Vietnam and America, October 1967* (New York: Simon & Schuster, 2003), p. 78.

157. Feminists have pointed out that Carmichael intended this remark to be a joke. See, for example, Wini Breines, *The Trouble between Us: The Uneasy History of White and Black Women in the Feminist Movement* (New York: Oxford University Press, 2006), p. 27.

158. Stern and Stern, *Sixties People*, p. 179.

159. Gitlin, *The Sixties*, p. 371.

160. Tiger, *Decline of Males*, p. 11.

161. Contrary to popular belief, feminist protestors at the Miss America Pageant never actually burned their bras, out of deference to Atlantic City's fire laws. Brownmiller, *In Our Time*, p. 37.

162. At a protest held in Washington, DC, at the time of Richard Nixon's inaugural in January 1969, Marilyn Webb told her listeners, "Women must take control of our bodies," only to have several men in the crowd yell comments such as "Take her off the stage and fuck her" and "Take off your clothes." Brownmiller, *In Our Time*, p. 57. During a nationwide Women's Strike for Equality on August 26, 1970, some male New Yorkers denounced marching females as "bra-less traitors," while in Los Angeles, one man called out, "The man is the king of the house, and we want our wives to be queens, not partners." Quoted in Terry H. Anderson, *The Movement and the Sixties* (New York: Oxford University Press, 1995), p. 360.

163. In the mid-1960s, some professors at prestigious universities such as Columbia refused to work with female graduate students. Brokaw, *Boom!* p. 220.

164. Quoted in Leslie Bennett, "Ivy League Women Face Social Barriers," *New York Times*, April 6, 1979.

165. Anthony Astrachan, *How Men Feel: Their Responses to Women's Demands for Equality and Power* (Garden City, NY: Doubleday, 1986), p. 38.

166. This emphasis on exclusively male activities typifies what the sociologist Michael S. Kimmel has characterized as the "masculinist" response to feminism. See Kimmel, "Who's Afraid of Men Doing Feminism?" in Tom Digby, ed., *Men Doing Feminism* (New York: Routledge, 1993), pp. 57–68.

167. Between 1967 and 1981, the number of reported forcible rapes in the United States tripled.

168. A poster carrying this phrase and the photo of three young women sitting cross-legged on a couch was often on display at antiwar rallies.

169. Letter of Marc B. Anderson to the *Daily Californian*, April 23, 1967, quoted in Adler, *Heretic's Heart*, pp. 172–73.

170. According to the psychiatrist Theodore Nadelson, "War preserves the social power of men over women." Nadelson, *Trained to Kill: Soldiers at War* (Baltimore: Johns Hopkins University Press, 2005), p. 153.

171. Adrienne Rich, "Caryatid," in *On Lies, Secrets and Silence: Selected Prose, 1966–1978* (New York: Norton, 1979), pp. 110, 115.

172. Susan Faludi, *Stiffed: The Betrayal of the American Man* (New York: Perennial, 2000), p. 27.

173. Ron Kovic, *Born on the Fourth of July* (New York: Akashic, 2005), p. 168. The psychiatrist Jonathan Shays found that many veterans felt betrayed by

their glory-seeking officers, who had violated the social contract among fighting men. Jonathan Shays, *Achilles in Vietnam: Combat Trauma and the Undoing of Character* (New York: Atheneum, 1994), pp. 14, 17, 19, 27. According to one estimate, as many as one in five US officers killed in Vietnam were victims of their own men.

174. Faludi, *Stiffed*, p. 356.

175. Quoted in John Spiller, et al., *The United States, 1763–2001* (London: Routledge, 2005), p. 234.

176. The writer and journalist Bob Greene documented many such incidents in his book *Homecoming: When the Soldiers Returned from Vietnam* (New York: G. P. Putnam's Sons, 1989).

177. During the late 1960s and early 1970s, polls showed that a majority of Americans felt too much money was being spent on the military. Alec M. Gallup and Frank Newport, eds., *The Gallup Poll 2005* (Lanham, MD: Rowman & Littlefield, 2006), p. 209.

178. A total of 680 US military personnel died of hostile and nonhostile causes in American overseas operations from 1980 to 1991. Table 2, "Worldwide U.S. Active Duty Military Deaths—Selected Military Operations," in Hannah Fischer et al., "American War and Military Operations Casualties," p. 7, http://fas.org/sgp/crs/natsec/RL32492.pdf (accessed August 15, 2009).

179. Kovic, *Born on the Fourth of July*, p. 148.

180. Ibid., p. 25.

181. Michael S. Kimmel, *Manhood in America: A Cultural History* (New York: Free Press, 1996), p. 262.

182. One study in the 1980s found that more than 30 percent of men who had served in Vietnam developed PTSD at some point. But this figure included those who had only experienced a "partial" form of this disorder. This survey also reported that combat veterans had a much higher incidence of depression, substance abuse, and personality disorders than soldiers who had been exposed to high "war-zone stress" or not served in Vietnam. See Richard A. Kulka et al., *Trauma and the Vietnam War Generation: Report of Findings from the National Vietnam Veterans Readjustment Study* (New York: Brunner/Mazel, 1990), pp. xxvii, 89, 99.

183. Kimmel, *Manhood in America*, p. 283.

184. Quoted in Anderson, *The Movement*, p. 419.

185. See, for example, Warren Farrell, *The Liberated Man: Beyond Masculinity—Freeing Men and Their Relationships with Women* (New York: Random House, 1974), and Jack Nichols, *Men's Liberation: A New Definition of Masculinity* (New York: Penguin, 1975).

186. By the 1980s, Wayne no longer appeared on lists of "most admired" American men.

187. Fig. 16.1, "Attitudes toward Morality of Sexual Activity" in Craig A. Rimmerman, Kenneth D. Wald, and Clyde Wilcox, eds., *The Politics of Gay Rights* (Chicago: University of Chicago Press, 2000), p. 413.

188. See, for example, George F. Gilder, *Sexual Suicide* (New York: Quadrangle, 1973).

189. Unhappiness with this "decentering" of white males is found, for example, in the novels of John Updike during the 1960s and 1970s. See Sally Robinson, *Marked Men: White Masculinity in Crisis* (New York: Columbia University Press, 2000), p. 25.

190. Susan Faludi, *Backlash: The Undeclared War against American Women* (New York: Crown, 1992), p. 9.

191. Some conservative pundits likened Carter to a woman president, who had revealed his "feminine spirit" after assuming office. Susan Jeffords, *Hard Bodies: Hollywood Masculinity in the Reagan Era* (New Brunswick, NJ: Rutgers University Press, 1994), p. 10.

192. In his speech at the 1976 GOP national convention, Reagan declared his belief that the banner of his party had "bold, unmistakable colors with no pale, pastel shades"—an implicit disavowal of feminine traits for masculine ones. Ronald Reagan, *The Greatest Speeches of Ronald Reagan* (West Palm Beach, FL: NewsMax, 2002), p. 45. Reagan's confronting Communist advances around the world conveyed the message that "real men were to venture forth because there was always the potential for a reward worth the risk and so the risk came to define manhood." David Paul Kuhn, *The Neglected Voter: White Men and the Democratic Dilemma* (New York: Palgrave Macmillan, 2007), p. 73.

193. In the 1981 cover image for this issue in which *Time* honored Reagan as "Man of the Year," the president, dressed in open shirt and Western-style slacks, looked more like Gary Cooper than a chief executive. See Jeffords, *Hard Bodies*, p. 2.

194. For example, in his two campaigns, George W. Bush also carried roughly 61 percent of this demographic group. Since 1980, Republican presidential candidates have garnered between 26 and 37 percent more white male votes than Democratic ones have. Kuhn, *Neglected Voter*, p. 4. A large part of this preference can be explained by the GOP's having appealed to the desire among many of these voters for a "truly" masculine leader.

195. For instance, one campaign bumper sticker in 1984 read, "Mondale Eats Quiche." Cited in Kimmel, *Manhood in America*, p. 296.

196. Faludi, *Backlash*, p. 239.

197. After this successful rescue of American medical students on the Caribbean island, Reagan declared, "Americans are now standing tall and firm." Quoted in Kimmel, *Manhood in America*, p. 291. Kimmel has characterized this

kind of military operation against weak enemies as reflecting a "bullying" and defensive masculinity.

198. The "Rambo" series, which debuted in 1982, reached its greatest commercial success in 1985, when *Rambo: First Blood Part II* grossed over $150 million in the United States, making it the second most popular movie of that year. President Reagan praised it for its depiction of an American military hero. As Susan Jeffords has noted, "the films that U.S. moviegoing audiences chose to see in large numbers during this period [the 1980s] were largely and consistently concerned with portrayals of white male action figures." Jeffords, *Hard Bodies*, p. 12.

199. Robert Bly, *Iron John: A Book about Men* (Reading, MA: Addison-Wesley, 1990), pp. 3, 85.

200. Stephen Wicks, *Warriors and Wild Men: Men, Masculinity and Gender* (Westport, CT: Bergin & Garvey, 1996), p. 4.

201. In William Golding's novel about a band of English schoolboys marooned on an island, one of them remarks: "This is our island. It's a good island. Until the grown-ups come to fetch us we'll have fun." Golding, *Lord of the Flies* (New York: Penguin, 1954), p. 35.

202. Jeff Madrick and Nikolaos Papinokaou, "The Stagnation of Male Wages," http://www.newschool.edu/cepa/publications/policynotes/Stagnation %20of%20Male%20Wages.pdf (accessed August 19, 2009).

203. Between 1990 and 2000, the marriage rate in the United States per 1,000 inhabitants, ages fifteen to sixty-four, fell from 14.9 to 12.5. It reached 11.2 in 2005. Table 132, "Marriage and Divorce Rates, by Country, 1990–2005," http://www.google.com/search?hl=en&rlz=1G1GGLQ_ENUS344&q= marriage+rate+united+states+statistics+1990+2000&aq=f&oq=&aqi= (accessed August 25, 2009). During this decade, the birth rate dropped from 16.7 per 1,000 to 14.7.

204. Faludi, *Backlash*, p. 9.

205. Not all conservatives backed this undertaking. Columnists Pat Buchanan, Robert Novak, and Rowland Evans, for instance, argued against it.

206. R. W. Apple, "Done: A Short, Persuasive Lesson in Warfare," *New York Times*, March 3, 1991.

207. *USA Today* polls showed 30 percent of Americans feared war against Iraq would be a mistake in January 1991, but only 15 percent regretted the decision by that July. By contrast, 60 percent felt the Vietnam War was a mistake, when polled in January 1973. "Poll Shows Support for Iraqi Pullout, Flag-Burning Amendment," *USA Today*, June 26, 2006, http://www.usatoday .com/news/washington/2006-06-26-poll-results_x.htm (accessed August 27, 2009). Public support for the war diminished when the number of projected

American casualties was increased. John Mueller, "American Public Opinion and Military Ventures Abroad: Attention Evaluation, Involvement, Politics, and the Wars of the Bushes," paper prepared for delivery at the 2003 Annual Meeting of the American Political Science Association, Philadelphia, August 28–31, 2003, p. 13, http://www.allacademic.com//meta/p_mla_apa_research _citation/0/6/4/5/6/pages64561/p64561–1.php (accessed August 22, 2009).

208. Public confidence in the US military rose from 63 percent in 1989 to 69 percent in 1991. Table 6–5, "Confidence in Institutions Trend," Barbara A. Bardes et al., *American Government and Politics Today: The Essentials—2008* (Florence, KY: Wadsworth, 2008), p. 212.

209. As a percentage of GNP, this rose 0.2 percent between 1991 and 1992, reversing a decline dating back to 1986. Table 1, "U.S. Military Spending as a Percentage of GDP, 1944–2003," http://www.truthandpolitics.org/military -relative-size.php (accessed August 24, 2009).

210. Eric Schmitt, "Ideas and Trends: The Gulf War Veteran; Victorious in War, Not Yet in Peace," *New York Times*, May 28, 1995. The proportion of young men ages sixteen to twenty-four who expressed interest in military service declined from 23 percent in 1990 to 22.5 percent in 1991 and 20 percent in 1992. Fig. 2–1, "Military Accessions and Applications with Ratio of Accessions to Applicants," FY 1776–2002, Office of Undersecretary of Defense, Personnel and Readiness, "Population Representation in the Military Services," FY 2005, p. 14. The high incidence of illnesses associated with the invasion of Kuwait ("Gulf War syndrome") also deterred some from joining the military after Operation Desert Storm.

211. Joshua S. Goldstein, *War and Gender: How Gender Shapes the War System and Vice Versa* (New York: Cambridge University Press, 2001), p. 94.

212. Eight of these died in traffic accidents, and five were killed when a Scud missile struck their barracks.

213. Fischer et al., "American War Casualties," p. 6.

214. Sara L. Zeigler and Gregory G. Gunderson, *Moving Beyond G.I. Jane: Women and the U.S. Military* (Lanham, MD: University Press of America, 2005), p. 49.

215. In a 1990 poll, 72 percent of civilian respondents said they would be in favor of women serving in combat units. Rosemary Skaine, *Women at War: Gender Issues of Americans in Combat* (Jefferson, NC: McFarland, 1999), p. 121.

216. A recent survey of 530 ROTC cadets found 55.7 percent of males opposed to women serving in the infantry. Table 2.2, "How Do You Feel about Women Serving in the Infantry?" Ziegler and Gunderson, *Moving Beyond G.I. Jane*, p. 23.

217. Gen. Volney F. Warner, preface to Erin Solaro, *Women in the Line of Fire: What You Should Know about Women in the Military* (Emeryville, CA: Seal Press, 2006), p. v.

218. *Gulf War and Health*, 6 vols., (Washington, DC: National Academies Press, 2008) 6:38.

219. Surveys of female veterans of the Vietnam conflict and First Gulf War carried out in 2004 and 2005 concluded that as many as 30 percent had been raped, and some 70 percent were the victims of other forms of sexual assault. Helen Benedict, *Lonely Soldier: The Private War of Women Serving in Iraq* (Boston: Beacon, 2009), p. 7. Even the Department of Defense concedes that only 10 percent of all such crimes are reported.

220. Shira Maguen, Michael Suvak, and Brett T. Litz, "Predictors and Prevalence of Posttraumatic Stress Disorder among Military Veterans," in Thomas W. Britt, Amy B. Adler, and Carl A. Castro, eds., *Military Life: The Psychology of Serving in Peace and Combat* (Westport, CT: Praeger, 2006), pp. 159–60.

221. Quoted in James E. Palombo and Randall G. Shelden, *Criminal to Critic: Reflections amid the American Experiment* (Lanham, MD: Lexington, 2009), p. 178. According to one source, only 8 percent of reported assaults on females in the military in 2007 resulted in court-martial, compared to the 40 percent of civilian cases that went to court that year. A woman who reports sexual harassment or assault is considered a "slut," "traitor," "weakling," or "liar." Benedict, *Lonely Soldier*, pp. 81, 90.

222. Some rapes of Iraqi women by US troops did occur at the Abu Ghraib prison.

223. Benedict, *Lonely Soldier*, p. 167.

224. William H. McMichael, "DoD: Sexual Assaults Increased in 2008," *Army Times*, March 18, 2009. Military officials attribute much of this increase to a greater willingness of female victims to come forward with their allegations.

225. Quoted in Benedict, *Lonely Soldier*, p. 4.

226. Rapes by British and other non-American troops have occurred, however. At least one English soldier was convicted of attempting to rape a female American in Kuwait in 2008. Allan Hall, "British Soldier Convicted of Attempted Rape of American Servicewoman in Toilet in Kuwait," *Daily Mail*, June 7, 2009.

227. An Israel Defense Force (IDF) study in 2003 found that 20 percent of female soldiers had reported that they had been victims of sexual harassment and another 7 percent had been sexually assaulted during the previous year. Rela Mazali, "'And What about the Girls?' What a Culture of War Genders out of

View," paper presented at a joint conference of the Women's Studies departments of major Israeli universities and the Israel Association of Feminist and Gender Studies, January 2002, p. 45, http://muse.jhu.edu/journals/nashim/v006/6.1mazali.pdf/ (accessed August 30, 2009).

228. Catherine Merridale, *Ivan's War: Life and Death in the Red Army, 1939–1945* (New York: Metropolitan, 2006), p. 241.

229. In his 2002 book, *Berlin: The Downfall, 1945*, Antony Beevor presented evidence of rape being carried out by Russian soldiers on countrywomen whom they had just freed from concentration camps. Daniel Johnson, "Red Army Troops Raped Even Russian Women as They Freed Them from Camps," *Daily Telegraph*, January 24, 2002, http://www.telegraph.co.uk/education/3293251/Red-Army-troops-raped-even-Russian-women-as-they-freed-them-from-camps.html (accessed August 15, 2009).

230. Quoted in John R. MacArthur, *Second Front: Censorship and Propaganda in the Gulf War* (New York: Hill & Wang, 1992), p. 108.

231. Ibid., p. 105.

232. After the First Gulf War, interest in joining the military declined. Between the fall of 1991 and 1996, the percentage of males considering joining the armed forces decreased from 26.2 to 20.7, with the greatest drop-off occurring among blacks. Many said they felt little motivation to participate in foreign wars after the end of the Cold War. Tom Philpot, "Interest in Military Service Wanes," *Proceedings: U.S. Naval Institute* 123, no. 9 (September 1997): 122.

233. Peter Singer, *Animal Liberation* (New York: HarperCollins, 1975), p. 25.

234. She made this comment during a 1992 television interview with her husband, prior to the New Hampshire presidential primary.

235. James Barron, "Thousands Feared Dead as World Trade Center Is Toppled," *New York Times*, September 11, 2001.

236. Quoted in Joyce Purnick, "Metro Matters; In a Crisis, the Giuliani We Wanted," *New York Times*, September 13, 2001.

237. Quoted in Robert D. McFadden, "After the Attacks, the President; Bush Leads Prayer, Visits Aid Crews; Congress Backs Use of Armed Force," *New York Times*, September 15, 2001.

238. Beth Gillin, "'Do Ya Think He's Sexy?' At Nearly 70, Rumsfeld Is TV's Newest Stud," *Philadelphia Inquirer*, December 29, 2001.

239. Ducat, *Wimp Factor*, pp. 230, 232.

240. Susan Faludi, *The Terror Dream: Fear and Fantasy in Post-9/11 America* (New York: Metropolitan, 2007), pp. 4, 9, 12.

241. Fox had made a pilot for the series, due for release in late September

2001, depicting an airplane taken over by hijackers and blowing up in mid-air. Ina Rae Hark, "Today Is the Longest Day of My Life: *24* as Mirror Image of 9/11," in Wheeler W. Dixon, ed., *Film and Television after 9/11* (Carbondale: Southern Illinois University Press, 2004), p. 121.

242. Faludi, *Terror Dream*, pp. 8, 23.

243. Ibid., pp. 6, 81, 87.

244. The army, navy, and Marines continued to meet their enlistment quotas up until 2005. "2003: Another Banner Military Recruitment and Retention Year," *American Forces News Service*, August 30, 2003, http://usmilitary .about.com/cs/joiningup/a/recruitgoals.htm (accessed August 31, 2009).

245. The percentage of white youths who were interested in joining the military rose from 16.2 percent in August 2001 to 21.6 percent in November, but then fell back sharply by the end of the year. Table 8.2, "Propensity for Military Service by Race/Ethnicity, and Time Period," Office of the Under Secretary of Defense, *Personnel and Readiness*, "Population Representation in the Military Services: Final Report" (March 2003), pp. 8–16. Many of the would-be volunteers after 9/11 were rejected as unqualified. Ibid., pp. 1–3. Cf. Jeff Reinking, "9/11 Recruits: They Enlisted When USA was Under Fire," *USA Today*, September 8, 2005.

246. In remarks at Chicago's O'Hare Airport on September 27, 2001, President Bush said, "Do your business around the country. Fly and enjoy America's great destination spots. Get down to Disney World in Florida. Take your families and enjoy life, the way we want it to be enjoyed."

247. This inner-city outreach was depicted in Michael Moore's 2004 film, *Fahrenheit 9/11*.

248. Bonuses for signing up rose sharply from $5,000 before the war in Iraq to $15,000–40,000 afterward. See Sarah Abruzzese, "Iraq War Brings Drop in Black Enlistments," *New York Times*, August 22, 2007. Since the United States has had an all-volunteer military, there has been a strong, consistent correlation between enlistment and the rate of unemployment among males ages sixteen to twenty-four. See Fig. 2, "High-Quality Enlistments and Youth Unemployment," Barbara A. Bicksler and Lisa G. Nolan, "Recruiting an All-Volunteer Force: The Need for Sustained Investment in Recruiting Resources," *Policy Perspectives* 1, no. 1 (September 2006): 3, http://www.defenselink.mil/prhome/docs/Bicksler%20 Recruiting%20Resources%20FINAL.pdf (accessed October 6, 2009).

249. For the impact of ideological factors, see John Eighmey, "Why Do Youth Enlist? Identification of Underlying Themes," *Armed Forces and Society* 32, no. 2 (January 2006): 307–28. See also Michael Massing, "The Volunteer Army: Who Fights and Why," *New York Review of Books*, April 23, 2008, http://www.nybooks.com/articles/21201 (accessed August 28, 2009); Ken Sug-

iura, "A Chance to Serve," *Atlanta Journal-Constitution*, February 13, 2007; and Leonard Wong, Thomas A. Kolditz, Raymond A. Millen, and Terrence M. Potter, "Why They Fight: Combat Motivation in the Iraq War" (Carlisle, PA: Strategic Studies Institute of the U.S. Army War College, July 2003), p. 19.

250. But the American military today is by no means made up overwhelmingly of men and women from poor families. See Fig. 12, "Distribution of Active-Duty Military Personnel, by Family Income Prior to Military Service," *The All-Volunteer Military: Issues and Performance* (Washington, DC: Congressional Budget Office, 2007), p. 30.

251. Kate Randall, "U.S. Poverty Rose Sharply in 2001," September 27, 2002, http://www.wsws.org/articles/2002/sep2002/pov-s27.shtml (accessed August 29, 2009).

252. Massing, "Volunteer Army." However, one study of enlistments has found that recruits have come from a wide range of socioeconomic backgrounds, suggesting that money alone is not the chief reason. Tim Kane, *Who Are the Recruits? The Demographic Characteristics of Military Enlistment, 2003–2005*, CDA06–09 (Washington, DC: Heritage Foundation, 2006).

253. Joshua Key, *The Deserter's Tale: The Story of an Ordinary Soldier Who Walked Away from the War in Iraq* (New York: Atlantic Monthly Press, 2007), p. 33. Other memoirs citing economic factors include Colby Buzzell's *Killing Time: My War in Iraq* and Kayla Williams's *Love My Rifle More Than You*.

254. Fig. 4.1, "Percentage Married Across All the Services," and Fig. 4.6, "Percentage Married Upon Accession Across All Active Services," Benjamin R. Karney and John S. Crow, *Families Under Stress: An Assessment of Data, Theory, and Research on Marriage and Divorce in the Military* (Santa Monica, CA: Rand, 2007), pp. 76, 79.

255. Chart 1, "Marital Status of Adult Americans," http://www.unmarried.org/statistics.html (accessed August 30, 2009).

256. These figures are cited in Chantelle Henneberry, "Women at War Face Sexual Violence," *BBC News*, April 17, 2009, http://news.bbc.co.uk/2/hi/americas/8005198.stm (accessed August 30, 2009).

257. In a recent survey, some 16 percent of females who had served in these wars had symptoms of PTSD. Sara Corbett, "The Women's War," *New York Times Magazine*, March 18, 2007.

258. See, for example, Steven Lee Myers, "Living and Fighting Alongside Men, and Fitting In," *New York Times*, August 17, 2009. Myers writes that the experiences of female soldiers in the Iraq and Afghanistan wars have "cultivated a new generation of women with a warrior's ethos." But he also notes that sexual harassment and assault remain problems, and that women are often viewed "derisively" in combat outposts.

BIBLIOGRAPHY

Abdul-Jabbar, Kareem, and Anthony Walton. *Brothers in Arms: The Epic Story of the 761st Tank Battalion, WWII's Forgotten Heroes.* New York: Broadway Books, 2004.

Abruzzese, Sarah. "Iraq War Brings Drop in Black Enlistees." *New York Times,* August 22, 2007.

Acemoglu, Daron, and David H. Autor. "Women, War and Wages: The Effect of Female Labor Supply on the Wage Structure at Mid-Century." *Journal of Political Economy* 112, no. 3 (May 12, 2003): 497–551. http://www.mit .edu/files1292 (accessed April 22, 2009).

Adams, David B. "Why Are There So Few Female Warriors?" *Behavior Science Research* 18, no. 3 (1983): 196–212.

Adams, Michael C. C. *Echoes of War: A Thousand Years of Military History in Popular Culture.* Lexington: University Press of Kentucky, 2002.

———. *Great Adventure: Male Desire and the Coming of World War I.* Bloomington: Indiana University Press, 1990.

Adler, Bill, ed. *Letters from Vietnam.* New York: Ballantine, 2003.

Alexander, Richard D. *Darwinism and Human Affairs.* Seattle: University of Washington Press, 1979.

Ambrose, Stephen E. *The Wild Blue: The Men and Boys Who Flew the B-24s over Germany.* New York: Simon & Schuster, 2001.

Anderson, Clarence E. *To Fly and Fight: Memoirs of a Triple Ace.* New York: St. Martin's Press, 1990.

Anderson, Karen. *Wartime Women: Sex Roles, Family Relations, and the Status of Women during World War II.* Westport, CT: Greenwood, 1981.

Anderson, Michael, ed. *British Population History: From the Black Death to the Present Day.* Cambridge: Cambridge University Press, 1996.

Anderson, William L., and Derek W. Little. "All's Fair: War and Other Causes of Divorce from a Beckerian Perspective (Statistical Data Included)." *American Journal of Economics and Sociology* 58, no. 4 (October 1999): 901–22.

Appy, Christian G. *Working-Class War: American Combat Soldiers and Vietnam.* Chapel Hill: University of North Carolina Press, 1993.

Atkinson, Rick. *In the Company of Soldiers: A Chronicle of Combat.* New York: Holt, 2004.

Babachenko, Arakady. *One Soldier's War.* New York: Grove Press, 2006.

Bacon, Alice Mabel. *Japanese Girls and Women.* Revised ed. London: Kegan Paul, 2001.

Bailey, Beth, and David Farber. *The First Strange Place: The Alchemy of Race and Sex in World War II Hawaii*. New York: Free Press, 1992.

Barash, David P. *The Whisperings Within*. New York: Harper & Row, 1979.

Barker-Benfield, Graham J. *The Horrors of the Half-Known Life: Male Attitudes toward Women and Sexuality in Nineteenth-Century America*, 2nd ed. New York: Routledge, 2005.

Barnhart, Michael A. *Japan Prepares for Total War: The Search for Economic Security, 1919–1941*. Ithaca, NY: Cornell University Press, 1988.

Bartov, Omer. *Hitler's Army: Soldiers, Nazis, and War in the Third Reich*. Oxford: Oxford University Press, 1992.

Bartow, Anne Llewelyn. Introduction to *War's Dirty Secret: Rape, Prostitution, and Other Crimes*, edited by Anne Llewelyn Bartow, pp. 5–23. Cleveland: Pilgrim Press, 2000.

Baskir, Lawrence M., and William A. Strauss. *Chance and Circumstance: The Draft, the War, and the Vietnam Generation*. New York: Knopf, 1978.

Bataille, Georges. *Death and Sensuality: A Study of Eroticism and the Taboo*. New York: Walker, 1962.

Baumeister, Roy F. "Is There Anything Good about Men?" Address before the American Psychological Association, San Francisco, August 24, 2007. http://www.fatherland.info/docs/is-there-anything-good-about-men -roy-baumeister.pdf (accessed June 14, 2009).

Baynes, John. *Morale: A Study of Men and Courage*. London: Cassell, 1967.

Bean, Lee L., Geraldine P. Mineau, and Douglas L. Anderton. *Fertility Change on the American Frontier: Adaptation and Innovation*. Berkeley: University of California Press, 1990.

Beck, Birgit. "Rape: The Military Trials of Sexual Crimes Committed by Soldiers of the Wehrmacht, 1939–1944." In *Home/Front: The Military, War and Gender in Twentieth-Century Germany*, edited by Karen Hagemann and Stefanie Schüler-Springorum, pp. 255–74. Oxford, New York: Berg, 2002.

———. *Wehrmacht und Sexuelle Gewalt: Sexualverbrechen vor Deutschen Militärgerichten, 1939–1945*. Paderborn: Schoningh, 2004.

Becker, Gary S. *A Treatise on the Family*. Cambridge: Harvard University Press, 1981.

Becker, Gary S., and Kevin M. Murphy. "Human Capital, Fertility, and Economic Growth." *Journal of Political Economy* 98, no. 5 (1990): S12–37.

Behling, Laura L. *The Masculine Woman in America, 1890–1935*. Urbana: University of Illinois Press, 2001.

Bennett, D. Scott, and Alan C. Stam. *The Behavioral Origins of War*. Ann Arbor: University of Michigan Press, 2004.

Besant, Walter. *The Revolt of Man*. London: Chatto & Windus, 1897.

Bissell, Tom. *The Father of All Things: A Marine, His Son and the Legacy of Vietnam*. New York: Pantheon, 2007.

Black, Jeremy. *Why Wars Happen*. London: Reaktion, 1998.

Blainey, Geoffery. *The Causes of War*. New York: Free Press, 1988.

Bloch, Kurt. "Urbanization of the Japanese People." *Far Eastern Survey* 10, no. 16 (August 25, 1941): 189–90.

Block, Josine. "Sexual Asymmetry: A Historiographical Essay." In *Sexual Asymmetry: Studies in Ancient Society*, edited by Josine Block and Peter Mason, pp. 1–58. Amsterdam: Gieben, 1987.

Bobbitt, Philip. *The Shield of Achilles: War, Peace, and the Course of History*. New York: Anchor, 2002.

Bouhdiba, Abdelhuhab. *Sexuality in Islam*. Translated by Alan Sheridan. London: Routledge & Kegan Paul, 1985.

Bourke, Joanna. *Dismembering the Male: Men's Bodies, Britain, and the Great War*. Chicago: University of Chicago Press, 1996.

———. *An Intimate History of Killing: Face-to-Face Killing in Twentieth-Century Warfare*. New York: Basic Books, 1999.

Bowman, Jannetta Ann, and Samuel H. Preston. "Two Centuries of Population Change in Central Japan: The Evidence from a Temple Death Register." *Population Studies* 45, no. 3 (November 1, 1991): 417–36.

Boyd, Cyrus F. *The Civil War Diary of Cyrus F. Boyd*. Edited by Mildred Throne. Baton Rouge: Louisiana State University Press, 1953.

Braudy, Leo. *From Chivalry to Terrorism: War and the Changing Nature of Masculinity*. New York: Knopf, 2003.

Braybon, Gail, and Penny Summerfield. *Out of the Cage: Women's Experiences in Two World Wars*. London: Pandora, 1987.

Breuer, William B. *War and American Women: Heroism, Deeds, and Controversy*. Westport, CT: Praeger, 1997.

Brittain, Melissa. "Benevolent Invaders, Heroic Victims and Depraved Villains: White Femininity in Media Coverage of the Invasion of Iraq." In *(En)Gendering the War on Terror: War Stories and Camouflaged Politics*, edited by Krista Hunt and Kim Rygiel, pp. 51–71. Burlington, VT: Ashgate, 2006.

Brittan, Arthur. *Masculinity and Power*. Oxford: Basil Blackwell, 1989.

Brooker, Paul. *The Faces of Fraternalism: Nazi Germany, Fascist Italy, and Imperial Japan*. Oxford: Clarendon Press, 1991.

Broyles, William, Jr. *Brothers in Arms: A Journey from War to Peace*. New York: Knopf, 1986.

Butz, William P., and Michael P. Ward. "The Emergence of Countercyclical U.S. Fertility." *American Economic Review* 69, no. 3 (June 1979): 318–28.

Buzzell, Colby. *My War: Killing Time in Iraq*. New York: G. P. Putnam's, 2005.

Call, R. A. Vaughn, and Jay D. Teachman. "Life-Course Timing and Sequencing of Marriage and Military Service and Their Effects on Marital Stability." *Journal of Marriage and the Family* 58, no. 1 (February 1996): 219–26.

Cameron, James. *1914*. New York: Rinehart, 1959.

Campbell, Anne. *Men, Women, and Aggression*. New York: Basic Books, 1991.

Campbell, Donald T., and Thelma H. McCormack. "Military Experience and Attitudes toward Authority." *American Journal of Sociology* 62, no. 5 (March 1957): 482–90.

Canetti, Elias. *Crowds and Power*. Translated by Carol Stewart. New York: Farrar, Straus & Giroux, 1984.

Caputo, Philip. *A Rumor of War*. New York: Holt, Rinehart and Winston, 1977.

Carlsson, Gosta. "The Decline of Fertility: Innovation or Adjustment Process." *Population Studies* 20, no. 2 (November 1966): 149–74.

Carreiras, Helena. *Gender and the Military: Women in the Armed Forces of Western Democracies*. London: Routledge, 2006.

Chagnon, Napoleon A. "Life Histories, Blood Revenge, and Warfare in a Tribal Population." *Science* 239, no. 4843 (February 26, 1988): 985–92.

Chang, Iris. "The Rape of Nanking." In *War's Dirty Secret: Rape, Prostitution, and Other Crimes*, edited by Anne Llewelyn Bartow, pp. 46–56. Cleveland: Pilgrim Press, 2000.

Childers, Thomas. *Wings of Morning: The Story of the Last American Bomber Shot Down Over Germany in World War II*. Reading, MA: Addison-Wesley, 2005.

Clinton, Catherine. *The Other Civil War: American Women in the Nineteenth Century*. New York: Hill & Wang, 1984.

Clinton, Catherine, and Nina Silber, eds. *Divided Houses: Gender and the Civil War*. New York: Oxford University Press, 1992.

Coale, J. Ansley. "Age Patterns of Marriage." *Population Studies* 25, no. 2 (July 1971): 193–214.

Cohen, Patricia. "Towers Fell, and Attitudes Were Rebuilt." *New York Times*, September 27, 2007.

Coleman, Penny. *Flashback: Posttraumatic Stress Disorder, Suicide, and the Lessons of War*. Boston: Beacon Press, 2006.

Connell, R. W. *Masculinities*. Berkeley: University of California Press, 1995.

Conover, Pamela J., and Virginia Sapiro. "Gender, Feminist Consciousness, and War." *American Journal of Political Science* 37, no. 4 (November 1993): 1079–99.

Cooke, Miriam, and Angela Woollacott, ed. *Gendering War Talk*. Princeton, NJ: Princeton University Press, 1993.

Cooper, Helen M., Adrienne Auslander Munich, and Susan Merrill Squier, eds. *Arms and the Woman: War, Gender, and Literary Representation*. Chapel Hill: University of North Carolina Press, 1989.

Copelon, Rhonda. "Surfacing Gender: Reconceptualizing Crimes against Women in Time of War." In *Woman and War Reader*, edited by Lois Ann Lorentzen and Jennifer Turpin, pp. 63–79. New York, London: New York University Press, 1998.

Corbett, Sara. "The Women's War." *New York Times Magazine*, March 18, 2007.

Courtwright, David T. *Violent Land: Single Men and Social Disorder from the Frontier to the Inner City.* Cambridge, MA: Harvard University Press, 1996.

Coyne, Kevin. *Marching Home: To War and Back with the Men of One American Town.* New York: Viking, 2003.

Cramer, James C. "Fertility and Female Employment: Problems of Causal Direction." *American Sociological Review* 45, no. 2 (April 1980): 167–90.

Crawford, John. *The Last True Story I'll Tell: An Accidental Soldier's Account of the War in Iraq.* New York: Riverhead, 2005.

Cronin, James E. *Industrial Conflict in Modern Britain.* London: Croom Helm, 1979.

Culleton, Claire A. *Working-Class Culture, Women, and Britain, 1914–1921.* New York: St. Martin's, 1999.

Damousi, Joy, and Marilyn Lake, eds. *Gender and War: Australians at War in the Twentieth Century.* New York: Cambridge University Press, 1995.

Darrow, Margaret H. *French Women and the First World War.* New York: Oxford University Press, 2000.

Davis, Kingsley. "Statistical Perspective on Marriage and Divorce." *Annals of the American Academy of Political and Social Science* 272 (November 1950): 9–21.

D'Emilio, John, and Estelle B. Freedman. *Intimate Matters: A History of Sexuality in America.* New York: Harper & Row, 1988.

Demos, John. *Past, Present, and Personal: The Family and the Life Course in American History.* New York: Oxford University Press, 1986.

Diamond, Stephen A. *Anger, Madness, and the Daimonic: The Psychological Genesis of Violence, Evil, and Creativity.* Albany: State University of New York Press, 1996.

Dollard, John, et al. *Frustration and Aggression.* New Haven, CT: Yale University Press, 1957.

Doms, Mark, and Ethan Lewis. "The Narrowing of the Male-Female Wage Gap." *FRBSF Economic Letter* 7, no. 17 (June 29, 2007): 1–3.

Dower, John W. *War without Mercy: Race and Power in the Pacific War.* New York: Pantheon, 1986.

Dubus, Andre III. *The Garden of Last Days.* New York: Norton, 2008.

Duellfer, Jost. *Nazi Germany, 1933–1945: Faith and Annihilation.* Translated by Dean Scott McMurry. London: Arundel, 1996.

Dugger, Celia. "Very Young Populations Contribute to Strife, Study Concludes." *New York Times*, April 4, 2007.

"Effect of War on Crime, Marriage, and Insanity." *Journal of Heredity* 9, no. 8 (1918): 365–67.

Ehrenreich, Barbara. *Blood Rites: Origins and History of the Passion of War*. New York: Holt, 1997.

Eighmey, John. "Why Do Youth Enlist? Identification of Underlying Themes." *Armed Forces and Society* 32, no. 2 (January 2006): 307–28.

Eisenstein, Zillah. *Hatreds: Racialized and Sexualized Conflicts in the 21st Century*. London, New York: Routledge, 1996.

———. *Sexual Decoys: Gender, Race and War in Imperial Democracy*. Melbourne: Spinifex Press, 2007.

Elder, Glen H., Jr., and Elizabeth C. Clipp. "Combat Experience and Emotional Health: Impairment and Resilience in Later Life." *Journal of Personality* 57, no. 2 (June 1989): 311–41.

Elkin, Henry. "Aggressiveness and Erotic Tendencies in Army Life." *American Journal of Sociology* 51, no. 5 (March 1946): 408–13.

Elshtain, Jean Bethke. *Women and War*. New York: Basic Books, 1987.

Elshtain, Jean Bethke, and Sheila Tobias, eds. *Women, Militarism, and War*. Savage, MD: Rowman & Littlefield, 1990.

Enloe, Cynthia. *Bananas, Beaches and Bases: Making Feminist Sense of International Politics*. Berkeley: University of California Press, 1990.

———. *Does Khaki Become You? The Militarization of Women's Lives*. London: Pluto Press, 1983.

———. *Maneuvers: The International Politics of Militarizing Women's Lives*. Berkeley: University of California Press, 2000.

———. *The Morning After: Sexual Politics at the End of the Cold War*. Berkeley: University of California Press, 1993.

Esposito, John. *Unholy War: Terror in the Name of Islam*. Oxford: Oxford University Press, 2002.

Evans, Richard J. *The Third Reich at War*. New York: Penguin, 2009.

Faludi, Susan. "America's Guardian Myths." *New York Times*, September 7, 2007.

———. *Backlash: The Undeclared War against American Women*. New York: Crown, 1992.Faust, Drew Gilpin. *This Republic of Suffering: Death and the American Civil War*. New York: Knopf, 2008.

———. *The Terror Dream: Fear and Fantasy in Post-9/11 America*. New York: Metropolitan, 2007.

Fausto-Sterling, Anne. *Myths of Gender: Biological Theories about Women and Men*. New York: Basic Books, 1992.

Fawaz, Gerges A. *Journey of the Jihadist: Inside Muslim Militancy*. Orlando: Harcourt, 2006.

Feeney, Griffin. "Fertility Rate in East Asia." *Science* 266 (December 2, 1994): 1518–23.

Ferrill, Arther. *The Origins of War: From the Stone Age to Alexander the Great.* Revised ed. Boulder, CO: Westview Press, 1997.

Fick, Nathaniel. *One Bullet Away: The Making of a Marine Officer.* Boston: Houghton Mifflin, 2005.

Fischer, Conan. *The Rise of the Nazis.* Manchester, UK: Manchester University Press, 1995.

Fisk, Robert. *The Great War for Civilization: The Conquest of the Middle East.* New York: Knopf, 2005.

Flynn, Robert. *A Personal War in Vietnam.* College Station: Texas A&M University Press, 1989.

Fornari, Franco. *The Psychoanalysis of War.* Translated by Alenka Pfeifer. Bloomington: Indiana University Press, 1975.

Foucault, Michel. *History of Sexuality*, vol. 1. New York: Pantheon, 1985.

Fraczek, Adam, and Horst Zumkley, eds. *Socialization and Aggression.* New York: Springer, 1992.

Frank, Paul Frederick. "Hysterical Men: War, Neurosis, and German Mental Health, 1914–1921." PhD dissertation, Department of History, Columbia University, 1996.

Frasier, Antonia. *Warrior Queens.* New York: Knopf, 1989.

Freud, Sigmund. *Civilisation, War, and Death.* Edited by John Rickman. Toronto: Hogarth Press and Institute of Psycho-Analysis, 1953.

Friedrich, Otto. *Before the Deluge: A Portrait of Berlin in the 1920s.* New York: Harper & Row, 1972.

Fromm, Erich. *The Anatomy of Human Destructiveness.* New York: Fawcett, 1973.

Frühstück, Sabine. *Colonizing Sex: Sexology and Social Control in Modern Japan.* Berkeley: University of California Press, 2003.

Funck, Marcus. "Ready for War? Concepts of Military Manliness in the Prusso-German Officer Corps before the First World War." In *Home/Front: The Military, War and Gender in Twentieth-Century Germany*, edited by Karen Hagemann and Stefanie Schüler-Springorum, pp. 43–67. Oxford: Berg, 2002.

Gabriel, Richard A. *No More Heroes: Madness and Psychiatry in War.* New York: Hill & Wang, 1987.

Gardiner, Marilyn. "Was It Easier Being a Mom in 1908?" *Christian Science Monitor*, May 8, 2008.

Gay, Peter. *Weimar Culture: The Outsider as Insider.* New York: Harper & Row, 1968.

Geen, Russell G. *Human Aggression.* Philadelphia: Open University Press, 2001.

The German Army and Genocide: Crimes against War Prisoners, Jews, and Other

Civilians, 1939–1944. Edited and translated by Hamburg Institute for Social Research. New York: Free Press, 1999.

Gerzon, Mark. *A Choice of Heroes: The Changing Faces of American Manhood.* Boston: Houghton Mifflin, 1982.

Ghiglieri, Michael P. *The Dark Side of Man: Tracing the Origins of Male Violence.* Reading, MA: Perseus Books, 1999.

Gilder, George F. *Naked Nomads: Unmarried Men in America.* New York: Quadrangle, 1974.

Gimbel, Cynthia, and Alan Booth. "Why Does Military Combat Experience Adversely Affect Marital Relations?" *Journal of Marriage and the Family* 56 (August 1994): 691–703.

Girard, Rene. *Violence and the Sacred.* Translated by Patrick Gregory. Baltimore: Johns Hopkins University Press, 1977.

Gittins, Diana. *Fair Sex: Family Size and Structure, 1900–1939.* London: Hutchinson, 1982.

Givens, Dale, and Martin A. Nettleship, eds. *Discussions on War and Human Aggression.* The Hague: Mouton, 1976.

Glatthaar, Joseph T. *General Lee's Army: From Victory to Collapse.* New York: Free Press, 2008.

Goldstein, Joshua S. *War and Gender: How Gender Shapes the War System and Vice Versa.* New York: Cambridge University Press, 2001.

Goodall, Felicity. *Voices from the Home Front.* Newton Abbot, UK: David & Charles, 2004.

Goode, William J. *After Divorce.* Glencoe, IL: Free Press, 1956.

Grass, Günter. "How I Spent the War." *New Yorker.* June 4, 2007.

Gray, J. Glenn. *Warriors: Reflections on Men in Battle.* New York: Harcourt Brace, 1959.

Greenberg, Gary A., Robert A. Rosenbeck, and Rani A. Desai. "Risk of Incarceration among Male Veterans and Nonveterans." *Armed Forces and Society* 33, no. 3 (April 2007): 337–50.

Greenwald, Maurine Weiner. *Women, War, and Work: The Impact of World War One on Women Workers in the United States.* Westport, CT: Greenwood, 1980.

Grew, Joseph G. *Ten Years in Japan: A Contemporary Record Drawn from the Diaries and Private and Official Papers of Joseph G. Grew, U.S. Ambassador to Japan.* New York: Simon & Schuster, 1944.

Grinker, Roy R., and John P. Spiegel. *Men under Stress.* Philadelphia: Blakiston, 1945.

Grossman, Attina. *Jews, Germans, and Allies: Close Encounters in Occupied Germany.* Princeton, NJ: Princeton University Press, 2007.

————. *Reforming Sex: The German Movement for Birth Control and Abortion Reform, 1920–1950.* New York: Oxford University Press, 1995.

Grossman, Dave. *On Killing: The Psychological Cost of Learning to Kill in War and Society.* Boston: Back Bay, 1996.

Hacker, J. David. "The Human Cost of War: White Population in the United States, 1850–1880." *Journal of Economic History* 61, no. 2 (June 2001): 486–89.

————. "Rethinking the 'Early' Decline of Marital Fertility in the United States." *Demography* 40, no. 4 (November 2003): 605–20.

Haines, Michael R. "Long-Term Marriage Patterns in the United States from Colonial Times to the Present." *History of the Family* 1, no. 1 (1996): 15–39.

Hajnal, John. "The Analysis of Birth Statistics in Light of the Recent International Recovery of the Birth-Rate." *Population Studies* 1, no. 2 (September 1947): 137–64.

Hall, Gwendolyn Midlo, ed. *Love, War, and the 96th Engineers (Colored): The World War II New Guinea Diaries of Captain Hyman Samuelson.* Urbana: University of Illinois Press, 1995.

Hall, Mitchell K. *Crossroads: American Popular Culture and the Vietnam Generation.* Lanham, MD: Rowan & Littlefield, 2005.

Halsey, A. H., ed. *Twentieth-Century British Social Trends.* New York: St. Martin's, 2000.

Hane, Mikiso, ed. *Reflections on the Way to the Gallows: Rebel Women in Prewar Japan.* Berkeley: University of California Press, 1988.

Havens, Thomas R. H. "Women and War in Japan, 1937–1945." *American Historical Review* 80, no. 4 (October 1975): 913–34.

Hedges, Chris. *War Is a Force That Gives Us Meaning.* New York: Public Affairs, 2002.

Herr, Michael. *Dispatches.* London: Picador, 1978.

Herzog, Dagmar. *Sex after Fascism: Memory and Morality in Twentieth-Century Germany.* Princeton, NJ: Princeton University Press, 2005.

Hess, Earl J. *The Union Soldier in Battle: Enduring the Ordeal of Combat.* Lawrence: University Press of Kansas, 1997.

Hetzel, A. M., and M. Cappetta. "Teenagers: Marriages, Divorces, Parenthood, and Mortality." *Vital Health Statistics* 21, no. 23 (August 1973): 1–42.

Heyder, D. W., and H. S. Wambach. "Sexuality and Affect in Frogmen." *Archives of General Psychiatry* 11 (September 1964): 286–89.

Higonnet, Margaret R., ed. *Behind the Lines: Gender and the Two World War.* New Haven, CT: Yale University Press, 1987.

Hillman, James. *A Terrible Love of War.* New York: Penguin, 2004.

Hirschfeld, Magnus. *The Sexual History of the World War.* New York: Panurge, 1934.

Hoffer, Eric. *The True Believer*. New York: Time, 1963.

Hoffert, Sylvia D. *When Hens Crow: The Woman's Rights Movement in Antebellum America*. Bloomington: Indiana University Press, 1995.

Holloway, Gerry. *Women and Work in Britain since 1840*. London: Routledge, 2005.

Holloway, Ralph L., Jr. "Human Aggression: The Need for a Species-Specific Framework." In *War: The Anthology of Armed Conflict and Aggression*, edited by Marvin Harris and Robert Murphy Morton Fried, pp. 29–48. Garden City, NY: Natural History Press (1968).

Hopper, Helen M. "'Motherhood in the Interest of the State': Baroness Ishimoto (Kato) Shiazue Confronts Expansionist Policies against Birth Control, 1930–1940." In *Japanese Women: Emerging from Subservience, 1868–1945*, edited by Hiroko Tomida and Gordon Daniels, pp. 40–56. Folkestone, Kent: Global Oriental, 2005.

Howard, Michael. *The Causes of Wars and Other Essays*. Cambridge, MA: Harvard University Press, 1984.

Hoyt, Edwin P. *Japan's War: The Great Pacific Conflict, 1853–1952*. New York: McGraw-Hill, 1986.

Hudson, Valerie M., and Andrea M. den Boer. *Bare Branches: Security Implications of Asia's Surplus Male Population*. Cambridge, MA: MIT Press, 2004.

Huesmann, L. Rowell, ed. *Aggressive Behavior: Current Perspectives*. New York: Plenum, 1994.

Hunt, Krista. "'Embedded Feminism' and the War on Terror." In *(En)Gendering the War on Terror: War Stories and Camouflaged Politics*, edited by Krista Hunt and Kim Rygiel, pp. 51–71. Burlington, VT: Ashgate, 2006.

Hunt, Krista, and Kim Rygiel. "(En)Gendered War Stories and Camouflaged Politics." In *(En)Gendering the War on Terror: War Stories and Camouflaged Politics*, edited by Krista Hunt and Kim Rygiel, pp. 1–24. Burlington, VT: Ashgate, 2006.

Hunt, William Ben. *Getting to War: Predicting International Conflict with Mass Media Indicators*. Ann Arbor: University of Michigan Press, 1997.

Hunter, Anne E., ed. *On Peace, War and Gender: A Challenge to Genetic Explanations*. New York: Feminist Press, 1991.

Huss, Marie-Monique. "Pronatalism in the Inter-War Period in France." *Journal of Contemporary History* 25, no. 1 (January 1990): 39–68.

Huston, Nancy. "Tales of War and Tears of Women." *Women's Studies International Forum* 5, nos. 3–4 (1982): 270–75.

Hynes, Samuel. *Flights of Passage: Reflections of a World War II Aviator*. New York: Beil, 1988.

Imaizumi, Yoko, Masatoshi Nei, and Toshiyuki Furusho. "Variability and Heritability of Human Fertility." *Annals of Human Genetics* 33, no. 3 (1970): 251–59.

James, William. *The Moral Equivalent of War and Other Essays*. New York: Harper & Row, 1971.

Janowitz, Morris. *The Professional Soldier: A Social and Political Portrait*. New York: Free Press, 1960.

Johnson, Allen W., and Timothy Earle. *The Evolution of Human Societies: From Foraging Group to Agrarian State*. Stanford, CA: Stanford University Press, 1987.

Johnson, Dominic D. P. *Overconfidence and War: The Havoc and Glory of Positive Illusions*. Cambridge, MA: Harvard University Press, 2004.

Johnson, Russell L. "'Volunteer While You May!': Manpower Mobilization in Dubuque, Iowa." In *Union Soldiers and the Northern Home Front: Wartime Experiences and Postwar Adjustments*, edited by Paul A. Cimbala and Randall M. Miller, pp. 30–68. New York: Fordham University Press, 2002.

Joseph, Ammu, and Kalpana Sharma, ed. *Terror, Counter-Terror: Women Speak Out*. London: Zed Books, 2003.

Joshi, Heather, and P. R. Andrew Hinde. "Employment after Childbearing in Post-War Britain: Cohort-Study Evidence on Contrasts Within and Across Generations." *European Sociological Review* 9 (1993): 203–27.

Kaelble, Helmut. "Eras of Social Mobility in 19th and 20th Century Europe." *Journal of Social History* 17, no. 3 (Spring 1984): 489–504.

Kagan, Donald. *On the Origins of War and the Preservation of Peace*. New York: Anchor, 1996.

Kantner, John F., and Melvin Zelnik. "Sexual Experience of Young Unmarried Women in the United States." *Family Planning Perspectives* 4, no. 4 (October 1972): 9–18.

Katz, Jesse. "The Recruit." *LA Magazine* 50 (March 2005): 3–98.

Keegan, John. *A History of Warfare*. New York: Vintage, 1993.

Keegan, John, and Richard Holmes. *Soldiers: A History of Men in Battle*. London: Hamilton, 1985.

Kent, Susan Kingsley. "The Politics of Sexual Difference: World War I and the Demise of British Feminism." *Journal of British Studies* 27, no. 3 (July 1988): 232–53.

Key, Joshua. *The Deserter's Tale: The Story of an Ordinary Soldier Who Walked Away from the War in Iraq*. New York: Atlantic Monthly Press, 2007.

Kidder, Tracy. *My Detachment: A Memoir*. New York: Random House, 2005.

Kienitz, Sabine. "Body Damage: War Disability and Construction of Masculinity in Weimar Germany." In *Home/Front: The Military, War and Gender in Twentieth-Century Germany*, edited by Karen Hagemann and Stefanie Schüler-Springorum, pp. 181–204. Oxford: Berg, 2002.

Kirk, Gwyn, and Margo Okazawa-Rey. *Women's Lives: Multicultural Perspectives.* 2nd ed. New York: McGraw-Hill, 2001.

Klima, John (pseud.). *Aggression: The Myth of the Beast Within.* New York: Wiley, 1988.

Knodel, John E. *The Decline of Fertility in Germany, 1871–1939.* Princeton, NJ: Princeton University Press, 1974.

Kobrin, Frances E. "The Fall of Household Size and the Rise of the Primary Individual in the United States." *Demography* 13, no. 1 (February 1976): 127–38.

Komarovsky, Mirra. *Dilemmas of Masculinity: A Study of College Youth*, 2nd ed. Walnut Creek, CA: AltaMira, 2004.

Kovic, Ron. *Born on the Fourth of July.* New York: Pocket Books, 1977.

Kroeber, Clifton B., and Bernard L. Fontana. *Massacre in the Gila: An Account of the Last Major Battle between American Indians.* Tuscon: University of Arizona Press, 1986.

Kuehne, Thomas. "Comradeship: Gender Confusion and Gender Order in the Germany Military, 1918–1945." In *Home/Front: The Military, War and Gender in Twentieth-Century Germany*, edited by Karen Hagemann and Stefanie Schüler-Springorum, pp. 233–54. Oxford, New York: Berg, 2002.

Kuhlman, Erika A. *Petticoats and White Feathers: Gender Conformity, Race, the Progressive Peace Movement, and the Debate over War, 1895–1919.* Westport, CT: Greenwood, 1997.

Kuhn, David Paul. *The Neglected Voter: White Men and the Democratic Dilemma.* New York: Palgrave Macmillan, 2007.

Kundrus, Birthe. "Gender Wars: The First World War and the Construction of Gender Relations in the Weimar Republic." In *Home/Front: The Military, War and Gender in Twentieth-Century Germany*, edited by Karen Hagemann and Stefanie Schüler-Springorum, pp. 159–80. Oxford, New York: Berg, 2002.

Laufer, Robert S., and M. S. Gallops. "Life-Course Effects of Vietnam Combat and Abusive Violence: Marital Patterns." *Journal of Marriage and the Family* 47, no. 4 (November 1985): 839–53.

Lee, Stephen J. *The Weimar Republic.* London: Routledge, 1998.

LeShan, Lawrence. *The Psychology of War: Comprehending Its Mystique and Its Madness.* Chicago: Noble, 1992.

Levy, Frank, and Richard J. Murname. "U.S. Earnings Levels and Earnings Inequality: A Review of Recent Trends and Proposed Explanations." *Journal of Economic Literature* 30 (September 1992): 1333–81.

Liddle, Joanna, and Sachiko Nakajima. *Rising Suns, Rising Daughters: Gender, Class and Power in Japan*, Bangkok: White Lotus, 2000.

Lilly, J. Robert. *Taken by Force: Rape and American GIs during World War II.* New York: Palgrave Macmillan, 2007.

Lingle, R. Christopher, and Ethel B. Jones. "Women's Increasing Unemployment: A Cross-Sectional Analysis." *American Economic Review; Proceedings of the Ninetieth Annual Meeting of the American Economic Association* 68, no. 2 (May 1978): 84–89.

Livingstone, Frank B. "The Effects of Warfare on the Biology of the Human Species." In *War: The Anthology of Armed Conflict and Aggression*, edited by Marvin Harris and Robert Murphy Morton Fried, pp. 3–15. Garden City, NY: Natural History Press, 1968.

Longman, Philip. *The Empty Cradle: How Falling Birth Rates Threaten World Prosperity and What to Do about It*. New York: Basic Books, 2004.

Lunden, Walter A. "War and Juvenile Delinquency in England and Wales, 1910 to 1943." *American Sociological Review* 10, no. 3 (June 1945): 390–93.

Lyons, Paul. *Class of '66: Living in Suburban Middle America*. Philadelphia: Temple University Press, 1994.

Maass, Peter. *Love Thy Neighbor: A Story of War*. New York: Knopf, 1996.

MacDonald, Lyn. *1914*. London: Michael Joseph, 1987.

———. *1914–1918: Voices and Images of the Great War*. London: Michael Joseph, 1988.

———. *1915: The Death of Innocence*. London: Headline, 1993.

Mack, Raymond. *Transforming America: Patterns of Social Change*. New York: Random House, 1967.

Mackie, Sarah. *Feminism in Modern Japan: Citizenship, Embodiment, and Sexuality*. Cambridge: Cambridge University Press, 2003.

Marks, Patricia. *Bicycles, Bangs, and Bloomers: The New Woman in the Popular Press*. Lexington: University Press of Kentucky, 1990.

Marran, Christine L. *Poison Woman: Figuring Female Transgression in Modern Japanese Culture*. Minneapolis: University of Minnesota Press, 2007.

Marty, Martin A. *Daily Life in the United States, 1960–1990: Decades of Discord*. Westport, CT: Greenwood Press, 1997.

Mason, Bobbi Ann. *In Country*. New York: Perennial, 1985.

Massad, Joseph A. *Desiring Arabs*. Chicago: University of Chicago Press, 2007.

Mass Rape: The War against Women in Bosnia-Herzogovina. Edited by Alexandra Stiglmayer. Translated by Marian Faber. Lincoln: University of Nebraska Press, 1994.

Mayer, Albert J., and Thomas Ford Hoult. "Social Stratification and Combat Survival." *Journal of Social Forces* 34, no. 2 (December 1955): 155–59.

McManus, John C. *The Deadly Brotherhood: The American Combat Soldier in World War II*. Novato, CA: Presidio Press, 1998.

McPherson, James M. *Battle Cry of Freedom: The Civil War Era*. New York: Oxford University Press, 2003.

———. *For Cause and Comrades: Why Men Fought in the Civil War*. New York: Oxford University Press, 1997.

Merridale, Catherine. *Ivan's War: Life and Death in the Red Army, 1939–1945*. New York: Metropolitan, 2006.

Milton-Edwards, Beverley. *Islam and Violence in the Modern Era*. New York: Palgrave Macmillan, 2006.

Mitchell, Richard H. *Thought Control in Prewar Japan*. Ithaca, NY: Cornell University Press, 1976.

Mitchinson, Wendy. *Giving Birth in Canada, 1900–1950*. Toronto: University of Toronto Press, 2002.

Modell, John, and Duane Steffey. "Waging War and Marriage: Military Service and Family Formation, 1940–1955." *Journal of Family History* 3, no. 1 (1988): 195–218.

Moghaddam, Fathali M. *From the Terrorists' Point of View: What They Experience and Why They Come to Destroy*. Westport, CT: Praeger, 2006.

Moller, Herbert. "Youth as a Force in the Modern World." *Comparative Studies in Society and History* 10, no. 3 (April 1968): 237–60.

Moon, Katherine H. S. *Sex among Allies: Military Prostitution in U.S.-South Korea Relations*. New York: Columbia University Press, 1997.

Moore, John Norton. *Solving the War Puzzle: Beyond the Democratic Peace*. Durham, NC: Carolina Academic Press, 2004.

Morgan, Carol E. *Women Workers and Gender Identities, 1835–1913: The Cotton and Metal Industries in England*. London, New York: Routledge, 2001.

Morgan, Robin. *The Demon Lover: On the Sexuality of Terrorism*. New York, London: Norton, 1989.

Morris, Madeleine. "In War and Peace: Rape, War, and Military Culture." In *War's Dirty Secret: Rape, Prostitution, and Other Crimes*, edited by Anne Llewelyn Bartow, pp. 167–203. Cleveland: Pilgrim Press, 2000.

Moskos, Charles C. *The American Enlisted Man: The Rank and File in Today's Military*. New York: Sage Foundation, 1970.

Moss, Mark. *Manliness and Militarism: Educating Young Boys in Ontario for War*. Oxford: Oxford University Press, 2001.

Mosse, George L. *Fallen Soldiers: Reshaping the Memory of the World Wars*. New York: Oxford University Press, 1991.

———. "Masculinity and the Decadence." In *Sexual Knowledge, Sexual Science: The History of Attitudes to Sexuality*, edited by Roy Porter and Mikulas Teich, pp. 251–66. Cambridge: Cambridge University Press, 1994.

———. *Nationalism and Sexuality: Respectability and Abnormal Sexuality in Modern Europe*. New York: Howard Fertig, 1985.

Nadelson, Theodore. *Trained to Kill: Soldiers at War*. Baltimore: Johns Hopkins University Press, 2005.

National Commission on Terrorist Attacks upon the United States. *The 9/11 Commission Report: Final Report of the National Commission on Terrorist Attacks upon the United States*. Washington, DC: Government Printing Office, 2004.

Nelson, Craig. *The First Heroes: The Extraordinary Story of the Doolittle Raid—America's First World War II Victory*. New York: Viking, 2002.

Nisbett, Richard E., and Dov Cohen. *Culture of Honor: The Psychiatry of Violence in the South*. Boulder, CO: Westview Press, 1996.

O'Connell, Robert L. *Ride of the Second Horseman: The Birth and Death of War*. New York: Oxford University Press, 1997.

O'Neill, William L. *A Democracy at War: America's Fight at Home and Abroad in World War I*. New York: Free Press, 1993.

Oppenheimer, Valerie Kincade. "Demographic Influence on Female Employment and the Status of Women." *American Journal of Sociology* 78, no. 4 (January 1973): 946–61.

Oren, Michael B. *Power, Faith, and Fantasy: America in the Middle East, 1776 to the Present*. New York: Norton, 2007.

Organski, A. F. K., and Jacek Kugler. *The War Ledger*. Chicago: University of Chicago Press, 1981.

Paddock, Troy R. E., ed. *Call to Arms: Propaganda, Public Opinion and Newspapers in the Great War*. Westport, CT: Praeger, 2004.

Paisley, Melvyn. *Ace! Autobiography of a Fighter Pilot, World War II*. Boston: Branden, 1992.

Palmer, Monte, and Princess Palmer. *At the Heart of Terror: Islam, Jihadists, and America's War on Terrorism*. London: Rowman & Littlefield, 2004.

Palmer, Robert K. *Army Ground Forces: The Procurement and Training of Ground Combat Troops*. Washington, DC: Department of the Army, 1948.

Patai, Raphael. *The Arab Mind*. New York: Scribner's, 1973.

Pavalko, Eliza K., and Glen H. Elder Jr. "World War II and Divorce: A Life-Course Perspective." *American Journal of Sociology* 95, no. 5 (March 1990): 1213–34.

Pedersen, Loren E. *Dark Hearts: The Unconscious Forces That Shape Men's Lives*. Boston: Shambhala, 1991.

Pedersen, Susan. "Gender, Welfare, and Citizenship in Britain during the Great War." *American Historical Review* 95, no. 4 (October 1990): 983–1006.

Philpott, Tom. "Interest in Military Service Wanes." *U.S. Naval Institute: Proceedings* 123, no. 9 (September 1997): 122.

Polachek, Solomon W., and John Robst. "Trends in the Male-Female Wage Gap: The 1980s Compared with the 1970s." *Southern Economic Review* 67, no. 4 (April 2001): 869–88.

Preston, Samuel H., and John McDonald. "The Incidence of Divorce within Cohorts of American Marriages Contracted since the Civil War." *Demography* 16, no. 1 (February 1979): 1–25.

Reardon, Carol. "'We Are All in This War': The 148th Pennsylvania and Home Front Dissension in Centre County during the Civil War." In *Union Soldiers and the Northern Home Front: Wartime Experiences and Postwar Adjustments*, edited by Paul A. Cimbala and Randall M. Miller, pp. 3–29. New York: Fordham University Press, 2002.

Reuter, Christopher. *My Life Is a Weapon: A Modern History of Suicide Bombing.* Translated by Helena Rags-Kirkby. Princeton, NJ: Princeton University Press, 2002.

Richardson, F. M. *Fighting Spirit: A Study of Psychological Factors in War.* New York: Crane, Russak, 1978.

Ricks, Thomas E. *Making the Corps.* New York: Touchstone, 1997.

Rieber, Robert W., ed. *The Psychology of War and Peace: The Image of the Enemy.* New York: Plenum, 1991.

Robb, George. *British Culture and the First World War.* London: Palgrave, 2002.

Robben, Antonius C. G. M. "Combat Motivation, Fear and Terror in Twentieth-Century Argentinian Warfare." *Journal of Contemporary History* 41, no. 2 (April 2006): 357–77.

Rodgers, Willard L., and Arland Thornton. "Changing Patterns in First Marriages in the United States." *Demography* 22, no. 2 (May 1985): 265–79.

Rotundo, E. Anthony. *American Manhood: Transformations in Masculinity from the Revolution to the Modern Era.* New York: Basic Books, 1993.

Rupp, Leila J. "I Don't Call That 'Volksgemeinschaft': Women, Class, and War in Nazi Germany." In *Women, War, and Revolution*, edited by Carol R. Berkin and Clara M. Lovett, pp. 37–54. New York: Holmes & Meier, 1980.

———. "Solidarity and Wartime Violence against Women." In *The Woman and War Reader*, edited by Lois Ann Lorentzen and Jennifer Turpin, pp. 303–307. New York: New York University Press, 1998.

Sack, John. *Lieutenant Calley: His Own Words.* New York: Viking, 1971.

Sanders, Helke, and Barbara Johr, ed. *Befreier und Befreite: Krieg, Vergewaltigungen, Kinder.* München: Kunstmann, 1992.

Sanderson, Warren C. "Quantitative Aspects of Marriage, Fertility and Family Limitation in Nineteenth-Century America: Another Application of the Coale Specifications." *Demography* 16, no. 3 (August 1979): 339–58.

Sato, Barbara Hamill. *The New Japanese Woman: Maternity, Media, and Women in Interwar Japan*. Durham, NC: Duke University Press, 2003.

Scanzoni, John. *Sexual Bargaining: Power Politics in the American Marriage*. 2nd ed. Chicago: University of Chicago Press, 1982.

Schmookler, Andrew Bard. *Out of Weakness: Healing the Wounds That Drive Us to War*. New York: Bantam Books, 1988.

Seibert, M. Therese, Mark A. Fossett, and Dawn M. Baunach. "Trends in Male-Female Status Inequality, 1940–1990." *Social Science Research* 26 (1997): 1–24.

Shay, Jonathan. *Achilles in Vietnam: Combat Trauma and the Undoing of Character*. New York: Atheneum, 1994.

Sheehan, James J. *Where Have All the Soldiers Gone? The Transformation of Modern Europe*. Boston: Houghton Mifflin, 2008.

Sherman, Nancy. *Stoic Warriors: The Ancient Philosophy behind the Military Mind*. Oxford: Oxford University Press, 2005.

Shils, Edward A., and Morris Janowitz. "Cohesion and Disintegration in the *Wehrmacht* in World War II." *Public Opinion Quarterly* 12 (Summer 1948): 280–315.

Silbey, David. *The British Working Class and Enthusiasm for the War, 1914–1916*. London: Cass, 2005.

Skaine, Rosemary. *Women at War: Gender Issues of Modern Women in Combat*. Jefferson, NC: McFarland, 1999.

Sklar, June, and Beth Berkov. "Teenage Family Formation in Postwar America." *Family Planning Perspectives* 6, no. 2 (Spring 1974): 80–90.

Smith, Howard L., ed. *British Feminism in the Twentieth Century*. Amherst: University of Massachusetts Press, 1990.

Snell, Mark A. "'If They Would Know What I Knew It Would Be Pretty Hard to Raise One Company in York': Recruiting, the Draft, and Society's Response in York County, Pennsylvania, 1861–1865." In *Union Soldiers and the Northern Home Front: Wartime Experiences and Postwar Adjustments*, edited by Paul A. Cimbala and Randall M. Miller, pp. 69–115. New York: Fordham University Press, 2002.

Soeters, Joseph, Cristina-Rodica Poponette, and Joseph T. Page. "Culture's Consequences in the Military." In *Military Life: The Psychology of Serving in Peacetime and Combat*, edited by Amy B. Adler, Carl Andrew Castro, and Thomas W. Britt, pp. 13–34. Westport, CT: Greenwood, 2006.

Soloway, Richard A. *Birth Control and the Population Question in England, 1877–1930*. Chapel Hill: University of North Carolina Press, 1982.

South, Scott J. "Economic Conditions and the Divorce Rate: A Times-Series Analysis of the Postwar United States." *Journal of Marriage and the Family* 47, no. 1 (February 1985): 31–41.

South, Scott J., and Kim M. Lloyd. "Marriage Markets and Non-Marital Fertility." *Demography* 29, no. 2 (May 1992): 247–64.

Stafford, David. *Ten Days to D-Day: Citizens and Soldiers on the Eve of the Invasion.* Boston: Little, Brown, 2003.

Stevens, Anthony. *The Roots of War and Terror.* London: Continuum, 2004.

Stevenson, Betsey, and Justin Wolfers. "Marriage and Divorce: Changes and Their Driving Forces." *Journal of Economic Perspectives* 21, no. 2 (Spring 2007): 27–52.

Stiehm, Judith Hicks. "The Protected, the Protector, the Defender." *Women's Studies International Forum* 5, no. 3/4 (1982): 367–76.

Stillman, Edmund, and William Pfaff. *The Politics of Hysteria: The Sources of Twentieth-Century Conflict.* New York: Harper & Row, 1964.

Stoddard, Lothrop. *The Rising Tide of Color against White World-Supremacy.* Honolulu: University Press of the Pacific, 2003.

Stoessinger, John G. *Why Nations Go to War.* 5th ed. New York: St. Martin's Press, 1990.

Stouffer, Samuel A., et al. *The American Soldier: Adjustment to Army Life.* Princeton, NJ: Princeton University Press, 1949.

Strachey, Alix. *The Unconscious Motives of War: A Psycho-Analytical Contribution.* London: Allen & Unwin, 1953.

Stromberg, Roland N. *Redemption by War: The Intellectuals and 1914.* Lawrence: Regents Press of Kansas, 1982.

Summerfield, Penny. *Women Workers in the Second World War: Production and Patriarchy in Conflict.* London: Routledge, 1984.

Surkis, Judith. *Sexing the Citizen: Morality and Masculinity in France, 1870–1920.* Ithaca, NY: Cornell University Press, 2006.

Szreter, Simon. *Fertility, Class and Gender in Britain, 1860–1940.* Cambridge: Cambridge University Press, 1995.

Taeuber, Irene B. "Demographic Research in Japan." *Pacific Affairs* 22, no. 4 (December 1949): 392–97.

———. *The Population of Japan.* Princeton, NJ: Princeton University Press, 1958.

Teitelbaum, Michael S. *The British Fertility Decline: Demographic Transition in the Crucible of the Industrial Revolution.* Princeton, NJ: Princeton University Press, 1984.

Teitelbaum, Michael S., and Jay M. Winter, *The Fear of Population Decline,* Orlando: Academic Press 1985.

Therborn, Göran. *Between Sex and Power: Family in the World, 1900–2000.* London: Routledge, 2004.

Theweleit, Klaus. *Male Fantasies*. 2 vols. Translated by Stephen Conway. Minneapolis: University of Minnesota Press, 1987–1989.

Thieme, Frederick P. "The Biological Consequences of War." In *War: The Anthology of Armed Conflict and Aggression*, edited by Marvin Harris, Robert Murphy, and Morton Fried, pp. 16–21. Garden City, NY: Natural History Press, 1968.

Thompson, Warren S. "The Demographic Revolution in the United States." *Annals of the American Academy of Political and Social Science* 262 (March 1949): 62–69.

Tiger, Lionel. *The Decline of Males*. New York: Golden Books, 1999.

———. *Men in Groups*. New York: Random House, 1969.

Tiger, Lionel, and Robin Fox. *The Imperial Animal*. New York: Holt, Rinehart & Winston, 1971.

Tolman, Edward C. *Drives toward War*. New York: Appleton, 1942.

Usborne, Cornelie. *The Politics of the Body in Weimar Germany: Women's Reproductive Rights and Duties*. Houndmills, UK: Macmillan, 1992.

Van Crefeld, Martin. *Men, Women and War*. London: Cassell, 2001.

Van Evera, Stephen. *Causes of War: Power and the Roots of Conflict*. Ithaca, NY: Cornell University Press, 1998.

Vasquez, John A. *The War Puzzle*. Cambridge: Cambridge University Press, 1993.

Vickers, Jeanne. *Women and War*. London: Zed Books, 1993.

Vinvovskis, Maris A. "'Have Social Historians Lost the Civil War?' Some Preliminary Demographic Speculations." *Journal of American History* 76, no. 1 (June 1989): 34–58.

Wattenberg, Ben J. *The Birth Dearth*. New York: Ballantine, 1987.

Weinstein, Laurie, and Christie C. White, eds. *Wives and Warriors: Women and the Military in the United States and Canada*. Westport, CT: Bergin & Garvey, 1997.

Wells, Lloyd M. *From Anzio to the Alps: An American Soldier's Story*. Columbia: University of Missouri Press, 2004.

Wessely, Simon. "Twentieth-Century Theories on Combat Motivation and Breakdown." *Journal of Contemporary History* 41, no. 2 (April 2006): 268–86.

Westhof, Charles F. "Differential Fertility in the United States: 1900 to 1952." *American Sociological Review* 19, no. 5 (October 1954): 549–61.

Whites, Lee Ann. *The Civil War as a Crisis in Gender: Augusta, Georgia, 1860–1890*. Athens: University of Georgia Press, 1995.

Wicks, Stephen. *Warriors and Wild Men: Men, Masculinity and Gender*. Westport, CT: Bergin & Garvey, 1996.

Wilkie, Jane Riblett. "The Decline of Men's Labor Force Participation and Income and the Changing Structure of Family Economic Support." *Journal of Marriage and the Family* 53 (February 1991): 111–22.

Williams, Kayla. *Love My Rifle More Than You.* New York: Norton, 2005.

Willmott, H. D. *Empires in the Balance: Japanese and Allied Pacific Strategies to April 1942.* Annapolis, MD: Naval Institute Press, 1982.

Winter, J. M. "The Demographic Consequences of the War." In *War and Social Change: British Society in the Second World War,* edited by Harold L. Smith, pp. 151–78. Manchester, UK: Manchester University Press, 1986.

———. *The Great War and the British People.* London: Macmillan, 1986.

Winters, Richard D. *Beyond Band of Brothers: The War Memoirs of Major Dick Winters.* New York: Caliber, 2006.

Wong, Leonard. "Combat Motivation in Today's Soldiers: U.S. Army War College Strategic Studies." *Armed Forces and Society* 32, no. 4 (July 1, 2006): 659–63.

Wong, Leonard, et al. "Why They Fight: Combat Motivation in the Iraq War." Strategic Studies Institute of the U.S. Army War College (July 1, 2003), http://www.bits.de/public/documents/iraq/3-seite/Wong_0703.pdf (accessed October 8, 2009).

Woodruff, Todd, Ryan Kelty, and David R. Segal. "Propensity to Serve and Motivation to Enlist among American Combat Soldiers." *Armed Forces and Society* 32, no. 3 (April 2006): 353–66.

Wrangham, Richard, and Dale Peterson. *Demonic Males: Apes and the Origins of Human Violence.* Boston: Houghton Mifflin, 1996.

Wright, Evan. *Generation Kill: Devil Dogs, Iceman, Captain America and the New Face of American War.* New York: Putnam, 2004.

Wright, Lawrence. *The Looming Tower: Al Qaeda and the Road to 9/11.* New York: Knopf, 2006.

Wright, Robert E. "The Easterlin Hypothesis and European Fertility Rates." *Population and Development Review* 15, no. 1 (March 1989): 107–22.

Zanotti, Barbara. "Patriarchy: A State of War." In *Reweaving the Web of Life: Feminism and Non-Violence,* edited by Pam McAllister, pp. 16–19. Philadelphia: New Society, 1982.

Zelnik, Marvin, and John F. Kantner. "First Pregnancies to Women Aged 15–19: 1976 and 1971." *Family Planning Perspectives* 10, no. 1 (January/February 1978): 11–20.

———. "The Resolution of Teenage First Pregnancies." *Family Planning Perspectives* 6, no. 2 (Spring 1974): 74–80.

———. "Sexual and Contraceptive Experience of Young Unmarried Women in the United States, 1976 and 1971." *Family Planning Perspectives* 9, no. 2 (March/April 1977): 55–71.

Zhang, David D., and Peter Brecke. "Global Climate Change, War, and Population Decline in Recent Human History." *Proceedings of the National Academy of Sciences (PNAS)* 104, no. 49 (December 4, 2007): 19214–19.

Zillman, Dolf. *Connections between Sexuality and Aggression.* Hillsdale, NJ: Erlbaum, 1983.

Zine, Jasmin. "Between Orientalism and Fundamentalism: Muslim Women and Feminist Engagement." In *(En)Gendering the War on Terror: War Stories and Camouflaged Politics*, edited by Krista Hunt and Kim Rygiel, pp. 27–49. Burlington, VT: Ashgate, 2006.

Zur, Ofer, and Andrea Morrison. "Gender and War: Reexamining Attitudes." *Journal of Orthopsychiatry* 59, no. 4 (October 1989): 528–33.

INDEX

459